THE OFFICIAL®

Directory to

U.S.
FLEA
MARKETS

THE OFFICIAL®

Directory to

U.S.
FLEA
MARKETS

Edited by
Kitty Werner

EIGHTH EDITION

House of Collectibles
The Crown Publishing Group • New York

Copyright © 2002 by Random House, Inc.

House of Collectibles is a registered trademark and the H colophon is a trademark of Random House, Inc.

Published by: House of Collectibles
The Crown Publishing Group
New York, New York

Distributed by the Crown Publishing Group, a division of Random House, Inc., New York, and simultaneously in Canada by Random House of Canada Limited, Toronto.

www.randomhouse.com

Printed in the United States of America

ISSN: 1073-208X

ISBN: 0-609-80922-9

Eighth Edition: May 2002

10 9 8 7 6 5 4 3 2 1

CONTENTS

INTRODUCTION

When using the listing of markets at the end of each state keep in mind that I have not personally checked each of these markets and cannot guarantee that they exist after this book is printed. For the 1996 book, one market sent in their listing and closed within a month! If the market is new to you, please call first, just in case. Quite a few markets have closed—some burned down, others had their land bought from under them. And just as many have opened since the Seventh Edition.

I was in Spain for a winter week one January and there in gorgeous Segovia was a local flea market covering about two blocks in the old part of town—no doubt the same place vendors have been selling for centuries. My children and I traveled around Europe for two summers and found that even in tiny villages in Provence, France, the Saturday market in my grandfather's hometown was similiar to the markets in tiny villages in northern Germany, near my husband's hometown. So much of the new merchandise is exactly the same as that sold here in the States. What makes a market different are the people, the atmosphere and the local produce and crafts. When you find a market that suits you—frequent it. Get to know its dealers and learn about the old treasures. Most of the dealers I have met love to talk about their wares and the history behind them.

In writing this book, I have spoken to hundreds of strangers in as many cities and towns around this country. I learned a great deal about flea markets in general, and collected some terrific stories. In this edition, more of these stories have been added to their respective market's listing. If you have a market story to share, send it along to me; my address is in the back of this book.

What I have gleaned from many conversations with these markets are these two basic facts:

1. The majority of people running flea markets are working for the fun of it, for the "family" a really good market becomes, and because they are, quite simply, dedicated to antiques, collectibles, and the treasures that may show up.

2. Those markets opened up "just to make a buck" quickly fold. It takes a lot of work and dedication to make a market work and grow, and more important to the market's survival, a healthy, loyal following of customers and dealers.

In fact, some of these markets become so "family" to dealers and customers that weddings and other major events are planned around market days. In one case, an elderly gentleman who lived at "his other home" for twenty-some years of the market's existence, seated at a different dealer's

1

booth each week, died just before the market reopened in April. His funeral happened to fall on opening day. As a tribute, his funeral procession drove slowly through the market in a final salute.

Two dealers we heard about, again, both elderly, died at their booth spaces, one while laughing with his customers. The other, an 87-year-old who had vowed to die on "his space," did so after having driven completely around the market, pulling into his accustomed space, and getting out of his car.

Another market, newly opened, became "family" so fast that when one dealer's husband required surgery, the other dealers kept her booth running for her so the family wouldn't go broke.

In a different vein, one market told me that one of their dealer spaces was lost/won (depending on your point of view) in a divorce settlement!

So, What Do You Sell?

When it came to asking about the merchandise sold, I asked the same question: What sort of things does your market sell? The answer is invariably the same: "You name it, we've got it!" Perhaps we should rename this book.

Occasionally I encountered a nagging question, "Was this market really a flea market?" Some markets are, of course, flea markets by any definition of the phrase. But still, what is the *real* definition of today's flea market? Do they sell only "old" items—a former qualification? Or is new merchandise fair game? Some markets have grown so large they have turned themselves into "malls." Quite a few of the "real malls" were removed from the book. However, some one-person antique shops were included, kept or added, simply because I felt that if you are hunting for antiques and collectibles, and these places were highly recommended, then they should be here for you, the dealer, looking to buy treasures.

Recent changes in markets and what they sell stem from the simple fact that there are only a finite amount of antiques and collectibles available— period. Chippendale lived only about 61 years and could create only a finite amount of furniture. The same goes for other "names" in the business. There were only so many baseball cards printed in any one year. That is what makes one card more valuable than another.

Trends make a difference too. Where sports cards were the rave several years ago, now it's something entirely different. Beanie Babies were hot. Collectible Barbies are hot. Star Wars is hot. Cards aren't.

More Is Less, or Is It More?

As more markets open for business, the fewer dealers there are to go around. If there are, in fact, more dealers (as more go into the business), there is still a "finite" number of goods to spread even more thinly.

As a result many markets have opened their stalls to "new merchandise." Still, the die-hards hold out and you can still find markets that deal only in antiques and collectibles. They are mentioned in the description of each market. But remember, to keep the market doors open, many markets that may have been more selective are now forced to sell the products the dealers have to sell—namely, new merchandise.

Many markets proudly boast about their size—"We are the largest in northeast Whatchamacallit!" Or "We are the largest Wednesday and Thursday market anywhere!" Sometimes you have to take such claims with a grain of sand. I had one man tell me he had the largest market in the business—"125,000 square feet!" I'm afraid I shattered his ego when I told him about a market that opened in an abandoned Ford factory (since gone out of business). Using only two of the six floors, they owned close to 750,000 square feet altogether. In fact, there are many markets in the 100,000-square-foot category. And just as many smaller ones—they seem to have the richest stories to tell. Bigger isn't always better. It simply depends on what you are looking for: a good time, your "other" family, a specific object, just to waste a day, a carnival atmosphere, whatever.

Many of the markets listed have turned into semi-carnivals to attract buyers, or to provide a more interesting place to visit as a getaway with the family. One market owner bought the contents of a former amusement park and has all the gnomes and creatures scattered around his property, including a 30-foot totem pole and twin pink elephants. Colonial Valley in Pennsylvania had a 26-inch-tall steer named Clyde (who unfortunately died). Mt. Sterling, Kentucky, celebrates the Third Monday Court Days, started in 1870 when the circuit court judge would pass through the towns of Maysville, Flemingsburg, and then Mt. Sterling doing his business—including the sentencing of some offenders to hang! The entire town shuts down and celebrates for three days (with over 2,000 dealers). Maysville and Flemingsburg joined in the act around 25 years ago, restarting their "Court Days." Sadly, Maysville has stopped doing their market. Those markets started Sunday after church and continued until the dancing ended on Monday night.

Two editions ago, I found the Texas Court Day markets and added most of them to my listings. Then the rest of the First Monday markets. Traditions die hard.

Educate Yourself

A neighbor of mine has found the greatest antique treasures in the local flea market, not noted for anything grand. She says you just have to look carefully and know what you are getting. Her house is furnished with numerous pieces of furniture, from chests and beds to baby high chairs, mostly culled from this one market. She has collected complete sets of china and silverware in five different patterns for each of her five children—all from flea markets.

A caution about being sure of what you want and knowing its value. There are numerous stories sprinkled throughout this book of surprise finds—the dealer who sold a frame for $75 only to hear later that the savvy buyer sold the old master in it for $250,000, and so on. Look carefully. You never know.

Do educate yourself if you are a serious buyer of antiques and collectibles. It obviously pays off.

Public Broadcasting Service (PBS) has been showing the Antique Road Show for several years now. It is a revelation to the uninitiated. If you haven't seen it, do try to see it. People bring in their curiosities, found stuff, and treasures to the show and expert antique appraisers and dealers tell the owner what their item is worth. Many times the owner doesn't realize that 1) it's a fake, 2) it is worthless, or more exciting, 3) it's a lost masterwork worth thousands upon thousands of dollars.

FLEA MARKETS: THEN AND NOW

Look at the history and development of the phenomenon of flea markets as an alternative to *shopping*—that is, going to town and wandering from store to store. The term "flea market," a direct translation from the French phrase *marché aux puces*, has come to signify a specially designated occasion for the purpose of exchanging a wide variety of goods—anything from valuable antiques to backyard junk.

In France, where the term was coined, fleas were found to accompany old furniture and clothing drawn from attics or barns. Today, some flea markets in the United States maintain a curious tie to this tradition by demanding that all furniture be either fumigated or else banned from the sale area entirely.

The flea market in the United States, however, has taken on other European customs—customs found not only in France but throughout the Continent. One custom is Market Day, a regularly scheduled time when a portion of town, usually the main square, is closed off from traffic as farmers, itinerant tradesmen, butcher and bone-men, and other dealers sell their merchandise—anything from produce and clothing to fresh meats and kitchen appliances—to the people of the town and surrounding area. From early in the morning—6:00 AM, even earlier—to the middle of the afternoon, buyers and sellers get together in a particular place for the single purpose of striking bargains. In America, where so many ancestors came from rural Europe, small towns have since the first settlement conducted fairs, animal shows, and farmers' markets as means of distributing locally made products. For early farmers, tool makers, and other craftsmen, the local market could prove an effective gateway to the larger markets of other cities and large towns in the region, as buyers from nearby districts would frequently come looking for special deals. The flea market in the United States, then, is a bit of a mongrel, with its Old World mixed parentage combined with that peculiarly American flair for the entrepreneurial. The giant flea markets like the Rose Bowl Flea Market in Pasadena, California, and the First Monday Trade Days in Canton, Texas, are cousins, and not very distant, to that of the antique shows and sales that keep popping up with increasing frequency throughout the country. The current popularity of flea markets large or small around urban centers, as well as in the deep country, suggests that these events have become a welcome and permanent part of our day-to-day lives.

A flea market may range in size from just a few sellers standing on the side of a highway trying to clean out the unwanted contents of their homes to a complex, labyrinthine structure of dealers' booths sprawled out across acres of open space indoors or outdoors or both. In other words, a flea market is rather like beauty—it is all in the eye of the beholder.

Thinking another way, it is not so much a particular kind of event (whether it's a "swap meet" or an antique show and sale), but rather an alternative to shopping at the mall—a place where the individual buyer is on equal terms with the individual dealer, where no prices are fixed, and the fun comes in finding just what you want and buying or selling it for a price that feels right to *you*.

In this seventh edition, our directory has grown to include the listings for all the markets we could find in business directories. That should bring our total number of markets to well in the thousands. Just be reminded that we didn't contact any of them listed in those sections. There simply wasn't enough time and space to do so. We do include just about any conceivable flea market from the one-man market to the gigantic San Jose market in California. One of my criteria was courtesy and friendliness. I didn't find every market that exists. I've been told that between Kansas and Texas there must be 4,000 flea markets alone! But I did find some obscure markets that are fund-raisers for churches, schools, and firehouses. According to the people who run these markets, you wouldn't believe the treasures that can be found there. One Texas market is simply the local residents' once-a-year garage sale. There is another market in Maryland doing the same thing.

There are some newer markets that have opened and grown tremendously since the seventh edition was published, and we've added them too.

I think you'll find this a wonderful mix. There are plenty of places that cater to families, providing rides, perhaps video arcades, games, petting zoos, and whatever they can think of that children might enjoy.

You could plan a vacation around many of the markets listed here. Don't be shy. The people I have talked with represent a rich cross-section of America, doing this because they loved the people who came as dealers and those who came as visitors. They are having fun and they want to share it. It's up to you.

BUYING AND SELLING
AT FLEA MARKETS

Coming Prepared

When shopping at flea markets—and this is as true for the fine antique shows as for the markets that feature new merchandise—be sure to distinguish between the valuable and not so valuable articles offered for sale. Keep in mind that flea markets trade in all kinds of things, not only antiques and fine collectibles, but also brand-new objects and some odds and ends that have ended up, somehow, in the dealer's hands. Notes promoter R. G. Canning of his early days organizing California's world-famous Pasadena Rose Bowl Flea Market and Swap Meet: "It was amazing to me that people would come to buy all that junk."

Of course, there is nothing wrong with your paying money for someone else's junk; it just depends on how much you value it. The flea market (in the most general sense of the term) is really not unlike a communal yard sale. It often provides the opportunity to sell things to other people who might be able to find a use for them—though they might be hard-pressed to say what that is exactly at the moment of purchase.

But whether it is a fine antique show or something as manic as the Rose Bowl Swap Meet, it is advisable to subject *all* merchandise to careful scrutiny, and not just the antiques and collectibles either. When shopping for "brand-name" items, be especially careful to check for fakes—some imitations are so masterful that they can fool a seasoned shopper. While imitations of brand-names appear to match the originals in craftsmanship and quality of materials, there have been many disappointed shoppers who have watched their "once-in-a-lifetime" bargains disintegrate in a matter of weeks or even days under normal use. Most flea markets monitor and insist that their dealers represent their goods honestly and use fair business practices. Several listed herein make known their policy of having their dealers not only stand behind their merchandise, but also offer refunds if the merchandise fails to please. This serves the double purpose of protecting both the buyer and the reputation of the market. Be sure to report any unfair or dishonest practices to the owner or operator of the market where this occurs. It is always best to be an alert and educated shopper.

Knowing When to Haggle

At flea markets, as with just about any kind of trade, a deal is made when both the seller and the buyer think they are getting a bargain.

Put a value on an item as soon as you can and stick to it, as best you can. Changing your mind in the middle of a sale is a sign of weakness and uncertainty—one that a hardened seller will be quick to take advantage of. The more sure you are in your initial assessments, the easier and more pleasant your overall shopping will be. And when you encounter an object that is not marked with a price, don't suggest one, but rather prompt the seller to give you one. After all, it is the obligation of the seller to have a price to quote for any item he sells.

And don't forget that a main activity at the flea market isn't so much shopping as bargaining. In other words, don't automatically assume that the first price you hear is final, whether offered by voice or by a price tag. In fact, you have a right as a potential buyer to ask for a "last price" before you make up your mind on an item. (Remember, though, that you can ask for a last price only once.) You are not necessarily being rude by passing up an object after hearing the final offer, so long as you are polite in your refusal and thank the seller for his/her offer.

Don't ever let a seller use intimidation to force you to buy an object. You alone can know whether you want an object and, if so, how much it is worth to you.

Carry lots of cash, best of all in small denominations. As a general rule, always be working toward a deal in your negotiations with flea market salespeople. After all, their business is to sell, not to talk. Do not ask for a price on an item unless you are genuinely interested.

If you want to haggle, be careful how you do it. Part of the trick is in knowing real value, of course. Even if something is already priced low, a deft haggler takes the position that it can be driven down further. If he's going to make an offer he'll make a considerably lower one, representing maybe 50 percent of the asking price or even less, figuring that the end result is likely to be a compromise.

The wrong way to ask for a discount is by deriding the merchandise or the price, by suggesting that the dealer does not know his business, or by doing anything which could trigger a negative reaction. For example, never say "The shop down the street is selling one just like this for $20 less." Or, worse, "You don't really expect to get $75 for this, do you?"

Remember that the sellers have heard every possible pitch for discounts. They hear them every day, the same ones over and over. After just a short time in business they get thoroughly turned off by most types of discount-seeking approaches, and by most of the typical "I-want-a-discount" customers.

The majority of such customers act as if the dealer owes them a favor. You need to be a little original in trying to obtain a discount and, above all, courteous. Be inventive, use your imagination, and, most important, make a good impression. As they say in showbiz, always leave 'em laughing. You may want to return someday, and you will want to be welcome next time.

Selling at Flea Markets

First of all, decide which markets you want to participate in. There may be several nearby. A beginner is apt to make his choice based on the wrong considerations, thinking in terms of which show offers the best rate on space, or how he can save $1.50 on gas by selling close to home. It's really useless to give much thought to these points. The important thing is, at which flea market are you likely to do the most selling? Visit different markets as a browser; look at what is going on. How many dealers are present? Are nearly all the spaces taken, or are the grounds half empty? Unless the flea market is a new one, or in some cases the season is winding down, empty ground space indicates an unsuccessful market. What are the sellers offering? What percentage of the sellers are offering collectors' items? If you're interested in collectibles, for example, it is unwise to take a space at a show where collectibles are seldom sold.

After deciding on the flea market at which to sell, make arrangements for a space well in advance. Talk to the manager and find out about the rules and regulations. They are more or less the same from one show to another, but there could be some differences. Every show has restrictions on what can and cannot be sold. With collectibles, you are not likely to run afoul of any taboos, except with firearms. Most flea markets do not permit the sale of firearms, antique or modern. Knives are almost always okay, except switchblades—some states have laws against them. Markets listed as "family" markets generally don't allow pornography, either.

Mostly you'll want to find out what you will be getting for your rental money. Does the management provide a table? What is the exact size of the space you'll get? Will you be required to collect sales tax? Is this show held rain or shine? If the show is canceled because of bad weather, do you get a refund or a raincheck for the next show?

Put some thought into what you are going to take to the show. It's always better to have a variety of merchandise than to go heavy on just a few kinds of items. Large items such as furniture will cut down your exhibit space. If you are going to show small things of moderate or high value, such as jewelry or scarce coins, try to get a display box with a glass top and a lock. This will reduce the risk of theft. Clean up merchandise before packing it off to the show. This does not mean an indiscriminate scrubbing that could lessen the value and desirability of an antique, but dusting and (where appropriate) polishing. It does not enhance sales value when items have a just-out-of-the-dustbin appearance. Try to arrange everything in a way that will make browsing as easy as possible. If you are selling magazines, stand them upright in a carton. That way customers can flip through them with a minimum of fuss. This will also help to keep the covers from tearing, which is sure to happen if they are just piled together in a heap. When selling magazines of high value, or old comic books, slip them into protective Mylar bags. Scarce coins should be displayed in 2" × 2" holders. Some items are, of course, more of a headache to display than others: with glassware and china you run the risk of breakage as a result of not only clumsy browsers but strong gusts of wind. If you are displaying a lot of breakables, you can take the precaution of making certain that your table is well anchored. One way of anchoring a table is by sinking the leg tips two or three inches into the ground, if this is feasible. Another is to place heavy stones or bricks on top for ballast. In any event, keep breakables toward the center of the table if you can, where they are not as likely to be swept away by an errant arm or sleeve.

Figure out how much you want to get for each item before the show and whether or not you are going to use price tags. Don't wait until somebody asks the price before you start thinking about it. Most flea market exhibitors mark prices on their merchandise, and this is probably the best course to follow, simply because many browsers just won't bother to ask the price, even if they are mildly interested. Of course, the marked price need not necessarily be the actual sum for which you would sell the item; you can leave yourself some leeway for bargaining, and it is usually a good idea to do this. But don't set your marked prices too much higher than what you would be willing to accept.

NATIONAL FLEA MARKET ASSOCIATION

by Jerry Stokes, Executive Director

The National Flea Market Association was founded in 1997 in Charlotte, North Carolina, to establish an organization for a major national industry that represents over one hundred million flea market shoppers and one million mom-and-pop businesses doing in excess of over five billion dollars in annual sales.

Flea Markets are known all over the world and have been in existence since civilization began with neighborly bartering. They are known by many names in the United States other than flea markets, such as swap meets, antiques markets, collectibles markets, First Monday, Traders Villages, special events and many others, but where there is a gathering of vendors, that is the definition of a flea market.

Millions of flea market vendors have performed invaluable services to the general public for hundreds of years. They provide a unique and exciting way of life for buyers of products and services of every kind imaginable, and each vendor is an example of a true entrepreneur. Markets are a great way to recycle and reuse items not needed but still useful—and to make money while selling unused goods.

Flea Market Vendors have no boundaries or barriers as long as what they sell is legal. They create their own style of business and live a life indescribable to a nondealer. They are men, women and children of all races, religion, faiths, colors and beliefs. They work long hours, getting up before dawn to go to yard sales for resale items or to setup at a flea market, and still work late into the night checking their inventory and doing their book work. Yet they always greet their customers with smiles, good manners and good deals. They do all this and more because they love what they do, not just because someone pays them to do it. They are the Protectors of the American Free Enterprise System and the unsung heroes of shopping lovers.

Flea Markets are unusual in many ways. They do not discriminate regarding age, gender, race, religion or any other difference. They are a place for any ethical and legal vendor looking for a place to offer his or her wares. Vendors are interesting people to talk with and they are personally involved with their sales. They take time to listen to you, and if you have the time, they can tell you some interesting stories. When asked by a reporter doing an article on flea markets why she worked there, a 84-year-old lady told the reporter, "Where else can an old 84-year-old lady make money to support herself while having so much fun?"

How We Started the NFMA

Having been involved in trade associations for over fifty years, in 1997, I spent a couple of years researching flea market vendors to organize a National Flea Market Vendors Association. I found out there were about one million vendors in the United States and none of them wanted to be on a board of directors. Most all of them said they did not want to be organized. Then I decided to organize the owners and managers with the idea of having them help organize the vendors but found the owners and managers wanted and needed a national organization to represent the flea market industry. I sent out about 3,000 invitations to an organizational meeting in Charlotte, North Carolina, on October 21, 1997. Peggy Alexander of the Peachtree Peddlers Flea Market in McDonough, Georgia, agreed to serve as our first president. We had 21 owners and managers from about 15 different states meet and vote to organize the National Flea Market Association. Our first Conference was held in April 1998 in Atlanta, Georgia. Since then, we have had annual conventions and trade shows in Las Vegas, Orlando, Dallas and San Diego.

Interesting Statistics

We represent about three thousand markets with annual payrolls in excess of one and a half billion dollars and annual sales in excess of five billion dollars. We pay over four hundred million dollars in taxes and provide over 80,000 staff jobs. Our mission is to protect the free enterprise system, develop entrepreneurs. We are the birthplace of small business. We promote tourism and benefit the local and national economy. The AP's survey reports 75% of customers have previously attended flea markets, 70% visit more than five times per year, 50% are male, 55% are married, 72% are younger than 45 years old, 62% make over $25,000 and 25% make over $50,000.

WHY THEY SHOULD JOIN NFMA

NFMA's objective is to serve the public interest and to benefit the flea market industry by fostering high standards of business conduct which merits public trust.

To disseminate information helpful to the flea market industry and to facilitate the exchange of ideas among members.

To encourage legislation and regulations constructive to the industry and to discourage legislation and regulations destructive to both the consumers and small businesses.

Abide by a Professional Code of Ethics.

Markets belonging to the NFMA are indicated by their logo:

PERIODICALS
OF INTEREST

Following is a selective list of periodicals with good coverage of flea markets. The approximate geographical scope of each publication is listed in parentheses after its name. The publications listed are produced either in tabloid newspaper or magazine format. This list, though far from complete, should help the reader find the most up-to-date listings for some of the many flea markets that, due to space limitations or our own oversight, have regrettably been omitted from this guide.

Antique Review (Midwest). PO Box 538, Worthington OH 43085-0538. Tel: (614) 885-9757. Monthly. Subscriptions are $20 per year. Web: www.krause.com or www.collect.com.

Antique Trader Weekly, The (Midwest). PO Box 1050, Dubuque IA 52004-1050. Tel: (319) 588-2073. Weekly. Subscriptions are $38 per year. Web: www.krause.com or www.collect.com.

Antique Week (Two editions: Eastern and Mid-Central). PO Box 90, Knightstown IN 46148-0090. Tel: (765) 345-5133. Weekly. Subscriptions are $32.95 per year each, and $59.75 for both; includes Antique Shop Guide issue.

Antiques & Art Around Florida, PO Box 2481, Ft Lauderdale FL 33303-2481. Order online. Email: aarf@shadow.net. Web: www.aarf.com.

Antiques & Auction News, Joel Sater's (Pennsylvania/Northeastern US). PO Box 500, Mount Joy PA 17552-0500. Tel: (717) 492-2541. Weekly. Subscriptions are $18 per year, third class; $45 for 6 months or $75 per year, first class mail.

Antiques & The Arts Weekly (New England/Northeastern US). The Bee Publishing Co, PO Box 5503, Newtown CT 06470-5503. Tel: (203) 426-8036. Weekly. Subscriptions are $62 per year. Email: subscriptions@thebee.com. Web: www.antiquesandthearts.com.

Arts & Antiques, 2100 Powers Ferry Rd, Atlanta GA 30339. Tel: (770) 955-5656. Subscriptions are $29.95 for 11 months. Email: subscriptions@artantiquesmag.com. Web: www.artantiquesmag.com.

Collector's Journal (Midwest). PO Box 601, Vinton IA 52349-0601. Tel: 1-800-472-4006. Weekly (except last two weeks in December and first week in January). Subscriptions are $26.95 per year. Email: antiquescj@aol.com. Web: www.collectorsjournal.com.

Collector Magazine and Price Guide. PO Box 1050, Dubuque IA 52004-1050. Tel: (319) 588-2073. Monthly. Subscriptions are $21.95. Web: www.krause.com or www.collect.com.

Collectors Mart. 700 E State St, Iola WI 54990-0001. Tel: 1-800-258-0929. Bi-monthly. Subscriptions are $40 a year. Web: www.krause.com.

Collectors News (National). 506 2nd St, Grundy Center IA 50638. Tel: 1-800-352-8039. Monthly. Subscriptions $28 per year US 2nd class. Email: collectors@collectors-news.com. Web: http://collectors-news.com.

Maine Antiques Digest (New England). PO Box 1429, Waldoboro ME 04572-1429. Tel: 1-800-752-8521. Monthly. Subscriptions are $43 per year, second class. Email: mad@maine.com. Web: www.maineantiquedigest.com.

New England Antiques Journal. 4 Church St, Ware MA 01082. Tel: 1-800-432-3505. Monthly. Subscriptions are $22.95 per year or $37.95 for two years. Email: visit@antiquesjournal.com. Web: www.antiquesjournal.com.

New York Antique Almanac, The (New York State). PO Box 2400, New York NY 10021-2400. Tel: (212) 988-2700. Published 9 times per year, including three bi-monthly issues. Subscriptions are $10 per year or $18 for two years.

New York–Pennsylvania Collector, The (Eastern and Mid-West US and Canada). 73 Buffalo St, Canandaiqua NY 14424. Tel: (585) 394-1712 or 1-800-836-1868. Monthly. Subscriptions are $21 per year; Canadian subscriptions are US$34 for one year. Email: collector@mpnewspapers.com. Web: www.ny-pacollector.com.

Renninger's Antique Guide (Eastern US). PO Box 495, Lafayette Hill PA 19444-0495. Tel: (610) 828-4614. Bi-weekly. Subscriptions are $15 a year for 25 issues or $28 for two years.

Treasure Chest. 564 Eddy St Ste 326, Providence RI 02903. 1-800-557-9662. Monthly. Subscriptions are $25 a year, first class.

Upper Canadian, The. PO Box 653, Smiths Falls, Ontario Canada K7A 4T6. Tel: (613) 283-1168. Bi-monthly. Subscriptions are US$27 for one year (C$26 in Canada), US$48 for two years (C$46 in Canada). Email: uppercanadian@recorder.ca. Web: www.uppercanadian.com.

Warman's Today's Collector, 700 E State St, Iola WI 54990-0001. Tel: 1-800-258-0929. Monthly. Subscriptions are $45 a year. Web: www.krause.com.

WEBSITES
OF INTEREST

There are many new websites being developed for those interested in flea markets and antiques and collectibles. For those of you new to the Internet, if you type in the main word of what you are looking for in the long, blank white line, i.e., *antiques*, the "search engine" will promptly go looking for anything with the word "antiques" in it, which can lead to some rather interesting finds. However, to get you started, here are some links that could be of interest.

www.about-antiques.com — Interesting site about antiques. Joe Cahall is an antique appraiser as well as dealer. He does this at the site, too.

www.antiqueandcollectible.com — A collection of antique and collectible associations, with listings of various organizations.

www.collectors.org — Collector's Organization. The official site of the National Association of Collectors. It has links to antique shows, flea markets, appraisers, and just about anything connected to the business. There is an eNews for flea markets on this site. Worth visiting.

www.fleamarketguide.com — Flea Market Guide of US Flea Markets has listings of markets around the country as entered by the markets themselves, so the information is somewhat "puffy" or not necessarily accurate since the listings aren't always updated.

www.fleamarkets.org — The official website of the National Flea Market Association. See their own page in this book. Great place for vendors and markets to check out what's happening in the markets.

www.fleamarketusa.com — Another state-by-state listing of markets; mostly names and addresses.

www.openair.org — The World Wide Guide to Farmers' Markets, Street Markets, Flea Markets and Street Vendors. Scattered information from around the world. Gets political.

www.pbs.org/wgbh/pages/roadshow — The Antiques Roadshow!

www.swapmeets.com — The Unofficial Swapmeet & Flea Market Directory is essentially advertising space plus some listings of markets.

www.iwily.com — A place that gathers information from many online auctions and offers a way for you to get the current prices offered.

HOW TO USE THIS BOOK

The flea markets listed in this book vary from those having fewer than 5 dealers to those with more than 2,000 dealers in some cases. The markets are listed alphabetically by state, and by town within each state. Each listing is broken down into the following subheadings:

DATES: Market days are listed here, including specific dates for 2002 where applicable. Rain dates are noted where applicable.

TIMES: Hours during which the flea markets are held are listed.

ADMISSION: If there is a cost to enter a market, the fee will be listed. Information about the availability and cost of parking is also presented.

LOCATION: A street address for the market is supplied where available; brief directions are provided for those traveling from out of town by car.

DESCRIPTION: This section discusses the size of the market, its age, the types of merchandise available, whether food is served on the premises, and any other interesting facts pertaining to its operation. All markets listed have restroom facilities on the premises or nearby, unless otherwise noted. It's the rare market that doesn't have food vendors.

DEALER RATES: This section provides the most complete information available at press time regarding costs of selling space at the market, and whether advance reservations are required.

CONTACT: Complete mailing address, telephone number, email and website of the market operator are supplied wherever possible for dealer or shopper inquiries.

The Official Directory to U.S. Flea Markets has been designed to provide essential information about flea markets across the country selected for variety of merchandise, number of dealers attending, or other information of interest to the bargain hunter. The at-a-glance format previously outlined aids in making this guide the easiest as well as the most up-to-date reference available on the subject.

ICONS USED

This year, we've introduced icons as quick guides to the market's services, in an effort to make the choice of market easier.

Indicates food is available, whether it be a full restaurant, snack bars, or wagons.

Restrooms of any usable sort. This could be from the full-fledged, everything restrooms to port-a-potties.

If the restrooms are handicapped-accessible, then the market is handicapped-accessible. There are a few markets that are simply fields and vendors. Could be a bit rough going for a wheelchair, although every market we spoke with would go out of their way to accommodate anyone using a wheelchair—even if it is not a requirement to do so. Festivals, in many states, are not required to be ADA compatible.

Member of the National Flea Market Association

IMPORTANT NOTICE

While the editors have made every effort to obtain the most exhaustive and accurate information available on a selection of flea markets from coast to coast in the continental United States, the reader is advised that in a work of this scope, inaccuracies may occur. House of Collectibles assumes no responsibility for any misprints or other errors found in this directory; all show dates, admission fees, dealer rates, etc. listed herein are subject to change at any time without notice. It is recommended that users of this directory call ahead or consult local sources whenever possible when planning a visit to a flea market.

FLEA MARKET
LISTINGS

ALABAMA

ATTALLA
Mountain Top Flea Market

DATES: Every Sunday, year round. Rain or shine.

TIMES: 5:00 AM until whenever.

ADMISSION: Free. Parking is free.

LOCATION: 11301 US Hwy 278 W, 6 miles west of Attalla. Hwy 278 W at 101 mile marker.

DESCRIPTION: Located on a mountaintop on 96 acres, this mostly outdoor flea market first started in 1971 and currently consists of approximately 1,000 dealers selling everything from antiques and collectibles to new merchandise (jewelry, clothing, shoes, tools, furniture), from handcrafted items from three states to fresh produce from local farmers. They describe themselves as "Alabama's longest market—with 2.6 miles of shopping." They average over 40,000 buyers every Sunday! Twelve snack bars are on the premises. Restrooms with handicap facilities are available.

DEALER RATES: $9 per 10' × 21' space outside per day, $10 for 10' × 10' booth inside (very limited inside space). Shed tops for rent at $2 per day, $4 for electric where available. Call the toll-free number for the latest information. Overnight camping with showers and restrooms is available. Reservations taken Monday 12:30 PM-4:00 PM, Tuesday through Thursday 8:00 AM-4:00 PM, Saturday 9:00 AM-6:00 PM.

CONTACT: Janie Terrell, Mountain Top Flea Market, 11301 US Hwy 278 W, Attalla AL 35954-7725. Tel: 1-800-535-2286. Email: mtopflea@hopper.net. Web: www.lesdeal.com/MTFM.

BESSEMER
Bessemer Flea Market

DATES: Every Friday, Saturday, and Sunday. Rain or shine.

TIMES: 8:00 AM-5:00 PM.

ADMISSION: Free. Parking is also free.

LOCATION: From Birmingham, take I-59 south to Bessemer Exit 112. Turn left under freeway, to Hwy 11, turn right and go 3 blocks to market on left behind McDonald's.

DESCRIPTION: Started in 1980, this "real old-fashion" indoor/outdoor market accommodates approximately 700 dealers on 16 acres. There are as many as 10-15,000 people attending these shows. A variety of goods from antiques to new merchandise can be found. A snack bar serves a variety of concession foods. Handicapped-accessible restrooms are available.

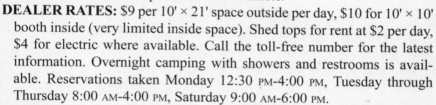

EALER RATES: $6 to $11 per day, depending on size and availability outside. Weekend rates are $16-$33 per space. Prepayment is required to reserve indoor space, outside is always available. There are overnight parking and shower facilities for traveling dealers.

CONTACT: Bessemer Flea Market, 1013 8th Ave N, Bessemer AL 35020-5417. Tel: (205) 425-8510.

Just Buzzing Around

Warned of a bunch of wasps swarming, the intrepid owners grabbed some wasp spray and decided to play hero. Arriving at the scene of noise, they realized they were facing honeybees—albeit a volleyball-size nest worth of the little critters. As one of their dealers raises bees, he was called upon to remove them. With his special bee vacuum, he safely removed the bees to his hives, where they thrive today.

BIRMINGHAM

The Flea Market at the Fairgrounds in Birmingham

DATES: First weekend of every month, year round, except during the Fair, plus the first and second weekends in December.

TIMES: Friday (first pick), 3:00 PM-7:00 PM. Saturday 9:00 AM-6:00 PM, and Sundays 9:00 AM-5:00 PM.

ADMISSION: Free. Parking is free.

LOCATION: Alabama State Fairgrounds. Exit 120 off I-20/59, follow the signs to the Alabama State Fair Complex.

DESCRIPTION: A Birmingham tradition for over 30 years, and now operating under its current management for 3 years, this market has 600 dealer spaces, mostly indoors. Billed as "Alabama's Largest Indoor Flea Market." Antiques; collectibles; European imports and home furnishings, furniture; oriental rugs; gold, silver, vintage and costume jewelry; gems; sterling silverware; glassware; vintage clothing; new clothing and accessories; purses; prints and framed art; gifts; ceramics; fishing gear; electronic equipment; golf clubs and accessories; automotive accessories; dolls; plants; tools; leather; toys; crafts; phones; make-up; bedding; coins; sport cards; comics; knives; books; CD's; cassettes; records; lamps; jewelry repair; crystal restoration; flowers; and "you name it!" There is an antique and collectibles only section. Some of their dealers have been there since the beginning of the market. There are concession stands and restrooms on the premises, all handicapped accessible.

DEALER RATES: $55-$60 per 10' × 10' indoor booth, per weekend; $30 for a "one-parking-space and a car-size parking space behind" area outdoors. The fairgrounds provide camping facilities for a fee. They are working to attract new businesses for their new building; please call for more information.

CONTACT: The Market 115, 130 Wildwood Pkwy Ste 108, Birmingham AL 35209. Tel: 1-800-3-MARKET (1-800-362-7538). Watch for their website.

Jefferson County Farmers' Market Flea Market

DATES: Daily.
TIMES: 8:00 AM-5:00 PM.
ADMISSION: Free. Parking is free.
LOCATION: 344 Finley Ave W.
DESCRIPTION: Now held on a field with 30 booths and open outdoor spaces, this flea market sells antiques, electronics, tools, belts, belt buckles, tapes, and assorted new and used merchandise. The Farmers' Market is open 24 hours a day next door, so there's plenty of produce at the market. Public restrooms, a snack bar and a store are on site; a restaurant is just down the road.
DEALER RATES: $8 per lock-up booth; $5 per open space. Reservations are not required for the open space, but there is a waiting list for the booths. Office hours are 7:00 AM-3:00 PM. Ask for Julie.
CONTACT: Jefferson County Farmers' Market, 344 Finley Ave W, Birmingham AL 35204. Tel: (205) 251-8737. Fax: (205) 251-8106.

COLLINSVILLE
Collinsville Trade Day

DATES: Every Saturday. Rain, shine or the occasional snowflake.
TIMES: 4:30 AM-2:30 PM.
ADMISSION: Free. $.50 for parking.
LOCATION: Hwy 11, S.
DESCRIPTION: Started in 1955 by Mrs. Harris on 4 acres of land, this market has grown to 65 acres after her son took over in 1979. They were written up in *National Geographic* in 1972. About 1,000 vendors sell antiques, collectibles, books, jewelry, used and new clothing and tools, stamps, cookware, toys, fresh produce, and new merchandise. Up on Coon Dog Hill livestock is traded and sold. There are 15 concessions and snack bars selling "festival food" to the hungry. Handicapped-accessible restrooms are available. When you visit, find Charles and say "Hi" for me! He does have good stories to tell.
DEALER RATES: $8 for covered space, $5 for open space. Reservations are suggested. Watch for their coming website.
CONTACT: Charles Cook, Collinsville Trade Day, PO Box 560, Collinsville AL 35961-0560. Tel: (256) 524-2536 or 1-888-524-2536.

CULLMAN
Cullman Flea Market

DATES: Saturday and Sunday.

TIMES: 8:00 AM–5:00 PM.

ADMISSION: Free. Parking is also free.

LOCATION: 415 Lincoln Ave SW. Next to I-65, on US Rt 278 at Exit 308.

DESCRIPTION: Opened in May 1989 and located on 40 acres of land
with nine acres just for parking, this market has 265 dealer spaces indoors and more space outdoors. Their dealers sell a variety of antiques,
collectibles, handmade and craft items, tools, hardware, jewelry, woodwork, handbags, glassware, baseball cards, coins, fresh produce, cheese
and dairy products, and new merchandise. Two concession stands with
seating areas provide food to hungry shoppers. Clean restrooms with
handicapped facilities are on the premises. They have added two antique
buildings since 1994, open Thursday through Monday. Also on the premises is Country Village, built of old barnboard, a collection of specialty
shops selling mostly antiques.

DEALER RATES: $22 and up per 9' × 10' booth for two days; $30 per
10' × 10' booth for two days. Reservations are required. RV hookups for vendors.

CONTACT: Frances Kilgo, Cullman Flea Market, PO Box 921, Cullman
AL 35056-0921. Tel: (256) 739-0910. Fax: (256) 739-5352.

DOTHAN
Sadie's Flea Market

DATES: Saturday and Sunday, year round.

TIMES: 8:00 AM-5:00 PM.

ADMISSION: Free. Parking is free.

LOCATION: On Rt 231 S, 5 miles south of Ross-Clark Circle in Dothan. From Rt 109, turn left on 231; market is a few hundred yards down the road.

DESCRIPTION: Open since May 1989, this market, located on 50 acres, has over 300 booths with 60 permanent dealers, but many times is full to capacity. Dealers sell a large variety of everything, including antiques, collectibles, crafts, produce, new and used merchandise—"real flea market stuff." A large Peanut Festival is held in the area in late October through early November. One large snack bar and a snack wagon quell any hunger, and two large handicapped-accessible restrooms are on the premises. There is a small RV park as part of the market. A local ultralight plane club has frequent fly-ins, attracting much local attention. Occasionally a sponsored local gospel group or a country band will perform here. There is usually musical entertainment every weekend.

DEALER RATES: Indoors: $55 per month for a 10' × 10' booth—if available; outside: $4 per day for a 4' × 8' table, or $4 per day for a 20' "parallel foot" setup BYOT. Reservations are preferred.

CONTACT: Sadie, Sadie's Flea Market, 7990 US 231 S, Dothan AL 36301-7836. Tel: (334) 677-5138.

FOLEY
Foley Indoor Flea Market

DATES: Saturday and Sunday.

TIMES: 9:00 AM-5:00 PM.

ADMISSION: Free. Parking is free.

LOCATION: 14809 Hwy 59, 1½ miles south of Summerdale, 3 miles north of Hwy 98 on Hwy 59.

DESCRIPTION: This "real friendly" market opened in July 1997 and is quickly growing, filling its 197 indoor booths. The 45,000-square-foot air-conditioned/heated building sits on 16 acres. There are at least 10 dealers specializing in antiques and collectibles. The rest sell plants, coffee, ceramics, wood crafts, collectibles, garage sale drag-ins, whatever comes along. A full restaurant offers food, including barbecue, during market hours. Handicapped-accessible restrooms are available.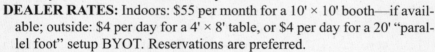

DEALER RATES: $40 per weekend inside space. Reservations are not required. There are RV setups with full hookups for the vendors.

CONTACT: Foley Indoor Flea Market, 14809 Hwy 59, Foley AL 36536. Tel: (334) 943-6349. Fax: (334) 943-6349.

HARPERSVILLE
Greater Shelby County Flea Market

DATES: Saturday and Sunday, year round.

TIMES: 9:00 AM-5:00 PM.

ADMISSION: Free. Parking is also free.

LOCATION: I-280 E to Hwy 25, exit at Harpersville about 4 miles south of Harpersville. On SR 25 between Harpersville and Wilsonville.

DESCRIPTION: Formerly the Dixie Land Flea and Farmer's Market. Opened in 1986 on 70 acres of land, this market has 400 booths inside a 70,000-square-foot building and acres of outside booths selling antiques, furniture, arts and crafts, jewelry, baseball cards, toys, evening gowns, fruits and vegetables, and plenty of new and used merchandise. Many of the dealers are permanent, and the market advertises heavily in newspapers, on radio and on television and hosts "live remotes" for on-air promotions. They have "everything and anything" in this country flea market. "In fact, there are some things we're not too sure about," says Steve Jones, the manager. Huge deer and wild turkeys roam around this market, driving hunters crazy during the appropriate seasons. This is a clean, well-run, friendly market. There is entertainment to keep the children busy. Plenty of food is available on the premises supplied by two restaurants and an ice cream parlor; and when needed, clean handicapped-accessible restrooms. Find Steve, say "Hi" for me, and ask him about all the stories I can't put in the book!

DEALER RATES: $7 per day includes table, plus electricity outside, but covered. Open outside space is $5 per day. Inside it starts at $12 per day. Campers can camp and hook up for $3 per day. There is full-time security, showers for dealers, and special handicapped facilities. Each booth has its own entrance with parking behind it.

CONTACT: Steve Jones, Greater Shelby County Flea Market, 33985 Hwy 25, Harpersville AL 35078. Tel: (205) 672-2022. Fax: (205) 672-2203.

All in a Day's Work
During the summer of 2000, they tried to grow watermelons on the grounds of the market. Well, that wasn't too successful—it seems the deer ate them! A self-described "gofer," Steve said he recently found himself with a soda in one hand, plunging a toilet with the other!

HIGHWAY 127
Highway 127 Corridor Sale

DATES: August, from the Thursday before the 3rd Sunday through Sunday for 4 days. 2002 dates: August 15-18.

TIMES: Whenever.

ADMISSION: Free. Parking is wherever you can find it—*off* the road.

LOCATION: All along US Hwy 127 through three states: Kentucky, Tennessee, and Alabama. When you see a collection of sellers, it's there.

DESCRIPTION: Started in 1987 as a way to get travelers off the interstate and back onto the country roads by Fentress County's former County Executive Mike Walker and some of his friends, this market of thousands of dealers in "oddities and antiques," yard sale unloaders, and whoever and whatever else shows up, sells everything old and/or crafty. They are trying to limit the offerings to antiques and oddities and eliminate "used clothes" and the like.

If you wish to travel the entire 450-mile route, start in Covington KY and work your way down to around Gadsden AL. There are plenty of food vendors. This has to be "the World's Longest Outdoor Sale."

Rules of the road: 1) *Drive Cautiously*—then you won't hit pedestrians or miss that goody you've been looking for. 2) Be *extremely* careful crossing the road! 3) Use your turn signals and don't stop suddenly for that goody (have a lookout who can give you ample warning). Otherwise, you may be dealing with insurance companies and wreckers rather than rare Ming.

DEALER RATES: Whatever the local landowner charges. Check out the website for a list of contacts in each state (it's huge) or call.

CONTACT: Southern Segment Coordinator at (205) 549-0391 for AL. Or Wanda (head coordinator), Fentress County Chamber of Commerce, PO Box 1294, Jamestown TN 38556-1294. Tel: (800) 327-3945. Web: jamestowntn.org.

JASPER
Kelly's Flea Market

DATES: Wednesday, Saturday and Sunday, year round, and the occasional holiday Monday.

TIMES: Sunup on Saturday to sundown on Sunday, really. Wednesday 7:00 AM-3:00 PM.

ADMISSION: Free. Parking is free.

LOCATION: Hwy 78. Just 3 miles east of the city limits of Jasper, 6 miles from the city center or 25 NW of Birmingham on US 78.

DESCRIPTION: Opened in April 1978, this outdoor market has 43 booths outside and under sheds with dealers selling antiques, produce, farm and home needs—described as "yard sale heaven." It is a "very laid-back, friendly, popular, family market." The market started when June wanted to stay home with her small child, quit work and had a yard sale at Mom's. Mrs. Kelly was so friendly that soon others joined her. No problem, it still grew!

DEALER RATES: $4 in the shed with electric, $2 for a table. If you want to reserve, do so, but if you don't, grab your spot by 7:00 AM or it will be gone! There are others waiting to use it.

CONTACT: Ray and June Fowler, 10016 Hwy 78, Jasper AL 35501-8158. Tel: (205) 483-6045.

KILLEN
Uncle Charlie's Flea Market

DATES: Every Saturday and Sunday.

TIMES: 9:00 AM-5:00 PM.

ADMISSION: Free. Ample free parking is available.

LOCATION: On Hwy 72 W, 5 miles east of Florence, in the Killen area.

DESCRIPTION: This indoor market started in 1982 and accommodates approximately 400 dealers. They exhibit a wide variety of items, including antiques, collectibles, arts and crafts, new merchandise and fresh produce. For your convenience, there are food and handicapped-accessible restrooms available on the premises.

DEALER RATES: $25 for 10' × 10' space per weekend. Reservations are required.

CONTACT: Tom Mabry, PO Box 190, Killen AL 35645. Tel: 1-800-542-2848. Day of show call or fax (256) 757-1771.

MADISON
Limestone Flea Market

DATES: Saturday and Sunday.

TIMES: 9:00 AM-5:00 PM.

ADMISSION: Free. Parking is free.

LOCATION: Hwy 72 at Burgreen Rd between Athens and Huntsville.

DESCRIPTION: Opened in July 1991, this indoor market of 450 booths filled with over 200 dealers sells antiques, collectibles, some garage sale goodies, furniture (with a separate Furniture Mart), crafts, coins, pool tables, oriental rugs, household goods and accessories, and lots of new merchandise. As Rosa says, "If it's 'hot,' it's here." In case of need, there are five concession stands and handicapped-accessible restrooms.

DEALER RATES: $41 for a 10' × 8' space for the weekend. There are also 10' × 9' and 10' × 10' spaces, as well. Reservations are required.

There are dealer showers and facilities, 2 camper hookups and overnight parking.

CONTACT: Limestone Flea Market Inc, 30030 US Hwy 72, Madison AL 35756. Tel: (256) 233-5183. Fax: (256) 233-1415. Email: info@limestone-fleamarket.com. Web: www.limestone-fleamarket.com.

MOBILE
Flea Market Mobile

DATES: Saturday and Sunday, year round. Rain or shine.
TIMES: 9:00 AM-5:00 PM.
ADMISSION: Free. Parking is free.
LOCATION: 401 Schillingers Rd N. Take I-10 to I-65, get off at Airport Blvd, about 8 miles west of I-65 take a right turn on Schillingers Rd. Follow the signs!

DESCRIPTION: Opened in 1988, this outdoor market is considered the largest in Alabama, with 700 dealers selling under cover. The goods run the gamut: antiques, collectibles, jewelry, new merchandise, "everything." There are three full-size concession stands serving the hungry.
DEALER RATES: $20-$25 per weekend for 8' × 10' space or $30-$35 for a larger size.
CONTACT: Flea Market Mobile, 401 Schillingers Rd N, Mobile AL 33608. Tel: (251) 633-7533. Fax: (251) 639-0570.

SCOTTSBORO
First Monday Flea Market

DATES: First Monday and preceding Sunday of each month.
TIMES: 8:00 AM until dark.
ADMISSION: Free. Parking is also free.
LOCATION: Courthouse Square in the center of downtown Scottsboro.
DESCRIPTION: Said to be the second-oldest market in the southeast, this is another classic 100-plus-year-old outdoor market started when the hanging judge showed up, held court and dispatched the bad guys, which of course brought all the locals to watch the show—and naturally, trade stuff. Although the court system has evolved somewhat, the market keeps going and going. From 250 dealers in winter to 300 dealers in the summer sell a variety of antiques, collectibles and secondhand items. For your convenience, food is served on the premises.

DEALER RATES: $15 per parking space. Availability of space is on a first-come, first-served basis.
CONTACT: Gayle Swafford, First Monday Flea Market, 23123 John T Reid Pkwy, Scottsboro AL 35768. Tel: (256) 574-4468. Fax: (256) 574-4339.

SELMA
Selma Flea Market

DATES: Every Saturday, year round. Rain or shine.
TIMES: 5:00 AM-until.
ADMISSION: Free. Parking is also free.
LOCATION: Selma By-Pass at River Rd.

DESCRIPTION: This market opened in 1986 in beautiful historic Selma. It attracts from 170 to 200 plus dealers in sheltered spaces selling about 50% antiques and collectibles; the rest is handmade crafts, fresh produce and meats, new merchandise, garage sale and household items. There is a snack bar on the premises, restrooms, as well as overnight parking and an RV park on site.
DEALER RATES: $8 per 10' × 10' booth. Reservations are requested.
CONTACT: Gary Maluda, Selma Flea Market, 606 River Rd, Selma AL 36703. Tel: (334) 875-0500.

SUMMERDALE
Highway 59 Flea Market

DATES: Saturday and Sunday, year round.
TIMES: 8:00 AM-4:00 PM.
ADMISSION: Free. Parking is also free.
LOCATION: On Hwy 59, between Foley and Robertdale, 13 miles north of Gulf Shores.

DESCRIPTION: This very busy market, "the best in this part of the country," has been in existence since the summer of 1985. Under new ownership since 2001, the market accommodates approximately 300 to 400 dealers outdoors but under cover, and 35 individual shops. They do not specialize in one particular area; instead they sell a wide variety of goods. Included are antiques, fine art, reproductions, and fresh produce, to name a few. The market is located on 33 acres, which also includes a 10,000- square-foot air-conditioned/heated mall. There is a restaurant on the premises with handicapped-accessible restrooms as well as a RV park with reasonable rates ($165/month for vendors) and full hookups.
DEALER RATES: $10 for 10' × 10' space per day, per table. Reservations are not required.
CONTACT: Don Phillips, Highway 59 Flea Market, 804 State Hwy 59 S, Summerdale AL 36580-4174. Tel: (334) 989-6642. Fax: (334) 989-6809.

OTHER FLEA MARKETS

We know or have heard about these markets, but have not personally contacted each one, as we have the markets with descriptions. If you plan to visit one of the markets listed below, *please call first* to make sure they are still open. Flea markets do come and go. While they were open when we went to press, they may not be later. We can't be responsible. *Call first!*

Alexander City: Flint Hill Flea Market, 4329 Dadeville Rd #A. Tel: (256) 234-2950.
Birmingham: Ensley Flea Market, 1924 Ave E. Tel: (205) 595-2666.
Birmingham: Tanniehill Flea Market, 1708 Ave D. Tel: (205) 780-9274.
Camp Hill: People's Flea Market, 161 S Main St. Tel: (256) 896-4006.
Centre: Castaways, 1470 W Main St Tel: (256) 927-7337.
Centre: Flea Market, 260 Cedar Bluff Rd. Tel: (256) 927-2117.
Centre: Garage Sale, 469 Cedar Bluff Rd. Tel: (256) 927-6442.
Cherokee: Cherokee Flea Market, Hwy 72. Tel: (256) 370-7858.
Childersburg: Cotney's Flea Market, 3160 Desoto Caverns Pkwy. Tel: (256) 378-5151.
Collinsville: Collinsville Trade Day, 1102 S Valley Ave. Tel: (256) 524-2127.
Cottonwood: Tri State Flea Market, 12657 S US Hwy 231. Tel: (334) 793-1144.
Deatsville: Oates Flea Market, 2351 US Hwy 31 N. Tel: (334) 358-1488.
Eclectic: Granny & Gramp's Flea Market, 647 Kowaliga Rd. Tel: (334) 541-2177.
Enterprise: Glover Ave Flea Market, 723 Glover Ave. Tel: (334) 393-7878.
Eufaula: Corner Flea Market, 439 S Randolph Ave. Tel: (334) 687-0071.
Gadsden: Flamingo Flea Market, 1818 US Hwy 431 S. Tel: (256) 492-0200.
Goodwater: Owen Flea Market, Railroad St. Tel: (256) 839-5158.
Hazel Green: Hazel Green Flea Market, 13954 Hwy 231 431 N. Tel: (256) 829-0900.
Heflin: I-20 Trade Day, 100 Cheaha State Park Dr. Tel: (256) 253-2286.
Huntsville: Huntsville Flea Market, 3515 Memorial Pkwy NW. Tel: (256) 858-8506.
Killen: North Alabama Flea Market, 7730 Hwy 72. Tel: (256) 757-1040.
Lanett: The Korner Flea Market, 1008 County Road 299. Tel: (334) 576-6054.
Leighton: Galaxy Flea Market, 8910 2nd St. Tel: (256) 446-5343.
Mobile: Stokes Flea Market, 236 S Wilson Ave. Tel: (334) 457-8130.
Montgomery: Crystal Palace Flea Market, 2373 Cong W L Dickinson Dr. Tel: (334) 279-1417.
Montgomery: Fantasy Land Flea Market, 3620 Atlanta Hwy. Tel: (334) 409-0017 or (334) 272-8841.
Montgomery: Southland Flea Market, 32 Perry Ct. Tel: (334) 288-9000.
Opelika: Station Point Flea Market, 931 S Railroad Ave. Tel: (334) 745-4000.

Phenix City: Valley Flea & Farmers Market, 3864 US Hwy 80 W. Tel: (334) 298-3728.

Smiths: Lee County Flea Market, Hwy 431 N & 280 W. Tel: (334) 291-7780.

Sylacauga: Coaling Road Flea Market, 1923 Coaling Rd. Tel: (256) 245-2867.

Sylacauga: Cotton Gin, 523 North Broadway Ave. Tel: (256) 245-1588.

Talladega: Coconuts, 204 Battle St W. Tel: (256) 362-5886.

Theodore: Hwy 90 Flea Market, 5751 Hwy 90 W. Tel: (334) 653-6589.

Tuscaloosa: Tuscaloosa County Flea Market, 1033 19th Ave E. Tel: (205) 553-9206.

Tuscumbia: B & J Flea Market, 5910 Hwy 43. Tel: (256) 381-8506.

Tuscumbia: Gene's Grocery & Flea Market, 17250 Hwy 72. Tel: (256) 381-3632.

Valley: Sam's Swap Shop, 10091 US Highway 29 N. Tel: (334) 756-7446.

Westover: 280 Flea Market, Hwy 442. Tel: 205-678-672?

Wetumpka: Blue Ridge Treasure Hunt, 2606 US Highway 231. Tel: (334) 514-0025.

Wetumpka: Goolsby Farmers & Flea Market, Hwy 231. Tel: (334) 567-5858.

Wetumpka: Santuck Flea Market, 7300 Central Plank Rd. Tel: (334) 567-7400.

ALASKA

ANCHORAGE

Anchorage Downtown Saturday Market

DATES: Every Saturday from mid-May through mid-September.

TIMES: 10:00 AM-6:00 PM.

ADMISSION: Free. Parking is free if you can find it, otherwise there are pay lots at $2 per day nearby.

LOCATION: In parking lot at 3rd and E Sts across from Hilton Hotel.

DESCRIPTION: This market, started in 1993, hosts approximately 285 vendors in 327 booths selling antiques and collectibles, new merchandise, jewelry, native arts, fine art (expensive stuff!), fancy feet (handmade and decorated footwear), crafts, and fresh produce. You can't possibly starve as there are 35 food vendors, including the enormously popular Kettle Corn (popcorn popped with sugar, really), and fresh seafood (seriously fresh!). After all the food sampling, the port-a-potties may come in handy.

DEALER RATES: $55 per 9' × 15' space per day, $40 per day under longer contract. There is a huge waiting list for spaces, so reservations are mandatory. However, there are usually up to 20 standby spaces if you get there early (before 5:30 AM, they might get a bit perturbed).

CONTACT: Bill Webb, Saturday Markets, PO Box 102440, Anchorage AK 99510. Tel: (907) 272-5634. Fax: (907) 272-5635. Email: saturdaymarket@alaskalife.net.

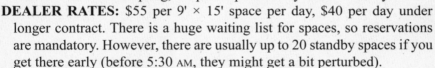

Anchorage Downtown Wednesday Market

DATES: Every Wednesday from Memorial Day through Labor Day Wednesday.

TIMES: 10:00 AM-6:00 PM.

ADMISSION: Free. Parking is free if you can find it, otherwise there are pay lots at $.50 per hour, maximum $5 per day nearby.

LOCATION: Covering 6 blocks along 4th Ave from C and F Sts, and along F and D Sts between 4th and 5th Sts.

DESCRIPTION: This market, started in 1999, hosts approximately 100-plus vendors in 150 booths selling antiques and collectibles, new merchandise, jewelry, native arts, fine art (expensive stuff!), fancy feet (handmade and decorated footwear), crafts, and fresh produce. You can't possibly starve, as there are 35 food vendors, including an open pit barbecue selling Huli Chicken and KC Ribs, the enormously popular Kettle Corn (popcorn popped with sugar), and fresh seafood (really fresh!). After all the food sampling, the port-a-potties may come in handy. (Yes, these are mostly the same vendors, same management, same almost everything, just different location.)

DEALER RATES: $95 per 10' × 10' space per day, $75 per day under longer contract. There is a huge waiting list for spaces, so reservations are mandatory. However, there are usually up to 20 standby spaces if you get there early (before 5:30 AM, they might get a bit perturbed).

CONTACT: Bill Webb, Wednesday Markets, PO Box 102440, Anchorage AK 99510. Tel: (907) 272-5634. Fax: (907) 272-5635. Email: saturdaymarket@alaskalife.net.

ARIZONA

CASA GRANDE
Shoppers Barn and Swap Meet
DATES: Saturday and Sunday.
TIMES: 7:00 AM-4:00 PM.
LOCATION: 13480 W Jimmie Kerr Blvd, off I10, Exit 198, between Tucson and Phoenix.
ADMISSION: Free. Parking is free.
DESCRIPTION: Open since 1983 under the same management, this outdoor market sells antiques, collectibles, new and used toys and merchandise, used auto parts, ceramics, and appliances. They are in the country, yet close to town, on a main road and next to many amenities. Restrooms are available.

DEALER RATES: $5 per day for center space, $7 per day for corner space, tables are $1 per day. First come, first served. There is security and the grounds are locked at night. Dealers can set up Friday morning. There are RV spaces available Friday through Sunday at $29 with electric.
CONTACT: Bud Gray, Shoppers Barn and Swap Meet, 13480 W Jimmie Kerr Blvd, Casa Grande AZ 85222-9433. Tel: (520) 836-1934. Fax: (520) 836-4938.

GLENDALE
Glendale 9 Swap Meet
DATES: Saturday and Sunday.
TIMES: 5:00 AM until.
LOCATION: At 5650 N 55th Ave. South of Bethany Home Rd on 55th Ave. Northwest of Phoenix.
ADMISSION: $.50 per person, children 11 and under free.
DESCRIPTION: This outdoor market of 300-400 in summer, 500-600 in winter on Sunday their big day (less on Saturdays), dealers sells about half new and half used merchandise including Indian crafts, antiques, collectibles, produce, used and new clothing, and garage sale treasures. There is a snack bar, 3 concessions and some hot dog, soda and coffee carts roaming the market. Handicapped-accessible restrooms may just come in handy.

DEALER RATES: $10 for a 27' × 15' space on Saturday, $15 on Sunday. Reservations are available on a monthly or yearly basis. Vendors enter from 4:00 AM.
CONTACT: Nancy Crane, Glendale 9 Swap Meet, 5650 N 55 Ave, Glendale AZ 85301. Tel: (623) 931-0877. Fax: (623) 931-8135.

GOODYEAR
Goodyear Market Place Swap Meet

DATES: Friday, Saturday and Sunday.

TIMES: 7:00 AM-4:00 PM.

ADMISSION: Free. Parking is free.

LOCATION: 17605 W McDowell Rd. Off I-10, Exit 124 Cotton Lane.

DESCRIPTION: Opened in 2000, this market has 1600 booth spaces filled with dealers selling just about everything, literally, under the sun, from antiques to the latest new stuff. There is plenty of food, as well as handicapped-accessible restrooms in Arizona's newest attraction.

DEALER RATES: $25 and up per space.

CONTACT: Tricia Curran, General Manager, Goodyear Market Place Swap Meet, 17605 W McDowell Rd, Goodyear, AZ 85338-6707. Tel: (623) 853-1488. Email: goodyearswap@aol.com. Web: www.fleaamerica.com/goodyear.html.

MESA
Mesa Market Place Swap Meet

DATES: Friday, Saturday and Sunday

TIMES: 7:00 AM-4:00 PM.

ADMISSION: Free. Parking is free.

LOCATION: 10550 E Baseline. East on Hwy 60 to Exit 193-Signal Butte Rd. Make a right at light to Baseline Rd, then turn right, entrance is on right.

DESCRIPTION: This covered market at the base of the Superstition Mountains is spread over 55 acres. To keep shoppers comfortable in the summer while shopping their 1,600 booths, there is a mister system (outside air conditioning!). The dealers sell just about everything from antiques to new merchandise, food, furniture, clothing, used goodies, whatever. One restaurant and six snack bars recharge the shopping batteries, while handicapped-accessible restrooms deal with other issues. So family oriented is this market that they hold special events to raise money for local non-profit organizations. Just in case you get bored (?), there is free entertainment.

DEALER RATES: $25 and up per space. Reservations are not required.

CONTACT: Mesa Market Place Swap Meet, 10550 E Baseline, Mesa AZ 85208. Tel: (480) 380-5572. Fax: (480) 380-5578. Email: mesamarke@aol.com. Web: www.fleaamerica.com/mesa.html.

MOJAVE
Mojave Swap Meet

DATES: Every day but Monday.

TIMES: 7:30 AM-6:00 PM. Saturday till 10:00 PM.

ADMISSION: Free. Parking is free.

LOCATION: 5005 Hwy 95, 12 miles south of Laughlin, Nevada or 12 miles north of Needles, California. One mile south of the Safeway.

DESCRIPTION: Started in 1987, this indoor/outdoor market has 150 dealers in winter and 30 dealers in summer selling antiques, collectibles, produce, coins, stamps, cards, garage sale goodies, crafts, furniture, toys, gift items, jewelry (custom gold), flowers, a fix-it shop (the manager's), appliances, and new merchandise. There are 18 stores in 6 buildings. Roberto's Tacos Restaurant and handicapped-accessible restrooms round out the facilities. Aiming for newer merchandise to accommodate the locals needs, as there isn't any other shopping nearby.

DEALER RATES: $10 per 12' × 24' space daily; $65 monthly; or $125 monthly for shed with a 12' × 24' space. Reservations are not required.

CONTACT: Mojave Swap Meet, 5005 Hwy 95, Mojave AZ 86426. Tel: (520) 768-3103.

PHOENIX
American Park N Swap

DATES: Every Wednesday, Friday, Saturday, and Sunday. Rain or shine.

TIMES: Wednesday 4:00 PM-10:00 PM; Friday 6:00 AM-2:00 PM; Saturday and Sunday 6:00 AM-4:00 PM.

ADMISSION: Friday free, otherwise $1 per person, 12 and under free. Parking is free.

LOCATION: 3801 E Washington St at 40th and Washington. From Loop 202 go south on 40th St.

DESCRIPTION: This show first opened in 1961. It is both an indoor and an outdoor market that accommodates from 1,500 dealers in summer to 2,500 in winter. Billed as "the largest open air flea market in the southwest." They added a shaded structure to cover half the total area of the market, making shopping a cooler experience. Whatever you want, you will probably find at this market. There are dealers selling art, crystal, jewelry, musical instruments, toys, clothes, pictures, housewares, garage sale items, weight loss products and tools. Finally, when you grow hungry from shopping, hit one of the many food courts, where there are many different types of foods available, from Mexican to Indian Fry Bread to American burgers and fries. Handicapped-accessible restrooms abound.

DEALER RATES: $15 and up per 9' × 21' booth per day, Wednesday, Saturday and Sunday, $5 and up on Friday. Reservations are suggested.

CONTACT: Richard K Hogue, PO Box 61953, Phoenix AZ 85034-1953. Tel: (602) 273-1250 ext 49 or 1-800-772-0852 out of state. Email: kpw26@aol.com. Web: www.americanparknswap.com.

Fairgrounds Antique Market

DATES: Third weekend of January, February, May, September, and November.

TIMES: Saturday 9:00 AM-5:00 PM; Sunday 10:00 AM-4:00 PM except in summer.

ADMISSION: $3 for adults; $2 seniors, 14 and under free with parent.

LOCATION: 1826 W McDowell Rd, State Fairgrounds, at the intersection of Grand Ave, 19th Ave and McDowell Rd.

DESCRIPTION: This show started in June 1986. The indoor market currently draws over 100 dealers in summer and 200 in winter. Dealers set up to sell a variety of antiques and collectibles. Food is served on the premises and there is full overnight RV camping.

DEALER RATES: $140 for a 16' × 10½' space. Additional spaces cost $35. $10 more for a corner space. Add on $45 for electricity. Tables and freestanding pegboards are $10. Reservations are strongly advised. They hold several other antiques only shows around Arizona.

CONTACT: Arthur or Linda Schwartz, Artlin, Inc & Jack Black Enterprises, PO Box 39005, Phoenix AZ 85069-9005. Tel: (602) 943-1766 within AZ or 1-800-678-9987 nationwide. Email: phxantique@jackblack.com. Web: www.jackblack.com.

Paradise Valley Swap Meet

DATES: Saturday and Sunday.

TIMES: 5:30 AM-3:30 PM.

LOCATION: 18615 Cave Creek Rd. Go 1 mile north of Bell Rd and Cave Creek Rd. On the northeast corner of Cave Creek Rd and Union Hills Rd.

ADMISSION: Free. Parking is free.

DESCRIPTION: This outdoor market, in operation for over 26 years, has 132 spaces and hosts from 40 dealers in summer to capacity in winter. They sell everything from antiques and collectibles to soaps, tools, jewelry, boxed foods, produce, t-shirts, garage sale, new merchandise, crafts, and the occasional reptile. There's a full concession stand to quell the munchies, and handicapped-accessible restrooms.

DEALER RATES: $10 per 10' × 10' or 10' × 29' space; corner space for $15; double space at $20 to $25 for 20' × 18' space; drop-off space at $10 for 10' × 10' or 10' × 15'. Reservations are a must in the winter, not required in the summer. Office is open Thursday and Friday 10:00 AM-1:00 PM.

CONTACT: Paradise Valley Swap Meet, 18615 N Cave Creek Rd, Phoenix AZ 85050. Tel: (602) 569-0052.

PRESCOTT VALLEY
Peddler's Pass, Inc

DATES: Friday (except during January and February), Saturday and Sunday, year round.

TIMES: Sunup to sundown.

ADMISSION: Free. Parking is free.

LOCATION: 6201 E Hwy 69, 6 miles east of Prescott on Hwy 69 in Prescott Valley.

DESCRIPTION: This market of 350 dealers in summer and 150 in winter started in 1987. The dealers feature a good mix of new and used merchandise and fresh produce with a strong market for antiques and collectibles. They even sell used cars! When the heat is too much in valley markets, dealers head up to the cooler mountains of Peddler's Pass. They are the "largest market in Northern Arizona," a clean, neat and well-organized "no hassle" market. They have added a 3,000-square-foot building to house a farmers' market pavilion. One big concession serves home-cooked food on the premises. There are handicapped-accessible restrooms on site.

DEALER RATES: $15 per 9' × 9' farmers' market space; $13 per 20' × 20'; $15-$18 per 25' × 20' corner and $23 per 40' × 20' space. The largest space also comes with electric and water hookups. Reservations are suggested. Vendors can camp out on their site from Thursday noon until the market closes 5:30 PM on Sunday.

CONTACT: Suzy Arnold, Peddler's Pass Inc, 2201 Clubhouse Dr, Prescott Valley AZ 86314-2921. Tel: (928) 775-4117 Wednesday through Sunday.

> **Versatility**
> Years ago, Ron, a dealer who painted pictures on trucks at the market, was approached by a neighboring dealer with a very sore tooth. Ron grabbed some pliers and removed the offending ivory. Later that same day, he married a young couple in the pavilion.

QUARTZSITE
The Main Event

DATES: The Big Show is held annually the last full two weeks in January. The area is open every day of the year, with 14 hearty vendors in 7 shops.

TIMES: 8:00 AM-6:00 PM (essentially dawn to just before dark).

ADMISSION: Free. Parking is $3.

LOCATION: On I-10 (Business 10), Mile Post 17.

DESCRIPTION: This Annual Gemboree first began in 1982. It is held on 100 acres of land with over 1,000 dealers from all corners of the globe and is well known as one of the largest gem sales in the country, as well as one of the most exciting flea markets. Dealers set up to sell a virtually limitless range of antiques and collectibles, including bottles, coins, hobby crafts, etc., along with lapidary equipment and thousands of specimens of gems and minerals from as far away as Brazil, Australia and Hong Kong. Food is served on the premises. Camping facilities for buyers as well as dealers with a fee for overnight parking.

DEALER RATES: Starts at $484.50-$612.50, including state sales tax for 18' × 32' space, which includes electric, water and sewer hookups, depending on space size and location. Reservations are absolutely necessary as they sell out early, as in years in advance for the best locations.

CONTACT: The Main Event, PO Box 2801, Quartzsite AZ 85346-2801. Tel: (928) 927-5213. Fax: (928) 927-4496. Email: mainevent@redrivernet.com. Web: www.quartzsite.com.

Tanque Verde Swap Meet

DATES: Thursday, Friday, Saturday and Sunday, year round, weather permitting.

TIMES: Thursday and Friday 3:00 PM-11:00 PM; Saturday and Sunday two sessions: 7:00 AM-3:00 PM and 3:00 PM-11:00 PM.

ADMISSION: Free. Parking is free.

LOCATION: 4100 S Palo Verde Rd. Just south of Ajo Way. Or take I-10 to Palo Verde N Exit 264B, go north 1 mile.

DESCRIPTION: This large outdoor family-owned market started in 1974 and is now considered a local tourist attraction as well as a city and county landmark. Its 800 dealers sell everything from antiques and collectibles to fresh produce, from unique Southwestern items to handcrafted treasures to new and used merchandise—"Everything from toothpicks to houses, except processed food." There are 12 restaurants and snack bars. A well-equipped cafeteria, The Food Mercado, creates homemade Mexican dishes and assorted specials every weekend, all at very reasonable prices. They just opened an outdoor barbecue facility and rebuilt their handicapped-accessible restrooms into big, fresh, clean facilities.

DEALER RATES: $12 per 11' × 26' space; $14 per 11' × 35' space; $16 per corner space. Reservations are not required, unless for monthly reservations.

CONTACT: Tanque Verde Swap Meet, PO Box 19095, Tucson AZ 85731-9095. Tel: (520) 294-4252. Fax: (520) 294-2358. Email: tanqueverdeswapmeet @tanqueverdeswapmeet.com. Web: www.tanqueverdeswapmeet.com.

Tohono O'Odham Swapmeet

DATES: Saturday and Sunday.

TIMES: 5:00 AM to whenever.

ADMISSION: Free. Parking is free.

LOCATION: 5721 S Westover Ave. On the corner of W Drexel and S Westover Aves.

DESCRIPTION: First started in the 1970s as the Westover Swap Meet and now under new management, this outdoor swap meet set on 185 acres attracts several hundred dealers in winter with 67 permanent monthly dealers and somewhat less in the hot summer. The rest is garage sale goodies, storage buy-outs, tailgate goods, collectibles, some antiques, produce, fruits, birds, lumber, paint, swords, knives, Indian crafts, and whatever. There is a Mexican concession and handicapped-accessible restrooms on site as well as plenty of vendors selling prepared foods throughout the market.

DEALER RATES: $10 per 18' × 28' space, $12 for a corner space. There is plenty of room for RVs. Reservations are not required.

CONTACT: Tohono O'Odham Swapmeet, 2161 W Drexel, Tucson AZ 85746. Tel: (520) 908-8646. Fax: (520) 908-8864.

YUMA
Yuma Park 'N Swap

DATES: Winter: Thursday through Sunday. Summer: Saturday and Sunday

TIMES: Winter: 6:00 AM-4:00 PM. Summer: 6:00 AM-2:00 PM.

ADMISSION: Free in summer, there is a fee in winter. Parking is free.

LOCATION: 4000 S 4th Ave at Yuma Greyhound Park. Take 4th Ave to 40th St. Call for exact directions if you need them.

DESCRIPTION: This family oriented, friendly open-air market is considered the "biggest and best flea market in Southwestern Arizona." In the busy winter months, when the weather is at its finest, this market is filled with over 1,000 vendors selling just about everything to an average of 15,000 buyers. Summers are quieter as the weather is hotter. However, the bargains are generally greater and the crowds are less large. There are plenty of food concessions and handicapped-accessible restrooms when needed.

DEALER RATES: $10 and up per day. First-come, first-served.

CONTACT: Sylvia Parada, Reservations, Yuma Park 'N Swap, 4000 S 4 Ave, Yuma AZ 85365. Tel: (602)726-4655 or outside AZ (800) 722-6811. Fax: (602) 344-0115. Email: bill@gresser.com. Web: www.ypns.com.

OTHER FLEA MARKETS

We know or have heard about these markets, but have not personally contacted each one, as we have the markets with descriptions. If you plan to visit one of the markets listed below, *please call first* to make sure they are still open. Flea markets do come and go. While they were open when we went to press, they may not be later. We can't be responsible. *Call first!*

Holbrook: Holbrook Flea Market, 1251 W Hopi Dr. Tel: (928) 524-9098.

Nogales: Swapmeet El Campo, 51 Maritza. Tel: (520) 761-4183.

Phoenix: El Gran Mercado 35th Ave, 1820 S 35th Ave. Tel: (602) 352-1228.

ARKANSAS

BATESVILLE
Old South Flea Market

DATES: Every Friday, Saturday and Sunday, year round. Rain or shine.
TIMES: Friday 9:30 AM-6:00 PM, Saturday 8:30 AM-6:00 PM, and Sunday 11:00 AM-6:00 PM.
ADMISSION: Free. Free parking is provided.
LOCATION: 661 Bethesda Rd, on Hwy 106.
DESCRIPTION: This indoor/outdoor market first opened in 1980, has recently relocated to their new building, currently accommodates about 140 dealers. Everything from antiques and collectibles to new merchandise, from fine art to fresh produce can be bought here. Snacks are served on the premises and handicapped-accessible restrooms round out the amenities.
DEALER RATES: Booth size is 10' × 10'; $10 per day, $25 per weekend, $60 for 4 weekends. Advance reservations are required during winter months.
CONTACT: Mark Davis, Old South Flea Market, 661 Bethesda Rd, Batesville AR 72501-6713. Tel: (870) 793-7508.

HOT SPRINGS
Higdon Ferry Flea Market

DATES: Daily.
TIMES: 10:00 AM-5:00 PM.
ADMISSION: Free. Parking is free.
LOCATION: 2138 Higdon Ferry Rd. Just off Rt 7 S. If you are coming from town, it's the first street on the right past and opposite the Hot Springs Mall and over the hill. If you are coming the other way, it's a left turn before the mall. Go behind the building, under the skating rink.
DESCRIPTION: Opened in 1986 on 11 acres, this market of over 70 dealers sells mostly antiques and collectibles, furniture, glassware, some reproductions and plenty of standard flea market fare. No food concessions, but two handicapped-accessible restrooms are on site.
DEALER RATES: $175 for a 12' × 24' single space per month. $75 a month for a 8' × 12' space, $125 for 8' × 20'. Reservations are requested. There are a few outdoor spaces for traveling dealers at $5 per day.
CONTACT: Higdon Ferry Flea Market, 2138 Higdon Ferry Rd, Hot Springs AR 71913-7202. Tel: (501) 525-9927.

JONESBORO
Farrville Flea Market

DATES: Daily, except Christmas.

TIMES: Weekdays 10:00 AM-5:00 PM, Saturday 10:00 AM-6:00 PM, Sunday 12:00 PM-6:00 PM.

ADMISSION: Free. Parking is free.

LOCATION: 5055 Hwy 49 N. Take Hwy 49N between Jonesboro and Brookland on Farrville curve.

DESCRIPTION: Opened in 1996, this indoor market houses 115 booth spaces, filled with 75-80 dealers selling antiques, collectibles, garage sale goodies, stamps, cards, coins, and new merchandise. About 90% old stuff with a retired banker selling only quality antiques. This is quite the "upper level" shopping experience. One vendor specializes in good, clean, used toys—not vintage.

DEALER RATES: $5-$25 per week depending on location in the store plus 10% commission. Reservations are a must, in case anything opens. $3 to set up outside if you are intrepid. January through March are the big months.

CONTACT: John or Merilyn Hancock, Farrville Flea Market, 5055 Hwy 49 N, Brookland AR 72417. Tel: (870) 931-9307.

JUDSONIA
Thackerland Flea Market

DATES: Saturday and Sunday.

TIMES: 7:00 AM-5:00 PM.

ADMISSION: Free. Parking is free.

LOCATION: 666 Hwy 367. Only 50 miles north of Little Rock.

DESCRIPTION: Open for 14 years, this market is noted for its wonderful antiques collected and auctioned on the first and third Thursdays by the owner. Hundreds of dealers set up indoors in two long newly air-conditioned buildings, outdoors and under sheds selling glassware, more antiques, collectibles, tools, coins, and more. This is a haunt for dealers looking to replenish their supplies. During the summer it's more like a carnival, with all the music and carryings-on. A small restaurant is on site and serves the vendors during non-market hours. Large restrooms will come in handy. On summer weekends there is entertainment and dancing for everyone. Gary is always adding to the market. They used to have dealers selling ostriches, pot-bellied pigs and other "exotic" animals during the appropriate fads, which was entertaining in itself. However, as the fads have fazed, the market has quietly enjoyed their newfound "peace and quiet." (There's still the awesome music!)

DEALER RATES: $12.50 inside space, $6 for outside space and it varies for the sheds depending on size. There is RV space with arrangements for vendors as well as bathing facilities. Reservations are suggested.

CONTACT: Gary Thacker, Thackerland Flea Market, PO Box 791, Judsonia AR 72081-0791. Tel: (501) 729-3063. Fax: (501) 729-3154.

LITTLE ROCK
Memphis Flea Market
The BIG One at Little Rock Expo Center

DATES: Saturday and Sunday, the second weekend of the month. There are special shows on other weekends, call for the schedule.

TIMES: 8:00 AM-6:00 PM.

ADMISSION: $1 per person. Children 12 and under free. Parking is free.

LOCATION: Little Rock Expo Center, 13000 I-30. From Memphis take I-40 to I-30 to Exit 128, then continue west 1 mile; market is on right.

DESCRIPTION: Over 500 vendors come to sell antiques, collectibles, clothing, garage sale goodies, books, crafts, furniture, used and new merchandise. There are concessions to feed you and handicapped-accessible restrooms when the time comes.

DEALER RATES: $40 per weekend for outside spaces, $60 for regular, $70 for premium. Reservations are required. Regular office hours are Monday through Friday 8:30 AM-5:00 PM. Also during the market week including Friday 9:00 AM-9:00 PM, Saturday and Sunday 7:00 AM-4:30 PM. Inside spaces are 10' × 10'. Outside spaces are available on a first-come, first-served basis. Tables are available for $6 each, per weekend, through the office.

CONTACT: Memphis Flea Market, Little Rock Expo Center, 13000 I-30, Little Rock AR 72209. Tel: (501) 455-1001 for tape, 455-1002 or fax: (501) 455-0162. Email: memflea@aol.com. Web: www.americanparknswap.com.

PRAIRIE GROVE
Daisies and Olives Antiques and Gifts Flea Market

DATES: Daily, except Thanksgiving, Christmas and Easter.

TIMES: 9:00 AM-5:00 PM, Sunday 10:00 AM-5:00 PM.

ADMISSION: Free. Plenty of free parking.

LOCATION: 129-135 E Buchanan St, on Hwy 62 W in Prairie Grove.

DESCRIPTION: Formerly known as The Battlefield Flea Market, this market opened in 1990. It is owned and managed by the Cooper-Ritchie family and has 50-plus dealers, located in two buildings (one a 90-year-old livery stable, the other a 105-year-old theater), are loaded with lots of antiques, collectibles, primitives, furniture, vintage clothing, and "dust collectibles." The market is named after "two poor ole ladies" just for the

record. Restrooms are on site and if you get hungry there is a café a half
block away or a fast-food place in the other direction a half block.

DEALER RATES: Call for rates. Reservations are required. There is a
waiting list.

CONTACT: Daisies and Olives Antiques and Gifts Flea Market, PO Box
688, Prairie Grove AR 72753-0688. Tel: (501) 846-1800. Email:
mritchie@pgtc.net.

Historical Note
The Battle of Prairie Grove was fought here during the Civil War.
   There is a state park next door commemorating the battlefield
   site.

SPRINGDALE
Oak Grove Flea Market

DATES: Saturday and Sunday, year round.

TIMES: 8:00 AM-4:00 PM.

ADMISSION: Free. Parking is also free.

LOCATION: 872 Oak Grove Rd. Corner of Oak Grove and Elm Springs
Rds.

DESCRIPTION: Considered one of the largest and oldest of northwest
Arkansas's flea markets, having opened in 1977, this indoor/outdoor market hosts between 60 and 100 dealers depending on the season. They sell
antiques, collectibles, furniture, fresh produce, crafts and new merchandise. Two concessions serve American or Mexican food. Handicapped-
accessible restrooms are available.

DEALER RATES: $8 per 12' × 14' space per day, outside; $85 per month
inside. Reservations are required for inside space; outside is first come,
first served.

CONTACT: Ramona or Bob Wallis, Oak Grove Flea Market, 872 Oak
Grove Rd, Springdale AR 72702. Tel: (501) 756-0697 or (501) 521-5791.

WEST MEMPHIS
Eastern Arkansas Flea Market

DATES: Thursday through Sunday.

TIMES: 10:00 AM-5:00 PM.

ADMISSION: Free. Parking is free.

LOCATION: 557 E Broadway St.

DESCRIPTION: Described as "an old-fashioned flea market," this market of 27 dealers inside and anywhere from "a couple of hardy souls" to

30 dealers outside, depending on the weather, sells antiques, lots of collectibles, computers, "a variety of stuff." Mostly old. One dealer "sells the most beautiful antique furniture." There are concession stands and the market is fully handicapped-accessible, including the restrooms.

DEALER RATES: Call, as there is quite a range of rates depending on location. Reservations are required for inside space.

CONTACT: Eastern Arkansas Flea Market, 557 E Broadway Street, W Memphis, AR 72301. Tel: (870) 735-9055.

West Memphis Flea Market

DATES: Thursday through Sunday.

TIMES: Thursday through Saturday 10:00 AM-6:00 PM. Sunday 11:00 AM-5:00 PM.

ADMISSION: Free. Parking is free.

LOCATION: 512 E Broadway. Easy access from either I-40 or I-55 from Exit 7 (both interstates), go to Broadway, right, 2 blocks to market on your right.

DESCRIPTION: Located along the Mississippi River, this market of 45 permanent and up to a total of 75 dealers sells everything from antiques and collectibles to household goods, glassware, new and vintage clothing, jewelry, the latest fads, and new merchandise. Other dealers come here to shop because the deals and merchandise are so good. They are near a RV park, a dog track for the bold, and only 7 miles from Memphis.

DEALER RATES: Inside there is a waiting list, outside is $6 for a 12' × 20' space under canopy. Reservations are necessary—really.

CONTACT: Virginia McNeely, West Memphis Flea Market, 512 E Broadway, W Memphis AR 72301-3201. Tel: (870) 735-1644 (leave message).

OTHER FLEA MARKETS

We know or have heard about these markets, but have not personally contacted each one, as we have the markets with descriptions. If you plan to visit one of the markets listed below, *please call first* to make sure they are still open. Flea markets do come and go. While they were open when we went to press, they may not be later. We can't be responsible. *Call first!*

Batesville: Trader B Flea Market, 901 Batesville Blvd. Tel: (870) 251-2894.

Beebe: Country Girl Flea Market, 1502 W Dewitt Henry Dr. Tel: (501) 882-2011.

Beebe: DO Drop In Flea Market, 316 W Center St. Tel: (501) 882-2424.

Benton: Benton Flea Market, 18325 Interstate 30. Tel: (501) 778-9011.

Benton: South Street Flea Market, 1229 W South St. Tel: (501) 315-6185.

Bryant: Collectors' Flea Market, 22430 I-30. Tel: (501) 847-6899.

Camden: Camden Flea Market, 1945 California Ave SW. Tel: (870) 836-9836.

Center Ridge: C & J's, 6868 Hwy 9. Tel: (501) 893-9878.

Clarksville: Westside Flea Market, 2206 W Main St. Tel: (501) 754-3484.

De Witt: De Witt Flea Market, 204 S Main St. Tel: (870) 946-2008.

El Dorado: Blackmon's Flea Market, 1332 W Hillsboro St. Tel: (870) 875-9000.

El Dorado: Ginger's Flea Market, 508 S Washington Ave. Tel: (870) 862-1935.

Fairfield Bay: A Wild Hare Flea Market, 134 Beaver Rd. Tel: (501) 884-4898.

Foreman: Foreman Flea Market, 107 Shuman St. Tel: (870) 542-6606.

Garfield: Martin's Flea Market, Hwy 62 & Oak. Tel: (501) 359-3782.

Garfield: Creek Flea Market, 18701 Hwy 62. Tel: (501) 359-3607.

Gravel Ridge: Northside Flea Market, 18801 Hwy 107. Tel: (501) 834-8060.

Gravelly: Gravelly Flea Market. Tel: (501) 299-4952.

Green Forest: Green Forest Flea Market, 224 Public Sq. Tel: (870) 438-5801.

Greenbrier: Picket Fence Flea Market, 6 N Broadview St. Tel: (501) 679-5589.

Harrisburg: Fran's Downtown Flea Market, 18719 Hwy 14 E. Tel: (870) 578-5870.

Harrisburg: Harrisburg Flea Market, 8142 Hwy 163. Tel: (870) 578-2598.

Harrisburg: White's Flea Market, 705 E Jackson St. Tel: (870) 578-3192.

Harrison: Early Bird Flea Market, 715 E Stephenson Ave. Tel: (870) 365-7276.

Harrison: Yellow Rose Flea Market, 4767 Hwy 65 N. Tel: (870) 743-9300.

Harrison: Lake Harrison Flea Market, 108 E Stephenson Ave. Tel: (870) 743-4287.

Hot Springs: Central City Flea Mart, 3310 Central Ave. Tel: (501) 623-4484.

Hot Springs: Central Park Flea Market, 5737 Central Ave. Tel: (501) 525-4430.

Hot Springs: Snow Springs Flea Market, 3628 Park Ave. Tel: (501) 624-7469.

Imboden: Finney's Flea Market, 1106 W 3rd St. Tel: (870) 869-1014.

Jacksonville: B & M Flea Market, 660 W Main St. Tel: (501) 985-1788.

Jacksonville: That Little Flea Market, 632 W Main St. Tel: (501) 985-0694.

Jacksonville: Look Out Flea Market, 100 N 1st St. Tel: (501) 985-0646.

Kingston: Grandpa's Flea Market. Tel: (501) 665-2642.

Knoxville: 64 Flea Mart, Hwy 64 W. Tel: (501) 885-6104.

Lowell: Magnolia House Flea Market Inc, 206 Spring Creek Rd. Tel: (501) 751-1787.

Magnolia: Downtown Flea Market, 105 N Jefferson St. Tel: (870) 234-7900.

Magnolia: Magnolia Flea Market, 1517 E Main St. Tel: (870) 901-6183.

Malvern: Cotten's Flea Market, Hwy 270 E. Tel: (501) 337-5772.

McGehee: Tess' Flea Market, 2206 Hwy 65 N. Tel: (870) 222-5887.

Mountain View: Jack's Flea Market, Hwy 14 E. Tel: (870) 269-4166.

Mountain View: Main Street Flea Market, 110 E Main. Tel: (870) 269-8986.

Mountain View: White Elephant Flea Market, 200 S Peabody. Tel: (870) 269-9375.

N Little Rock: Treasure Trove Flea Market, 8325 Mac Arthur Dr. Tel: (501) 753-4145.

Newport: Campbell Station Flea Market, 6601 N Hwy 67. Tel: (870) 523-4466.

Osceola: Hillbilly's Flea Market, 213 W Hale Ave. Tel: (870) 563-2788.

Paragould: 7 Acres Flea Market, 2607 E Kingshighway. Tel: (870) 236-1922.

Paragould: Overpass Flea Market, 200 E Kingshighway. Tel: (870) 239-4478.

Perry: Oppelo Flea Market, 287 Hwy 9. Tel: (501) 354-2640.

Pine Bluff: Pinecrest Flea Market, 407 N Blake St. Tel: (870) 536-3532.

Pleasant Plains: Pleasant Plains Flea Market, 452 Main St. Tel: (501) 345-2720.

Pocahontas: AAA Fleamarket, 5642 Hwy 67 S. Tel: (870) 248-1411.

Pocahontas: Double D Flea Market, 5241 Hwy 67 S. Tel: (870) 248-9500.

Prairie Grove: Tea Pot Flea Market, Hwy 62 W. Tel: (501) 267-4440.

Rogers: Bear Creek, 15790 E Hwy 12. Tel: (501) 925-2327.

Rogers: Pioneer Flea Market, 1018 N 2nd St. Tel: (501) 631-6150.

Sherwood: Hilltop Flea Market & Antique, 7311 N Hills Blvd. Tel: (501) 833-9557.

Springdale: Betty's Homestyle Flea Market, 4556 N Thompson St. Tel: (501) 872-0355.

Springdale: Big Blue Flea Market, 452 E Henri De Tonti Blvd. Tel: (501) 361-9211.

Springdale: Monterey Flea Market, 331 E Emma Ave. Tel: (501) 872-7791.

Springdale: Tontitown Flea Market, 831 E Henri De Tonti Blvd. Tel: (501) 361-9902.

Springdale: 412 Flea Market, 2298 W Henri De Tonti Blvd. Tel: (501) 361-9118.

Stuttgart: Stuttgart Flea Market, 1606 S Vine St. Tel: (870) 673-2224.

Van Buren: Crawford County Flea Market, 4400 Alma Hwy. Tel: (501) 410-4014.

Walnut Ridge: Ma & Pa's Flea Market, 712 Hwy 67 N. Tel: (870) 886-7737.

Wynne: Southside Flea Market, 1556 S Falls Blvd. Tel: (870) 238-2312.

CALIFORNIA

ANDERSON
Jolly Giant Flea Market

DATES: Saturday and Sunday, year round.
TIMES: 6:30 AM-3:00 PM.
ADMISSION: $1.25 for a family, $.50 general, $.35 seniors, 6 and under free.
LOCATION: 6719 Eastside Rd. Take I-5 to Anderson. At Junction 273, exit off I-5; the market is 4 miles north of Anderson. The cross street is Latona Rd.
DESCRIPTION: Started in 1979, this indoor/outdoor market has 90,000 square feet of merchandise for sale. As they describe it, "More fun than you can bargain for." Their 150-250 dealers sell antiques, produce, cards, coins, furniture, garage sale goodies, tools and new and used merchandise. When you wilt from hunger, try one of their two restaurants. When the need hits, there are handicapped-accessible restrooms too.
DEALER RATES: $6 for 10' × 10' space on Saturday; $8 on Sunday. Reservations are suggested, but not needed.
CONTACT: Office Staff or Jim or Patti Smith, Jolly Giant Flea Market, 6719 Eastside Rd, Anderson CA 96007. Tel: (916) 365-6458. Fax: (916) 365-6450.

BAKERSFIELD
Bakersfield Fairground Swap Meet

DATES: Tuesday, Saturday and Sunday.
TIMES: Tuesday 6:00 AM-2:00 PM, Saturday 6:00 AM-3:00 PM, Sunday 5:00 AM-3:00 PM.
ADMISSION: Tuesday $.50, Saturday $.75, Sunday $1. Parking is free.
LOCATION: At the Kern County Fairgrounds, at the intersection of Ming and Union, right on the corner.
DESCRIPTION: This outdoor market, open since 1986, attracts 300 to 400 dealers year round selling antiques, collectibles, crafts, produce, new merchandise, farm tools, cars, boats, motor homes, used merchandise and "everything under the sun." Loads of snack bars and handicapped-accessible restrooms add to the amenities. Their logo is "a bargain of treasures..." so look for them.
DEALER RATES: Tuesday $7, Saturday $11, Sunday $14 for a 20' × 20' space. Reservations are not required. First come, first served. There are monthly reservations if you want them.
CONTACT: Ed Murphy, Bakersfield Fairgrounds Swap Meet, 312 Stable, Bakersfield CA 93307. Tel: (661) 397-1504 or (661) 833-1733.

Pacific Swap-O-Rama

DATES: Sundays. Rain or shine.

TIMES: 8:00 AM-4:00 PM.

ADMISSION: $.75, children under 12 free. Free parking is available. There is $1 parking as well.

LOCATION: 4501 Wible Rd. Take Fwy 99, Exit White Ln and Wible Rd, 2 blocks south.

DESCRIPTION: This show opened in 1971. It is an outdoor market accommodating anywhere from 450 to 550 dealers. The dealers sell approximately 90% new merchandise, modern clothes, etc. for the mostly Hispanic shoppers. There is also an assortment of secondhand goods. Fresh produce is available in season. For your convenience, there is Mexican food available (including menudo to help sober people up after too much time at the beer garden), the beer garden, picnicking under the trees, a barbershop, plenty to keep the kids happy, and live music. Handicapped-accessible restrooms are on site.

DEALER RATES: $15 reserved space, $20 for non-reserved. Reservations are suggested. The office is open Friday for reservations from 9:00 AM-3:00 PM and Saturday 9:00 AM-5:00 PM. Dealers can setup at 6:00 AM.

CONTACT: Pacific Swap-O-Rama, 4501 Wible Rd, Bakersfield CA 93313. Tel: (661) 831-9342. Fax: (661) 831-2158.

BERKELEY
Berkeley Flea Market

DATES: Saturday and Sunday, year round.

TIMES: 7:00 AM-7:00 PM.

ADMISSION: Free. Parking is free.

LOCATION: Ashby Bart Station. Located off of Hwy 80, take the Ashby Ave Exit and go straight up. The market is located on Ashby Ave and Martin Luther King Way at the Ashby BART station.

DESCRIPTION: Open since 1973, this multi-cultural flea market is operated by Community Service United, a non-profit organization with proceeds shared by local charitable social service agencies. It accommodates up to 280 dealers (but hey, many take more than one space, so average is 190) selling antiques, collectibles, used furniture, electronics/appliances, musical instruments, tools, new and used clothing, books, international items, household goods, and ethnic products. They encourage used items. There is a produce section and a snack bar. They were voted "Best of the Bay" Flea Market by the *Bay Guardian* in 1999 and 2000, as a truly classic flea market in the bay area.

DEALER RATES: $20 per day, $19 if paid in advance. Reservations can be made in the office Thursdays 5:00 PM-7:00 PM, Fridays 12:00 PM-3:00 PM, Saturday 7:00 AM-4:00 PM, Sundays 7:00 AM to 4:00 PM. Weekends, the office closes for lunch from 12:00-1:30 PM. Office closes at 2:30 on the second Saturday of each month. Reservations are not required, but are suggested.

CONTACT: Charisse Cronland, Berkeley Flea Market, 1937 Ashby Ave, Berkeley CA 94703. Tel: (510) 644-0744. Email: findme@berkeleyfleamarket.com. Web: www.berkeleyfleamarket.com.

BLOOMINGTON
Bel-Air Swap Meet

DATES: Wednesday, Friday, Saturday and Sunday.
TIMES: 6:00 AM-3:00 PM.
ADMISSION: $.50. Parking is free.
LOCATION: 17565 Valley Blvd.
DESCRIPTION: Open since 1986 and moved down the road in June 1997, this outdoor market averages 638 dealers year round selling antiques, collectibles, crafts, produce, furniture, coins, produce stamps, cards, garage sale goodies, and new merchandise. A snack bar and restrooms are on site.

DEALER RATES: Wednesday or Friday $15 and up, Saturday or Sunday $25 and up. Space size: 18' × 25'. Reservations are required with a sellers permit.
CONTACT: Bel-Air Swap Meet, 17565 Valley Blvd, Bloomington CA 92316. Tel: (909) 875-3000. Fax: (909) 877-1633.

CAMPBELL
Second Saturday Flea Market

DATES: Second Saturday of every month, weather permitting.
TIMES: 7:00 AM-dusk.
ADMISSION: Free. Parking is also free.
LOCATION: South from Santa Cruz on Hwy 17, turn west at Hamilton; then travel ½ mile to Winchester Blvd; then turn left and go ½ block to Campbell Center Shopping Center.
DESCRIPTION: This show started in 1971. The outdoor market accommodates 60-70 dealers. You can find almost anything here from antiques and collectibles to fine art and a bare minimum of new merchandise— "whatever dealers bring that is legal to sell." Mostly, the dealers are selling good old flea market stuff, garage sale goodies, much more old than new. "This is still an old fashion flea market." John, a record dealer, has been here since anyone can remember. He has found or sold "any record you can imagine." There are several restaurants in the shopping center, although you just might want to try Jerseys, with "the best cheese steak this side of the Delaware River." This market is noted for the friendliness

of their people. "It's like a family. When one gets sick, the others help out." Some of the vendors have been here every weekend since the market opened.

DEALER RATES: $10 for 10' × 10' space (a parking space). Reservations are not accepted—first come, first served.

CONTACT: Second Saturday Flea Market, c/o Jerseys Cheese Steak Co, 1781 S Winchester Blvd, Campbell CA 95008. Tel: (408) 374-1415.

CONCORD
Solano Drive-In and Swap Meet

DATES: Saturday and Sunday.

TIMES: 6:00 AM-4:00 PM.

ADMISSION: Saturday $.25, Sunday $1. Free parking.

LOCATION: Solano Drive-In Theater, 1611 Solano Way. Just off Hwy 4.

DESCRIPTION: This 12-year-old outdoor market, one of the largest and oldest in the Northbay area, draws about 200 dealers on Saturday and up to 500 dealers on Sunday selling lots of garage sale goodies and household treasures, some antiques, collectibles, storage buyouts, bulk items, household stuff, new and used stuff, junk, produce, and whatever. There is a snack bar on site as well as handicapped-accessible restrooms.

DEALER RATES: Saturday $5, Sunday $15; monthly and yearly rates available. Otherwise, first come, first served.

CONTACT: Solano Swap Meet, 1611 Solano Way, Concord CA 94520-5307. Tel: (925) 687-6445. Web: Watch for their website.

COSTA MESA
The Orange County Market Place

DATES: Saturday and Sunday except during the Orange County Fair (in late July).

TIMES: 7:00 AM-4:00 PM.

ADMISSION: $2; children under the age of 12 are admitted free.

LOCATION: Orange County Fairgrounds, 88 Fair Dr. Take 55 Fwy W Exit at Fair Dr and go right on Fair Dr, or 405 Fwy Exit at Fairview and follow the signs to the Orange County Fairgrounds.

DESCRIPTION: Since 1969, an average of 40,000 to 50,000 shoppers per week come to buy from their 1,000-plus vendors spread over 60 acres in this exceptionally clean, outdoor market. In 2000, they added a classic car museum, called the Automotive Road of Dreams, recounting the history of automobiles from the 1900s to present. Some of their treasures include Charlie Chaplins' Pierce-Arrow, valued at over $250,000, a 1976 Cadillac Bicentennial Eldorado with 6 miles on it, a Buick hearse, and one of only 2 Cadillac Tulip Sedans, and one Edsel. They have added a manufacturers outlet center with great discounts on leather clothing, brand-name apparel for everyone, computers, as well as a new produce area with veggies, fruit, bakery, fresh flowers, and nuts. This is the largest weekly event in Southern California, its emphasis is on family and fun. They do so well, they attract about 2 million visitors a year. It's also a great place for celebrity sitings, from movies to sports figures. There are plenty of food concessions, an ice cream parlor, authentic TX barbecue, and I'm told not to forget their "legendary fresh cinnamon rolls." Aren't you just too grateful for the handicapped-accessible restrooms? This is such an affluent market, there are attendants in the restrooms! Have a roll for me, and find Jeff and tell him "thank you."

DEALER RATES: $45 per day for 15' x 27' space. Office hours Monday through Friday 9:00 AM-4:00 PM.

CONTACT: Orange County Fairgrounds, 88 Fair Dr, Costa Mesa CA 92627. Tel: (949) 723-6606 (for vendor info) or 723-6660 office or shopper's hot line: (949) 723-6616. Fax: (949) 723-6659. Email: telphil@earthlink.net. Web: www.ocmarketplace.com.

CUPERTINO
DeAnza College Flea Market

DATES: First Saturday of every month. Rain or shine.

TIMES: 8:00 AM-4:00 PM.

ADMISSION: Free. Parking is $3 on campus.

LOCATION: 21250 Stevens Creek Blvd. Take Hwy 280 north or south to Hwy 85 west, then to DeAnza College via Stevens Creek Blvd.

DESCRIPTION: This outdoor market began in 1972 and is operated by the student government and the student activities committee, with proceeds benefitting the student body. There are over 900 booths selling antiques, fine art, arts and crafts, collectibles, and new merchandise. From 15-20,000 people attend this event each day! Food is served on the premises and handicapped-accessible restrooms are available.

DEALER RATES: $25 for two parking spaces approximately 18' × 20' as selling area; $50 for four spaces approximately 36' × 20'. Reservations must be made one month in advance.

CONTACT: DeAnza Flea Market, 21250 Stevens Creek Blvd, Cupertino, CA 95014-5702. Tel: (408) 864-8414 or 864-8964 if that's working. Web: www.deanza.fhda.edu/depts/studact/dasbflea.html or just go to www.deanza.fhda.edu and go for Friends and Visitors to Flea Markets.

ESCONDIDO
Escondido Swap Meet

DATES: Wednesday through Sunday.

TIMES: Wednesday and Thursday 6:30 AM-4:00 PM; Friday 1:30 PM-9:30 PM; Saturday and Sunday 6:00 AM-5:00 PM.

ADMISSION: Wednesday $.75, Thursday $.35, Friday, Saturday and Sunday $1. Parking is free.

LOCATION: 635 W Mission Ave. Take 78 east to Centre City Parkway S, take second right at Washington Ave. The market is on the right side after Quince St.

DESCRIPTION: Since 1970, on the site of an historical drive-in movie theater, this indoor/outdoor market is generally fixed stands with electricity and set prices. There is mostly new merchandise with a heavy Mexican accent and lots of used goods. Some of the merchandise seen for sale is: tools, electronics, loads of clothes, books, music instruments, tapes, and more. Fourteen concessions include seven restaurants: Mexican, Mediterranean, Italian, fish and chips, barbeque, chicken, and a bakery. A snack bar serves a wide variety of sandwiches, snacks and breakfast. The Farmer's Market section sells inexpensive fresh produce, cheeses and dairy products, and meats.

DEALER RATES: Per 18' × 20' booth: Wednesday $11, Thursday $8, Friday $22, Saturday $17, Sunday $20. Reservations are not required; it's a first-come, first-served market. For serious sellers monthly reservations are available.

CONTACT: Raul Palomino, 635 W Mission Ave, Escondido CA 92025. Tel: (760) 745-3100 Monday thru Friday, or during the days of event (760) 757-5286.

EUREKA
Flea Mart by the Bay

DATES: Every Friday, Saturday and Sunday.

TIMES: Friday 8:00 AM-4:00 PM, Saturday and Sunday 8:00 AM-5:00 PM.

ADMISSION: Free. Parking is free.

LOCATION: 1200 W Del Norte, off Hwy 101. They are next to the public fishing pier.

DESCRIPTION: Since 1981, this indoor market of 50-70 dealers has been selling collectibles, crafts, coins, cards, video games, tools, toys, garage sale goodies, furniture, and new merchandise. When the need hits, there is one snack bar and handicapped-accessible restrooms. During December, they hold drawings for prizes and giveaways.

DEALER RATES: $5 per 3' × 8' table daily. $10 for the weekend; $56 for an 8' × 10' enclosed booth monthly. Reservations are suggested, but otherwise first come, first served.

CONTACT: Leah Patton, Flea Mart by the Bay, 1200 W Del Norte St #3, Eureka CA 95503. Tel: (707) 443-3103. Email: lindystar3@aol.com.

FOLSOM
Annual Peddlers' Fair and Antique Market

DATES: Antique Fair (spring) is the third Sunday in April and Peddlers' Antique and Collectible Fair (fall) is third Sunday in September. Rain or shine. 2002: April 21, September 15.

TIMES: 8:00 am-4:00 PM.

ADMISSION: Free. Some parking is free, some paid. There is a free shuttle service available.

LOCATION: On Sutter St in historic Folsom. From Hwy 50, take Folsom Blvd Exit, turn left, 2.9 miles to Sutter St.

DESCRIPTION: Started in 1966, this outdoor market in the Sierra foothills now accommodates 300 dealers selling antiques and collectibles. No new merchandise is allowed. More than 20,000 people attend this semi-annual fair. In the heart of "gold country," this fair is located in the middle of some fascinating history: the Folsom Powerhouse was the first commercial transporter of long-distance electricity; there are the logging and gold mining histories; Chinese diggings; special exhibits of early Indian life at the History Museum on Sutter Street and more. They hold a live antique auction during these events. Food is plentiful and there are handicapped-accessible restrooms when needed.

DEALER RATES: $100 for 10' × 10' space. Reservations are required; set-up starts at 3:00 AM.

CONTACT: Attn: Grissi Kolto-Merchant, Kolmer Productions, 620 Pemberton Ln, Folsom CA 95630. Tel: (916) 353-1198. Email: kolmerevents@aol.com. Web: www.kolmeronline.com.

FRESNO
Cherry Avenue Auction, Inc

DATES: Open every Tuesday and Saturday.

TIMES: 7:00 AM-3:00 PM.

ADMISSION: Free. Parking is $1 per car, Tuesday; $2 per car on Saturday.

LOCATION: 4640 S Cherry Ave. Take Hwy 99 to Jensen Ave exit (Jensen is 2 miles south of downtown Fresno); then go west 1 block to Cherry; then go south to yard. Cherry Auction is on Cherry Ave between Central and American Aves. Or take Fwy 41 to American Ave east to Cherry Ave.

DESCRIPTION: This show began over 60 years ago. Now there are over 3 acres of vendor spaces and walkways under sheds or canopy and 15 acres total vendor area. The 800-plus dealers who attend this market sell

"1,000 + 1 items," from antiques and collectibles to new merchandise and fresh produce—it can all be bought. This is one of the oldest outdoor markets in the area. Their motto is "shopping made fun." There is a variety of food available on the premises as well as clean handicapped-accessible restrooms.

DEALER RATES: Reservations are taken only by the month. The cost for dealer space is $13 per 10' × 20' space on Saturday; $8 per space on Tuesday (Tuesday is a 2 for 1 deal). Reservations are not required.

CONTACT: Cherry Avenue Auction Inc, 4640 S Cherry Ave, Fresno CA 93706. Tel: (559) 266-9856. Fax: (559) 266-9439.

FULLERTON

Orange County Register Antiques and Collectibles Round-Up

DATES: The first Sunday in May and October. Rain or shine.

TIMES: 9:00 AM-2:00 PM.

ADMISSION: $5, children under 12 free with adult. Parking is free. Dealers can get in early (from 6:00 AM to 9:00 AM) to buy for $10. A special preview VIP admission from 5:00 AM to 7:30 AM is $15.

LOCATION: Cal State University just off the 57 Fwy at Nutwood Ave exit. Turn west on Nutwood and at the first light into the Cal State Fullerton campus and follow the signs.

DESCRIPTION: This outdoor show, started in 1962 and recently moved to this location, is sponsored by the Register Charities (Orange County Register newspaper), with all profits going to charity. The 800 dealers sell antiques and collectibles. It is the largest antique-related event in Orange County. Food is available on the premises and there are handicapped-accessible restrooms.

DEALER RATES: $50 for 8' × 18' booth. Reservations are recommended.

CONTACT: RG Canning, PO Box 400, Maywood CA 90270-0400. Tel: (323) 560-7469 ext 15. Fax: (323) 560-5924. Office hours Mondays and Wednesdays 10:00 AM-5:00 PM. Email: rgc@rgcshows.com or website: www.rgcshows.com.

GALT

Galt Market

DATES: Every Tuesday and Wednesday, except Christmas Day.

TIMES: 6:00 AM until everyone packs up (usually around 3:00 PM).

ADMISSION: Free. Parking is free.

LOCATION: Approximately half way between Stockton and Sacramento on Hwy 99. From the south: take the Central Galt Exit, turn left across the bridge and at the bottom of the bridge, turn left at the stop light. From the north: take the Central Galt Exit, turn right at the stop sign, at the bottom of the bridge, turn left at the stop light. The Galt Market is located directly behind the Marion O Lawrence Library and parking is available to the left or right.

DESCRIPTION: This is two distinct outdoor markets, with the Tuesday market specializing in new merchandise, crafts, clothing, home decor items, jewelry, statuary, wood products, pictures/frames, dried flowers, awnings, oriental rugs, and loads more. The Wednesday market is the "old" flea and produce market and deals in antiques, collectibles, crafts, garage sale goodies, and the like. The produce market is considered quite awesome with plenty of ethnic specialties. There are 860 dealer spaces on over 10 acres, with an average of 400-plus dealers. This market draws vendors from throughout California and the surrounding states as well as a number of foreign countries. Many of their vendors attend trade shows around the United States and some make regular buying trips to Europe, the Middle East and the Orient. Food vendors provide plenty of eatables. The entire market is handicapped accessible, right down to the restrooms. Market advice: "Wear good walking shoes and shop until you drop!" Grab a market guide as you enter. Customer carry-out services are offered to adjacent parking lots and loading zones. The market is exceptionally busy during Spring Break and the summer, so get there before 9:30 AM for good parking and selections.

DEALER RATES: Tuesday: $30 for non-food vendors for a 10' × 30' space; food vendors pay $70 for a 20' × 30' space. Tuesday dealers must have a State of California Board of Equalization Seller's Permit and a City of Galt Business License to sell. Wednesday: $20 for non-food vendors for a regular space; food vendors pay $70 for a regular space. Wednesday vendors selling at the market more than two times per year are required to have a State of California Board of Equalization Seller's Permit. All vendors selling prepared or packaged food or plants on either day, and all Wednesday produce, are required to have Sacramento Country Environmental Health Permits. Please check their website, call or write for their vendor brochure.

CONTACT: Galt Market, c/o 380 Civic Dr, Galt CA 95632. Tel: (209) 745-2437 for a tape message, or if you want a human when the tape starts touch "0" during office hours—Monday through Wednesday. Or call (209) 745-4695. Fax: (209) 745-9794. Email: clerk@ci.galt.ca.us. Web: www.ci.galt.ca.us.

GLENDALE
Glendale Community College Swap Meet

DATES: Every third Sunday of the month.
TIMES: 8:00 AM-3:00 PM.

ADMISSION: Free. Parking is free.

LOCATION: Glendale Community College, upper parking lot. Take the Glendale 2 Fwy north, exit on Mountain St, take a left; it is on the right side of the road just behind the bridge.

DESCRIPTION: There are approximately 150-200 spaces. From a reader who visited this market and was impressed: only antiques and collectibles are sold here, no new stuff. Goodies include: stamps, coins, books, crystal, dishes, glasses, knickknacks, some clothing and fabric. You can still make a deal. Snacks are available and there are restrooms.

DEALER RATES: $35 for a 3-parking-stall space per Sunday. You must park your vehicle in that space. If you are not considered an occasional seller, you must get a "seller's permit" from any local State of California Board of Equalization office. Reservations are an excellent idea, although if any spaces are empty, they are let on a first-come, first-serve basis. Gates open for vendors at 6:00 AM.

CONTACT: Jon Harris, GCC Swap Meet Office, 1122 E Garfield Ave, Glendale CA 91205. Tel: (818) 240-1000 ext 5805, Monday through Thursday 8:00 AM-6:00 PM. Email: jharris@glendale.cc.ca.us.

GOLETA
Santa Barbara Swap Meet

DATES: Sunday.

TIMES: 6:00 AM-2:00 PM.

ADMISSION: $1. Children under 12 free. Parking is free.

LOCATION: 907 S Kellogg Blvd. Going south on Hwy 101, get off at Fairview, left on Hollister, right on S Kellogg, stay on S Kellogg until the end of the road. Going north on Hwy 101, get off on 217 Junction, right on Hollister, left on S Kellogg, stay on until the end of the road.

DESCRIPTION: This outdoor market, open since 1967 on the site of an old drive-in theater, is crammed with 200 dealers selling antiques, collectibles, crafts, furniture, garage sale goodies, cards, old coins, and new merchandise. There is plenty of fresh produce. About 70% of the merchandise is new. Many locals do their weekly shopping here even though, as the manager describes it, "This is a secluded place." A snack bar and concessions feed the famished. And handicapped-accessible restrooms are most welcome.

DEALER RATES: $20 per 16' × 16' space. First come, first served. If you wish to reserve space, it costs $30 more per month, daily $5. Electricity is available; bring your own setup. Must have a California Resellers License.

CONTACT: Santa Barbara Swap Meet, 907 S Kellogg, Goleta CA 93117. Tel: (805) 964-9050 for tape information, (805) 967-4591 on Sunday. Fax: (805) 683-3601.

HEMET
Maclin's Hemet Open-Air Market

DATES: Saturdays, year round.

TIMES: 7:30 AM-2:00 PM.

ADMISSION: Free. Parking is free.

LOCATION: 27400 Ramona Bowl Rd at the Ramona Pageant. From Hwy 74, to south on Girard. Follow up to Ramona Bowl Rd.

DESCRIPTION: Opened in 2001, this Maclin's market has 50-100 dealers selling new and used merchandise, produce and crafts.

DEALER RATES: Saturday $15 per 21' × 21' space. Bring your own setup.

CONTACT: Maclin's, 7407 Riverside Dr, Ontario CA 91761. Tel: (909) 984-5131. Or toll-free in California 1-800-222-7467. Fax: (909) 988-8041. Email: info@maclinmarkets.com. Web: maclinmarkets.com.

HUNTINGTON BEACH
Golden West College Swap Meet

DATES: Saturday and Sunday, year round. Rain or shine.

TIMES: 8:00 AM-3:00 PM.

ADMISSION: Free. Parking is free.

LOCATION: Golden West College Campus. Between Golden West St and Edinger Ave.

DESCRIPTION: This 22-plus-year-old market operates to benefit the college programs and operations. The Saturday market is mostly old goods, antiques, collectibles and whatever. Sunday's market is old and new merchandise. Some of the 680 dealer spaces sell fresh produce, records and music memorabilia, as well as the usual flea market goodies. My market visitor was impressed with this market, saying you can still get good deals.

DEALER RATES: $25 per space reserved. $30 for same day (i.e. grabbing space at the last minute). Cash only.

CONTACT: Golden West College Swap Meet, 15744 Golden West St, Huntington Beach CA 92647-3197. Tel: (714) 898-SWAP (7927) for tape message, or (714) 895-8737 Monday-Friday during office hours 8:00 AM-5:00 PM.

INDIO
Maclin's Indio Open Air Market

DATES: Every Wednesday and Saturday night.

TIMES: 4:00 PM-10:00 PM.

ADMISSION: $.50, children under 12 free. Parking is free.

LOCATION: 46-350 Arabia St. From Hwy 111 take Monroe south, then east on Dr. Carreon to Arabia.

DESCRIPTION: Unlike any of their other markets, this Maclin's Market is open evenings. There is plenty of "locally grown and nationally fa-

mous" produce and baked goods, music, handcrafted arts and jewelry and just about anything and everything for your home, family, pets, or car. This place is described as one big fair, especially on Wednesdays. Night shopping here is a treat, as it is much cooler in the evenings.

DEALER RATES: Wednesday $20 per space, Saturday $15. Just show up the day of the market by 4:00 PM to get your space. Gates open at 2:00 PM for set up. Get there early if you want a space; it goes quickly.

CONTACT: Maclin's, 7407 Riverside Dr, Ontario CA 91761. Tel: (909) 984-5131 or 1-800-222-7467 in California. Fax: (909) 988-8041. Email: info@maclinmarkets.com. Web: maclinmarkets.com.

KING CITY
King City Rotary Flea Market

DATES: First Sunday in April. Rain or shine.

TIMES: 7:00 AM-4:00 PM.

ADMISSION: $3 for adults. $1 for children age 12 and under. Parking is free.

LOCATION: Salinas Valley Fairgrounds. Take Hwy 101 to Canal St, then follow signs to Fairgrounds.

DESCRIPTION: This show began in 1969 and is both an indoor and outdoor market that accommodates approximately 150 dealers selling new merchandise as well as some antiques, crafts, collectibles, and fresh produce. There is also a variety of foods available, including Mexican, American, and Oriental. Handicapped-accessible restrooms come in handy.

DEALER RATES: $15 for 10' × 15' space. $10 for each additional space. Reservations are required.

CONTACT: Chris Davis, King City Rotary, PO Box 611, King City CA 93930-0611. Tel: (831) 385-0414. Day of show call the fairgrounds (831) 385-3243.

LANCASTER
Lancaster Chamber of Commerce
Semi-Annual Flea Market

DATES: First Sunday in May; first Sunday in October. Rain or shine. (They say it always shines.)

TIMES: 9:00 AM-4:00 PM.

ADMISSION: $5 per adult, $3 seniors and military, children 12 and under free. Parking is free.

LOCATION: Antelope Valley Fairgrounds. 155 East Ave I. Take the 14 Fwy (Palmdale/Lancaster) to Ave I exit and head east approximately 2 miles to the intersection of Ave I and Division St.

DESCRIPTION: This indoor/outdoor market has been operating since May 1966 as the fundraiser for the local Chamber of Commerce. From 300 to 450 dealers from four states are attracted to this well-organized market selling antiques, arts and crafts, collectibles, home improvements, novelties, clothing and commercial sales. Available food goodies: Mexican, Oriental, and American sold by 10-20 vendors. Handicapped-accessible restrooms are available. When this market first opened, vendors would wait impatiently until the gates were thrown open, then race for whatever spot they could get. Now it is a finely tuned event run by 300 volunteers.

DEALER RATES: $70 for 10' × 10' premium space inside; $60 per 10' × 10' outdoor premium or park and sell premium; or $50 per 15' × 15' standard area; odds and ends zone $25 per 20' × 20' space. Space sold up to the day of the event. Setup time 5:00 AM.

CONTACT: Special Event Administrator, Antelope Valley Chambers of Commerce-Lancaster/Rosamond, 554 W Lancaster Blvd, Lancaster CA 93534-2534. Tel: (661) 948-4518 or fax: (661) 949-1212. Email: lcoc@avfleamarket.org. Web: www.avfleamarket.org.

LODI
Lodi Street Faire

DATES: First Sunday in May and October. Rain or shine.

TIMES: 8:00 AM-4:00 PM.

ADMISSION: Free. Parking is free.

LOCATION: Downtown Lodi on School St, between Lodi Ave and Lockeford St.

DESCRIPTION: This semi-annual fundraiser attracts over 550 dealers selling antiques, collectibles, arts and crafts, and new merchandise. Food vendors sell a variety of treats in two Food Alleys. One parking lot is devoted to tables and chairs for those eating or resting. Over 40,000 attend this fair. There are volunteers roaming the fair in golf carts waiting to be flagged down by weary or overloaded shoppers looking for a lift. Roving entertainment is provided.

DEALER RATES: $80 for 13' × 13' space, $115 for 13' × 13' corner space. Reservations are required.

CONTACT: Lodi District Chamber of Commerce, 35 S School St, Lodi CA 95240. Tel: (209) 367-7840. Day of show contact workers in on-site information booth.

Cover Your Cup?

One vendor spray paints pictures while you wait. Buyers appreciated her more *after* she was moved away from their line of fire.

Apparently, she's quite good at painting, too.

LONG BEACH
Outdoor Antique and Collectible Market

DATES: Third Sunday of every month. Rain or shine. Special shows in 2002: April 7 and September 29.

TIMES: 6:30 AM-3:00 PM.

ADMISSION: $4.50 for adults. No fee for children under 12. Free parking.

LOCATION: Veterans Stadium at Lakewood Blvd and Conant St. Take Lakewood Blvd N exit from Fwy 405, turn right onto Lakewood Blvd, go north approximately 2 miles, turn right on Conant St.

DESCRIPTION: This outdoor market opened in 1982 and is the largest regularly scheduled antique and collectible show in the west. It draws over 800 dealers selling antiques, collectibles, "home furnishings, decorative items, country collectibles and hidden treasures" spread over 20 acres. Please note that only antiques and collectibles may be sold here. Because of its proximity to Hollywood, it attracts quite a few celebrities. You never know! And it has a Good Housekeeping Seal of Approval, no less. There is plenty of food available

DEALER RATES: Booths measure 19' × 16' and range in cost from $50, $60, and $70, with corners at $90. Advance reservations are required.

CONTACT: Americana Enterprises Inc, PO Box 69219, Los Angeles CA 90069. Tel: (323) 655-5703. Email: info@longbeachantiquemarket.com. Web: www.longbeachantiquemarket.com.

> **Don't You Wish**
> Recently a customer bought a 1960's battery-operated Japanese-made toy robot for $300. It was listed and sold for $60,000 at a toy auction about the same time. Lucky, lucky!

LOS ALTOS HILLS
Foothill College Flea Market

DATES: Third Saturday of each month, year round.

TIMES: 8:00 AM-3:00 PM.

ADMISSION: Free. Parking is $2.

LOCATION: 12345 El Monte Rd at the college, parking lot F.

DESCRIPTION: Since 1980 this market, located in the foothills and surrounded by eucalyptus trees, has been a fundraiser for the well-known Foothill College Theatre Guild. The 200 or so dealers enjoy a terrific reputation for their antiques, collectibles, fine art items, great crafts, books, vintage clothing and jewelry, and affluent garage sale items—from affluent shoppers, of course.

DEALER RATES: $18 for a single space of 16' × 16', with corner spots available for $25 (no discounts and quite limited). Vendor spaces available for Seniors, Foothill College students and staff rent for $15. Reservations definitely suggested though some standby space is available the day of the market.

CONTACT: Foothill College Flea Market, 12345 El Monte Rd, Los Altos Hills CA 94022-4504. Tel: (650) 948-6417.

MARYSVILLE
Marysville Flea Market

DATES: Sundays.
TIMES: 5:30 AM-4:00 PM.
ADMISSION: Free. Parking is free.
LOCATION: 1468 Simpson Ln. Off Hwy 70, 45 minutes north of Sacramento.
DESCRIPTION: Billed as "one of California's oldest flea markets," this outdoor, but under cover, market of 400 dealers sells antiques, collectibles, fishing supplies, jewelry, stereos, clothing, cards, furniture, produce, and new merchandise. One large snack bar, two beer booths, one sno-cone booth and handicapped-accessible restrooms relieve the necessaries. As the management describes this market, "we are small enough to be well traveled, large enough to hunt for bargains with friendly management and vendors."
DEALER RATES: $10 per 16' × 18' with 2 tables, or $10 per 20' × 20' with no tables; $15 under cover. Reservations are suggested.
CONTACT: Misty Sinnott, Marysville Flea Market, 1468 Simpson Ln, Marysville CA 95901-9747. Tel: (530) 743-8713. Fax: (520) 742-2124.

MORGAN HILL
Morgan Hill Flea Market

DATES: Every Saturday and Sunday, year round.
TIMES: 7:30 AM-6:00 PM.
ADMISSION: Free. Parking is also free.
LOCATION: 140 E Main St in Morgan Hill, 25 miles south of San Jose.
DESCRIPTION: This show began in 1964. The market is held outdoors and consists of over 200 dealers selling under shade trees. Shoppers may find antiques and collectibles, as well as new and used merchandise and fresh produce. Food is served on the premises.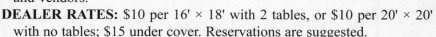
DEALER RATES: $12 for 3' × 10' table on Saturdays and $15 on Sundays. Reservations are not required.
CONTACT: Morgan Hill Flea Market, 140 E Main St, Morgan Hill CA 95037-3734. Tel: (408) 779-3809.

NILES
Niles Antique Fair and Flea Market

DATES: Last Sunday in August.

TIMES: 4:00 AM-4:00 PM. Flashlight shopping allowed!

ADMISSION: Free. Parking is $6 and is run as a Boy Scout fundraiser. Some free parking is available early.

LOCATION: In the Niles Business District. Take Hwy 680 to Mission Blvd north to Niles Blvd; or take Hwy 880 to Alvarado/Niles Blvd east.

DESCRIPTION: This one-day event has been a successful fundraiser for many local non-profit organizations since 1925. Most of Niles Blvd and side streets are closed as over 500 dealers turn Niles into antique heaven. Buyers may start arriving as early as 4:00 AM and continue to shop throughout the day. Antiques, arts and crafts, and a variety of collectibles can be found. Niles itself is an historic landmark, home of the former Essanay Studios (of Charlie Chaplin, Ben Turpin fame), Vallejo's Mill (the first flouring mill) and its Railroad Depot Museum with a large railroad layout. Non-profit organizations run the many food concessions as their fundraiser and there are handicapped-accessible restrooms available. In 2001, there were 120,000 visitors!

DEALER RATES: $135 for 10' × 12' space with early reservations, $150 for later reservations. Reservations are suggested. First come, first served.

CONTACT: Niles Main Street Association, PO Box 2038, Fremont CA 94536-2038. Tel: (510) 742-9868. Email: info@niles.org. Web: www.niles.org.

NIPOMO
Nipomo Swap Meet and Flea Market

DATES: Every Friday, Saturday, and Sunday. Indoors year round, outdoors weather permitting.

TIMES: 6:00 AM-6:00 PM.

ADMISSION: Free. Parking is $1 Saturday and $2 Sunday.

LOCATION: 263 N Frontage Rd, 101 Fwy, off-ramp is Tefft St.

DESCRIPTION: Open since 1974 and rejuvenated under new ownership since 1997, this market's 300 or so dealers sell lots of antiques and collectibles (try Dean Wright's Collectibles), clothing, jewelry, crafts, GT wireless, hot tubs, new and used furniture, new and used merchandise, and tons of fresh produce. There are seven food vendors and plenty of handicapped-accessible restrooms. There are 100 indoor spaces in buildings that comprise the flea market area; outdoors is the swap meet with tons of garage sale goodies.

DEALER RATES: $3 on Friday, $6 Saturday, $12 Sunday, $18 for all three. $85 monthly, guaranteed in your place. Flea market buildings $125-$175 for 14' × 20' building monthly.

CONTACT: Nipomo Swap Meet and Flea Market, 263 N Frontage Rd, Nipomo CA 93444. Tel: (805) 929-7000. Fax: (805) 929-7007.

Say What?
There is on-site security for vendors, but one night the guard dog took off with an unsecured $300 cowboy boot. The vendor admitted it was his fault. The boot was later found gnawed and buried.

NORTHRIDGE
Northridge Antique Swap Meet

DATES: The fourth Sunday of every month, as well as the fifth Sunday when there is one—and there are four a year.
TIMES: General admission 8:00 AM-2:00 PM. Early birds from 5:00 AM.
ADMISSION: $5 between 5:00 AM-8:00 AM, $3 after. Parking is free.
LOCATION: Cal State Northridge University. From the 405 Fwy take Devonshire west, turn left on Lindley, go 1 block to Lassen St.
DESCRIPTION: This open-air market is described by a reader as a "very nice antique market with only old stuff, collectibles, many garage sales and very positive dealing." The 150-300 dealers sell, among the other things: antique furniture, paintings, rugs, bronzes, lighting, pottery, porcelain, clocks and watches, postcards, stamps, coins, fishing equipment, and toys. Food is available on site. The fifth Sunday market is huge and quite popular.
DEALER RATES: $50 per 25' × 17' inline space, corner spaces $70. Reservations are suggested.
CONTACT: Daryll Fisher, Antique Attractions, 17041 Lakewood Blvd, Bellflower CA 90706-5522. Tel: (562) 633-3836.

OAKHURST
Mountain Peddler's Show

DATES: The Saturdays and Sundays of Memorial Day and Labor Day weekends. Rain or shine.
TIMES: Saturday 8:00 AM-8:00 PM, Sunday 8:00 AM-4:00 PM.
ADMISSION: Free admission. Free parking.
LOCATION: State Hwy 49 and Junction Dr. Oakhurst is located in the Sierra Nevada foothills on California State Hwy 41, 36 miles north of Fresno, and 16 miles south of Yosemite National Park.
DESCRIPTION: Initiated as a revenue source for the Chamber of Commerce, the first flea market was held in 1978. There were 186 booths and

a crowd of 10,000. Today, there are 20,000 buyers cruising through 300 booths selling antiques, collector's items, high-quality antique furnishings, glassware, pottery, clocks, porcelain, vintage, estate and costume jewelry, and arts and crafts. Food vendors offer everything from "tri-tip" to deli sandwiches and beer for the visitors. Live entertainment, free to the public, is provided. Handicapped-accessible toilets are available around the market.

DEALER RATES: Starting at $100 for an inline and $125 corner booth and up per 10' x 10' booth. The earlier you make a reservation, the less expensive. There is a late fee of $25 per space added to the rates, usually within 30 days of the market date. Set up Friday at 3:00 PM. Set up varies depending upon booth location. Security is on premises.

CONTACT: Eastern Madera County Chamber of Commerce, 49074 Civic Circle Drive, Oakhurst CA 93644. Tel: (559) 683-7766. Fax: (559) 683-0784. Email: chamber@sierratel.com. Web: www.sierratel.com/chamber.

OAKLAND
Coliseum Swap Meet

DATES: Tuesday through Sunday.

TIMES: 6:30 AM to whenever the dealers pack up.

ADMISSION: Tuesday $.25, Wednesday and Thursday $.50, Friday $.75, Saturday $1, and Sunday $1.50. Parking is free.

LOCATION: 5401 Coliseum Way. At I-880 and Coliseum Way, ½ mile south of the Oakland Coliseum.

DESCRIPTION: Next door to the Oakland "A's," this market averages 400 dealers on weekends, much less during the week, selling "everything" including loads of antiques and collectibles, fruits, vegetables, used and new merchandise, and craft items during the holidays. This place is known for the antiques, with many antique dealers prowling the place first thing every day, just to nab the good stuff! (Get there early if you like antiques.) More antiques dealers are selling on weekends than weekdays. Plenty of south-of-the-border fruits are sold here. Food is served on the premises and there are handicapped-accessible restrooms.

DEALER RATES: $5 on Tuesday, $10 Wednesday through Friday, $18 on Saturday and $20 on Sunday. They only handle monthly or yearly reservations. You must come in person to make your reservations.

CONTACT: Coliseum Swap Meet, 5401 Coliseum Way, Oakland CA 94601-5021. Tel: (510) 534-0325 for a recording or (510) 533-1601 to speak to someone.

OCEANSIDE
Oceanside Drive-In Swap Meet

DATES: Every Saturday, and Sunday, and holiday Mondays. Rain or shine.

TIMES: 6:00 AM-3:00 PM.

ADMISSION: Mondays and Saturdays $.75 fee; Sundays $1. Parking is free.

LOCATION: 3480 Mission Ave, 3 miles east of IF-5.

DESCRIPTION: Started in 1971, there are now more than 600 dealers featured in this outdoor market in a former drive-in theater. There were four theaters; now two are the market, and two are the parking area. Their goods range from antiques and collectibles to car parts, kitchen and household goods, music, jewelry, clothing, dry goods, ceramics (including Thailand China), toys, sporting goods, and whatever. Three lunch trucks served the famished, with "awesome Mexican food!" There are handicapped-accessible restrooms when needed. Occasionally the circus shows up, there are frequent giveaways, clowns come on Saturday to entertain the children (of all ages).

DEALER RATES: Saturday $16; Sunday $25; Monday $10 for 18' × 24' space. Reservations are not required for daily sales. Monthly reservations are available. There are 50 storage buildings for rent as well.

CONTACT: Oceanside Drive-In Swap Meet, 635 W Mission Ave, Escondido CA 92025. Tel: (760) 745-3100. Fax: (760) 741-5748. Day of show call (760) 757-5286, Saturday and Sunday.

ONTARIO
Maclin's Chino Open Air Market

DATES: Every Tuesday, Saturday and Sunday.

TIMES: 7:30 AM-3:00 PM.

ADMISSION: $.50, children under 12 free. Parking is free.

LOCATION: 7407 Riverside Dr. From points west, take Fwy 60 east to Euclid south, then east on Riverside Dr. From points east, take Fwy 60 west to Grove south, then west on Riverside Drive.

DESCRIPTION: This unique place to sell and shop has been serving the public since 1936. It is a cross between a swap meet, a mall, and a country fair, with not just dealers but exotic foods and children's attractions. There is a genuine livestock auction on Tuesdays and a restaurant with a 40s beer and wine bar and a wide-screen TV. Between 350 and 500 dealers sell everything from antiques and collectibles to clothing and gold jewelry, as well as new merchandise. One area has only used and collectible goodies. There are even children's pony rides. There is also a fish market on the premises. Live entertainment is provided by musicians who come to entertain and sell their music. Handicapped-accessible restrooms are available.

DEALER RATES: Rates are from $7 to $25. We suggest dealers come between 7:00 AM and 7:30 AM to get a space.

CONTACT: Maclin's, 7407 Riverside Dr, Ontario CA 91761. Tel: (909) 984-5131. Or toll-free in California 1-800-222-7467. Fax: (909) 988-8041. Email: info@maclinmarkets.com. Web: maclinmarkets.com.

PALMDALE
Antelope Valley Swap Meet at Four Points

DATES: Saturday and Sunday, year round.

TIMES: Saturday 7:00 AM-4:00 PM; Sunday 6:00 AM-4:00 PM.

ADMISSION: $1 Saturday; $1.50 Sunday. Parking is free.

LOCATION: 5550 Pearblossom Hwy. Intersection of Hwy 138 and Pearblossom Hwy. Five miles east of Palmdale.

DESCRIPTION: "Everything under the sun!" describes this swap meet opened in 1977. About 350 dealers sell antiques, collectibles, crafts, garage sale goods, old and new merchandise, tools, fresh produce and "soup to nuts." Great food is easily found, including homemade tamales and corn dogs, authentic Mexican food, buffalo burgers, three beer gardens, and biscuits and gravy, to mention a mouth watering few. This market, with its country/western atmosphere, live country and Mexican music every Sunday and pony rides for the kids, seems to offer more than something for everyone. In 1997 they upgraded their facilities for the comfort of their patrons and dealers. After all that food, the handicapped-accessible restrooms will come in handy.

DEALER RATES: Saturday: $10 per 20' × 20' booth; Sunday $20 per booth. Storage sheds are available from $125-$250 per month. Reservations are not required; first come, first served. RV'ers are welcome to stay overnight. Office opens 7:00 AM on Saturday, 6:00 AM on Sunday.

CONTACT: Joyce Bruce, Antelope Valley Swap Meet, PO Box 901807, Palmdale CA 93590. Tel: (661) 273-0456. Fax: (661) 273-5465. Email: info@swapmeetat4points.com. Web: www.swapmeetat4points.com.

PANORAMA CITY
Valley Indoor Swap Meet

DATES: Wednesday through Monday.

TIMES: Weekdays 11:00 AM-7:00 PM, weekends 10:00 AM-6:00 PM.

ADMISSION: Free. Parking is free.

LOCATION: 14650 Parthenia St. Take 101 Fwy to Van Nuys Blvd, go north 4 miles to Parthenia St.

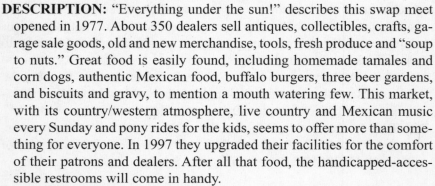

DESCRIPTION: Started in 1986 and the only major retailing center to survive the Northridge earthquake, this indoor market of 250 dealers sells all new merchandise, including collectibles, crafts, furniture, toys, shoes, and lots of clothing. Three snack bars quell the munchies and handi-capped-accessible restrooms are on site. They hold promotional events every month, including: health fairs, carnivals, circus, Halloween costume contests, bands, and more.

DEALER RATES: $500 monthly per 9' × 13' space. Reservations are required.

CONTACT: Valley Indoor Swap Meet, 14650 Parthenia St, Panorama City CA 91402. Tel: (818) 893-8234 or fax: (818) 894-5676. Email: info@indoorswap.com. Web: www.indoorswap.com.

PASADENA
Rose Bowl Flea Market

DATES: Second Sunday of each month. Rain or shine.

TIMES: 9:00 AM-3:00 PM.

ADMISSION: $7 per person, children under 12 free with an adult. Free parking, and VIP parking for a fee. Early admission for $10 from 7:30 AM-9:00 AM, and very early VIP admission is $20 from 6:00 AM-7:30 AM.

LOCATION: Pasadena Rose Bowl, at the corner of Rosemont Ave and Aroyo Blvd. Well marked. Close to the freeway junctions of 210 Foothill, 134 Ventura and 110 Pasadena Fwys.

DESCRIPTION: This monthly market ranks among the largest and best known in the country. It has operated outdoors on the grounds of the Rose Bowl Stadium since 1968 and currently hosts over 2,200 sellers and approximately 20,000 shoppers at each sale. Virtually anything under the sun can be found here, from antiques and collectibles to new merchandise and arts and crafts. Buyers often include Hollywood celebrities. Vendors may not sell food, animals, drug-related items or ammunition. Food and beverages and handicapped-accessible restrooms complete the amenities.

DEALER RATES: $40-$100 per 10' × 20' space per day depending upon location. Advance reservations strongly suggested.

CONTACT: RG Canning Enterprises, PO Box 400, Maywood CA 90270. Tel: (323) 560-7469 ext 11. Office hours Mondays and Wednesdays 10:00 AM-5:00 PM. Fax: (323) 560-5924. Email: rgc@rgcshows.com or website: www.rgcshows.com.

POMONA
Collector's Street Faire

DATES: Last Saturday of odd months.

TIMES: 8:00 AM-5:00 PM.

ADMISSION: Free. Parking is free.

LOCATION: 2nd St, downtown Pomona, between the 100 and 200 blocks of Pomona's Antique Row.

DESCRIPTION: Held in the historic 1920s buildings of downtown Pomona since 1985, with 500 vendors in the historic buildings and another 100 along the sidewalks. This is an antique and collectibles only market. There is plenty of food available and handicapped-accessible restrooms around. Plenty of movies are made in this area.

DEALER RATES: $35-$65 per space depending on location. Space is always available, first come, first served. But reservations are a good idea, too. They don't turn any one away.

CONTACT: RG Canning Enterprises, PO Box 400, Maywood CA 90270. Tel: (323) 560-7469 ext 14. Fax: (323) 560-5924. Office hours Mondays and Wednesdays 10:00 AM-5:00 PM. Email: rgc@rgcshows.com or website: www.rgcshows.com.

Valley Indoor Swap Meet

DATES: Daily except Tuesday.

TIMES: 10:00 AM-6:00 PM.

ADMISSION: Free. Parking is free.

LOCATION: 1600 East Holt Blvd. Take San Bernardino Fwy (10) to Indian Hill Blvd, go south 1 mile to Holt Blvd. Indian Hill ends at the swap meet.

DESCRIPTION: Started in 1986, this air-conditioned indoor market of 400 dealers and services offers ethnic crafts, furniture, a pet store, one-hour photo service, electronics, an optometrist, a dentist, new merchandise, porcelain, and loads of the latest fashion clothing, shoes and accessories. This is considered the largest indoor swap meet in the Inland Empire, with unique displays of Mexican and American merchandise. A snack bar quells the munchies and handicapped-accessible restrooms ease the other necessities. There are giveaways for children, live entertainment on weekends, and other fun things to do. On the third Saturday of every month there is a free food giveaway for needy families (the No More Empty Shelf program). You can literally buy or do anything business-wise under this roof.

DEALER RATES: $470 monthly for a 10' × 10' space. Reservations are required. There is a multiple space discount after 2 spaces, i.e. first 2 are $470 each, the third and beyond are $370 each space.

CONTACT: Valley Indoor Swap Meet, 1600 E Holt Blvd, Pomona CA 91767. Tel: (909) 620-1449 or 620-5083; for taped information 620-4792. Fax: (909) 620-5790.

PORTERVILLE
Porterville College Swap Meet

DATES: Every Saturday, weather permitting.

TIMES: 5:00 AM-4:00 PM.

ADMISSION: $.50. Parking is also free.

LOCATION: From Bakersfield: Go north on Hwy 99 to Hwy 65. Then 50 miles to Hwy 190, then east 1 mile to college. From Fresno, go south on Hwy 99 to Hwy 190, then go east 17 miles to college.

DESCRIPTION: Started in 1981, this market has an average of 300 dealers attending. There is always plenty of elegant junk available along with an ample supply of antiques, arts and crafts, collectibles, jewelry, the occasional snake, and music tapes, along with new merchandise and fresh produce. This market is run for the benefit of the student scholarship fund and is a Foundation function. There is always plenty of food available on the premises, as well as handicapped-accessible restrooms.

DEALER RATES: $15 for 24' × 36' space (electricity costs an additional $1). Reservations are advised but not necessary.

CONTACT: Bill Goucher, Porterville College Swap Meet, 150 E College Ave, Porterville CA 93257-5901. Tel: (559) 791-2200 (college) or Mr Goucher at (559) 784-9161.

REDDING
Epperson Brothers Auction and Flea Market

DATES: Saturday and Sunday, year round. Rain or shine.

TIMES: Sunup to sundown. Also, auctions are held at 6:30 PM every Wednesday and at 1:00 PM every Sunday.

ADMISSION: $1 per carload Sundays; Saturdays admission is free.

LOCATION: 21005 Fig Tree Ln, 1 mile south of Redding International Airport, off Airport Rd.

DESCRIPTION: The market, located on 20 acres of trees, first opened in 1962 and now consists of 100 to 150 dealers selling their goods both indoors and outdoors. Antiques, collectibles, arts and crafts, and new and used furniture can be purchased. Food, beer (had to mention that!), plenty of parking and handicapped-accessible restrooms are available on the premises.

DEALER RATES: $5 for 4' × 8' table (plus space for vehicle) on Saturday. $10 per space on Sunday.

CONTACT: Jack L Epperson, 21005 Fig Tree Ln, Redding CA 96007. Tel: (530) 365-7242 or Karen Bloom. Fax: (530) 365-3159.

ROSEVILLE
Denio's Roseville Farmers' Market and Auction, Inc

DATES: Every Friday through Sunday. Rain or shine.

TIMES: Friday 8:00 AM-2:00 PM for the open-air market only. Weekends 7:00 AM-5:00 PM.

ADMISSION: $.50 walk-ins or parking is $2 per car.

LOCATION: 1551 Vineyard Rd. Take I-80 to Roseville/Riverside exit, turn left on Cirby Way, right on Foothill Blvd to Vineyard, right on Vineyard Rd.

DESCRIPTION: Denio's is a family owned and operated business in the same location since 1947, serving northern California, southern Oregon, and western Nevada. It averages 1,500 to 2,000 dealers selling everything imaginable—antiques, collectibles, comics, clothing, rugs, electronics, motor homes and vans, hats, toys, handmade/craft items, fresh produce and new merchandise. About 50% of the market is old stuff and garage sale goodies. Friday is their open-air market only. Delicious corn dogs and international foods are available on the premises. Just in case of need, there are handicapped-accessible restrooms.

DEALER RATES: Start at $20 per space, about 18' × 20'. Reservations are required for weekends. Reservations are taken on Friday of the weekend you wish to sell. The rental office is open market hours.

CONTACT: Rental Office, Denio's Roseville Farmers' Market, 1551 Vineyard Rd, Roseville CA 95678-2000. Tel: (916) 782-2704. Web: www.denios.org

SACRAMENTO
Folsom Boulevard Flea Market

DATES: Every Saturday and Sunday. Rain or shine.

TIMES: 7:00 AM-5:00 PM.

ADMISSION: Free. Parking is free.

LOCATION: 8521 Folsom Blvd. Use Hwy 50 going to Lake Tahoe, take Watt Ave south to Folsom Blvd, turn right, go .8 miles to market on right.

DESCRIPTION: This show first opened in 1966. It accommodates 400 dealers in both an indoor and outdoor market. Four barns house fresh produce, antiques and collectibles in permanent space. This is said to be the longest-operating flea market within the city limits of Sacramento. Seven restaurants, including Mexican, Chinese and a deli, operate on the premises. Handicapped-accessible restrooms add to the amenities.

DEALER RATES: $20 for one 4' × 8' table, $15 for the second table, $10 for each additional table. Reservations are accepted Wednesday through Friday 9:00 AM-5:00 PM.

CONTACT: Emil, Jr and John Magovac, Owners, Folsom Boulevard Flea Market, 8521 Folsom Blvd, Sacramento CA 95826. Tel: (916) 383-0880 or (916) 383-0950.

SAN BERNARDINO
San Bernardino Outdoor Market

DATES: Every Sunday. Rain or shine.

TIMES: 6:00 AM-2:00 PM.

ADMISSION: $1, children under 13 are free with an adult. Free and paid parking is available.

LOCATION: National Orange Showgrounds. Directly off the 215 Fwy. Take the Orange Show Road exit and follow the signs.

DESCRIPTION: There are almost 800 dealers attending this, the area's largest weekly outdoor show. An enormous selection of merchandise can be found, about half new and half used. Antiques, collectibles, crafts and new merchandise are just some of the items to be ferreted out. Many sellers are "the average guy cleaning out his garage." From one reader: "Worth visiting every several months to keep in touch." For your convenience, food is also available on the premises.

DEALER RATES: $7 to $35 depending on location of space. Reservations are suggested. They claim to never turn anyone away. If you are more than a two-time seller, you need a Sales Tax Permit from the State Board of Equalization.

CONTACT: RG Canning, PO Box 400, Maywood CA 90270-0400. Tel: (909) 888-0394 Monday or Wednesday between 10:00 AM-5:00 PM. Email: rgc@rgcshows.com or website: www.rgcshows.com.

SAN DIEGO
Kobey's Swap Meet at the San Diego Sports Arena

DATES: Friday through Sunday and every day of the week prior to Christmas.

TIMES: 7:00 AM-3:00 PM.

ADMISSION: Friday $.50 per person, weekends $1, children under 12 free. Parking is free.

LOCATION: Sports Arena at 3500 Sports Arena Blvd.

DESCRIPTION: Opened in 1976, this outdoor market of 1,000 spaces hosts 700 vendors selling antiques, collectibles, crafts, produce, coins, stamps, cards, garage sale finds, furniture and new merchandise. Food kiosks and restrooms are available.

DEALER RATES: Weekends $25 and up for a 16' × 18' space ($20 unreserved); $8 for Friday. Reservations are recommended during holiday or peak seasons. Reservations must be made in person Wednesday through Sunday; Wednesday at the office, Thursday through Sunday at the main entrance at 3500 Sports Area Blvd.

CONTACT: Kobey Swap Meet, 3350 Sports Area Blvd #K, San Diego CA 92110. Tel: (619) 226-0650 (24-hour information) or (619) 523-2700 Monday through Friday from 9:00 AM-5:00 PM. Fax: (619) 523-2715. Email: kim@kobeyswap.com. Web: www.kobeyswap.com.

SAN FRANCISCO
"America's Largest" Antique & Collectible Shows

DATES: 2002: February 16-17, September 21-22. Call or visit their website for 2003 dates.

TIMES: Saturday 8:00 AM-6:00 PM; Sunday 9:00 AM-5:00 PM.

ADMISSION: $5, $2 under 17, free under 12. Parking is $5.

LOCATION: Cow Palace. Cow Palace exit off Hwy 101, San Francisco.

DESCRIPTION: This indoor market opened in 1988 and attracts over 350 dealers selling antiques and collectibles only, including estate jewelry, rare books, bakelite jewelry, Western Americana, toys, art, advertising pottery, militaria, glass, decorating items, movie memorabilia, autographs and vintage clothing to over 8,000 shoppers per show. Food and restrooms are available on the premises.

DEALER RATES: $140 per 10' × 10' booth. Reservations are required.

CONTACT: Palmer/Wirfs & Associates, 4001 NE Halsey Ste 5, Portland OR 97232. Tel: (503) 282-0877. Fax: (503) 282-2953. Email: palmerwirfs@qwest.net. Web: www.palmerwirfs.com.

SAN JOSE
Capitol Flea Market

DATES: Thursday through Sunday.

TIMES: 6:00 AM-5:30 PM, Friday only 7:00 AM-5:30 PM.

LOCATION: 3630 Hillcap Ave. Capitol Expwy at Monterey Hwy.

ADMISSION: 50¢ on Thursday, Friday free, Saturday $1.25, Sunday $1.50. Children under 12 free. Parking is free.

DESCRIPTION: This outdoor market, in business since 1982, hosts from 500 to 900 dealers depending on the season. They sell mostly antiques, collectibles, and garage sale specials (self-billed as the "World's Largest Garage Sale"). Very little new merchandise is sold here. They describe themselves as an "old-fashioned" flea market in the best sense of the word. Covering 35 acres in a drive-in theater, they park from 4,000 to 12,000 cars a day! "We are crammed!" says their manager. He advises you to "Come early for the bargains." They cater to families. There is a gigantic used car and truck sale every weekend selling vehicles at $12 a set of wheels! They've added a huge farmers' market produce area (with 40-50 vendors here alone) featuring farm fresh fruits and vegetables at bargain prices. Live music and free raffles liven the weekends. There are restaurants and snack bars on site with a wide range of food available.

DEALER RATES: $14 on Thursday, $10 on Friday, $15-$25 on Saturday, $20-$25 on Sunday. Although spaces may vary, they all accommodate a car or truck and ample selling space. Reservations are not required. Monthly reservations are available.

CONTACT: Dwight Price, Capitol Flea Market, 3630 Hillcap Ave, San Jose CA 95136-1344. Tel: (408) 225-5800.

The Flea Market, Inc
DATES: Wednesday through Sunday, year round.
TIMES: Dawn to dusk.
ADMISSION: Free. Parking is $5 Saturday and Sunday; $1 Wednesday through Friday.
LOCATION: 1590 Berryessa Rd between Hwys 680 and 101.
DESCRIPTION: Started in 1960, with 20 vendors on an old feedlot on a country lane in what is now called Silicon Valley, this humongous market is billed as the "Original Flea Market" and is probably the world's largest, covering 120 acres with well over 2,000 dealers selling everything—from antique and collectible, to abused and garage sale. They have a quarter-mile-long produce row, 8 miles of aisles, 30 snack bars, 60 roving food carts, clean, well-attended handicapped-accessible restrooms and an average of 80,000 visitors each weekend. Watch for their special events: the Salsa Festival including contest (you can eat yourself to death on the sauces and chips!), Octoberfest, Cinque de Mayo, Holiday Crafters Fair (just before Thanksgiving), Bicycle Fairs, whatever! Wednesdays are good days for mid-week bargains, Thursday and Friday for the neighborhood swap meet atmosphere. Weekends are wild.

DEALER RATES: Per 17' × 20' space per day: Wednesday regular space $15, corner $20; Thursday and Friday $10; Saturday regular space $25, corner $50; and Sunday regular space $30, corner $65. No reservations are necessary, but suggested if you have a preference for a space. For a garage sale special: $10 for the first Saturday of the month. There are monthly rates; ask at the office. Reservations is open Friday, 8:30 AM to 1:00 PM; Saturday, 8:30 AM to 3:00 PM; Sunday 9:00 AM to 3:00 PM. 1-800-BIG-FLEA or 1-(408) 453-1110 x 246. Gates open at 5:00 AM.
CONTACT: Reservations Manager, The Flea Market Inc, 1590 Berryessa Rd, San Jose CA 95133-1003. Tel: (408) 453-1110 or 1-800-BIG-FLEA. Fax: (408) 437-9011. Email: john@sjfm.com. Web: www.sjfm.com.

SAN JUAN BAUTISTA
San Juan Bautista Annual Flea Market
DATES: First Sunday in August. Rain or shine.
TIMES: 8:00 AM-5:00 PM.
ADMISSION: Free. Some parking lots nearby are free, some aren't.
LOCATION: In downtown San Juan Bautista, 40 miles south of San Jose on Hwy 101.
DESCRIPTION: This show first began in 1963, and nowadays over 200 vendors from 9 states and 100 California cities come to participate in this

event, all conducting their business outdoors on the main streets of the town. Antiques and collectibles can be purchased. This market claims to be the oldest and largest one-day street show in California and has been named one of the top four flea markets in California by *Good Housekeeping* magazine. There are 10 restaurants and plenty of street vendors providing food.

DEALER RATES: $185 for 10' × 20' space. Reservations are required. Dealers start arriving as early as 1:00 AM.

CONTACT: Chamber of Commerce, PO Box 1037, San Juan Bautista CA 95045. Tel: (831) 623-2454. Fax: (831) 623-0674.

SANTA CLARITA (SAUGAS)
Saugus Swap Meet

DATES: Every Sunday and Tuesday. Rain or shine.

TIMES: Sunday 7:00 AM-3:00 PM. Tuesday 7:00 AM-2:00 PM.

ADMISSION: $1 for adults on Sunday only, children under 12 are admitted free. Parking is free.

LOCATION: 22500 Soledad Canyon Rd. From Los Angeles, take I-5 to Valencia Blvd exit, turn right on Valencia Blvd, go 3¼ miles. Market is on the right.

DESCRIPTION: This show began in 1965. There are approximately 650 dealers conducting their business outdoors and selling everything from antiques and collectibles to new merchandise and fresh produce. The market is held on the grounds of movie star Hoot Gibson's former ranch, and formerly the Saugas Speedway. Food is available on the premises. From one reader: "...garage sales were good quality, good dealing available. About 60/40 percent new/collectibles. Many businesses come to advertise." There is pottery, carpets, home repair, remodeling, florals, electronics collectibles, and live entertainment.

DEALER RATES: Tuesday market $10 per space. Sundays $30 for 20' × 16' space. Assigned location space is available from $25-$60 a day. Reservations are not required. Park on space. Setup starts at 6:00 AM.

CONTACT: Saugus Swap Meet, Box 901, Santa Clarita CA 91380-9001. For information contact office Tuesday through Friday 8:00 AM-3:00 PM. Tel: (818) 716-6010 for tape information or (661) 259-3886. Fax: (661) 259-8534. Email: sspeedwy@pacbell.net. Web: www.saugusspeedway.com.

SANTA FE SPRINGS
Santa Fe Springs Swap Meet

DATES: Wednesday through Sunday.

TIMES: Wednesday 5:30 AM-3:30 PM, Thursday 5:30 AM-2:00 PM, Friday night 5:00 PM-10:00 PM, Saturday 5:30 AM-4:00 PM, and Sunday 5:30 AM-4:30 PM.

ADMISSION: $.50 on Wednesday; free on Thursday; $.50-$1 on Friday (seasonal); $1 Saturday and Sunday. Parking is free.

LOCATION: 13963 Alondra Blvd. Take Valley View exit off I-5. The market is located 1 block west of Valley View.

DESCRIPTION: This market began in 1960 and is said to be the first swap meet in Southern California. Held at a former drive-in theater, this market averages 650 dealers on weekends selling everything from arts and crafts, pop collectibles, fine art, new and used merchandise, and fresh produce. There are a Himalaya roller coaster ride, bumper boats (seasonal) and a video arcade to keep children busy. There are plenty of special events, including petting zoos, magicians, performing clowns, rock-climbing apparatus, kiddie slides and haunted houses. Each weekend, a large, outdoor barbecue is open and live entertainment performs in the snack bar area. Food, from a snack bar and catering trucks, is served on the premises and there are handicapped-accessible restrooms.

DEALER RATES: $10 Wednesday; free on Thursday; $15-$40 Friday nights (seasonal pricing); $25-$30 per space on Saturday and Sunday. Day-of-event sales are possible on a first-come, first-served basis. Monthly Reserve spaces are available for all days. Garage sale rates: $5 on Saturday; $10-$15 Friday night; $10 Sunday. (Subject to availability.)

CONTACT: Santa Fe Springs Swap Meet, 13963 Alondra Blvd, Santa Fe Springs CA 90670. Tel: (562) 921-4359 (then dial 0 for a live person) or (562) 921-9996 for tape message. Fax: (562) 921-1706. Email: info@sfsswapmeet.com. Web: www.sfsswapmeet.com.

SANTEE
Santee Swap Meet

DATES: Saturday and Sunday. Rain or shine.

TIMES: 6:30 AM-2:00 PM.

ADMISSION: $.75. Parking is free.

LOCATION: 10990 Woodside Ave N. Take 67 north to Riverford Rd exit. Turn left at exit, then left at Riverford Rd, left at Woodside Ave N. Market is on the right side at the drive-in theater.

DESCRIPTION: Open since 1984, this outdoor market draws large crowds of buyers as well as sellers. Many a garage is cleaned out here. Vendors sell new merchandise, antiques, collectibles, crafts and produce. This is a fast-growing market which holds special events on Saturdays. The second Saturday special event is strictly antiques and collectibles. It is held next to the main swap meet. A snack bar serves a wide variety of sandwiches, snacks and breakfasts.

DEALER RATES: Saturday $11 per 20' × 20' booth, Sunday $13 per 20' × 20' booth. Reservations are not required; it's a first-come, first-served market.

CONTACT: Joe Crowder, Escondido Swap Meet Associates, 635 W Mission Ave, Escondido CA 92025. Tel: (760) 745-3100. Day of show (619) 449-7927.

SEBASTOPOL
Midgley's Country Flea Market

DATES: Saturday and Sunday, year round. Weather permitting.
TIMES: 6:30 AM-4:30 PM.
ADMISSION: Free. Parking is free.
LOCATION: 2200 Gravenstein Hwy S. Off Hwy 101 to Gravenstein Hwy or Hwy 116. Market is about 5 miles down the road. Only 50 miles north of San Francisco.

DESCRIPTION: This family friendly outdoor market, run by the same family, has been open since 1972. There are up to 250 dealers filling 500 spaces during the summer and anywhere from 150 to 200 dealers selling their goods during the winter months. At least 50% of this market is still "bonafide flea market" goodies. There is a large variety of antiques, collectibles, crafts, new merchandise and even fresh produce available. Basically anything new or used is sold, including clothes, books, pictures, jewelry, tires, and furniture, just to name a few. Two snack bars and handicapped-accessible restrooms deal with issues other than browsing.
DEALER RATES: Currently $13 for 4' × 8' table and parking for one vehicle. Weekly, monthly and seasonal rates available. Reservations are not required.
CONTACT: Midgley's Country Flea Market, 2200 Gravenstein Hwy S, Sebastopol CA 95472-4854. Tel: (707) 823-7874 or 1-800-800-FLEA in California. Email: dwade@sonic.net.

> ### Lost and Found
> Years ago, a rather strange piece of denture was turned into the office as lost. The odd piece sat in the lost and found box for months, but the owners couldn't imagine that this curious piece could actually fit someone. Sure enough, one day a man asked if anyone had turned in any dentures. Well, they said, yes . . . is this what you are looking for? The fellow took the proffered piece and fitted it in his mouth perfectly.

STANTON
International Market Place (Indoor Swapmeet of Stanton)

DATES: Daily except Tuesday.
TIMES: Weekends 10:00 AM-6:00 PM; weekdays 10:00 AM-7:00 PM.
ADMISSION: Free. Parking is free.
LOCATION: 10401 Beach Blvd, 2 miles south of Knott's Berry Farm.

DESCRIPTION: This two-story indoor market has 200 spaces with 75 vendors selling crafts, new merchandise, jewelry, perfumes, sportswear, athletic shoes, luggage, clothing, computer stuff, electronic appliances, gifts, nail and beauty salon, groceries, caps, embroidering, silk flowers and more. One snack bar, a restaurant, and handicapped-accessible restrooms are on site.

DEALER RATES: $275-$600 for 4 weeks or 28 days depending on the location for a 8' × 12' space. Reservations are not required.

CONTACT: Jila Ilami, Manager, Indoor Swapmeet of Stanton, 10401 Beach Blvd, Stanton CA 90680. Tel: (714) 527-1112 or (714) 527-1234 or fax: (714) 527-1595. Email: indoorswapofstanton@sbcglobal.net.

TORRANCE
Roadium Open Air Market

DATES: Daily, except Christmas and New Year's Day.

TIMES: 7:00 AM-3:00 PM.

ADMISSION: Weekends: $1.50 per car and driver, plus $.50 per person up to $3.50 maximum. Monday and Friday $1 per car and driver, $.50 per person; Wednesday $1.25 per person; Tuesday and Thursday $.50 per person. Children are free.

LOCATION: 2500 Redondo Beach Blvd. From Long Beach and the south, take the San Diego Fwy (405) to Crenshaw. Go right to Redondo Beach Blvd, turn right into the market. From the north, take 405 to the Redondo Beach Blvd Exit and go east to the market.

DESCRIPTION: For over 40 years the Roadium has been a fixture in Torrance with 470 dealers, spread over 15 acres, offering fresh produce, plenty of new and pre-owned merchandise and some antiques and collectibles. There is a snack bar, roving snack carts, restrooms, and an ATM.

DEALER RATES: $14-$55 per space depending on location and day of week; reservations requested. Office hours: 5:30 AM-3:00 PM.

CONTACT: John Schoen, Roadium Open Air Market, 2500 Redondo Beach Blvd, Torrance CA 90504. Tel: (323) 321-3709 or within California 1-800-833-0304. Fax: (323) 321-0114. Email: roadium@earthlink.net. Web: www.Roadium.com.

TURLOCK
Turlock Sales Yard Flea Market

DATES: Tuesdays only.

TIMES: 4:00 AM-dark.

ADMISSION: Free. Parking is $1.

LOCATION: At the corner of East Ave and N Johnson Rd.

DESCRIPTION: This historic, real old-time flea market on 10 acres of selling space and 15 acres of parking evolved into a hugely popular hit with 400-500 dealers nabbing all 750 spaces selling 5 acres of antiques, collectibles, and just used stuff; 2½ acres of produce; and 2½ acres of new merchandise. This is a great place to buy "used" treasures for resale. In case of famishment, there is a small restaurant doing the burger thing, plus 12 food wagons (selling tacos, Chinese) roaming the market, quelling thirsts as well. Handicapped-accessible restrooms come in handy if you sample too much.

DEALER RATES: $20 per 12' × 24' space, take as many as you need. No reservations taken. For regular dealers with a preference for a space, they will hold it only until 6:30 AM.

CONTACT: Scott Linn, Turlock Sales Yard Flea Market, PO Box 25, Turlock CA 95380-0025. Tel: (209) 667-4441. Email: ssslll@aol.com.

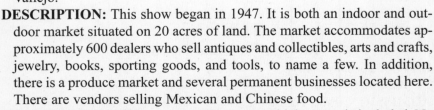

The Beginnings

In 1938, Scott's grandfather sold horses off a street corner. Gradually, others came to buy and auction off their livestock, then boxed household items. This market exploded into a flea market in the 1970s, the livestock market was sold off and the whole shebang was moved to its current location.

A few years ago, three paintings were puchased for $80, taken to the San Francisco area, sold around there until some savvy seller got them and sold them through Butterfields—for $80,000.

VALLEJO

Napa-Vallejo Flea Market and Auction

DATES: Every Sunday. Rain or shine.

TIMES: 5:00 AM-5:00 PM.

ADMISSION: Free. $3 parking fee.

LOCATION: 303 Kelly Rd, off Hwy 29, halfway between Napa and Vallejo.

DESCRIPTION: This show began in 1947. It is both an indoor and outdoor market situated on 20 acres of land. The market accommodates approximately 600 dealers who sell antiques and collectibles, arts and crafts, jewelry, books, sporting goods, and tools, to name a few. In addition, there is a produce market and several permanent businesses located here. There are vendors selling Mexican and Chinese food.

DEALER RATES: $20 per 10' × 20' space; vehicle space is included. No reservations are accepted. Sellers should arrive and set up between 5:00 AM-10:00 AM.

CONTACT: Tom Harding, Napa-Vallejo Flea Market and Auction, 303 Kelly Rd, Vallejo CA 94590-9647. Tel: (707) 226-8862.

VENTURA
Ventura Flea Market

DATES: 2002: February 3, April 28, June 2, August 18, September 22, November 3. Call for 2003 dates, or check the website.

TIMES: 9:00 AM-2:00 PM, although you can shop while the vendors pack up until 4:30 PM. Advice: come early for the best parking.

ADMISSION: $5, children under 12 are free with an adult. Parking is free or paid. Early dealer and collector's hours start at 6:00 AM for an $8 admission.

LOCATION: Ventura County Fairgrounds, aka Seaside Park at 10 W Harbor in Ventura, just off the 101 Ventura Fwy at California St.

DESCRIPTION: There are over 800 dealers attending this outdoor show. Everything from antiques to collectibles to crafts and new merchandise to garage specials can be found here. It is one of California's most popular markets, with approximately 8,000 buyers. For your convenience, there are also food and handicapped-accessible restrooms available on the premises. As one shopper describes this market: "95% collectibles and garage sales, only 5% new stuff. Very good dealers who want to make a deal. Bargains can still be found here."

DEALER RATES: $30, $40, or $50 per 20' × 20' space. Reservations are suggested.

CONTACT: RG Canning, PO Box 400, Maywood CA 90270-0400. Tel: (323) 560-7469 ext 13. Office hours are Monday and Wednesday 10:00 AM-5:00 PM. Email: rgc@rgcshows.com or website: www.rgcshows.com.

VICTORVILLE
Maclin's Victorville Open-Air Market

DATES: Every Saturday and Sunday.

TIMES: 6:00 AM-2:30 PM.

ADMISSION: $1, children 12 and under free. Seniors $.75. Parking is free.

LOCATION: San Bernardino County Fairgrounds, 14800 Seventh St. Located off the 15 Fwy on Roy Rogers exit.

DESCRIPTION: Opened in 1997, this market has 150-200 dealers selling household goods, clothing, new and used merchandise, collectible and specialty items. There is "great on-site" food service. Live entertainment is provide by local musicians.

DEALER RATES: Saturday $15 for any space; Sunday $12 for everything. Spaces are 20' × 20'. Bring your own setup. You can prepay Friday evening from 3:00 PM-5:00 PM.

CONTACT: Maclin's, 7407 Riverside Dr, Ontario CA 91761. Tel: (909) 984-5131. Or toll-free in California 1-800-222-7467. Fax: (909) 988-8041. Email: info@maclinmarkets.com. Web: maclinmarkets.com.

VISALIA
Visalia Sales Yard, Inc

DATES: Thursday and Sunday, year round.
TIMES: 6:00 AM-3:00 PM.
ADMISSION: Free. Parking is also free.
LOCATION: 29660 Rd 152, 1½ miles east of Visalia.

DESCRIPTION: This show began in 1948 and is currently an all-outdoor market that accommodates approximately 300 dealers. Among the items to be found here are antiques and collectibles, new merchandise, and fresh produce. A snack bar serves hot dogs, burritos, breakfasts and other delights, and handicapped-accessible restrooms take care of other needs.
DEALER RATES: $8 per 10' × 10' space. Monthly reservations are available, otherwise first come, first served.
CONTACT: Karen Green, Visalia Sales Yard Inc, 29660 Rd 152, Visalia CA 93291-9152. Tel: (559) 734-9092.

WOODLAND HILLS
Valley Indoor Swap Meet

DATES: Friday through Sunday.
TIMES: 10:00 AM-6:00 PM.
ADMISSION: Free. Parking is free.
LOCATION: 6701 Variel Ave. Take 101 Fwy to Desoto Ave, go north 1½ miles to Kittridge St, left 2 blocks.

DESCRIPTION: Opened in 1983, this is the first of three Valley Indoor Swap Meets in California (see Pomona and Panorama City). Housed in two buildings, their 500 dealers sell new merchandise and specialize in clothing and accessories. These markets are huge and sell just about anything you can think of. One of the buildings is open weekends only, the other from Friday through Sunday. Claimed to be "the most famous, well-known indoor swap meet in southern California. Selling high-end merchandise. Many movie and TV celebrities can be seen attending on almost any weekend." Handicapped-accessible restrooms alleviate the load from too many stops at the many snack bars offering all the usual goodies.
DEALER RATES: $320 in the 2-day building, $420 in the 3-day building, monthly for a 10' × 10' space. Reservations are required.
CONTACT: Dena Weingart, Valley Indoor Swap Meet, 6701 Variel Ave, Woodland Hills CA 91303. Tel: (818) 340-9120 or 340-9123. Fax: (818) 340-5413. Email: info@indoorswap.com. Web: www.indoorswap.com.

YUCCA VALLEY
Sky Village Outdoor Marketplace

DATES: Saturday and Sunday, year round.
TIMES: 5:30 AM-2:00 PM.
ADMISSION: Free. Parking is free.
LOCATION: 7028 Theater Rd, near the intersection of S Hwys 62 and 247.
DESCRIPTION: This family owned, still old-fashioned, "not overly commercialized" swap meet's 200 dealers sell a mix of antiques and collectibles, old tools, and new and used merchandise—described as from "junk to gems." As it is so easy to rent and set up here, many locals bring in tons of garage sale goodies. In fact, many items you might be looking for elsewhere and can't find are probably here! The Sky Cafe serves homemade breakfast and lunch. Clean restrooms are on site.

DEALER RATES: Saturday: $10 for a 20' space, Sunday $9. Reservations are not required. Gates open at 5:30 AM. You can stay overnight next to your merchandise.
CONTACT: Bob and Elizabeth Carr, Sky Village Outdoor Marketplace, PO Box 1808, Yucca Valley CA 92288-1808. Tel: (760) 365-2104. Web: www.desertgold.com/sky/sky.html.

OTHER FLEA MARKETS

We know or have heard about these markets, but have not personally contacted each one, as we have the markets with descriptions. If you plan to visit one of the markets listed below, *please call first* to make sure they are still open. Flea markets do come and go. While they were open when we went to press, they may not be later. We can't be responsible. *Call first!*

Alameda: Norcal Swap Meet, 1150 Ballena Blvd. Tel: (510) 769-7266.
American Canyon: Flea Market & Auction, 303 S Kelly Rd. Tel: (707) 226-8862.
Anderson: Happy Valley Flea Mart, 17820 Strawberry Ln. Tel: (530) 365-3644.
Aromas: Red Barn Flea Market, 1000 Hwy 101. Tel: (831) 726-3101.
Atwater: Atwater Open Air Market, 2877 Atwater Blvd. Tel: (209) 358-8040.
Berkeley: Berkeley Flea Market, 1937 Ashby Ave. Tel: (510) 644-0744.
Castroville: Castroville Flea Market, 10900 Merritt St. Tel: (831) 633-0369.
Chico: Silverdollar Swap Meet, Silver Dollar Fair Grounds. Tel: (530) 892-9205.
Clearlake: Clearlake Flea Market, 16080 Davis Ave. Tel: (707) 995-7070.
Fresno: Big Fresno Flea Market & Swap, 1641 S Chance Ave. Tel: (559) 268-3646.
Gerber: Gerber Flea Market, 8795 San Benito Ave. Tel: (530) 385-2919.
Kerman: Country Fair, 14443 W Whitesbridge Ave. Tel: (559) 846-9172.

Lancaster: Lancaster Flea Market, 554 W Lancaster Blvd. Tel: (661) 948-4518.

McKinleyville: Redwood Flea Market. Tel: (707) 839-3049.

Merced: Merced Flea Market, 2824 Park Ave. Tel: (209) 723-3796.

Merced: Merced Swap Meet, Childs Ave & G St. Tel: (209) 382-0808.

Modesto: Crow's Landing Flea Market, 3113 Crows Landing Rd. Tel: (209) 538-3363.

Modesto: Modesto Flea Market, 1107 S 7th St. Tel: (209) 522-7762.

Oakland: San Pablo Flea Market II, 6100 San Pablo Ave. Tel: (510) 420-1468.

Orland: Old Town, 424 Colusa St. Tel: (530) 865-3347.

Orosi: Orosi Swap-Meet, 41286 Rd 124. Tel: (559) 528-2288.

Oroville: Palermo-70 Flea Market, 842 Palermo Rd. Tel: (530) 534-3768.

Perris: Lake Perris Old Time Swap Meet, Lake Perris Fairgrounds. Tel: (909) 657-1569.

Roseville: Auction Town, 100 Atkinson St. Tel: (916) 783-0138.

Salinas: Skyview Flea Market, 925 N Sanborn Rd. Tel: (831) 757-3532.

San Francisco: Far East Flea Market, 729 Grant Ave. Tel: (415) 989-8588.

San Francisco: Mission's Flea Market, 2260 Mission St. Tel: (415) 552-7047.

Selma: Selma Flea Market, 10951 E Mountain View Ave. Tel: (559) 896-3243.

Soquel: Skyview Flea-Market, 2260 Soquel Dr. Tel: (831) 462-4442.

Stockton: Stockton Flea Market, 2542 S El Dorado St. Tel: (209) 465-9933.

COLORADO

COLORADO SPRINGS
The Flea Market

DATES: Saturday and Sunday, year round.
TIMES: 7:00 AM-4:00 PM.
ADMISSION: $1, children are free. Parking is free.
LOCATION: 5225 E Platte Ave. On Platte Ave 1 mile east of Academy Blvd.
DESCRIPTION: Started in 1965, this "super clean" outdoor market has
up to 500 dealers in summer and 200 dealers in winter selling antiques,
collectibles, crafts, produce, coins, stamps, cards, garage sale finds, furniture, and new merchandise on 35 acres of paved and landscaped grounds.
They have a great view of Pikes Peak to boot! Five service carts, an
outdoor patio snack bar, a walk-up bar, one restaurant (I'm told "great
food" and open for breakfast and lunches) and handicapped-accessible
restrooms complete the amenities. They do hold events for children and
families, including pony rides.
DEALER RATES: $15 per 20' × 20' space Saturday, $17 on Sunday. Reservations are first come, first served or reservations can be made in the
summer only, Friday (12:00 PM-4:00 PM), Saturday and Sunday during
market hours. No trailer drop-offs.
CONTACT: Bob Zippfel, The Flea Market, PO Box 7229, Colorado Springs
CO 80933-7229. Tel: (719) 380-8599. Fax: (719) 380-8585. Web:
www.csfleamarket.com.

DENVER
Mile High Flea Market, Inc

DATES: Every Wednesday, Saturday and Sunday, year round.
TIMES: 7:00 AM-5:00 PM.
ADMISSION: $2 per person weekends, $1 per person Wednesdays, under
12 free.
LOCATION: I-76 and 88th Ave.
DESCRIPTION: This indoor/outdoor flea market started in 1977 and is
currently America's third-largest flea market and Colorado's largest flea
market. It brings over 1.5 million bargain hunters to 80 paved acres of
brand name, close-out, garage sale and seasonal merchandise. It features
from 1,800 dealers in summer to 1,500 in winter selling antiques, fine
art, collectibles, new merchandise, sports shoes, socks and underwear,
clothing, silk plants, crystals, sunglasses, tires, auto parts, tools, luggage,
furniture, bicycles, fishing tackle, cowboy boots, baby clothes, army sur-

plus, antique train bells, hog greasers, steam ship whistles, one left manne-
quin leg, bowling balls, jackalopes, and seasonal merchandise, including
bedding plants, Christmas trees, pumpkins and farm-fresh produce. About
800 of the dealers are cleaning out their garages, and 700 to 1,000 vendors
are regulars. A new family midway features rides for children and adults
alike. This is billed as a family event with plenty of parking for motor homes
and tour buses. A restaurant, 5 food stands, 2 beer tents, corn roasters, outdoor grills and a fleet of 15 mobile food carts provide ample food and beverage. You can also rent shopping carts, wheelchairs and wagons.

DEALER RATES: $20 per 12' × 25' space per day for Saturday and Sun-
days; $10 per day on Wednesday. There is a $3 per space per day advance reservations fee. Reservations taken all week beginning Monday
afternoons for the following Wednesday and/or weekend (by phone with
MasterCard or Visa). Monthly reservations are also available. Tables and
storage containers are available for rental.

CONTACT: Jim Hurrell, Marketing Director, 7007 E 88 Ave, Henderson
CO 80640. Tel: (303) 289-4656 or 1-800-861-9900. Fax: (303) 286-1922.

FORT COLLINS
Foothills Indoor Flea Market

DATES: Daily.

TIMES: 10:00 AM-6:00 PM.

ADMISSION: Free. Free parking is available.

LOCATION: Just off I-25, between Fort Collins and Loveland on Hwy
287.

DESCRIPTION: This show opened in 1982. It accommodates approximately
100 dealers. This indoor markets contain over 500,000 different items stashed
in 26,000 square feet of space. Sold here are antiques, arts and crafts, and
collectibles. There is no food available on the premises aside from popcorn;
however, we're told there is a great restaurant next door. There are three
more markets in this area—DJs, Itchy's, and Sidekick.

DEALER RATES: $140 plus a 7% fee per 100-square-foot space, per
month. Reservations are required; monthly rates only are available.

CONTACT: Foothills Indoor Flea Market, 6300 S College, Fort Collins
CO 80525-4044. Tel: (970) 223-9069.

Fort Collins Flea Market

DATES: Daily.

TIMES: 10:00 AM-6:00 PM.

ADMISSION: Free. Free parking is available.

LOCATION: Just off I-25, between Fort Collins and Loveland on Hwy 287.

DESCRIPTION: This market opened in 1985. They accommodate approximately 85 dealers selling antiques, arts and crafts, collectibles, fur-

niture, collectible glassware, clothing, groceries, and more. There is also a selection of new merchandise. While no food is served, there are handi-capped-accessible restrooms. There is a restaurant just down the road.

DEALER RATES: $150 plus a 6% fee per 100-square-foot space, per month. Reservations are required; monthly rates only are available.

CONTACT: Vince and Joy Barnhart, Fort Collins Flea Market, 6200 S College, Fort Collins CO 80525-4046. Tel: (970) 223-6502. Email: fcfmarket@qwest.net.

Itchy's Flea Market

DATES: Daily.

TIMES: Monday through Saturday 9:00 AM-6:00 PM, Sunday 10:00 AM-6:00 PM.

ADMISSION: Free. Parking is free.

LOCATION: 6132 S College Ave, Hwy 287.

DESCRIPTION: Opened in 1991, this family-run indoor market of 60 deal-ers sell "everything" literally, from antiques, collectibles, sports cards (a huge sports card shop), furniture, books, novelties, knives and swords, household stuff, small kitchen stuff, new merchandise, groceries, garage sale stuff (no junk allowed), and whatever else the dealers can drag in that is loadable and legal. Candy and drinks are available and handicapped-accessible restrooms.

DEALER RATES: $140 per month, per 100 square feet, plus 6% com-mission. You don't have to be there to sell your goods, and the manage-ment pays the dealers every two weeks.

CONTACT: Itchy's Flea Market, 6132 S College Ave, Fort Collins CO 80525. Tel: (970) 226-4150.

Sidekick Flea Mart

DATES: Daily. Closed Easter, Thanksgiving, Christmas.

TIMES: 10:00 AM-6:00 PM.

ADMISSION: Free. Parking is free.

LOCATION: 6024 S College Ave.

DESCRIPTION: Opened in 1993, this indoor market of 50-75 dealers sells mostly collectibles: toys, cap guns, Hallmark, teakwood, furniture, antiques, videos, Beanie Babies, and the like. Handicapped-accessible restrooms are available. This is one of many flea markets in this few-block area of Ft. Collins.

DEALER RATES: $1.65 per square foot plus 7% commission per month. Reservations are required.

CONTACT: Sidekick Flea Mart, 6024 S College Ave, Fort Collins, CO 80525. Tel: (970) 226-3210.

LAFAYETTE
Lafayette Flea Market

DATES: Daily, year round.

TIMES: 10:00 AM-6:00 PM.

ADMISSION: Free. Parking is free.

LOCATION: 130 E Spaulding, just behind the Conoco gas station on the corner of South Public Rd and Spaulding St.

DESCRIPTION: This market opened April 1, 1990, with 20,000 square feet in a climate-controlled, heated and cooled former bowling alley. They were ranked 12th out of 50 of the "Biggest and Best" Flea Markets in the US in the March 1994 issue of *Good Housekeeping* magazine. Antique stores are two blocks away. There are 116 dealer spaces, with 90 dealers specializing in glassware, hobbies, stamps, coins, antique furniture, collectibles, sports cards, secondhand items, jewelry, and consignments. Since they've been counting visitors, they average 3,500 per week and sell about 7,000 items per month. Not bad!

DEALER RATES: $1.50 per square foot per month or $150 per month for a 10' × 10' booth plus a 10% commission. Reservations are required.

CONTACT: Bill Hopkins, Lafayette Collectibles & Flea Market, 130 E Spaulding, Lafayette CO 80026-2148. Tel: (303) 665-0433. Email: Lafayetteflea@aol.com.

> **Ugly Is as Ugly Does:**
> Recently, a dealer here had a cast-iron door stop priced at $35 on sale in her space for over a year. No takers. Then she read about that particular door stop in *Country Living* magazine—with a price tag of $450. She raced back to the store to snag it back. There it was in all its glory. Ugly as sin, but worth a small bundle. It has since been sold on eBay for $350. As Bill says, "See what happens when you judge a book by its cover?"

LONGMONT
Front Range Indoor Flea Market

DATES: Monday through Saturday.

TIMES: Monday, Wednesday, Friday and Saturday 10:00 AM-6:00 PM. Tuesday and Thursday 9:00 AM-7:30 PM.

ADMISSION: Free. Parking is also free.

LOCATION: 1420 Nelson Rd. West off US 287 on Colorado Rt 119. Approximately 2 blocks east of Boulder County Fair Campgrounds.

DESCRIPTION: This growing market opened in 1989 and currently has over 70 dealers. Housed in a 25,000-square-foot building, these dealers sell new merchandise, collectibles, antiques, jewelry, furniture, sports cards, clothing, and "a lot of everything. We are one of the premier flea markets in the Denver/Boulder area." No food is available, but restrooms are on site.

DEALER RATES: $1.85 per square foot plus 10%. Reservations are required as there is a waiting list.

CONTACT: Vicky Andrew or Marj Sater, Front Range Indoor Flea Market, 1420 Nelson Rd, Longmont CO 80501-6352. Tel: (303) 776-6605.

OTHER FLEA MARKETS

We know or have heard about these markets, but have not personally contacted each one, as we have the markets with descriptions. If you plan to visit one of the markets listed below, *please call first* to make sure they are still open. Flea markets do come and go. While they were open when we went to press, they may not be later. We can't be responsible. *Call first!*

Aurora: Colorado Indoor Flea Market, 9605 E Colfax Ave. Tel: (303) 367-2790.

Aurora: Kim's Gifts, 9333 E Colfax Ave. Tel: (303) 344-1885.

Aurora: Old Town Gift Shop, 9425 Montview Blvd. Tel: (303) 363-8190.

Aurora: Reina Mini Mart, 1440 Havana St. Tel: (303) 739-9669.

Aurora: Las Siete Luminarias, 10061 E Colfax Ave. Tel: (303) 366-7771.

Canon City: Treasures, 322 Main St. Tel: (719) 275-7542.

Cortez: Hoppy's Flea Market & Storage,116 Henry St. Tel: 970-565-6016. Open Thursday through Monday, 12 PM-6 PM, Sat 8 AM-8 PM.

Denver: Federal Indoor Flea Market, 830 Federal Blvd. Tel: (303) 534-1778.

Denver: Mississippi Flea Mart, 2915 W Mississippi Ave. Tel: (303) 727-9091.

Denver: Young's Market, 270 S Federal Blvd. Tel: (303) 922-4268.

Englewood: Cinderella Outdoor Flea Market, South Platte River Dr. Tel: (303) 783-9496.

Englewood: Mini Flea Mart, 3441 S Broadway, CO 80110. Tel: (303) 761-5118. Open Tuesday through Saturday, 10 AM-5 PM.

Estes Park: Such A Deal, 425 W Elkhorn Ave. Tel: (970) 586-2460.

Evans: United Flea Market, 922 37th St. Tel: (970) 330-4143.

Fort Collins: D & J Antiques & Collectibles, 6012 S College Ave. Tel: (970) 226-6070.

Holyoke: This & That, 118 N ½ Interocean Ave. Tel: (970) 854-4503.

Lamar: Lamar Flea Market, 110 E Sherman St. Tel: (719) 336-0333.

Loveland: Everybody's Flea Market, 210 E 4th St. Tel: (970) 669-9575.

Loveland: Loveland Flea Market, 851 S Lincoln (US 287). Tel: (303) 669-9972. Open weekends.

Loveland: Moe's Flea Market & Antiques, 339 E 4th St. Tel: (970) 663-4355.

Loveland: North Fork Antique Flea Market, 3121 W Eisenhower Blvd. Tel: (970) 203-1522.

Monte Vista: Monte Vista's Indoor Flea Market, 206 Adams St. Tel: (719) 852-6996.

Pueblo: Anthony's Lake Ave Mini Storage & Flea Market, 2220 Lake Ave. Tel: (719) 561-3832.

Pueblo: Fiesta Mart, 755 Desert Flower Blvd. Tel: (719) 542-3434.

Pueblo: JUN Indoor Flea Market, 728 East 4th St. Tel: (719) 545-2902.

CONNECTICUT

COVENTRY
Coventry Indoor Outdoor Flea Market

DATES: Every Sunday, year round except Christmas Sundays.
TIMES: 9:00 AM-4:00 PM.
ADMISSION: Free. Parking is free.
LOCATION: 44 Lake St. Junctions of Rts 31 and 275.
DESCRIPTION: Open since October 1990, this indoor/outdoor market of approximately 80 dealers sells sports cards, comics, antiques and collectibles with dealers specializing in jewelry, furniture, records (40 feet worth!), military items, paper, linens, glass, coins, and books. "We will always have dealers with the latest collectibles, tag sale items, fine antique furniture and just plain junk." In 1993, they opened the Coventry General Store selling Coventry-made products: vinegars, dried flowers, furniture, and Westerwald pottery from Pennsylvania with the Coventry pattern. There is a "great clean snack bar with more than hot dogs" as well as handicapped-accessible, clean restrooms.
DEALER RATES: $12 to $25 depending on size and location. Reservations are requested.
CONTACT: Joseph and Rose Fowler, Coventry Flea Market, 110 Wall St, Coventry CT 06238-3143. Tel: (860) 742-9362. Day of market call: (860) 742-1993.

EAST HARTFORD
Connecticut Comic Book Flea Market

DATES: Sundays, generally the fourth Sunday monthly except January. Call for dates.
TIMES: 11:00 AM-5:00 PM.
ADMISSION: $.99 fee. Parking is free.
LOCATION: Elks Hall at 148 Roberts St. Take Exit 58 from I-84, follow the signs.
DESCRIPTION: This show started in 1974 and has approximately 30 dealers. It is an indoor market that sells collectibles, antiques, new merchandise, as well as pulp magazines, science fiction, collectibles, gum cards, and movie items, but they specialize in comic books for collectors. Food is served on the premises.
DEALER RATES: $45 for an 8' table. Advance reservations are required.
CONTACT: Harold E. Kinney, c/o The Bookies Bookstore, 155 Burnside Ave, E Hartford CT 06108. Tel: (860) 289-1208 in afternoons. Email: hal2000@snet.net.

FARMINGTON
Farmington Antiques Weekend

DATES: Second weekend in June and Labor Day weekend. 2002: June 7 & 8, August 31–September 1.

TIMES: 10:00 AM–5:00 PM. Early admission 7:00 AM.

ADMISSION: $7 for adults for the weekend, $5 for Sunday alone. Parking is free. Early admission fee $25.

LOCATION: At the Farmington Polo Grounds, 10 miles west of Hartford and 3 miles from Exit 39 off I-84.

DESCRIPTION: This national antiques event opened in 1980 and is held both outdoors and under tents. Jenkins Management now runs this show as of 2000. There are around 600 dealers at each show selling antiques, fine art, and collectibles, but this market specializes in antiques from rural America. This claims to be the #1 large antiques and better collectibles event in the United States, and it draws approximately 30,000 people per show. All merchandise is guaranteed to be as represented: no new merchandise, no reproductions. Excellent gourmet grille fare will sate your hunger and handicapped-accessible restrooms will come in handy.

DEALER RATES: $275 on the lawns, $350 and up under the tents. Reservations are required well in advance as there is a long waiting list. Write for map and motel list, or check their website.

CONTACT: Farmington Antiques Weekend Inc, Box 580, Fishers IN 46038. Tel: (317) 598-0012. Fax: (317) 598-9007. Week of show call (860) 677-7862. Email: JonJIndpls@aol.com. Email: showinfo@farmington-antiques.com. Web: www.farmington-antiques.com.

HARTFORD
Hartford Marketplace

DATES: Every Saturday and Saturday, plus Memorial Day, July 4 and Labor Day. The Friday after Thanksgiving starts their winter season.

TIMES: 9:00 AM–4:00 PM.

ADMISSION: Adult $1, children under 15 free. Parking is free.

LOCATION: On Market St, at the intersection of Rt 84 and Rt 91.

DESCRIPTION: This upscale market of 200–300 vendors sells antiques, collectibles, food concessions, fresh produce, and used and new merchandise. The site is handicapped-accessible. Clean restrooms on site.

DEALER RATES: Saturday and Sunday $50–$85 per 12' x 25' space. Antiques $40 per space. Reservations are a good idea.

CONTACT: Meadowlands Marketplace, 1 Selleck St, Norwalk CT 06855. Tel: 1-888-445-6543. Fax: (203) 866-4318. Email: info@meadowlandsfleamarket.com. Web: www.meadowlandsfleamarket.com.

JEWETT CITY
College Mart Flea Market

DATES: Every Sunday.

TIMES: 9:00 AM-4:00 PM.

ADMISSION: Free. Parking is free.

LOCATION: Wedgewood Dr. Exits 84 and 85 off I-395.

DESCRIPTION: Started in 1982 in the old Slater Textile Mill, this market now hosts 140 vendors indoors and outdoors selling antiques, glassware, clothing, collectibles, toys, crafts, furniture, all types of old and new jewelry, gold, silver, and new merchandise. Food is available on the premises.

DEALER RATES: $15 for a half space (5' × 10') to $30 for a full space (10' × 10'). Outdoor space is $20. Reservations are strongly recommended.

CONTACT: Bob Leone, College Mart Flea Market, Wedgewood Dr, Jewett City CT 06351. Tel: (860) 376-3935 or (860) 642-6248.

MANSFIELD
Mansfield Drive-in Theater and Marketplace

DATES: Sundays, year round, rain or shine, but call first if it snows.

TIMES: 9:00 AM-3:00 PM.

ADMISSION: Free. Parking is $2 from 8:00 AM-9:00 AM; $1 after that.

LOCATION: Mansfield Drive-In Theatre at 228 Stafford Rd. At the junction of Rts 31 and 32.

DESCRIPTION: Operating since 1975 (formerly Eastern Connecticut Flea Market), and one of the first markets in Connecticut, this now indoor and outdoor market's 200-plus dealers sell antiques, clothes, collectibles, new and used books, tools, toys and more—from "antiques to high tech" with a computer vendor on site. Breakfast and lunch are served at the market, or bring your own. This market is held at a thriving three-screen drive-in theater and its concession is open during the market.

DEALER RATES: Outdoors: $20 for a 14' × 14' space weekly; or $17.50 per week on a monthly basis. Indoors: $20-$25 per week. Rental tables (32" × 7') are $3-$4 a day, if you need one. Reservations are taken on a monthly basis only; otherwise, first come, first served. Setup starts at 7:30 AM and no sales (by local law) before 8:00 AM.

CONTACT: Michael Jungden, Mansfield Marketplace, 228 Stafford Rd, Mansfield CT 06250. Tel: (860) 456-2578.

NAUGATUCK
Peddlers Market

DATES: Every Sunday from the first Sunday in April to the end of November. Weather permitting.

TIMES: Dawn to dusk.

ADMISSION: Free. Parking is free.

LOCATION: On Rt 63 (New Haven Rd) between Waterbury and New Haven.

DESCRIPTION: This market began operation in 1969 on 9 hilly, beautiful acres. There are anywhere from 75 to 80 dealers at this family oriented outdoor market. You can find most anything here from antiques and collectibles to new merchandise and fresh produce, including fishing equipment, furniture, and household items. It is located in a beautiful setting near the highway. This clean market's food vendors sell delicious egg sandwiches, fried dough, Italian sausage and mushroom sandwiches, and other special foods that are so popular people come for the food alone! There are clean, modern portable toilet facilities on the premises. As a civic service, non-profits are allowed to set up and sell for fundraisers.

DEALER RATES: $25 for up to 30' front per day. These are quite generous spaces as there is plenty of room. Reservations are not required.

CONTACT: Thomas Murray, 51 Gunntown Rd, Naugatuck CT 06770-3626. Tel: (203) 729-6339; or Gerald Garceau, 33 Hazel Ave, Naugatuck CT 06770. Tel: (203) 729-7762.

You Never Know What It's Worth

Mr. Murray bought a lovely piece of cherrywood furniture for $30 off a dealer's truck. It would make a lovely gift for his wife. Shortly, another dealer approached him and offered him $100 for it. No, not for sale. A few hours later the dealer approached him again, offering $200. No, not for sale. A few hours later, Mr. Murray was again approached with a $300 offer. No, that's final. *Really!*

NEW HAVEN
Boulevard Flea Market

DATES: Saturday and Sunday, year round.

TIMES: 7:00 AM-4:00 PM.

ADMISSION: Free. Parking is $1.

LOCATION: 500 Ella T Grasso Blvd. Northbound: I-95, take Exit 44 Kimberly Ave. Bear right off exit, go left at traffic light at ET Grasso Blvd (Rt 10). Market is ¾ mile on the left. Southbound: I-95, Exit 45 Rt 10, bear right down ramp, go straight, market is still ¾ mile on left.

DESCRIPTION: Opened in 1949, this outdoor market has to be the oldest in Connecticut. Depending on the weather (if it's raining, the market is open but not overwhelmed), their 100-plus dealers sell about 80% new merchandise, including clothes, tapes, produce (in season), and loads of "tag sale" or garage finds. Although not many antiques appear, plenty of collectibles do find their way here. On a good day up to 15-18,000 customers roam and buy. Several snack carts and vendors feed the famished and there is a handicapped-accessible port-o-let when needed.

DEALER RATES: $30 Saturday, $50 for Sunday per 20' space, with plenty of vehicle space. There is always space for dealers. Reservations are not required.

CONTACT: Chuck, Boulevard Flea Market, 500 Ella T Grasso Blvd, New Haven CT 06519. Tel: (203) 772-1447 or toll-free (877) 228-7554. Email: info@fleact.com. Web: www.fleact.com.

NEW MILFORD
Elephant's Trunk Flea Market

DATES: Sundays only, in 2002: March 24 through Sunday before Christmas, except Easter Sunday.

TIMES: 7:00 AM-3:30 PM. Early buyers can get in at 5:45 AM until 7:00 AM at $20 per person.

ADMISSION: General admission $1 adults, children 13 and under free. Parking is free and plentiful. No pets allowed! Early bird admission is $20 and allows you in at 5:45 AM.

LOCATION: Rt 7. Exit 7 from I-84, 7 miles north of Danbury.

DESCRIPTION: This market started in 1977. The 300-plus dealers break down their sales as approximately 65% antiques and collectibles, 35% general line merchandise and everything else, including plants, fruits, and new merchandise. Lately, far more antiques and collectibles have been coming in, making this a great place to treasure-hunt. There are dealers who have been with this market since the beginning and buyers who return the same time every weekend and have, over the years, become friends. There are 55 acres with room for 500 dealer spaces. Food is available on the premises.

DEALER RATES: $35 per 25' × 20' space. All dealers are urged to have a Connecticut tax number. Reservations are not required. Vendors enter at 5:00 AM and stay until 4:00 PM.

CONTACT: Contact Greg Baecker by telephone: (860) 355-1448. Web: www.elephanttrunck.com.

Maplewood Flea Market

DATES: Saturday and Sunday.

TIMES: 8:30 AM-4:00 PM.

ADMISSION: Free. Parking is free.

LOCATION: 458 Danbury Rd, Rt 7 N.

DESCRIPTION: Opened in 1991, this indoor market of 100-plus dealers (in a 25,000-square-foot building with dealers usually hogging more than one space) offers antiques, collectibles, glass, antique jewelry, used fur-

niture, and new merchandise. One snack bar with handicapped-accessible restrooms serves the famished in its own food court. This market is especially handicapped-accessible and visited by the busload.

DEALER RATES: $55 per 12' × 6' single space per weekend, $95 per double space. Double-space vendors can leave their merchandise overnight. There is complete security on the premises. Reservations are suggested for the "winter" season as they get "crammed."

CONTACT: Sandy Modzelewski, Maplewood Flea Market, 458 Danbury Rd, New Milford CT 06776. Tel: (860) 350-0454.

> **Don't Even Think of It!**
> Occasionally, someone has dropped off furniture in their parking lot. Dumb idea. The market dragged it in—and sold it! Of course, they kept the profits for themselves, as the "gift" was anonymous. Then again, there was a painting purchased here, as well as a table, that when offered through Sotheby's in New York brought in quite a lot of money!

NIANTIC
Between the Bridges Antique and Collectibles Flea Market

DATES: Thursday through Tuesday, year round.

TIMES: 10:00 AM-5:00 PM. Sunday 12:00 PM-5:00 PM.

ADMISSION: Free. Parking is free.

LOCATION: 65 Pennsylvania Ave. Take Exit 74 off I-95, turn right, 3 miles.

DESCRIPTION: Opened in May 1991, this new market (OK, it's really a store) has 60 dealers and a waiting list selling just antiques, collectibles and used furniture. No new merchandise or crafts. There is an antique radio and television restorer next door.

DEALER RATES: $30 for 65 square feet of space. You don't have to be there to sell. There is a waiting list, so call first.

CONTACT: John and Diane Deer, 65 Pennsylvania Ave, Niantic CT 06357-3224. Tel: (860) 691-0170.

OLD MYSTIC
Old Mystic Antique Flea Market

DATES: Every Sunday, weather permitting.

TIMES: 8:00 AM-5:00 PM.

ADMISSION: Free. Parking is free.

LOCATION: Rt 27 in Old Mystic. Across from the southern entrance to I-95, at the Mystic Visitor and Transportation Center.

DESCRIPTION: This market, in business since 1974, has co-op dealers in winter, to 25 dealers in the summer. While the market deals mostly in antiques, there is some new merchandise sold as well, including toys. One dealer specializes in antique Matchbox cars. Mystic Seaport is less than one mile away. Breakfast, lunch and snacks are available on the premises.

DEALER RATES: $25 per Sunday for 14' × 22' space. Reservations are strongly recommended.

CONTACT: Sonny Hendel, 6 Hendel Dr, Old Mystic CT 06372. Tel: (860) 536-0646.

TORRINGTON
Wright's Barn and Flea Market

DATES: Saturday and Sunday, year round.

TIMES: 10:00 AM-4:30 PM.

ADMISSION: Free. Parking is free.

LOCATION: Wright Rd off Rt 4, between Torrington and Goshen. Follow the large signs on Rt 4.

DESCRIPTION: This indoor market opened in 1981 in a huge 10,000-square-foot dairy barn with 40 dealers selling mostly antiques and some collectibles. Most of their dealers are permanent (12 dealers have been there over 19 years) and come from over 20 miles away. There is a snack bar and a fireplace to keep you warm in winter.

DEALER RATES: $20 for 10' × 14' booth, Saturday and Sunday. Reservations are required.

CONTACT: Milly Wright, Wright's Barn, 149 Wright Rd, Torrington CT 06790-2625. Tel: (860) 482-0095.

WALLINGFORD
Redwood Country Flea Market

DATES: Every Saturday and Sunday, and some holidays, year round, weather permitting (even in snow!).

TIMES: 6:00 AM-2:30 PM.

ADMISSION: Free. Parking is also free.

LOCATION: At 170 Hartford Tnpk in Wallingford. Take Exit 13 off I-91, or take Exit 64 off Wilbur Cross Pkwy.

DESCRIPTION: This show began in 1973, making 2002 their 30th big one. There are approximately 75 to 90 dealers at this outdoor market selling almost anything from antiques and collectibles to new merchandise and fresh produce. They do extensive advertising in area papers and trade magazines. The Dubars have a restaurant on the premises that is well known to the rich and famous whose pictures cover the walls. Walter

Dubar, the original founder of this market, has retired, leaving his son and grandsons to run this unique place. However, if you can find Walter, he has some wonderful stories to tell! Hi Walter! Hi Ken! Hi Steven!

DEALER RATES: Spaces measure 20' × 10', but it's best to call for their reasonable rates, as they vary. Reservations are suggested.

CONTACT: Ken Dubar and Steven Hugo, Redwood Country Flea Market, 170 S Turnpike Rd, Wallingford CT 06492. Tel: (203) 269-3500 between 1:00 PM-7:00 PM weekdays or all day Saturday and Sunday.

They Aren't Kidding
It isn't unheard of to have large snowstorms in Connecticut. Out come the snowplows and the market continues.

WESTBROOK
Westbrook Flea Market

DATES: Saturday and Sunday, year round.

TIMES: 7:00 AM-4:00 PM.

ADMISSION: Free. Parking is free.

LOCATION: Boston Post Rd (Rt 1). Take I-95 to Exit 64 to Rt 1, Boston Post Rd.

DESCRIPTION: Open since 1980, this outdoor market of 50 dealers sells antiques, collectibles, crafts, coins, stamps, cards, garage sale goodies, furniture, choice junk, and new merchandise. According to the owner, 90% of the vendors display collectibles, while the remaining 10% display "choice junk" reclaimed from the town dump! Surprisingly, he says, these sell the best. Marty says, "Look for the nautical raunch! Hey, we are on the shore." One restaurant feeds the famished and handicapped-accessible restrooms deal with other necessities.

DEALER RATES: Saturday $10 per space, Sunday $15. Reservations are not required.

CONTACT: Westbrook Flea Market, 110 Boston Post Rd (PO Box 1065), Westbrook CT 06498-1065. Tel: (860) 664-1737.

WOODBURY
Woodbury Antiques and Flea Market

DATES: Saturday, mid-March to mid-December, weather permitting.

TIMES: 7:00 AM-1:00 PM.

ADMISSION: Free. Parking is free.

LOCATION: Junction of Rts 6 and 64. Off I-84, take Exit 15, go 3½ miles on Rt 6E to market.

DESCRIPTION: For over 33 years this outdoor market has been considered one of the best antiques markets in Connecticut. Located in a beautiful country setting, their 90 to 140 dealers sell primarily antiques, collectibles, furniture, memorabilia, coins, antique tools, jewelry, books, military items, art and a constantly changing assortment of fascinating items. New merchandise includes tools, jewelry, clothes, household goods, over-the-counter products, plants and new surprises every week. It is described as the "#1 Saturday market in Connecticut" with "great browsing and buying in Woodbury, the Antiques Capital of Connecticut." This market has a strong following because of the quality of the goods sold and its pleasant setting. One restaurant and two food vendors feed the starving.

DEALER RATES: $30 for a 20' × 20' space. Reservations are not required, but recommended. They can be made up until 9:00 PM on Thursday, or by email. Check the website for more information.

CONTACT: Don and Diane Heavens, PO Box 184, Woodbury CT 06798. Tel: (203) 263-2841. Email: wdbyflea@aol.com. Web: www.woodburyfleamarket.com.

DELAWARE

DOVER
Spence's Bazaar and Auction and Flea Market
DATES: Every Tuesday and Friday. Rain or shine.
TIMES: 8:00 AM-8:00 PM.
ADMISSION: Free. Parking is free.
LOCATION: 550 S New St, 2 blocks west of Kent General Hospital.

DESCRIPTION: This indoor/outdoor market first began in 1933. With a variety of shops on site and 200 dealer tables, a shopper can find antiques, collectibles, household and secondhand items. Also on the premises are a farmers' market selling cheeses, meats, produce, pizza, ice cream and loads more, as well as a restaurant and restrooms. Auctions are held at 3:00 PM selling all sorts of stuff.
DEALER RATES: $17 for a 3-table setup. Reservations are not necessary.
CONTACT: Gregory Spence or Jack Scott, Spence's Bazaar, 550 S New St, Dover DE 19904-3536. Tel: (302) 734-3441.

LAUREL
Bargain Bill Indoor/Outdoor Flea Market
DATES: Every Friday, Saturday and Sunday.
TIMES: Friday 8:00 AM-4:00 PM; Saturday and Sunday 6:00 AM-5:00 PM. November through March hours on weekends 8:00 AM-5:00 PM.
ADMISSION: Free. Free parking is provided.
LOCATION: At the intersection of US 13 Dual and Rt 9 E, 14 miles north of Salisbury. From Washington DC, take Rt 50 W to Rt 404 E, then Rt 13 south.
DESCRIPTION: This indoor/outdoor show began in 1978 and is located just 30 minutes from the Atlantic Ocean and listed as a Delaware tourist attraction. People come from all over the United States to buy from the 200 (in winter) to 500 dealers (in summer) who sell everything from antiques to new merchandise, from collectibles to fresh produce—all tax free! Other items to be found are: electronics, books, air-brush artist, baked goods, records, jewelry, vacuums, new and used clothing and tools, wicker, doors, portable buildings, and groceries, among others. There's a unique covered market with skylights to illuminate the merchandise where vendors can park next to their treasures. When this market first opened, vendors laid their merchandise on the ground. Now they have a 400' air-conditioned/heated indoor market with over 800 tables. Talk about having everything—in December 1992, they had a wedding here complete

with wedding gown, tuxedo, minister, cake and music. A large restaurant serves a fantastic breakfast and lunch and there are handicapped-accessible restrooms when needed.

DEALER RATES: $26 and up per 8' × 10' indoor space. $17 and up per 16' frontage outdoor space, includes two 8' tables. Reservations are not required but are nice. Overnight camping with electric hookups and air-conditioned and heated restrooms.

CONTACT: Bill & Leslie Brown, 10912 County Seat Hwy, Laurel DE 19956. Tel: (302) 875-9958 or (302) 875-2478. Fax: (302) 875-1830. Email: fleamkt@magpage.com. Website: www.bargainbill.com.

Route 13 Outlet Market

DATES: Friday, Saturday and Sunday, year round.
TIMES: Friday and Saturday 9:00 AM-7:00 PM; Sunday 9:00 AM-6:00 PM.
ADMISSION: Free. Parking is also free.
LOCATION: Rt 13 at SR 462.
DESCRIPTION: Started in 1985, they now have over 100 vendors selling collectibles, as well as items ranging from clothing to jewelry in this 84,000-square-foot building. There are plenty of collectibles. One vendor has loads of new tools that are "priced less than Wal-Mart." Another sells all sorts of electronics: stereos, telephones, car radios and accoutrements. Thirty-two vendors sell sportswear and clothing, others jewelry. You can't possibly starve—15 restaurants, including Thai, Chinese, several down-home country, pizza and Italian, and some hot dog purveyors feed the famished. Their huge Amish market and restaurant is one of the big draws of the market selling fresh cheeses, meats, deli and baked goods. Ninety-five percent of the merchandise is new and 80% of the vendors have been with this market from the beginning. Over the last few years much of the merchandise has become even more high-end, top-quality goods. If an item fails to satisfy, it is quite common to be able to return it to the original vendor.

DEALER RATES: $65 per 12' × 18' space per weekend and up. Reservations are not required.

CONTACT: Merrill Gravener, Route 13 Outlet Market, PO Box 32, Laurel DE 19956-0032. Tel: (302) 875-4800. Fax: (302) 875-7535.

NEW CASTLE
New Castle Farmers' Market

DATES: Friday, Saturday and Sunday, year round.
TIMES: Friday and Saturday 10:00 AM-10:00 PM; Sunday 10:00 AM-6:00 PM.
ADMISSION: Free. Parking is also free.
LOCATION: Rt 13 and Hares Corner.

DESCRIPTION: Started in 1954, this indoor/outdoor market is really two markets in one. The outside is the flea market for antiques and collectibles, and restricted to used items only; the inside market is the farmers' market with over 60 merchants. This is said to be one of the premier markets on the East Coast with genuine Pennsylvania Dutch merchants selling outstanding quality beef, pork, poultry, cheeses and homemade baked goods. The produce stands are works of art. Delicious food is available on the premises. Handicapped-accessible throughout.

DEALER RATES: Friday $13 per day; Saturday and Sunday $17 per day. First come, first served.

CONTACT: New Castle Farmers' Market, 110 N DuPont Hwy, New Castle DE 19720. Tel: (302) 328-4102. Fax (302) 328-9525.

DISTRICT OF COLUMBIA

Capitol Hill Flea Market at Eastern Market

DATES: Sundays, March through Christmas.

TIMES: 10:00 AM-5:00 PM.

ADMISSION: Free. Parking is where you find it.

LOCATION: 7th and N Carolina Aves SE, only ½ block from the Metro Eastern Market station.

DESCRIPTION: This outdoor market of up to 175 dealers sells antiques, collectibles, arts and crafts, imports, and produce in season. Started in 1983, adding farmer's row in 1987, and a school playground in 1992, this is a continuation of the selling along these streets that has been going on for more than 125 years. There is plenty of food nearby, both at the market itself, and in adjoining Capitol Hill business district. Check out the crab cakes at the Market Lunch, worth the long line, but short wait (they are quick). The management advertises in *The Washington Post* and other selected publications, although with the publicity they get locally, it seems unnecessary. After all, they are an institution around here.

DEALER RATES: $20 per table space, $30 for two 6' tables (½ spaces), $40 for roughly 100 square feet (single space), $55 in double spaces of about 200 square feet, or super spaces—larger than doubles—for $20 more per 100 square feet. Setup begins at 8:30 AM. Prepayment is required. The market is fully booked with a waiting list for permanent exhibitors. However, vacancies are sometimes available. BYOT and setup. Be prepared for lousy weather.

CONTACT: Tom Rall, The Flea Market at Eastern Market, 1101 N Kentucky St, Arlington VA 22205. Tel: (703) 534-7612. Email: marketflea@aol.com. Web: http://easternmarket.net, where more information, including a reservation form, is available.

Georgetown Flea Market

DATES: Every Sunday, year round.

TIMES: 9:00 AM-5:00 PM.

ADMISSION: Free. Limited street parking is free.

LOCATION: Parking lot of Hardy Middle School on Wisconsin Ave across from the Safeway, between S and T Sts NW.

DESCRIPTION: Started in 1971, this outdoor market has become a legend since its inception. Author Larry McMurtry (of *Lonesome Dove* fame) based his novel *Cadillac Jack* on this market. The owner, Michael Sussman, describes his market's wares as "good, solid, antiques and collectibles. This is where the antique dealers come to restock their shops on their way to fancy shows, and decorators come with their clients to decorate their homes," with many a great bargain to be had. His 70-plus good exhibitors, many of whom are regulars, sell fine antiques, collectibles, antique and Deco furniture, vintage clothing, antique silver, crafts, homemade furniture, and other fine items. Don't worry about food; there are plenty of places to chow down in Georgetown. Mary Randolph Carter, an avid collector, and Ralph Lauren, ad exec and author of *American Junk*, love this market and raid it occasionally. Diane Keaton comes to buy vintage clothing. The local papers (i.e., *The Washington Post*) are forever writing this place up. Restroom facilities and food are at the Safeway across the street. If you find Michael at the market, say "Hi" and tell him "we still miss the Phoenix"; he'll understand.

DEALER RATES: $30-$50 depending on space and if you have your vehicle with you. Reservations are an excellent idea, but Michael will try to squeeze you in, if necessary. No reservations will be made by phone. Setup starts at 6:00 AM. Ask for Bill, the manager.

CONTACT: Michael Sussman, 2109 N St NW, Washington DC 20037. Tel: (202) 296-4989. Fax: (202) 223-0289. Web: www.georgetownfleamarket.com.

Great Shopping

Someone bought a painting here for $300 that was worth $9,000. Stickley chairs have gone for $15. Well-known antiques dealer Guy Bush shops here every Sunday morning.

Georgetown Flea Market at U Street

DATES: Saturday and Sunday.

TIMES: 9:00 AM-5:00 PM.

ADMISSION: Free. Parking is free where you can find it.

LOCATION: 1345 U St in the Shaw area of DC, between 13th and 14th Sts on U St. Next to the U Street-Cardoza Metro station.

DESCRIPTION: This market opened in 1999 when the Georgetown market site was being repaved. Forty vendors sell LPs (jazz is big), some collectibles, and new merchandise. Food vendors will keep you energized.

DEALER RATES: $15-$20 depending on space and if you have your vehicle with you. Reservations are an excellent idea, but Michael will try to squeeze you in, if necessary. No reservations will be made by phone. Setup starts at 6:00 AM.

CONTACT: Michael Sussman, 2109 N St NW, Washington DC 20037-3017. Tel: (202) 296-4989. Fax: (202) 223-0289. Web: www.georgetownfleamarket.com.

FLORIDA

APOPKA
Three Star Flea Market
DATES: Every Saturday and Sunday. Rain or shine.
TIMES: Dawn to dusk.
ADMISSION: Free. Free parking is available.
LOCATION: 2930 S Orange Blossom Trail. Hwy 441.
DESCRIPTION: This market began in 1966. About 60 dealers sell their antiques, collectibles, handicrafts, garage sale items and produce from covered stalls outdoors. They are only 18 miles from Disney World. There is a food wagon on the premises.
DEALER RATES: $10.80 per space and parking per day. They provide tables and clothes racks. Reservations are required.
CONTACT: Mary C Markeson, Owner, c/o Three Star Flea Market, 2390 S Orange Blossom Trail, Apopka FL 32703-1870. Tel: (407) 293-2722.

AUBURNDALE
International Market World
DATES: Every Friday, Saturday, and Sunday. Rain or shine.
TIMES: 8:00 AM-4:00 PM.
ADMISSION: Free. Free parking is available on 30 acres.
LOCATION: 1052 Hwy 92 W Auburndale. Between Orlando and Tampa, just east of Lakeland. Near Cypress Gardens.
DESCRIPTION: This market opened in 1981 and currently attracts anywhere from 750 (summer) to 1,000-plus (winter) dealers in indoor or outdoor spaces. A new building was added in 1991 adding another 200 stalls. As one of Florida's largest markets, Market World attracts customers from throughout Central Florida as it is only a short 45-minute drive from either Tampa or Orlando down I-4. There is an endless variety of merchandise from antiques and collectibles to new merchandise and fresh produce. Several attractions include karaoke Saturday and Sunday afternoons, a fishing pond, a 1909 antique carousel, alligator display, buffalo farm, and exotic animal rehab-zoo featuring Florida panthers, to name a few. There is a delightful country atmosphere and an eager-to-please management. There are numerous concessions serving a variety of foods on the premises. Handicapped-accessible restrooms are available.
DEALER RATES: Friday open air spaces $10-$15 depending on location, Saturday or Sunday $17-$25 per space or $40-$55 per 8' × 10' space per three-day weekend; $155-$200 monthly for indoor or under cover,

and open air spaces are $125 a month. Reservations are not required, but can be made Wednesday or Thursday between 9:00 AM-4:00 PM. Dealers may start setting up shop at 7:00 AM Friday through Sunday.

CONTACT: International Market World, 1052 Hwy 92 W, Auburndale FL 33823-9585. Tel: (863) 665-0062. Fax: (863) 666-5726.

BONITA SPRINGS
Flamingo Island Flea Market

DATES: Friday through Sunday.

TIMES: 8:00 AM-4:00 PM.

ADMISSION: Free. Parking is free.

LOCATION: 11902 Bonita Beach Rd. Take I-75 to Exit 18W. Go 2/10 mile west, the market is on the north side.

DESCRIPTION: This new market opened in 1999 with up to 200 dealers selling antiques, collectibles, crafts, produce, meats, coins, stamps, cards, garage sale goodies, furniture, man-made waterfalls, jewelry (14k-18k gold, estate, and costume), and new merchandise. In case of hunger, there are seven restaurants and three snack bars. If needed, there are handi-capped-accessible restrooms.

DEALER RATES: Space is either Blue or Red depending on location. The Red space is the higher price. Per month: $100-$120 per 8' × 32' aisle space, $200-$240 per 10' × 10' space, $300-$360 per 10' × 20' space. Reservations are required, especially in winter. There may be some sum-mer daily space available; if interested, ask.

CONTACT: Gene Vacarro or Glenda Farrow, Flamingo Island Flea Market, 11902 Bonita Beach Rd, Bonita Springs FL 34135. Tel: (941) 948-7799 or 495-9500. Fax: (941) 947-7882. Email: gvacarro@flamingoisland.com. Web: flamingoisland.com.

BRADENTON
Red Barn Flea Market Plaza

DATES: Entire market Wednesday, Saturday and Sunday; Fridays also, November through April. Plaza area Tuesday through Sunday.

TIMES: Wednesday, seasonal Fridays, Saturday and Sunday 8:00 AM-4:00 PM; Tuesday, Thursday and Friday 10:00 AM-4:00 PM.

ADMISSION: Free. Parking is free.

LOCATION: 1707 1st St E. Located on US 41 and US 301 at 17th Ave. From I-75 take Exit 42 W on SR 64 (Manatee Ave) to US 41. Take a left on US 41, go approximately 2 miles. The market is on the east side.

DESCRIPTION: The original market opened in May 1981 followed by the plaza in May 1985. On October 21, 1996, the entire market was de-stroyed by a devastating fire. It reopened July 1998 with 23 retail stores and approximately 400 covered and over 200 uncovered booths with a variety of new and used merchandise, including antiques, collectibles, crafts, clothing, produce, meats, coins, cards, garage sale goodies, and furniture. The market spreads over 20 acres with 125,000 square feet under roof. This market is crammed with a variety of goods and services. There are courtesy carts to and from the parking lots. There are special shows year round, but Antique Weekends every fourth weekend, May through September, where you can bring your favorite antique and have it appraised. When the munchies strike, pick from five restaurants and an ice cream stand. Handicapped-accessible restrooms provide relief. A popular, clean, high-traffic market located near the Gulf Coast, it has over 50 peacocks in the trees on the hill. Security patrolled by uniformed off-duty deputies.

DEALER RATES: All spaces are approximately 10' × 10'. Inside booths are $27.50 plus tax per day, outside covered booths $25 and tax per day, and outside uncovered booths are $22 plus tax per day. Outside under roof are $20 plus tax per day. Tables are $1 plus tax each per day. Rates are less off season. Please check. Their website has more information.

CONTACT: Red Barn Rental Office, 1707 1 St E, Bradenton FL 34208. Tel: (941) 747-3794 or 1-800-274-FLEA. Fax: (941) 747-6539. Email: info@redbarnfleamarket.com. Web: www.redbarnfleamarket.com.

Pets and Mascots

The Red Barn has very unique mascots in their beautiful peacocks roaming the grounds. Many customers have their pictures taken with the tame birds. Occasionally, when the market is closed, the peacocks roam the aisles playing "customer" until gently ushered back into their "home" among the giant oaks and oleanders. During these strolls, they can be caught admiring themselves in the glass doors. Among the flock is a rare white peacock.

BROOKSVILLE
Airport Flea Market and Farmers' Market

DATES: Every Saturday and Sunday. Rain or shine.

TIMES: 8:00 AM-3:00 PM.

ADMISSION: Free. Parking is also free.

LOCATION: 17375 Spring Hill Dr. Six miles south of Brooksville, just off US 41.

DESCRIPTION: This market started in 1977. A new owner took over the market in 1998, repaved it, added a new pole barn with 105 new spaces, upgraded the facilities and cleaned the place up. The market accommo-

dates approximately 400 dealers and is held both indoors and outdoors. There are no specialties but rather a large assortment of goods is offered, including antiques, fine art, arts and crafts, collectibles, new merchandise, used household items, and tools. The farmers' market is open daily, 8:00 AM-5:00 PM. Food concessions offer breakfasts and lunches, including Italian and barbecue, and the handicapped-accessible restrooms just may come in handy.

DEALER RATES: $73 for 8' × 12' space indoors, per month: $10 for Saturday, $9 for Sunday or $17 for the weekend for three-table set up under covered space outdoors, per day; or $7 Saturday, $6 Sunday, $12 for the weekend or $45 monthly for open-air space. Reservations are required except during the summer.

CONTACT: Bob Murch, Airport Flea Market, 17375 Spring Hill Dr, Brooksville FL 34609-8195. Tel: (352) 796-0268. Fax: (352) 796-1099.

CHIEFLAND
Chiefland Farmer's Flea Market

DATES: Friday through Sunday, year round. Rain or shine.

TIMES: 7:00 AM-3:30 PM.

ADMISSION: Free. Parking is free.

LOCATION: US Hwy 19 and 98, Alt 27 N. Market located across from ABC Pizza and Best Western Motel.

DESCRIPTION: Since 1983, this indoor flea market has expanded four times on its 23 acres and is in the Suwannee River area, in the center of town, near motels. The market was sold two years to Sonny, who has done a remarkable job of improving it, drawing in scads of new dealers. There are a total of 310 selling spaces, all under one roof, with concrete floors and screens. Water and electricity are available to each booth, as well as RV electricity. Dealers can park their RV in the back of their booth. Currently the market attracts approximately 200 dealers in the summer and 250 in the winter selling antiques, collectibles including NASCAR and Disney, handmade crafts, produce stand, plants, flowers, new and used furniture, plenty of used and new merchandise among other treats. In addition, there is a small grocery store (weekends only), glassware, tools, leather craft shop, Indian shop, appliances, and carpet and vinyl store. Two restaurants feed the hungry, and handicapped-accessible restrooms.

DEALER RATES: $6 per 10' × 10' booth on Friday and $8 on Sunday; $10 on Saturday; $20 for three days. Reservations are suggested.

CONTACT: Sonny Griffeth, Chiefland Farmer's Flea Market Inc, 316 NW 11th Ave, Chiefland FL 32646. Tel: (352) 493-2022.

COCOA
Frontenac Flea Market

DATES: Friday, Saturday and Sunday.

TIMES: 8:00 AM-4:00 PM.

LOCATION: 5605 N US Hwy 1, midway between Cocoa and Titusville, right on US 1.

ADMISSION: Free. Parking is free.

DESCRIPTION: In operation since 1976, this market has an average of 450 dealers selling antiques, collectibles, new and used merchandise, silk flowers, and a farmers market selling fresh fruits and vegetables. One of the several food concessions sells a "famous quarter-pound hot dog." Just in case you need them, there are handicapped-accessible restrooms. This market is close to the Kennedy Space Center and beaches so you can see the shuttles take off.

DEALER RATES: $18.02 per day for a 10' × 8' space indoors; $13.78 for a 10' × 20' space outdoors. First come, first served.

CONTACT: Ronnie Christian, Frontenac Flea Market, PO Box 10, Sharpes FL 32959-0010. Tel: (321) 631-0241. Fax: (321) 631-0246.

DAYTONA
Daytona Flea Market

DATES: Friday, Saturday, and Sunday, year round. Rain or shine.

TIMES: 8:00 AM-5:00 PM.

ADMISSION: Free. Parking is free.

LOCATION: Southwest corner of I-95 and US 92.

DESCRIPTION: This indoor/outdoor market opened in 1981 just five miles from the "World's Most Famous Beach," attracting 2.5 million visitors. Over 1,000 booths on 40 acres sell antiques, collectibles, home furnishings, clothes, jewelry, used and new merchandise, produce, plants and just about everything imaginable. Two sections of the market are fully air-conditioned, including the entire undercover section cooled by a one-of-a-kind outdoor unit. Two sit-down restaurants and nine snack bars provide ample food for the hungry.

DEALER RATES: For a 10' x 7' booth undercover with a table, $15 and up for Saturday and Sunday, $8 and up on Friday. Ninety percent of this market is under roof. Reservations are suggested, in some cases required.

CONTACT: Lisa Wilson, Rental Agent, 2987 Bellevue Rd, Daytona Beach FL 32124. Tel: (386) 253-3330 x 14. Email: lisa@daytonafleamarket.com. Web: www.daytonafleamarket.com.

DELRAY BEACH
Delray Swap Shop

Warning: This market is almost impossible to talk to. After many repeated attempts to speak with someone, they never returned my calls. They are open, but their voicemail is impenetrable and when you do get through, no one will speak with you. So the rental information may be outdated.

DATES: Thursdays through Monday.

TIMES: 9:00 AM-4:00 PM.

ADMISSION: Free. Parking is $1.

LOCATION: 2001 N Federal Hwy. Take I-95 to Atlantic Ave in Delray Beach to N Federal Hwy, north 3 miles to Swap Shop.

DESCRIPTION: This market has been open since 1976, with 430 dealer spaces mostly outdoors. Items for sale are mostly new merchandise, including: health and beauty aids, clothing, jewelry, hats, pictures and frames, household goods, and vegetables in season. Several snack bars serve the hungry. Handicapped-accessible restrooms are on site.

DEALER RATES: Monday and Thursday $10 per space, Friday $15; Saturday and Sunday from $25 to $100 for 11' × 15' spaces. For the antique mall: Monday, Thursday, and Friday $5; $8 Saturday and Sundays, each day. Reservations are required. There is a wait list for no-shows, at $25 for space at the last minute with no guarantees. Watch for their website.

CONTACT: Loretta Shaw, Manager, Delray Swap Shop, 2001 N Federal Hwy, Delray FL 33483. Tel: (561) 276-4012. Fax: (561) 276-9019.

FORT LAUDERDALE
Oakland Park Boulevard Flea Market

DATES: Every Wednesday through Sunday, year round.

TIMES: Friday and Saturday 10:00 AM-9:00 PM; Wednesday, Thursday and Sunday 10:00 AM-7:00 PM.

ADMISSION: Free. Parking is plentiful and free.

LOCATION: 1½ miles west of I-95, and ½ mile east of SR 7, at 3161 W Oakland Park Blvd.

DESCRIPTION: This popular market has been a landmark in Fort Lauderdale since 1971. "This is the place where the neighborhood shops," as well as Fort Lauderdale's original indoor flea market. Over 200 dealers sell only all-new merchandise although some collectibles can be found. There are many clothing and fine jewelry merchants in this modern, clean and air-conditioned facility. Local residents and tourists alike make frequent visits to this market located near major highways, airports and cruise-ports. It is a bit of southern charm that makes this flea market such a success. Handicapped-accessible restrooms, two snack bars and a restaurant serving home-cooked fare add to the amenities.

DEALER RATES: $600 and up per space per month includes utilities, advertising and plenty more. Reservations are required. Currently they are accepting applications for the waiting list.

CONTACT: Leonard Bennis, Manager, Oakland Park Boulevard Flea Market Inc, 3161 W Oakland Park Blvd, Ft Lauderdale FL 33311-1229. Tel: (954) 733-4617. Fax: (954) 731-1150.

Swap Shop of Ft. Lauderdale

DATES: Every day including holidays, year round. Rain or shine.

TIMES: Monday through Thursday 6:00 AM-5:30 PM; Friday 6:00 AM-6:00 pm; weekends 6:00 AM-6:30 PM.

ADMISSION: Free. Free parking is available in the south lot. Preferred parking Thursday, Saturday and Sunday is $1-$2.

LOCATION: 3291 W Sunrise Blvd, between I-95 and the Turnpike.

DESCRIPTION: This well-known show began in 1967. Over 2,000 dealers sell both indoors and out on 88 acres of grounds. All sorts of things can be found here—antiques, crafts and collectibles, new and used items, produce, watches, electronics, clothing, plants—you name it! All new merchandise comes with a full guarantee. They say they are "the largest flea market in the Eastern United States." Free circus shows are presented daily, and they feature 17 international restaurants in their air-conditioned 180,000-square-foot entertainment center. At night they have the world's largest 13-screen drive-in, showing first-run movies nightly.

DEALER RATES: Call for current rates. Reservations are advised during the winter season. Reservations are open daily from 9:00 AM-4:00 PM. Call (954) 791-SWAP (7927) ext 204.

CONTACT: Reservation Office, c/o Swap Shop, 3291 W Sunrise Blvd, Fort Lauderdale FL 33311. Tel: (954) 791-SWAP (7927). Fax: (954) 792-7962.

FORT MYERS
Fleamasters Fleamarket

DATES: Friday, Saturday and Sunday, year around.

TIMES: 8:00 AM-4:00 PM.

LOCATION: 4135 Dr Martin Luther King Jr Blvd.

ADMISSION: Free. Parking is free.

DESCRIPTION: Opened in 1985, this completely undercover outdoor market, billed "as the largest market in southwest Florida," hosts an average of 1,200 dealers year round in 400,000 square feet of space. Their dealers sell everything "from fruit to nuts," including antiques, collectibles, clothing, new merchandise, wheelchair rentals and more. The food courts provide an ample feast from pizza to ice cream, Mexican, and good-old-

USA fast food. In fact, this market is so popular it has become a tourist attraction in its own right with over 1 million visitors annually. They hold car shows, mother-daughter look-alike contests, boxing matches, and numerous other cool events throughout the year, even shooting Santa out of a cannon for Christmas fun. (One year, Santa had a broken leg— before the firing!)

DEALER RATES: $45-$68, plus tax and license, per 10' × 12' booth for a 3-day weekend, depending on location. There are daily and monthly rates available. Reservations are not required—first come, first served—although dealers can continue to hold the same spot week after week as long as the space is paid for.

CONTACT: Donna Matthew, Fleamasters Fleamarket, 4135 Dr Martin Luther King Jr Blvd, Ft Myers FL 33916. Tel: (941) 334-7001. Fax: (941) 334-2087. Email: DianeL@fleamall.com. Web: www.fleamall.com.

HOMOSASSA SPRINGS
Howard's Flea Market

DATES: Friday, Saturday and Sunday, year round.

TIMES: 7:00 AM-3:00 PM.

ADMISSION: Free. Parking is free.

LOCATION: Hwy 19, 3 miles south of Homosassa.

DESCRIPTION: Open since 1969, this market of 700 to 800 dealers occupies 50 acres full of antiques, collectibles, some new merchandise, clothes, typical flea market fare, produce and occasionally dairy products (cheeses), and one aisle devoted to garage sale goodies. A polebarn structure houses many of the dealers while the rest are outdoors. Their many concession stands are "excellent," the office assures me. They hold special events with the proceeds used to raise funds for local children's charities. At Christmas, they hold "Adopt-a-Baby" where the dealers "adopt" a needy child for Christmas. Like their sister market in Webster, they hold car shows.

DEALER RATES: Daily including tax: Covered $14.84 per 10' × 12' space with 3 tables. Outside $8.48 per 10' × 10' space, or $11 to $14 per 10' × 30' space depending on location. Reservations are suggested, although, if you do show up they will manage to find you a spot somehow. The office is open for reservations on Thursday and Friday.

CONTACT: Teri Davis, Howard's Flea Market, 6373 S Suncoast Blvd, Homosassa FL 34446-3005. Tel: (352) 628-4656 (office) or (352) 628-3532. Fax: (352) 628-7443. Email: office@howardsfleamarket.com. Web: www.howardsfleamarket.com.

JACKSONVILLE
Beach Boulevard Flea Market

DATES: Saturday and Sunday.
TIMES: 7:00 AM-6:00 PM.
ADMISSION: Free. Parking is free.
LOCATION: 11041 Beach Blvd.
DESCRIPTION: This market averages 550 dealers selling antiques, collectibles, crafts, clothes, shoes, oriental goods, garage sale goodies, new and used furniture, fresh produce, and plenty of new merchandise. There are four snack bars, a restaurant and handicapped-accessible restrooms on site. Twenty vendors are open daily, including a printing setup, a computer dealer, and an embroiderer.
DEALER RATES: Outdoors: $17 per 10' × 9' open space, $27 with cover. $110 and $185 respectively monthly. Table space only: $10 per 3' × 8' space with table daily under cover, $99 monthly. They don't take reservations.
CONTACT: Beach Boulevard Flea Market, 11041 Beach Blvd, Jacksonville FL 32246-4809. Tel: (904) 645-5961.

Playtime Drive-In Flea Market

DATES: Wednesday, Friday through Sunday, weather permitting.
TIMES: 5:00 AM-2:00 PM.
ADMISSION: Free. Free parking is available.
LOCATION: 6300 Blanding Blvd. Just north of 295 Exit.
DESCRIPTION: Opened in 1960, this market of 300 dealers on Wednesday and 150 or so on weekends sells about 50-75% garage sale goodies and new merchandise, and a huge produce market. There's a big concession selling food, and handicapped-accessible restrooms when you need them.
DEALER RATES: $7 Wednesday, $6 Friday through Sunday per 12' x 20'. First come, first served.
CONTACT: Robert, Playtime Drive-In Flea Market, 6300 Blanding Blvd, Jacksonville FL 32210. Tel: (904) 771-2300.

Ramona Flea Market

DATES: Saturday and Sunday, year round.
TIMES: 8:00 AM-5:00 PM.
ADMISSION: $.50 per adult. Parking is free.
LOCATION: 7059 Ramona Blvd. From I-295 take I-10 east to first Exit 54, Lane Ave, go south. The first intersection is Ramona Blvd. Turn right. They are 3 blocks down the road on the right.
DESCRIPTION: Started in 1971, this indoor/outdoor market has 600 to 800 dealers (depending on the season) selling crafts, produce, coins, new

merchandise, garage sale goodies, and furniture. Four snack bars and three restaurants, including a beer garden and an ice cream parlor, fill the famished. And yes, handicapped-accessible restrooms are available.

DEALER RATES: $7.52 to $14.91 (includes tax) depending on the location of the 10' × 7' space. They have open or under cover with 2 tables, electricity for inside spaces at $2 per day. The office is open for reservations Wednesday and Thursday from 9:00 AM-5:00 PM and Friday from 9:00 AM-6:00 PM. They recommend reserving space at least 2 weeks in advance. They open for vendors to set up at 6:30 AM.

CONTACT: Rick Waller, General Manager, or Joan Wade, Reservation Manager, 7059 Ramona Blvd, Jacksonville FL 32205. Tel: (904) 786-3532 or 1-800-583-3532 (FLEA). Fax: (904) 783-1661. Email: fleaman@jax-inter.net.

KEY LARGO
Key Largo Warehouse Market

DATES: Saturday and Sunday.

TIMES: 8:00 AM-5:00 PM.

ADMISSION: Free. Free parking is available.

LOCATION: On US Rt 1, at Mile Marker 103.5.

DESCRIPTION: This small, selective but excellent market has 60 dealers selling "everything you could want," with an emphasis on antiques and collectibles. Charlie's vegetables are said to be "the best on the Keys." A sampling of some of their dealers' specialties are baskets, bathing suits, marine and fishing gear, orchids and exotic plants, ceramic goods and bikes. A snack bar serves American dishes to the hungry. This is the only market open all year long on the Keys. They place a high value on "treating our people right."

DEALER RATES: $357 monthly for a front-row 10' × 40' space if you are lucky enough to get one; $210.05 for a second-row 10' × 30' space; and $102.07 for a 10' × 10' space. Reservations are most necessary.

CONTACT: Key Largo Warehouse Market, Key Largo Storage, 103530 Overseas Hwy, Key Largo FL 33037-2839. Tel: (305) 451-0677.

KISSIMMEE
Osceola Flea and Farmers' Market

DATES: Friday through Sunday. Rain or shine.

TIMES: 8:00 AM-5:00 PM.

ADMISSION: Free. Parking is free.

LOCATION: 2801 E Irlo Bronson Memorial Hwy.

DESCRIPTION: Started in 1987, this market averages 900-plus vendors selling antiques, collectibles, jewelry, new merchandise, new and used

furniture, tools, produce, garage sale goodies, sports equipment, clothing, shoes, pets, household and DIY goods, and whatever else shows up.
There is one restaurant, three snack bars, handicapped-accessible
restrooms, and live entertainment to keep you busy between shopping
forays.

DEALER RATES: $17.50 daily per 10' × 10' under roof. Other rates avail-
able; call or hit the website for more information. The office is open
Thursday 9:00 AM-5:00 PM, and during regular flea market hours. No,
they don't take reservations, but you can call about space availability.

CONTACT: Osceola Flea & Farmers' Market, 2801 E Irlo Bronson Hwy,
Kissimmee FL 34744. Tel: (407) 846-2811. Fax: (407) 846-3392. Email:
osceola@fleaamerica.com or USAFlea@aol.com. Web: www.fleaamerica.com.

LAKE CITY
Lake City Flea Market

DATES: Every Saturday and Sunday. Rain or shine. Closed from mid-
October to mid-November for Columbia County Fair.

TIMES: 7:00 AM-4:00 PM.

ADMISSION: Free. Free parking is available.

LOCATION: Columbia County Fairgrounds, 1 mile east of I-75 on US 90
at SR 247 (Branford Hwy).

DESCRIPTION: This indoor/outdoor market opened in 1980 and changed
hands in 2001. It accommodates approximately 100 to 150 dealers selling everything from antiques and collectibles to new merchandise and
fresh produce. There are 1,500 motel rooms available at reasonable rates
located within a half mile of the flea market. There is a snack bar serving
flea market "fare," and handicapped-accessible restrooms.

DEALER RATES: Call for the latest rates; they were unavailable at press
time. In 2000: $9 per 10' × 10' space indoors, per day; $6 and up per day
outdoors. Reservations for space indoors are required and all reservations must be prepaid. No reservations are taken by phone.

CONTACT: Lake City Flea Market, Hwy 247, Lake City FL 32024-8637.
Tel: (386) 752-8822.

LAKELAND
Lakeland Farmers' Market

DATES: Saturday and Sunday. Rain or shine.

TIMES: 8:00 AM-3:00 PM.

ADMISSION: Free. Free parking is available.

LOCATION: 2701 Swindell Rd. Take I-4 to W Memorial Blvd exit, then
go 1 mile. At the intersection of Swindell Rd and W Memorial Blvd at
Kathleen High School.

DESCRIPTION: This market, originally a "Curb Market" in the 1930s, moved to its present location in 1971 where local farmers and craftsmen could sell their goods; some of these original sellers still work here. The market now accommodates from 225 to 350 dealers that sell collectibles, arts and crafts, new merchandise, used items, clothing, tools, household necessities, used farm- and work-related items and fresh produce and meats. This is a rustic, down-to-earth flea market with a museum, free of charge, on the premises. There are five restaurants and snack bars to choose from.

DEALER RATES: Saturday $11 per 10' × 10' space under cover, Sunday $15. Rates in the open field are $8 per 25' × 15' space. Reservations are first come, first served. The office opens at 6:00 AM.

CONTACT: Jim Wilbanks, 2701 Swindell Rd, Lakeland FL 33805-3815. Tel: (863) 682-4809.

LAKE WORTH
Lake Worth High School Flea Market

DATES: Saturday and Sunday, year round. Rain or shine.

TIMES: 4:00 AM-3:00 PM. Really.

ADMISSION: Free. Parking is free.

LOCATION: 1701 Lake Worth Rd at Lake Worth High School parking lot. At I-95 and Lake Worth Rd, under the I-95 overpass next to the Tri-Rail Station. From Florida Tnpk: Exit 93E 6 miles. From I-95: Exit 6th Ave S, right to "A" St to Lake Worth Rd or Exit 10th Ave N, left to "A" St, right to Lake Worth Rd.

DESCRIPTION: So how does a high school raise funds for scholarships for needy students and other necessaries? Hold a flea market! Since the mid-'80s this market has contributed more than $1 million dollars to student scholarships. Not bad. In fact, the market is so popular it has been repeatedly written up in Florida papers. Every weekend, their 300 dealers spread out across the school parking lot selling wonderful books, antiques, collectibles, produce, new and used merchandise, rugs, luggage, garage sale goodies, and discount groceries. This place is the local "weekend mall" for locals.

DEALER RATES: $10 per spot. First come, first served.

CONTACT: Betty and Ralph Milone, Lake Worth High School Flea Market, PO Box 6592, Lake Worth FL 33466-6592. Tel: (561) 439-1539. Fax: (561) 439-8742. Email: LWHSFlea@aol.com.

MARGATE
Margate Swap Shop

DATES: Saturday, Sunday and Tuesday.

TIMES: 5:00 AM-2:30 PM.

ADMISSION: Free. Parking is $1.
LOCATION: 1000 N SR 7 (US 441). West of Pompano Beach; west of Florida Tnpk and I-95 (Atlantic Blvd to Rt 441 then north several blocks).
DESCRIPTION: This family type indoor/outdoor market opened in 1976 and has grown to 300 to 550 dealers selling antiques, collectibles, new and used merchandise, lots of garage sale goodies, glassware, crystal, clothing, flowers, vitamins, t-shirts, and fresh produce. This flea market has one of the largest produce sections around. The Lake Shore Motel is on the property. Two snack bars and handicapped-accessible restrooms are on site.
DEALER RATES: $8 per 10' × 20' space. Reservations are required for monthly, daily—first come, first served. Their rates fluctuate with the seasons; this rate is the current winter rate. Summer should be less.
CONTACT: Manager, Margate Swap Shop, 1000 N SR 7, Margate FL 33063. Tel: (954) 971-7927. Fax: (954) 979-3729.

MELBOURNE
Super Flea and Farmers' Market
DATES: Friday, Saturday and Sunday.
TIMES: 9:00 AM-4:00 PM.
ADMISSION: Free. Parking is free.
LOCATION: 4835 W Eau Gallie Blvd. At the corner of I-95 and Eau Gallie Blvd, Exit 72.
DESCRIPTION: Opened in 1987, this market of 200-350 dealers sells antiques, collectibles, cars, crafts, produce, coins, cards, garage sale goodies, new merchandise, furniture (new and used), quality 14K and silver jewelry, ruby and gem mining, and a huge selection of professional chef and restaurant supplies. Their dealers set up in the open, under cover or in shops. Hungry? Their food courts include Gyros, Buffalo-style wings, New York-style pizza, homemade donuts, whatever. Get this: the weekend before Thanksgiving Day they hold their Annual Turkey Bowl. People actually bowl frozen turkeys down a bowling lane to win a free turkey, sodas and other prizes. They have been told that their handicapped-accessible restrooms are the cleanest of any flea market.
DEALER RATES: $5 per day and up for 10' × 8' space; $164 and up monthly. Enclosed units are available. Reservations are suggested.
CONTACT: Susan Jerome, Manager, Super Flea, 4835 W Eau Gallie Blvd, Melbourne FL 32934. Tel: (321) 242-9124 Thursday through Saturday. Email: sj@superfleamarket.com. Web: www.SUPERFLEAMARKET.com.

MIAMI
Opa Locka/Hialeah Flea Market

DATES: Daily.

TIMES: 5:00 AM-7:00 PM.

ADMISSION: Free and $1 plus parking available Saturday and Sunday.

LOCATION: 12705 NW 42nd Ave. Take I-75 south to Opa Locka exit. I-95 to NW 103st St, Exit west 4 miles to NW 42nd Ave and north 1 mile, market is on both sides. The market is just 15 minutes north of Miami International Airport on Le Jeune Rd (NW 42nd Ave) at 127th St.

DESCRIPTION: Opened in 1985, this indoor/outdoor market boosts 1,000-plus dealers selling collectibles, new merchandise, produce, meats, garage sale goodies, furniture, clothing, you name it. Thirteen restaurants and handicapped-accessible restrooms add to the amenities.

DEALER RATES: $30 and up per 20' × 20' space per week. Reservations are not required.

CONTACT: Scott Miller, Opa Locka/Hialeah Flea Market, 12551 NW 42 Ave, Opa Locka, FL 33054. Tel: (305) 688-0500. Fax: (305) 687-8312.

MOUNT DORA
Florida Twin Markets

DATES: Saturday and Sunday, except for the 3-day extravaganzas held the third full Friday through Sunday of November, January and February.

TIMES: Flea market 8:00 AM-4:00 PM; antique market 9:00 AM-5:00 PM. Extravaganza Fridays 10:00 AM-5:00 PM.

ADMISSION: Free on regular dates. Extravaganzas: $10 on Friday, $5 on Saturday, $3 on Sunday. Parking is free.

LOCATION: East of Mt. Dora, 25 miles north of Orlando on new Hwy 441, just past intersection of Hwy 441 over Hwy 46 at the bottom of the hill on the right.

DESCRIPTION: These markets, started in 1983, are sister markets to the highly successful Pennsylvania Renninger's markets. Sitting on 117 acres, they are actually two distinct and separate markets about 900 feet apart. One is devoted to antiques with over 150 dealers, the other is a farmers and flea market with over 500 dealers. However, during Extravaganzas the antique dealers numbers swell to over 1,200. In addition, they have eight Antique Fairs from March through October on the third full Saturday and Sunday. As you can imagine, they sell just about anything and everything at these two markets. Four restaurants and handicapped-accessible restrooms add to the amenities.

DEALER RATES: Flea Market: $13.50 per 10' × 10' space under roof, $7 per 15' × 25' space outside. Extravaganza rates run from $130 and up depending on where the space is. Reservations are required.

CONTACT: Florida Twin Markets Inc, PO Box 1699, Mt Dora FL 32757-1699. Tel: (352) 383-8393 Antiques, (352) 383-3141 Flea Market or 1-800-522-3555 for either market. Email: manager@renningersflorida.com. Web: www.renningers.com.

NAPLES
Naples Drive-In Flea Market
DATES: Saturday and Sunday, year round; Fridays October through April.
TIMES: 7:00 AM-3:00 PM.
ADMISSION: Free. Parking is free.
LOCATION: 7700 E Davis Blvd. Off Exit 15 from I-75.
DESCRIPTION: Open since 1975, and under new ownership/management, this outdoor market of 200-350 dealers is half flea market, half farmers' market, with loads of produce and loads of garage sale goodies. Antiques, collectibles, souvenirs, furniture and new merchandise can be found here. One big restaurant and handicapped-accessible restrooms add to the amenities.
DEALER RATES: Summer, May through October, $6 or $10 per 10' × 20' space; winter, November through April, $10 or $15 per space. Reservations are first come, first served. Canopies and tables are available.
CONTACT: Jack, Naples Drive-In Flea Market, 7700 E Davis Blvd, Naples FL 33942-5311. Tel: (941) 774-2900. Fax: (941) 774-2900.

NORTH FORT MYERS
North Side Drive-In Flea Market
DATES: Wednesday, Friday through Sunday, weather permitting.
TIMES: 5:00 AM-2:00 PM.
ADMISSION: Free. Free parking is available.
LOCATION: 2521 N Tamiami Trail. On Old Rt 41 N, in the old business district. Off Exit 26 from I-75.
DESCRIPTION: This outdoor market began before 1980. Wednesday is their big day as it is the only Wednesday market around. It accommodates approximately 250-350 (they did squeeeeze 396 dealers in one Wednesday) dealers selling antiques, glass, arts and crafts, collectibles, fresh produce, and both new and used merchandise. Art reckons the ratio is 60/40 old to new. One snack bar (trust me, you won't starve) serves homemade cooked-to-order breakfast. After that you may need their handicapped-accessible restrooms.
DEALER RATES: Wednesday $8-$10 depending on the season, winter is higher; Friday $3; Saturday and Sunday $6-$8. Reservations are not required. Do reserve for Wednesday—it fills quickly!
CONTACT: Art, North Side Drive-In and Flea Market, 2521 N Tamiami Trail, N Ft Myers FL 33903-2348. Tel: (941) 995-2254.

NORTH FORT PIERCE
Biz-E-Flea Market

DATES: Saturday and Sunday, year round.

TIMES: 7:00 AM-closing (up to 3:00 PM).

ADMISSION: Free. Parking is also free.

LOCATION: 3252 N US 1, 1 mile north of St. Lucie Blvd (Airport Rd) and 11 miles south of Oslo Rd, Vero Beach.

DESCRIPTION: This covered outdoor market first opened in 1980. There are anywhere from 50 dealers during the summer to 90 dealers during the winter selling antiques, collectibles, crafts, tools, electronic equipment, carpeting and new and good used merchandise. Fresh vegetables are also sold. This is a family style market boasting sidewalks for easy walking. One complete concession with seating and restrooms add to the amenities.

DEALER RATES: For a 10' × 10' space daily: $10 uncovered with 3 tables, no electric; $12 covered with electric and 3 tables. Weekly and monthly rates are available. Reservations are not necessary, but suggested.

CONTACT: Biz-E-Flea Market, 3252 N US 1, Ft Pierce FL 34946. Tel: (561) 466-3063.

NORTH MIAMI
North Miami Flea Market

DATES: Every Wednesday through Sunday; open daily Thanksgiving through Christmas.

TIMES: Wednesday and Sunday 10:00 AM-7:00 PM; Thursday-Saturday; 10:00 AM-9:00 PM.

ADMISSION: Free. Free parking is available.

LOCATION: 14135 NW 7th Ave, 1 block west of I-95 off N 135th St. (The Blue Building.)

DESCRIPTION: This is South Florida's original indoor flea market, and it all began in 1967. Between 70 and 80 (formerly up to 200) dealers sell a variety of goods, including antiques as well as new merchandise, fine art, and fresh produce. There is also clothing for the entire family, housewares, electronics, toys—the list goes on. The indoor market is clean and air-conditioned and features deluxe snack bars, a new ice cream shop and a restaurant.

DEALER RATES: $250 and up (plus tax) for 10' × 15' space monthly with annual lease preferred. Includes telephone service, advertising, security service, electric and maintenance.

CONTACT: Market Manager, North Miami Flea Market, 14135 NW 7 Ave, N Miami FL 33168-6897. Tel: (305) 685-7721. Fax: (305) 685-7722.

OAK HILL
Oak Hill Flea Market

DATES: Tuesday, Friday, Saturday and Sunday.

TIMES: 7:00 AM till around 1:00-3:00 PM.

ADMISSION: Free. Parking is free.

LOCATION: 351 US 1, 28 miles south of Daytona and 40 miles north of Cocoa. Via I-95: From Daytona, take the Edgewater Exit and go south 8 miles on US 1; from Cocoa, take the Oak Hill Scottsmoor Exit and go north 8 miles on US 1.

DESCRIPTION: Opened in 1986, and surrounded by palm trees and sand, this indoor/outdoor market of 70-250 dealers, depending on the season (winter is higher and often sells out of space), sells antiques, collectibles, plants, canned goods, household items, clothing, toys, tools, hardware, produce, appliances, and new merchandise. The ratio of sale items is only 20% new, 10% produce, and the rest is garage sale goodies, and antiques and collectibles. During the winter months, a food concession trailer is set up on the grounds to join the Back to the '50s Restaurant. Baby Boomers, take note—a '50s joint with hand-dipped ice cream, shakes, sundaes, breakfast. Bring back memories? They hold special events during the year: Antique Radio Collectors Annual Meet and Flea Market, Antique Tool Collectors Meet and Flea Market, and the New Car Show and Sale.

DEALER RATES: Per 8' table: Tuesday $3, Friday $5, Saturday $7, Sunday $7. Same price for inside or outside tables, or 10' wide spaces outside with no table. Reservations are recommended, particularly from September thru May. There are 180 spaces inside under roof, 100 spaces available outside and 5 enclosed permanent stalls.

CONTACT: Edith Layton, Flea Market Manager, PO Box 116, Oak Hill FL 32759-0116. Tel: (386) 345-3570. Fax: (386) 257-9531. Email: roaringtwnties@ns.gemlink.com. Web: members.tripod.com/~roaring_twenties/index-6.html or maxpages.com/maxpage.cgi/roaringtwnties.

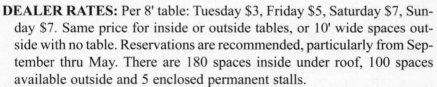

Local History
Oak Hill Flea Market and Back to the '50s Restaurant was originally a busy truck stop and restaurant back in the 1950s and '60s when the Kennedy Space Center was being built. In those pre-I-95 days, US 1 was the main route for travelers and workers. It is still a preferred route for many folks going to Spacecoast to see a lift-off.

OCALA
Ocala Drive-In Flea Market

DATES: Saturday and Sunday, year round. Rain or shine.

TIMES: 6:00 AM-4:00 PM.

ADMISSION: Free admission and free parking.

LOCATION: 4850 S Pine Ave (South 441-301-27).

DESCRIPTION: Started in 1979, the Ocala Flea Market is located at the only drive-in theater in the county, which is open on Friday, Saturday, and Sunday. Approximately 300 dealers occupy selling space in the summer and 450 in the winter, offering antiques, collectibles, handmade crafts, vegetables, tools, clothes, plants, birds, and new merchandise. There is a pawnshop on the premises. Food is available, as are handicapped-accessible restrooms.

DEALER RATES: $10.50 per day for a 10' × 10' booth under roof; $8 per day for a 10' × 10' booth outside. Reservations are suggested.

CONTACT: Ocala Drive-In Flea Market, 4850 S Pine Ave, Ocala FL 34480-9105. Tel: (352) 629-1325 or (352) 629-1666.

OKEECHOBEE
The Market Place Flea Market

DATES: Saturday and Sunday, year round.

TIMES: Winter: 8:00 AM-4:00 PM. Summer: 8:00 AM-3:00 PM.

ADMISSION: Free. Parking is free.

LOCATION: 3600 Hwy 441 S. From I-95: go west on Hwy 710, then west on Hwy 70, then south on Hwy 441. They are approximately 3 miles down the road on the left across from Scotty's.

DESCRIPTION: This family owned and operated market has been filling the need of "everything and anything" market for the locals as well as the transient workers from this area. Their 550 dealers (in season) sell some antiques and collectibles, tons of fresh produce (just picked) and loads of new merchandise (tends towards the flashy stuff, electronics, jewelry, hair decorations), clothing and new furniture. The entire market is under cover on pavement. There are six snack bars and two Mexican restaurants, just in case you can't wait to eat. Local advice: "Bring your fishing gear!" They are located on the north end of Lake Okeechobee.

DEALER RATES: Winter: $25 per 10' × 10' space and table per weekend. Summer: $17 per 10' × 10' space and table per weekend. Lock-down stores are available, some with air conditioning. Reservations are strongly recommended, especially in winter as they get full quickly. Dealers may stay overnight in self-contained rigs as water, electric, showers, laundry room and a dump station are available on site. A huge KOA Campground is next door.

CONTACT: The Market Place Flea Market, 3600 Hwy 441 S, Okeechobee FL 34974-6235. Tel: (863) 467-6639. Fax: (863) 467-0645.

OLDSMAR
Oldsmar Flea Market

DATES: Saturday and Sunday, year round.

TIMES: 9:00 AM-5:00 PM.

ADMISSION: Free. Free parking available.

LOCATION: 180 N Racetrack Rd, at the corner of Hillsboro Ave and Racetrack Rd.

DESCRIPTION: This market began in 1980. About 1,100 dealers sell to the public. Ninety-five percent of them are indoors and offer antiques, collectibles, handmade and craft items, produce, meats, and cheeses. New merchandise is also sold. In addition, there are two bakeries, two nurseries, and even beauticians, as well as handicapped-accessible restrooms on the premises. Ten snack bars provide plenty of food and refreshment.

DEALER RATES: Prices vary from $12 plus tax daily with one table and parking; rented on a first-come, first-served basis. Their office is open Thursday and Friday 9:00 AM-3:00 PM, and weekends 7:00 AM-5:00 PM. Reservations can be made only one week in advance provided you show up in person and pay in advance.

CONTACT: Oldsmar Flea Market, PO Box 439, Oldsmar FL 34677-0439. Tel: (813) 855-5306 (during market days) or (813) 855-2587 office. Fax: (813) 855-1263. Web: home.att.net/~ad-man/oldsmar.htm.

PALMETTO
Midway Flea Market

DATES: Friday, Saturday and Sunday, year round. October through June: Thursday through Sunday, weekly yard sales.

TIMES: 8:00 AM-4:00 PM. Yard sales: 7:00 AM-3:00 PM.

ADMISSION: Free. Parking is free.

LOCATION: 10816 US 41 N. Take Exit 45 from I-75 west to US41. Market is midway between Tampa and Sarasota, near Sun City.

DESCRIPTION: Since 1987 this indoor/outdoor market's 375-plus dealers have been selling antiques, collectibles, produce, coins, cards, new merchandise, clothes, furniture, crafts, plants, groceries and garage sale goodies. When the munchies strike pick from three restaurants or the concession trailer. And yes, there are handicapped-accessible restrooms. This market is busy from October through May. The new management maintains an exceptionally clean market and prides itself on its friendliness.

DEALER RATES: 1-year leases available. Reservations are necessary for indoors, recommended for outdoors. They have RV hookups for dealers and guests who just can't bear to leave.

CONTACT: Paul A Semanco or Heather Smith, Midway Flea Market, 10816 US 41 N, Palmetto FL 34221. Tel: (941) 723-6000. Fax: (941) 723-9093.

PENSACOLA
T & W Flea Market

DATES: Saturday and Sunday. Rain or shine.

TIMES: Dawn to dusk.

ADMISSION: Free. Free parking is available.

LOCATION: 1717 N T St, on the west side of Pensacola.

DESCRIPTION: This indoor/outdoor market started in 1979. There are 400 dealers per weekend selling a variety of objects, including antiques, fine art, arts and crafts, new merchandise, fresh produce, etc.—it's all here. They have made many improvements in this market including concrete aisles. Four snack bars provide food for the hungry. Handicapped-accessible restrooms complete the amenities.

DEALER RATES: $10 and up. Reservations are required for the more desirable spaces.

CONTACT: Red Cotton, T & W Flea Market, 1717 N T St, Pensacola FL 32505-6000. Tel: (850) 433-4315 weekends or 433-7030 mid-week.

PINELLAS PARK
Wagonwheel Flea Market

DATES: Saturday and Sunday.

TIMES: 7:30 AM-4:00 PM.

ADMISSION: Free. Parking is $1.

LOCATION: 7801 Park Blvd, at 74th Ave, between Belcher and Starkey Rds. Off I-275 Exit 28W (was 15W).

DESCRIPTION: Opened in 1967, this market of 1200-1800 vendors sells a few antiques and collectibles, crafts, fresh produce, but mostly new merchandise. There is a food court, 30 snack concessions, handicapped-accessible restrooms, a courtesy tram, stroller and wheelchair rentals among other amenities.

DEALER RATES: $6 per 10' × 10' open space, $9.50 under cover. First come, first served. Although the office is open Tuesday through Friday for reservations, should you want to reserve a good spot.

CONTACT: Wagonwheel Flea Market, 7801 Park Blvd, Pinellas Park FL 33781-3708. Tel: (727) 544-5319. Fax: (727) 541-4005. Web: zipmall.com/wagonwheel.htm.

> **Dolphin Watch!**
> This market is located five miles inland from the Gulf of Mexico, but on the Intercoastal Waterway. A while ago, three dolphins ambled into their lake and hung around. Eventually, two decided it wasn't big enough and left. The third fellow is still there, enjoying his personal lake and audience.

PLANT CITY
Country Village Flea Market

DATES: Every Wednesday. Rain or shine.

TIMES: 7:00 AM-2:00 PM.

ADMISSION: Free. Free and paid ($1) parking is available.

LOCATION: 3301 Paul Buchman Hwy. On corner of State Rd 39 (now called Paul Buchman Hwy) and Sam Allen Rd, 1 mile north of I-4. (Tampa area.)

DESCRIPTION: This market began in 1979 and currently ranks among the largest Wednesday markets. It accommodates dealers outdoors, selling plenty of used goods. Also available are antiques, collectibles, and fresh produce. Food is served on the premises. Their Wednesday market is so popular that they have turned away dealers for lack of room! There is a wholesale produce market seven days a week from 6:00 AM to whenever. In fact, the produce market grew so big, it took over all the buildings!

DEALER RATES: $7 for 24' outdoor space. No reservations are required and there are no advance shopping hours for dealers.

CONTACT: Country Village Flea Market, 3301 Paul Buchman Hwy, Plant City FL 33565-5051. Tel: (813) 752-4670.

PORT RICHEY
USA Fleamarket

DATES: Friday, Saturday and Sunday.

TIMES: 8:00 AM-4:00 PM.

ADMISSION: Free. Parking is free.

LOCATION: 11721 US Hwy 19, 200 yards south of SR 52 on US Hwy 19.

DESCRIPTION: Started in 1980, this market, now completely under cover, runs from 600 dealers in summer to crammed full in winter. Their dealers sell antiques, collectibles, crafts, produce, jewelry, western wear, records, tapes, hobby supplies, tools, clothing, perfumes, pewter, scrubs, purses, clocks, art, appliances, silk flowers, sneakers, lamps and other new and used merchandise. There is a dollar shop, an automotive shop, a beauty salon, hobby shop, and seven snack bars as well. Look for their humongous electronic sign at the entrance ("you can't miss it!")—"One of the best flea markets on the west coast of Florida."

DEALER RATES: From $13 for aisle tables, and $14 and up daily for booths from 9' × 12' to 12' × 36'. There are weekly and monthly rates available as well as shed rentals. Vendors set up at 7:00 AM, vacate by 5:00 PM.

CONTACT: USA Fleamarket Inc, 11721 US Hwy 19, Port Richey FL 34668. Tel: (727) 862-3583. Fax: (727) 862-5724.

ST AUGUSTINE
St Johns Flea Market

DATES: Saturday and Sunday.

TIMES: 9:00 AM-5:00 PM.

ADMISSION: Free. Parking is free.

LOCATION: I-95 and SR 207, Exit 94.

DESCRIPTION: This market opened in 1985 and has 500 spaces indoors and out with dealers selling "everything"; antiques, collectibles, new and used merchandise, produce, plants, and more. It is all under roof. Located in historic St. Augustine, the country's oldest city and a major tourist attraction. Food is available on the premises as are clean handicapped-accessible restrooms and RV facilities.

DEALER RATES: $12 per day, or depending on dealer's needs. Reservations are suggested.

CONTACT: St Johns Flea Market, PO Box 1284, St Augustine FL 32085-1284. Tel: (904) 824-4210. Fax: (904) 824-9287.

SANFORD
Flea World

DATES: Every Friday, Saturday, and Sunday. Rain or shine.

TIMES: 9:00 AM-6:00 PM.

ADMISSION: Free. Free parking is available for 4,000 cars.

LOCATION: 4311 Hwy 17-92. From I-4, take Exit 50 east to Hwy 17-92, turn right 1 mile.

DESCRIPTION: This market started on May 20, 1982, with just a 12-acre tract. It has now grown to accommodate 1,700 dealers on 104 acres of land. There is an "all-under-one-roof" building with 1,700 booths and three other air-conditioned buildings. Shoppers really can get it all here from antiques and collectibles to the unusual: a lawyer, an optometrist, a barber and beauty shop, and an exotic pet shop. The Friday market features $5 garage sales free before 9:00 AM. Fifteen fun food stops quell hunger and a Family Fun Park is located next door. Bingo and other events are held every weekend including circus acts and Elvis impersonators.

DEALER RATES: $14.50-$15.50 per space and up. Reservations are required and must be made in person. The rental office is open Thursday from 8:30 AM-5:00 PM.

CONTACT: Rental Manager, Flea World, 4311 Hwy 17-92, Sanford FL 32773. Tel: (407) 330-1792 ext. 224. Email: RENTALS@fleaworld.com. Web: www.fleaworld.com.

STUART
B & A Flea Market

DATES: Saturday and Sunday. Rain or shine.

TIMES: 8:00 AM-3:00 PM.

ADMISSION: Free. Parking $1.

LOCATION: South US Highway 1, just north of Indian Street, across from Home Depot.

DESCRIPTION: This market first opened in 1975. It accommodates over 600 dealers both indoors and outdoors who assemble to sell just about everything including antiques, collectibles, fine art, arts and crafts, new merchandise, and everything else imaginable. A farmers' market sells fresh produce. Hot dog carts roam the market and with a deli and other concessions quell hunger. Handicapped-accessible restrooms are on site.

DEALER RATES: Starting at $14 daily for an uncovered space, $24 for a covered space. Spaces are 10' × 10' to 10' × 20'. Reservations must be made in person and paid for by 7:00 AM the day of the market.

CONTACT: Mary Sue Davis, Flea Market Manager, B & A Flea Market, 2201 SE Indian St, Stuart FL 34997. Tel: (561) 288-4915. Fax: (561) 288-2140. Email: baindust@onearrow.net. Web: www.bafleamarket.com.

TAMPA
Big Top Flea Market

DATES: Saturday and Sunday, year round.

TIMES: 9:00 AM-4:30 PM.

ADMISSION: Free. Parking is free.

LOCATION: Take I-75 south to Fowler Ave (SR 582), Exit 54, heading east. Market is 500 yards east of I-75.

DESCRIPTION: The Big Top Flea Market, opened in October 1990, was built in a unique hub and spoke design so that every booth is well traveled and easily accessible. The market is named after the 27,000-square-foot center core that resembles a huge circus tent. It houses 1,000 booths with over 200,000 square feet of both covered and enclosed spaces. Eventually the Market will have over 1,100 spaces. While there is a wide variety of merchandise including produce, fine jewelry, antiques, collectibles and crafts, this market is keeping the true spirit of a flea market: value, bargains and fun. A full food court and handicapped-accessible restrooms add to the amenities.

DEALER RATES: Daily rates from $16-$25.50 plus tax per space depending on location and season (20% lower in summer). Monthly and weekend rates are available. Office is open Monday 1:00 PM-4:00 PM, Friday 9:00 AM-4:00 PM. Yard sales rates at $9.50 per space.

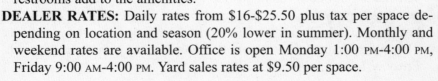

CONTACT: Big Top Flea Market, 9250 E Fowler Ave, Thonotosassa FL 33592. Tel: (813) 986-4004. Fax: (813) 986-6296. Email: info@bigtopfleamarket.com. Web: www.bigtopfleamarket.com.

THONOTOSASSA
301 North Flea Market

DATES: Tuesday through Sunday.
TIMES: 9:00 AM-5:00 PM.
ADMISSION: Free. Parking is free.
LOCATION: 11802 N 301. Just take I-75 to Fowler Ave. Exit and head east or travel east on Fowler from 56th St. Turn left (north) on Hwy 301. You can't miss them: they are just past the Machinery Auction on the left-hand side of the road.

DESCRIPTION: Opened in 1980 (the oldest flea market in Hillsborough County), this indoor market has 100 booths, full on weekends, with dealers selling antiques, collectibles, tools, furniture, glassware, books, and loads of yard sale stuff. There is a snack bar run by Jim, who retired from 35 years in the fast-food business, and restrooms. During the week, only the shops are really open (video, appliance, and book shops). It is one of the last of the "old-tyme" flea markets.
DEALER RATES: Inside rates start at $100 per month. Reservations are needed.
CONTACT: Jim Shafer, North 301 Flea Market, 11802 N 301 Hwy, Thonotosassa FL 33592. Tel: (813) 986-1023. Office hours: Tuesday-Sunday 9:00 AM-7:00 PM. Fax: (813) 986-1023.

WALDO
Waldo Farmers' and Flea Market

DATES: Every Saturday and Sunday. Rain or shine.
TIMES: 7:30 AM-4:30 PM.
ADMISSION: Free. Free parking available.
LOCATION: Located on Hwy 301 N, north of Waldo on both sides of the road—at the traffic light.

DESCRIPTION: This Farmers' and Flea Market attracts an average of 750 dealers in the summer and 900 dealers during the winter selling antiques, collectibles, vegetables, tools, new merchandise and "much more." The market has been running since 1973. There is a huge antique mall here, open every day. There is a snack bar on the premises. "Look for the big chair, windmill and the Big Horse." They describe themselves as: "The old-fashioned flea market. A country market with big city crowds. Friendly folks."

DEALER RATES: $8 and up per 10' × 10' space. The majority of spaces are under covered sheds; however, outside space and lock-up stalls are also available. Dealers may stay overnight and city licenses are included in the booth rental. The office is open Thursday through Sunday.

CONTACT: Waldo Farmers' and Flea Market, 17805 NE US Hwy 301, Waldo FL 32694-4629. Tel: (352) 468-2255.

WEBSTER

Sumter County Farmers' Market, Inc

DATES: Every Monday year round, except Christmas Day. Rain or shine.

TIMES: 8:00 AM-3:00 PM.

ADMISSION: Free. Free parking is provided on market grounds.

LOCATION: On Hwy 471 in Webster. Accessible from Hwy 50, Hwy 301, or Hwy 98.

DESCRIPTION: This market opened in 1937 and currently attracts between 1,200 (summer) and 2,000 (winter) dealers who sell a range of antiques, collectibles, craft items, new and used merchandise, and fresh produce, including citrus and flower plants. This market is well known for its selection of antique items and locally grown vegetables. There is a large wholesale area on site as well. Snack food, as well as a sit-down restaurant, are available on the premises.

DEALER RATES: $10 per 10' × 10' booth, covered with 2 tables; $8 per 12' × 12' booth, open with 2 tables. Cancellations are done by a lottery system at 7:00 AM. All dealers must have city and county licenses, available at office every Monday between 7:30 AM and 9:30 AM, for $7 per day or $35 for the year.

CONTACT: Margie Hayes, Office Manager, PO Box 62, Webster FL 33597-0062. Tel: (352) 793-3551. Fax: (352) 793-9474. Web: www.websterfleamarket.com.

Webster Westside Flea Market

DATES: Mondays, year round.

TIMES: 6:00 AM-3:00 PM.

ADMISSION: Free. Parking is $2.

LOCATION: 516 NW 3rd St. On Hwy 478 at NW 3rd St. On the west side of town.

DESCRIPTION: Considered the oldest flea market in the state, they opened as an outdoor market in 1931. Many of the dealers are under cover, although not really indoors. Also known as "Antique Alley" for their quality antiques and collectibles, this market's 800 or so dealers also sell some new merchandise, produce, and whatever. They bill themselves as an "antique, collectible, new, used and unusual market." They hold Car Shows the first Sunday of the month, with a three-day Extravaganza in

February. They tried an antiques-only car and bike show one weekend in 1997 and found it was so successful that they were doing them on the first Sunday of the month. Watch for the advertisements as to the dates. Plenty of concessions dot the market and handicapped-accessible restrooms abound. Howard's Flea Market in Homosassa is their sister market and headquarters.

DEALER RATES: Daily including tax: Covered with 2 tables: $16.09 per 10' × 10' space. Small field: $10.70 per 10' × 10' with 1 table. Big field: $27 per 30' × 15' space, no tables. Reservations are suggested, although if you do show up they will manage to find you a spot somehow. The office is open for reservations on Thursday and Friday.

CONTACT: Howard's Flea Market, 6373 S Suncoast Blvd, Homosassa FL 34446-3005. Tel: (352) 628-4656 for HQ or (352) 568-0494 or 793-9877 for the market. For a tape of Webster-only information and their voicemail, call 1-800-832-7396. Email witha2@scia.net. Web: www.howardsfleamarket.com and click on Sister Market.

ZEPHYRHILLS
Zephyrhills Flea Market

DATES: Friday, Saturday, and Sunday.

TIMES: 8:30 AM-3:30 PM.

ADMISSION: Free. Parking is free.

LOCATION: 39336 Chancey Rd. Follow Rt 301 to the south side of Zephyrhills, turn east on Chancey Rd. Go about 1½ miles; the market is on the right.

DESCRIPTION: Started in 1991, this indoor/outdoor market has 340 or so spaces with 100 or more dealers depending on who takes up how much room. The outdoor sellers are under roof on concrete paths. They sell antiques, collectibles, baked goods, ceramics, watches, coins, plants, household goods, yard sale items, oldies music, and from one dealer, motorized scooters for the handicapped. Food wagons quell hunger and there are handicapped-accessible restrooms on site. This market has been noted for its cleanliness and friendly people.

DEALER RATES: Outside: about $16 for a proper space depending on the season, special rates for yard sales. Indoors: $165-$185 per month (there are 64 spaces).

CONTACT: Dee, Zephyrhills Flea Market, 39336 Chancey Rd, Zephyrhills FL 33540-6559. Tel: (813) 782-1483.

OTHER FLEA MARKETS

We know or have heard about these markets, but have not personally contacted each one, as we have the markets with descriptions. If you plan to visit one of the markets listed below, *please call first* to make sure they are still open. Flea markets do come and go. While they were open when we went to press, they may not be later. We can't be responsible. *Call first!*

Avon Park: Broken Spoke Flea Market, 2 E Main St. Tel: (863) 453-0078.
Bartow: Bartow Flea Market, 1705 US Hwy 17 S. Tel: (863) 519-0602.
Belleview: Market of Marion, 12888 SE US Hwy 441. Tel: (352) 245-6766.
Big Pine Key: Big Pine Key Flea Market, US Hwy 1 Mm 30.5. Tel: (305) 872-4103.
Blountstown: Southside Flea Market, 15015 Hwy 71 S. Tel: (850) 674-6110.
Blountstown: Trading Post, 1508 N Pear St. Tel: (850) 674-2630.
Bradenton: Bayshore High Flea Market, 703 65th Avenue Dr W. Tel: (941) 755-6339.
Bradenton: Roma Flea Market, 5715 15th St E. Tel: (941) 756-9036.
Bushnell: Sumter Drive In Flea Market, 7368 SR 471. Tel: (352) 793-3581.
Clearwater: 49ER Flea Market, 10525 49th St N. Tel: (727) 573-3367.
Cocoa: Jumping Flea Market, 2507 N Cocoa Blvd. Tel: (321) 636-9664.
Crawfordville: Coyote Dogs Flea Market, 892 Woodville Hwy. Tel: (850) 210-1155.
Crestview: Super Flea, 300 Rasberry Rd. Tel: (850) 689-0100.
De Land: Deland Flea Market, 1570 7th Ave. Tel: (386) 740-9432.
De Funiak Spgs: De Funiak Flea Market, 2653 Hwy E. Tel: (850) 892-3668.
Delray Beach: Carnival Flea Market At Delray, 5283 W Atlantic Ave. Tel: (561) 499-9935.
Ellenton: Enterprise Flea Market, 2408 US Hwy 301 N. Tel: (941) 723-9424.
Eustis: Lake County Fairgrounds, 2101 N Cty Road 452. Tel: (352) 357-9692.
Eustis: Bill Cox Flea Market, 510 E Washington Ave. Tel: (352) 483-0105.
Fort Myers: Flea Market of Ortiz Ave, 1501 Ortiz Ave. Tel: (941) 694-5019.
Gulf Breeze: Flea Market, 5760 Gulf Breeze Pkwy. Tel: (850) 934-1971.
Homestead: Bargain Town Flea Market, 24420 S Dixie Hwy. Tel: (305) 257-4335.
Hudson: Hudson Flea Market, 9411 Denton Ave. Tel: (727) 869-0650.
Indialantic: Thomas W Rill Flea Market, 401 N Riverside Dr. Tel: (321) 726-9718.
Interlachen: Rodriquez Flea Market, 1300 Hwy 20. Tel: (386) 684-4969.
Jacksonville: ABC Flea Market, 10135 Beach Blvd. Tel: (904) 642-2717.
Jacksonville: Golfair Flea Market, 3854 Sandy Shores Dr. Tel: (904) 765-8744.

Jacksonville: Liberty Street Flea Market, 3805 N Liberty St. Tel: (904) 634-8824.

Jacksonville: Market Place, 7059 Ramona Blvd. Tel: (904) 786-3532.

Jacksonville: Pecan Park Flea/Farmers Market, 614 Pecan Park Rd. Tel: (904) 751-6770.

Key Largo: Flea Market, 103530 Overseas Hwy. Tel: (305) 451-0677.

Lake Wales: Sunshine Flea Market, 4449 N US Hwy 27. Tel: (863) 679-1015.

Lecanto: Stokes Flea Market, 5220 W Gulf To Lake Hwy. Tel: (352) 746-7200.

Leesburg: North Lake Flea Market Inc, 2557 US Hwy 441. Tel: (352) 326-9335.

Marianna: Trading Post, 6052 Hwy 90. Tel: (850) 592-3373.

Melbourne: Greg Piacentino Flea Market, 2820 Caribbean Isle Blvd. Tel: (321) 960-5771.

Miami: 7th Ave Flea Market, 13995 NW 7th Ave. Tel: (305) 681-9973.

Miami: Hallandale Flea Market, 21301 Biscayne Blvd. Tel: (305) 931-7223.

Miami: Liberty Flea Market, 7900 NW 27th Ave. Tel: (305) 836-9848.

Miami: Tropicaire Drive-In Flea Mkt, 9769 S Dixie Hwy 201. Tel: (305) 663-6570.

Milton: I-10 Flea Market & Antiques, 3524 Garcon Point Rd. Tel: (850) 623-6349.

Monticello: Hamm's Flea Market, 925 E Washington St. Tel: (850) 997-5114.

Naples: Bass & Bass Flea Mart, 230 Industrial Blvd. Tel: (941) 643-4424.

Newberry: Weeks Flea Market, 8979 SE 80th St. Tel: (352) 472-2061.

Ocala: I-75 Super Flea Market, 4121 NW 44th Ave. Tel: (352) 351-9220.

Odessa: Gunn Highway Flea Market, 2317 Gunn Hwy. Tel: (813) 920-3181.

Okeechobee: Market Place Flea Market, 3600 Hwy 441 S. Tel: (863) 467-6639.

Okeechobee: Trading Post Flea Market, 3100 Hwy 441 S. Tel: (863) 763-4114.

Opa Locka: 183rd Street Flea Market, 18200 NW 27th Ave. Tel: (305) 624-1756.

Orlando: K K Flea Market, 1325 W Washington St #2. Tel: (407) 841-0736.

Orlando: Orlando Flea Market, 5022 S Orange Blossom Trl. Tel: (407) 857-0048.

Orlando: Three Star Flea Market, 2390 N Orange Blossom Trl. Tel: (407) 293-2722.

Orlando: William L Chiesa Flea Market, 4721 Ethans Glenn Ave. Tel: (407) 275-0213.

Pace: Big Oak Flea Market, 4132 Hwy 90. Tel: (850) 995-9181.

Pace: Pea Ridge Flea Market, 5186 Hwy 90. Tel: (850) 994-8056.

Palmetto: Country Fair-Flea Market, 512 10th St E. Tel: (941) 722-5633.

Palmetto: Midway Flea Market, 10816 US Hwy 41 N. Tel: (941) 723-6000.

Panama City: 15th Street Flea Market, 2233 E 15th St. Tel: (850) 769-0137.

Pensacola: B & B Flea Market, 3721 W Navy Blvd # B. Tel: (850) 455-3200.

Pensacola: Chicken Nest Flea Market, 1316 N New Warrington Rd. Tel: (850) 456-3226.

Pensacola: I-10 Flea Market, 3205 E Olive Rd #141. Tel: (850) 478-0107.

Perry: Perry Flea Market, 3609 S US Hwy 19. Tel: (850) 838-1422.

Plant City: Country Village Flea Market, 3301 Paul Buchman Hwy. Tel: (813) 752-4670.

Plant City: Frenchmen's Flea Market, 102 N Collins St. Tel: (813) 754-8388.

Port St Joe: Big Barn, 412 Monument Ave. Tel: (850) 227-7410.

Port Charlotte: Rainbow Flea Market, 4628 Tamiami Trl. Tel: (941) 629-1223.

Port Charlotte: Sun Flea Market Inc, 18505 Paulson Dr # C6. Tel: (941) 255-3532.

St Augustine: St Johns County Flea & Farmers, 2495 SR 207. Tel: (904) 824-4210.

Tallahassee: Tallahassee Flea Market, 200 Capital Cir SW. Tel: (850) 877-3811.

Tampa: Pender Grass Flea Market, 3522 W Azeele St. Tel: (813) 353-2266.

Waldo: Trading Post, 17500 NE US Hwy 301. Tel: (352) 468-2622.

West Palm Beach: Beach Drive-In Theater, 1301 Old Dixie Hwy. Tel: (561) 844-0330.

West Palm Beach: Dr Flea's Intl Flea Market, 1200 S Congress Ave. Tel: (561) 965-1500.

West Palm Beach: Forty Fifth Street Flea Market, 1710 45th St. Tel: (561) 863-6424.

West Palm Beach: Uptown-Downtown Flea Market, 5700 Okeechobee Blvd. Tel: (561) 684-5700.

GEORGIA

ACWORTH
Highway 41 Flea Market
DATES: Saturday and Sunday.
TIMES: 5:30 AM-5:30 PM.
ADMISSION: Free. Parking is free.
LOCATION: 3352 N Cobb Pkwy. Take I-75 N to Barrett Pkwy. Turn left. Go down to Hwy 41. Then turn right. Go exactly 6 miles to the market.

DESCRIPTION: Opened in 1975, this market averages 450-500 dealers selling antiques, collectibles, garage sale goodies, produce, and lots of new and used merchandise. It's a clean market with four concession stands, two lemonade stands, two boiled peanut stands, and when needed handicapped-accessible restrooms. There are 19 buildings with 1,400 tables here, covering about 42 acres.
DEALER RATES: $12 per day for a 8' × 8' space with table. Reservations are suggested and you can go in on Friday during office hours to reserve. Otherwise, first come, first served.
CONTACT: Robert Davenport, Highway 41 Flea Market, 3352 N Cobb Pkwy, Acworth GA 30101-8304. Tel: (770) 975-0100.

Lake Acworth Antique and Flea Market
DATES: Every Saturday and Sunday.
TIMES: 8:00 AM-5:00 PM.
ADMISSION: Free. Parking is free.
LOCATION: 4375 Cobb Pkwy NW, approximately 35 miles north of Atlanta and 5 miles west of I-75, off Hwy 92, Exit 278. Follow Hwy 92 to Cobb, turn right, go approximately 1 mile. Market is on the left.
DESCRIPTION: Started in 1978, this flea market was formerly known as Delight's. It is held indoors, in the open air, and under cover. There are 400 dealers exhibiting antiques, arts and crafts, fresh produce, collectibles, and new merchandise. Wendell, the manager, figures there's about a third of the market in antiques and collectibles, a third in yard sale goodies, and the rest is new merchandise. Located near Allatoona Lake on Lake Acworth, the average daily attendance ranges between 2,000 and 3,000 people. Here you will find something for everyone. Three concession stands feed the famished and handicapped-accessible restrooms are on site.
DEALER RATES: $5 for outside space with 1 table, $8 for under cover space. Inside space with lock-up is charged at $75 per month per 100 square feet of space. Reservations are necessary for inside. No vendor's license required.

138

CONTACT: James Little, Lake Acworth Antique and Flea Market, 4375 Cobb Pkwy North NW, Acworth GA 30102-4219. Tel: (770) 974-5896 (Saturday and Sunday only).

ALBANY
Kitty's Flea Market

DATES: Saturday, and Sunday, year round.
TIMES: 7:00 AM-6:00 PM.
ADMISSION: Free. Parking is also free.
LOCATION: 3331 Sylvester Rd. On US 82, 3 miles north of Albany.
DESCRIPTION: This market opened in 1985 in the middle of a pecan orchard and accommodates 320 regular dealers under roof and another 350 in the open or under shade, adding new tables all the time. "Anything you can think of" is sold here, including produce, furniture, clothes and jewelry. It is described by one regular as real "country, very laid back" and agreeable. This market is doing a booming business. If you love pecans, you can even pick your own! Four concession stands quell the screaming munchies, handicapped-accessible restrooms provide relief and a new 42-spot RV park provides camping facilities for dealers. Come for the Sunday's occasional Gospel singing, or you might be there when the clown shows up!
DEALER RATES: $6 per table under the shed, $4 outside space. Reservations are required under the shed only. Outside dealers can set up outside with no reservation.
CONTACT: Jim Andrews, Kitty's Flea Market, PO Box 51324, Albany GA 31703-1324. Tel: (229) 432-0007.

ATLANTA
Lakewood Antiques Market

DATES: Second weekend of every month, Friday-Sunday, year round. An Extravaganza is held in November for five days.
TIMES: Friday 9:00 AM-6:00 PM; Saturday 9:00 AM-6:00 PM; Sunday 10:00 AM-5:00 PM.
ADMISSION: $3. Parking is free. Thursday is early buyers day for $5.
LOCATION: 2000 Lakewood Way. Take I-75-85 S, Exit 243 E and follow the signs.
DESCRIPTION: Since 1969, this market has been hosting from 800 to 1,200 dealers selling at least 75% antiques and collectibles. Their historic buildings are situated on 117 acres of land with a fully equipped bar and restaurant and dealer camping spots on site. They have added new air-conditioned and heated buildings.

DEALER RATES: $110 per 8' × 10' booth inside space; $75 per 14' × 15' outside space. After advance reservations are filled, it is first come, first served.
CONTACT: Ed Spivia, PO Box 6826, Atlanta GA 30315-0826. Tel: (404) 622-4488. Day of show contact Diane Dominick at above number.

Scott Antique Market Antiques & Collectibles Show
DATES: Second weekend of every month.
TIMES: Friday and Saturday 9:00 AM-6:00 PM, Sunday 10:00 AM-4:00 PM.
ADMISSION: Free. Parking is $3.
LOCATION: Atlanta Exposition Centers, North and South Facilities at 3650 Jonesboro Rd. Take Exit 40 (Jonesboro Rd) off I-285, 3 miles east of Atlanta Airport.

DESCRIPTION: Since 1986 this indoor/outdoor market has 2,400 dealers selling the finest in antique and collectibles only. Exhibitors from all over the U.S. feature fine antique furniture, jewelry, time pieces, china, pottery, books, coins, silver, glassware, textiles, linens, advertising items, military items, paintings, and much more. Four snack bars and one restaurant supply the energy to keep you browsing. Handicapped-accessible restrooms are on site.
DEALER RATES: Indoors: $125 for a 8' × 10' space; outdoors: $95 for a 10' × 10' space. There is an open field space for $55 for a 15' × 20' space to park and display. Reservations are required. Tables, chairs, pegboards, showcases, and safes are available for rent.
CONTACT: Scott Antique Markets, PO Box 60, Bremen OH 43107-0060. Tel: (740) 569-4112. Fax: (740) 569-7595. During the show call (404) 361-2000.

AUGUSTA
South Augusta Flea Market
DATES: Saturday and Sunday.
TIMES: 7:30 AM-6:00 PM.
ADMISSION: Free. Parking is free.
LOCATION: 1562 Doug Barnard Rd (formerly New Savannah Rd), Hwy 56. Bobby Jones Exit 10, left, first building on the right.

DESCRIPTION: This market opened April 4, 1977 making 2002 its 25th anniversary! Half their 650 dealers are in permanent spaces filling a 110' × 1000' building and the rest in temporary spaces. They sell everything from antiques, collectibles, Avon, produce, loads of yard sale goodies, pets, animals, new merchandise and whatever else comes in. The ratio is about 40% old to 60% newer. Their restaurant opens at 7:30 AM serving a breakfast buffet, there are two snack bars, lemonade stands, and handi-capped-accessible restrooms to handle all necessities. This is a clean, friendly, very successful market.
DEALER RATES: $5 per temporary space, $1 per table. First come, first served. Gates open at 6:00 PM on Friday, or line up the next morning.

CONTACT: South Augusta Flea Market, 1562 Doug Barnard Pkwy, Augusta GA 30906-9271. Tel: (706) 798-5500.

CARROLLTON
West Georgia Flea Market

DATES: Saturday and Sunday.
TIMES: 8:00 AM-4:30 PM.
ADMISSION: Free. Parking is free.
LOCATION: 3947 Hwy 27N, I-20W Exit 11 and go south 2.4 miles.
DESCRIPTION: This "old time" flea market is one of the oldest and largest in Georgia. There are approximately 400 dealers in 600-700 spaces selling about half old and half new merchandise—"a good mix," says the manager. Plenty of garage sale goodies make it here, as well as collectibles, crafts, new and used furniture, fresh produce, new and used merchandise. The market consists of buildings, a pole barn and all spaces are under cover. Three snack bars with full menus and handicapped-accessible restrooms take care of essential shopping needs.

DEALER RATES: Weekend rates: $20 per 10' × 8' outside space (dirt floor) with table, $26 inside with concrete floor. Reservations are highly recommended for the better spaces.
CONTACT: West Georgia Flea Market, 3947 N Hwy 27, Carrollton GA 30017-7924. Tel: (770) 832-6551 or toll-free 1-866-882-2455. Email: westgaflea@netzero.net or reservations to westgeorgiaflea@hotpop.com. Web: www.WestGeorgiaFlea.com.

CLEVELAND
129 Flea Market

DATES: Every weekend, plus holidays.
TIMES: 9:00 AM-6:00 PM.
ADMISSION: Free. Parking is free.
LOCATION: 1612 Hwy 129, 1 mile south of Cleveland.
DESCRIPTION: Under new management since 2001, formerly the Red, White and Blue Flea Market, this indoor/outdoor market of 75-112 dealers sells antiques, collectibles, books, new and used merchandise, tools, clothing, western gear, vacuums, jewelry, and fresh produce in season. There is a snack bar as well as handicapped-accessible restrooms.

DEALER RATES: $10 outside covered shed, $17.50-$25 inside per space per day. Monthly rates available. Reservations are requested. Camping facilities are available for dealers; please call.
CONTACT: 129 Flea Market, 50 Hale Ct, Maysville GA 30558. Tel: (706) 865-1716. Email: mikeandsonscomputers@alltel.net.

DARIEN
Ya'll Come Flea Market

DATES: Saturday and Sunday.

TIMES: Saturday 8:00 AM-6:00 PM. Auctions on Saturday at 7:00 PM. Sunday 8:00 AM-5:00 PM.

ADMISSION: Free. Parking is free.

LOCATION: I-95 and Hwy 251, Exit 49 (Darien Exit), 1 mile west of Exit 49 on Hwy 251, on the right side of road.

DESCRIPTION: Admittedly small in vendor number (their dealers tend to fill up to 15 booths apiece) but large in size, this rural indoor/outdoor market is housed in a 19,000-square-foot building. Opened in 1997, there are from 8 (during the worst of the heat) to 23 vendors filling their 75 booths selling used merchandise, books, pottery, crafts, produce, furniture, garage sale goodies, flowers, and whatever shows up. Their occupancy rate is 95-100%. A snack bar serves cool food and drink in the summer and hot homemade meals in the winter; and in case you need them, there are handicapped-accessible restrooms. In 2001, they added climate-control to their auction and dining room—too cool! Saturday's auction features callers from all over the South, selling new, old stuff, furniture, and more whatevers. Find Laverne in the snack bar, or Duke, and say "Hi!"

DEALER RATES: $14 inside 10' × 10' space, $10 outside per day. Friday is setup day 10:00 AM-4:00 PM. Reservations are required for inside space (they have to make the space for you) and not for outside space.

CONTACT: Laverne or Duke, Ya'll Come Flea Market, Rt 3 Box 3599, Townsend GA 31331. Tel: (912) 437-5650. Fax: (912) 437-3504.

DECATUR
Kudzu Antique Flea Market

DATES: Friday, Saturday and Sunday.

TIMES: Friday and Saturday 10:30 AM-5:30 PM; Sunday 12:30 PM-5:30 PM.

ADMISSION: Free. Parking is also free.

LOCATION: 2874 E Ponce de Leon. Off I-285, Exit 31.

DESCRIPTION: This dealer's paradise opened in October 1980. Their 27 dealers, in 27,000-square-foot barn-like building, sell mostly American antiques, collectibles, and furniture. There is very little new merchandise sold here and what comes in is exceptionally good. No food available on premises.

DEALER RATES: Rarely any vacancies; call for information.

CONTACT: Kudzu Antique Flea Market, 2874 E Ponce de Leon, Decatur GA 30030-2337. Tel: (404) 373-6498.

EAST POINT
Greenbriar Flea Market

DATES: Thursday through Monday, year round.

TIMES: Monday and Thursday 11:00 AM-8:00 PM; Friday and Saturday 10:00 AM-9:00 PM; Sunday 12:00 PM-7:00 PM.

ADMISSION: Free. Parking is also free.

LOCATION: 2925 Headland Dr. Across from the Greenbriar Mall.

DESCRIPTION: Opened in 1983, this friendly market hosts 136 dealers selling all new merchandise, including jewelry, clothes, hats, fragrance, shoes, photos, and endless amounts of more at very reasonable prices. They remodeled the entire market in 1993 adding 10,000 square feet, a few retail stores and a little restaurant to handle all your hunger problems; handicapped-accessible restrooms handle other needs.

DEALER RATES: $225 and up per month. Reservations are suggested, especially around the holidays. They can accommodate traveling dealers passing through. Just ask.

CONTACT: Greenbriar Flea Market, 2925 Headland Dr, East Point GA 30344-1906. Tel: (404) 349-3994.

MACON
Smiley's Flea Market

DATES: Saturday and Sunday.

TIMES: 7:00 AM-5:00 PM.

ADMISSION: Free. Parking is free.

LOCATION: 6717 Hawkinsville Rd. On US 129/GA 247, 4 miles south of Macon.

DESCRIPTION: Opened in 1985, this indoor/outdoor market's several hundred dealers sell everything from "antiques to zebras" and everything in between, new and pre-owned. Plenty of yard sale stuff comes in as well. There are three snack concessions to satisfy the munchies, and clean handicapped-accessible restrooms. RV parking is available. There are another two new buildings added in September 2001, adding another 15,000 square feet of selling space. As Cindy says, "Come grow with us!"

DEALER RATES: $7 for 9' × 9' outside space with table in parking lot area, inside the fence with a 10' × 10' space and one table $11 per day, $20 for the weekend. Lock-up buildings are available by the month. Reservations are recommended. Office hours are Thursday and Friday 9:00 AM-5:00 PM; Saturday and Sunday 7:00 AM-5:00 PM.

CONTACT: Smiley's Flea Market, 6717 Hawkinsville Rd, Macon GA 31206-6805. Tel: (478) 788-3700. Fax: (478) 788-5344. Email: info@smileysworld.com. Web: www.smileysworld.com.

MCDONOUGH
Peachtree Peddler's Flea Market

DATES: Saturday and Sunday, year round. Also Fridays from Thanksgiving to Christmas.

TIMES: Saturday 9:00 AM-6:00 PM; Sunday 10:00 AM-6:00 PM. Friday 10:00 AM-5:00 PM.

ADMISSION: Free. Parking is free.

LOCATION: 155 Mill Rd. Off I-75, Exit 221.

DESCRIPTION: This market of approximately 250 dealers inside and 50 or so outside during good weather sells antiques, crafts, collectibles, leather, fine to cheap art, ethnic goods, garage sale goodies, used and new clothes, fishing and sports gear, and used and new merchandise. They bill themselves as "The largest indoor flea market, in the heart of Georgia" with 80,000 square feet of climate-controlled shopping, outside selling, three snack bars and handicapped-accessible restrooms. There is a special Free Flea Fridays where locals can bring their yard sale stuff and sell it for free on Friday, generally from May through September (weather permitting). They have recently added a 12,000-square-foot Peachtree Antique Centre antique mall—all pre-1970 antiques—that is open daily.

DEALER RATES: $65 for a 10' × 12' space per weekend inside, $15 per 10' × 20' space outside per day. Reservations are required for inside space; outside is first come, first served.

CONTACT: Peachtree Peddler's Flea Market, 155 Mill Rd, McDonough GA 30253-5918. Tel: (770) 914-2269 or 1-888-661-3532. Fax: (770) 914-0911. Email: henrycomktplace@mindspring.com. Web: www.peachtreepeddlers.com.

PENDERGRASS
Pendergrass Flea Market

DATES: Saturday and Sunday.

TIMES: 9:00 AM-5:00 PM.

ADMISSION: Free. Parking is free.

LOCATION: At I-85 Exit 157. 50 miles north of Atlanta, between Gainesville and Athens.

DESCRIPTION: Opened in 1988, this indoor/outdoor market of 300-plus dealers sells antiques, collectibles, new and used furniture, books, crafts, garage sale goodies, fresh produce, watches, and new merchandise. Their climate-controlled building is 205,000 square feet, and there are two large covered outdoor selling areas for the garage sales, produce, plants and the like. Another large covered area for pets and animals. There is a food court as well as handicapped-accessible restrooms on site.

DEALER RATES: $10-$42.50 per space depending on how much and where. Reservations are accepted beginning the Monday preceding the weekend the vendor plans to sell. Office is open every day except Wednesday, 9:00 AM-5:00 PM.

CONTACT: Pendergrass Flea Market, 5641 Hwy 129 N, N Pendergrass GA 30567. Tel: (706) 945-1900 or (770) 945-1900. Fax: (706) 693-4506. Email: info@pendflea.com. Web: www.pendflea.com.

SAVANNAH
Keller's Flea Market

DATES: Saturday and Sunday, year round.
TIMES: 8:00 AM-6:00 PM.
ADMISSION: Free. Parking is free.
LOCATION: 5901 Ogeechee Rd. From I-95 take Exit 94 for 1 mile east towards Savannah. Take Hwy 17 exit off 204.
DESCRIPTION: This outdoor market hosts 400-500 dealers selling antiques, collectibles, garage sale goodies, produce, plants and new merchandise either under cover or in enclosed buildings. Janie Arkwright's Kitchen feeds the famished.
DEALER RATES: $15 or $20 depending on where, per day. Setup starts Friday between 8:00 AM-6:00 PM. The office is open the same hours Friday through Sunday. Reservations are not accepted; first come, first served.
CONTACT: Keller's Flea Market, 5901 Ogeechee Rd, Savannah GA 31419-8905. Tel: (912) 927-4848. Fax: (912) 925-2638.

OTHER FLEA MARKETS

We know or have heard about these markets, but have not personally contacted each one, as we have the markets with descriptions. If you plan to visit one of the markets listed below, *please call first* to make sure they are still open. Flea markets do come and go. While they were open when we went to press, they may not be later. We can't be responsible. *Call first!*

Albany: Albany Flea Market, 1540 N Washington St. Tel: (229) 438-9933.
Alpharetta: Euclid Fleamarket, 5330 Derby Chase. Tel: (515) 237-8293.
Athens: J & J Flea Market, 11661 Commerce Rd. Tel: (706) 613-2410.
Atlanta: Buford Highway Flea Market, 5000 Buford Hwy. Tel: (770) 452-7140.
Atlanta: Ultimate Flea Market, 3685 Chamblee Dunwoody Rd. Tel: (770) 454-0484.
Atlanta: Flea Market USA, 1919 Metropolitan Pkwy SW. Tel: (404) 763-3078.

Atlanta: Kirkwood Flea Market, 1986 Hosea L Williams Dr. Tel: (404) 377-2425.

Augusta: Kings Flea Market, 3035 Milledgeville Rd,, GA 30904. Tel: (706) 738-9555.

Bainbridge: Joe's Flea Market, 1329 W 3rd St. Tel: (229) 243-9585.

Baxley: S & R Trading Post, 9942 Golden Isles W. Tel: (912) 367-3532.

Blakely: Blakely Flea Market, 556 N Main St. Tel: (229) 723-6056.

Braselton: Braselton Flea Market & Auction, 115 Harrison St. Tel: (706) 658-2664.

Bremen: Highway 78 West Flea Market, 5063 US Hwy 78. Tel: (770) 537-0170.

Brunswick: Brunswick Flea & Farmers Market Inc, 208 Ponderosa. Tel: (912) 267-6787.

Cairo: C & C Flee Market, 221 1st Ave NE. Tel: (229) 377-8906.

Canton: Flea Extravaganza, 1063 Marietta Rd. Tel: (770) 345-4000.

Canton: Pine Ridge Trading Post, Cumming Hwy. Tel: (770) 479-5402.

Cedartown: Cedar Creek Flea Market, 591 West Ave. Tel: (770) 748-6916.

Clarkston: Clarkston Flea Market, 4222 E Ponce De Leon Ave. Tel: (404) 292-0059.

Columbus: Flea Market City, PO Box 12212. Tel: (706) 685-1943.

Commerce: Banks Crossing Flea Market, Ridgeway Rd. Tel: (706) 335-6541.

Cumming: A New Concept In Flea Markets, Hwy 9 GA 400. Tel: (770) 889-3400.

Cumming: Georgia 400 Flea Market. Tel: (770) 889-3400.

Dalton: Big D Flea Market, 3451 Cleveland Rd. Tel: (706) 259-3269.

Decatur: Glenwood Flea Market, 3900 Glenwood Rd. Tel: (404) 284-9139.

Decatur: Flea Mart-Candler, 1954 Candler Rd. Tel: (404) 289-0804.

Eastman: Eastman Flea & Antiques Mart, 1107 Herman Ave. Tel: (478) 374-7868.

Flowery Branch: Gainesville Flea Market, 5540 Atlanta Hwy. Tel: (770) 967-9080.

Fort Oglethorpe: Bitter Creek, 791 Battlefield Pkwy. Tel: (706) 858-1616.

Grantville: M & M Flea Market, 6450 Hwy 29. Tel: (770) 583-3800.

Hampton: Sweetie's Flea Market, Hwy 19-41. Tel: (770) 946-4721.

Jesup: Back Yonder Flea Market, 3343 Odum Hwy. Tel: (912) 588-0143.

Lagrange: Bailey's Flea Market, 1308 Hogansville Rd. Tel: (706) 883-7902.

Lagrange: Moss Flea Market, 3069 Westpoint Rd. Tel: (706) 883-6762.

Lake Park: Bargainville Flea Market, I-75 Exit 2 & Mill S, Tel: (229) 559-0141.

Lexington: Willis Flea Market, Hutchinson Rd. Tel: (706) 743-8965.

Lithia Springs: Bill's Flea Market, 4085 Bankhead Hwy. Tel: (770) 949-1188.

Loganville: Flatcreek Flea Market, 3084 Hwy 78. Tel: (770) 466-4223.

Macon: Billingsley's Trading Center, 3097 Joycliff Rd. Tel: (478) 745-2009.

Macon: Carter's Flea Market, 6230 Hawkinsville Rd. Tel: (478) 785-0866.

Matthews: Matthews Flea Market, 7600 Campground Rd. Tel: (706) 547-2229.

McDonough: A New Concept In Flea Markets, 155 Mill Rd. Tel: (770) 914-2269.

Milledgeville: Midway Flea Market, 395 Allen Memorial Dr SW. Tel: (478) 452-5099.

Milledgeville: Sunshine Flea Market, 321 Harrisburg Rd SW. Tel: (478) 454-4149.

Millen: Highway 25 Flea Market, 425 US Hwy 25 S. Tel: (478) 982-3532.

Millen: Tisha's Flea Market, 512 US Hwy 25 N. Tel: (478) 982-7733.

Oxford: Brenda's Flea Market, 5503 Hwy 138 SW. Tel: (770) 787-8173.

Pine Mountain: Mountain Top Flea Market, 6590 Hamilton Rd. Tel: (706) 663-4848.

Rabun Gap: Rabun Flea Market, Hwy 441 N. Tel: (706) 746-2837.

Reynolds: Warehouse Flea Market, 131 Sumter St. Tel: (478) 472-8683.

Roswell: Roswell Antique Mall & Flea Market, 700 Holcomb Bridge Rd. Tel: (770) 993-7200 or (770) 642-6964.

Rutledge: Rutledge Trading Post Flea Market, 7170 Atlanta Hwy. Tel: (706) 557-1800.

Sasser: Porky's Flea Market, 8125 Albany Hwy. Tel: ((229) 698-4578.

Savannah: John's Barn & Flea Market, 103 Sunshine Ave. Tel: (912) 238-3532.

Screven: J & A Flea Market, 207 J L Tyre St. Tel: (912) 579-2408.

Smyrna: New Windy Hill Flea Market Inc, 1000 Windy Hill Rd SE. Tel: (770) 319-0444.

Talking Rock: Stagecoach Flea Market, Hwy 136. Tel: (706) 636-3483.

Thomaston: Cecil's Flea Market, 3131 Barnesville Hwy. Tel: (706) 647-2258.

Thomaston: Crosswinds, 407 N Center St. Tel: (706) 647-3162

Thomaston: Fanny's Flea Market, 197 Triune Mill Rd. Tel: (706) 646-2915.

Warner Robins: Crossroads, 101 Elberta Rd. Tel: (478) 918-0440.

Washington: Flea Market, 324 Hospital Dr. Tel: (706) 678-7195.

Waycross: Chrystal's Fleamarket, 1631 Genoa St. Tel: (912) 283-9808.

HAWAII

AIEA
Kam Super Swap Meet
DATES: Wednesday, Saturday, Sunday and most holidays. Rain or shine.
TIMES: 5:00 AM-3:00 PM.
ADMISSION: $.50, children under 12 free. Parking is free.
LOCATION: 98-850 Moanalua Rd, across from the Pearlridge Shopping Center.
DESCRIPTION: This outdoor meet started in 1966. There are hundreds of dealers in Polynesian and Hawaiian crafts and collectibles, new items, slightly used items, fresh produce, milk caps, ethnic delicacies, fresh island fish, and much more. You will also find a varied assortment of clothes and Polynesian-made arts and crafts. Food is available on the premises and handicapped-accessible restrooms.
DEALER RATES:
Unreserved Sellers: $10 per stall Saturday and Sunday, $9 Wednesday and weekday holidays.
Reserved Sellers: Monthly reservations are $19 per stall per day of the week, for an entire month (i.e., a month of Sundays, a month of Wednesdays). There is also a daily charge for reserved sellers: $8 per Saturday and Sunday, $7 per Wednesday and weekday holiday.
Marketplace Sellers: $75 per stall per day per month (i.e., a month of Sundays, etc.) for Saturdays and Sundays; $60 per stall per day per month for Wednesdays.
CONTACT: Kam Super Swap Meet, Kam Drive-In Theatre, 99-500 Salt Lake Blvd, Aiea HI 96701. Tel: (808) 483-5933 recorded message and instructions or (808) 483-5535 between 7:30 AM-1:30 PM to speak to someone. Fax: (808) 847-9270.

HONOLULU
Aloha Flea Market
DATES: Wednesday, Saturday, Sunday and some holidays.
TIMES: 6:00 AM-3:00 PM.
ADMISSION: $.50 per person. Children 12 and under are free. Parking is free.
LOCATION: Aloha Stadium. Right across the street from the Arizona Memorial in Pearl Harbor. Fifteen minutes from Waikiki.
DESCRIPTION: This market opened in 1979 and averages 1,200 vendors selling shirts, antiques, collectibles, diving gear, tools, sporting goods,

148

shoes, and new and used merchandise. During the holiday season, the dealer ranks swell to monumental proportions. Rows of shade trees line the market, so it stays cool. Of course, it offers the ideal weather. No flammables are allowed. Food and restrooms are on the premises. This is the largest market in the state of Hawaii and "on a per capita basis, the largest in the US." Recently, both these markets came under the same management.

DEALER RATES: $10-$50 per space. One of the four stall sizes is 18' × 20'. Reservations are not required.

CONTACT: Aloha Flea Market, 99-500 Salt Lake Blvd, Aiea HI 96701. Tel: (808) 486-6704. Web: www.AlohaFleaMarket.com.

IDAHO

BOISE
Spectra's Flea Market

DATES: Saturday and Sunday, usually the second or third week of September through March. Do call, as the dates depend on the availability of the Fairgrounds buildings. 2002: January 19-20, February 23-24, April 13-14 for starters.

TIMES: Saturday 9:00 AM-6:00 PM. Sunday 10:00 AM-4:00 PM.

ADMISSION: $1. Parking is free.

LOCATION: West Idaho Fairgrounds. From Chinden Blvd to the corner of Glenwood and Chinden. Look for the market.

DESCRIPTION: This exceptionally clean indoor market has been around for "15-20" years with 130-180 dealers selling mostly antiques, collectibles, memorabilia, candy, jerky, furniture, Tupperware® and some new merchandise. There are snack bars and handicapped-accessible restrooms on site as well as special access. Their markets coincide with other big shows held at the same time.

DEALER RATES: $50 per 10' × 10' "in-line" space, $60 for a corner space. Reservations are required, as well as a 50% deposit. Table and electric are available at $10 each. Setup starts Friday 11:00 AM-8:00 PM.

CONTACT: Sam Jones, Spectra Productions, PO Box 333, 834 E State St, Eagle ID 83616-4439. Tel: (208) 939-6426 or 1-800-635-2274. Fax: (208) 939-6437.

CASCADE
Cascade Flea Market

DATES: Daily if the dealers want to, mid-May through the first weekend in October. But mainly Friday through Sunday.

TIMES: 9:00 AM-6:00 PM.

ADMISSION: Free. Parking is free.

LOCATION: In front of the Cascade Airport, Hwy 55. Out of Boise north on Hwy 55 to Cascade. Watch for all the state flags flying!

DESCRIPTION: Opened in 1992, this small growing market of 40 vendors is held outdoors next to an airport. They have a nice, clean, family oriented market with vendors selling antiques, collectibles, Indian crafts and jewelry, old license plates and bumper stickers, clothes, music tapes and CDs, and whatever. Most of their vendors return every year, bringing pals along. When the necessaries are needed, there are handicapped-accessible restrooms on site as well as a snack bar. Located in a tourist's paradise of hunting, fishing (serious trout fishing here, folks), hiking—the usual extraordinary mountain pleasures—this market has plenty of new faces visiting all the time.

DEALER RATES: $25 per 20' × 40' space outside for Friday through Sunday, plus the cost of electric if needed. $8-plus (depends on electric costs) per day with electric if the dealer wants to stay all week. Reservations are suggested if you wish to use electric. Thursday is a free day, used for setup. There are RV facilities nearby for dealers who wish to stay all week, but only if selling during the entire stay.

CONTACT: Ron and Glenna Young, Cascade Flea Market, PO Box 399, Cascade ID 83611-0399. Tel: (208) 382-4894 (Young's home) or 382-3600 during the season.

Mushies!!
Note: You may find that a dealer isn't at his or her post—as the Morell mushrooms hide around here. Many have been known to bug-out in search of the delicacies. So, if you see dealers sneaking off, you have an idea where they are going. Follow them!

KETCHUM-SUN VALLEY— WARM SPRINGS VILLAGE
Antique Peddler's Fair Antique Show

DATES: July 4 and Labor Day weekends, each year. Rain or shine.
TIMES: 9:00 AM-7:00 PM.
ADMISSION: Free. Free parking is available.
LOCATION: In Warm Springs Village, Ketchum-Sun Valley. On world-famous Picaboo St at the base of the ski lift.
DESCRIPTION: This show first opened in 1970 in the heart of Wood River Valley, Ketchum and Sun Valley. It is Idaho's largest antique market, with over 125 dealers coming from Maine to California bringing wonderful antiques, Oriental carpets, rare books and fine art. There is always a large selection of furniture, Indian and Oriental collectibles, china, high-end jewelry, loads of silver, and vintage clothes, to name a few. Their Labor Day Weekend show is "Wagon Days Celebration" with parades of wagons, rodeo, "shoot-'em outs" and plenty to keep everyone busy (including buying awesome goodies).

Because of its extraordinary natural beauty, this area has become a summer playground offering guided pack and river trips, hiking, swimming, fantastic fishing and ice shows featuring the champions. These shows attract many famous people, including Olympic athletes and some Hollywood stars who have homes in the area. Food is served on the premises.

DEALER RATES: $195 per 10' × 12' space, for all three days. Reservations are required. Bring your own canopy and booth setup.

CONTACT: Jan Perkins or Jeffrey, 2902 Breneman St, Boise ID 83703. Tel: (208) 345-0755 or 368-9759.

Interesting Note

Jan wants you to know that "Sun Valley is the first destination ski resort in the country, started by the Union Pacific Railroad and Averill Harriman—and had the first chair lifts in the world." (Betcha Mad River Glen has the oldest still-running original chair lift in the world. Heaven help the person who tries to change it!)

SAGLE
Sagle Flea Market

DATES: Saturday, Sunday and holidays, May through September.

TIMES: Whenever, but at least 8:00 AM to dark.

ADMISSION: Free. Parking is free.

LOCATION: 130 Algoma Spur Rd. Just 40 miles north of Coeur d'Alene in the panhandle of Idaho.

DESCRIPTION: Opened in 1979, this market has 100 dealer spaces full of dealers (some hog more than one space) selling "anything used," including garage sale goodies, livestock (not too badly worn), crafts, and produce. When they say "livestock" they aren't kidding—llamas were the big thing in 1999. There is a snack bar and handicapped-accessible restrooms on site. Occasionally, antique donkey engines show up, as well as a "Wilfred Brimley" look-alike dealer selling tools who threatens to charge for the autographs, he gets so much attention. Allen assures me that their "ice cream scoops will bug your eyes out."

DEALER RATES: Up to $15 for open 10' × 12' space per day, $12 per 12' × 12' space covered per day. Reservations are preferred.

CONTACT: Allen or Sonny, Sagle Flea Market, 130 Algoma Rd, Sagle ID 83860-9387. Tel: (208) 263-2244. Email: asbond@sisna.com.

Hot Doggity

Several years ago, the owners purchased a new batch and type of hot dog from the local meat-packing plant for their snack bar. It was so popular that locals started calling the plant looking for the "Sagle" hot dog. The packing plant hadn't a clue—at first.

ILLINOIS

ALSIP
Tri-State Swap O Rama

DATES: Wednesday, Saturday and Sunday. Rain or shine.
TIMES: Wednesday 7:00 AM-2:00 PM, Saturday and Sunday 7:00 AM-4:00 PM.
ADMISSION: $1 per person. Free parking available for 5,000 cars.
LOCATION: 4350 W 129th St. Take I-294 to Cicero Ave (Rt 50) south to 131st, east to Door or Pulaski Rd to 129th west.
DESCRIPTION: The Tri-State Swap O Rama is held both indoors and outdoors. Started in 1979, there are now 700 to 900 dealers selling antiques, fresh produce, meats, collectibles, and new merchandise. In 1997, they added another 1,000 parking spaces and a new wing accommodating 200 more dealers. Food is served on the premises.
DEALER RATES: $20 for space that measures 8' × 12' indoors or $20 per 12' × 24' outdoor booth. Advance reservations are suggested.
CONTACT: Jim Pierski, Swap O Rama, 4600 W Lake St, Melrose Park IL 60160-2747. Tel: (708) 344-7300.

BLOOMINGTON
3rd Sunday Market

DATES: Third Sunday May through October.
TIMES: 8:00 AM-4:00 PM.
ADMISSION: $5, children under 13 free. Parking is free. Early-bird Saturday admission: $25 for one, $40 for two people.
LOCATION: Interstate Center at the McLean County Fairgrounds. Take Exit 160B off I-39, or I-74, or I-55.
DESCRIPTION: Started in 1987, this market of 450 dealers sells only antiques and collectibles. There are 275 antiques dealers inside an Expo Center that is 2½ acres under roof, the rest either under a polebarn or in the open. There is plenty of food available and handicapped-accessible restrooms. Because Don and Carol are experts on antiques and collectibles themselves, the market is consistent in its quality of goods.
DEALER RATES: Expo Center: $95-$240 per space. Polebarn: $110-$125. Outside: $75-$120. Reservations are suggested.
CONTACT: Don and Carol Raycraft, PO Box 396, Bloomington IL 61761-0369. Tel: (309) 452-7926.

Serendipity

One cold, miserable, market day, an older man approached Don carrying a paper bag and looking quite stunned. Don, noticing his demeanor, asked him what happened. The gentleman explained that he collected tobacco tins. For 40 years he had searched for the elusive yellow one. He had heard about them, read about them, but had never seen one, much less owned one. Tobacco tins come in red, green and the elusive yellow. The yellow ones are rare and worth $1500, according to the gent. And he had plenty of red and green ones. It was that yellow prize that eluded him.

Until that day. He had come into the market on early-bird admission, just to see what was there. As he turned to look at something else—a yellow spot caught his eye.

Yes! His heart pounding, he reached for the prized yellow tin. Quite prepared to lay out $1500 for this gem, he turned the tin over—and marked on the bottom was $12.95. *Hunh?*

Trembling, he inquired of the dealer as to how much the dealer *really* wanted.

The dealer took back the tin and turned it over, "$11 bucks." Sold.

Authors Note:

Don and Carol have written 55 books on antiques and collectibles. Have any questions? And yes, some of the book dealers at the market sell their books. Their latest was published by Wallace Homestead, *Price Guide to American Country Antiques* in November 1999.

CHICAGO
Ashland Avenue Swap O Rama

DATES: Thursday, Saturday and Sunday.

TIMES: Thursday 7:00 AM-5:00 PM; Saturday and Sunday 7:00 AM-4:00 PM.

ADMISSION: $1 per person; free parking.

LOCATION: 4100 S Ashland Ave, 1 mile west of I-94, near White Sox Park.

DESCRIPTION: Started in 1990, there are now 1,000 indoor and outdoor dealers exhibiting fresh produce and new and used merchandise. Described as "very ethnic and cosmopolitan," this market now claims to be the largest in the Chicago area. Three restaurants serve the hungry.

DEALER RATES: $22 per 12' × 8' inside space; $25 per 24' × 12' outside space. Reservations are required.

CONTACT: Jim Pierski, Swap O Rama, 4600 W Lake St, Melrose Park IL 60160. Tel: (708) 344-7300.

New Maxwell Street Market

DATES: Sundays, year round.

TIMES: 7:00 AM-3:00 PM.

ADMISSION: Free. Parking is free where you can find it. Or there is $3 parking on Clinton and 14th Pl.

LOCATION: Canal and Roosevelt Sts on Canal between Taylor St and Depot Pl.

DESCRIPTION: The New Maxwell Street Market is a continuation of the former one started blocks away in the early 1900s. From 350 to 500 dealers sell just about anything you could imagine. However, if you love antiques and fine collectibles, get there especially early and follow or race ahead of the other dealers scarfing up the real treasures. There is plenty of clothing, Mexican and African art and crafts, tons of food including the famous Maxwell Street Polish sausages, tools, toys, household necessities—just about anything. There are the appropriate relief facilities dotted around the market, as well as security. Plenty of great music from renowned blues artists adds to the festivities.

DEALER RATES: $10 for a table and table-sized space, if lucky enough to get one. $30 for a selling space with place for a vehicle. You must have a license before you can sell. Reservations are mandatory. This is how they are done: The first Thursday of the month the fax line is used only for "alternate" dealers (non-permanent, or those without assigned spaces) to call in and get put on the Alternate List for the month. When a permanent dealer doesn't take the assigned spot that weekend, then the alternates are called in order. Keeps people from lining up for 12 hours just to get a space. The office is open to get your license Wednesday through Friday 10:00 AM-6:00 PM; Saturday 7:00 AM-1:00 PM; Sunday 5:00 AM-2:00 PM.

CONTACT: Job Menchaca, New Maxwell Street Market Office, 548 W Roosevelt Rd, Chicago IL 60607-4917. Tel: (312) 922-3100. Fax: (312) 922-3169 (also used solely for reservations the first Thursday of the month). Web: www.openair.org/maxwell/newmax.html.

MELROSE PARK
Melrose Park Swap O Rama

DATES: Every Friday, Saturday and Sunday.

TIMES: 7:00 AM-4:00 PM Saturday and Sunday; Fridays 8:00 AM-3:00 PM.

ADMISSION: $1 per person. Free parking is available for 1,000 cars.

LOCATION: 4600 W Lake St, at corner of Lake St (Rt 20) and Mannheim Rd (Rt 45).

DESCRIPTION: Started in 1975, 450 dealers both indoors and outdoors offer antiques, fine art, arts and crafts, fresh produce, collectibles, and new merchandise. Food is served on the premises.

DEALER RATES: $20 per 12' × 8' space inside, and $19 per 12' × 24' space outside. Reservations are suggested.

CONTACT: Jim Pierski, Swap O Rama, 4600 W Lake St, Melrose Park IL 60160. Tel: (708) 344-7300.

Wolff's Indoor Flea Market

DATES: Saturday and Sunday. Outdoors open Saturday and Sunday, April through October.

TIMES: 7:00 AM-4:00 PM.

ADMISSION: $1, $.50 seniors and children 6-12, under 6 are free. Parking is free.

LOCATION: 2031 N Mannheim Rd. Just north of North Ave, 6 miles straight south of their Rosemont market.

DESCRIPTION: Opened in 1999, and part of a large antique mall housed in a new 100,000 square foot building, this market of 350 dealers inside and more outside sells new and used merchandise, clothing, toys, tools, jewelry, collectibles, antiques, crafts, furniture, coins and plenty more. There are 100 dealers in the antique mall open every day but Tuesday and Wednesday. Their restaurant, Topper's Dogs, will satisfy your hunger, and there are handicapped-accessible restrooms when needed.

DEALER RATES: $20 Saturday, $25 Sunday per 8' x 12' space. Reservations are not required.

CONTACT: David Wolff, 970 Arkansas Dr, Elk Grove Village IL 60007. Tel: (847) 524-9590. Fax: (708) 345-9763. Email: Info@WolffsFleaMarket.com. Web: www.wolffsfleamarket.com.

PECATONICA

The "Pec-Thing" Antique and Flea Market

DATES: Third Sunday weekend in May and September.

TIMES: 8:00 AM-5:00 PM.

ADMISSION: $2 per person. Plenty of free parking is available.

LOCATION: Winnebago County Fairgrounds, 7th and 4th St entrances. One mile north of US Rt 20 on Pecatonica Rd.

DESCRIPTION: Started in 1980, this market operates both indoors and out. Over 400 dealers sell antiques, collectibles, handmade crafts, and new and used items. All food must pass Fair Board approval. Several local homes are listed in the National Registry. Breakfast and lunch are served on the premises by one restaurant and six snack bars. Just in case, there are handicapped-accessible restrooms.

DEALER RATES: Outside Spaces: $25 (20' × 25' frontage by 10' × 15' deep). Open Shed Spaces: $35 (24' × 8', roof over top, dirt floor). Inside Spaces: $50 (average 16' × 10', cement floor). Table Rental: $7 (8' tables, advanced rental only). Vendor setup on Friday before show from 9:00 AM until 9:00 PM. Gates open to vendors at 6:00 AM Saturday and Sunday. Full payment is required to reserve space. Space may be available at the gate during setup hours on a first-come, first-served basis. Cash only at the gate. Visa/MasterCard accepted.

CONTACT: Manager, PO Box K, Pecatonica IL 61063. Tel: (815) 239-1641 or 1-800-238-3587. Fax: (815) 239-1653. Web: www.winnebagocountyfair.com.

ROCKFORD
Sandy Hollow Antique and Flea Market

DATES: Every Saturday and Sunday. Rain or shine.
TIMES: 8:00 AM-5:00 PM.
ADMISSION: Free admission and parking.
LOCATION: Alpine/Sandy Hollow Rd at 3913 Sandy Hollow Rd. Take Hwy 20 to Alpine exit, go north to Sandy Hollow, then west 1½ blocks.
DESCRIPTION: Started in 1976 at Alpine Village. At the current location, this market has room for 200 dealers outside and 60 indoors, offering antiques, fresh produce, collectibles (books, records, coins, baseball cards, etc.), and new merchandise. A food grill serves the famished, and just in case, there are handicapped-accessible restrooms.

DEALER RATES: $25 per weekend for space measuring 10' × 12' inside (dealers must furnish own tables). Reservations are required in advance for indoor space only. $10.00 setup fee outdoors.
CONTACT: Carol A Fritsch, 6350 Canyon Wood Dr, Rockford IL 61109-2745. Tel: (815) 397-6683.

ROSEMONT
Wolff's Flea Market

DATES: Sundays, April through October.
TIMES: 7:00 AM-3:00 PM.
ADMISSION: $1 adults, $.50 seniors and children 6-12, under 6 free. Parking is free.
LOCATION: Allstate Arena (formerly the Rosemont Horizon), 6920 N Mannheim. Between Touhy and Higgins. Take I-90 west to Lee St Exit near intersection of I-90 and I-294. Literally on the Chicago city line, just 2 miles from Chicago.

DESCRIPTION: This outdoor summer market started in 1991 and has over 500 dealers selling antiques, collectibles, crafts, produce, coins, stamps, cards, garage sale goodies, furniture, and new merchandise. Two snack bars and handicapped-accessible restrooms add to the amenities.

DEALER RATES: $27 per 25' × 18' space. Open at 5:00 AM for setup. Reservations are not required.

CONTACT: David Wolff, 970 Arkansas Dr, Elk Grove Village IL 60007. Tel: (847) 524-9590. Fax: (708) 345-9763. Email: Info@WolffsFleaMarket.com. Web: www.wolffsfleamarket.com.

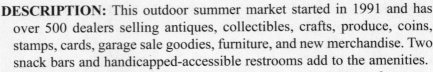

Pricey Fads

Someone sold a Peanuts royal blue elephant Beanie Baby here for over $5,000!

SANDWICH

Sandwich Antiques Market

DATES: Held six times each summer, May through October. 2002: May 19 (3rd Sunday), June 23 (4th Sunday), July 28 (4th Sunday), August 18 (3rd Sunday), September 22 (4th Sunday) , October 27 (4th Sunday). Check for the same Sundays each year.

TIMES: 8:00 AM-4:00 PM.

ADMISSION: $5 per person. Parking is free.

LOCATION: The Fairgrounds, SR 34. From I-88, Sugar Grove Exit to Rt 30 to Hinckley. Follow signs on west side of Hinckley. Just 60 miles west of Chicago.

DESCRIPTION: Started in 1988, this 160-acre shaded indoor-outdoor market attracts 550 dealers selling only top-quality antiques and collectibles. It is the only market in Illinois where dealers must give a 10-day money-back guarantee that the merchandise is as represented. There is a furniture delivery service available. A cafeteria and several snack concessions recharge the shopping batteries making handicapped-accessible restrooms welcome.

DEALER RATES: $100 per 25' × 25' outside booth: $95 per 10' × 10' inside booth. Reservations are required.

CONTACT: Robert C Lawler, Show Manager, Sandwich Antiques Market, 1510 N Hoyne, Chicago IL 60622-1804. Tel: (773) 227-4464. Day of show call: (815) 786-3337. Fax: (773) 227-6322. Email: robert@antiquemarkets.com. Web: www.antiquemarkets.com.

ST CHARLES
Kane County Flea Market

DATES: First Sunday of every month and preceding Saturday afternoon. Unless the Sunday falls on Easter or New Year's Day, then it is the following weekend. Rain or shine. 2002: January 5-6, February 2-3, March 2-3, April 6-7, May 4-5, June 1-2, July 6-7, August 3-4, 31-September 1, October 5-6, November 2-3, 30-December 1.

TIMES: Saturday 12:00 PM-5:00 PM; Sunday 7:00 AM-4:00 PM.

ADMISSION: $5, children under 12 with parents are free. Free parking is available.

LOCATION: Kane County Fairgrounds (Randall Rd); west side of St Charles between Rt 64 and Rt 38.

DESCRIPTION: Having started with a humble 35 dealers in 1967, there are currently as many as 1,400 dealers (average 1,200 in summer, 800 in winter) selling antiques, fine art, collectibles, coins, fancy "junque" and the occasional new merchandise. Dealers, shoppers and collectors have come from as far away as Korea and all over the United States to shop here. "If you can't find it at Kane County, it was probably never made." There are four indoor buildings for winter months, and nine indoor buildings and seven sheds for summer months. This market has been listed in *Good Housekeeping* as one of the top 25 markets in the United States. So popular is this market, it prompted a local minister to ask: "Would Jesus skip church to shop at the Kane County Flea Market?" Plenty of good food, served by two restaurants and several snack bars, including country-style breakfast, is served on the premises.

DEALER RATES: Shed space at $105, North Main building $125, Stripe Buildings at $105 per space; $115 per weekend for a 10' × 20' space outdoors (cash only). Advance reservations are required for space under cover only; outside space is first come, first served. Setup Saturday at 9:00 AM. There is a parking lot in back for dealers.

CONTACT: Helen Robinson, Kane County Flea Market Inc, PO Box 549, St Charles IL 60174-0549. Tel: (630) 377-2252. Fax: (630) 377-2989. Web: www2.pair.com/kaneflea.

SYCAMORE
Antique, Craft, and Flea Market

DATES: The last full weekend in October.

TIMES: 9:00 AM-5:00 PM.

ADMISSION: $2 for adults; $1 senior citizens and students K-12; under 5 free. Free parking is available.

LOCATION: At the Sycamore High School. Take Rt 23 south through downtown Sycamore to the south edge of town. Turn onto Spartan Trail at stop light on Rt 23. Sycamore is only 65 miles northwest of Chicago on Rt 64.

DESCRIPTION: This indoor craft fair and flea market, started in 1973 and currently consisting of 155 dealer booths, is operated by the Sycamore Music Boosters. It is run in conjunction with Sycamore's Annual Pumpkin Festival, which includes a variety of activities on that weekend, such as carved and decorated pumpkins on the Court House lawn (approximately 1,000), 10K race on Sunday, food booths, carnival, craft shows, and a giant parade Sunday afternoon. Proceeds from all activities associated with the weekend are used to support non-profit organizations in the community. It is estimated that approximately 100,000 people visit the community over Pumpkin Festival weekend. The Antique, Craft and Flea Market is a juried show which in the past has had handcrafted items, candies, handcarved wood products and other goods produced by artists. There are antiques and collectibles as well as the usual flea market fare. Food is available on the grounds, and there are handicapped-accessible restrooms. A shuttle bus provides transportation between the school and the downtown area for $.50 per person. A "stroller park" is available, with attendants, as strollers are not allowed in the market.

DEALER RATES: $85 for a 9' × 12' or 10' × 12' booth; reservations required.

CONTACT: Sycamore Music Boosters, PO Box 432, Sycamore IL 60178-0432. (Show chairmen change yearly.) Tel: (815) 895-2678, Jenny Thornton, show manager.

TOWANDA
Towanda Antique Flea Market

DATES: Every July 4. Rain or shine.

TIMES: 9:00 AM-5:00 PM.

ADMISSION: Free. Free parking is available.

LOCATION: Northwest of Bloomington, Illinois, on I-55. Take Exit 171.

DESCRIPTION: Started in 1968, the show has grown larger every year and currently features 250 dealers outdoors selling antiques, arts and crafts, collectibles, and new merchandise. This market has become known as a buyer's market because of the fair prices. Food is available on the premises. Since this is a July 4 activity, expect the usual festivities and fireworks.

DEALER RATES: $30 per 12' × 12' space. Reservations are required.

CONTACT: Linda Potts, PO Box 103, Towanda IL 61776. Tel: (309) 728-2384.

WHEATON
All-Night Flea Market
DATES: The weekend after the third Sunday in August.
TIMES: 5:00 PM-9:00 AM.
ADMISSION: $5. Parking is free.
LOCATION: DuPage County Fairgrounds, 2015 Manchester Rd. I-88 west to Naperville Rd, north to Rt 38, west to County Farm Rd, north to Manchester.
DESCRIPTION: This is the original outdoor overnight flea market. Hundreds of dealers come to sell whatever they can, from old to new stuff. Many concessions will refill you for more shopping, and handicapped-accessible restrooms provide relief. As they say, "Come for dinner, shop until breakfast."
DEALER RATES: $90-$130 for a 20' × 25' space. Reservations are necessary.
CONTACT: All-Night Flea Market, PO Box 32, Itasca IL 60143-0032. Tel: (630) 833-8280.

DuPage Antique & Collectible Market
DATES: Third weekend of every month, except no show in July.
TIMES: 7:00 AM-3:00 PM.
ADMISSION: $3. Parking is free.
LOCATION: DuPage County Fairgrounds, 2015 Manchester Rd. From O'Hare Airport, take 294 south to I-88 west to Naperville Rd. North to Rt 38 or Roosevelt Rd. West to County Farm Rd. North to Manchester Rd to the fairgrounds.
DESCRIPTION: Started in 1972, this indoor/outdoor market has approximately 200 dealers selling strictly antiques and collectibles inside several buildings (80% of the market) and whatever is allowed outside. There are handicapped-accessible restrooms and a food concession on site.
DEALER RATES: Outside: $25 per space. Inside: $60-$75 per space depending on size and location. Some is BYOT; the $75 includes tables and chairs. Reservations are needed for inside space.
CONTACT: DuPage Antique & Collectible Market, PO Box 32, Itasca IL 60143-0032. Tel: (630) 833-8280.

Just Stepping Off
The market butts up to the railroad line heading into Chicago. A couple of years ago during the market they noticed the conductor, after taking the coal train into Chicago, had hopped another train back to the market to go shopping!

OTHER FLEA MARKETS

We know or have heard about these markets, but have not personally contacted each one, as we have the markets with descriptions. If you plan to visit one of the markets listed below, *please call first* to make sure they are still open. Flea markets do come and go. While they were open when we went to press, they may not be later. We can't be responsible. *Call first!*

Bolingbrook: Montana Charlie's Flea Market, IH 55 & Joliet Rd. Tel (630) 739-4338.

Chicago: Massey's Flea Market, 3637 S Giles Ave. Tel (773) 536-2720.

East St Louis: Fairmont Flea Market, 5410 Collinsville Rd. Tel: (618) 271-9885.

Elgin: Elgin Flea Market, 840 N State St. Tel: (847) 622-9696.

Grafton: Jacob's Flea Market, 128 E Main St. Tel: (618) 786-3689.

Joliet: Derald's Indoor Flea Market, 219 Maple St. Tel: (815) 723-0700.

Marion: Tri-County Flea Market, 1021 N Market St. Tel: (618) 993-6721.

Rockford: Alpine Flea Market, 3291 S Alpine Rd. Tel: (815) 874-4145.

Rockford: Sandy Hollow Flea Market, 3913 Sandy Hollow Rd. Tel: (815) 397-6683.

Tinley Park: I-80 Flea Market, 19100 Oak Park Ave. Tel: (708) 532-8238.

Waukegan: Waukegan Flea Market, 1700 N Lewis Ave. Tel: (847) 662-9665.

INDIANA

BROOKVILLE
White Farmers' Market

DATES: Every Wednesday. Rain or shine.
TIMES: Daylight (really) to noon.
ADMISSION: Free. Free parking is available.
LOCATION: White's Farm on Holland Rd, 3 miles southeast of town on Hwy 52, 30 miles northwest of Cincinnati, Ohio.
DESCRIPTION: A combination flea market and livestock auction, this market was originally started by the present owner's grandfather in 1937. Currently there are between 350 and 400 dealers in summer and between 50 and 75 dealers in the winter selling antiques, arts and crafts, fresh produce and fruits, collectibles and new merchandise on a 260-acre farm. Amish baked goods are offered as well as farm fresh eggs and small animals such as ducks, rabbits and chickens. Don't miss the Chicken Man—he is amazing—as is his flock of creatures. Look for the fellow with a head full of feathers. Next door to the farm one can see and visit the oldest church in Indiana on its original foundation. The market is located in the scenic Whitewater Valley. Indoor setups are located in the farm's original granary and tobacco barns. The buildings have been refurbished in the original antique atmosphere. They have added more storage buildings for inside setups. Special events are held throughout the year.
DEALER RATES: $10 per 20' × 22' space outdoors. Reservations are not necessary for outside space, but are required for inside space. Inside spaces from $10 to $20, depending on size and location.
CONTACT: Dave or Paula White, 6119 Little Cedar Rd, Brookville IN 47012-9291. Tel: (765) 647-3574 (business) or (765) 647-5360 if desperate.

CANAAN
Canaan Fall Festival & Pony Express Mail-Run Celebration

DATES: Second weekend in September. Rain or shine.
TIMES: Friday and Saturday 9:00 AM-10:00 PM; Sunday 9:00 PM-5:00 PM.
ADMISSION: Free. Free parking is available.
LOCATION: On the Canaan Village Square.
DESCRIPTION: Publicized as an old-fashioned event, this outdoor festival draws a very large crowd to this small village. Approximately 160 dealers sell a range of items from antiques and collectibles to craft items, fresh produce, and some new merchandise. Highlights include the longest-running annual Pony Express in the United States, plus many games,

contests (including frog jumping and largest/smallest contest), and stage entertainment. On Saturday, the old-fashioned parade starts at 10:30 AM and features floats, bands, horses, a Postal Representative swearing in the Pony Express rider, and other events. The Fire Department's food concession does something special with its fish dish; it's a perennial favorite. The Kremer House Museum with three generations of furnishings was donated to the town in 1980 and is open to the public during this festival. For those of you who need more exercise, they have added the 6K Yellow Britches Valley/Indian Trails Run/Walk. Enjoy! Oh, and find Gale and say "Hi" for me!

DEALER RATES: $40 per 20' × 20' space per event plus $5 for electric.

CONTACT: Gale H Ferris, President, Canaan Restoration Council Inc, 9713 N State Rd 62, Canaan IN 47224. Tel: (812) 839-4770.

Wandering Pets

Years ago, a buffalo got loose from Rising Sun, a town in Ohio County, and wandered across two more counties, and through the Canaan Fall Festival. He didn't seem to be a problem, just visiting, but he really had people wondering. By the time the wanderer got to the Proving Grounds, he was deemed a hazard to the population and killed. But the people of Canaan haven't forgotten their buffalo visitor.

CEDAR LAKE
Barn and Field Flea Market

DATES: Saturday and Sunday. Indoors year round, and outdoors weather permitting.

TIMES: 8:00 AM-4:00 PM.

ADMISSION: Free. Parking is free.

LOCATION: 15049 Parrish Ave. W 151st Ave at corner of Parrish Ave, 1 mile east of Rt 41.

DESCRIPTION: Opened well over 20 years ago and housed in a 100-plus-year-old barn with permanent dealers, this country market specializes in antiques and collectibles, used merchandise, used furniture, glassware, lamps, and garage sale goodies. It's a great place for dealers to stock up for their travels. The number of dealers ranges from 20-150 or so, depending on the weather.

DEALER RATES: $5 per day for whatever space is needed outside. Just roll on in! Inside space is permanently rented, but they do have the occasional vacancy. If you wish to rent inside, call Pat for more information. There is overnight camping for dealers.

CONTACT: Pat, Barn and Field Flea Market, PO Box 411, Cedar Lake IN 46303-0411. Tel: (219) 696-7368.

Uncle John's Flea Market

DATES: Saturday and Sunday, year round. Outdoors, weather permitting.

TIMES: 8:00 AM-4:00 PM in the buildings; anytime after 5:00 AM for outdoor sales.

ADMISSION: Free. Parking is free.

LOCATION: 15205 Wicker Ave, Rt 41, 9 mi south of Rt 30. Approximately 20-25 miles south of I-80-94 on Hwy 41 (Indianapolis Blvd) and approximately 10 miles west of I-65, between Rt 30 and SR 2.

DESCRIPTION: This market averages over 150 outdoor dealers in the summer, and over 200 dealers, year round, in 11 buildings selling antiques, collectibles, new and used furniture, jewelry, books, produce, clothing, crafts, and new merchandise. When you get peckish, try the family owned and operated diner, and when you need them there are handicapped-accessible restrooms.

DEALER RATES: $10-$15 per day for outdoor space. $60 and up per month per 12' × 12' for indoor space. Reservations are not required.

CONTACT: Uncle John's Flea Market, 15205 Wicker Ave, Cedar Lake IN 46303-9367. Tel: (219) 696-7911. Email: uncjohns@pla-net.net.

FRANKLIN
Gray Goose Collector's Fair

DATES: Second Saturday and Sunday, September through April, except the first weekends in November and December due to other fairground schedules.

TIMES: 9:00 AM-4:00 PM.

ADMISSION: Free admission and free parking.

LOCATION: At the Johnson County Fairgrounds on Fairgrounds St. Take I-65, Exit 90 (Rt 44), go west to Fairgrounds St, turn right.

DESCRIPTION: This indoor show began operation in 1994. It is southern Indiana's largest. Although a small market with 48-52 dealers, they carry a variety of strictly antiques and collectibles, including lots of primitives, and collectible jewelry. This is a very friendly market with good dealers who are willing to go out of their way to help their customers. In fact, many of the dealers have been thanked for setting up! Concessions and a full kitchen provide hot-plate lunches and homemade pies on the premises, and there are handicapped-accessible restrooms. Watch for a summer one-day outside show, as the one they held in 2001 was quite successful. Dates are not confirmed yet, so call first.

DEALER RATES: $65 for a 12' × 10' area and 2 tables inside; outside is $20. Reservations are required for indoor space only.

CONTACT: Doris and Carl Hubbell, 753 Hillcrest Dr, Greenwood IN 46142-1830. Tel: (317) 881-5719.

FRIENDSHIP
Friendship Flea Market

DATES: Two nine-day shows. 2002: June 8-16; September 14-22. Call for 2003 dates. Generally, starting the second Saturday through the following Sunday a week later. Rain or shine.

TIMES: All day and night, really. At least by 9:00 AM.

ADMISSION: Free admission. Parking is available at $3 per vehicle.

LOCATION: On Hwy 62, 6 miles west of Dillsboro.

DESCRIPTION: Started in 1968, this indoor/outdoor market consists of approximately 500 dealers selling antiques, arts and crafts, fresh produce, collectibles such as guns, knives, and beads, and new merchandise. It is located on the grounds adjoining the National Muzzle Loading Rifle Association. Up to 100,000 people attend this event. Food is served on the premises. In 1984, this market was listed by *Good Housekeeping* magazine as one of the 25 best flea markets in the United States. It is the largest of the four markets within a half mile of each other. Every night of the market, a campfire is crackling with country music entertainment. They really mean it is open day and night!

DEALER RATES: $150 for 9 days per 10' × 10' space indoors or a 20' × 20' space outdoors. Advance reservations are required.

CONTACT: Tom Kerr or Jan Schnell, 946 Kyles Lane, Covington KY 41017. Tel: (859) 341-9188. Fax: (859) 363-8184. Days of the show call the flea market at (812) 667-5645.

Ft Wayne Indiana Flea Market

DATES: 2002 dates: January 11-13, February 22-24, April 19-21, and November 22-24. Call for 2003 dates.

TIMES: Friday 3:00 PM-9:00 PM; Saturday 10:00 AM-7:00 PM; Sunday 11:00 AM-5:00 PM.

ADMISSION: $1. Parking is $2.

LOCATION: Allen County War Memorial Coliseum. Corner of Coliseum and Parnell Aves.

DESCRIPTION: This market started in 1991 with 400 dealers selling antiques, collectibles, and the usual flea market everything. Already it is quite successful. Food is available on the premises.

DEALER RATES: $85 per 14' × 8' space; $128 per 21' × 8' space; $170 per 28' × 8' space. Reservations are required.

CONTACT: Stewart Promotions, 2950 Breckinridge Ln Ste 4A, Louisville KY 40220. Tel: (502) 456-2244 except Tuesday and Friday. Email: sp2950@home.com. Web: www.stewartpromotions.com.

GARY
Market City

DATES: Friday, Saturday and Sunday.

TIMES: 9:00 AM-5:00 PM.

ADMISSION: Free. Parking is free.

LOCATION: 4121 Cleveland St at 41st St.

DESCRIPTION: This market opened in 1990 and has been full ever since, with all 250 inside booths filled. There is plenty of room outside for dealers, with at least 20 hanging around through snow and good weather. In good weather, they average 60-100 dealers outside. Inside dealers sell about 80% new merchandise to 20% old, including electronics, clothing, shoes, jewelry, leather, and other new items. Outside is a grab-bag of garage sale goodies, clean-outs, and whatever happens by. Their inside kitchen serves meals and snacks, and just in case, there are handicapped-accessible restrooms.

DEALER RATES: Outside: $7 per day in the open area, $12 per day under roof. $50 and up per day inside—if they have room. Reservations are suggested only if you want to be under cover outside. If you are interested in the inside space, call Roger.

CONTACT: Roger VanSelow, Market City, 4121 Cleveland St, Gary IN 46408-2427. Tel: (219) 887-3522.

INDIANAPOLIS
Indiana Flea Market

DATES: 2002: January 18-20, February 15-17, March 8-10, April 12-14, June 14-16, July 19-21 September 6-8, November 1-3, November 29-December 1, December 13-15. Usually the second weekend each month, depending on availability of the fairgrounds. Check first!

TIMES: Friday noon to 7:00 PM; Saturday 10:00 AM-7:00 PM; Sunday 11:00 AM-5:00 PM. New Year's: Friday and Saturday 10:00 AM-7:00 PM; Sunday 11:00 AM-5:00 PM.

ADMISSION: Free. Parking $2.

LOCATION: Indianapolis State Fairgrounds.

DESCRIPTION: This indoor market opened in 1976 and hosts between 400 to 1,000 dealers depending on the seasons. There are special Antique and Country Craft shows scattered throughout their schedule in addition to the flea markets. Some of these scheduled events fill three buildings! The dealers sell mostly antiques, collectibles and flea market treasures. Food is available on the premises.

DEALER RATES: $85 per 14' × 8' space; $128 ($128 New Year's) per 21' × 8' space; $170 per 28' × 8'. Reservations are required.

CONTACT: Stewart Promotions, 2950 Breckinridge Ln Ste 4A, Louisville KY 40220. Tel: (502) 456-2244 (except Tuesday and Friday). Email: sp2950@home.com. Web: www.stewartpromotions.com.

Liberty Bell Flea Market

DATES: Friday through Sunday, year round.

TIMES: Friday 12:00 PM-8:00 PM; Saturday 10:00 AM-7:00 PM; Sunday 10:00 AM-5:00 PM.

ADMISSION: Free. Free parking is available.

LOCATION: 8949 E Washington St (US 40).

DESCRIPTION: This indoor/outdoor show has been operating for over 25 years. Over 88 dealers spread over 200 spaces (they like this market!) sell everything and anything from antiques, collectibles, carpet, furniture, a delightful fellow making leather goods, and new merchandise to produce (in season), meats, cheese, and handmade items. There is a snack bar on the grounds.

DEALER RATES: $45 per 12' × 14' booth per weekend. No advance reservations required, but call to make sure there is space. Inside in the winter gets pretty full, so call.

CONTACT: Noble Hall, Liberty Bell Flea Market, 8949 E Washington St, Indianapolis IN 46219-6829. Tel: (317) 898-3180.

LAPORTE
Wildwood Park Flea Market

DATES: Saturday and Sunday, April 1 through October.

TIMES: 9:00 AM to whenever.

ADMISSION: Free. Parking is free.

LOCATION: At the junction of I-94—Hwy 20 and Hwy 35, Exit 40A, off I-94.

DESCRIPTION: Opened in 1978, this outdoor summer market, on lovely park-like grounds covered with oak and maple trees, hosts 120 dealers selling basically antiques, collectibles, produce and coins. There is an indoor antique mall on the grounds. A snack bar and handicapped-accessible restrooms are on site.

DEALER RATES: $10 per 20' × 25' space. Reservations are not required.

CONTACT: Wildwood Flea Market, 4938 W US Hwy 20, LaPorte IN 46350-8268. Tel: (219) 879-5660. Fax: (219) 879-0297.

LAWRENCEBURG
Tri-State Antique Market

DATES: Always the first Sunday of the month, from May through October.

TIMES: 7:00 AM-3:00 PM DST.

ADMISSION: $2.50 per adult. Free parking is available.

LOCATION: On Rt 50, 1 mile west from Exit 16, off I-275.

DESCRIPTION: Started in 1986, this indoor/outdoor market now draws 250-300 dealers from three surrounding states. The promoter of this show has said that this is where many shop owners come to stock their shelves and floor space, buying both furniture and small items. "Lots of good treasures." Only antiques and old collectibles are sold. Bruce describes this as "the largest antiques and vintage collectibles-only market in the state of Indiana." Food is served on the premises and handicapped-accessible restrooms are located at both the front and rear of the property.

DEALER RATES: $45 per 20' × 30' outside space paid in advance, 12' × 15' undercover space in open-sided barn or shelter, or 10' × 10' space indoors. All spaces are $50 paid day-of-show, subject to availability. Advance reservations are suggested. Early birds are admitted for advance shopping at 5:00 AM.

CONTACT: Bruce Metzger, PO Box 35, Shandon OH 45063-0035. Tel: (513) 738-7256. Email: bmetzger@fuse.net. Web: www.queencityshows.com.

Classic Market Tales

In 1989, there was a "dust devil" during the show. Hypnotized, the vendors and buyers watched this little mini-tornado form at the end of the fairgrounds. Slowly, it moved down the midway street of the market flipping tables, toppling cupboards, lifting cast iron ware and dropping it through glass showcases, scattering the "smalls" and lightweight merchandise. After traveling about 100 feet, the twister stood still, lifted off the ground and retreated back to the rear of the grounds, leaving choking dust in the air and wreckage marking its route.

An editor of *Antique Week* was there holding down a table full of smalls to keep them from being sucked up in the twister. Unfortunately for him, protecting the smalls prevented him from shooting pictures of the incredible event!

Says Bruce Metzger, the promoter of this show: "No one was injured in this occurrence, although some merchandise sustained damage and some was just plain lost. It's a hell of a thing to be remembered for, but people still like to talk about the dust devil at Lawrenceburg."

METAMORA
Canal Days Flea Market

DATES: The first full weekend in October, Friday through Sunday. Rain or shine.

TIMES: All day Saturday and Sunday.

ADMISSION: Free. Parking is available at $3 to $5 per vehicle.

LOCATION: From Indianapolis, take US 52 east. From Cincinnati, go west on I-74 to Exit 169, then west on US 52, and then go 8 miles west of Brookville.

DESCRIPTION: An estimated 175,000 people attend this October weekend initiated as a continuation of the time, in the 1800s, when local farmers would set up along Main Street to unload their farm surplus. In 1969 a couple of guys got together and thought they'd restart an old tradition by setting up a few card tables next to the canal. The idea took over and grew. Obviously, its time had come. Currently over 700 dealers set up to sell antiques, fine art, arts and crafts, collectibles, and a little bit of new merchandise. Metamora is a lovely old town with a canal and canal boat pulled by horses, and there is an old grist mill which still operates. There are over 130 shops open May until December, and a passenger train runs on the weekends. There is a handicapped-accessible port-a-potty on site.

DEALER RATES: From $150 per 10' × 10' space for the three-day weekend and up depending on size space. Reservations are required. Setup on Thursday, but you can't conduct business until Friday.

CONTACT: Al and Pat Rogers, PO Box 76, Metamora IN 47030-0076. Tel: (765) 647-2194.

Historical Note
A local gift shop was once the Farmers Merchants Bank, robbed by John Dillinger, who left a bullet hole on an inside wall. Go look for it.

MUNCIE
Greenwalt's Flea Market

DATES: First weekend of every month September through May, except when September's first weekend falls on Labor Day, when it is the second weekend. 2002 dates: January 5-6, February 2-3, March 2-3, April 6-7, May 4-5, September 7-8, October 5-6, November 2-3, December 7-8.

TIMES: 9:00 AM-4:00 PM on Saturday; 9:00 AM-3:00 PM on Sunday.

ADMISSION: Free admission and free parking.

LOCATION: At Delaware Fairgrounds-Memorial Building. Take I-69 to Muncie/Frankton Exit 332. Go approximately 7 miles (becomes McGalliard Ave) to Wheeling Ave, then turn south and go 7 blocks to the Fairgrounds.

DESCRIPTION: This indoor market, which opened in 1976, houses approximately 65-70 dealers selling antiques, collectibles, handmade/craft items, toys, jewelry, baseball cards and new merchandise. Food is available on the premises.

DEALER RATES: $40 a weekend for a 10' × 10' booth. Advance reservations are required.

CONTACT: Mary Greenwalt, 604 N Kettner Dr, Muncie IN 47304-9776. Tel: (765) 289-0194.

NASHVILLE
Westward Ho! Flea Market

DATES: Saturday and Sunday, April through October. Three-day weekends on Memorial Day and Labor Day.

TIMES: 9:00 AM-5:00 PM.

ADMISSION: Free. Parking is free.

LOCATION: 4469 SR 46 E. Located 4½ miles east of Nashville on SR 46.

DESCRIPTION: This market features eight acres of shopping both in 100 shops or under roof on concrete floors. Priding themselves on being completely handicapped accessible, their dealers sell antiques, collectibles, leather, lace, hardware goods, ball cards, belts, buckles, paper goods, custom t-shirts, sweats, wicker baskets, perfumes, concrete lawn ornaments, jewelry, crocheted doilies, western wear, ribbons, craft supplies, spices and flavorings and more. There is plenty of food served by Larry under shady trellises or in the open.

DEALER RATES: $13.50 per day per 14' × 14' space, electric included. Reservations would be nice.

CONTACT: Phyllis J Thompson, Westward Ho! Flea Market, PO Box 1167, Nashville IN 47448-1167. Tel: (812) 988-0750. Email: westwardhoflea@hotmail.com. Web: www.westwardhofleamarket.com.

SCOTTSBURG
Saw Mill Hill Flea Market

DATES: Wednesday through Sunday, year round.

TIMES: 8:00 AM-5:00 PM.

ADMISSION: Free. Parking is free.

LOCATION: Hwy 56 W. From I-65 take Exit 29 to Hwy 56 W about ¼ mile off the interstate.

DESCRIPTION: Opened in 1990, this indoor market hosts 50 dealers. The dealers sell a fair amount of antiques and collectibles, tools, musical instruments, loads of household goods and whatever comes in. Their motto is: "If we ain't got it, it ain't worth having."

DEALER RATES: $23 per weekend inside. Reservations are suggested.

CONTACT: Michael E Davisson, Saw Mill Hill Flea Market, 1621 McClain Ave, Scottsburg IN 47170-1161. Tel: (812) 752-3551.

SHIPSHEWANA
Shipshewana Auction and Flea Market

DATES: Every Tuesday and Wednesday, May through October. Rain or shine.

TIMES: Tuesday 7:00 AM-5:00 PM, Wednesday 7:00 AM-3:00 PM.

ADMISSION: Free. $2 per car parking during June, July and August.

LOCATION: On SR 5 on the southern edge of Shipshewana, 160 miles north of Indianapolis, 50 miles east of South Bend and 100 miles south of Grand Rapids.

DESCRIPTION: This show first opened in 1922 selling six pigs, seven cows, and several head of young cattle. It moved to its present location in 1947. It is held both indoors and outdoors and accommodates approximately 1,000 dealers (fewer in winter) and has room for more. Just about anything you might want can be found at this market, from antiques and collectibles, to fine art, arts and crafts, to new merchandise, to fresh produce. There is also a Miscellaneous and Antique Auction every Wednesday at 8:00 AM, and a livestock auction at 11:00 AM. The widely known Horse and Tack Sale is held on Fridays at 9:00 AM and always draws a full house of spectators. One full-service and four fast-food restaurants, one snack bar and four drink stands take care of any possible hungers, and after that you'll find their handicapped-accessible restrooms useful.

DEALER RATES: Approximately $36 per 20' × 25' space outdoors, for two days; $45 per 8½' × 10' space indoors, for two days. Reservations are required.

CONTACT: Kevin Lambright, PO Box 185, Shipshewana IN 46565-0185. Tel: (219) 768-4129. Fax: (219) 768-7041. Email: tradingplace@shipshenet.com. Web: www.tradingplaceamerica.com.

OTHER FLEA MARKETS

We know or have heard about these markets, but have not personally contacted each one, as we have the markets with descriptions. If you plan to visit one of the markets listed below, *please call first* to make sure they are still open. Flea markets do come and go. While they were open when we went to press, they may not be later. We can't be responsible. *Call first!*

Bedford: Pat's Flea Market, SR 37. Tel: (812) 278-8764.
Evansville: Diamond Flea Market, 1250 E Diamond Ave. Tel: (812) 464-2675.
Evansville: Giant Flea Market, 2600 S Kentucky Ave. Tel: (812) 421-8274.
Evansville: Kawlagi Flea Market, 400 N Main St. Tel: (812) 424-4543.
Evansville: Southlane Flea Market, 2608 S Kentucky Ave. Tel: (812) 424-2608.
Friendship: Friendship Downtown Flea Market, 5874 Friendship Main St. Tel: (812) 667-5322.
Gas City: Mick's Flea Market, 212 E Main St. Tel: (765) 677-0281.
Hartford City: Hartford City Flea Market, 101 N High St. Tel: (765) 348-1163.
Indianapolis: East Indy Flea Market, 8101 Pendleton Pike. Tel: (317) 898-4322.
Indianapolis: Irvington Flea Merket, 6301 E Washington St. Tel: (317) 375-1885.
Indianapolis: South Indy Flea Market, 3825 S East St. Tel: (317) 782-1887.
Indianapolis: Town & Country Flea Market, 4435 N Keystone Ave 9. Tel: (317) 545-5608.
Indianapolis: West Washington Flea Market, 6445 W Washington St. Tel: (317) 244-0941.
Laurel: Pioneer Flea Market, 22211 US Hwy 52. Tel: (765) 698-1210.
Madison: Craig Flea Market, 248 Clifty Dr. Tel: (812) 273-0044.
Marion: Marion Flea Market, 3316 S Nebraska St. Tel: (765) 674-7083.
Michigan City: Wildwood Park Community Farm, 4938 W US Hwy 20. Tel: (219) 879-5660.
Montgomery: Main Street Flea Market, RR 3. Tel: (812) 486-3214.
Montgomery: Montgomery Flea Market, Cty Rd 650 E. Tel: (812) 486-3977.
Muncie: Westside Flea Market, 1313 S Batavia Ave. Tel: (765) 741-9901.
Nashville: Olde Time Flea Market, 5400 SR 46 E. Tel: (812) 988-2346.
New Albany: Pine Ridge Flea Market, 3328 Corydon Pike. Tel: (812) 941-1111.
North Vernon: Green Meadows Flea Market, N Hwy 7. Tel: (812) 346-9945.

Paoli: Mellie's Flea Market, 201 SE 1st St. Tel: (812) 723-5666.

Veedersburg: Dalle's Folle Flea Market, 2302 S US Hwy 41. Tel: (765) 798-2315.

Veedersburg: Steam Corner Flea Market, 2164 S US Hwy 41. Tel: (765) 798-5710.

Veedersburg: Steamcorner Flea Market, Hwy 41 & SR 32. Tel: (765) 294-2202.

Versailles: Friendship Flea Market, 6491 E SR 62. Tel: (812) 667-5645.

Washington: Hometown Flea Market, 401 E Main St. Tel: (812) 257-1043.

IOWA

DUBUQUE
Dubuque Flea Market

DATES: Three times yearly, call for dates. Generally Sundays the middle of February, April and October. Do call to check first. 2002: February 10, April 14, October 27.

TIMES: 8:00 AM–3:00 PM.

ADMISSION: $1 for 12 and over, 11 and under free. Parking is free.

LOCATION: Dubuque County Fairgrounds, 5 miles west of town on Hwy 20.

DESCRIPTION: This indoor/outdoor market began in 1970. Approximately 100 to 140 dealers sell a variety of antiques, collectibles, art objects, music, furniture, stamps, trains, coins, and crafts. Among the local attractions are a dog track and river boats. There is food available on the premises and restrooms when the times comes. As Jerome describes it, "It's a good place to bring the family. Over the course of 30 years of running this market, I've made many good friends of the people who come here." So, find Jerome and make a new friend!

DEALER RATES: $14 per 8' space inside including a table; wall space is $16; $20 per 20' × 20' space outside with no table. Reservations are required for inside space. Outside is first come, first served.

CONTACT: Jerome F Koppen, 260 Copper Kettle Ln, E Dubuque IL 61025-9528. Tel: (815) 747-7745.

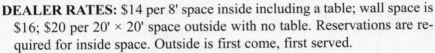

LAKE OKOBOJI AT MILFORD
Treasure Village Flea Market and Antiques Shows

DATES: Memorial Day Weekend (Saturday through Monday); July 4 weekend (Thursday through Sunday); Labor Day weekend (Saturday through Monday); and first weekend in August (Saturday and Sunday). Call for specific dates as July 4 falls on different days each year. In 2002 the dates are: May 25-27, July 4-7, August 3-4, August 31-September 2.

TIMES: 8:00 AM–6:00 PM.

ADMISSION: Free. Parking is also free.

LOCATION: Treasure Village, 2033 Hwy 86, 3 miles northwest of Milford.

DESCRIPTION: Held outdoors under the trees, this market generally limits its dealers to about 80. They show a variety of toys, coins, collectibles, primitives, antiques, sports cards, crafts, tools, and novelties, among other treasures. To amuse the children there is a children's theatre and for everyone miniature golf. Hand-dipped ice cream, sandwiches, and the usual

concession fare are available. This is a real family affair and social gathering for tourists and the local residents. Lake Okoboji is one of only three "blue-water lakes" in the world; the others are Lake Geneva in Switzerland and Lake Louise in Canada. It is also the number-one tourist attraction in Iowa.

DEALER RATES: $80 for a 20' × 20' space Memorial Day and Labor Day—the 3-day events; $90 for July 4, a 4-day event; August first weekend $35. Reservations are required. Pre-paid reservations are allowed a discount—deduct $10 for 3- and 4-day events, $5 for the 2-day event if paid one month before the show.

CONTACT: Garth and Bonnie Neisess, Manager, 2033 Hwy 86, Milford, IA 51351-7348. Tel: (712) 337-3731.

SPIRIT LAKE
Annual Antique Show and Flea Market at Vick's Corner

DATES: Memorial Day (Saturday through Monday), July 4, and Labor Day weekends. For 2002: May 25-27, July 4-7 (Thursday through Sunday), August 31-September 1-2 (Saturday through Monday).

TIMES: 8:00 AM-6:00 PM.

ADMISSION: Free. Parking is also free.

LOCATION: Junction of Hwys 9 and 86 at Vick's Corner.

DESCRIPTION: This market started the Spirit Lake market corner in 1966. Ninety dealers from 10 different states sell antiques, collectibles and primitives. Absolutely no junk is allowed. People plan their vacations around these market days as the dealers who come here are famous throughout the country for the quality of their goods. This is a 10-acre grove area all grassed and kept up like a golf course. Vick's Corner is a general store established in 1930 and a well-known landmark in the area. Food concessions and restrooms are on site.

DEALER RATES: $85 per booth for one show. Reservations are highly recommended.

CONTACT: LW Vick, Vick's Corner, RR Box 9131, Spirit Lake IA 51360. Tel/fax: (712) 336-1912 or (712) 336-1496 or 336-5602. Email: vickscorner@lakescable.com. Web: http://vickscorner.com/antique.htm.

WHAT CHEER
Collectors Paradise Flea Market

DATES: First Sunday and preceding Saturday in May, August, and October. 2002 dates: May 4-5, August 3-4, October 5-6.

TIMES: 7:00 AM to whenever.

ADMISSION: $1 per person per day, 12 and under free with adult. Free parking is available. Early bird admission $2 per day before Saturday.

LOCATION: At the Keokuk County Fairgrounds in What Cheer. Take Exit 201 off I-80 and drive south 20 miles on Hwy 21.

DESCRIPTION: According to local shoppers, Larry Nicholson's Collectors Paradise is well named. Having started this indoor/outdoor market in 1977, Mr. Nicholson has raised dealer attendance up to around 500, with some dealers showing up for setup as early as the Wednesday before the show. Dealers come from all of the Midwest. This market is one of the major antique and collectible markets in the Midwest. Shoppers, who can number as high as 7,000, are invited to get an early chance to browse through the innumerable bargains on the Saturday preceding the main sale day for the same early bird $2 fee. Antiques and collectibles of every shape and size are to be found here, including glassware, toys, tools, coins, jewelry, stamps, baseball cards, postcards, primitives, furniture, and more. Among the foods served is funnel cake, a favorite among local flea marketeers. Lunch is available.

DEALER RATES: $40 for outside space for the weekend. Reservations are required.

CONTACT: Larry D Nicholson, Collectors Paradise Inc, PO Box 413, What Cheer IA 50268-0413. Tel: (641) 634-2109. Email: plnsk@kdsi.net.

KANSAS

HUTCHINSON
Mid-America Flea Markets
DATES: First Sunday of each month, October through June. 2002 only: The February show will held January 27 due to remodeling of the building.
TIMES: 9:00 AM-4:00 PM.
ADMISSION: $.50 per person. Free parking is available.
LOCATION: At the Kansas State Fairgrounds, well marked in Hutchinson.
DESCRIPTION: This indoor market first opened its doors in 1964. Currently there are approximately 200 dealers that specialize in a variety of types of antiques and collectibles, exhibiting miscellaneous items at a wide range of prices. A concession stand and handicapped-accessible restrooms are available on the premises.
DEALER RATES: $17 per 10' × 12' space. Reservations are required.
CONTACT: Av Hardesty, Mid-America Markets, PO Box 1585, Hutchinson KS 67504-1585. Tel: (620) 663-5626. Day of show call: (620) 663-9000.

OPOLIS
Opolis Flea Market
DATES: Saturdays and Sundays, and Monday by chance; year round.
TIMES: Daylight hours.
ADMISSION: Free, with free parking.
LOCATION: On the Kansas-Missouri State Line; junction of US 171 and 57.
DESCRIPTION: Since 1978 this relatively small flea market has only antiques and collectibles, including miscellaneous Volkswagen autos and parts, all of it collected by two antique fanatics. This collection of treasures is housed in several warehouses and is a haunt of dealers looking to replenish their stocks. They have had other dealers with them in the past, but the whole situation is in flux. Call first. Say Hi to Louie and Norma for me!
DEALER RATES: Call for availability, as there wasn't any space available as we went to press. But you never know.
CONTACT: Louie and Norma Kukovich, Box 42, Opolis KS 66760. Tel: (620) 231-2543.

SPARKS
Sparks Antiques and Collectibles Flea Market
DATES: Three shows a year: 1) the first Sunday in May plus the preceding three days for a 4-day show; 2) the second weekend in July, Friday through

Sunday for a 3-day show; 3) Labor Day weekend the preceding two days for a 4-day show. In 2002: May 2-5, July 12-14, August 29-September 1.

TIMES: Most dealers open between 7:00-8:00 AM and close up by 6:00 PM.

ADMISSION: Free. Parking is free on 4 acres next to the market as well as around town.

LOCATION: K-7 Hwy and old US 36, now known as Mission Rd. Just 23 miles west of St. Joseph, MO or 19 miles east of Hiawatha, KS on Old US 36 Hwy or 24 miles north of Atchison, KS or 11 miles south of White Cloud, KS on K-7 Hwy.

DESCRIPTION: Of this market's over 400 dealers, 325 sell antiques. You can count on plenty of quality antiques and collectibles as they are 95% antiques. (Get here early!) Started in 1982, this market is on the way to several other markets held the same weekend and together they draw 75,000 people trolling for treasures—this, in a town population of 9 the rest of the year, described by Ray as "officially a ghost town." Plenty of food is available either at the market or around town. You can't starve. There are 16 food vendors, including Mexican, German, Indian, and barbecue among the myriad choices. Find Ray and give him a hardy "Howdy and Thank You!" for me. Besides, he is full of cool stories!

DEALER RATES: $55-$70 for 20' × 30' outside space or $75-$90 for 10' × 15' inside space for the week. There are larger spaces available. Electricity is $5 a day extra. Table rental is $5 per table for the entire show. Setup starts on Wednesday, Thursday is dealer day. Don't miss it!

CONTACT: Ray Tackett, PO Box 223, Troy KS 66087-0223. Tel: (785) 985-2411 except during market hours, when Ray can be reached at the market: (785) 442-5589.

Another Sparks Special from Ray

Although we have signs up on the highway and all over town that say "Sparks Flea Market" I hear these comments all the time and have to laugh about it afterwards. The main two comments are "My, how big White Cloud has grown! [The neighboring town.]" and, "I am too tired to go to Sparks after going through this market."

Apparently, the town of Sparks' population is small enough that the town will officially be dropped off maps. Or as Ray says, "We will be dropped off the road maps soon as we have been officially declared a ghost town." You'll just have to look for the Sparks Flea Market signs!

WELDA
Old School Flea Market

DATES: Daily, except Monday and Tuesday.
TIMES: Sunday 12:00 PM-6:00 PM, otherwise 10:00 AM-6:00 PM.
ADMISSION: Free. Parking is free.
LOCATION: 511 Commercial St.

DESCRIPTION: Opened in an old high school in 1995, this market of 50 dealers sells lots of old, used, and collectible stuff, including estate sale finds. About 75% of the merchandise is old. No food here, but plenty of restrooms! This is quite a place for filling up your trunk with treasures.
DEALER RATES: Inside: $5 for shelves, up to $30 for 8' × 8' space per month. For visiting vendors, setup outside is free. Inside reservations are needed to find space.
CONTACT: Old School Flea Market, 511 Commercial St, Welda KS 66091. Tel: 785-448-3367.

WICHITA
Village Flea Market

DATES: Every Friday, Saturday and Sunday. Rain or shine.
TIMES: 9:00 AM-5:00 PM.
ADMISSION: Free. Parking is also free.
LOCATION: 2301 S Meridian.

DESCRIPTION: This indoor/outdoor market first opened in 1974. Their 125 to 150 dealers sell everything from antiques and collectibles to hand-made craft items, tools, toys, clothing, and jewelry. An interesting variety of garage-sale items are also available with several dealers who go out scouting for the stuff. There are great bargains here. For your comfort the 100,000 square-foot building is heated as well as air-conditioned. It is also equipped with a modern security system. Cooper says they have a great restaurant and handicapped-accessible restrooms as well. Some of their dealers have been here 25 years and seem to be doing very well indeed. When you find Cooper, say "Hi" for me!
DEALER RATES: $45 per 10' × 10' booth for the 3-day weekend. Space is rented on a first-come, first-served basis. There is a full-time security police officer on duty all weekend.
CONTACT: Dale Cooper, Village Flea Market, 2301 S Meridian, Wichita KS 67213. Tel: (316) 942-8263.

Mid-America Flea Markets

DATES: Irregular Sunday dates, one per month, except for July and August. 2002: January 20, February 3, March 24, April 14, May 19, June 23, September 15, October 22, also 27 (in Pavilion II) November 17,

December 15. They try for the same weekends, but it doesn't always work. Call for 2003 dates.

TIMES: 9:00 AM-4:00 PM.

ADMISSION: $1 per person. Free parking is available.

LOCATION: At the Kansas Coliseum, at the intersection of 85th St and I-135 N, Exit 17.

DESCRIPTION: This indoor market opened in 1978 and accommodates approximately 650 dealers. Visitors come to view the large selection of antiques and collectibles; there is always a wide variety to choose from, at a wide range of prices. About 40% of the items sold are new merchandise including clothing, jewelry and gifts. A concession stand and handicapped-accessible restrooms are on the premises.

DEALER RATES: $17 per 8' × 10' space. Reservations are required.

CONTACT: Av Hardesty, Mid-America Markets, PO Box 1585, Hutchinson KS 67504-1585. Tel: (620) 663-5626. Show date phone: (620) 755-2560.

OTHER FLEA MARKETS

We know or have heard about these markets, but have not personally contacted each one, as we have the markets with descriptions. If you plan to visit one of the markets listed below, *please call first* to make sure they are still open. Flea markets do come and go. While they were open when we went to press, they may not be later. We can't be responsible. *Call first!*

Chanute: East Oak Flea Market, 120 E Oak St. Tel: (620) 431-3198.

Chanute: Evergreen Antique Mall & Flea, 612 S Central Ave. Tel: (620) 431-4314.

Chanute: Proctors Flea Market, 319 W 3rd St. Tel: (620) 431-7655.

Coffeyville: B & K Pecans & Flea Market, 802 E 11th St. Tel: (620) 251-6887.

Derby: Derby Flea Market, 327 Red Powell Dr. Tel: (316) 789-9500.

Dodge City: Happy Trail Flea Market, 317 W Trail St. Tel: (620) 227-2168.

Emporia: Flea Market, 329 Commercial St. Tel: (620) 342-5333.

Eudora: Eudora Main Street Fleamarket, 714 Main St. Tel: (785) 542-3934.

Fredonia: Valley Flea Market, RR 4 Box 196F. Tel: (620) 378-4479.

Garden City: Sanjuan Flea Market, 902 E Fulton St. Tel: (620) 276-6049.

Great Bend: 281 Bypass Flea Market, 1135 US Hwy 281 Byp. Tel: (620) 793-7660.

Hutchinson: Bernard's Flea Market, 1211 E Blanchard Ave. Tel: (620) 665-4062.

Kansas City: Merriam Lane Flea Market, 1270 Merriam Ln. Tel: (913) 677-0833.

La Cygne: Lucky Penny Flea Market, 310 Chestnut St. Tel: (913) 757-2675.

Osawatomie: Old Country Store Flea Market, 510 Main St. Tel: (913) 755-6595.

Pleasanton: Big G's Flea Market, 6th & Main. Tel: (913) 352-6113.

Topeka: A & A Ministorage & Flea Market, 914 SE Jefferson St. Tel: (785) 232-1414.

Topeka: C & F Flea Market, 2305 SE 10th Ave. Tel: (785) 233-9797.

Topeka: Four Day Flea Market, 5907 SW 21st St. Tel: (785) 273-9425.

Topeka: Lane St Flea Market, 1425 SW Lane St. Tel: (785) 232-6737.

Wichita: Midtown Flea Market, 509 E Harry St. Tel: (316) 262-7150.

Wichita: Village Flea Market, 2301 S Meridian Ave. Tel: (316) 942-8263.

KENTUCKY

ASHLAND
Hillbilly Flea Market

DATES: Thursday, Friday, Saturday and Sunday.

TIMES: 8:00 AM-5:00 PM.

ADMISSION: Free. Parking is free.

LOCATION: Russell Rd, Rt 23, north of Ashland.

DESCRIPTION: Opened in 1985, this indoor/outdoor market of 100-150 dealers sells antiques, collectibles, clothing, crafts, jewelry, fresh produce, new and used merchandise. The 21,000-square-foot building is heated and air-conditioned. Their restaurant serves up home-cooked meals and when needed there are handicapped-accessible restrooms.

DEALER RATES: Thursday and Friday: $5 per 10' × 25' space, Saturday and Sunday $7 per space, inside depends on square footage.

CONTACT: Elwood Gibbs, Hillbilly Flea Market, 100 W Main St, Greenup KY 41144. Tel: (606) 329-1058 or 1-800-357-1058.

> **Strangest Object at the Market**
> This one has to take the prize: the jawbone of an ass! As Elwood says, "It sold!"

BOWLING GREEN
Flea Land of Bowling Green

DATES: Saturday and Sunday, year round.

TIMES: 9:00 AM-6:00 PM.

ADMISSION: Free. Parking is free.

LOCATION: 1100 Three Springs Road, adjacent to I-65, Exit 22.

DESCRIPTION: Opened in 1994, this indoor/outdoor market of 300 indoor booths has dealers selling everything from antiques and collectibles, NASCAR, to used and new merchandise. Plenty of food and handicapped-accessible restrooms add to the amenities.

DEALER RATES: $7 per day outside, $43 per 10' × 15' space per weekend. Reservations are required for inside space only; outside is first come, first served.

CONTACT: Flea Land of Bowling Green, 1100 Three Springs Road, Bowling Green KY 42104. Tel: (270) 843-1978.

CORBIN
Cumberland Parkway Flea Market

DATES: Saturday and Sunday.

TIMES: 9:00 AM-5:00 PM.

ADMISSION: Free. Parking is free.

LOCATION: 305 W Cumberland Gap Pkwy. Take Exit 29 off I-75.

DESCRIPTION: Opened in 1996, this market of 150-160 dealers sells collectibles, crafts, stamps, cards, coins, produce, furniture, garage sale goodies, appliances, TVs, and new merchandise. There is one snack bar and handicapped-accessible restrooms on site.

DEALER RATES: $36 per weekend for 10' × 15' space. Reservations are not required.

CONTACT: Cumberland Pkwy Flea Market, PO Box 999, Corbin KY 40702-0999. Tel: (606) 526-9712. Fax: (606) 526-1629.

ELIZABETHTOWN
Bowling Lanes Flea Market

DATES: Saturday and Sunday.

TIMES: 8:00 AM-5:00 PM.

ADMISSION: Free. Parking is free.

LOCATION: 4547 N Dixie, US 31W; 35 miles south of Louisville on I-65 and 8 miles south of Fort Knox.

DESCRIPTION: This indoor/outdoor market of 300-500 dealers sells antiques, collectibles, new and used merchandise, clothing, jewelry, furniture, crafts, and fresh produce. There are two booths of antiques in one of the two buildings, handicapped-accessible restrooms, a snack concession, shed space and hundreds of dealers in open-air spaces, depending on the weather. Garage sale goodies are mostly outside with loads of new stuff every weekend. Inside is mostly newer merchandise.

DEALER RATES: $7 per 10' × 12' in the open per day, $8 for either inside 8' × 8' space, or under shed per 10' × 10' space per day. Reservations are needed for shed or inside space, not for outside. Do check in with the market just in case. They do fill up.

CONTACT: Bowling Lanes Flea Market, 4547 N Dixie Hwy, Elizabethtown KY 42701-8857. Tel: (270) 737-5755 or the bowling alley at (270) 737-7171.

FLEMINGSBURG
Annual Old-Fashioned Court Day

DATES: Second Monday and preceding weekend of October, rain or shine. (Essentially Columbus Day weekend and Monday.) For 2002: October 12-14.

TIMES: Saturday, sunup to whenever; Sunday noon until Monday whenever.

ADMISSION: Free. Parking is wherever you find it; some is free, some isn't.

LOCATION: The entire town of Flemingsburg! In the center of town, on Main St.

DESCRIPTION: Started in 1969 to continue the tradition of the circuit judge plying his trade (trials and hangings), this town turns into a huge market centered in downtown Flemingsburg. About 100 outside vendors sell everything and anything you can imagine—old, new and otherwise. They do try to have a booth or two of unusual things like games and rides for kids, clogging, and live entertainment. This shebang ends with a good old-fashioned square dance on Monday night. This event is the fundraiser for the local Rescue Squad who sponsors this market.

DEALER RATES: Setup anytime after 6:00 PM Friday. $75 per 10' × 10' space for three days. Reservations are strongly recommended.

CONTACT: Annual Old-Fashioned Court Day, Chamber of Commerce, 114 Water St, Flemingsburg KY 41041. Tel: (606) 845-1223. Email: flemingchamber@pqisp.net.

FREDONIA
Old Fredonia School Flea Market

DATES: Friday through Sunday, year round.

TIMES: Friday and Saturday 8:00 AM-5:00 PM. Sunday 1:00 PM-5:00 PM.

ADMISSION: Free. Parking is free.

LOCATION: Fredonia School on Hwy 641.

DESCRIPTION: Located in an old school building on a major highway, this market opened in 1992. There are 9 dealers spread around 11 rooms and all hallways of the old school selling antiques, collectibles, crafts, cards, stamps, garage sale goodies, clothing, ceramics, pictures, furniture, horse tack, horse-drawn equipment, antique tools, vintage car parts, memorabilia and some new merchandise. No food, but handicapped-accessible restrooms are in the school. Mary and her dealers do appreciate their visitors and love to welcome them.

DEALER RATES: $100 per month for a 22' × 27' room and Mary will sell for you if you can't be there, no commissions. There is a waiting list for inside space.

CONTACT: Mary Boone, Old Fredonia School Flea Market, 306 Cassidy Ave, Fredonia KY 42411. Tel: (270) 545-9115 (business) or 545-3982 (home).

Hysterical Note
What would you do with an old school put up for auction? Buy it.
Then what? Turn it into a flea market. That's what Malcolm Boone
bought, and Mary did with it. Not only does it have items for sale,
but it has displays of local history. There is an old still (no, you
can't have it, and doesn't make stuff anymore), a broom-making
setup and all sorts of odds and ends tucked everywhere. If you want
to hold a really big event there, rent the gym!

GREENVILLE
Luke's Town and Country Flea Market
DATES: Monday and Tuesday, year round, weather permitting.
TIMES: 8:00 AM-dark Monday; 6:00 AM-2:00 PM Tuesday.
ADMISSION: Free, with some free parking; $1 parking is available nearby.
LOCATION: Hwy 62 W, 1 mile from Greenville city limits.

DESCRIPTION: This outdoor market has been operating since May 1979.
On Monday about 25 to 100 dealers show. Tuesdays are busier, with
between 200 and 400 dealers selling antiques, collectibles, crafts, new
merchandise, and produce, as well as poultry and livestock. The surrounding area is rustically scenic, with Lake Malone and many other
state parks nearby. There is a real family atmosphere here and a large
antique display and collection to view (but not for sale) and several antique shops nearby. Food is available on the grounds.
DEALER RATES: $3 and up per 8' × 10' space per day Tuesdays and
Monday holidays; $2 on non-holiday Mondays. Reservations are appre-
ciated but not necessary.
CONTACT: Wayne and Judy Rice, Managers, Luke's Town and Country
Flea Market, 2006 US Hwy 62 W, Greenville KY 42345. Tel: (270) 338-
4920 or (270) 338-6284.

HIGHWAY 127
Highway 127 Corridor Sale
DATES: August, from the Thursday before the third Sunday through Sun-
day for 4 days.
TIMES: Whenever.
ADMISSION: Free. Park in designated parking areas along the route. Call
the Kentucky Office of Public Affairs, tel: (502) 564-4890 for locations.
Or check their website: www.kytc.state.ky.us.
LOCATION: All along US Hwy 127 through three states: Kentucky, Ten-
nessee and Alabama. When you see a collection of sellers, it's there.

DESCRIPTION: Started in 1987 as a way to get travelers off the inter-state and back onto the country roads by Fentress (TN) County's former County Executive Mike Walker and some of his friends, this market of thousands of dealers in "oddities and antiques," yard sale unloaders, and whoever and whatever else shows up sells everything old and/or crafty. If you wish to travel the entire 450-mile route, start in Covington KY and work your way down to around Gadsden AL. There are plenty of food vendors. This has to be "the World's Longest Outdoor Sale."

Rules of the road: 1) Drive Cautiously—then you won't hit pedestrians or miss that goody you've been looking for. 2) Be extremely careful cross-ing the road! 3) Use your turn signals and don't stop suddenly for that goody (have a lookout who can give you ample warning). Otherwise, you may be dealing with insurance companies and wreckers rather than rare Ming.

DEALER RATES: Whatever the local landowner charges. Check out the website for a list of contacts in each state (it's huge) or call.

CONTACT: Fentress County Chamber of Commerce, PO Box 1294, Jamestown TN 38556-1294. Tel: (800) 327-3945. Web: jamestowntn.org.

LEITCHFIELD
Bratcher's Flea Market

DATES: Wednesday and Saturday, year round, weather permitting.

TIMES: Dawn to 2:00 PM.

ADMISSION: Free admission and parking, including overnight before show days.

LOCATION: On Hwy 62, 1 mile east of Leitchfield.

DESCRIPTION: This market opened over 30 years ago and is now run by the granddaughter of the founder. Approximately 150 dealers sell their antiques and collectibles outdoors. Handicrafts, new merchandise, and produce in season are also for sale. This is a well-managed, well-run market. There is a food concession at the market.

DEALER RATES: $7-$8 per 8' × 10' space per day. Reservations for the month are suggested.

CONTACT: Carol Heffley, Bratcher's Flea Market, PO Box 396, Leitchfield KY 42754-0396. Tel: (270) 259-5948.

LONDON
Flea Land Flea Market

DATES: Saturday and Sunday, year round.

TIMES: 9:00 AM-5:00 PM. Extended holiday shopping days Thanksgiving through Christmas.

ADMISSION: Free. Parking is free.

LOCATION: 235 Barbourville Rd. Take London Exit 38 off I-75, 2 miles east. Follow the signs.

DESCRIPTION: Opened in 1990, this indoor/outdoor market of 400 dealers sells antiques, collectibles, crafts, produce, coins, cards, garage sale goodies, furniture, gold, jewelry, all sorts of home furnishings, rugs, NASCAR items, and new merchandise. Their building is a heated and cooled 80,000 square feet of selling space with one restaurant, a concession stand, and handicapped-accessible restrooms—"the largest in the state of Kentucky." They say they are "known as one of the cleanest and best."

DEALER RATES: $38.50 per 10' × 15' space weekly; $43.50 per 10' × 19' space weekly; or $12 per 10' × 10' outside space. Reservations are required.

CONTACT: Brenda Hail, Flea Land Flea Market, PO Box 862, London KY 40741. Tel: (606) 864-3532.

London Tobacco Warehouse Flea Market

DATES: Friday, Saturday and Sunday, year round.

TIMES: 9:00 AM-5:00 PM.

ADMISSION: Free. Parking is free.

LOCATION: 420 Tobacco Rd. Off the London Bypass. Watch for the signs.

DESCRIPTION: Since 1981, this market's 80 dealers have been selling antiques, collectibles, garage sale goodies, some new merchandise, and produce in season. There are handicapped-accessible restrooms and a concession stand on site.

DEALER RATES: $33 per weekend or $11 per day for a 12' × 16' space. Reservations are an excellent idea, as the market is usually full.

CONTACT: Carl Tuttle, London Tobacco Warehouse Flea Market, 420 Tobacco Rd, London KY 40741-2311. Tel: (606) 878-7726 (flea market) or 878-9000 (office). Fax: (606) 864-6195.

LOUISVILLE
Derby Park Trader's Circle

DATES: Saturday and Sunday, year round. Rain or shine.

TIMES: 9:00 AM-5:00 PM.

ADMISSION: Free. Free parking for public.

LOCATION: I-264 to Taylor Blvd N exit. Turn right on Taylor and go 3 stoplights. Turn left on Arcade. At light make a left onto 7th Street Rd and the market is on the right at 2900 7th St Rd.

DESCRIPTION: Located 7/10 of a mile from Churchill Downs, this indoor air-conditioned 100,000-square-foot market with 150 outside booths has been operating since 1985. They have dealers in approximately 480 indoor spaces selling antiques, collectibles, handmade crafts, vegetables, furniture, clothing, knives, guns, toys, carpet, baseball cards and new merchandise. They had an "Outrageous Giveaway Promotion" culminating with the winner driving off in a 1969 Rolls Royce Silver Shadow. Wonder what they'll do next time? Four snack bars provide food on the premises and handicapped-accessible restrooms complete the amenities.

DEALER RATES: $36 per 6' × 20' or 10' × 12' indoor booth for the weekend; $45 per weekend for 18' × 10' booth; $10 per outdoor booth per day. Reservations are first come, first served.

CONTACT: Art Enoch or Keith Age, Derby Park Traders Circle Flea Market, 2900 S 7th Street Rd, Louisville KY 40216-4126. Tel: (502) 636-3532. Fax: (502) 634-0094. Email: derbyparkfleamkt@aol.com. Web: http://fleamarkets.com/derbypark/index.html.

Kentucky Flea Market

DATES: 2002: January 25-27, March 1-3, April 5-7 April 26-28, May 24-27, July 4-7, July 26-28, August 30-September 2 (Labor Day), September 27-29, October 25-27, December 13-15 (Christmas show) December 27-30 (New Year's). Please double-check the schedule, just in case the dates change. It can be found on their website, or call.

TIMES: Friday 12:00 PM-7:00 PM; Saturday 10:00 AM-7:00 PM; Sunday 11:00 AM-5:00 PM. Memorial Day, Labor Day, and New Years: Friday 12:00 PM-7:00 PM; Saturday 10:00 AM-7:00 PM; Sunday 11:00 AM-6:00 PM; Monday 10:00 AM-5:00 PM. July 4: Thursday 12:00 PM-7:00 PM; Friday 10:00 AM-7:00 PM; Saturday 10:00 AM-6:00 PM; Sunday 11:00 AM-5:00 PM.

ADMISSION: Free. $3 for parking in 15,000 spaces.

LOCATION: Kentucky Fair and Exposition Center. Junctions of I-264 and 65. Follow the signs.

DESCRIPTION: Started in 1972, and housed in a 250,000-square-foot climate-controlled building, this market consists of 1,000 to 2,000 dealers selling antiques, fine arts, arts and crafts, collectibles, and new merchandise. It is promoted as one of the largest indoor flea markets in the United States, in one of this country's finest facilities. On regular show days the market draws between 30,000 and 50,000 shoppers; on holidays, the crowds can swell to 100,000 or more. Food is served on the premises, and when the need arises, there are handicapped-accessible restrooms.

DEALER RATES: $85 ($100-$110 holidays) per 14' × 8' space per show; $128 ($150-$165 holidays) per 21' × 8' space; $170 ($200-$220 holidays) per 28' × 8' space. Larger spaces are available. Higher holiday rates. Reservations are required well in advance.

CONTACT: Stewart Promotions, 2950 Breckinridge Ln Ste 4A, Louisville KY 40220. Tel: (502) 456-2244 (except Tuesday and Friday). Email: sp2950@home.com. Web: www.stewartpromotions.com.

MT STERLING
October Court Days

DATES: The weekend of and including the third Monday in October, annually.

TIMES: 6:00 AM Saturday through 6:00 PM Monday, non-stop.

ADMISSION: Free admission; parking from $5 per day or wherever you can find it.

LOCATION: The entire town of Mt Sterling! Take Exit 110 off I-64, 30 miles east of Lexington; or take Exit 113 off I-64, 100 miles west of Ashland.

DESCRIPTION: Mt Sterling has always been a big trading center. Around 1796, it was traditional for the local county judge to hang convicted offenders on the third Monday in October, which naturally started people trading over the entire weekend. People came from miles away to buy and sell cows, horses, dogs, produce, tools, and other farm goods. This market attracts 2,000 dealers officially and averages 175,000 shoppers. Even now, during Court Days, people bring objects of all shapes and sizes for sale or trade—more dogs and other farm animals (to Preston), guns, axe handles, hammer handles, and antiques of all kinds that defy cataloging. Among the various foods for sale are corn meal and real Kentucky sorghum molasses, which is still made right in this mountain area.

DEALER RATES: Average rate is $200 plus $20 for city license per 20' × 20' space for three days. Reservations are required in advance.

CONTACT: October Court Days, Montgomery County Tourism Dept, 51 N Maysville, Mt Sterling KY 40353. Tel: (859) 498-8732. Fax: (859) 498-3947. Email: mtourism@mis.net. Web: mountsterling-ky.com.

Historical Notes

Mt Sterling Court Days are so popular that the market has a life of its own. While the official market is an eight-block area in the center of town—having started at the courthouse originally, then moved to the street, then to the stockyards (now in Preston)—they have since just plain spread all over town, much of it quite independent of the official function.

When the city fathers decided that having lots of animals in the center of town wasn't healthy, neighboring Preston, in Bath County, took over that part of the market and started their own Preston Court Days, about 15 miles east of Mt Sterling.

One section along the creek is just for trading guns and knives. Visitors to that area are rather startled to feel that they have stepped back in time about 200 years with local mountaineers walking around with several shotguns parked on their shoulders. Yet never has a shot been fired or any injury happened.

RICHWOOD
Richwood Flea Market

DATES: Tuesday, Saturday and Sunday, year round.

TIMES: Saturday and Sunday 9:00 AM-5:00 PM; Tuesday outdoors, day-break to 1:00 PM, weather permitting.

ADMISSION: Free. $1.50 per car for parking.

LOCATION: 10915 US 25, Richwood exit. I-75 to Exit 175, north on US 25, 15 minutes south of Cincinnati.

DESCRIPTION: Opened in 1980, this market has about 300 indoor and 100 outdoor sellers. The indoor sellers are housed in a former tobacco warehouse over three acres big. There are many antiques, collectibles, craft items, sporting goods, tools, guns and knives, shoes, general merchandise as well as farm goods, jewelry, and new merchandise to be found. The Tuesday market is a genuine old-fashioned flea and farmers' market with loads of in-season produce and used stuff.

Newly remodeled in 1997, they added two food courts with a big-screen television and local entertainment. Their fried chicken is considered the best around and they added a meat smoker and feature fresh pork and chicken barbecue every weekend. Handicapped-accessible restrooms add to the amenities.

DEALER RATES: Inside spaces per weekend: $75 per 16' × 15' space, $50 per 16' × 8' space, or $45 per 8' × 15' space. Outdoor covered spaces: $20 per day for Saturday and Sunday, Tuesdays are 2 spaces for $15. Reservations are suggested for indoor or their new covered outdoor spaces. Outdoor: $15 for a 3-car parking space outdoors on Tuesday; $15 for 2 spaces for weekends. First come, first served.

CONTACT: Mike Stallings, PO Box 153, Florence KY 41022-0153. Tel: (859) 371-5800. Fax: (859) 371-5680. Email: richflea10@aol.com. Web: www.richwoodfleamarket.com.

Ask Mike about those special urinal screens. . . . too funny!

SIMPSONVILLE
Shelby County Flea Market

DATES: Saturday and Sunday.

TIMES: 9:00 AM-5:00 PM.

ADMISSION: Free. Parking is free.

LOCATION: 820 Buck Creek Rd. I-64, exit 28; west of Lexington.

DESCRIPTION: Since 1985, this market of 350 inside vendors and up to 150 outside vendors (depending on the weather) sells antiques, col-

lectibles, garage sale goodies, clothing, furniture, jewelry, books, crafts, fresh produce, used and new merchandise. The merchandise mix is generally 70% new to 30% old on the inside, and mostly old and garage sale goodies on the outside. There is a major concession stand with several satellite stands nearby (ice cream, Chester's fried chicken, and more) as well as handicapped-accessible restrooms. This is probably the largest weekly flea market in Kentucky.

DEALER RATES: $43.50 per 10' × 12' space inside per weekend, $12 per 10' × 20' space outside per day. Reservations are required inside, as they fill up quickly and generally have a waiting list after the summer season. Outside is first come, first served.

CONTACT: Dana Smith, Shelby County Flea Market, 820 Buck Creek Rd, Simpsonville KY 40067-6629. Tel: (502) 722-8883. Fax: (502) 722-8881.

SOMERSET
Lake Cumberland Flea Market

DATES: Saturday and Sunday, year round.

TIMES: Saturday 9:00 AM-6:00 PM, Sunday 10:00 AM-6:00 PM. Extra hours during Christmas season.

ADMISSION: Free. Parking is free.

LOCATION: 95 Super Service Dr. Right off 914, aka New Southern By-Pass or Veterans Memorial Hwy.

DESCRIPTION: Opened in 1993, this indoor market's 100-plus dealers, in 260 booths, sell antiques, collectibles, crafts, produce, furniture, garage sale goodies, books, herbs and oils, clothes, tools, and new merchandise. There is one restaurant on the premises with handicapped-accessible restrooms. They pride themselves on their clean market.

DEALER RATES: $34 per 10' × 15' space per weekend, $68 per 20' × 15' space. First come, first served.

CONTACT: Anna Gutting or Vertrees Warner, Lake Cumberland Flea Market, 95 Super Service Dr, Somerset KY 42501-6146. Tel: (606) 678-0250 or 1-800-246-4062. Fax: (606) 678-0250.

WINCHESTER
Winchester Flea Market

DATES: Saturday and Sunday.

TIMES: 8:00 AM-5:00 PM.

ADMISSION: Free. Parking is free.

LOCATION: 4400 Relivo Rd, I-64 Exit 94.

DESCRIPTION: Open since 1986, this indoor/outdoor market of 50 dealers sells antiques, collectibles, crafts, coins, cards, garage sale goodies, fur-

niture, records, books, glassware, skillets, hardware, and new merchandise. There is a snack bar and handicapped-accessible restrooms on site.
DEALER RATES: $7 per 12' × 12' space per day or $14 for the weekend; first come, first served.
CONTACT: Raymond C Huls, Winchester Flea Market, 1417 W Lexington Ave, Winchester KY 40391. Tel: (859) 745-4332.

OTHER FLEA MARKETS

We know or have heard about these markets, but have not personally contacted each one, as we have the markets with descriptions. If you plan to visit one of the markets listed below, *please call first* to make sure they are still open. Flea markets do come and go. While they were open when we went to press, they may not be later. We can't be responsible. *Call first!*

Bowling Green: Flea Land, 1100 Three Springs Rd. Tel: (270) 843-1978.
Butler: Crossroads Flea Market, 2105 Hwy 27. Tel: (859) 472-6952.
Campbellsville: Campbellsville Flea Market, 426 Woodlawn Ave. Tel: (270) 789-0708.
Clay City: Industrial Park Flea Market, Hwy 15 W. Tel: (606) 663-9297.
Corbin: Corbin Indoor Flea Market, US Hwy 25-W S. Tel: (606) 528-3091.
Georgetown: Country World Flea Market, 3010 Paris Pike. Tel: (502) 867-0831.
Georgetown: Georgetown Flea Market, 150 Edwards Ave. Tel: (502) 868-0858.
Guthrie: Dale's Flea Market, 425 State St. Tel: (270) 483-1999.
Guthrie: Southern Kentucky Flea Market, 52 Cypress Ln. Tel: (270) 483-2166.
Hagerhill: Super Flea Market, 7280 S Ky Rt 321. Tel: (606) 789-9799.
Hazard: Hazard Village Flea Market, 368 Dawahare Dr. Tel: (606) 439-2529.
Irvine: Countryside Flea Market, 1984 Winchester Rd. Tel: (606) 723-8086.
Irvington: Linda's Flea Market, 224 N 1st St Hwy 79. Tel: (270) 547-4811.
Louisa: Larry's Flea Market, US Hwy 23 N. Tel: (606) 638-4433.
Louisville: Country Fair Flea Market, 3502 7th Street Rd. Tel: (502) 368-6186.
Louisville: Preston Flea Market, 6201 Preston Hwy. Tel: (502) 968-8582.
Maceo: Hog Heaven Flea Market, 8424 US Hwy 60 E. Tel: (270) 264-4420.
Maysville: King's Market, 1171 Progress Way. Tel: (606) 759-8036.
Morehead: Moorehead Flea Market, 530 Fraley Dr. Tel: (606) 784-2444.
Mt Sterling: Queen Street Flea Market, 107 S Queen St. Tel: (859) 497-9100.
Mt Sterling: South Queen Street Flea Market, 109 S Queen St. Tel: (859) 499-0330.
Mt Washington: Cherokee's Flea Market & Antiques, 810 N Bardstown Rd. Tel: (502) 538-2456.
Murray: Gray's Flea Market, 609 S 4th St. Tel: (270) 753-7047.
Owensboro: Farm Store Flea Market, 2430 E 4th St. Tel: (270) 686-3001.

Paducah: Traders Mall Flea Market, 6900 Benton Rd. Tel: (270) 898-3144.

Shepherdsville: Awesome Flea Market, 165 Dawson Dr. Tel: (502) 543-7899.

Shepherdsville: Bullitt County Stock Yard, 3000 S Preston Hwy. Tel: (502) 543-3852.

Shepherdsville: Rountree's Flea Market, 2385 N Preston Hwy. Tel: (502) 543-1731.

Simpsonville: Shelby County Flea Market, 820 Buck Creek Rd. Tel: (502) 722-8883.

Stanford: Stanford Drive In Flea Market, 1645 Hustonville Rd. Tel: (606) 365-1317.

West Paducah: Pirate's Cove Flea Market, 8940 US Hwy 60 W. Tel: (270) 744-6873.

Winchester: Goff's Corner Flea Market, 12449 Ironworks Rd. Tel: (859) 842-3803.

LOUISIANA

ARCADIA
Bonnie & Clyde Trade Days, Inc

DATES: The weekend before the third Monday of each month, Friday through Sunday. 2002: April 12-14, May 17-19, June 14-16, July 12-14, August 16-18, September 13-15, October 18-20, November 15-17, December 13-15.

TIMES: Dawn to dark.

ADMISSION: Free. Parking is $3.

LOCATION: Take I-20, Exit 69 and go south 3½ miles to market.

DESCRIPTION: Since its opening in September 1990, this outdoor show has grown from the original 635 dealers to over 800 dealer spaces. The grounds feature three stocked lakes for free fishing, a restaurant, amphitheater and stage, 100 RV hookups and facilities. There are dozens of concessions and dealers selling just about anything and everything. They have added both a washateria and free shower facilities for vendors.

DEALER RATES: $40-$80-$100 per booth depending on size and location. Booths are rented by the month. Reservations are suggested.

CONTACT: Bonnie & Clyde Trade Days Inc, PO Box 243, Arcadia LA 71001-0243. Tel: (318) 263-2437 or 1-888-835-6112. Fax: (318) 263-9803. Email: info@bonnieandclydetradedays.com. Web: www.bonnieandclydetradedays.com.

BATON ROUGE
Deep South Flea Market

DATES: Every Friday, Saturday and Sunday. Rain or shine.

TIMES: 10:00 AM-6:00 PM.

ADMISSION: Free. Parking is also free.

LOCATION: 5905 Florida Blvd.

DESCRIPTION: This indoor market began in 1974. Approximately 275 dealers sell everything from antiques and collectibles, to a variety of crafts and artwork, to secondhand merchandise and produce. A restaurant and handicapped-accessible restrooms add to the amenities.

DEALER RATES: $60 per 8' × 10' space, per weekend. Reservations are not required.

CONTACT: Bill Vallery, 5905 Florida Blvd, Baton Rouge LA 70806. Tel: (225) 923-0142 or 923-0333 for a tape.

Greater Baton Rouge Flea Market

DATES: Saturday and Sunday.

TIMES: 9:00 AM-5:00 PM.

ADMISSION: Free. Parking is free.

LOCATION: 15545 Airline Hwy. On US 61 (Airline Hwy) between Baton Rouge and New Orleans. From I-10 Exit 173 East, go 2½ miles to Airline Hwy, turn right, go ¾ miles to market.

DESCRIPTION: Opened in October 1975, this market of 250 dealers under roof sell "everything from apples to Zydeco," with a ratio of old stuff to new about 50/50. They describe themselves as "the largest old-fashioned modern flea market in Southern Louisiana." The market is entirely handicapped-accessible, the food is apparently quite awesome—genuine Gonzales Jambalaya for a start—and they have clean restrooms.

DEALER RATES: $25 and up per space, depending on size and location. Reservations are suggested.

CONTACT: Keith Bryan, Greater Baton Rouge Flea Market, 15545 Airline Hwy, Prairieville LA 70769. Tel: (225) 673-2682. Fax: (225) 673-9348.

GREENWOOD/SHREVEPORT
Greenwood Flea Market

DATES: Saturday and Sunday, year round.

TIMES: 9:00 AM-6:00 PM.

ADMISSION: Free. Parking is free.

LOCATION: 9249 Jefferson-Paige Rd. I-20, Exit 5.

DESCRIPTION: This unusual market started in 1982, with 150 dealer spaces inside, 25 railroad boxcars and numerous outside setups. Their dealers sell antiques, collectibles, primitives, baseball cards, glassware, furniture, jewelry, and everything old and new. One of the owners saw the railroad boxcars sitting around a Texas siding and decided they would be fun and brought them over to Louisiana. Handicapped-accessible restrooms and a snack bar are available on the premises.

DEALER RATES: $27.50 per weekend; $110 per month. $110 per railroad car plus electric. $8 per day outside. Reservations are required.

CONTACT: Larry Milligan, Greenwood Flea Market, 9249 Jefferson-Paige Rd, Greenwood LA 71033. Tel: (318) 938-7201.

JEFFERSON
Jefferson Flea Market

DATES: Friday through Sunday, year round.

TIMES: 10:00 AM-6:00 PM.

ADMISSION: Free. Parking is free.

LOCATION: 5501 Jefferson Hwy. Three blocks west of Clearview, off the Huey P Long Bridge.

DESCRIPTION: This market, under new management, opened in 1978, occupies an old 90,000-square-foot building supply warehouse with 70-75 dealers specializing in antiques, collectibles and awesome old stuff. Very little is new. (Maybe some reproductions? They do make furniture here.) Some of their dealers are nationally known for their expertise. "Chef Tommy" holds court in the snack bar serving the "finest hot dogs in the South." The loading dock area is used by the locals for their garage sale goodies and for transient dealers.

DEALER RATES: Permanent dealers: $200-$250 for an average-sized space. Daily is $15 in the dock area.

CONTACT: Louis, Jefferson Flea Market, 5501 Jefferson Hwy, Jefferson LA 70123. Tel: (504) 733-0011.

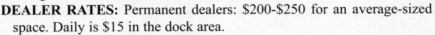

LACOMBE
190 Trading Post Flea Market

DATES: Every Saturday and Sunday. Rain or shine.

TIMES: 9:00 AM-5:00 PM.

ADMISSION: Free. Free parking is available.

LOCATION: 31160 Hwy 190 W. On Hwy 190, 4 miles east of Lacombe and 6 miles west of Slidell.

DESCRIPTION: Started in 1958, this indoor/outdoor market is said to be the oldest in Louisiana, having been in continuous operation since that time. There are 20 dealers selling antiques, fine art, arts and crafts, fresh produce, collectibles, new merchandise, appliances, and furniture, as well as unusual items such as farm equipment, American-made tools, etc. One can find anything and everything here, even hard-to-find items. Food is available nearby.

DEALER RATES: From $6 to $65 depending upon size of space. First-come, first served.

CONTACT: Mary and Harold Fayard, 31160 Hwy 190 W, Lacombe LA 70445. Tel: (985) 882-6442.

NEW ORLEANS
French Market Community Flea Market

DATES: Daily.

TIMES: 7:00 AM-7:00 PM.

ADMISSION: Free. Parking is where you find it, or in paid lots.

LOCATION: 1235 N Peters St. Located on the riverfront behind the old US Mint (yes, coins were minted here) between the Mint and Café du Monde. It is quite the tourist attraction.

DESCRIPTION: This has got to be the great-granddaddy of all flea markets, started in 1791! Located in a historic part of New Orleans, this market (and the adjoining markets that sort of just run together) has around 300 dealers selling just about everything: African clothes and artifacts, antiques, collectibles, quilts, Guatemalan clothes, tie-dye clothing, t-shirts, stained glass, purses, dolls, toys, ceramics, glasses, masks, furniture, stones and rocks, jewelry, plenty of produce, seafood and whatever. Many of the dealers are permanent fixtures, some are seasonal.

DEALER RATES: Weekdays: $7-$23 a space; weekends: $13-$40 a space, depending on what is available. Spaces are given out by tenure on a weekly basis. All vendors must have city and state licenses and current photo ID and social security number.

CONTACT: Antoinette Guiton, French Market Office, 1008 N Peters St, New Orleans LA 70116. Tel: (504) 522-2621 or (504) 596-3420 (market office). Fax (504) 596-3427. Web: www.frenchmarket.org.

OTHER FLEA MARKETS

We know or have heard about these markets, but have not personally contacted each one, as we have the markets with descriptions. If you plan to visit one of the markets listed below, *please call first* to make sure they are still open. Flea markets do come and go. While they were open when we went to press, they may not be later. We can't be responsible. *Call first!*

Alexandria: Dantzler's Flea Market, 204 Ragan Dr. Tel: (318) 443-1589.

Bastrop: Jeff's Flea Market, 124 N Vine St. Tel: (318) 556-0099.

Baton Rouge: Flea Market, 5905 Florida Blvd. Tel: (225) 923-0333.

Bossier City: USA Flea Mart, 6201 E Texas St. Tel: (318) 741-0055.

Boyce: Crossroad Flea Market, 505 Saint Clair Rd. Tel: (318) 793-5690.

Breaux Bridge: Cecilia Flea Market, 1018 Anse Broussard Hwy. Tel: (337) 667-7066.

Cheneyville: Loren One Flea Market. Tel: (318) 279-2641.

Crowley: Dupont's Flea Market, 667 Standard Mill Rd. Tel: (337) 785-2009.

Elton: Flea Market of Elton, 913 Main St. Tel: (337) 584-3325.

Eunice: Cajun Flea Market, 1051 W Laurel Ave. Tel: (337) 457-7274.

Franklinton: Trading Post, 1329 Washington St. Tel: (985) 839-2866.

Harrisonburg: Harrisonburg Flea Market, 12529 Hwy 124. Tel: (318) 744-5994.

Independence: Something Old, Something New, 301 SW Railroad Ave. Tel: (985) 878-6464.

Iowa: A-Bear's Fleamarket, 310 W Hwy 90. Tel: (337) 582-6017.

Iowa: Cormier's Flea Market, 15311 Hwy 165. Tel: (337) 582-6752.

Kenner: Sante Fe Flea Market, 623 Maria St. Tel: (504) 463-5701.

Lafayette: Dud Arnaud Flea Markets, 1016 Cameron St. Tel: (337) 235-4345.
Lafayette: Pinhook Flea Market, 3131 W Pinhook Rd. Tel: (337) 234-1538.
Lake Charles: Cornerstone Flea-Market, 2001 Ryan St. Tel: (337) 436-1660.
Lake Charles: Family Flea Market, 100 Widgeon St. Tel: (337) 439-0101.
Lake Charles: Front Porch Flea Market, 2012 Ryan St. Tel: (337) 430-0606.
Lake Charles: Rainbow Flea Market, 2913 Ryan St. Tel: (337) 439-2575.
Leesville: Little Willie's Flea Market, 14004 Lake Charles Hwy. Tel: (337) 537-3000.
Longville: O'Kelley's Flea Market Inc, 124 Conner Rd. Tel: (337) 725-6393.
Many: Lagniappe Trade Days, 23 Circle R Rd. Tel: (318) 256-0240.
Maurice: Maurice Flea Market, 8701 Maurice Ave. Tel: (337) 898-2282.
Metairie: Good Times Fancy Flea Market, 4815 Thrush St. Tel: (504) 888-8471.
Natalbany: Doug's Flea Market, 47411 N Morrison Blvd. Tel: (985) 345-8277.
Natalbany: Natalbany Flea Market, Hwy 51. Tel: (985) 542-7018.
Pierre Part: Pierre Part Flea Market, 2600 Hwy 70 S. Tel: (985) 252-1263.
Prairieville: Greater Baton Rouge Flea Mrkt, 15545 Airline Hwy. Tel: (225) 673-6365.
Ragley: Weekend Flea Market, 7231 Hwy 190. Tel: (337) 725-6215.
Shreveport: Dunn & Dunn Flea Market, 1854 S Brookwood Dr. Tel: (318) 687-1840.
Shreveport: Dunn's Flea Market, I-20. Tel: (318) 687-1501.
Shreveport: Tradedays Market, 1020 Shreveport Barksdale Hwy. Tel: (318) 868-3800.
Shreveport: Traders Corner Fleamarket, 4711 Greenwood Rd. Tel: (318) 635-3355.
Turkey Creek: Turkey Creek Trading Post, 14644 Veteran Memorial Hwy. Tel: (337) 461-2380.
Vidalia: Super Flea Market, 5222 Hwy 84 W. Tel: (318) 336-5555.
Ville Platte: Soileau's Flea Market, 3012 Opelousas Rd. Tel: (337) 363-7154.
Welsh: Sanford & Son Fleamarket, 716 E Russell Ave. Tel: (337) 734-2794.
Zachary: Zachary Crossroads Flea Market, 20130 Plank Rd. Tel: (225) 658-9566.

MAINE

BRUNSWICK
Waterfront Flea Market

DATES: Saturday and Sunday, year round.

TIMES: 8:00 AM-5:00 PM.

ADMISSION: Free. Parking is free.

LOCATION: 14 Maine St. It's the huge 4-story brick mill building down by the Androscoggin River Bridge. You really can't miss this one.

DESCRIPTION: Opened in 1996 in a very old 1830s textile mill, this building houses 70 dealers selling literally everything from antiques and collectibles, cards and books, to new merchandise. The ratio is about 70% old. There is a snack bar as well as restrooms when the need arises. Next door is a 140-dealer antique mall, a candle factory and outlet store as well as other shops. (Lock up your wallet!)

DEALER RATES: $12 per day for 10' × 10' space, including 1 table. Reservations are necessary, as there is a waiting list for space.

CONTACT: Gloria Woods, Waterfront Flea Market, 14 Maine St, Brunswick ME 04011. Tel: (207) 729-0378. Fax: (207) 725-9500.

OXFORD
Undercover Antiques

DATES: Daily, including *all* holidays.

TIMES: 8:00 AM to last customer.

ADMISSION: Free. Parking is also free.

LOCATION: Rt 26. One-half mile north of Oxford Plains Speedway on left. Only 30 minutes from I-95 Gray exit and 45 minutes from Conway.

DESCRIPTION: Under new ownership since June 1997, this market originally opened in 1970. There are over 100 dealers inside, year round, selling antiques, collectibles, sports cards, primitives, advertising items, videos and paperbacks (40,000 of them!). They do have handicapped-accessible restrooms plus a wheelchair if anyone needs it. They accept major credit and debit cards.

DEALER RATES: $100-$140 a month for a 8' × 10' booth, tables $60 a month and the market does the selling.

CONTACT: Bert Morin, Undercover Flea Market, 960 Main St, Oxford ME 04270. Tel: (207) 539-4149.

SACO
Cascade Flea Market

DATES: Weekends, May through October. Daily from mid-June through Labor Day.

TIMES: 7:00 AM-5:00 PM, or as late as the customers hang around.

ADMISSION: Free. Parking is free.

LOCATION: Rt 1. Take Exit 5 off Maine Tnpk. After the toll take Exit 2B; sign will read Rt 1N, Portland Rd. Take that exit, go approximately 2 miles north on Rt 1. On the right-hand side at the corner of Rt 1 and Cascade Rd.

DESCRIPTION: This outdoor market has been operating since 1979 near Old Orchard Beach and Funtown-Splashtown USA. The dealers, numbering anywhere from 100 to 350 (depending on who hogs how much space), sell plenty of antiques, collectibles, crafts, produce and new merchandise. Two snack concessions serve the hungry. Restrooms are on site.

DEALER RATES: Spaces, 15' frontage (with tables): Monday through Friday $8, Saturday $18, Sunday $20. Tables and their little spaces, each: Monday through Friday $4, Saturday $9, Sunday $10. Reservations are suggested, as they are usually full.

CONTACT: Betty O'Donnell, Cascade Flea Market, 885 Portland Rd. Saco ME 04072. Tel: (207) 282-8875. Fax: (207) 883-9033.

SCARBOROUGH
Scarborough Downs Flea Market & Craft Show

DATES: Saturday and Sunday, mid-September to mid-May.

TIMES: 8:00 AM-4:00 PM.

ADMISSION: Free. Parking is free.

LOCATION: Scarborough Downs Race Track. Exit 6, Maine Tnpk or Rt 1.

DESCRIPTION: This indoor market, opened in 1997, hosts 100-150 dealers at 300 tables. They sell antiques, collectibles, occasional produce (some from Florida), some garage sale goodies, used vacuums and TVs, and new merchandise. There is a concession stand as well as handicapped-accessible restrooms on site.

DEALER RATES: $20 per table per day, or $30 for the weekend, but there are discounts for more than one table. Reservations are required.

CONTACT: Scarborough Downs Flea Market & Craft Show, PO Box 468, Scarborough ME 04070-0468. Tel: (207) 883-4331 ext. 1014. Fax: (207) 657-2965.

SEARSPORT
Hobby Horse Flea Market

DATES: Friday, Saturday, Sunday and holidays. Every day but Tuesday, when some of the dealers are open anyway.

TIMES: 8:00 AM-5:00 PM.

ADMISSION: Free. Parking is free.

LOCATION: Rt 1, Bangor Rd, 3 miles north of Searsport.

DESCRIPTION: This indoor/outdoor market of 30 dealers sells mostly antiques and collectibles, including coins, old books, plenty of used goods, some furniture, jewelry, crafts, clothing, even Native American stuff from Arizona, gas pumps, cans and auto stuff, as well as a little new merchandise. The dealers are housed in 16 small buildings, one medium and one larger building as well as 40 tables under canopies for the outdoor dealers. There is a lunch wagon on weekends and holidays, as well as a restroom. They have been written up in several papers in Maine.

DEALER RATES: $6 per table. There are 40 tables to choose from. The indoor spaces are rented by the season.

CONTACT: Mary Harriman, Hobby Horse Flea Market, PO Box 215, Stockton Springs ME 04981. Tel: (207) 548-2981. Email: hobbyhcoll@aol.com.

> **Movie Goodies**
> One of the coffins from the film of Stephen King's *Pet Sematary* was sold here, along with other items from the movie set. A local cemetery was used for the shoot.

WOOLWICH
Montsweag Flea Market

DATES: Wednesday, Saturday and Sunday, May through October. Also, Friday, June through August.

TIMES: 6:30 AM-3:00 PM.

ADMISSION: Free. Free parking is available.

LOCATION: On Rt 1 in Woolwich, 5 miles north of Bath.

DESCRIPTION: The promoter tells us that this market, started in 1977, is rated number one in Maine and number three in New England. It is pictured in the book *Coastal Maine, A State of Mind*. There are about 85-100 dealers selling antiques, arts and crafts, fresh produce, collectibles, new merchandise, tools, plants and seedlings, early primitives, and fine jewelry. This market mainly deals with antiques and collectibles. The market is held outdoors and there is food served on the premises.

DEALER RATES: $8 and $10 for 3' × 8' tables, depending on market day. Advance reservations are requested.

CONTACT: Norma Scopino, 6 Hunnewell Ln, Woolwich ME 04579-4852. Tel: (207) 443-2809. Email: fleamkt@gwi.net.

> **Great buys**
> Norma tells of a vinegar cruet bought here for $7 that was later valued at $2500, although sold to another dealer for $1800. A dealer bought a picture at a yard sale for $3 and sold it here for $1500. Then there are the movies made at this location, including *Lonesome* and *Made in Maine*.

OTHER FLEA MARKETS

We know or have heard about these markets, but have not personally contacted each one, as we have the markets with descriptions. If you plan to visit one of the markets listed below, *please call first* to make sure they are still open. Flea markets do come and go. While they were open when we went to press, they may not be later. We can't be responsible. *Call first!*

Augusta: Augusta Flea Market & Crafts, 145 Bangor St. Tel: (207) 621-6353.

Brunswick: Waterfront Flea Market, 14 Maine St. Tel: (207) 729-0378.

Gardiner: West Gardiner Flea Market, 899 Hallowell Litchfield Rd. Tel: (207) 724-3952.

Island Falls: Two Potato Flea & Farmers Market, Rt 159. Tel: (207) 463-3532.

Poland: Evergreen Flea Market, 291 Mechanic Falls Rd. Tel: (207) 345-3521.

Waterboro: Granite Ridge Fleamarket, Rt 202. Tel: (207) 247-5628.

MARYLAND

BALTIMORE

North Point Drive-In Outdoor/Indoor Flea Market

DATES: Every Saturday and Sunday. Rain or shine.

TIMES: 7:00 AM-2:00 PM.

ADMISSION: $.25 per person. Parking for 800 cars is free.

LOCATION: 4001 N Point Blvd. Take the Baltimore Beltway 695, off at Exit 41, bear left, go to the McDonald's; they are across the street on the right.

DESCRIPTION: Started in 1971, this indoor/outdoor market runs year round in a 24,000-square-foot building next to a drive-in theater. It is claimed it's the oldest and one of the largest flea markets in the area. On Saturdays, 150-200 dealers (300 on Sunday) sell antiques, arts and crafts, fresh produce, collectibles, new merchandise, used items, junk, plants, furniture, etc. One snack bar inside, a hot dog stand outside and handicapped-accessible restrooms add to the amenities.

DEALER RATES: $10 on Saturday inside or out, $10 inside per table, $15 per table inside or per space outside on Sundays. Please call for information. Reservations are helpful. Sundays, for $20 the back gate opens at 4:00 AM.

CONTACT: Dottie Stevens, North Point Drive-In Flea Market, 7721 Old Battlegrove Rd, Baltimore MD 21222. Tel: (410) 477-1337.

Patapsco Flea Market

DATES: Saturday and Sunday. Rain or shine.

TIMES: 8:00 AM-5:00 PM.

ADMISSION: $.25. Parking is free.

LOCATION: Corner of 1400 W Patapsco Ave and Annapolis Blvd.

DESCRIPTION: Started in 1982 in a former "strip mall," this market has over 700 dealers indoors (140,000 square feet) and outdoors selling "everything"—a few antiques, new and used merchandise, collectibles, garage sale goodies, and more. They are growing constantly, adding buildings as needed. There are weekly bingo games, an international food court, deli, ice cream parlor, carry-out lunch counters, barbecue pit, hot dog stand, handicapped-accessible restrooms, and more.

DEALER RATES: $10 and up for large outdoor space; $20 and up table space inside; $75 and up for a large store. Reservations are not required. Office and vendor stocking hours are 9:00 AM-2:00 PM Thursday and Friday.

CONTACT: Bob Lomonico, Patapsco Flea Market, 1400 W Patapsco Ave, Baltimore MD 21230. Tel: (410) 354-5262 or 354-3040 or office at 354-3041. Fax: (410) 354-3876.

> **The sign says OFFICE**
> No, the office isn't a bank, nor can you pay other bills up there, nor
> can you buy lottery tickets, nor can you place bets on the horses!
> It's an *office!*

BALTIMORE/DUNDALK
Plaza Flea Market & Pennsylvania Dutch Farmer's Market
DATES: Saturday and Sunday.
TIMES: Saturday 7:00 AM-3:00 PM; Sunday 7:00 AM-4:00 PM.
ADMISSION: Free. Parking is free.
LOCATION: 2401 North Point Blvd, just off Exit 40 of Baltimore Beltway
I-695. Just across the street from the Wal-Mart.
DESCRIPTION: Opened in 1986 as a farmers' market, it grew to the
Plaza Flea Market by 1989, "one of the largest flea markets in Mary-
land." Within their 170,000 square feet are over 600 dealers selling liter-
ally everything, from baby stuff, dolls and doll houses, leather goods,
Avon, toys, tools, coins, sports cards, office supplies, electronics, an-
tiques, clothing, whatever. The amish produce market is in the Farmer's
Market and sells meats, ice cream and pretzels, along with their baked
goods and hot chicken. Heck, they even have a Bingo parlor! Obviously,
there is plenty of food and the market, including the restrooms, is com-
pletely handicapped-accessible.
DEALER RATES: Saturday $10; Sunday $15. Tables come with space
rental. Permanent spaces are $70 and up. Office hours are 9:00 AM-4:00
PM Thursday and Friday or during market hours.
CONTACT: Mike Miller, Brian Miller, or Darlene Miller, Plaza Flea Market, 2401 N Point Blvd, Baltimore MD 21222. Tel: (410) 285-4504. Email:
michael-1949@excite.com. Web: www.plazafleamarket.com.

BETHESDA
Bethesda Flea Market
DATES: Every Sunday, April through November.
TIMES: 8:00 AM-5:00 PM.
ADMISSION: Free. Free parking is available.
LOCATION: Two miles south of I-495 at 7155 Wisconsin Ave in Bethesda
(northwest Washington DC area).
DESCRIPTION: Started in 1932 by 50 farm women to sell their produce
to local Washington residents, the market became the Bethesda Flea Mar-

ket in 1974, with 50 to 60 outside dealers now sell antiques, collectibles, and furniture. Great sales are available at the Montgomery County Farm Women's Market.

DEALER RATES: $15 per 10' × 20' space. Reservations are not required.

CONTACT: James R Bonfils, Bonfils & Associates, 4539 Alton Pl NW, Washington DC 20016. Tel: (202) 966-3303 or for a taped message (301) 652-0100. Web: www.bethesdafleamarket.com.

COLUMBIA
The Columbia Market

DATES: Every Sunday, mid-April through October. Rain or shine. 2002: April 14-October 27.

TIMES: 8:00 AM-3:00 PM.

ADMISSION: Free. Parking is available and is also free.

LOCATION: Between Baltimore and Washington DC. Off I-95, Exit 41 W to Rt 175, at the mall on the JCPenney's side.

DESCRIPTION: This market first opened in 1972. It is held outdoors on the parking decks, but protected from weather, and accommodates up to 300 dealers—200 undercover and 100 in the open. Super Sundays are held the first Sunday of the month and take up all three levels of the parking garage with the open spaces on the top level. Regular Sunday markets are just the bottom level. There is a huge variety of antiques, collectibles, and crafts for sale. Food is available at the mall as well as handicapped-accessible restrooms.

DEALER RATES: Super Sunday: $60 per 16' × 16' space undercover pre-paid, $25 per space unprotected, pre-paid. Regular Sunday: $35 under cover. Call for more rates. Reservations are suggested.

CONTACT: Bellman Promotions Inc, 11959 Philadelphia Rd, Bradshaw MD 21021. Tel: (410) 679-2288. Fax: (410) 679-6919.

ELDERSBURG
Freedom Lions Club Flea Market & Craft Show

DATES: 2002: May 4.

TIMES: 8:00 AM-3:00 PM.

ADMISSION: Free and parking is free.

LOCATION: In Carroll County, 2 miles south of Eldersburg at the Freedom District Fire Company Carnival Grounds. Only 20 minutes NW of Baltimore and about 8 miles north of I-70.

DESCRIPTION: This market is the fundraiser for the Freedom District Lions Club and benefits the Wilmer Eye Institute and Low Vision Research Center at Johns Hopkins Hospital. Among the treasures sold are: antiques, collectibles, baseball cards, homemade dolls, tools, and spring flowers. There is a variety of food to please everyone.

DEALER RATES: $15 for a 24' × 24' space outdoors. Reservations are required.
CONTACT: Ruth Howsden, 6111 Oklahoma Rd, Eldersburg MD 21784. Tel: (410) 795-0984.

FORESTVILLE
Uncle Jack's Flea Market

DATES: Friday through Sunday.
TIMES: Friday and Sunday 12:00 PM-6:00 PM, Saturday 9:00 AM-6:00 PM.
ADMISSION: Free. Parking is free.
LOCATION: 7756 Marlboro Pk. Take the Beltway (I-495), Exit 11B, turn right at the first light, right at the second light, quick left into the Ames Plaza (the Big Apple) shopping center.
DESCRIPTION: This indoor/outdoor market features 35-40 dealers year round selling antiques, collectibles, crafts, coins, stamps, cards, new merchandise and brand-new furniture "at flea market prices." The new furniture section is now a 20,000-square-foot showcase. No food, but handicapped-accessible restrooms are on site.
DEALER RATES: $20 per table. Reservations are not required.
CONTACT: Jack Kalin, Uncle Jack's Flea Market, 7756 Marlboro Pike, Forestville MD 20747-4410. Tel: (301) 736-JACK (5225). Fax: (301) 736-4778.

INDIAN HEAD
Village Green Flea Market

DATES: Saturdays April through October. Rain or shine.
TIMES: 7:00 AM-1:00 PM.
ADMISSION: Free. Parking is also free.
LOCATION: On the Village Green. From out of town take Indian Head Hwy S (formerly known as I-210 S) to the very end. Village Green is located on the right just outside the main entrance to the Naval Surface Warfare Center, off Lackey Dr and Pye St.
DESCRIPTION: Started in 1987 by the Town of Indian Head as a way for local residents to have a flea market and a place to have yard sales, this market usually has about 30-35 dealers and residents selling flea market goods, yard sale items, some new merchandise, wood crafts, and local fresh produce. There are handicapped-accessible restrooms at the site.
DEALER RATES: $7 per space, collected on site. Reservations are not required. Local permit required for food sales (excludes produce). Pet sales/giveaways not permitted. Pre-packaged food sales allowed by permit only.
CONTACT: Town of Indian Head Community Affairs, Attn: Karen L-Williams, 4195 Indian Head Hwy, Indian Head MD 20640. Tel: (301) 753-6633 or (301) 743-5574. Fax: (301) 743-9008.

NORTH EAST
North East Auction Galleries and Flea Market

DATES: Every day. Rain or shine.

TIMES: 8:00 AM-dusk.

ADMISSION: Free. Ample free parking is provided.

LOCATION: Off I-95, on the corner of Rt 40 and Mechanics Valley Rd.

DESCRIPTION: This market has been in operation since 1973, and currently attracts between 50 dealers in winter and 150 in summer who sell a variety of goods, including antiques, collectibles, craft items, new merchandise, auto parts, furniture, household goods, appliances, baseball cards, oriental rugs and fresh produce. The market is located at the head of the picturesque Chesapeake Bay, in a high-traffic area near state parks, marinas, campgrounds, yacht clubs, and other local attractions. In addition, a consignment auction is held every Tuesday evening and an automobile auction is held every Thursday evening. Food is available on the premises, as are handicapped-accessible restrooms.

DEALER RATES: $15 per 8' × 10' table inside; outside tables are $10. Reservations are suggested for inside; outside first come, first served.

CONTACT: R C Burkheimer, North East Auction Galleries, PO Box 551, North East MD 21901-0551. Tel: 1-800-233-4169. In Maryland, call (410) 287-5588. Fax: (410) 287-2029. Email: colonel50@hotmail.com. Web: www.rcburkheimer.com.

RISING SUN
Hunter's Sale Barn, Inc

DATES: Every Monday. Rain or shine.

TIMES: 3:00 PM-9:00 PM, auction at 6:00 PM.

ADMISSION: Free. Free parking is available.

LOCATION: Take Exit 93 off I-95, then go north 2½ miles to a dead end, turn right on Rt 276; market is 2½ miles down on the right.

DESCRIPTION: Originally this business was a livestock market. The flea and farmers' market started in 1975, and the livestock sales stopped in 1985. This indoor/outdoor market has 120 dealers selling antiques, arts and crafts, fresh produce, collectibles, and new merchandise. This is a family oriented market kept clean and very pleasant. In addition, an auction is also conducted at the market at 6:00 PM selling eggs, produce and general merchandise. Monday night is Sale Barn Auction Night for the county. There is a full restaurant on the premises. This is a well-attended market drawing 300-plus people to the auction alone. As a result of a nasty Easter Sunday fire burning down their auction house, they have built a new state-of-the-art heated/air-conditioned 17,500-square-foot building to replace the old one.

DEALER RATES: $15 per 4' × 8' space, $25 for a 16' × 16' space. First come, first served.

CONTACT: Norman E Hunter and Carol A or Ronda L Hunter, PO Box 427, Rising Sun MD 21911. Tel: (410) 658-6400 or fax: (410) 658-3864.

OTHER FLEA MARKETS

We know or have heard about these markets, but have not personally contacted each one, as we have the markets with descriptions. If you plan to visit one of the markets listed below, *please call first* to make sure they are still open. Flea markets do come and go. While they were open when we went to press, they may not be later. We can't be responsible. *Call first!*

Baltimore: One Flea Market, 10 E 21st St. Tel: (410) 837-0200.

Baltimore: Hilltop Indoor Flea Market, 5504 Park Heights Ave. Tel: (410) 578-0002.

Boonsboro: Rt 65 Flea & Farmers Market, 7445 Sharpsburg Pike. Tel: (301) 432-7793.

Boonsboro: Auction Square Flea Market, 7700 Old National Pike. Tel: (301) 416-2788.

Elkridge: Flea Market World, 6675 Amberton Dr. Tel: (410) 796-1025.

Elkridge: US1 Flea Market, 7540 Washington Blvd. Tel: (410) 799-8301.

Emmitsburg: Emmittsburg Flea Market, 17319 N Seton Ave. Tel: (301) 447-2300.

Hagerstown: First Inner-City Flea Market, 13617 Pennsylvania Ave. Tel: (301) 791-6408.

Hagerstown: Treasure Island, 50 E Franklin St # 1. Tel: (301) 745-3244.

Havre De Grace: Bonnie Braie Flea Market, 1301 Pulaski Hwy. Tel: (410) 679-6895.

Hebron: Route 50 Flea Market, 26379 Ocean Gtwy. Tel: (410) 341-7100.

Joppa: Pulaski Flea Market, 12420 Pulaski Hwy. Tel: (410) 679-3206.

Laurel: Teen Challenge of Maryland, 13919 Baltimore Ave # 9. Tel: (301) 604-2400.

Lexington Park: J S Flea Market, 21779 Tulagi Pl. Tel: (301) 866-1900.

St Leonard: Chesapeake Market Place, 5015 Saint Leonard Rd. Tel: (410) 586-3725.

Temple Hills: Market, 6337 Old Branch Ave. Tel: (301) 449-5535.

MASSACHUSETTS

BRIMFIELD

Brimfield always opens the second Tuesday in May, first Tuesdays after July 4 and Labor Day, and runs through the following Sunday. The only exception is when a Jewish holiday falls during the week after Labor Day, when it is pushed back a week.

Brimfield, a small town in Massachusetts, turns into a huge and justly famous antiques- and collectibles-only show three times a year. It has its own website for more information at: www.brimfieldshow.com.

Crystal Brook Antique Show

DATES: 2002: May 14-18, July 9-13, and September 10-14. This market Tuesday through Saturday of the Brimfield show.

TIMES: Literally from dawn Tuesday to 5:00 PM on Saturday.

ADMISSION: Free. However, they don't have any parking area as they are so small.

LOCATION: On Rt 20. Take the Palmer exit off the Massachusetts Tnpk, to Rt 20, then 10 miles east to Brimfield. Or Sturbridge exit on Massachusetts Tnpk, then 10 miles west of Sturbridge on Rt 20.

DESCRIPTION: It is an outdoor market that accommodates approximately 35 dealers. This is considered a relatively small market, but there are many quality antiques and collectibles sold.

DEALER RATES: Call for current rates.

CONTACT: Maureen Ethier, 4 Palmer Rd, Brimfield MA 01010-0354. Tel: (413) 245-7647.

J & J Promotions Antiques and Collectibles Shows

DATES: 2002: May 17-18, July 12-13, and September 13-14. Generally, the same Friday and Saturday of each Brimfield show.

TIMES: Friday 6:00 AM-5:00 PM; Saturday 9:00 AM-5:00 PM.

ADMISSION: Friday $5 per person, Saturday $3. $5 parking fee. Oversized vehicles are $10.

LOCATION: From Boston: take Massachusetts Tnpk west to Exit 9 at Sturbridge; follow Rt 20 west to Brimfield for approximately 7 miles to Auction Acres. From New York City: take I-95 north to I-91 north. Go through Hartford to I-84 east to Sturbridge and Rt 20 west for about 6 miles. Or, I-95 north to I-91 through Hartford to Springfield to I-291 east to I-90 (Massachusetts Tnpk) east to Exit 8 at Palmer, go beyond exit booth and turn right at stop light, then left to Rt 20 east for approximately

6 miles. Look for tan colonial house with red shutters and a big red barn located on southern side of Rt 20.

DESCRIPTION: This outdoor show first opened in 1959. Auction Acres is the home of Gordon Reid's original Antique Market. Now owned by his two daughters, this prestigious property covers 40 acres at the center of Brimfield. Today, antiques and collectibles enthusiasts from all over the world continue to visit this famous market. Dealers and exhibitors alike have, year after year, relied on the experience and quality in the organization and presentation of these shows of antiques and collectibles. A "fully-featured food pavilion with dining area and 24-hour service" is on site along with handicapped-accessible restrooms and portable potties around the site.

DEALER RATES: Space size and prices vary. Please call for more information.

CONTACT: Jill Reid Lukesh and Judith Reid Mathieu, J & J Promotions, Auction Acres, PO Box 385, Brimfield MA 01010-0385. Tel: (413) 245-3436 or (978) 597-8155. Email: info@jandj-brimfield.com. Web: www.jandj-brimfield.com.

For Sale
One Push-Me-Pull-You from Dr Doolittle fame.

Angus, Where Are You?
During one market, Angus went missing. This little white male dog got "lost" at the market and his prim Scottish owner put out a $500 reward for his safe return. Reports came flying in from all corners of tiny Brimfield that Angus was seen with this female dog, then that one, then another—*for 2½ days!* All the time, she, the owner, would wail in her brogue, that "wee Angus wouldn't be doing *that*." Naturally, the market personnel were frantically trying to deal with the market while trying to help alleviate Mommy Angus' worst fears.

Looking for the reward, streams of people came in with dogs on leashes, none of which fitted Angus's tiny white-bodied description. To top that off, there is a no-pets and animals policy here, for fairly obvious reasons.

Finally, Angus wandered back to Mama, looking extremely worse for wear—filthy, mud-spattered, lumpy coat—just awful looking. "Ah, me Angus," brogued Mommy, "Angus had a *dirrrrty* weekend."

Now, when things go awry at Brimfield, it's known as an "Angus" day.

New England Motel Antiques Market, Inc

DATES: This market operates Wednesday through Sunday of Brimfield week. 2002: May 15-19, July 9-14, September 11-15.

TIMES: Wednesday opening days 6:00 AM-dusk; other days, 8:00 AM to dusk.

ADMISSION: $5, opening day only. Parking is $5.

LOCATION: Rt 20, Palmer Rd in the center of the Mart.

DESCRIPTION: This show started in 1986 and is said "to have the finest and freshest merchandise in the Brimfield's." About 400 reputable dealers from the United States, Canada and Europe sell quality antiques and collectibles in the center of the Northeast's greatest outdoor show. A pavilion houses 24 of their finest dealers. There is a huge food court on the premises and handicapped-accessible restrooms.

DEALER RATES: $250 for a 20' × 24' booth. Reservations are required. Parking is also available. There are camping facilities, and this is located on the grounds of a motel, if you are lucky enough to get a room.

CONTACT: Marie Doldoorian, PO Box 186, Sturbridge MA 01566. Tel: (508) 347-2179. Fax: (508) 347-3784. Day of show call: (413) 245-3348. Email: kikdanjo@aol.com or info@antiques-brimfield.com. Web: www.antiques-brimfield.com.

Shelton Antique Shows

DATES: 2002: May 14-19, July 9-14, and September 10-15. 2003: May 8-13, July 10-15, September 4-9. This market is open for the entire Brimfield show.

TIMES: Daybreak on.

LOCATION: 34 Main St aka Rt 20 (aka Palmer Rd). Between Exit 9 Sturbridge or Exit 8 Palmer off Massachusetts Tnpk. Exit Sturbridge Rt 86 from Connecticut.

ADMISSION: Free. Parking is $4-6 a day.

DESCRIPTION: This market started in 1975 and is located on 1-mile strip of the largest outdoor antique event in the United States. Approximately 175 dealers sell antiques and collectibles. There are dealer showers, food service, and table rentals available. Pets are welcome.

DEALER RATES: From $250 per 20' × 20' booth. Reservations are required. One-day rates offered after opening day.

CONTACT: Lois J Shelton, PO Box 124, Brimfield MA 01010-0124. Tel: (413) 245-3591. Fax: (413) 245-7905. Email: sheltons@prodigy.net.

> **Weird**
> An antique hearse was sold here after a hot bidding war. It was the only item brought in by the dealer.

CHARLETON

Charleton Antique and Flea Market, Inc

DATES: Every Sunday indoors and outdoors, year round. Rain or shine. April through November, Saturdays outdoors, weather permitting.

TIMES: Saturday 7:00 AM-3:00 PM. Sunday 7:00 AM-4:00 PM.

ADMISSION: Saturdays free; Sundays, adults $.50; children under 12 free.

LOCATION: 90 Worcester Rd, Rt 20, Trolley Crossing, at the junctions of Rts 20 and 31. From the east: I-290 or I-395, Exit 7A or I-90 Exit 10, to Rt 20 W 8 miles. From the west: I-90 Exit 9 to Rt 20 E 9 miles to Rt 31 S.

DESCRIPTION: This indoor/outdoor market has been open since 1975 and recently moved to this location from Auburn with many of the same dealers. It accommodates approximately 100 dealers indoors, and 75-plus dealers outdoors and in new kiosk-style sheds. Many items such as antiques, arts and crafts, collectibles, new merchandise, and even fresh produce can be found. Many dealers also sell a variety of stamps, coins, and baseball cards. One snack bar feeds the wilting; there are handicapped-accessible restrooms on site.

DEALER RATES: $30 per 9' × 9' space, indoors, with 1 free table. $20 per space outdoors on Sundays, $15 on Saturdays—with 1 free table. Additional tables are $3 each. Reservations are required for indoor space. Weekly storage space, 15' × 22' is available. Kiosk-style sheds rent for $45 per weekend.

CONTACT: Charleton Antique & Flea Market, 90 Worcester Rd, Charleton MA 01507. Tel: (508) 248-5690.

> **Just try it!**
> A dealer came in trying to flog a tombstone he had purchased at a garage sale. It was a great tombstone, very clear names and dates, in great condition. Only trouble was, it's against the law to sell them. It was confiscated by the police, who came to the market to do so!

EAST DOUGLAS

Douglas Flea Market, Antiques, and Collectibles

DATES: Saturday, Sunday and Monday holidays.

TIMES: Saturday 10:00 AM-4:00 PM; Sunday 8:00 AM-4:00 PM; Monday holidays 10:00 AM-2:00 PM.

ADMISSION: Free. Parking is free.

LOCATION: Northeast Main St. From Providence or Worcester: take Rt 146 to Rt 16, and follow the State's Blue Attraction signs #146 and #16.

DESCRIPTION: This indoor/outdoor market is housed in an historic dairy barn on 50 acres. Dealer tables replace the cows and the silo houses the Snack Bar serving all homemade foods including breakfast, snacks and

meals. They have added a new tea room and tavern serving beer and wine. Furniture is sold in the hayloft. Other treasures sold include antiques, memorabilia, glassware, antique toys, country goods, cards, and garage sale goodies. Handicapped-accessible restrooms add to the amenities of this unique and friendly market.

On Columbus Day weekend, they hold an outdoor Antique/Collectible show with an appraiser on site, charging $2 per item appraised. The appraiser also comes the first Sunday of each winter month, December through April.

DEALER RATES: Outside: $2 per car length, with table $5. Inside: $10 per week. Reservations are required for inside only.

CONTACT: Marlene Bosma, PO Box 634, E Douglas MA 01516. Tel: (508) 278-6027 or weekends at (508) 476-3298. Email: mabcob@gis.net. Web: www.douglasfleamarket.com.

GRAFTON
Grafton Flea Market, Inc

DATES: Every Sunday. Rain or shine.

TIMES: 6:00 AM-4:00 PM.

ADMISSION: $.50 for an adult, children free. Free parking is available.

LOCATION: On Rt 140 near the Grafton-Upton town line. Take the Massachusetts Tnpk to Rt 495 south, then take Upton Exit 21B to Rt 140.

DESCRIPTION: This show first opened in 1970. There are approximately 300 dealers attending this market, which is held both indoors and outdoors. A variety of items such as antiques, collectibles, arts and crafts, new merchandise, and fresh produce can be found. There is also a selection of baseball cards, stamps, and coins. There is catered food available on the premises.

DEALER RATES: $20 per space, outdoors. $30 per space, indoors. Reservations are required for indoor space only.

CONTACT: Harry Peters, PO Box 206, Grafton MA 01519-0206. Tel: (508) 839-2217.

HADLEY
Olde Hadley Flea Market

DATES: Every Sunday from the third Sunday in April through the first Sunday in November, weather permitting.

TIMES: 6:00 AM-4:00 PM.

ADMISSION: Free. Free parking is available.

LOCATION: On Rt 47 S, Lawrence Plain Rd. Take Exit 19 off Rt 91 north. Or, take Exit 20 off Rt 91 south. Follow Rt 9 east to center of Hadley, then 2 miles south on Rt 47.

DESCRIPTION: This show opened in 1980. There are 200-plus dealers selling their goods at this outdoor market. There is everything from antiques and collectibles, from new merchandise to fresh produce sold here including maple sugar, honey and plants. Excellent catered food is available on the premises. This flea market has a beautiful country setting at the foot of the Mount Holyoke Range. Special features of this flea market include antique auto viewing and the Silver Eagle Hot Air Balloon lift-off. There is also the Old Hadley Museum, Skinner State Park, Mitch's Marina, as well as shopping malls and many fine restaurants nearby. Do say "Hi" to Ray and his border collie, Jessie, as they travel around the market in his golf cart.

DEALER RATES: $20 per 25' × 25' space. Reservations are not required. First come, first served. There are advance shopping hours for dealers starting at 6:00 AM. Gates open Saturday at 3:00 PM so dealers can stay overnight. Bring a flashlight!

CONTACT: Raymond and Marion Szala, 45 Lawrence Plain Rd, Hadley MA 01035. Tel: (413) 586-0352.

Know your goods!
A sterling silver compote purchased here for $75 was sold on eBay for $8300. Just a slight profit!

HUBBARDSTON
Rietta Ranch Flea Market

DATES: Sundays, April through October. Rain or shine.
TIMES: 7:00 AM-til.
ADMISSION: Free admission and free parking.
LOCATION: On Rt 68.
DESCRIPTION: Opened in 1967, this market attracts 600 dealers who offer antiques, collectibles, handmade/craft items, vegetables, and new merchandise. They offer a full concession with indoor and outdoor dining offering fried dough, hamburgers, hot dogs, and they even have a liquor license. Plenty of handicapped-accessible restrooms and 20 acres of parking make this an easy place to spend the day. They are in the process of restoring a complete antique train with a 1915 steam engine for display.
DEALER RATES: Dealers are charged $15 for outside space about the size of a large car, including one table. $15 for two tables on the inside. First come, first served or reserve for the season only.
CONTACT: Raylene, Rietta Ranch Flea Market, PO Box 35, Hubbardston MA 01452-0035. Tel: (978) 632-0559.

LEOMINSTER
Four Seasons Flea Market

DATES: Saturday and Sunday.

TIMES: 9:00 AM-4:00 PM.

ADMISSION: Free. Parking is free.

LOCATION: 38 Spruce St. Only minutes from Rt 2, I-190 and Rt 12 and Rt 13 off Mechanic St just 2 blocks from the center of town.

DESCRIPTION: Opened in 1994, this indoor market of 30 dealers in summer (vacation time, doncha know) and 80-90 dealers in winter (now, we're down to business!) sells antiques, collectibles, coins, stamps, cards, garage sale goodies, furniture, and new merchandise. The ratio is considered 30% old to 70% new. The snack bar also has handicapped-accessible restrooms to add to the amenities.

DEALER RATES: $25 per 10' × 6' space per weekend. Reservations are suggested. There are special rates for multiple spaces.

CONTACT: Joe Sans, Four Seasons Flea Market, 38 Spruce St, Leominster MA 01453-3233. Tel: (978) 534-3890 or 1-800-926-9997.

RAYNHAM
Raynham Flea Mart

DATES: Every Sunday, and Saturdays Thanksgiving through Christmas.

TIMES: 8:00 AM-6:00 PM.

ADMISSION: $1 adults, $.50 for seniors. Free parking is available.

LOCATION: At junction of Rt 24 and Rt 44.

DESCRIPTION: This show began in 1974. There are 500 dealers indoors in a 60,000-square-foot one-story building and over 400 dealers outdoors on 10 acres of land. This market screens its dealers to ensure variety and quality of items. These include antiques, arts and crafts, collectibles, jewelry, new merchandise, fresh produce and more. There are six snack bars, a full restaurant, handicapped-accessible restrooms and parking for thousands of cars.

DEALER RATES: Outside $25 and up per space, inside $35 and up. Call for rates, as they vary according to location and size. Reservations are recommended.

CONTACT: J Mann, Raynham Flea Market, Judson and South St, Raynham MA 02767. Tel: (508) 823-8923. Email: raynhmflea@aol.com. Web: www.raynhamflea.com.

ROWLEY
Todd Farm Famous Old-Fashioned Flea Market

DATES: Sundays, mid-April through the Sunday preceding Thanksgiving.

TIMES: 5:00 AM to whenever. Flashlights welcome.

ADMISSION: Free. Parking is free.

LOCATION: Rt 1A. I-95 Exit 54, go east on Rt 133. Then north on Rt 1A 1 mile.

DESCRIPTION: This classic flea market, opened in 1973, features up to 240 dealers, depending on the month, selling mostly antiques, collectibles, and especially furniture. There are a number of antique shops in the barn and at the farmhouse. One snack bar inside and one out. Restrooms are available.

DEALER RATES: $30 per generous 30' × 20' space per day. First come, first served.

CONTACT: Todd Farm, PO Box 342, Rowley MA 01969-0342. Tel: (978) 948-3300. Email: toddfarm@toddfarm.com. Web: www.toddfarm.com.

> One year a dealer came and laid in a circle the contents of a late dentist's lab. There were all those nasty little picks and scrapers— as well as some false teeth and stuff. The little picks and tools went quickly, as they are great for furniture restorers to get into those hard-to-reach places. Just like our teeth!

TAUNTON
Taunton Expo Center Flea Market

DATES: Saturday and Sunday, plus some holiday Mondays.

TIMES: Saturday 8:00 AM-4:00 PM, Sunday 7:00 AM-5:00 PM.

ADMISSION: $1 per adult. Parking is free.

LOCATION: Mill River Place Mall, 1 Washington St, in the center of Taunton.

DESCRIPTION: Opened under management and enlarged in 1987, the entire market burned to the ground on September 15, 2001. The outdoor market remained open to the end of the season. Happily, it is reopening indoors at this new location. This market attracts 500-800 dealers selling antiques, collectibles, crafts, jewelry, clothing, coins, fresh produce, seafood, furniture, garage sale goodies, and new merchandise. There are plenty of food outlets as well as handicapped-accessible restrooms on site.

DEALER RATES: Outside: $30 per weekend. Inside: $250 and up monthly. Reservations are required for inside space, not for outside.

CONTACT: Armand Gagne, Taunton Expo Center Flea Market, PO Box 68, Taunton MA 02780-0068. Tel: (508) 880-3800. Fax: (508) 880-5100.

WELLFLEET
Wellfleet Drive-In Flea Market

DATES: Every Saturday, Sunday and holiday Mondays, April through October. Also open every Wednesday and Thursday during July and August. Rain or shine.

TIMES: 8:00 AM-4:00 PM.

ADMISSION: $2 per carload Saturday, Sunday and Wednesday. $1 per carload Thursday and off-season Saturdays.

LOCATION: On Rt 6 towards Provincetown, on Wellfleet-Eastham line. Once you are on Cape Cod, just follow the road to Provincetown.

DESCRIPTION: This show started about 30 years ago in the Cape Cod National Seashore at Wellfleet. They have 26 acres of family entertainment. Depending upon the season, there can be anywhere from 50 to 250 dealers at this outdoor market. They specialize in antiques, collectibles, furniture and new merchandise. There are also arts and crafts vendors, artists, and anything else that is legal. For your convenience, food is available on the premises. The owners of this market pride themselves on running a very clean market with a very fine reputation.

DEALER RATES: $20 per 18' × 22' space. Reservations are not required.

CONTACT: Eleanor Hazen, Wellfleet Drive-In Flea Market, PO Box 811, Wellfleet MA 02667-0811. Tel: (508) 349-0541 or in Eastern MA 1-800-696-3532. Fax: (508) 349-2902.

> **Just for the record:**
> All you connoisseurs of fine music and instruments: a Stradivarius violin was found here! Obviously, the dealer didn't know what he had.
>
> Eleanor reports that many of her vendors who had tried eBay are selling better here and have given up on eBay to boot!

OTHER FLEA MARKETS

We know or have heard about these markets, but have not personally contacted each one, as we have the markets with descriptions. If you plan to visit one of the markets listed below, *please call first* to make sure they are still open. Flea markets do come and go. While they were open when we went to press, they may not be later. We can't be responsible. *Call first!*

Chicopee: Pioneer Valley Flea Market, 725 Meadow St. Tel: (413) 592-0188.
Dracut: Dracut Flea Market, 1 Mill St. Tel: (978) 957-4242.
Lawrence: Jolly Flea, 73 Winthrop Ave. Tel: (978) 682-2020.
Leominster: Four Seasons Flea Market, 38 Spruce St. Tel: (978) 534-3890.
Newburyport: Oldies Marketplace, 27 Water St. Tel: (978) 465-0643.
North Oxford: Oxford Flea Market, Rt 20 & Hwy 56. Tel: (508) 987-5098.
Peabody: Peabody Flea Market, 26 Howley St. Tel: (978) 531-1902.
Revere: Revere Flea Market, 565 Squire Rd. Tel: (781) 289-7100.
Springfield: Flea Market, 946 Worthington St. Tel: (413) 732-9168.
Stoughton: Stoughton Flea Market, 1202 Washington St. Tel: (781) 341-9714.
Worcester: Kelley Square Flea Market, 149 Washington St. Tel: (508) 755-9040.

MICHIGAN

ARMADA
Armada Flea Market

DATES: Tuesday and Sunday, mid-April through October.

TIMES: 6:00 AM-2:00 PM, or total exhaustion, whichever comes first.

ADMISSION: Free. Parking is free.

LOCATION: 25381 Armada Ridge Rd. Take M97 (Groesbeck Hwy aka North Ave) north to Village of Armada. Turn right at the four-way stop; they are approximately 1 mile down the road.

DESCRIPTION: Started in a stockyard in the 1940s, this outdoor market gradually became a flea market in the 1960s. Depending on the weather, they will have up to 300 dealers selling mostly antiques and collectibles, a few crafts, produce in season and some new merchandise. There is a snack bar when the munchies hit, and handicapped-accessible restrooms when needed.

DEALER RATES: Tuesday $10 and up for a single space, $15 and up for a double space. Sunday $15 and up. And no, they don't take reservations. Just come on down!

CONTACT: Armada Flea Market, PO Box 525, Armada MI 48005-0525. Tel: (586) 784-9604.

Interesting Visitors

There is a couple from Florida who come up and sing a bit of country western and gospel at the market. It started when their car broke down several years ago.

Pamela Anderson came here to visit Kid Rock, then came down to visit the market.

CENTREVILLE
Centreville Antiques Market

DATES: Held five times each summer. May through August and October. Call for exact dates.

TIMES: 7:00 AM-3:00 PM.

ADMISSION: $4. Handicapped-accessible parking is available.

LOCATION: At St Joseph's County Fairgrounds on M-86. In the heart of Michigan's Amish area, halfway between Chicago and Detroit, 150 miles from either city.

DESCRIPTION: This show opened in 1973. It is both an indoor and outdoor market that accommodates approximately 500 dealers. This show is limited to antiques, fine art, and select collectibles. There is also plenty of food available on the premises. This show provides a chance to "slip back in time and visit a part of small-town America." One can stroll around the 174 acres on the fairgrounds and recheck the merchandise, or walk to the fence near the viewing stand and watch a driver take a practice run around the track. This show is well thought out and well planned. Although this is a rather large market, Robert Lawler, the show manager, has done his very best to maintain a cozy, family like environment.

DEALER RATES: $80 per 25' × 25' space. Inside space for $75 for 10' × 10' space. Reservations are required.

CONTACT: Robert C Lawler, Show Manager, 1510 N Hoyne, Chicago IL 60622-1804. Tel: (773) 227-4464. Email: cvl@antiquemarkets.com. Web: www.antiquemarkets.com. (Watch that you get the address correctly, there are several other web addresses that are similar.)

COPEMISH
Copemish Flea Market and Auction

DATES: Every Friday, Saturday and Sunday from May through October.

TIMES: 9:00 AM-6:00 PM.

ADMISSION: Free. Parking is free.

LOCATION: On M-115, 10 miles west of Mesick on M-115, 10 miles east of Benzie and US 31 on M-115.

DESCRIPTION: Started in 1940, this outdoor market of 25 dealers sells antiques, collectibles, crafts, produce, coins, stamps, cards, garage sale goodies, furniture, and new merchandise. One snack bar and handicapped-accessible restrooms complete the amenities. There is a Dollar Store open daily on the premises.

DEALER RATES: $7 per day for a 20' × 25' space, or $15 per week. First come, first served. Reservations are available.

CONTACT: Attn: Sally, Copemish Flea Market and Auction, PO Box 116, Copemish MI 49625-0116. Tel: (231) 378-2430. Fax: (231) 378-2430.

FLAT ROCK
Flat Rock Historical Society Antique and Flea Market

DATES: First Sundays in May and October. Rain or shine.

TIMES: 7:00 AM-4:00 PM.

ADMISSION: Free. Parking is free.

LOCATION: At the Flat Rock Speedway, 1 mile south of Flat Rock on Telegraph Rd.

DESCRIPTION: This outdoor market opened in 1973 and accommodates about 250 dealers. There are a variety of antiques, arts and crafts, and collectibles. The money from this show is used to support the Flat Rock Historical Society Museum. Food is served on the premises.

DEALER RATES: $35 for a 20' × 20' space. Reservations are not required.

CONTACT: Flat Rock Historical Society, PO Box 337, Flat Rock MI 48134-0337. Tel: (734) 782-5220.

LEXINGTON
Lexington Harbor Bazaar

DATES: Saturday and Sunday.

TIMES: 10:00 AM-6:00 PM.

ADMISSION: Free. Parking is free.

LOCATION: 5590 Main St, 2 blocks south of stop light on US 25 (Main St).

DESCRIPTION: Open since 1987, this indoor market of about 50 dealers sells only antiques and collectibles. Auctions are held about every four to six weeks. They also sell online, if you hit their website. Handicapped-accessible restrooms add to the amenities.

DEALER RATES: $27 per booth per week. Reservations are required.

CONTACT: Main Office, Lexington Harbor Bazaar, 5590 Main St, Lexington MI 48450. Tel: (810) 359-5333 from 10:00 AM-5:00 PM daily. Fax: (810) 359-5333. Email: bazaar@tias.com. Web: www.harborbazaar.com.

MT CLEMENS
Gibraltar Trade Center North

DATES: Friday through Sunday, year round.

TIMES: Friday 12:00 PM-9:00 PM, Saturday 10:00 AM-9:00 PM, Sunday 10:00 AM-6:00 PM.

ADMISSION: $2 a carload.

LOCATION: I-94 to Exit 237 N River Rd, go 1 mile down on right-hand side.

DESCRIPTION: Opened in 1990, this market has 1,200 dealer spaces and 250,000 square feet of selling space indoors. Only new merchandise is sold indoors, "everything from A to Z" literally. Dealers also sell through special shows: Sports Cards, Sportsman, Computer, Antiques, Home Improvement, Boat & Fishing, Arts and Crafts, etc. Watch for the ads with the listing as to what show is on for the weekend. There is plenty of food available in snack bars and restaurants, and clean, handicapped-accessible restrooms.

DEALER RATES: Starting at $78 for a 12' × 6' space, $88.50-$125 for 12' × 8' space, and up depending on size of booth and location. Outdoors, April through October only, for a 10' × 8' booth under canopy: to sell new merchandise spaces are $10 a day; used items, produce, plants, antiques or collectibles—$5 per day.

CONTACT: Gibraltar Trade Center North Inc, 237 N River Rd, Mt Clemens MI 48043. Tel: (586) 465-6440. Fax: (586) 465-0458. Email: mtclemens@gibraltartrade.com. Web: www.GibraltarTrade.com.

MUSKEGON
Golden Token Flea Market

DATES: Saturdays.

TIMES: 6:00 AM-2:00 PM.

ADMISSION: Free. Parking is also free.

LOCATION: 1300 E Laketon Ave, 1 block west of US 31 on Laketon Ave.

DESCRIPTION: Started in 1985, this growing market of about 75 dealers fills two rooms selling whatever—from antiques and collectibles to whatever comes in. In summer the market is held outside; it moves inside the first weekend in October. Breakfast, fountain sodas, hot dogs to shrimp dinner, are available on the premises, making the handicapped-accessible restrooms welcome.

DEALER RATES: $5-$6 per table. Reservations are not required, but can be made. Yearly rates are available. There is plenty of room!

CONTACT: Golden Token, 1300 E Laketon Ave, Muskegon MI 49442. Tel: (231) 773-1137. Fax: (231) 722-4646. Email: mummum56@hotmail.com.

Muskegon Flea Market

DATES: Wednesdays, mid-May through mid-October.

TIMES: 5:00 AM-3:00 PM.

ADMISSION: Free. Parking is free.

LOCATION: Seaway Dr at Eastern Ave, ½ mile north of downtown Muskegon; take US 31 Business N/Seaway Dr to Eastern Ave.

DESCRIPTION: This outdoor market of 300 dealers started in 1965. Antiques, collectibles, produce, cards, garage sale finds, ethnic clothing and music as well as new merchandise is sold. Two snack bars and handicapped-accessible restrooms add to the amenities. When Cheri comes around, say Hi for me!

DEALER RATES: $7 per 10' × 15' covered space; $6 per 10' × 30' asphalt space; $5 per 10' × 40' field space. Overflow area is available if usual space is filled. Reservations are required for specific spaces only, but encouraged. Otherwise first come, first served and they will tap you for the fees.

CONTACT: Cheri Burdick, Manager, c/o City of Muskegon, 933 Terrace St, Muskegon MI 49443. Tel: (231) 722-3251.

Select Auditorium Flea Market

DATES: Saturday, year round.

TIMES: 6:00 AM-2:00 PM.

ADMISSION: Free. Parking is free.

LOCATION: 1445 East Laketon Ave. At US 31 and Laketon Exit; easy on and off crossway.

DESCRIPTION: Opened in 1975, this indoor/outdoor market of 75-100 dealers sells antiques, collectibles, crafts, coins, stamps, cards, garage sale finds, some furniture, new merchandise and bingo supplies. They hold bingo games after the market. One snack bar and handicapped-accessible restrooms add to the amenities. The market is held outdoors in summer, indoors in winter.

DEALER RATES: $6 for 2 parking spaces outdoors, or $7 per 4' × 8' table inside. Reservations are required for inside only.

CONTACT: Terry Durham, Select Auditorium, 1445 E Laketon Ave, Muskegon MI 49442. Tel: (231) 726-5707.

PAW PAW
Reits Flea Market

DATES: Saturdays, Sundays and summer holidays, from April through October. Rain or shine.

TIMES: 8:00 AM-4:00 PM.

ADMISSION: Free. Free parking is available.

LOCATION: Five miles west of Paw Paw on Red Arrow Hwy, Exit 56 off I-94.

DESCRIPTION: This outdoor market opened in 1965 and currently accommodates approximately 500 dealers. There are many garage sale items along with antiques, toys, tools, household items, jewelry, collectibles, art, and much more. Corey says that about 75% of the goods are old. This is a clean and well-managed family market with events all summer long, including a wine feast. One full-service restaurant and two concession stands, the Pavilion and the Rest Stop, provide breakfast all day (rather famous for their "Southern omelets with home-made gravy") and lunches, as well as handicapped-accessible restrooms.

DEALER RATES: $12 per 22' × 20' space per day, outdoors. Reservations are not required. New dealers welcome. Dealers can spend the night on the premises; this is a licensed campground. Electric will be available soon.

CONTACT: Corey Sinkovics and Bob Hixenbaugh, Reits Flea Market, 45146 Red Arrow Hwy, Paw Paw MI 49079. Tel: (616) 657-3428. Web: www.reitsfleamarket.com

PIERSON
B & K Storage and Flea Market

DATES: Saturday and Sunday, May through October.

TIMES: 8:30 AM-3:00 PM.

ADMISSION: Free. Parking is free.

LOCATION: 4833 Maple Hill Rd. 131 Hwy, north of Grand Rapids to Exit 114 (Cannonsville Rd), turn right to Federal Rd, turn left, go 1½ mile to Kendaville Rd, turn left and go to the first road on the left, Maple Hill Rd.

DESCRIPTION: This indoor/outdoor market of 3 dealers started in 1996 selling antiques, collectibles, crafts, coins, cards, garage sale goodies, books (old and collectible), Hot Wheels, clothing, good used furniture, general household, home decorating items and new merchandise. No food, but there are restrooms available.

DEALER RATES: $10 per 12' × 16' space per day. Reservations are suggested.

CONTACT: Karon Miesiaczek, B & K Storage & Flea Market, 4833 Maple Hill Rd, Pierson MI 49339-9504. Tel: (231) 937-9255 or 937-9256. Email: bkflea@pathwaynet.com.

Lost and Found Again

An elderly woman haunted the market for three weeks looking for a specific book from her childhood. There was a poem in the book she couldn't remember completely. On her third visit, the book was located. With her new treasure, she stood in front of the building and recited the entire poem. Many shoppers stopped to listen to her recitation. She told her audience that "this was the best thing that had happened to her."

She hasn't been seen since.

SAGINAW
Giant Public Market

DATES: Friday, Saturday and Sunday.

TIMES: Saturday 10:00 AM-7:00 PM; Sunday 10:00 AM-6:00 PM.

ADMISSION: Free. Parking is free.

LOCATION: 3435 Sheridan Ave, I-75 exit 144B, then right onto State St, then left onto Williamson, then right about 3 miles to the market.

DESCRIPTION: This market averages 80 to 100 indoor dealers selling antiques, collectibles, new furniture, tools, sports, electronics, games, clothing, garage sale goodies, and new merchandise. Their snack bar makes one heck of a burrito; the handicapped-accessible restrooms could come in handy.

DEALER RATES: $36 weekend for 100 square feet. No reservations taken.

CONTACT: Marie or Ken, Giant Public Market, 3435 Sheridan Ave, Saginaw MI 48601-4458. Tel: (517) 754-9090. Fax: (517) 754-7465.

TAYLOR
Gibraltar Trade Center

DATES: Friday through Sunday, year round.

TIMES: Friday 12:00 PM-9:00 PM, Saturday 10:00 AM-9:00 PM, Sunday 10:00 AM-6:00 PM.

ADMISSION: $2 a carload.

LOCATION: I-75 and Eureka Rd (Exit 36).

DESCRIPTION: Opened in 1980, this market has 1,200 dealer spaces (occupied by 500 or so dealers) and 50,000 square feet of selling space indoors. Regular dealers sell mostly new merchandise, clothes, electronics, shoes, leather goods, and so forth. There are special shows every weekend: Sports Cards, Antiques, Home Improvement, Boat & Fishing, Arts and Crafts, etc. There is plenty of food available in snack bars and restaurants, and clean, handicapped-accessible restrooms.

DEALER RATES: Starting at $80 and up depending on size and location. Outdoors for a 10' × 8' booth under canopy April through October only: to sell new merchandise spaces are $15 a day—no used items can be sold outside anymore.

CONTACT: Gibraltar Trade Center Inc, 15525 Racho Rd, Taylor MI 48180-5213. Tel: (734) 287-2000. Fax: (734) 287-8330. Email: showtlr@gibraltartrade.com. Web: www.GibraltarTrade.com.

WARREN
Country Fair Flea Market

DATES: Every Friday, Saturday and Sunday, year round.

TIMES: Friday 4:00 PM-9:00 PM, Saturday and Sunday 10:00 AM-6:00 PM.

ADMISSION: Free. Parking is also free.

LOCATION: 20900 Dequindre Blvd, 2 blocks north of Eight Mile Rd.

DESCRIPTION: This indoor show began in 1978 and currently has about 300 dealers exhibiting antiques, collectibles, produce, sports memorabilia, crafts, new merchandise, 14-carat gold and silver jewelry, leather, Amish furniture, Hush-Puppy shoes, and brass items. One snack bar and handicapped-accessible restrooms add to the amenities. A good portion of the market is antiques housed in Antique Village. Their dealers take great pride in their merchandise.

DEALER RATES: $63 per 5' × 10' space per weekend or $123 for a double-size space. Reservations are suggested.

CONTACT: Mike and Katie Holland, Country Fair Flea Market, 20900 Dequindre, Warren MI 48091. Tel: (586) 757-3740 or 757-3741. Fax: (586) 757-3742.

Zeb's Michigan Flea Market

DATES: Friday through Sunday.

TIMES: Friday 4:00 PM-9:00 PM, Saturday 10:00 AM-9:00 PM, Sunday 10:00 AM-6:00 PM.

ADMISSION: Free. Parking is free.

LOCATION: 24100 Groesbeck Hwy. Just 1½ miles east of I-696.

DESCRIPTION: Opened 15 years ago and now under new management, this market of 35 dealers sells antiques, collectibles, crafts, coins, stamps, cards, garage sale goodies, furniture, and new merchandise. One snack bar feeds the famished, and handicapped-accessible restrooms come in handy.

DEALER RATES: $45 per 8' × 8' space. Reservations are not required.

CONTACT: Zeb's Michigan Flea Market, 24100 Groesbeck Hwy, Warren MI 48089-4716. Tel: (586) 771-3535.

WATERFORD
Dixieland Flea Market

DATES: Friday, Saturday, and Sunday.

TIMES: Friday 4:00 PM-9:00 PM; Saturday and Sunday 10:00 AM-6:00 PM.

ADMISSION: Free. Parking is free.

LOCATION: On corner of Dixie Hwy and Telegraph Rd.

DESCRIPTION: It is nice to discover a market that hangs on to local color. Since 1975 and under its present ownership since 1986 this indoor/outdoor market has over 200 dealers selling antiques, collectibles, jewelry, glassware, new and used merchandise. It has been described as being like a giant outdoor garage sale in summer with 20-100 dealers. Four restaurants (Pizza, Coney Island, Mexican and Chinese) across the back of the market create a small food court, making the handicapped-accessible restrooms a necessary visit.

DEALER RATES: $50 and up for inside space. Reservations are required inside. Outdoors is $20 per day per 15' x 18' space.

CONTACT: Dixieland Flea Market, 2045 Dixie Hwy, Waterford MI 48328. Tel: (248) 338-3220. Fax: (248) 338-3221.

OTHER FLEA MARKETS

We know or have heard about these markets, but have not personally contacted each one, as we have the markets with descriptions. If you plan to visit one of the markets listed below, *please call first* to make sure they are still open. Flea markets do come and go. While they were open when we went to press, they may not be later. We can't be responsible. *Call first!*

Benton Harbor: Rosaiah Flea Market, 1220 M 139. Tel: (616) 926-4048.

Cheboygan: Treasure Hunt Flea Market, 405 Duncan Ave. Tel: (231) 627-6080.

Cheboygan: Treasure Hunt Flea Market, 10917 N Straits Hwy. Tel: (231) 627-2092.

Detroit: American Flea Market, 11500 E 8 Mile Rd. Tel: (313) 371-2130.

Detroit: Metro Flea Market, 6665 W Vernor Hwy. Tel: (313) 841-4890.

Detroit: Piquette Trade Ctr Flea Market, 285 Piquette St. Tel: (313) 875-5531.

Fort Gratiot: Wurzel's Flea Market, 4189 Keewahdin Rd. Tel: (810) 385-4283.

Grayling: Ernie's Flea Market, M 72 W. Tel: (989) 348-5695.

Harrison: Parkview Flea Market, 3033 N Clare Ave. Tel: (989) 539-3507.

Holland: Unique Flea Market, 5970 136th Ave. Tel: (616) 399-1982.

Lansing: Flea Market, 2016 E Michigan Ave. Tel: (517) 372-5356.

Lansing: Jackie's I-69 Super Flea, 5555 Lansing Rd. Tel: (517) 645-7700.

Milan: Milan Flea Market, 11204 Ann Arbor Rd. Tel: (734) 439-4901.

Mio: Mio Flea Market, 317 S Mount Tom Rd. Tel: (989) 826-8822.

Newaygo: Newaygo Flea Market, 8566 Mason Dr. Tel: (231) 652-2114.

Niles: Downtown Flea Market, 115 E Main St. Tel: (616) 684-2866.

Pinconning: Bargain Barn, 300 N Huron Rd. Tel: (989) 879-2873.

Portage: Mary's Flea Market, 8139 Portage Rd. Tel: (616) 324-4056.

Potterville: Bob's Flea Market, 214 W Main St. Tel: (517) 645-2270.

Ravenna: Sullivan Flea Market & Auction, 11851 Heights Ravenna Rd. Tel: (231) 853-2435.

Romulus: Greenlawn Grove Flea Market, 16447 Middlebelt Rd. Tel: (734) 941-6930.

Royal Oak: Royal Oak Farmers Market, 316 E 11 Mile Rd. Tel: (248) 548-8822.

Saginaw: Saginaw Trade Ctr Inc, 2885 Bay Rd. Tel: (989) 498-8000.

Warren: Van Dyke Flea Market, 23524 Van Dyke Ave. Tel: (810) 757-5883.

Warren: Warren Community Trade Ctr, 2300 E 10 Mile Rd. Tel: (810) 756-7660.

MINNESOTA

ANNANDALE
Wright County Swap Meet

DATES: Saturday, from the first Saturday in April until the last of October.
TIMES: 8:00 AM-2:00 PM.
ADMISSION: Free. Parking is free.
LOCATION: 13594 100th St NW. Annandale-West Hwy 55, go 3 miles, turn north on County Rd 136, go 1¾ miles, turn east on 100th St, go ¼ miles to market.

DESCRIPTION: Located in the small town of Annandale near lots of lakes, this outdoor, fresh-air market of 150 dealers sells antiques, collectibles, crafts, produce, coins, stamps, cards, garage sale goodies, furniture, and new merchandise. One restaurant and three snack bars feed the famished and there are handicapped-accessible restrooms, just in case.

DEALER RATES: $12 per 30' × 20' space. First come, first served.
CONTACT: Gladys Miller, Wright County Swap Meet, 13594 100 St NW, South Haven MN 55382-3327. Tel: (320) 274-9005 or 274-8071.

DETROIT LAKES
Shady Hollow Flea Market

DATES: Sundays from Memorial Day to the Sunday after Labor Day. Three-day shows Saturday through Monday on Memorial Day and Labor Day weekends. Two-day show near July 4.
TIMES: 7:00 AM-5:00 PM.
ADMISSION: Free. Parking is free.
LOCATION: On Hwy 59, 5 miles south of Detroit Lakes.

DESCRIPTION: Started in 1970, this outdoor market averages 75-100 dealers selling antiques, collectibles, furniture, junk, crafts, produce, cards, and coins. Eighteen cabins are rented for entire season by dealers. Several lunch wagons serve the market.
DEALER RATES: $15 and up, depending on size. Reservations are not taken.
CONTACT: Ardis Hanson or Monte Jones, Shady Hollow Flea Market, 1760 E Shore Dr, Detroit Lakes MN 56501. Tel: (218) 847-9488 (Hanson) or 847-5706 (Jones).

Talk About Success!

Years ago, a one-shot-a-year vendor called early on in the season to request her special, coveted shady spot for Labor Day Sunday. She arrived early with a loaded truck and set up.

Around 8:00 AM she came to the market managers asking for her money back, as she had sold out and was leaving!

DULUTH
31ˢᵗ Annual Studebaker Drivers Club
Swap Meet, Flea Market and Classic Car Show

DATES: Annually, the second Sunday in August. Rain or shine.

TIMES: 8:00 AM-4:00 PM.

ADMISSION: $2 per person, children under 12 and seniors (65 and older) free. $2 parking per car.

LOCATION: Lake Superior College, 2101 Trinity Rd, 2 miles south of Miller Hill Mall.

DESCRIPTION: This show opened in 1972. It is both an indoor and outdoor market that accommodates anywhere from 35 spaces inside to 200 spaces outside. You can buy anything from antiques and collectibles to junk, coins, gifts, crafts, glass, hobbies and new merchandise. Many old and restored antique cars are on display for the Car Show (200 cars). There are also old car parts for all makes and models on sale. Food is served on the premises. There is a car corral with usually 50 cars for sale.

DEALER RATES: $10 per 10' × 20' space outdoors; $10 per 10' × 10' space indoors. Reservations are recommended. There are advance shopping hours for dealers on the Saturday before the show.

CONTACT: North Land Wheels Chapter, PO Box 1004, Duluth MN 558101004. Tel: (218) 722-8533, 722-4855, or 624-5932.

HINCKLEY
Hinckley Flea Market

DATES: Thursday through Sunday, May through the first weekend in October.

TIMES: 8:30 AM-6:00 PM.

ADMISSION: Free. Parking is free.

LOCATION: Just west of Grand Casino Hinckley. Take 35W north to Hinckley Exit 183. Take a right on Hwy 48. The market is located on the left side of the road about ½ mile down the road.

DESCRIPTION: This market is an indoor and outdoor summer market with 35 or so dealers inside and more outside (depending on the weather!) selling antiques, collectibles, crafts, furniture, cards, garage sale stuff, clothes, and new merchandise. There are food wagons on the premises, as well as handicapped-accessible restrooms.

DEALER RATES: Outside: $10 per 10' × 15' space with 1 table per day; inside $38-$51 per 10' × 15' space with 1 table. Reservations are not required, but do get discounts.

CONTACT: Gus Afrooz, Hinckley Flea Market, 803 Hwy 48, Hinckley MN 55037. Tel: (763) 754-3200, (320) 384-9911 or 1-888-442-2042. Fax: (320) 384-6589.

> **Wedding Bells**
> Two young people working at the market met here, fell in love here, and decided that here was the place to hold their wedding. They did marry here—holding a "shotgun wedding" with their vendor friends dressed in hillbilly attire and their poodle acting as ringbearer.

ORONOCO
Downtown Oronoco Gold Rush, Inc

DATES: Third Saturday and Sunday in August. Rain or shine.

TIMES: Sunup to sundown.

ADMISSION: Free. Parking is also free. The town provides free outlying parking with bus transportation into town. Parking costs you in town.

LOCATION: The entire downtown Oronoco!

DESCRIPTION: Started in 1972, the entire town participates in this weekend-long flea market. The main street is closed off to traffic and over 1,500 dealers set up selling antiques, collectibles, flea market goodies, crafts, unfound and refound treasures; as one organizer says "if they don't have it here in those two days, you can't find it!" Some residents sell right out of their garages. Over 40,000 people come through here each day. The money raised is used to help the City of Oronoco finance their First Response system, the fire department, plant new trees, fix the community center, fireworks for July 4 and whatever else is needed. Ample food is available.

DEALER RATES: $60 per 15' × 15' space for the weekend. Reservations are required. Many spaces are reserved well in advance.

CONTACT: Oronoco Gold Rush, PO Box 266, Oronoco MN 55960-0266. Tel: (507) 367-4405 City Clerk's Office. Fax: (507) 367-4982.

PARK RAPIDS
Summerset Market

DATES: Thursdays from Memorial Day to Labor Day.

TIMES: 7:00 AM-4:00 PM.

ADMISSION: Free. Parking is free.

LOCATION: 3 miles east of Park Rapids on Hwy 34.

DESCRIPTION: Opened in 1972, this neat, clean, and friendly market of 50 or so dealers (depending on the weather) sells antiques, garage sale goodies, collectibles, crafts, and some new merchandise. There is a snack bar selling the usual fare. Restrooms are available.

DEALER RATES: $10 per 16' × 22' space per day. Reservations are not needed.

CONTACT: Summerset Market, 17770 State 34, Park Rapids MN 56470. Tel: (218) 732-5570. Email: denment@wcta.net.

WABASHA
Wabasha Indoor/Outdoor Flea Market

DATES: Saturday and Sunday, year round.

TIMES: 9:00 AM-5:00 PM.

ADMISSION: Free. Parking is also free.

LOCATION: Hwy 61 and Industrial Ct.

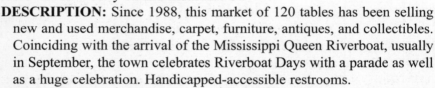

DESCRIPTION: Since 1988, this market of 120 tables has been selling new and used merchandise, carpet, furniture, antiques, and collectibles. Coinciding with the arrival of the Mississippi Queen Riverboat, usually in September, the town celebrates Riverboat Days with a parade as well as a huge celebration. Handicapped-accessible restrooms.

DEALER RATES: $10-$12.50 per table. Reservations are required.

CONTACT: Doc Carlson, Wabasha Indoor/Outdoor Flea Market, PO Box 230, Wabasha MN 55981-0230. Tel: (651) 565-4767.

OTHER FLEA MARKETS

We know or have heard about these markets, but have not personally contacted each one, as we have the markets with descriptions. If you plan to visit one of the markets listed below, *please call first* to make sure they are still open. Flea markets do come and go. While they were open when we went to press, they may not be later. We can't be responsible. *Call first!*

Park Rapids: Country Flea Market, Hwy 34 E. Tel: (218) 732-5570.

Rochester: 21st Century Flea Market, 2130 S Broadway. Tel: (507) 287-8373.

South Haven: Wright County Swapper's Meet, 13594 100th St NW. Tel: (320) 274-9005.

MISSISSIPPI

JACKSON
Fairgrounds Antique Flea Market

DATES: Saturday and Sunday, year round.

TIMES: Saturday 8:00 AM-5:00 PM; Sunday 10:00 AM-5:00 PM.

ADMISSION: $1 per person. Free parking.

LOCATION: 900 High St. Take High St exit off I-55 to 890 Mississippi St at the State Fairgrounds. In the big "steel building."

DESCRIPTION: This indoor flea market is in its 17th year and has over 200 dealers in antiques, collectibles, crafts, produce, and new merchandise. There are also some primitives and books. This is a very well-rounded flea market. A little bit of everything, but about 60% antiques and collectibles. A complete concession provides food on the premises and there is a concession area with handicapped-accessible restrooms. Camper electrical hookups are available.

DEALER RATES: $40 for a wall booth, $50 for an aisle booth, $5 each for tables. Reservations are required one week in advance only.

CONTACT: Frank Barnett, Fairgrounds Antique Flea Market, PO Box 23579, Jackson MS 39225. Tel: (601) 353-5327.

Birthday Surprise

Years ago, a young man was celebrating his 21st birthday with two buddies at the market. Each gave him a present, but he had to guess what was in the box before he was allowed to open it.

As the presenter of the first box handed his over, the birthday boy guessed candy as the dad had a candy store. He was right.

As the second box was handed over, the birthday boy shook it gently, knowing this pal's dad owned a liquor store. Liquid dripped out the bottom, and guessing it was vodka, the kid licked it. No, said the giftor, it's not vodka, try again.

Another wee shake, more liquid, another lick. Champagne! Wrong again.

It was a puppy.

MCNEIL
McNeil Flea Market

DATES: Friday through Sunday.

TIMES: 8:00 AM to dark.

ADMISSION: Free. Parking is free.

LOCATION: 2 Cemetery Rd, on Hwy 11 and Cemetery Rd. Only 70 miles from New Orleans.

DESCRIPTION: This little market of 25 dealers, housed in a garage and in the parking lot, offers antiques, collectibles, garage sale goodies, and used stuff. This is quite a weekend adventure for the collectors from New Orleans who come here for the treasures. There are snacks available on site as well as handicapped-accessible restrooms.

DEALER RATES: $10 per table either under shelter or in the parking lot, per day.

CONTACT: McNeil Flea Market, 212 Larow Dr, McNeil MS 39426. Tel: (601) 798-0350.

PHILADELPHIA
Williamsville Flea Market

DATES: Friday and Saturday. Rain or shine.

TIMES: 6:00 AM-6:00 PM.

ADMISSION: Free. Parking is free.

LOCATION: 10031 Rd 606. Located at the intersection of Hwy 15 and Hwy 16, across from McDonald's and Key West Inn. Just 5 miles from the Silverstar Casino.

DESCRIPTION: This outdoor market averages 35 dealers selling antiques, collectibles, crafts, produce, furniture, garage sale goodies, tools, clothes, Indian jewelry and baskets, rugs and new merchandise. There is a concession stand and restrooms. The best months to visit are July and August as the last weeks of July celebrate the Choctaw Indian Fair and the first week in August is the Neshoba County Fair. Apparently, the entire town shuts down to attend this fair with concerts every night, horse races, a rodeo, beauty pageant, and the flea market.

DEALER RATES: $8 per 10' × 10' space, or several little 10' × 10' buildings, some with space in front from $135 per month. First-come, first served.

CONTACT: Lee Harris or Tom McCullough, Williamsville Flea Market, 10031 Rd 606, Philadelphia MS 39350-8601. Tel/fax: (601) 656-8428.

RIPLEY
Ripley First Monday Flea Market and Trade Day

DATES: Saturday and Sunday preceding the first Monday of each month.

TIMES: Dawn to dusk.

ADMISSION: Free. $2 parking fee.
LOCATION: 10590 Hwy 15 S, On Hwy 15, 65 miles from Memphis and 45 miles from Tupelo.
DESCRIPTION: This outdoor market has operated since 1893, ranking it among the nation's most venerable. Drawing in 30,000 shoppers monthly and accommodating an average of 500 dealers over 50 acres, there is everything from antiques, collectibles, fresh produce, and new merchandise to a variety of crafts and reproduction oak furniture available. Food, from corn dogs to catfish, is served on the premises. There are handicapped-accessible restrooms as well.
DEALER RATES: $25 for a 18' × 18' booth, $40 for a covered spot. Reservations are suggested.
CONTACT: Wayne or Betty Windham, Ripley First Monday Trade Days, 10590 Hwy 15 S, Ripley MS 38663. Tel: 1-800-4-RIPLEY Monday through Friday, (662) 837-4051 or 837-7442. Fax: (662) 837-7080. Email: hww@dixie-net.com. Web: www.firstmonday.com.

TUPELO
Tupelo's Gigantic Flea Market

DATES: Friday, Saturday and Sunday, the second full weekend of the month, except February and August.
TIMES: Friday evening 6:00 PM-9:00 PM, Saturday 9:00 AM-7:00 PM, Sunday 10:00 AM-5:00 PM.
ADMISSION: $1 per person, under 12 free. Parking is free.
LOCATION: Tupelo Furniture Market Buildings I & II at 1879 N Coley Rd.
DESCRIPTION: Started in 1992, this market hosts over 800 dealers selling "everything" (they all say that, and usually mean it!), from antiques and collectibles, to new merchandise. From high-end to low-end—it's all here. Housed in two large heated and cooled buildings with outside spaces as well. Concession stands feed the famished.
DEALER RATES: $65 for the full 3-day weekend. Spaces are 9' × 11'. Reservations are preferred.
CONTACT: Tupelo's Gigantic Flea Market, 1879 N Coley Rd, Tupelo MS 38801. Tel: (662) 842-4442. Fax: (662) 844-3665. Email: fleamarket@tupelomarket.com.

Old Story
It is said that a picture and frame were sold for $5 at an auction in Mississippi. The new owner took the picture and frame to another auction and sold it for $115 and thought he did real well! The savvy New York buyer took it back to New York and reportedly she sold it for over $50,000.

OTHER FLEA MARKETS

We know or have heard about these markets, but have not personally contacted each one, as we have the markets with descriptions. If you plan to visit one of the markets listed below, *please call first* to make sure they are still open. Flea markets do come and go. While they were open when we went to press, they may not be later. We can't be responsible. *Call first!*

Amory: 41 Flea Market, 30025 Hwy 41 W. Tel: (662) 837-5453.
Bogue Chitto: Tucker's Flea Market, 743 Hwy 51 SE. Tel: (601) 833-1802.
Booneville: Booneville Indoor Flea Market, 406 Adams St. Tel: (662) 720-1200.
Canton: Canton Flea Market Inc, 3332 N Liberty St. Tel: (601) 859-8055.
Carthage: Pearl River Flea Market, 1037 Hwy 35 S. Tel: (601) 267-4140.
Florence: Magnolia Flea Market, 3965 Hwy 49 S. Tel: (601).845-4655.
Foxworth: Flea Mart, 1767 Hwy 98 W. Tel: (601) 731-5892.
Hattiesburg: 49 Flea Market, 19 Dewitt Carter Rd. Tel: (601) 583-4554.
Hurley: Hurley Flea Market, 8510 Hwy 614. Tel: (228) 588-6766.
Laurel: Calhoun Flea Market, 5035 Hwy 84 W. Tel: (601) 649-0462.
Lucedale: Tri County Flea Market, Hwy 98 E. Tel: (601) 947-9699.
Lucedale: Commerce Street Flea Market, 194 Commerce St. Tel: (601) 766-9941.
McComb: Georgia Avenue Flea Market, 205 E Georgia Ave. Tel: (601) 684-0633.
McComb: Mc Comb Flea Market Inc, 131 N Front St. Tel: (601) 249-0290.
Meridian: Carol's Flea Market, 2604 State Blvd. Tel: (601) 693-0760.
Natchez: Main Street Market Place, 613 Main St. Tel: (601) 445-8479.
Natchez: Washington Flea Market, 445 Morgantown Rd. Tel: (601) 445-9365.
New Albany: New Albany Flea Market, 510 W Bankhead St. Tel: (662) 534-0380.
Poplarville: Deep South Flea Market, 3838 Hwy 26 W. Tel: (601) 772-9764.
Prentiss: Virginia's Flea Markets, 2303 Columbia Ave. Tel: (601) 792-5110.
Quitman: Desoto Flea Market, 341 Cty Rd 690. Tel: (601) 776-2224.
Seminary: Country Trading Post, 1087 Hwy 49. Tel: (601) 722-9432.
Shannon: Shannon Flea Market, 5954 Hwy 145. Tel: (662)767-9050.
Sumrall: Flea Market, 920 Hwy 42. Tel: (601) 758-4154.
Sumrall: Lake Serene Flea Market, 95 Piney Woods Ln. Tel: (601) 268-7888.

MISSOURI

COLONY
Colony #1 Flea Market

DATES: First and second weekends of every month from March through October, and the first weekend in November.

TIMES: Daylight.

ADMISSION: Free. Parking is free.

LOCATION: Rt V off Rt K, 1½ miles northwest of town. In the NE corner of Knox County. The closest "big" town is Kirksville about 35 miles west.

DESCRIPTION: This 20-year-old market (the one with the row of flags in front, aka the second largest flea market in the area) boasts about 170 dealers hogging 300 spaces selling antiques, collectibles, some crafts, garage sale goodies, tools, trinkets, the occasional hedgehog or other livestock (big and little), produce, fresh baked goods, and new merchandise. They hold auctions on Friday nights at 7:00 PM. There is a snack vendor and restrooms at the market.

DEALER RATES: $15 per 20' × 30' space per weekend, $7 extra for electricity. There are hot showers and water available for vendors hanging around. Thursday is setup day. First come, first served.

CONTACT: Danny or Dawnetta White, Colony Flea Market, RR1 Box 64A, Rutledge MO 63563. Tel: (660) 434-5504. Email: ddwhite@marktwain.net.

FARMINGTON
Farmington Flea Market

DATES: Friday through Sunday.

TIMES: 8:00 AM-4:00 PM.

ADMISSION: Free. Parking is free.

LOCATION: Hwy 67, 1 mile north of Farmington.

DESCRIPTION: This indoor/outdoor market has been operating about 17 years and recently moved from the fairgrounds to this location next to an antique mall. There are two buildings housing mostly permanent dealers (there is a waiting list), but outside has plenty of space. The 80-100 dealers sell antiques, collectibles, crafts, new and used furniture, books, new merchandise, pottery, tools, household items and garage sale goodies. Snacks are sold on the premises, and there are handicapped-accessible restrooms.

DEALER RATES: $3 per day outside, $120 and up for inside 26' × 10' when available. Reservations are a must inside (that waiting list!) but not outside.

CONTACT: Farmington Flea Market, 4618 US Hwy 67, Farmington MO 63640. Tel: (573) 756-1691.

JOPLIN
Joplin Flea Market

DATES: Every Saturday and Sunday, year round. Rain or shine.

TIMES: 8:00 AM–5:00 PM.

ADMISSION: Free admission and free parking.

LOCATION: 1200 block of Virginia Ave in the Old City Market; 1 block east of 12th and Main Sts.

DESCRIPTION: Started in 1977, this indoor/outdoor market comprises 200 dealers selling all kinds of curios and antiques. There are crafts, collectibles, new and used merchandise, produce, meats and cheeses, primitives, stamps and coins, tools, jewelry, clothing, postcards, and the list goes on. An entire city block, indoors, of flea market space has grown behind this market with new heating units to keep the dealers warm year round. They added another shed with roof in 1996. There is a snack bar and handicapped-accessible restrooms.

DEALER RATES: Call for reasonable rates on 10' × 18' space per day outside with parking space by booth or 9' × 20' space inside. There are open butler sheds with asphalt paving, and open space for dealers with their own canopies. Free storage for the following week is provided for inside dealers with advance payment. Reservations are suggested.

CONTACT: Laverne Miller, Joplin Flea Market, 2572 Markwardt Ave, Joplin MO 64801. Tel: (417) 623-3743.

A Tad of History
This market was built in the 1930s for the City of Joplin by the WPA to house their produce market. It was the largest watermelon distribution center in the entire United States, with trucks parked all around it awaiting their turn. Laverne Miller purchased the property from the city in 1977 to open the area's first flea market. She has since bought up much of the property around here to enlarge her flea market, upgrading the area in the process.

PEVELY
The Big Pevely Flea Market

DATES: Every Saturday and Sunday, year round. Rain or shine.

TIMES: 8:00 AM–5:00 PM.

ADMISSION: Free admission and free parking.

LOCATION: 8773 Commercial Blvd. Take I-55 south from St Louis to Exit 180. Take a left at the bottom of the ramp, go to the third stoplight and turn right for ¼ mile to market.

DESCRIPTION: This indoor/outdoor market opened in 1969 in an old drive-in theater. Over the years they have added two buildings housing about 200 dealers each. Altogether, their 500 to 600 dealers in 750 spaces sell antiques, collectibles, crafts, cards, clothing, garage sale goodies, vegetables, plants, and new merchandise. Building 1 now houses a furniture and bedding outlet. Snack bars serve the hungry, including their "famous farmer's breakfast" and freshly made hamburgers, and in the summer, there's entertainment on the patio. Outdoor vendors are under cover. Building 2 is now a Flea Market Mall open daily where the market sells for the vendors. Just in case, there is an ATM machine on site.

DEALER RATES: Outside $12 per 10' × 20' per day, covered spaces an additional $5 per day. Inside: $18 per 5' × 12' single space, $40 for an end-cap double space. Reservations are requested indoors. Outdoor space can be reserved, or is allocated on a first-come, first-served basis. At the Mall: call for rates, the market does the selling. Open every Friday from 8:00 AM-6:00 PM. Overnight camping for dealers on Friday and Saturday nights only; shower facilities available.

CONTACT: The Big Pevely Flea Market, PO Box 419, Pevely MO 63070-0419. Tel: (636) 479-5400 or 475-3215. Fax: (636) 479-7680. Email: pevelyfleamkt@jcn1.com. Web: www.pevelyfleamarket.com. NFMA

SAINT LOUIS
Frison Flea Market

DATES: Every Friday, Saturday and Sunday.

TIMES: 9:00 AM-5:00 PM.

ADMISSION: $1. Parking is free.

LOCATION: 7025 St Charles Rock Rd. Next door to the Metro Link at Rock Rd Station.

DESCRIPTION: Open since 1982, this market has 370 spaces filled with dealers selling some antiques and collectibles, and lots of clothing, jewelry, appliances, and plenty of new merchandise. There is a snack bar, a produce stand, and handicapped-accessible restrooms.

DEALER RATES: $15 per 10' × 10' space with out-of-town vendors getting preference. First come, first served.

CONTACT: Frison Indoor Flea Market Inc, 7025 St Charles Rock Rd, St Louis MO 63133. Tel: (314) 727-0460 or pager (314) 582-0446.

Recent History
To build this Metro Link, the government took away two acres of their parking lot. At least it is convenient!

SIKESTON
Tradewinds Flea Market

DATES: Every Friday through Sunday, rain or shine.

TIMES: All day.

ADMISSION: Free. Free parking is available.

LOCATION: 875 W Malone. Sikeston is 150 miles south of St Louis, 150 miles north of North Memphis.

DESCRIPTION: This indoor/outdoor market opened in 1974 and now accommodates approximately 300 dealers. There is everything here from antiques and collectibles to arts and crafts to new merchandise. Tools, toys, fresh produce, as well as chickens, turkeys, guinea pigs, and rabbits are available. The Tradewinds Restaurant is in the middle of the market. This market has been growing steadily since it began, as more and more dealers are coming from all over the United States to sell their goods.

DEALER RATES: $7 per space, per day; Sundays are free. Reservations are first come, first served.

CONTACT: Tradewinds Flea Market, 875 W Malone, Sikeston MO 63801. Call the Tradewinds Restaurant at (573) 471-3965.

SPRINGFIELD
I-44 Swap Meet

DATES: Saturday and Sunday, March through November, rain or shine.

TIMES: Daylight to dark.

ADMISSION: $1 per car admission and parking.

LOCATION: 2600 E Kearney at Neergard, across from the Bass Pro plant. Then ½ mile north on Neergard.

DESCRIPTION: "Sooner or later it's out there, if you want it." Started in 1984, this swap meet has from 200 to 300 dealers selling everything! It is on 30 acres right along I-44. Live bands and 5 snack bars liven things up. Free camping on Friday and weekends.

DEALER RATES: For a 30' × 20' space: $8 on Saturday; $10 Sundays. First come, first served.

CONTACT: Butch Koonce or Bob Nelson, 2743 W Kearney, Springfield MO 65803. Tel: (417) 866-7493 (Butch) or (417) 833-2728 or (417) 864-6508 (office).

OTHER FLEA MARKETS

We know or have heard about these markets, but have not personally contacted each one, as we have the markets with descriptions. If you plan to visit one of the markets listed below, *please call first* to make sure they are still open. Flea markets do come and go. While they were open when we went to press, they may not be later. We can't be responsible. *Call first!*

Aldrich: Oak Forrest Flea Market, 5299 Hwy 123. Tel: (417) 694-3046.

Anderson: Anderson Main Street Flea Market, 111 Main St. Tel: (417) 845-7383.

Appleton City: K & J Flea Market, RR 1 Box 136. Tel: (417) 876-3084.

Aurora: Houn' Dawg Flea Market, 16 W Olive St. Tel: (417) 678-4555.

Aurora: Madison Place Flea Market, 330 S Madison Ave. Tel: (417) 678-6307.

Barnhart: Kohler City Flea Market, 7045 US Hwy 61/67. Tel: (636) 464-2322.

Bertrand: Bertrand Flea Market, Hwy 62 W. Tel: (573) 683-6345.

Bolivar: Downtown Flea Markets, 110 W Jackson St. Tel: (417) 777-2288.

Bolivar: Hidden Treasures Flea Market, 3100 S Morrisville Rd. Tel: (417) 326-4499.

Bolivar: Super Flea Market, 2869 W Broadway St. Tel: (417) 326-6360.

Bowling Green: 3-G Flea Market, 224 W Main St. Tel: (573) 324-2929..

Branson: Branson Heights Flea Market, 1139 W State Hwy 76. Tel: (417) 335-3165.

Branson: Cadwell's Downtown Flea Market, 114 E Main St. Tel: (417) 334-5051.

Branson: Coffelt Country Flea Market, 675 State Hwy 165. Tel: (417) 334-7611.

Buffalo: Heaven's Tears Flea Market, 118 N Ash St,. Tel: (417) 345-7068.

Buffalo: Country Folk Flea Market, 1047 Blaine Dr. Tel: (417) 345-7778.

Butler: Hummingbird Flea Market, RR 5 Box 30. Tel: (660) 679-6016.

Cabool: Cabool Flea Market, 711 Roberts St. Tel: (417) 962-4258.

Cainsville: Flea Market, 1108 Enterprise St. Tel: (660) 893-5354.

Cape Girardeau: Doris' Flea Market, 631 Good Hope St. Tel: (573) 651-1665.

Carl Junction: Carl Junction Flea Market, 118 S Main St. Tel: (417) 649-7131.

Cassville: Highway 112 Flea Market, RR 2. Tel: (417) 847-5778.

Cassville: Hilltop Flea Market, RR 4 Box 4450. Tel: (417) 847-3029.

Centralia: Hobby Horse Flea Market, 105 W Hwy 22. Tel: (573) 682-3311.

Columbia: Ice Chalet Flea Market, 3411 Old 63 S. Tel: (573) 449-5596.

Crane: Another Darn Flea Market, 208 N Main. Tel: (417) 723-5404.

Cuba: Seller's Flea Market, RR 2 Box 2542. Tel: (573) 732-4106.

De Soto: Redfield's Flea Market, 500 S Main St. Tel: (636) 586-3456.

Doniphan: Sue's Poorboy Fleamarket, RR 8 Box 6808. Tel: (573) 996-4086.

Farmington: Farmington Flea Market, 4602 US Hwy 67. Tel: (573) 756-1967.

Farmington: Farmington Outdoor Flea Market, 4618 US Hwy 67. Tel: (573) 756-1691.

Fredericktown: Cherokee Pass Frontier Market, 6696 Hwy 67. Tel: (573) 783-7700.

Fredericktown: M & M Flea Market, 3103 E Hwy 72. Tel: (573) 783-8474.

Fulton: E T's Flea Market, 512 E 8th St. Tel: (573) 642-5571.

Goodman: Kelly Springs Flea Market, S 71 Hwy. Tel: (417) 364-7799.

Goodman: Ole Yeller Barn Flea Market, 21009 Gateway Dr. Tel: (417) 364-7227.

Granby: Granby Flea Market, 799 W Valley St. Tel: (417) 472-3532.

Greenfield: K & P Flea Market, 13 N Allison Ave. Tel: (417) 637-2207.

Greenville: Poor Boys Flea Market, 127 Front St. Tel: (573) 224-5272.

Hayti: Quinn's Flea Market, 305 E Washington St. Tel: (573) 359-2565.

Hermitage: Hermitage Flea Market, W Hwy 54. Tel: (417) 745-2200.

Highlandville: Eagle's Nest Flea Market, 6922 US Hwy 160 S. Tel: (417) 443-7710.

Houston: Indian Creek Flea Market, 16280 Indian Creek Trl. Tel: (417) 967-5355.

Hunnewell: Stone's Family Auction Barn, 8951 Hwy 36. Tel: (573) 983-2228.

Imperial: Barnhart Flea Market, 6850 US Hwy 61/67. Tel: (636) 464-5503.

Independence: KC Flea Market, 4545 S Noland Rd. Tel: (816) 478-7007.

Joplin: Kentucky Street Flea Market, 315 Commercial Aly. Tel: (417) 624-8810.

Kansas City: Adrienne's Midtown Flea Mkt, 3308 Troost Ave. Tel: (816) 561-3532.

Kansas City: Super Flea, 6200 Saint John Ave. Tel: (816) 241-5049.

Kansas City: Westport Flea Market & Bar, 817 Westport Rd. Tel: (816) 931-1986.

Kennett: W W Flea Market, 804 Independence Ave. Tel: (573) 888-0078.

Kimberling City: Flea Country, 11966 Hwy 13. Tel: (417) 739-5505.

Knob Noster: Big Hubba's Flea Market, 95 NE D Hwy. Tel: (660) 563-3639.

Lincoln: E & W Flea Market, 138 E Main St. Tel: (660) 547-2322.

Macon: Colonel Flea Market, 304 S Missouri St. Tel: (660) 385-2497.

Madison: Serendipity Antique Flea Mrkt, 112 W Broadway St. Tel: (660) 291-8777.

Malden: Randy's Flea Market, 105 S Madison St. Tel: (573) 276-2111.

Malden: This N That Flea Market, 132 S Madison St. Tel: (573) 276-2166.

Malden: Downtown Flea Market, 100 E Main St. Tel: (573) 276-3141.

Miller: Minnie's Flea Market, 201 S Gilmore St. Tel: (417) 452-3313.

Mountain Grove: Hills Flea Market, Bus Hwy 60. Tel: (417) 926-7525.

Mountain View: East Side Flea Market. Tel: (417) 934-6997.

Mountain View: Red Barn Flea Market, 500 E 7th St. Tel: (417) 934-5606.

Neelyville: Tink's Cotton Patch Flea Market, Rt 5. Tel: (573) 989-4076.

Neosho: Plew's Flea Market, Hwy 175. Tel: (417) 451-1053.

Neosho: South Elwood Flea Market, RR 5. Tel: (417) 451-5140.

Oak Grove: Oak Grove Flea Market, 1120 S Broadway St. Tel: (816) 625-7595.

Osage Beach: Osage Beach Flea Market, 965 Hwy 42. Tel: (573) 348-5454.

Osage Beach: Village Flea Market, 1071 Main St # A. Tel: (573) 348-5616.

Ozark: Ozark Flea Market, 905 W Jackson St. Tel: (417) 581-8544.

Ozark: Riverview Plaza Flea Market, 1025 N 10th Ave. Tel: (417) 581-3080.

Pineville: Pineville Flea Market, Main St. Tel: (417) 223-7473.

Poplar Bluff: Bluff City Trade Fair, 902 S Hwy 53. Tel: (573) 686-9968.

Poplar Bluff: Country Junction Flea Market, Hwy 67 S. Tel: (573) 686-2275.

Poplar Bluff: Doug's Flea Market, 522 N G Street. Tel: (573) 686-3606.

Poplar Bluff: Fifth Street Flea Market, 1712 S Broadway St. Tel: (573) 686-5852.

Poplar Bluff: Flea Market, 1020 S Broadway St. Tel: (573) 686-8490.

Poplar Bluff: Jordan's Lake Road Flea Market, Hwy 60 & T. Tel: (573) 686-4542.

Republic: West County Flea Market, 4896 S Douglas Dr. Tel: (417) 732-8415.

Rocky Comfort: Highway 76 Flea Market, Hwy 76. Tel: (417) 652-3681.

Rolla: I-44 Flea Market. Tel: (573) 762-3532.

Seligman: Tom's Flea Market, Hwy 37. Tel: (417) 662-3205.

Sikeston: Sikeston Trade Fair Flea Market, 330 State Route H. Tel: (573) 472-9964.

Sikeston: Sikeston Trade Center Flea Market, 2022 E Malone Ave. Tel: (573) 472-9933.

South West City: Chicken Coop Flea Market. Tel: (417) 762-3311.

Springfield: Country Corner Flea Market, 351 N Boonville Ave. Tel: (417) 862-1597.

Springfield: Ferguson Flea Market, 7327 E Farm Road 132. Tel: (417) 863-6699.

Springfield: Frisco Flea Market, 1601 W Division St. Tel: (417) 862-1510.

Springfield: Frisco Flea Market II, 3000 W Chestnut Expy. Tel: (417) 869-2148.

Springfield: M J Flea Market, 208 E Commercial St. Tel: (417) 831-9441.

Springfield: Park Central Flea Market, 429 N Boonville Ave. Tel: (417) 831-7516.

Springfield: Scenic Hill Flea Market, 605 S Scenic Ave,. Tel: (417) 865-1800.

Springfield: STD Flea Market, 505 E Trafficway St. Tel: (417) 831-9110.

Springfield: STD Flea Market, 651 S Kansas Ave. Tel: (417) 831-6331.

Springfield: STD Storage & Flea Market, 1820 E Trafficway St. Tel: (417) 831-6367.

St Louis: A & P Super Flea, 6104 Page Blvd. Tel: (314) 721-6693.

St Louis: Bel-Ridge Flea Market, 8943 Natural Bridge Rd. Tel: (314) 426-7848.

St Louis: Big Top Flea Market, 9971 Lewis and Clark Blvd. Tel: (314) 388-3943.

St Louis: Lou's Flea Market, 8919 Natural Bridge Rd. Tel: (314) 423-6335.

Stockton: Indian Treasure Flea Market, 303 State Hwy 32 W. Tel: (417) 276-2050.

Sullivan: Attic Flea Market, 24 Taylor St. Tel: (573) 468-5800.

Sullivan: Main Street Flea Market, 12 W Main St. Tel: (573) 468-4555.

Troy: Gateway Frontier Flea Market, 23 N Star. Tel: (636) 528-0816.

Ulman: Ulman Flea Market, 360 Hwy C. Tel: (573) 369-2730.

Union: Mason Dixon Line Flea Market, I-44 & 50. Tel: (636) 583-2014.

Van Buren: Riverways Flea Market, Main and Oliver. Tel: (573) 323-8628.

Walnut Grove: Cat's Eye Flea Market, 109 S Washington Ave. Tel: (417) 788-2939.

Wappapello: American Way Flea Market, HC 2 Box 2194. Tel: (573) 222-8432.

Wellsville: THC Flea Market, 101 N 1st St. Tel: (573) 684-3223.

West Plains: Donlo's Flea Market, 5016 US Hwy 160. Tel: (417) 256-7586.

Wheatland: Galmey Flea Market, Hwy 254. Tel: (417) 282-5472.

Willow Springs: Junk-Shun Barn Flea Market, 2296 County Road 1270. Tel: (417) 469-3339.

Willow Springs: Traders Village USA, 3649 US Hwy 63. Tel: (417) 469-4494.

MONTANA

BILLINGS
Big Sky Flea Market

DATES: Saturday and Sunday, mid-March through mid-October.

TIMES: 7:00 AM-5:00 PM.

ADMISSION: Free. Parking is free.

LOCATION: 2221 Old Hardin Rd. Off I-90 between Exits 452 and 455. Market is on Old Hardin Rd (S Frontage Rd), across from the Tour America RV Center.

DESCRIPTION: Opened in 1997, this market of 15 dealers sells antiques, collectibles, produce, furniture, garage sale goodies, tools, knives, and new merchandise. One snack bar feeds the famished and there is a port-a-let when needed.

DEALER RATES: $10 per 10' × 20' space. Reservations are not required.

CONTACT: Jacque or Tom Moore, 1333 Maurine St, Billings MT 59101. Tel: (406) 252-6789.

NEBRASKA

BROWNVILLE
Spring Flea Market/Fall Flea Market

DATES: Spring: Memorial Day weekend, Friday through Monday. Fall: Last full weekend in September, Saturday and Sunday.

TIMES: 8:00 AM-5:00 PM.

ADMISSION: Free. Parking is free.

LOCATION: Main St. From I-29, exit for Hwy 136, 5 miles to Brownville. Only 70 miles south of Omaha, 80 miles from Topeka or Kansas City. Brownville is next to the Missouri River.

DESCRIPTION: Started in 1957 as a fundraiser for the Brownville Historical Society to preserve its heritage, this market increases the town population of 148 to 10,000 on market days. Their 260 dealers sell mostly antiques, collectibles, attic finds, some crafts and new merchandise. Several food concessions aid and abet the hungry. Restrooms are available.

DEALER RATES: $35 for 22' × 15' space for the each event. Reservations are recommended.

CONTACT: The Head Flea, Brownville Historical Society, PO Box 1, Brownville NE 68321-0001. Tel: (402) 825-6001 or 825-4751 (Zac Vice, current Head Flea).

Local History

Brownville, the oldest town in Nebraska (founded in 1854) and located on the Missouri River, was a starting point for immigrants on the Oregon Trail. Wagons would gather, up to 176 at a time, to await a leader to take them out west. In its heyday, 30 packet boats a day would unload their supplies for the wagon trains and later the Denver Gold Rushers in their quests for new lands and riches. The population would grow to 5,000 until the wagons left, then it shrank until the next train formed.

Most of the town is registered on the National Historic Register and was recently included as one of 25 towns in a book on Historic Towns in America. An excursion boat still operates from spring until mid-summer. To top all this off, think of Brownville along with "sister cities" San Francisco and Rome; all are built on seven hills.

GRAND ISLAND
Great Exchange Flea Market

DATES: Daily, except major holidays.

TIMES: 10:00 AM-5:00 PM, except Sundays 12:00 PM-5:00 PM.

ADMISSION: Free. Parking is free.

LOCATION: 3235 Locust St at intersection with Hwy 34; I-80 Exit 312 onto Rt 281 and go north 5 miles to Hwy 34, then 2 miles east to S Locust.

DESCRIPTION: Opened in 1988, this market of 60 dealers sells antiques, collectibles, crafts, sports cards, garage sale goodies furniture, books (through The Paper Route), and new merchandise.

DEALER RATES: These are all permanent vendors. Call for vacancies.

CONTACT: Great Exchange Flea Market, 3235 S Locust St, Grand Island NE 68801-8816. Tel: (308) 381-4075.

OMAHA
Blue Ribbon Flea Market

DATES: Daily.

TIMES: 9:00 AM-6:00 PM.

ADMISSION: Free. Parking is free.

LOCATION: 6606 Grover St. Take I-80 60th St Exit or 72nd St Exit to Grover St. It's the first traffic light north of I-80.

DESCRIPTION: Opened in 1994, this indoor market of 175 dealers sells antiques, furniture, cards, garage sale goodies, and a wide selection of new merchandise. There isn't any food in here, but there are handicapped-accessible restrooms.

DEALER RATES: $50 and up, monthly, starting with a 5' × 5' booth size. There is locked showcase space as well as shelf rentals. Reservations are necessary.

CONTACT: Blue Ribbon Flea Market, 6606 Grover St, Omaha NE 68106-3631. Tel: (402) 397-6811. Email: geolapole@earthlink.net.

WALTHILL
NE Nebraska's Scenic View Flea Market & Hillbilly Auction

DATES: First full weekend of each month, from April through October first and last weekend.

TIMES: Morning to whenever.

ADMISSION: Free. Parking is free.

LOCATION: South of Winnebago—go 4 miles south on Rt 75, then 1 mile east.

DESCRIPTION: Open since 1993, this indoor/outdoor market of 50 dealers sells antiques, collectibles, crafts, produce, coins, garage sale goodies, dogs and poultry (do they mix?), and new merchandise. There is food available on the premises as well as restrooms. Saturday's auction is the Hillbilly Auction; Sunday's auction is a consignment affair. According to Don, there is plenty to see around here with gorgeous scenery (hills, timber) and horses pulling wagons, stray deer and turkeys roaming... Worth a stop.

DEALER RATES: $100 yearly for a 30' × 40' or $10 per weekend. Electricity is $5 additional.

CONTACT: Don Nottelman, Flea Market, RR 1, Walthill NE 68067-9801. Tel: (402) 846-9150 or 349-9320 (pawnshop).

OTHER FLEA MARKETS

We know or have heard about these markets, but have not personally contacted each one, as we have the markets with descriptions. If you plan to visit one of the markets listed below, *please call first* to make sure they are still open. Flea markets do come and go. While they were open when we went to press, they may not be later. We can't be responsible. *Call first!*

Grand Island: Great Exchange Flea Market, 3235 S Locust St. Tel: (308) 381-4075.

Lincoln: Indian Village Flea Market, 3235 S 13th St. Tel: (402) 423-5380.

North Platte: R J Flea Market, W Hwy 30. Tel: (308) 534-0138.

Omaha: Blue Ribbon Flea Market, 6606 Grover St. Tel: (402) 397-6811.

South Sioux City: Siouxland Fleamarket Inc, 2111 Dakota Ave. Tel: (402) 494-3221.

NEVADA

LAS VEGAS
Fantastic Indoor Swap Meet

DATES: Friday, Saturday and Sunday, year round. Also open additional days during Christmas season.

TIMES: 10:00 AM-6:00 PM.

ADMISSION: $1, seniors $.50. Children 12 and under free with paying adult. Parking is free on 15 acres. Monkeys are free. Ask Berny about this one.

LOCATION: 1717 S Decatur at Oakey Blvd.

DESCRIPTION: Opened in 1990, this huge market (200,000 square feet) has dealers in 600 booths selling all new merchandise, crafts, "the most wonderful things" from satellite dishes to more usual fare. There are four snack bars selling American, New York City food and a variety of other delectable edibles. They have a lounge for ball-game viewing, so the men can watch the ball games while their wives shop. Then there are the handicapped-accessible restrooms when you need them—after all that game watching. And really, go look for the monkeys.

DEALER RATES: From $445 and up for four 3-day weekends. Advance reservations are required as there is a two-week waiting period to get a city license. All sellers must have a state tax permit. Office hours: Thursday 10:00 AM-3:00 PM.

CONTACT: Berny Krebs, Rentals, Fantastic Indoor Swap Meet, 1717 S Decatur, Las Vegas NV 89102. Tel: (702) 877-0087 or fax: (702) 877-3102. Email: admin@fantasticswap.com Web: www.fantasticswap.com.

> **Berny's Babies**
> Berny brought in a pair of little chimps and gave them their own booth (it's quite protected and it's the chimps' "game room"). They are literally Berny's children. The little guys are quite an attraction, not only in the market, but in Las Vegas too. The MGM Grand wants to show them too. No, no, no. . . .

Silver State Flea Market

DATES: Third weekend of the month, year round.

TIMES: 7:00 AM-3:00 PM.

ADMISSION: $1 for those 13 years and over, free for kids 12 and under. Parking is free. Active military with proper ID are admitted free.

LOCATION: Sam Boyd Stadium, on the grounds of University of Nevada, Las Vegas.

DESCRIPTION: This market's grand opening was November 2001 as an open-air market based on the most successful Orange County Market Place in Costa Mesa, California, and owned by the same family, the Tellers. Their aim is to bring high-quality merchandise to their customers, and offer a clean, fun family-atmosphere—as they do in California. The market will feature several hundred vendors offering top-of-the-line merchandise and services at better than retail prices, arts and crafts, manufacturers' outlet specials, fresh produce and flowers, food to go items, antiques and other treasures. There will be entertainment, plenty of food and handicapped-accessible restrooms.

DEALER RATES: $10 per 15' × 30' space that includes seller's vehicle as an introductory rate on a first-come, first-served basis. If you wish to make reservations, or the market gets very popular, very fast, then reservations may be a good idea. They can be made over the web, by mail, or in person.

CONTACT: Silver State Market Place, 1930 Village Center Circle 3-349, Las Vegas NV 89143. Tel: (702) 386-7927 or (702) FUN-SWAP. Fax: (702) 386-7926. Email: VendorInfo@SilverStateMarketPlace.com. Web: www.SilverStateMarketPlace.com.

NORTH LAS VEGAS
Broadacres Open Air Swap Meet

DATES: Friday, Saturday and Sunday, year round. Rain or shine.

TIMES: 6:30 AM to whenever.

ADMISSION: $.50 on Friday, otherwise $1 per person weekends, children under 12 free.

LOCATION: 2960 Las Vegas Blvd, Las Vegas Blvd N at Pecos. Four miles north of the Union Plaza Hotel on Las Vegas Blvd N.

DESCRIPTION: Opened in November 1977, this outdoor market is in its 24th year of business. Their 700 dealers in the summer attract 18,000 buyers weekly, and 1,500 dealers attract 25,000 buyers during the winter months. Antiques, collectibles, tools, toys, crafts, produce, and new merchandise are available. There are plenty of shade trees and clean restrooms.

DEALER RATES: The charge for a booth measuring 15' × 30' is $20 on Saturday and Sunday and $8 on Friday. Make your reservations during business hours. They have 1,000 reserved spaces and only 500 daily unreserved spaces. Office hours: Friday 6:30 AM-12:30 PM, weekends 6:30 AM-2:00 PM.

CONTACT: Jake Bowman, Broadacres Open Air Swap Meet, PO Box 36-4059, N Las Vegas NV 89036-4059. Tel: (702) 642-3777.

SPARKS
El Rancho Flea Market

DATES: Saturdays and Sundays, year round, weather permitting.

TIMES: Summer from 5:30 AM-4:30 PM: winter from 6:00 AM to whenever.

ADMISSION: $.50 per person; children under 12 free, includes parking.

LOCATION: 555 El Rancho Dr at the El Rancho Drive-In Theater. Off I-80 at the "G" St exit, go east 2 blocks on Prater then 2 blocks north on El Rancho Dr, turn left on G St. If you are on El Rancho Dr, you can't miss them; they are next to Paradise Park.

DESCRIPTION: Located in Sparks, well known for gambling casinos, near Lake Tahoe. Twin city to Reno. Opened in 1978, this outdoor flea market attracts 200-250 dealers selling antiques, collectibles, fresh produce, new merchandise, and garage sale items. There are plenty of food carts roaming the market, a barbecue stand with made-to-order goodies, a beer garden (they do card you) and handicapped-accessible restrooms.

DEALER RATES: Start at $16 per space, call for other rates and sizes. Reservations are not required—first come, first served—although some space is reserved until 8:00 AM.

CONTACT: El Rancho Swap, 555 El Rancho Dr, Sparks NV 89431. Tel: (775) 358-6920. Fax: (775) 358-2833.

NEW HAMPSHIRE

DERRY
Grand View Flea Market
DATES: Saturday and Sunday, year round. Rain or shine.
TIMES: Saturday 9:00 AM-3:00 PM, Sunday 7:00 AM-4:00 PM.
ADMISSION: Sunday only: $.50 for adults; children under 12 free.
LOCATION: At the junction of Rt 28 and Bypass 28 S.
DESCRIPTION: This show, established more than 30 years ago, is one of northern New England's first and finest. In the center of the market is a pond with a 30-foot-tall Indian totem pole. It also has a strange collection of statuary, including two very large elephants, a bear and several genies, purchased from an old amusement park. From 40-100 dealers outside depending on the weather and 50 or so inside sell all sorts of antiques, collectibles, crystals, books, novelties, jewelry, gifts, appliances, fabric and lace, new and used furniture, handmades, and new items. Food and handicapped-accessible restrooms are available on the premises. A golf driving range is next door.
DEALER RATES: Indoors: Saturdays $10, Sundays $20 per 12' × 8' space including 3 tables. Outdoors: Saturday $5 includes tables, Sunday $15 per "large car length" space plus $1 per table. Reservations are not required.
CONTACT: Kathi Taylor, Grand View Flea Market, 34 S Main St, Derry NH 03086. Tel: (603) 432-2326.

HOLLIS
Hollis Country Store and Flea Market
DATES: Every Sunday, first Sunday of April through the second Sunday of November, plus Labor Day. Weather permitting.
TIMES: 7:00 AM-4:00 PM.
ADMISSION: Free. $2 parking fee.
LOCATION: On Silver Lake Rd (Rt 122). Take Exit 7W off Rt 3 (in Nashua) to 101A west. Go 8 miles, then turn left onto Rt 122S. Market is 2½ miles on the right.
DESCRIPTION: Opened in 1965, this outdoor market now attracts over 250 dealers selling antiques and collectibles as well as new merchandise and some fresh produce. This is a well-attended, busy market, attracting dealers and customers from all over New England and as far as California. They have an excellent reputation for quality goods at reasonable prices. A snack bar serves up the goodies and there are restrooms when needed.

DEALER RATES: $20 per 15' × 20' space. Reservations are preferred.
CONTACT: Alice Prieto, 436 Silver Lake Rd, Hollis NH 03049. Tel: (603) 465-7813 or 882-6134. Fax: (603) 882-0927. Email: hollisflea@aol.com.

This'll Get 'em Department
A woman brought in a trailer with a shed on it loaded with over $10,000 worth of power tools—and sold it all for $10. She was divorcing her husband.

Just Married
One of their dealers asked if he could hold his wedding and reception at the market. Thinking the wedding itself wasn't appropriate to the market, but a reception was; the reception was held at the market, with a neighboring dealer creating a beautiful wedding cake for the event. Other dealers pitched in with punch and ice cream.

Many shoppers that day participated in an unexpected celebration.

LEBANON
Colonial Antiques and Flea Market
DATES: Daily indoors, Sundays outdoors, weather permitting.
TIMES: 9:00 AM-5:00 PM. However, Sundays during the dark months the whole market opens at 8:00 AM, and during the light months they open at 6:00 AM.
ADMISSION: Free. Parking is free.
LOCATION: Rt 12A at Exit 20 off I-89 at Colonial Plaza.
DESCRIPTION: Opened in 1976, and under new management since mid-June 1995, this market's over 90 dealers sell antiques, collectibles, estate jewelry, furniture, old books, old clothes, dolls, old tools, postcards, stamps, fine glassware, paintings, bottles, crafts and much more. Many of their dealers are recognized authorities in their field. There are "loads of fine treasures, a bargain hunters paradise," with fine smalls and rare prints among other found prizes. This market strives for the finest quality available. They have a reputation as the "first and oldest and funnest market in New England."
DEALER RATES: $33.50 for about 7' × 10' space weekly inside. Outdoors is $14 for 2 parking spaces. Reservations are mandatory for inside, as there is a waiting list. No reservations for the outside space.
CONTACT: Colonial Antiques and Flea Market, 5 Airport Rd, W Lebanon NH 03784. Tel: (603) 298-7712 or 298-8132.

Okay, I Believe That Department

A woman came in looking for a Christmas present for her doctor husband and "hit" on an 1820 anatomy book published in Edinburgh, Scotland. She leafed through the pages with their copper-plate pictures and found a handsome adult male skeleton. Obviously intrigued, she asked, "Who is this?" The dealer, without hesitation, replied, "George Washington." That didn't faze her. Then she happened upon another skeleton picture of an infant. "Who's this?" she asked. Again, without a blink, the dealer replied, "George Washington—as an infant."

She didn't buy the book.

MEREDITH
Burlwood Antique Center

DATES: Daily, May 1-October 31.

TIMES: 10:00 AM-5:00 PM.

ADMISSION: Free. Free parking is available.

LOCATION: 194 Daniel Webster Hwy. On Rt 3. From I-93, take Exit 23, then go east on Rt 104, 9 miles to Rt 3, then turn right to get to Burlwood Antique Center.

DESCRIPTION: This 3-story indoor market opened in 1983 and currently accommodates over 175 dealers. There is a variety of quality antiques and collectibles sold. Fine art and plenty of costume and fine jewelry, smalls, Shaker items and primitives are also available, as well as an antique lighting and furniture gallery. Because they are open only six months a year, all the merchandise is fresh each year. This is a great place for dealers to stock up for other markets, as most of their shoppers are dealers.

DEALER RATES: $150 per 5' × 3' × 8' space per month with a seasonal contract required.

CONTACT: Mark Diette or Mary Di Maria, 194 Daniel Webster Hwy, Meredith NH 03253. Tel: (603) 279-6387. Email: info@burlwood-antiques.com. Web: www.burlwood-antiques.com.

Wonder What They Will Do With That?

One dealer sold a vintage 1880s portable folding mortician's table. Would you like to try it?

OTHER FLEA MARKETS

We know or have heard about these markets, but have not personally contacted each one, as we have the markets with descriptions. If you plan to visit one of the markets listed below, *please call first* to make sure they are still open. Flea markets do come and go. While they were open when we went to press, they may not be later. We can't be responsible. *Call first!*

Chichester: Jim's Flea Market, 263 Dover Rd. Tel: (603) 798-5603.
Londonderry: Londonderry Gardens Flea Mkt, 5 Avery Rd. Tel: (603) 880-9935.
Pelham: Moe's Flea Market, 12 Bridge St. Tel: (603) 635-1800.
Salem: Salem NH Flea Market Inc, 20 Hampshire Rd. Tel: (603) 893-8888.
Woodstock: Woodstock Flee Market, Woodstock Plz. Tel: (603) 745-2816.

NEW JERSEY

BELVIDERE
Five Acres

DATES: Every Saturday and Sunday, weather permitting (ice is a problem).
TIMES: 8:00 AM until everyone is gone.
ADMISSION: Free. Parking is also free.
LOCATION: 421 Rt 46 E. On Rt 80, take Exit 12 south to Rt 46, go east 1,500 feet. Market is on right.

DESCRIPTION: This outdoor flea market opened in 1965. There are between 75 and 100 dealers selling anything from antiques and collectibles to arts, crafts and new merchandise. Fresh produce is also available in season. There is a bar on premises. They opened a small antiques mall on the premises in the spring of 1999. Say Hi to Totsy for me!
DEALER RATES: $15 per 10' × 20' space. Reservations are not required. If interested in selling in the new antique building, contact Totsy.
CONTACT: Totsy Phillips, PO Box 295, Belvidere NJ 07823-0295. Tel: (908) 475-2572.

BERLIN
Berlin Farmers' Market

DATES: Thursday, Friday, Saturday and Sunday. Rain or shine.
TIMES: 8:00 AM-4:00 PM outside flea market Saturday and Sunday only, weather permitting. Farmers' Market Thursday-Friday 11:00 AM-9:30 PM; Saturday 10:00 AM-9:30 PM; Sunday 10:00 AM-6:00 PM inside.
ADMISSION: Free. Free parking is available.
LOCATION: 41 Clementon Rd. Just off Rt 30, Rt 73 or Rt 42 about 40 minutes from either Atlantic City or Philadelphia.
DESCRIPTION: This market started in 1930 as a livestock auction. Today it is located on about 60 acres of land. These spacious accommodations house the outdoor flea market and parking lot. The indoor shopping market is in a building ¼ mile long. Between their indoor and outdoor market, on any given weekend there are anywhere from 700 to 800 dealers. The types of merchandise to be found are unlimited: from antiques to new merchandise, from quality new and used furniture, arts and crafts to fresh produce. Seen and sold: clothing of all kinds, gold stuff, toys, tools, hardware, health and beauty aids, furniture, sports cards, video games and tapes, etc. Once a customer brought in a house on a trailer—and sold it! There are two snack bars and three other food vendors inside, and eight food vendors outside. This flea market is proudly owned and operated by the third generation of the Giberson family.

DEALER RATES: For flea market vendors: $20 per 12' × 30' booth—strictly used merchandise for 2 days ($15 for one day); $35 per 12' × 30' booth for all new merchandise. Reservations are suggested. Office is open Thursday and Friday.

CONTACT: Stan Giberson, Jr or Ron Smith, 41 Clementon Rd, Berlin NJ 08009. Tel: (856) 767-1284 or (856) 767-1246. Fax: (856) 767-8435.

CHERRY HILL
Garden State Park Flea Market

DATES: Sunday, mid-March through December, weather permitting (very rare).

TIMES: 8:00 AM-3:00 PM.

ADMISSION: Free. Parking is $1.

LOCATION: Garden State Park Race Track, Hwy 70. Rt 295, Exit 34B to Rt 70 W exit for Cherry Hill; 3 miles on the right. Use the main entrance on Rt 70.

DESCRIPTION: This outdoor market, opened in 1989, consists of 500-1,200 dealers (depending on the season) selling 99% new merchandise. It's considered a good upscale market. Two food courts with 12-14 vendors at each court and handicapped-accessible restrooms will take care of all your needs. Arthur treats his vendors and customers as human beings, as he has 20 years experience as a vendor. He considers this a fun market. They do a lot of advertising.

DEALER RATES: $35 per space, daily. $115 per month of Sundays. Reservations are needed depending on the season, so call. There will be special discounted rates for antiques and used merchandise dealers at $10 per day. Please call Arthur about those.

CONTACT: Arthur, Garden State Park Flea Market, PO Box 1024, Somerset NJ 08873-1024. Tel: (856) 665-8558 or cell (732) 558-5016. Email: aeloudon@aol.com.

COLUMBUS
Columbus Farmers' Market

DATES: Every Thursday, Friday, Saturday and Sunday. Rain or shine.

TIMES: Inside hours: Thursday and Saturday 8:00 AM-8:00 PM; Friday 10:00 AM-8:00 PM; Sunday 8:00 AM-5:00 PM. Outside hours: Thursday, Saturday and Sunday dawn to whenever!

ADMISSION: Free. Free parking is available.

LOCATION: On Rt 206, 5 miles south of Exit 7 off the New Jersey Tnpk.

DESCRIPTION: This outdoor market began in 1929. This indoor/outdoor market accommodates from 400 dealers in winter to 1,700 dealers in summer selling antiques and collectibles as well as new merchandise and fresh produce. There are 70 permanent stores, including seven restaurants, shoe repair, sewing machine repair, a Chinese food shop and all types of specialty shops. Food is served on the premises.

DEALER RATES: Thursday $30 per 12' × 30' space; Saturday $10; Sunday $30 per 12' × 30' booth—new items; $20 per 12' × 30' booth—used items. Reservations are not required; spaces are assigned by the management.

CONTACT: Columbus Farmers Market, 2919 US Hwy 206, Columbus NJ 08022-0322. Tel: (609) 267-0400.

DOVER
Dover Marketplace

DATES: Sundays, April through December.

TIMES: 9:00 AM-5:00 PM.

ADMISSION: Free. Parking is free.

LOCATION: 18 W Blackwell St. Rt 80 Exit 35A. Near the Chester Lions Club.

DESCRIPTION: Opened in 1998, covering 12 city blocks plus an antique center and shops, this market of 200 dealers is a good old-fashioned street fair—"the only continuously operating street fair," according to its owner—as it runs weekly. Averaging 95% new merchandise versus old goodies, and 10-12,000 shoppers, this market also has plenty of food vendors on site, plenty of restaurants nearby, and handicapped-accessible restrooms.

DEALER RATES: $50 per Sunday, yearly rate. Daily rate $85. Spaces for the daily rate are very limited, so you must call ahead to determine if your merchandise category is open. Reservations are essential.

CONTACT: Bob Brumale, Dover Marketplace, 18 W Blackwell St, Dover NJ 07073. Tel: (973) 989-7870. Email: solonpond@aol.com. Web: fleamarketsusa.com (notice the plural, as there is another site with a similar name).

EAST BRUNSWICK
Route 18 Flea Market

DATES: Every Friday, Saturday, and Sunday.

TIMES: Friday 11:00 AM-9:00 PM; Saturday 10:00 AM-9:00 PM; Sunday 11:00 AM-6:00 PM. Additional December hours: Monday through Thursday 12:00 PM-9:00 PM.

ADMISSION: Free. Parking is free.

LOCATION: At 290 Rt 18; NJ Tnpk Exit 9, take Rt 18 south to Prospect St, make U-turn and go back north 1 block.

DESCRIPTION: Open since 1977 and described as a "poor man's mall," this indoor market of over 150 vendors sells antiques, collectibles, fresh produce, deli items, coins, cards, furniture, framing and art galleries, and plenty of new merchandise, including many quality gold jewelry dealers. Ten restaurants in an international food court (Greek, Chinese, Mexican, etc.) feed the famished, and when you need them there are handicapped-accessible restrooms. There is weekly entertainment with live bands, wrestlers, soap stars, car shows and monthly sports card auctions.

DEALER RATES: Daily, weekend and monthly rates for a 10' × 10' basic space are available upon request. Prices range depending on where and how long. Reservations are suggested.

CONTACT: Barbara Passwaters, Route 18 Indoor Market, 290 Route 18, E Brunswick NJ 08816-0905. Tel: (732) 254-5080 or 254-5082. Fax: (732) 254-1761. Email: Route18Market@aol.com. Web: www.route18market.com.

EAST RUTHERFORD
Meadowlands Marketplace

DATES: Every Thursday and Saturday, plus Memorial Day, July 4 and Labor Day; Saturdays only January through March. The Friday after Thanksgiving starts their winter season.

TIMES: 9:00 AM-4:00 PM.

ADMISSION: Adults $1, children under 15 free. Parking is free.

LOCATION: At Giants Stadium parking lot 17 on Rt 3 W at the New Jersey Sports Complex.

DESCRIPTION: This upscale market of 700-800 vendors sells antiques, collectibles, fresh produce, seafood, and used and new merchandise. There are food concessions and the site is entirely handicapped-accessible.

DEALER RATES: Thursday $30, Saturday $50-$85 per 18' × 36' space. Antiques $40 per space. Reservations are a good idea.

CONTACT: Meadowlands Marketplace, 1 Selleck St, Norwalk CT 06855. Tel: (201) 935-5474 or 1-888-445-6543. Fax: (201) 935-5495 or (203) 866-4318. Email: info@meadowlandsfleamarket.com. Web: www.meadowlandsfleamarket.com.

EDISON
Mid-Winter Antiques & Collectibles Classic

DATES: February 9-10, July 27-28, November 23-24, 2002. The last two dates are tentative, so call first, or check their website.

TIMES: Saturday 10:00 AM-6:00 PM, Sunday 11:00 AM-5:00 PM.

ADMISSION: $5. Parking is free.

LOCATION: New Jersey Convention Center. Raritan Center, Expo Hall, 97 Sunfield Ave.

DESCRIPTION: February 2002 will be their first show in New Jersey with dealers in over 500 booths selling only quality antiques and collectibles. Food is available as well as handicapped-accessible restrooms.

DEALER RATES: $120 per 8' × 10' space. $65 for electric. Tables are available for $8 each. Reservations and prepayment are required.

CONTACT: D'Amore Promotions, 2125 McComas Way Ste 102, Virginia Beach VA 23456. Tel: (757) 430-4735. Fax: (757) 430-4738. Email: sales@bigfleamarket.com. Web: www.damorepromotions.com.

New Dover United Methodist Church Flea Market

DATES: Every Tuesday, mid-March through mid-December. Rain or shine (unless there is a severe threatening storm).

TIMES: 7:00 AM-1:00 PM.

ADMISSION: Free. Free parking is available at the rear of the church.

LOCATION: 687 New Dover Rd. Take Exit 131 on Garden State Parkway, bear right, go to first light (Wood Ave), turn right, go to second light (New Dover Rd), and finally, turn left.

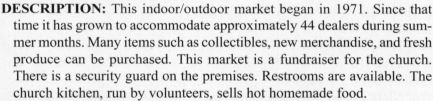

DESCRIPTION: This indoor/outdoor market began in 1971. Since that time it has grown to accommodate approximately 44 dealers during summer months. Many items such as collectibles, new merchandise, and fresh produce can be purchased. This market is a fundraiser for the church. There is a security guard on the premises. Restrooms are available. The church kitchen, run by volunteers, sells hot homemade food.

DEALER RATES: $20 per table, inside with table or outside parking space size. Reservations are required, as most of their vendors are permanent. New vendors should arrive by 6:30 AM for space and setup.

CONTACT: New Dover United Methodist Church, 687 New Dover Rd, Edison NJ 08820. Tel: (732) 381-7904.

ENGLISHTOWN
Englishtown Auction Sales Flea Market

DATES: Saturday and Sunday, year round; also open Good Friday, Labor Day, and Friday after Thanksgiving.

TIMES: Saturday 7:00 AM-4:00 PM; Sundays and holidays 9:00 AM-4:00 PM.

ADMISSION: Free, with free parking available.

LOCATION: 90 Wilson Ave; New Jersey Tnpk Exit 9; access from Rt 18 S and Rt 527 S.

DESCRIPTION: Since 1929 this market has been known as "shopping at its best for the entire family." This combination indoor/outdoor show is held in five buildings and on 40 acres of outside dealer space. Their hundreds of dealers sell antiques and collectibles, jewelry, hubcaps, clothing, housewares, furniture, as well as new merchandise. Food items are restricted, but three food courts and an air-conditioned tavern as well as handicapped-accessible restrooms add to the amenities. Their mascot Sunny roams the markets on weekends entertaining kids of all ages. Check out their Internet site for specials.

DEALER RATES: Spaces start at $5-$7 a day outdoors. $160 and up per month for a single 12' × 15' booth inside. Monthly reservations are suggested. Office hours: Saturday 7:00 AM-4:00 PM, Sunday and holidays 9:00 AM-4:00 PM, and Mondays and Fridays 10:00 AM-2:00 PM.

CONTACT: Manager, Englishtown Auction Sales, 90 Wilson Ave, Englishtown NJ 07726. Tel: (732) 446-9644. Fax: (732) 446-1220. Email: info@englishtownauction.com. Website: www.englishtownauction.com.

FARMINGDALE/COLLINGWOOD PARK
Collingwood Auction and Flea Market

DATES: Every Friday, Saturday and Sunday.

TIMES: Outside opens every day at 7:30 AM. Inside: Friday 12:00 PM-8:00 PM, Saturday 10:00 AM-8:00 PM, Sunday 10:00 AM-5:00 PM.

ADMISSION: Free. Parking is free.

LOCATION: On St Hwy 33 and 34, ½ mile west of Collingwood traffic circle, 4 miles south of Colts Neck.

DESCRIPTION: Opened around 1950 with 40 acres of selling space, this indoor market of 125 vendors and outdoor market of up to 600 vendors sells antiques, collectibles, crafts, garage sale goodies, jewelry, clothing, furniture, fresh produce, and new and used merchandise—ratio of about 50/50 old to new. Saturday night is Antique Auction night, first and third Wednesday nights are the tailgate auctions at 5:00 PM. The first Tuesday at 6:00 PM is the car and truck auction, not to forget Saturday's tree and shrub auction, which I'm assured is quite popular. There is a snack bar and handicapped-accessible restrooms on site.

DEALER RATES: Outside: Friday $2, Saturday $6, Sunday $9 per space. Inside $200 and up monthly with reservations. Outside, white tables, are first come, first served. Everything else is reservations only.

CONTACT: Collingwood Auction & Flea Market, 1350 Hwy 33, Farmingdale NJ 07727. Tel: (732) 938-7941. Fax: (732) 938-4652.

Really Old and Unique
There was an antique bamboo pole fly-fishing set with many tips sold here for $750. This is quite a unique find.

FLEMINGTON
The Flemington Fair Flea Market

There may be some zoning changes affecting the property this market uses. As it stands at press time, the market will be held April through November. However, that could all change.

DATES: Every Wednesday, April until there is a decision made on the zoning. Call or email for more information.

TIMES: 6:00 AM-4:00 PM.

ADMISSION: Free. Free parking is available.

LOCATION: On Hwy 31, 22 miles north of Trenton; 18 miles north of New Hope, PA; 30 miles southeast of eastern Pennsylvania; 45 miles west of New York City.

DESCRIPTION: Started in 1980, this market now accommodates anywhere from 75 to 120 dealers outdoors as well as 16 indoor shops. Although the majority of vendors sell antiques and collectibles, fine art, arts and crafts, new merchandise, plants, clothing, fresh produce and everything under the sun can be found. Situated in the beautiful, historic country setting of the Flemington Fairgrounds, this can be a fun day for the entire family!

DEALER RATES: $6 per 8' × 20' space outdoors; $500 per season per 10' × 12' indoor shop which includes 10' × 30' outdoors. Reservations are required for indoor space only. Vendors set up at 6:00 AM on Wednesday.

CONTACT: Melissa L Yerkes, 25 Kuhl Rd, Flemington NJ 08822. Tel: (908) 782-7326 after 5:00 PM. Day of show call main office at (908) 782-2413. Email: gourd55@yahoo.com.

JEFFERSON
Jefferson Township Fire Company #2 Flea Market

DATES: Saturday from April through October.

TIMES: 6:30 AM to whenever.

ADMISSION: Free. Parking is free.

LOCATION: Rt 15 S, across from the Pathmark. Take I-80 W to Exit 34B (Rt 15 N), go down 3 traffic lights. Go down Pathmark ramp and cut across through Pathmark.

DESCRIPTION: Opened around 1989 as a fundraiser for the Fire Department, this market of 30-50 dealers sells antiques, collectibles, crafts, produce in season, trading cards, Ts and sweats—whatever comes in. The Fire Department runs the food concession.

DEALER RATES: $15 for a "oh, car-sized-wide" space daily, $60 monthly, or $300 for a full season. Reservations are suggested and appreciated. Tables for $5.

CONTACT: Jefferson Township Fire Company, PO Box 5, Lake Hopatcong NJ 07849. Tel: (973) 663-5810.

LAKEWOOD
Route 70 Flea Market

DATES: Friday, Saturday and Sunday, year round.

TIMES: Friday 8:00 AM-2:00 PM. Saturday and Sunday 7:00 AM-4:00 PM.

ADMISSION: Free. Parking is free.

LOCATION: 117 Rt 70, between Garden State Pkwy and Rt 9. From the South: Take GSP north to Exit 83. Take Rt 9 north to Rt 70 E. Bear right after the golf course, go down to the stop sign, make a left. Go to the traffic light, turn left to the market. From the North: Take GSP south to Exit 88. Pay the toll, turn right onto Rt 70 W. Follow Rt 70 W a few miles and market will be on the right.

DESCRIPTION: Opened in 1980, this indoor/outdoor "true flea market" of 700-1,000 dealers sells antiques, collectibles, crafts, fresh produce, meats, seafood, coins, stamps, cards, clothing, jewelry, garage sale goodies, furniture, and new merchandise. There are snack bars for the hungry and handicapped-accessible restrooms when needed.

DEALER RATES: $9 per 8' table on weekends, $4 on Friday, ground spaces start at $10. Reservations are not required.

CONTACT: Michael Gingrich, General Manager, Rt 70 Flea Market, 117 Hwy 70, Lakewood NJ 08701-5820. Tel: (732) 370-1837. Fax: (732) 840-5684. Email: Yeahohk@aol.com.

LAMBERTVILLE
Golden Nugget Antique Flea Market

DATES: Every Wednesday, Saturday and Sunday, outdoors, year round. Rain or shine. Indoor shops are open on weekends.

TIMES: Outdoors: 6:30 AM-4:00 PM; indoors 8:30 AM-4:00 PM.

ADMISSION: Free. Parking is $1 on Sundays, otherwise free.

LOCATION: Rt 29, 2 miles south of Lambertville, 5 miles north of Exit 1 on I-95.

DESCRIPTION: This indoor/outdoor market began its operation in 1960 and currently accommodates 40 indoor shops and 200 tables outdoors. The main building offers 15,000 square feet of space and is air-conditioned for year-round use. Dealers offer antiques and collectibles such as furniture, glassware and porcelain, craft items, and new merchandise. A snack bar restaurant serves breakfast, lunch, soups and "you name it." This market is located within a few miles of several historic sites: Washington Crossing, New Hope-Lahaska and Lambertville.

DEALER RATES: $8 for a 8' × 4' table on Wednesday, $15 on Saturday, $25 on Sunday. Reservations are required for Sunday. Please reserve in person or via the tape on the phone number.

CONTACT: Angelo Peluso, Manager, Golden Nugget Antique Flea Market, 1850 River Rd, Lambertville NJ 08530. Tel: (609) 397-0811.

> **Movie News**
> In September 1997, Dan Rather for *CBS Eye on America* filmed a segment on a falcon figurine sold at the market in 1990. Unusual about the falcon, it had the initials "WB" on the bottom. The purchaser believes it is the figurine used as a prop in the Humphrey Bogart film *Maltese Falcon* filmed by Warner Bros. If true then the falcon, purchased for $8, is estimated to be worth $400,000. Oh, what a return on investment!

Lambertville Antique Flea Market, Inc
DATES: Wednesday, Saturday and Sunday. Rain or shine.
TIMES: Outdoors: 6:00 AM till they leave (closing). Indoors: 8:00 AM-4:00 PM.
ADMISSION: Free. Free parking is available.
LOCATION: On Rt 29, 1 mile south of Lambertville, along the Delaware River.

DESCRIPTION: Opened in 1967, this is both an indoor and outdoor market, with a pavilion covering for 49 of its spaces outside. In total, there are close to 150 dealers who attend selling strictly antiques and collectibles. This market was listed in *Good Housekeeping* as one of the 25 best antique markets in the United States. Indoors there are 15 showcases, and three buildings with different dealers selling furniture, pottery, estate jewelry, vintage clothing, sterling, bronzes, and sports memorabilia. The Market Grill serves homemade specials, and handicapped-accessible restrooms add to the amenities.
DEALER RATES: Wednesdays $14 for a 2-table space under the pavilion, or $8 for a 2-table setup outside. Sundays $48 for a 2-table space under the pavilion and $40 outside; Saturday $32 under the pavilion, $22 outside. Reservations for anything on Sunday, and for Wednesday and Saturday pavilion space are required. Office hours: Wednesday through Friday 10:00 AM-4:00 pm, weekends 8:00 AM-4:00 PM.
CONTACT: Heidi or Rob, Lambertville Antique Flea Market Inc, 1864 River Rd, Lambertville NJ 08530. Tel: (609) 397-0456.

MANAHAWKIN
Manahawkin Flea Mart
DATES: Friday, Saturday and Sunday, year round. Outdoors, weather permitting.
TIMES: 9:00 AM-5:00 PM.
ADMISSION: Free. Parking is free.

LOCATION: 657 E Bay Ave, off Rt 9. Take Garden State Pkwy to Exit 63 Manahawkin Exit. Follow signs to Manahawkin Business District, Bay Ave. Mart is on the right-hand side of the road.

DESCRIPTION: This good year-round show started in 1977 and hosts 100 outdoor and 45 indoor dealers featuring antiques, collectibles, produce, meats, new merchandise, and stained glass items. One snack bar and handicapped-accessible restrooms add to the amenities. They are located within 2 miles of Long Beach Island on the Atlantic Ocean, a popular tourist spot.

DEALER RATES: Outdoors: Friday $5 per 22' × 19' space, weekends $20 per space per day; $160 monthly. Inside rates vary. Reservations are not required outdoors, but are for indoors. BYOT and show up by 7:00 AM to be directed to a spot.

CONTACT: Manahawkin Flea Mart, PO Box 885, Manahawkin NJ 08050-0885. Tel: (609) 597-1017.

NESHANIC STATION
Neshanic Flea Market

DATES: Every Sunday, March through December. Rain or shine.

TIMES: 6:00 AM–5:00 PM.

ADMISSION: Free. $.50 parking donation to the Neshanic Volunteer Fire Company.

LOCATION: Midway between Somerville and Flemington, off Hwy 202.

DESCRIPTION: This outdoor market opened in 1970 and currently draws approximately 100 dealers. Some of the types of items you can find include antiques and collectibles, fine art, and arts and crafts, as well as new merchandise and fresh produce. There is a snack bar on the premises. This friendly market is family owned and operated, and is located in a beautiful historic village.

DEALER RATES: $15 per 4' × 8' space, $23 for two spaces. BYOT (bring your own table). Reservations are not required.

CONTACT: Mary and Jack Weiss, Neshanic Flea Market, 100 Elm St, Neshanic Station NJ 08853. Tel/fax: (908) 369-3660.

Talk about a Family Market

The Weisses' daughter, Chris, has grown up at this market—the market and Chris are about the same age. Many of the dealers have been there as long as the market, making them ersatz parents. So when Chris had a baby last year, her daughter acquired "500 grandparents!"

NEW EGYPT
New Egypt Auction and Flea Market Village

DATES: Every Wednesday and Sunday, year round.

TIMES: 7:00 AM-2:00 PM. (Some vendors leave after noon.)

ADMISSION: Free. Free parking is available.

LOCATION: On Rt 537 between Rts 528 and 539. Take Exit 7 or 7A off the New Jersey Tnpk. Six miles west of Great Adventure/Six Flags Amusement Park.

DESCRIPTION: This "lively, friendly, and unique" indoor/outdoor flea market village has been in existence since 1959. There are approximately 100 dealers in 60 buildings large and small, including 12 antique shops or at tables of all sizes buying and selling antiques, collectibles, produce, new and used clothing, tools, hardware, coins, books, furniture, metals recycling, and lots of other used items and oddities. Don't expect all the vendors to be there all the time—this is a unique experience folks. If the weather is iffy, call before going! Food is served on the premises. Track down Les for me and say, "Hello, Les!" See their story at the end of this chapter. It's wonderful!

DEALER RATES: $6 per 5' × 12'-20' table on Wednesday; $7 per table on Sunday. Prices include parking space. Reservations are not required.

CONTACT: Les Heller, New Egypt Flea Market Village, 933 Rt 537, Cream Ridge NJ 08514. Tel: (609) 758-2082.

PALMYRA
Tacony-Palmyra Swap N' Shop Flea Market

DATES: Every Saturday, Sunday, and selected holidays, year round, weather permitting.

TIMES: 6:00 AM-3:00 PM.

ADMISSION: Free. Free parking is available.

LOCATION: On Rt 73. From New Jersey follow Rt 73 to Tacony-Palmyra Bridge. From Pennsylvania take I-95 exit and follow signs to Tacony-Palmyra Bridge.

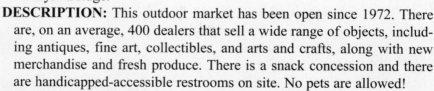

DESCRIPTION: This outdoor market has been open since 1972. There are, on an average, 400 dealers that sell a wide range of objects, including antiques, fine art, collectibles, and arts and crafts, along with new merchandise and fresh produce. There is a snack concession and there are handicapped-accessible restrooms on site. No pets are allowed!

DEALER RATES: $40 and up per 18' × 18' space. Additional reserved spaces are available. Reservations are not required. Dealers must have a valid NJ sales license. There is a reserved line; if interested call.

CONTACT: Lauresia Phillips, PO Box 64, Palmyra NJ 08065-0064. Tel: (856) 829-3001. Day of show call the general line at (856) 829-3000. Fax: (856) 768-8419.

RAHWAY
Rahway Italian-American Club Flea Market

DATES: Wednesday and Friday, year round.

TIMES: 7:00 AM-3:00 PM.

ADMISSION: Free. Parking is also free.

LOCATION: 530 New Brunswick Ave in Rahway. Corner of Inman and New Brunswick Aves.

DESCRIPTION: This market has been held for 26 years, featuring 35-40 dealers outdoors selling antiques, collectibles, crafts, designer clothes, baseball cards, jewelry, and new merchandise. A snack bar featuring homemade food serves the hungry, and handicapped-accessible restrooms come in handy.

DEALER RATES: Wednesday $10, Friday $15 per 12' booth. Reservations are suggested.

CONTACT: Angelo, Rahway Italian-American Club Flea Market, 530 New Brunswick Ave, Rahway NJ 07065-2929. Day of show call (732) 574-3840 (the club number).

RANCOCAS WOODS
William Spencer's Antique Show

DATES: Second Sunday of the month, March through December. Rain date the following Sunday.

TIMES: 8:00 AM-4:00 PM.

ADMISSION: Free. Free parking is available.

LOCATION: On Creek Rd, 1 mile from the Rancocas Woods exit off I-295.

DESCRIPTION: This very popular market first opened in 1950. There are over 150 dealers attending this outdoor market set in a beautiful, wooded area. They specialize in antiques and collectibles, and they also have a craft show on the fourth Saturday of every month from March through November. Antique show items include jewelry, glass, vintage clothing, furniture, etc. Craft show items include handicrafts, quilted gifts, handmade toys, etc. They were written up in the *New York Times* in 1993 and people are still coming because of the recommendation. The show is outside a collection of buildings, some of which are log cabins. There are two small restaurants and handicapped-accessible restrooms at this special market.

DEALER RATES: They request that you call for more information, as there are too many variations on size and show to list here. Reservations are required.

CONTACT: Isabel Michalski, c/o William Spencer, 118 Creek Rd, Rancocas Woods NJ 08054. Tel: (856) 235-1830.

Local News
During the winter of 1996/97 some locals decided that they had had enough of the "traffic and noise" of this still-growing market. When a Zoning Board meeting was held to decide the market's fate, the attendance at the meeting was close to unanimous in favor of continuing the market with slight modifications as to parking and location of stands and how early the vendors can set up. It seems that many local merchants profit from the market's crowds, keeping the area alive and healthy.

VINELAND
U-Sell Flea Market

DATES: Friday, Saturday and Sunday, year round.
TIMES: 6:00 AM-5:00 PM.
ADMISSION: Free. Parking is free.
LOCATION: 2896 S Delsea Dr. From Philadelphia go south on SR 55 to Sherman Ave exit. Turn left, proceed 2 miles to SR 47 Delsea Dr. Turn right; market is 300 feet down on the right.
DESCRIPTION: Opened in 1974, this market hosts up to 350 dealers under steel canopies on a 15-acre blacktop. Some antiques and collectibles, clothing, toys, tools, sports cards, fresh produce, "you name it" are sold here. Three food courts dispense breakfast and lunch, and handicapped-accessible restrooms are available. Lately, their customer count has been growing as the area has built up.
DEALER RATES: $12 Friday, $18 Saturday and Sunday for a 10' × 26' space and one 8' × 4' table. Reservations are not required.
CONTACT: Tim, U-Sell Flea Market, 2896 S Delsea Dr, S Vineland NJ 08361. Tel/fax: (856) 691-1222.

WARREN
Washington Valley Fire Company Flea Market

DATES: Every Sunday, Easter to Christmas, weather permitting.
TIMES: 7:30 AM-4:00 PM.
ADMISSION: Free. Free parking is available, although a $1 donation is much appreciated.
LOCATION: 140 Washington Valley Rd. Go north from Greenbrook 1½ miles from Rt 22 west on Warrenville Rd to first traffic light, turn left, go 1 mile.
DESCRIPTION: Formed in 1971, this outdoor market's 150 to 200 dealers sell antiques and collectibles as well as new merchandise. All this is

done by and for the volunteers of the Washington Valley Fire Company so that they can provide their own fire-fighting equipment. Food is served on the premises. They hold a shrub auction twice a year. So successful was a visit from a psychic reader, she returns for almost every show!

DEALER RATES: $15 per 10' × 20' space, including a table; additional tables at $7 per table. Reservations are not required. Monthly rates are 25% less.

CONTACT: Jerome Boschen, 12 Washington Valley Rd, Warren NJ 07059. Tel: (732) 469-2443.

WOODSTOWN
Cowtown Bawl, Inc

DATES: Every Tuesday and Saturday, year round.

TIMES: 8:00 AM-4:00 PM.

ADMISSION: Free. Free parking is available.

LOCATION: On Rt 40. From South Delaware Memorial Bridge 8 miles east of the bridge, take Atlantic City Exit to Rt 40 and go 8 miles to Cowtown. From North 295, take Exit 4 onto Rt 48, go east 6.5 miles until joining Rt 40. Market is 2 miles on right.

DESCRIPTION: This market opened in 1926 in the center of Woodstown and moved to this location in 1940, as they had outgrown their original spot. Nearly 700 dealers sell anything from antiques, arts and crafts, and collectibles to fresh produce, meats, cheeses, and new merchandise. This market is held both indoors and outdoors. Plenty of concession stands and handicapped-accessible restrooms add to the amenities. They draw anywhere from 15,000 to 40,000 people a day. Election Day is very popular here. Maybe it has something to do with the livestock market on Tuesdays. They sell cattle, the occasional buffalo. . . or as the boss says, "If it walks in here, we'll sell it!" During the summers, there is a professional rodeo every Saturday night.

DEALER RATES: $15-$35 per space. Reservations are not required.

CONTACT: Robert Becker, Manager, Cowtown Bawl Inc, 780 Rt 40, Pilesgrove NJ 08098-2909. Tel: (856) 769-3000 or 3202.

Keeping It in the Family
The current owner, Grant Harris, is the fourth generation of his family to own and run this market. It grew from the traditional Colonial markets held in New Jersey, officially and legally, on Tuesdays, which, of course, explains the popularity of Tuesdays at the Cowtown Bawl!

The strangest thing sold here was a Chinese wedding bed. No one knew quite what it was, this beautifully carved, gigantic structure, but it did sell.

Not from Here

But the news stories were full of the tale of a fellow who, looking through a box of rocks for sale, bought a big chunk of something for about $3. It was later proved to be one of the largest uncut emeralds in the world. The dealer tried to bring a lawsuit against the buyer to get his rock back. No go. The courts ruled that he had sold it, fair and square.

OTHER FLEA MARKETS

We know or have heard about these markets, but have not personally contacted each one, as we have the markets with descriptions. If you plan to visit one of the markets listed below, *please call first* to make sure they are still open. Flea markets do come and go. While they were open when we went to press, they may not be later. We can't be responsible. *Call first!*

Avenel: Avenel Flea Market, 1488 Rahway Ave. Tel: (732) 388-8868.
Bayonne: St Vincents Flea Market, 28 W 47th St. Tel: (201) 823-3032.
Camden: Jerry's Flea Market, 2701 Mt Ephraim Ave. Tel: (856) 338-0088.
Chester: Chester Lion Club Flea Market. Tel: (908) 879-4408.
Elmer: Circle 40 Flea Market, 770 US Hwy 40. Tel: (856) 358-8183.
Ventnor City: Sand Flea Market, 6003 Atlantic Ave. Tel: (609) 823-7713.
Villas: Bayside Flea Market, 901 Sunset Plz. Tel: (609) 889-4550.

From the New Egypt Auction and Farmers Market Animal Kingdom Outpost

by Fritz Davis

In the more than 43-year history of the market, animals have played as interesting a part as the management, merchants, and customers. Aside from merchants' and customers' pets, brought along for a day's outing, there have been "regulars" who came on their own.

Most memorable of these was Herman, a little three-legged mutt of a vaguely wirehair ancestry, who would show up early every market day, rain or shine, with or without his master, and stay late. In time he became the market's official closer. When Herman would finally stop, late in the day, look up and down the empty aisles and then turn reluctantly homeward, you could hear merchants calling back and forth among themselves: "Herman's going home—the market's over!"

Many merchants' pets, too, are well remembered, especially Gaby, a toy poodle of somewhat irascible disposition who belonged to Bill H., a dealer in coins, jewelry, and small antiques. It was hard to tell just when Gaby might develop a dislike to someone, and once convinced of that person's undesirability, never forgot and never forgave. Because I was a very good friend of her master's, she tolerated me, but just barely. For years I lingered on the "pending approval list," until the matter was settled once and for all—not to my advantage.

It was at the close of market day. Bill and Gaby were visiting me in my shop. I closed up, and Bill and I set off for a final cup of coffee and a rehash of the day's events. Unfortunately, by accident, I had locked Gaby in the shop.

Eventually we realized what had happened and I freed her, but it was too late. I had been put on the "no-good" list. Gaby rushed out as soon as I opened the door, grabbed my pants cuff, twisting it savagely, growling ferociously. From then on, she had to be forcibly restrained—all 8½ pounds of her—whenever I came in view.

We had a merchant, a devoted cat-lover, whose family developed allergies to his pets. He begged to be allowed to rent a facility at the market for their use as he couldn't bear the thought of being parted from them. After some hesitation, the management, cat-lovers themselves, agreed and an "apartment" was set up, complete with comfortable beds, heat, food and water bowls, toilet facilities, and private entrance. The merchant came every day and visited with his feline friends and everybody was happy. Naturally, it became a running joke among the regulars that we were the only flea market in the country with a "cat house."

One day a merchant showed up peddling a variety of odds and ends, including a snapping turtle—a large and very fine specimen, completely trussed up with rope. Perspective buyers were supposed to make soup, purportedly a gourmet's delight, from this poor creature. I felt so sorry for it, exposed as it was to the hot cruel sun, I dug into my pocket and produced the necessary ten dollars and bought its freedom. A six-year-old friend shared my feelings, and we placed the turtle in his toy wagon, took it down to the creek that runs along the western edge of the market, and after some quick and fancy maneuvering to avoid its impressive jaws, set it free. This made a great impression on the merchant who had sold the turtle, and for years after, he pointed me out to anyone who would listen as the true eccentric, though he used another term, one who actually paid ten dollars for a turtle and then let it go! Whether he thought this strange and aberrant behavior on my part commendable or possibly dangerous, I was never sure.

Soon we will be putting up bat houses at the market as part of a national voluntary effort to help preserve and restore this important and greatly misunderstood creature, so important for pollination and insect control. When this is done, I guess it can be truthfully said that we have finally gone batty at the New Egypt Market.

Courtesy
Fritz Davis
New Egypt Auction and Farmers Market
reprinted from the 1996 edition

NEW MEXICO

ALBUQUERQUE
Indoor Mercado

DATES: Friday, Saturday and Sunday, year round.

TIMES: Friday 12:00 PM-6:00 PM; weekends 10:00 AM-6:00 PM.

ADMISSION: Free. Parking is free.

LOCATION: 2035 12th St and I-40.

DESCRIPTION: This market opened in September 1991 and has 50-75 dealers selling new merchandise, plenty of imports, some southwestern arts and crafts and jewelry, ceramics, toys, new clothes, books, art and the "usual fare." They have a psychic and an air brush artist to round out the goodies. There is a food court, a snack bar and handicapped-accessible restrooms just in case.

DEALER RATES: $180 to $190 for a 10' × 10' space per month depending on length of reservation. Three and six months leases required. There is some daily space available for $15 per day, $40 for the whole weekend. There is some first-come, first-served space.

CONTACT: Indoor Mercado, 2035 12 St NW, Albuquerque NM 87104-2301. Tel: (505) 243-8111. Fax: (505) 243-8419.

New Mexico State Fair Flea Market

DATES: Saturday and Sunday, except for September during State Fair.

TIMES: 7:00 AM-5:00 PM.

ADMISSION: Free. $2 parking fee.

LOCATION: New Mexico State Fairgrounds at Louisiana and Central Sts NE, at Gate 9, the main entrance.

DESCRIPTION: This market opened in 1979 and currently has between 100 and 1,200 dealers depending on the weather selling everything: antiques, collectibles, arts and crafts, saddles, tools, boots, iron work, sand paintings, t-shirts, new merchandise—everything! Probably the largest market in New Mexico. Known for a lengthy jewelry row and one section of Native American arts and crafts. There's a new casino, and occasionally live horse racing next door coincides with the market. Excellent food, including American, Italian, barbecue, and Mexican, is available on the premises, as well as handicapped-accessible restrooms.

DEALER RATES: $12 per space. Reservations are not required. There are monthly rates at a discount.

CONTACT: New Mexico State Fair Flea Market, PO Box 8546, Albuquerque NM 87198-8546. Tel: (505) 265-1791 ext 305. Fax: (505) 266-7784.

North Valley Indoor Flea Market

DATES: Tuesday through Saturday.

TIMES: 9:00 AM-5:00 PM.

ADMISSION: Free. Parking is free.

LOCATION: 1026 Candelaria NW. From I-40, 12th St Exit to Candelaria. Located at 12th and Candelaria.

DESCRIPTION: Opened in 1993, this indoor market of 20 vendors sells antiques, collectibles, Native American artifacts, crafts, garage sale goodies, coins, stamps, cards, furniture, and new merchandise. One snack bar relieves the munchies and handicapped-accessible restrooms may come in handy. "Many treasures are found in this market." For that alone, it might be worth the trip.

DEALER RATES: $100-$160 per month depending on location and size. Reservations are required.

CONTACT: Gloria or Richard Gould, North Valley Indoor Flea Market, 1026 Candelaria Rd NW, Albuquerque NM 87107-2413. Tel/fax: (505) 344-2130.

FARMINGTON
Farmington Flea Market

DATES: Every Friday through Sunday. Rain or shine.

TIMES: 6:00 AM-8:00 PM during summer; 7:00 AM-7:00 PM during winter.

ADMISSION: Free. Free parking is available.

LOCATION: On Hwy 550, halfway between Farmington and Aztec, at 7701 E Main St.

DESCRIPTION: This outdoor market opened in 1970 and currently accommodates up to 300 dealers during peak season. Among the articles available are antiques and collectibles, fine art, crafts, household items, furniture, new merchandise, and fresh produce. A notable feature of this market is that it also offers animals such as horses, goats, pigs, dogs, cats—and a duck or two. One food concession building and handicapped-accessible restrooms add to the amenities.

DEALER RATES: $4 per 12' × 26' space Friday and Sunday; $8 per space on Saturday. Reservations are required March through August only. Self-contained trailers may stay on the grounds Friday through Sunday night for no additional fee. Food is served on the premises.

CONTACT: Cathey Wright, Owner, 4301 Holiday Dr, Farmington NM 87402. Tel: (505) 325-3129.

LAS CRUCES
Big Daddy's Market Place, Inc

DATES: Saturday and Sunday, year round.

TIMES: 6:30 AM-3:00 PM.

ADMISSION: Free. Parking is also free.

LOCATION: 7320 N Main (Hwy 70 E).

DESCRIPTION: Since 1981 there have been approximately 400 dealers every weekend selling antiques, collectibles, new and used merchandise, anything and everything. A convenience store and Laundromat are on the premises. To satisfy the munchies, there are one international and two Mexican restaurants on the premises.

DEALER RATES: $9 per space under giant metal sheds, outside $7 per space. They supply the tables. Reservations are not required. They do take reservations on Fridays from 8:00 AM-5:00 PM. Motor homes may stay overnight Friday and Saturday for $5 a night including hookup.

CONTACT: Manager, Big Daddy's Market Place Inc, PO Box 1954, Las Cruces NM 88004-1954. Tel: (505) 382-9404 or 382-1055.

ROSWELL
Monterey Markets

DATES: Daily, except Tuesday and Wednesday.

TIMES: 10:00 AM-5:00 PM.

ADMISSION: Free. Parking is free.

LOCATION: 1400-I W 2nd St.

DESCRIPTION: Opened in 1991, this indoor/outdoor market of 40-50 dealers sells antiques, collectibles, crafts, furniture, garage sale goodies, and new merchandise. There is a restaurant, run by the Egg-Roll Queen (a lady from Vietnam), open on weekends only, and handicapped-accessible restrooms. I'm told ERQ's egg rolls are superb. Say Hi to Stormy for me! P.S. Stormy adds, "Find your space alien souvenirs here!"

DEALER RATES: $1 per 12' × 12' space outside daily, $15 per month. Inside: spaces start at $80 for approximately 12' × 12' space. Outside: first come, first served. Inside reservations are required.

CONTACT: Stormy, Monterey Flea Market, 1400-I W 2 St, Roswell NM 88201-2066. Tel: (505) 622-4430.

Hysterical Note
As to the real fun stuff: Yes, this is the famous (infamous?) Roswell, NM, where the alleged UFOs landed on July 4, 1947. Find Stormy and ask him about this!

OTHER FLEA MARKETS

We know or have heard about these markets, but have not personally contacted each one, as we have the markets with descriptions. If you plan to visit one of the markets listed below, *please call first* to make sure they are still open. Flea markets do come and go. While they were open when we went to press, they may not be later. We can't be responsible. *Call first!*

Albuquerque: A Bit of Everything, 4000 Central Ave SW. Tel: (505)352-6737.
Albuquerque: Antiques & Things, 4710 Central Ave SE, Tel: (505)268-1313.
Albuquerque: Flea Market Things & Collectibles, 200 San Mateo Blvd SE. Tel: (505)268-1122.
Albuquerque: Star Flea Market, 543 Coors Blvd SW. Tel: (505)831-3106.
Albuquerque: Things Etc-The Indoor Flea Mkt, 1138 San Mateo Blvd SE. Tel: (505)268-1717.
Carlsbad: Seven Rivers Enterprises, 101 E Fiesta Dr. Tel: (505)887-5880.
Clovis: Carnival, 105 S Martin Luther King. Tel: (505)749-2085.
Moriarty: Moriarty Flea Market, 707 Rt 66 E. Tel: (505)832-5048.
Ruidoso Downs: Prime Time Flea Market, 1432 E Hwy 70. Tel: (505)378-8369.

NEW YORK

BOUCKVILLE
Bouckville Antique Pavilion

DATES: Every Sunday, from the last Sunday of April through the last Sunday of October. Special shows run by the Bonos (former operators): June Two-Day Show (first weekend in June, maybe), August Six-Day Show (third weekend in August, Tuesday through Sunday).

TIMES: 7:00 AM-4:00 PM.

ADMISSION: Free. Parking is also free.

LOCATION: On Rt 20, in the center of Bouckville, 100 miles west of Albany, 35 miles east of Syracuse, 25 miles west of Utica.

DESCRIPTION: This market, started in 1984, is located "in the heart of antique country." There are 41 shops as well as 6 multi-dealer co-ops included in this show. Close to 200 dealers specialize in antiques and collectibles, including furniture, glass, toys, jewelry, paintings, baseball cards, lamps, military items, coins, dishes, dolls, and tools. During the August show, there will be around 2,000 dealers in town for this one show. Whether you are shopping outdoors or under cover, all booths are conveniently protected from the mud if it rains. When you need a break from shopping, plenty of food is available on the premises, as well as handicapped-accessible restrooms.

DEALER RATES: $15 for 20' × 25' space outdoors; $20 for 12' × 12' tent space plus 12' × 20' space for vehicle. Reservations are advised.

CONTACT: Jack Malone, Antique Pavilion, PO Box 46, Bouckville NY 13310-0046. Tel: (315) 893-7411. For the two special shows only: Steve and Lynda Bono, Rt 20, Bouckville NY 13310. Tel: (315) 893-7483.

CALLICOON
Callicoon Flea Market

DATES: Weekends May through December; also Monday, Thursday and Friday during June through August.

TIMES: Saturdays 10:00 AM-5:00 PM; other days 11:00 AM-3:00 PM.

ADMISSION: Free. Parking is also free.

LOCATION: 43 Lower Main St, Route 17B W from Monticello, New York. Or Rt 97 from Port Jervis or Hancock, NY.

DESCRIPTION: This market began in 1980 in the historical town of Callicoon in sight of the Delaware River. It is privately run with a variety of interesting collectibles, antiques, crafts, lighting fixtures, depression and carnival glass, some new merchandise, furniture, and the occasional railroad and jewelry collectibles. The owner tries to have a bit of something for everyone. Many of the original buildings in town are wonderful examples of 1800s architecture. There is camping and canoeing nearby, as well as local bed-and-breakfast inns.

DEALER RATES: Not applicable.

CONTACT: Carol Kay, Callicoon Flea Market, PO Box 278, Callicoon NY 12723. Tel: (845) 887-5411. Call for seasonal hours.

CHEEKTOWAGA
Super Flea and Farmers' Market

DATES: Every Saturday and Sunday. Rain or shine.

TIMES: 9:00 AM-6:00 PM.

ADMISSION: Free. Parking is free.

LOCATION: Off New York State Thruway, Exit 52 E, at 2500 Walden Ave.

DESCRIPTION: Begun in 1975, this is the largest indoor and outdoor flea market in western New York, with 300 dealers outside in the summer and another 200 inside year round. Offered are a wide range of antiques, collectibles, crafts, new merchandise, as well as fresh produce, meats, and dairy products. The Super Flea and Farmers' Market boasts four fast-food restaurants on the premises, as well as handicapped-accessible restrooms.

DEALER RATES: $25 per 2-table space per weekend, the most common, call for other sizes and rates; $15 per 11' × 22' booth outside per day. Space is available on a first-come, first-served basis.

CONTACT: Ronald A Wagner, General Manager, Super Flea and Farmers' Market, 2500 Walden Ave, Cheektowaga NY 14225. Tel: (716) 685-2902. Fax: (716) 685-9605.

> Bob does tell of the chap who brought in pet burial vaults to sell. He doesn't know how well the dealer did, but notes that at the end of the day, there was a busted one in the trash pile. Makes one wonder what they tried to stuff it with. . . .

CLARENCE
Kelly's Antique World

DATES: Every Sunday, year round.

TIMES: 8:00 AM-4:00 PM.

ADMISSION: Free. $1 parking from May through October, free the rest of the time.

LOCATION: 10995 Main St, 15 miles east of Buffalo and 40 miles west of Rochester on Main St (Rt 5).

DESCRIPTION: There are over 400 dealers in winter and over 800 dealers in summer displaying their merchandise. Four buildings on the premises help to separate the various sale items. Two buildings are exclusively for antiques and collectibles. The other two buildings' dealers sell new merchandise, gift items, collectibles and more. There is an enormous variety of items with everything from antiques and collectibles to new merchandise, meats, and cheeses for sale. They hold Great American Garage Sales the first Sunday of each month from June through September. Special shows are scheduled during the year, including a twice yearly EXPO featuring 500 of the finest antique and collectible dealers from 22 states and Canada. There are admission charges for these special shows. There are five restaurants and handicapped-accessible restrooms scattered around the market.

DEALER RATES: Flea market rates are $20 per 21' × 20' space outdoors; $25-$30 per 9' × 9' booth indoors. Reservations are not required outside but are required for inside space.

CONTACT: Katy Toth, Kelly's Antique World, 10995 Main St, Clarence NY 14031. Tel: (716) 759-8483 or outside NY 1-800-959-0714. Fax: (716) 759-6167. Email: antiques@pcom.net. Web: www.antiqueworldmarket.com.

LEVITTOWN
Tri-County Flea Market

DATES: Thursday through Sunday.

TIMES: Thursday and Friday 12:00 PM-9:00 PM; Saturday and Sunday 10:00 AM-6:00 PM.

ADMISSION: Free. Parking is also free.

LOCATION: 3041 Hempstead Tnpk.

DESCRIPTION: Opened in 1981, this indoor market has 400 dealers selling literally everything—all new merchandise and collectibles, including shoes, leather, toys, plants, jewelry, flags, and all sorts of clothing. You could furnish your house and clothe a family from the merchandise sold here. There is one floor containing a newly expanded "America's Largest" Jewelry Exchange, and another at mezzanine level has a collectible card show and a huge wicker furniture display. They have 55,000 square feet of display area loaded with just furniture. For all merchandise purchased here, there is a seven-day money-back guarantee, except on special orders. A food court provides food to starving patrons and handicapped-accessible restrooms are there when the need arises.

DEALER RATES: $800 to $900 for a very large space for 16 working days (about one month). Reservations are required.

CONTACT: Barbara Eve, Tri-County Flea Market, 3041 Hempstead Tnpk, Levittown NY 11756. Tel: (516) 579-4500 or fax (516) 579-6715.

MONTICELLO
Alan Finchley's Flea Market at Monticello Raceway

DATES: Saturday and Sunday, from July 4th weekend through Labor Day weekend.

TIMES: 9:00 AM-5:00 PM, weather permitting.

ADMISSION: Free. Parking is free.

LOCATION: On Route 17B, just off Rt 17 (future I-86), Exit 104.

DESCRIPTION: Established in 1976, this is New York State's original upscale outdoor marketplace. About 100 vendors sell mostly new merchandise with a smattering of collectibles each week on a blacktop surface. As new vendors arrive weekly, there is always new merchandise. "We are a friendly, informal market that is well known for honest, friendly management and vendors." This is definitely a family oriented market. Food carts and handicapped-accessible restrooms add to the amenities.

DEALER RATES: $30 per weekend: pay for Saturday, get Sunday free. Monthly and seasonal discounts available. Most vendors may park in their selling space. A limited number of tables are available on a first come basis for $5 per day. Bring your own canopies and tents. Electric not available.

CONTACT: Alan Finchley, 750 Lido Blvd #6A, Lido Beach, NY 11561. Tel: (516) 897-5396 or (845) 796-1000. Web: www.monticellofleamarket.com.

NEW YORK CITY
The Annex Antiques Fair and Flea Market

DATES: Every Saturday and Sunday, year round.

TIMES: 9:00 AM-5:00 PM.

ADMISSION: $1 for antique market. Flea market is free. Ample parking is available, but not free.

LOCATION: Avenue of the Americas, between 24th and 26th Sts in Manhattan.

DESCRIPTION: This show began over 30 years ago and is claimed to be the longest running outdoor show in the metropolitan area. The market accommodates 600 to 700 dealers who come from all over the United States, Canada, and Europe to sell an amazing variety of merchandise, including antique jewelry, vintage clothing, bronzes, Art Deco, porcelain, and rugs. There are three outdoor selling areas and an indoor selling area—The Garage—that holds 150 dealers. Restaurants are nearby. There are relief facilities around the market, and handicapped-accessible restrooms in The Garage. In September 1999, *Country Living* magazine held a "What Is It? What Is It Worth?" event at this market.

DEALER RATES: Per 10' × 10' booth: T-Lot (flea market) Saturday: $110, Sunday $160; Antique Fair Saturday $135, Sunday $160. X-Lot per 9' ×

12' booth Saturday and Sunday $60. The Garage is $170 for a 10' × 10' space for the weekend. Reservations are preferred. Office hours are Monday through Friday 9:00 AM-5:00 PM.

CONTACT: Michael, Annex Antique Fair, New York NY (don't send mail, call). Tel: Michael (212) 243-5343 or for the Garage at (212) 647-0707. Fax: (212) 463-7099. Day of show call (212) 243-7922. Email: michael@metropolitanevents.com.

GreenFlea at IS 44

DATES: Every Sunday, year round. Rain or shine.

TIMES: 10:00 AM-6:00 PM.

ADMISSION: Free. Parking space is not provided. Garages are available nearby at standard city rates.

LOCATION: Columbus Ave at 77th St. Across the street from the Museum of Natural History.

DESCRIPTION: This show first opened in 1980 as a benefit for the school. Over 350 dealers attend this market, selling their merchandise both indoors and outdoors. This market is known for its quality antiques, fine art, arts and crafts (many special orders and made-to-orders by metalworkers, wood carvers and the like), vintage clothing and jewelry, and collectibles. Of special interest are the fruits, vegetables, baked goods and fresh flowers that are available from their farmers' market, an extension of the famous GreenMarket at Union Square. Proceeds are used directly for the benefit of the children, with over $300,000 given to the school each year. This market is unique as one of the first of its kind in the country whose purpose was education and support of the public school system. It is now a community event with a following of many thousands of people attending every Sunday. Beverly Sills, the famous opera diva, said this is one of her favorite places to visit.

DEALER RATES: $25 up to $100 for space depending on size. Reservations are required in advance.

CONTACT: GreenFlea Inc, 162 W 72nd St, New York NY 10023-3300. Tel: (212) 721-0900. Day of show call: (212) 734-3578. Email: greenflea@aol.com.

Honey?

Their Honey Man is quite famous for his New York honey—which comes from the flowers in Central Park, no less. Honey Man keeps his beehives on the top of his apartment building in northern Manhattan! This is definitely a "must-try" delicacy.

GreenFlea at PS 9

DATES: Every Saturday, year round. Rain or shine.

TIMES: 10:00 AM-6:00 PM.

ADMISSION: Free. Parking space is not provided. Garages are available nearby at standard city rates.

LOCATION: 84th St just west of Columbus Ave.

DESCRIPTION: This show first opened in September 2001 as a benefit for the school. Over 100 dealers attend this market, selling their merchandise both indoors and outdoors. This market is known for its quality antiques, fine art, arts and crafts, vintage clothing and jewelry, and collectibles. Many of the vendors are overflow from their Sunday IS 44 market. Of special interest are the fresh vegetables, fruits, and fresh flowers that are available from their farmers' market, an extension of the famous GreenMarket at Union Square. Proceeds are used directly for the benefit of the schoolchildren. There are some interesting versions of "fast food" provided here by vendors, and I'm not talking "hot dogs" either. Of course, there are handicapped-accessible restrooms when the time comes.

DEALER RATES: $25 up to $100 for space depending on size. Reservations are required in advance.

CONTACT: GreenFlea Inc, 162 W 72 St, New York NY 10023-3300. Tel: (212) 721-0900. Day of show call: (212) 721-1233. Email: greenflea@aol.com.

PS 183 Antique Flea and Farmers' Market

DATES: Every Saturday, year round. Rain or shine.

TIMES: 6:00 AM-6:00 PM.

ADMISSION: Free. Parking space is not provided. Garages are available nearby at standard city rates.

LOCATION: 419 E 66th; or 67th St between First and York Aves.

DESCRIPTION: This show first opened on August 12, 1979, and is now back with its original operator. From 100 to 150 dealers attend this indoor/outdoor market, selling antiques, collectibles, jewelry (from Georgian and Victorian eras, and fine estate to retro costume), textiles, laces, vintage clothing, pottery, china, silver, furniture and more. This is a great family place with plenty of homemade foods. Of special interest is the farmer's market selling smoked meats, fruits, vegetables, fish, cheeses, plants and fresh flowers from farmers in the tri-state area.

DEALER RATES: $50 inside space; $45 outside space. All tables and chairs provided. Reservations are required in advance.

CONTACT: Bob DiTroia, 98-30 67 Ave, Forest Hills NY 11374. Tel: (718) 897-5992. Fax: (718) 997-8192.

> So popular is Bob, the manager, that when he returned to run the market (he was outbid for four years), signs were draped around, "Bob's back!"

The Showplace

DATES: Saturday and Sunday, year round. An antiques gallery is open daily on the second floor and lower level.

TIMES: 8:30 AM-5:30 PM. Upstairs antique gallery weekdays 10:00 AM-6:00 PM.

ADMISSION: Free. On weekends, parking around the market is available on the streets.

LOCATION: 40 W 25th Street, between Sixth Ave and Broadway.

DESCRIPTION: This hugely successful market opened January 23, 1993, and moved to larger quarters. Their 135 dealers on three floors with 31,000 square feet of selling space specialize in antiques and collectibles only. In addition, The Antique Gallery has 65 dealers selling daily on the top floor. They were featured in the *New York Times* two months after their opening when they were the hot topic during the famous 1993 blizzard. The flea market scenes of Barbra Streisand's movie *The Mirror Has Two Faces* were filmed here. If it's old it's probably here: furniture, lamps, jewelry, paintings, silver, toys, clothing, timepieces, books, comics, whatever. They do plenty of advertising and as a result the market draws in buyers by the thousands each weekend. Lines form here early every weekend before opening looking for the as-yet-unfound bargains. And they have been found here. An espresso bar offers sandwiches, coffee and teas, and excellent light foods.

DEALER RATES: $250 for a 8' × 9' space (larger spaces available) for the weekend. Reservations are required. Galleries are available for $800-$1500 per month.

CONTACT: Amos Balaish, The Showplace, 40 W 25 St, New York, NY 10001. Tel: (212) 633-6063. Fax: (212) 633-6064.

NORWICH

37th Annual Antique Auto Show and Flea Market

DATES: Annually, the Saturday and Sunday of Memorial Day.

TIMES: 8:00 AM-5:00 PM.

ADMISSION: $4 daily. Shuttle buses run from city parking lots to the site. There is no on-site parking; it's already full of antique cars and dealers. There is parking in the school adjacent to the fairgrounds.

LOCATION: Chenango County Fair Grounds, E Main St.

DESCRIPTION: This market is a car buff's dream with proud owners and dealers showing and selling antique cars (Sunday), muscle cars (Sat-

urday), and show cars—and then the regular antique flea market, crafts, car parts sales (huge business, this), and auctions. There were over 700 antique cars on display in 1995, and over 300 muscle cars, which is about the norm. They hold two auctions on site: the Car Auction and then the "2+2" Auction, nicknamed the Poor Man's Auction. At the 2+2, the buyer and seller each pay the auctioneer $2 as a fee. All sorts of odds and ends are sold during this auction including "cheap" cars. Naturally, the fabulous cars are sold during the Car Auction.

DEALER RATES: All spaces are $30 for two days reserved by May 15; after that all spaces are $40. They do have a few spaces for the unregistered. However, please pre-register for your own peace of mind, and theirs. It's infinitely easier on everyone.

CONTACT: Ray Hart, PO Box 168, Norwich NY 13815-0168. Tel: (607) 334-4044.

PORT CHESTER
Empire State Flea Market Mall

DATES: Friday, Saturday and Sunday, year round. Also from the day after Thanksgiving through Christmas Eve, daily with extended hours.

TIMES: Friday 12:00 PM-8:00 PM; Saturday, Sunday 10:00 AM-6:00 PM.

ADMISSION: Free. Parking is also free.

LOCATION: Kohl's Shopping Center at 515 Boston Post Rd. At the intersection of I-95, Exit 21 and I-287, Exit 11.

DESCRIPTION: This market started in 1976 and is New York State's original upscale year-round indoor flea market mall. Featured are over 150 new merchandise vendors and the region's only "and largest" fine jewelry exchange. A uniform cash refund policy is offered by all merchants and supported by on-site management. Handicapped-accessible parking and entrances. One-level, climate-controlled shopping with approximately 10,000 shoppers per weekend.

DEALER RATES: Space is sold on a monthly basis only. Rentals average $500 per month per 10' × 10' space. All vendors must have or acquire a NY State Sales Tax Certificate.

CONTACT: Alan Finchley, 515 Boston Post Rd, Port Chester NY 10573. Tel: (914) 939-1800. Fax: (914) 939-5046. Email: AlanFinchley@empirestatefleamarket.net. Web: www.empirestatefleamarket.net.

QUEENS
Aqueduct Flea Market

DATES: Tuesday, Saturday and Sunday, March through Christmas.

TIMES: 9:00 AM-5:00 PM.

ADMISSION: $2 per car load. $1 per walk-in.

LOCATION: Ozone Park. Take Belt Parkway to Exit 18B Lefferts Blvd, go north to Rockaway Blvd, then a left to 108th St.

DESCRIPTION: This outdoor market first opened in 1974. There is a wide variety of merchandise to choose from, including hardware, electronics, clothing, jewelry, household items, linens and leather to shoes and sneakers. Everything from antiques and collectibles to new merchandise and fresh vegetables can be found. They boast of over 1,000 friendly merchants and thousands of customers from all over the world. There are all types of prepared foods available when you need a break from shopping, as well as handicapped-accessible restrooms.

DEALER RATES: $75 and up per 12' × 25' booth depending on location. Monthly rates available. Daily vendors can just show up, or make reservations for longer terms.

CONTACT: Aqueduct Flea Market, c/o Plain and Fancy Shows, 1550 Old Country Rd, Westbury NY 11590. Tel: (516) 222-1530 or (516) 745-5706. Email: info@aqueductfleamkt.com. Web: www.aqueductfleamkt.com.

RHINEBECK
Rhinebeck Antiques Fair

DATES: Three shows annually on the Saturday and Sunday of Memorial Day weekend in May, fourth Saturday in July (one-day show) and Columbus Day weekend in October. In 2002: May 25-26, July 27, October 12-13.

TIMES: Saturday 10:00 AM-5:00 PM. Sunday 11:00 AM-4:00 PM. July show only 9:00 AM-5:00 PM.

ADMISSION: $7 for Memorial and Columbus weekend shows for the weekend; $6 for the July show. Parking is free.

LOCATION: Indoors on the Dutchess County Fairgrounds, on Rt 9 at northern edge of Rhinebeck. From New York Thruway, take Exit 19 to Rhinecliff Bridge, cross bridge and continue 1 mile to Rt 9G, then south 1 mile to Rt 9, and then south to Fairgrounds.

DESCRIPTION: 2002 marks the 26th year of this casual, eclectic and extraordinary antiques fair. This indoor market attracts approximately 200 (175 for July) dealers and 8,200 buyers exhibiting a wide variety of quality antiques at a variety of prices, literally, from $25 into the thousands. Delicious food is served on the premises, making the handicapped-accessible restrooms handy. Find Jimi, bring him coffee, and say "Hi!" for me.

DEALER RATES: $510 per space and up. Reservations are required. There is a waiting list from which dealers are first chosen.

CONTACT: Jimi Barton, Rhinebeck Antiques Fair, PO Box 838, Rhinebeck NY 12572-0838. Tel: (845) 876-1989. Saturday only at the fair: (845) 876-6403. Email: RhbAntFair@aol.com. Web: www.rhinebeckantiquesfair.com.

Jimi tells of the spring 2001 fair when a dealer brought in two life-size zinc statues from an old (unidentified) cathedral. They were marked at $600,000 for the pair. They didn't sell and went to auction, but, says Jimi, "Everyone got to see those beautiful statues."

SCHENECTADY
White House Flea Market

DATES: Wednesday through Sunday. Rain or shine.

TIMES: 9:00 AM-5:00 PM.

ADMISSION: Free. Free parking is also available.

LOCATION: 3901 State St.

DESCRIPTION: This indoor market has been held every weekend since 1985. Approximately 40 dealers sell antiques, collectibles, handmade craft items, furniture, books, records and toys, as well as new merchandise. This is the area's largest indoor, year-round market and an excellent place for dealers to find great treasures. There are restrooms, if needed.

DEALER RATES: Average $27 per week. Advance reservations are required. Permanent dealers usually fill this market.

CONTACT: White House Flea Market, 3901 State St, Schenectady NY 12307. Tel: (518) 346-7851.

STATEN ISLAND
Antiques, Arts and Crafts Market

DATES: Three shows per year. First Sunday in June; Sunday after Labor Day in September, first Sunday in October. Rain dates, the following Sundays.

TIMES: 10:00 AM-5:00 PM.

ADMISSION: $2. Parking is free.

LOCATION: At the Staten Island Historical Society, Historic Richmond Town, 441 Clarke Ave. From Verrazano Narrows Bridge, follow New Jersey W Rt to Richmond Rd/Clove Rd Exit; proceed to the second light and turn left onto Richmond Rd, about 5 miles ahead turn left onto St. Patricks Place, and finally, turn right on Clarke Ave. From St. George, take bus #74.

DESCRIPTION: This show has been in existence since 1970. It is an outdoor market that accommodates approximately 140 dealers from Staten Island, Manhattan, Brooklyn, Long Island, New Jersey, Pennsylvania, and Connecticut. They sell antiques, collectibles, stamps, coins, old photographs, books, baseball cards, oil and water-color paintings, plants, handmade crafts, and much more. Hot dogs, soda, donuts and coffee are available for hungry shoppers. This show attracts crowds of over 3,000 visitors. For an additional fee visitors will also have the opportunity to see the exhibit buildings and museum.

DEALER RATES: $50 per 10' × 19' space. Reservations are required.

CONTACT: Historic Richmond Town, 441 Clarke Ave, Staten Island NY 10306-1198. Tel: (718) 351-1611 ext. 280. Fax: (718) 351-6057.

Yankee Peddler Day

DATES: First Sunday in May. Rain date is third Sunday in May.

TIMES: 10:00 AM-5:00 PM.

ADMISSION: $2. Parking is free.

LOCATION: At the Staten Island Historical Society, Historic Richmond Town, 441 Clarke Ave. From Verrazano Narrows Bridge, follow New Jersey W Rt to Richmond Rd/Clove Rd exit; proceed to the second light and turn left onto Richmond Rd, about 5 miles ahead turn left onto St. Patricks Place, and finally, turn right on Clarke Ave. From St. George, take bus #74.

DESCRIPTION: This outdoor market began in 1968. It hosts over 150 dealers from New York, New Jersey, Connecticut, and Pennsylvania who sell antiques, arts and crafts, silver, glass, furniture, jewelry and collectibles. The Women's Auxiliary at the Staten Island Historical Society is responsible for this fundraising event. This is claimed to be the first large outdoor flea market on the Island. This show is always well attended by dealers and buyers alike. Food is served on the premises.

DEALER RATES: $50 per 10' × 19' space. Reservations are required.

CONTACT: Historic Richmond Town, 441 Clarke Ave, Staten Island NY 10306-1198. Tel: (718) 351-1611 ext. 280. Fax: (718) 351-6057.

STORMVILLE

Stormville Airport Antique Show and Flea Market

DATES: Held annually on the last Sunday of April, May (Memorial weekend), first Sundays of July (July 4 weekend), August, September (Labor Day weekend), the second Sunday in October (Columbus weekend) and their Christmas show the first Sunday in November. Rain or shine.

TIMES: 7:00 AM-5:00 PM.

ADMISSION: Free. Parking is free.

LOCATION: At the airport. On Rt 216 in Stormville.

DESCRIPTION: This massive outdoor market began in 1970. Over 700 dealers attend their shows. A variety of purchases can be made, including antiques, arts and crafts, and collectibles. Shopping for new merchandise and fresh produce can also be accomplished at this market. Food is served

on the premises. (I'm told by friends who visited here that the goodies go real fast early on Saturday. Step lively!)

DEALER RATES: $65 pre-paid per 20' × 20' space or $80 at the gate. Reservations are suggested.

CONTACT: Pat Carnahan, PO Box 125, Stormville NY 12582-0125. Tel: (845) 221-6561. Fax: (845) 226-4766.

YONKERS
Yonkers Raceway Market

DATES: Sundays, last Sunday in March through the Sunday before Christmas.
TIMES: 9:00 AM-4:00 PM.
ADMISSION: $2 per car.
LOCATION: Yonkers Racetrack. Cross the George Washington Bridge, take the Major Deegan Expressway to New York Thruway Exit 2, right there. From the other direction, from the New York Thruway take Exit 4 (Central Ave) to the racetrack.

DESCRIPTION: This outdoor market's 400 dealers sell mostly new merchandise, although when there are enough dealers (40 or more) in antiques and collectibles one corner will be put aside for their wares exclusively. There are loads of different foods available: bratwurst, fish and chips, pizza, sausages, and lots more on traveling food trucks and snack bars. Naturally, there are clean handicapped-accessible restrooms for your convenience.

DEALER RATES: $40 for a 9' × 28' space with reservations; $50 without reservations.

CONTACT: Marty McGrath, Yonkers Raceway Market Inc, Yonkers Raceway, 810 Central Ave, Yonkers NY 10704. Tel: (914) 963-3898 or 968-4200 ext 216. Fax: (914) 968-1121.

OTHER FLEA MARKETS

We know or have heard about these markets, but have not personally contacted each one, as we have the markets with descriptions. If you plan to visit one of the markets listed below, *please call first* to make sure they are still open. Flea markets do come and go. While they were open when we went to press, they may not be later. We can't be responsible. *Call first!*

Addison: Chemung Flea Market, 1009 Fountain Ln. Tel: (607) 767-1206.
Avon: 9 Mart, 2688 Lakeville Rd. Tel: (716) 226-6870.
Avon: East Avon Flea Market, 1520 W Henrietta Rd. Tel: (716) 226-8320.
Belfast: Belfast Flea Market, Routes 305 & 19. Tel: (716) 365-9989.
Bridgeport: South Shore Flea Market, Rt 31. Tel: (315) 633-9766.

Bronx: Mike's Flea Market, 656 Prospect Ave. Tel: (718) 401-0023.
Brooklyn: Brighton Bazaar Inc, 272 Brighton Beach Ave. Tel: (718) 648-1815.
Brooklyn: Diana's Flea Market, 379 Rockaway Ave. Tel: (718) 385-1388.
Brooklyn: Margarita's Flea Market, 1231 Surf Ave. Tel: (718) 946-5188.
Brooklyn: Market Square, 1815 85th St. Tel: (718) 234-8830 .
Brooklyn: R & J Flea Market, 4119 Church Ave. Tel: (718) 469-7023.
Buffalo: American Park 'n Swap, 40 Fountain Plz # 700. Tel: (716) 858-5000.
Conklin: Jimay's Flea Market, 1766 Conklin Rd. Tel: (607) 775-4039.
Cortland: Riverside Flea Market, 160 Clinton Ave. Tel: (607) 758-4962.
Flushing: Genesis Flea Market, 9905 37th Ave. Tel: (718) 457-5391.
Levittown: Surinder Arneja Flea Market, 3041 Hempstead Tpke. Tel: (516) 520-1553.
Lowman: Lowman Flea Market, Rt 17. Tel: (607) 734-3670.
Malone: Ed's Flea Market, 91 W Main St. Tel: (518) 481-5371.
North Tonawanda: Main Street Flea Market, 140 Main St. Tel: (716) 692-7885.
Oneonta: Country Club Flea Market, Country Club Rd. Tel: (607) 436-9171.
Patterson: Patterson Flea Market, 3163 Rt 22. Tel: (845) 878-0001.
Plattsburgh: Bob's Flea Market, 15 Clinton St. Tel: (518) 566-0309.
Plattsburgh: South End Flea Market, 133 Sharron Ave. Tel: (518) 561-6926.
Pottersville: Dick's Flea Market, Route 9. Tel: (518) 494-4931.
Pulaski: Hillside Markets-Flea & Farm, 7753 SR 3. Tel: (315) 298-4085.
Ravena: Leisure Time Flea Market, 2532 US Rt 9W. Tel: (518) 756-8772.
Ravena: Ravena Barn Flea Market, 29 Old State Rd. Tel: (518) 756-7778.
Savona: Traders Market, 6250 SR 415. Tel: (607) 583-2328.
Sayville: Attia's Flea Market, 5750 Sunrise Hwy. Tel: (631) 244-5755.
Schenectady: Colonial Flea Market, 2948 Guilderland Ave. Tel: (518) 356-7065.
Schoharie: Cater's Flea Markets, Grand St. Tel: (518) 295-8057.
Springwater: Springwater Flea Market, Mill. Tel: (716) 669-2646.
Syracuse: Central NY Regional Market, 2100 Park St #101. Tel: (315) 422-8647.
Syracuse: Lennox Flea Market, 400 N Midler Ave. Tel: (315) 463-2196.
Valley Stream: Flea Market, 41 Green Acres Rd. Tel: (516) 593-3131..

NORTH CAROLINA

ALBEMARLE
Albemarle Flea Market
DATES: Friday, Saturday and Sunday, year round.
TIMES: Friday and Saturday 10:00 AM-8:00 PM, Sunday 10:00 AM-6:00 PM.
ADMISSION: Free. Parking is free.
LOCATION: Stony Gap Rd. Take Hwy 52 south from Albemarle, at the former skating rink. Between Hwys 52 and 2427.

DESCRIPTION: Located in an air-conditioned former dance hall and skating rink, this market houses 50 dealers selling treasured antiques to yard sale stuff including collectibles, old beer signs and advertisements, depression glass, leather, tools, new merchandise, Avon, army surplus, and crafts. It is said that Fats Domino performed on their stage during the dance hall years. Handicapped-accessible restrooms and a snack bar are on site.
DEALER RATES: $24 for space along the wall with peg boards, $18 for non-wall space. Reservations are required, as there is a waiting list.
CONTACT: Lyman Jones, Albemarle Flea Market, 1100 NC Hwy 109S, Mt Gilead NC 27306. Tel: (704) 982-5022.

CHARLOTTE
Metrolina Expo
DATES: First full weekend based on the first Saturday of the month, Thursday through Sunday.
TIMES: Thursday through Saturday 8:00 AM-5:00 PM, Sunday 9:00 AM-5:00 PM.
ADMISSION: $5, seniors $3. $10 (Early Buyers Day), $15 (4-day pass) per person for regular shows. Extravaganzas $6, $10, $50 (depending on which day you go) and a four-day pass issued Thursday for $15 per person.
LOCATION: 7100 Statesville Rd (Hwy 21). Exit 16A off I-77.
DESCRIPTION: This market, started in 1971, has grown from 800 to 2,000 exhibitors devoted to selling antiques and antique collectibles only. The grounds include 20 buildings, two malls, as well as dealers on the ground. There are restaurant areas, vendors and all sorts of food available, as well as handicapped-accessible restrooms. Twice a year, in April and November, they add 30 big top tents to the grounds, adding 5,000 dealer spaces. Dealers come from all across the U.S., Canada, Europe and South America for this big one. They are known as the Metrolina Antique and Fine Collectibles Shows.

DEALER RATES: $80-$120 depending on location and size of space. Reservations are required. Contact Metrolina Expo for the latest information.
CONTACT: Lydia Stainback, Metrolina Expo, PO Box 26652, Charlotte NC 28226-6652. Tel: (704) 596-4643 or 1-800-824-3770. Fax: (704) 598-8786. Email: info@metrolinaexpo.com. Web: www.metrolinaexpo.com.

DALLAS
I-85/321 Flea Market

DATES: Saturday and Sunday.
TIMES: 8:00 AM-4:00 PM.
ADMISSION: Free. Parking is free.
LOCATION: 3867 High Shoals Hwy. From I-85 in Gastonia head north on Rt 321 for 3 miles to Cherryville exit, turn right at traffic light to Old 321 and turn right and market is 2 miles ahead on right.
DESCRIPTION: Operating since 1983, this indoor/outdoor market boasts 500 or so dealers filling 750 spaces and tables. There are 300 indoor booths, 200 outside under cover, and 250 open tables. Items sold include plenty of garage sale goodies, some antiques, collectibles, plenty of fresh produce, new and used furniture, crafts, jewelry, clothing, and loads of new merchandise. There are 10 food outlets and handicapped-accessible restrooms when needed.
DEALER RATES: $8 per table outside, $15 per 10' × 10' space outside under cover, and $20 per 12' × 12' space inside daily. Reservations are required for inside and covered spaces. Outside is first come, first served.
CONTACT: David Stewart, I-85/321 Flea Market, PO Box 402, Dallas NC 28034-0402. Tel: (704) 922-1416, pager (704) 834-8093. Fax: (704) 922-4525. Email: fleabit85@hotmail.com.

DEEP GAP
Wildcat Flea Market

DATES: Friday through Sunday, May through October.
TIMES: Friday 9:00 AM-5:00 PM; Saturday and Sunday 8:00 AM-6:00 PM. Auction every Saturday at 6:00 PM. Antique auctions one Tuesday a month.
ADMISSION: Free. Parking is free.
LOCATION: 8156 US Hwy 421 S, 7 miles east of Boone.
DESCRIPTION: High in the Blue Ridge Mountains, along the Blue Ridge Pkwy, this family run flea market has been in business since 1972. From 70-80 dealers sell antiques, collectibles, discount groceries, candles, crafts, old and new glassware including depression, old and new gold jewelry, novelties, tools, hardware, new merchandise, coins, cards, furniture, computers and electronics and whatever. From 3,000-5,000 buyers show up

in this market every weekend. There is an auction every Saturday night at 6:00 PM, year round. Special Antique and Estate Auctions are held as needed. There is a wonderful restaurant on premises serving full breakfast, lunch and dinner. Large, clean restrooms are on site. Located in the rafters of the main building is a "Hanging Museum," representing 32 years of collecting antiques and primitives, said to make the most die-hard collector "envious."

DEALER RATES: Outside rates $5 a day for a shed (except free on Friday). Inside and more permanent space available from $65 per month; please call for more information. Reservations are required, as most space is reserved for the season. Full-hook up RV sites rent by the day, week or month. Mini storage units are available from $40 per month.

CONTACT: Elaine, Jack or Kevin Richardson, PO Box 163, Deep Gap NC 28607. Tel: (828) 264-7757.

Historical Note
The original market was built in 1972, and as they were putting the finishing touches on the roof—it collapsed! The builders had to build the entire structure again. Obviously, it stayed up this time. They've used it for 30 years.

A piece of depression glass was purchased here for $5 and later re-sold for $240.

International Folk recording artist "Doc" Watson makes his home in Deep Gap and can occasionally be found inside the main building "pickin" with his childhood friend and local dealer, Denver Cheek.

FLETCHER
Smiley's Flea Market and Antique Mall

DATES: This market is open every Friday, Saturday and Sunday, year round. Antique mall is open daily.

TIMES: Hours are 7:00 AM-5:00 PM. Antique mall is open 10:00 AM-5:00 PM.

ADMISSION: Free with over 10 acres of free parking.

LOCATION: Halfway between Asheville and Hendersonville on Rt 25. Take Exit 13 off I-26, then travel north ½ mile on Rt 25.

DESCRIPTION: This indoor/outdoor market began in 1984. The market provides over 11,000 square feet of space in the antique mall with 250 shops and over ½ mile of 600 spaces of covered selling spaces and daily spaces under a shed in the flea market. It attracts an average of more than 250 dealers. A large variety of items can be found, including antiques, collectibles, handicrafts, fresh produce, and some new merchandise. This place is known as the "Baseball Card and Beanie Baby Capital of Western North Carolina." Five snack bars serve the hungry. RV parking available.

DEALER RATES: $12 per 10' × 10' space per day inside the flea market area with two tables. Outside space $9 each. 10' × 25' lockable units are available at $161 per month. $115 per 10' × 12' space per month in the antique mall. Reservations are not required outside. RV space rents for $8 per day for electric and sewer.

CONTACT: Wade McAbee, Smiley's Flea Market and Antique Mall, PO Box 458, Fletcher NC 28732. (828) 684-3532 or Polly Hickling at the antique mall 684-3515. Fax: (828) 684-5651.

FOREST CITY
74 By-Pass Flea Market

DATES: Friday, Saturday and Sundays, year round.

TIMES: 6:00 AM-4:00 PM.

ADMISSION: Free. Parking is free.

LOCATION: 180 Frontage Rd. Eight miles east of Rutherfordton and 15 miles west of Shelby, exit Forest City off 74 By-Pass.

DESCRIPTION: This indoor/outdoor market opened in 1986 and hosts up to 240 dealers in summer and 100 in winter. They sell antiques, ball cards, racing cards, collectibles, electronics, CDs and DVDs (these come in before Wal-Mart gets them!), groceries and fresh produce, cheeses, baked goods, clothing, leather goods, tools, jewelry, and new merchandise. The outside tables invite garage sale goodies. Three snack bars and handicapped-accessible restrooms add to the amenities.

DEALER RATES: $7 per 10' × 10' inside booth; $8 outside under shed; $4 in the open. Reservations are required for inside space as there is a 4-page waiting list. Otherwise suggested.

CONTACT: Gary Hardin, 180 Frontage Rd, Forest City NC 28043-4348. Tel: (828) 245-7863 anytime.

What a Buy—Update

One buyer/dealer picked up a 1950s-vintage Buddy L car for $5. When he looked it up on the catalog to price it, it was worth $550. As Gary says, he spent an hour polishing that little thing until it gleamed.

Update 2001: A little visitor to the market saw the little car on the dealer's table and thought it was a great play toy. Unfortunately, the car zoomed off the table, crashing to the ground and chipping a chunk off the front end—devaluing it immediately by half.

FUQUAY-VARINA
Fuquay Flea Market

DATES: Saturday and Sunday.

TIMES: 8:00 AM-5:00 PM.

ADMISSION: Free. Parking is free.

LOCATION: 6109 NC Hwy 55. Hwy 55E. From Raleigh, take Rt 401S to Hwy 55E, then left on 55E, go ¼ mile and market is on left.

DESCRIPTION: This indoor market of 130 dealers, housed in a 130,000-square-foot building, sells antiques and collectibles, crafts, new and used furniture, jewelry, and fresh produce. As their customers are predominately Hispanic, their merchandise is geared to the needs of their customers. Snack bars feed the famished and handicapped-accessible restrooms are available.

DEALER RATES: Call for rates, as reservations are needed.

CONTACT: Fuquay Flea Market, 6109 NC Hwy 55, Fuquay Varina NC 27526. Tel: (919) 552-4143.

GREENSBORO
"Super Flea" Flea Market

DATES: Usually scheduled for the second weekend every month. But call to make sure.

TIMES: Saturday 8:00 AM-5:00 PM; Sunday 10:00 AM-5:00 PM.

ADMISSION: $2 per person, children under 12 are free. $3 for parking.

LOCATION: Greensboro Coliseum Complex, Exhibit Hall. 1921 W Lee St. Follow signs posted in town.

DESCRIPTION: This very successful indoor market, started in 1976, recently attracted as many as 10,000 shoppers on a weekend, with 500 dealers selling various types of antiques and collectibles, estate and costume jewelry, garage sale goodies, along with arts and crafts and about 30% new merchandise. They even sold tires once! Food is served on the premises and there are handicapped-accessible restrooms.

DEALER RATES: $70 per 8' × 10' space, 1 table and 2 chairs for the weekend, additional tables are $8. Reservations are required in advance.

CONTACT: Smith-Tomlinson Co, PO Box 16122, Greensboro NC 27416. Tel: (336) 373-8515. Email: info@superflea.com. Web: www.superflea.com.

HICKORY
Springs Road Flea Market

DATES: Saturday and Sundays, year round.

TIMES: 8:00 AM-4:00 PM.

ADMISSION: Free. Parking is free.

LOCATION: 3451 Springs Rd.

DESCRIPTION: This indoor/outdoor market opened in the former Springs Road Drive-In Theater in 1981. From 200 to 300 dealers sell anything and everything imaginable, including antiques, arts and crafts, collectibles and new merchandise. There is a heated building 500' long for indoor sales which has proved so popular they added 2 outdoor sheds. Two concessions provide food to the hungry.

DEALER RATES: $6 per day for a 20' × 20' outdoor space (2 car parking spaces), $8 under a shed with 2 tables, and $60-$90 per month for a 10' × 12' or 20' × 12' space inside, if available (there is a waiting list). Reservations are a good idea for the shed spaces, necessary to check for inside space availability; first come, first served for the outside.

CONTACT: Springs Road Flea Market, 3451 Springs Rd, Hickory NC 28601. Tel: (828) 256-7669.

HIGH POINT
The Triad Antique & Collectible Market

DATES: February 16-17, 2002.

TIMES: Saturday 10:00 AM-6:00 PM. Sunday 11:00-5:00 PM.

ADMISSION: $5. Parking is free.

LOCATION: Showplace Arena. 218 East Commerce Ave.

DESCRIPTION: A new show in 2001, and back by popular demand, with over 300 dealers selling antique jewelry, glass and porcelain, textiles and vintage clothing, furniture from the 18th, 19th and 20th century, artwork and decorative accessories, silver, antique toys, primitives and Americana, country store, antique advertising, architectural and gardening accessories, Victorian ladies items, hunting and fishing collectibles, and more. There is plenty of food and handicapped-accessible restrooms.

DEALER RATES: $100 per space 8' deep by 10' wide. Tables $8 each, electric $25. Reservations are a must.

CONTACT: D'Amore Promotions, 2125 McComas Way Ste 102, Virginia Beach VA 23456. Tel: (757) 430-4735. Fax: (757) 430-4738. Email: sales@damorepromotions.com. Web: www.damorepromotions.com.

LEXINGTON
Farmers' Cooperative Livestock and Flea Market

DATES: Tuesday and Wednesday, year round. Rain or shine.

TIMES: Tuesdays: Early (say daybreak?) until everyone drops (usually after dark). Really! Wednesdays: 6:30 AM-5:00 PM.

ADMISSION: Free. Parking is free.

LOCATION: 366 Livestock Market Rd.

DESCRIPTION: Since the 1930s this market has been running a livestock and flea market. The flea market has around 400 vendors selling antiques, collectibles, new merchandise, garage sale goodies, lots of produce, clothes, tools and whatever comes in. Wednesday mornings they hold a Poultry Auction and a "Junk Sale Auction" at 10:00 AM, then the goat and cattle auction at 1:00 PM. For a 20% commission, they sell the stuff you don't want to! There is a café with appropriate restrooms on site.

DEALER RATES: $6 per space. Reservations not required.

CONTACT: Davidson Farmers Cooperative Inc Office & Sales, PO Box 558, Lexington NC 27293. Tel: (336) 248-2173. Contact Dan York the day of the markets to reserve at (336) 248-5208.

Farmers' Market and Flea Market

DATES: Monday and Tuesday. Rain or shine.

TIMES: Monday 7:30 AM-6:00 PM (wholesale only—must have a resale license to get in); Tuesday 7:00 AM-1:00 PM (wholesale and retail).

ADMISSION: Free into retail market; wholesale requires membership. Free parking is available.

LOCATION: On Old Hwy 64 W, ¾ mile off of the I-85 business loop.

DESCRIPTION: This outdoor market has been in business since 1973 and is now under new ownership. It attracts 300 dealers selling a full range of antiques and collectibles, as well as new merchandise, farm produce, and tag sale items. There is also a wholesale market that operates on Mondays and Tuesdays at this same location. They have over 100 wholesale vendors selling all new merchandise: new clothing, novelties, toys, jewelry, crafts and other assorted goodies. "Wholesale Alley" is not open to the general public and requires a state sales tax ID to be able to enter the area. The Wholesale Alley has been a real success story here.

DEALER RATES: $12 for a 10' × 10' sheltered booth to $7 per 12' × 16' outside space per day. Wholesale Alley are rented by the month, all for prices. Reservations are suggested.

CONTACT: Kevin or Sarah Berkley, 308 Berrier Ave, Lexington NC 27295. Tel: (336) 248-2157.

Market Toys?
Former owner Tim bought an empty grenade shell for his young son
from an army surplus dealer. Unknown to his mother, Tim's son
took it to his kindergarten Show and Tell at school, wrapped in a
bag. When his teacher opened the bag, she naturally freaked.
"Cleaned the whole school out," says Tim. The sheriff's department was called, and of course, Tim and his wife were summoned.
The janitor, fearing for his life I'm sure, carefully took the grenade
out to the middle of the playing field and guarded it there. The
cops arrived and did their thing. Of course, Tim's son was terribly
upset that the officials were taking his favorite toy. Tim duly arrived, went to the field and pocketed the harmless casing. But not
before catching a severe lecture from the deputy and the school
principal.

MORGANTON
Jamestown Flea and Farmers' Market

DATES: Saturday and Sunday, year round. Rain or shine.
TIMES: 7:00 AM-5:00 PM.
ADMISSION: Free admission and free parking.
LOCATION: Jamestown Rd. One half mile off I-40 at Exit 100.
DESCRIPTION: This flea market, which attracts 300-400 dealers year
round, has been held since 1983. Dealers sell antiques, collectibles, handmade crafts, vegetables, and new merchandise. There are clean handicapped-accessible restrooms, spacious parking, storage, showers, and security available. Seasonally, up to five restaurants and several snack bars
take care of hunger problems (and boost the calorie count).
DEALER RATES: $60 for a 10' × 10' booth for 4 weeks; advance reserva-
tions are very nice, especially during holiday seasons, but not always
necessary.
CONTACT: Bob Smith, Manager, Jamestown Flea Market, PO Drawer
764, Morganton NC 28655-0764. Tel: (828) 584-4038.

Unexpected Visitors
They once had a skunk walk through the market that decided it
really didn't want to be there. "It disrupted the equilibrium of quite
a few, but did no harm."

RALEIGH
North Carolina State Fairgrounds Flea Market

DATES: Every Saturday and Sunday, except the month of October during State Fair.

TIMES: 9:00 AM-5:00 PM.

ADMISSION: Free. Parking is free.

LOCATION: North Carolina State Fairgrounds at the intersection of Hillsborough St and Blue Ridge Blvd. Take I-40 to Wade Ave, Exit 289 or 290, Rt 54 east to Hillsborough St.

DESCRIPTION: They must be doing something right, as they have 500 dealers inside and out in a total of 200,000 square feet of selling space—indoors in climate-controlled buildings. They particularly welcome antiques and have been known for the quality and quantity of their selection. Among the items sought after by loyal customers are the quality antiques, collectibles, craft items, fresh produce and a huge variety of new merchandise and services (framing, jewelry and bike repairs and more). The 1853 Grill serves up plenty of homemade soups and sandwiches and awesome Italian pizza. There are outside food vendors, an indoor snack bar and handicapped-accessible restrooms. The park-like fairgrounds boast benches and quiet places. For the kids, the pet dealers have plenty of animals to pet and love.

DEALER RATES: $16 per 10' × 20' outside space, including vehicle. There is a waiting list for inside space. Inside space is by the square foot. Outside space is first come, first served.

CONTACT: Joan Long, Fairgrounds Flea Market, PO Box 33517, Raleigh NC 27636. Tel/fax: (919) 829-3533. Email: cfmi@mindspring.com. Web: www.ncstatefair.org.

Watson's Flea Market

DATES: Saturday and Sunday, year round.

TIMES: 8:00 AM-5:00 PM.

ADMISSION: Free. Parking is free.

LOCATION: 1436 Rock Quarry Rd, I-40, Exit 300.

DESCRIPTION: Open since 1985, this indoor/outdoor market of 170 outside and 60 inside dealers sells everything from rummage and garage sale goodies to new merchandise; from fine furniture to antique furniture, old and new clothing, tools, electronics, carpets, household items, computers, food and produce, jewelry and repair, pictures, flowers, "you name it." Two snack bars, and a taco stand feed the famished, handicapped-accessible restrooms, and an ATM may come in handy. Ingrid describes the market as a "real old-fashioned flea market."

DEALER RATES: Outside: $8 per day per 10' 20' space, inside rates vary depending on size and location. Reservations for inside only, as there is a long waiting list; outside is first come, first served.

CONTACT: Ingrid Watson, Watson's Flea Market, 1436 Rock Quarry Rd, Raleigh, NC 27610. Tel: (919) 832-6232. Fax: (919) 832-1637. Watch for their website and email.

SALISBURY
Webb Road Flea Market

DATES: Saturday and Sunday, year round. Rain or shine.

TIMES: 8:00 AM-5:00 PM.

ADMISSION: Free admission and free parking.

LOCATION: 905 Webb Rd. Six miles south of Salisbury on I-85 at Webb Rd, Exit 70. Just 30 miles north of Charlotte.

DESCRIPTION: This flea market was started in 1985 and attracts 300 to 400 dealers. They sell antiques, collectibles, handmade crafts, vegetables, new merchandise, and coins, and specialize in jewelry, furniture, glass, tools, auto accessories, books and just about anything. Most of the merchandise is new. There's a restaurant on site selling mostly soup and sandwiches and the occasional plate lunch. There are clean handicapped-accessible restrooms, spacious parking, storage, and 24-hour security. Find John, the manager, and ask him about his dental jobs, and say Hi for me!

DEALER RATES: $60 per 10' × 10' booth for four weeks inside. Advance reservations are suggested inside. Outside rates: $6 for open 10' × 10' space, $7 for sheltered space.

CONTACT: John Nash, Manager, Webb Road Flea Market, 905 Webb Rd, Salisbury NC 28146-8536. Tel: (704) 857-6660.

Sitting In It—
John and his wife also have a shop at an antique mall. One of his offerings was a dental chair. While he was sitting in it, during non-market hours, of course, a couple of fellows came into the shop. As John describes it, he offered to do dental work, as he did that when he wasn't at the market. Turns out—one of the fellows *was* a dentist!

WINSTON-SALEM
The Original Cooks Flea Market

DATES: Saturday and Sunday.

TIMES: Saturday 8:00 AM-5:00 PM; Sunday 9:00 AM-5:00 PM.

ADMISSION: Free. Parking is free.

LOCATION: 4290 N Patterson Ave. Hwy 52N and Germantown Rd.

DESCRIPTION: Originally opened in 1991, then reopened in 1998, then combined with their second market in April 2001, this market has "hundreds of dealers in 500 spaces in 155,000 square-feet of selling space" selling literally "everything" from antiques and collectibles to loads of new merchandise and garage sale goodies. Snack bars, food vendors and handicapped-accessible restrooms add to the amenities.

DEALER RATES: $38 per 12' × 12' space per weekend. Reservations are a must, as there is a waiting list!

CONTACT: The Original Cooks Flea Market, 4290 N Patterson Ave, Winston-Salem NC 27105. Tel: (336) 661-0610. Fax: (336) 661-1918.

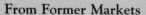

From Former Markets

Ashland's Dreamland Flea Market

They used to have a part-time deputy sheriff on site just to keep things in order while Dusty and his staff worked inside their office. One day an excited man burst into the office to announce that one of the dealers had brought a lion! Dusty and his partner decided to check this out. After three walks through the market, they still hadn't seen this lion. Then Dusty noticed a school bus taking up three to four spaces with something rather lion-like next to one wheel. Upon closer inspection it proved to be a young male, about 100 pounds, just growing his mane and fortunately on a very short chain. "The deputy pitched a fit!" The dealer put the lion in the school bus for the duration of the market and was never seen again.

It was here that someone bought a WWII artillery shell, took it home, fiddled around with it—and found $400 stashed in the base. You never know what you'll find.

OTHER FLEA MARKETS

We know or have heard about these markets, but have not personally contacted each one, as we have the markets with descriptions. If you plan to visit one of the markets listed below, *please call first* to make sure they are still open. Flea markets do come and go. While they were open when we went to press, they may not be later. We can't be responsible. *Call first!*

Ahoskie: Daniel's Flea Market, 301 Main St E. Tel: (252) 209-9144.
Asheboro: Ramseur Flea & Farmer's Market. Tel: (336) 625-4688.
Asheville: Dreamland Flea Market, McArthur Ln. Tel: (828) 258-0999.
Biscoe: Biscoe Flea Market, 215 S Main St. Tel: (910) 428-3500.
Burlington: West Webb Flea Market, 1413 W Webb Ave. Tel: (336) 229-9783.
Charlotte: Flea Market of Pineville, 3674 Hwy 51. Tel: (800) 527-4117.
Clinton: Clinton Flea Market, 1555 Turkey Hwy. Tel: (910) 592-3289.
Clinton: Sampson County Flea Market, 1480 Hobbton Hwy. Tel: (910) 592-7425.
Connellys Spgs: New Forty Flea Market, 5550 Paradise Ave. Tel: (828) 879-8841.
Eden: Eden Flea Market, 122 N Van Buren Rd. Tel: (336) 627-9440.
Elizabethtown: White Lake Flea Market, US Hwy 701 N. Tel: (910) 872-0085.
Elkin: Ye Olde Flea Market, 1046 Benham Church Rd. Tel: (336) 957-2361.
Faison: Faison Flea Market, 121 N NC 50 Hwy. Tel: (910) 267-1000.
Fayetteville: Bragg Boulevard Flea Market, 3315 Bragg Blvd. Tel: (910) 868-3100.
Franklin: Franklin Flea & Craft Market, Highlands Rd. Tel: (828) 524-6658.
Goldsboro: Artis Flea Market, 117 W Walnut St. Tel (919) 736-8590.
Goldsboro: Downtown Flea Market & Auction, 217 N Center St. Tel: (919) 734-0641.
Goldsboro: Goldsboro Flea Market, 2102 Wayne Memorial Dr. Tel: (919) 736-4422.
Graham: Graham Flea Market, 614 W Elm St. Tel: (336) 227-0505.
Greensboro: Flea, 3220 N Ohenry Blvd. Tel: (336) 621-9210.
Greenville: 43 South Flea Market, 1906 Fox Trot Ln. Tel: (252) 321-5575.
Greenville: Greenville Flea Market, 2400 S Memorial Dr. Tel: (252) 355-3646.
Hamptonville: 421 Flea Market, 3134 US Hwy 421. Tel: (336) 468-2376.
Hamptonville: Vintage Village Flea Market, 2832 US Hwy 421. Tel: (336) 468-8434.
Hayesville: Dan's Flea Market, 3998 Old Hwy 64 E. Tel: (828) 389-9725.
Henderson: Harris' Flea Market, 48 Allison Cooper Rd. Tel: (252) 438-5816.
Hendersonville: Trader's Junction, 706 Brooklyn Ave. Tel: (828) 697-1664.
Hertford: Dail's Flea Maket, 405 W Grubb St. Tel: (252) 426-4060.

Holden Beach: Bridgeside Flea Market, 3506 Holden Beach Rd SW. Tel: (910) 842-2080.

Holly Ridge: D & F Flea Market, 1324 NC Hwy 172. Tel: (910) 329-0155.

Jamestown: Westchester Flea, 715 W Main St. Tel: (336) 454-5706.

Lenoir: Foothills Flea Market, 2330 Blowing Rock Blvd. Tel: (828) 754-1224.

Louisburg: West River Road Flea Market, 44 W River Rd. Tel: (919) 496-1737.

Lumberton: Country Flea Market, 1102 Kite Rd. Tel: (910) 738-2823.

Lumberton: Lumberton Flea Market, 3561 Lackey St. Tel: (910) 738-4519.

Lumberton: T & A Flea Market, 91 Asa Rd. Tel: (910) 739-1885.

Lumberton: Traders Station Flea Market, 8750 NC Hwy 41 N. Tel: (910) 618-0004.

Maxton: Maxton Flea Market & Auction, 108 S 1st St. Tel: (910) 844-5595.

Maysville: Belgrade Flea Market, 7484 New Bern Hwy. Tel: (910) 743-3143.

Mebane: Buckhorn Jockey Lot & Market, 508 Buckhorn Rd. Tel: (919) 563-9420.

Monroe: Sweet Union Flea Market, 4420 W Hwy 74. Tel: (704) 283-7985.

Mt Airy: Felts Flea Market, 2290 Park Dr. Tel: (336) 786-6668.

Mt Airy: Mayberry Flea Market, 1275 US Hwy 52 N. Tel: (336) 789-0920.

Mt Olive: Southern Wayne Flea Market, 5460 US Hwy 117 Alt. Tel: (919) 658-8228.

Murfreesboro: Inside Outside Flea Market, 904 W Main St. Tel: (252) 398-8198.

Murphy: Foster's Flea Market, Junction 19129. Tel: (828) 837-9089.

New Bern: Cabbage Rose Flea Market, 2403 Trent Rd. Tel: (252) 635-1235.

New Bern: Poor Charlie's Flea Market, 210 Hancock St. Tel: (252) 633-4841.

Raleigh: Watson's Flea Market, 1436 Rock Quarry Rd. Tel: (919) 832-6232.

Randleman: Randleman Flea Market, 130 S Main St. Tel: (336) 495-6470.

Rich Square: Cecil's Flea Market, 151 N Main St. Tel: (252) 539-2476.

Roanoke Rapids: Flea Market, 260 Roanoke Ave. Tel: (252) 537-1258.

Rockingham: Airport Road Flea Market, 560 Airport Rd. Tel: (910) 895-0505.

Rocky Mount: Pack House Flea Market, RR 2. Tel: (252) 446-6910.

Rocky Point: Wells Rocky Point Flea Market, 1535 Hwy 133. Tel: (910) 675-0311.

Rocky Point: Stallings Flea Market, 12025 US Hwy 117 S. Tel: (910) 675-3023.

Rolesville: Rolesville Flea Market, 105 E Young St. Tel: (919) 556-3226.

Sanford: Sanford Flea Market, 405 Wicker St # A. Tel: (919) 776-7041.

Smithfield: Trader's Flea Market, 1505 US 70 Bus Hwy W. Tel: (919) 989-6026.

Southport: Dosher Hospital Volunteer Flea Market, 129 E Moore St. Tel: (910) 457-5620.

Spring Lake: 210 Flea Market, 14230 NC Hwy 210 S. Tel: (910) 960-8112.

Spring Lake: P J's Flea Market, 14170 N C 210. Tel: (910) 436-2334.

Tarboro: Dee's Flea Market, RR 3. Tel: (252) 823-3716.

Tarboro: P J's Flea Market, 1205 W Northern Blvd. Tel: (252) 823-4993.

Thomasville: Eleven Acre Flea Market, 825 Julian Ave. Tel: (336) 472-0244.

Vanceboro: Vance Mill Flea Market, 206 1st Ave. Tel: (252) 244-2800.

Walkertown: 66 Flea Market, 2800 Old Hollow Rd. Tel: (336) 595-4800.

Wallace: Wallace Flea Market, 1562 N Norwood St. Tel: (910) 285-3642.

Washington: Poor Man's Flea Market, E Hwy 264. Tel: (252) 975-9956.

Whittier: Gateway Flea Market, US Hwy 441 N. Tel: (828) 497-9664.

Whittier: Uncle Bill's Flea Market, 5427 Hwy 74 W. Tel: (828) 586-9613.

Wilkesboro: Autrey's Flea Market, 4641 W US Hwy 421. Tel: (336) 973-4470.

Wilmington: Old Dairy Road Flea Market, 6 Old Dairy Rd. Tel: (910) 397-2833.

Wilmington: Star Way Flea Market, 2346 Carolina Beach Rd. Tel: (910) 763-5520.

Wilson: Dee's Flea Market 3, 2028 S Goldsboro St. Tel: (252) 293-1136.

Wilson: Nichol's Big Flea, 1817 US Hwy 301 S. Tel: (252) 234-2008.

Wilson: P & G Flea Market, 3122 US Hwy 301 S. Tel: (252) 237-0411.

NORTH DAKOTA

MANDAN
Dakota Midwest Flea Market and Antique Show
DATES: First weekend of every month, except January.
TIMES: Saturday 9:00 AM-5:00 PM; Sunday 10:00 AM-4:00 PM.
ADMISSION: $1 per person age 10 and older. Free parking.
LOCATION: At the Mandan Community Center, 901 Division St. Take Exit 152 off I-94, then travel south on 6ᵗʰ Ave northwest to Division St. Signs are posted.
DESCRIPTION: This show has operated indoors since 1984 and currently attracts an average of 80 dealers who sell a wide range of items, including antiques and collectibles and fine artworks. One snack bar and handicapped-accessible restrooms add to the amenities. The market is close to historic Fort Abraham Lincoln, which was once the home of General Custer and has been restored as a national landmark.
DEALER RATES: $10 per 8' × 4' table per weekend. There are special rates for more tables. Reservations are required.
CONTACT: Barb and Bruce Skogen, 2512 93 St SE, Bismarck ND 58504. Tel: (701) 223-6185. Day of show call the Community Center at (701) 667-3260. Fax: (701) 223-9537.

MINOT
Magic City Flea Market
DATES: Second Saturday and Sunday of every month, except January and July. Call to make sure, just in case.
TIMES: Saturday 8:00 AM-4:00 PM, Sunday 10:00 AM-4:00 PM.
ADMISSION: $1 per person. Free parking is available.
LOCATION: On State Fairgrounds. Well marked in downtown Minot.
DESCRIPTION: This indoor market first opened in 1967 and currently accommodates an average of 75 dealers. There is a variety of antiques, collectibles, and crafts available at this market. This is an old-fashioned flea market with plenty of treasures dragged out of local attics and basements. Lots of old primitives, crockery and some Victorian treasures are still to be found. There is a concession stand and handicapped-accessible restrooms when needed.
DEALER RATES: $24 per 8' × 10' space per weekend, includes table and chairs. Reservations are required.

CONTACT: Richard Timboe, Manager, PO Box 1672, Minot ND 58701-1672. Tel: (701) 852-1289 at home or at the antique shop (701) 838-1150.

Drat!

When a former salesman died his family came across loads of his old samples: pipes, combs, sunglasses, condoms, razors and other "stuff" from his cases. Stuff that was sold to the likes of cigar shops, billiard halls and barbershops. Three truckloads of this still-in-original-packaging stuff was taken to the local dump. Some was left on the side of the road for anyone to help themselves. Eventually, some of this 1940s treasure made it to the flea market.

Another customer bought an old rolltop desk and took it home. Stashed away by one of its former owners: $17,000.

Richard was called to handle an estate sale and found a pristine iron lung, 60 brass fire extinguishers, advertising signs, early time clocks, a copper boiler, and dozens of cream cans among other wild items the former owner of a scrap metal place had stashed. Do ask him about it!

OHIO

BEACH CITY
Shady Rest Flea Market

DATES: Every Sunday, from the last Sunday in April through the second Sunday in October.

TIMES: Dawn to dusk.

ADMISSION: Free. The ample parking is free. No dogs or other pets are allowed on the grounds. Please!

LOCATION: Rts 250 and 93.

DESCRIPTION: Held under the trees, this old-fashioned outdoor market, started in the late 1960s by the late Mike Vukich, who ran the market with Mildred's help until his death in 2000 at 97, averages about 75-100 dealers and offers a range of miscellaneous items, including produce, collectibles, new merchandise, and handmade crafts. This is the oldest flea market in Tuscarawas County. In 1997, they considerably updated their facilities. Food and toilet facilities are available. Mildred is 82 herself, but will continue to run the market in Mike's memory. Thank you, Mildred.

DEALER RATES: $7 per day per dealer. Advance reservations not required. There are Dumpsters for the leftovers.

CONTACT: Mildred Dinger Miller, 1762 Johnstown Rd NE, Dover OH 44622. Tel: (330) 343-9508.

BLOOMFIELD
Bloomfield Farm and Flea Market

DATES: Every Thursday, year round. Rain or shine.

TIMES: 7:00 AM-3:00 PM.

ADMISSION: Free. Parking is free.

LOCATION: One-half mile west of N Bloomfield on Rt 87.

DESCRIPTION: Now under new ownership, this market claims to have been in business since 1943, making it one of the oldest markets in the state of Ohio. They are located in the heart of Amish country, attracting Amish dealers as well as buyers. There is a buggy parking area away from the car parking. It draws 150-300 dealers who sell both indoors (100) and outdoors (up to 200). Among the offerings are two meat markets (fresh and smoked), a discount cheese outlet, fresh farm products, Amish baker, tools, bulk spices, candles, canned goods, socks, candy, collectibles, lots of garage sale goodies, as well as crafts, new goods and antiques. Food concessions (3-5) and toilet facilities are available. There is a consignment auction at 9:00 AM to buy or sell.

DEALER RATES: $9 per 10' × 12' stall outside; inside, when available, $11. Reservations are required for some stalls.

CONTACT: Jo or Bill Herman, PO Box 51, Kinsman OH 44428-0051. Tel: (330) 876-7233. Day of market call (440) 685-9791.

COLUMBUS
Livingston Court Indoor Flea Market

DATES: Friday, Saturday and Sunday year round.

TIMES: 10:00 AM-7:00 PM.

ADMISSION: Free. Parking is also free.

LOCATION: 3575 E Livingston Ave. Just west of Courtright Rd.

DESCRIPTION: Opened in 1988, this market has about 300 dealers selling antiques, collectibles, arts and crafts, flea market fare and new merchandise. One snack bar and handicapped-accessible restrooms add to the amenities.

DEALER RATES: Starting at $15 per day or $30 per weekend. Reservations are preferred.

CONTACT: Bill Marcum, Rainbow Enterprises, 865 King Ave, Columbus OH 43212. Tel: (614) 291-3133. Day of show call Bill Marcum at: (614) 231-7726.

Scott Antique Market

DATES: 2002: January 19-20, February 16-17, March 23-24, April 27-28, November 29-December 1, December 21-22. Watch for about the same weekends in 2003.

TIMES: Saturday 9:00 AM-6:00 PM, Sunday 10:00 AM-4:00 PM.

ADMISSION: Free. Parking is $4.

LOCATION: Ohio Exposition Center. Off I-71, Exit 111, 17th Ave.

DESCRIPTION: This market opened in 1989 with 1,200 dealers (1,600 in November) selling exclusively antiques and collectibles. Considered "a treasure hunter's paradise," their dealers sell antique furniture, jewelry, silver, glassware, textiles, linens, advertising items, military items, paintings and more. There is a restaurant to perk up the weary shopper. Handicapped-accessible restrooms are also available. There is a sister market held in Atlanta, Georgia, the second weekend of every month.

DEALER RATES: $93 for a 10' × 10' space in the Multi-Purpose and Celeste buildings.

CONTACT: Scott Antique Markets, PO Box 60, Bremen OH 43107-0060. Tel: (740) 569-4112. Fax: (740) 569-7595.

South Drive-In Theatre Flea Market

DATES: Every Wednesday, Saturday and Sunday, April through October.
TIMES: 7:00 AM-2:00 PM.
ADMISSION: $.50 per carload includes parking.
LOCATION: 3050 S High St. Take I-71 south to Frank Rd; east on Frank Rd to High St; south on High St about 1 mile.
DESCRIPTION: In business since 1975, with an average of 350 dealers, outdoors only. Crafts, fresh produce, and new merchandise complement general flea market fare. Food and restrooms are available.

DEALER RATES: $5 for a 20' × 20' space, Saturdays and Sundays; $1 on Wednesdays. Reservations not required.
CONTACT: Don Smith, Rainbow Enterprises, 865 King Ave, Columbus OH 43212. Tel: (614) 291-3133 or 491-6771.

Westland Indoor Flea Market

DATES: Friday through Sunday.
TIMES: 10:00 AM-7:00 PM.
ADMISSION: Free. Parking is free.
LOCATION: 4170 W Broad St at Georgesville Rd.
DESCRIPTION: This newer market has 400 spaces for dealers selling everything from antiques and collectibles to newer merchandise. It is a sister market to three others in the Columbus area that cover North, East, and South, and this one covers the West side. Two snack bars and handicapped-accessible restrooms add to the amenities.

DEALER RATES: $5 per space per day outdoors. Indoor $17 per day, $33 per weekend. Reservations not recommended.
CONTACT: Peggy Morehouse, Rainbow Enterprises, 865 King Ave, Columbus OH 43212. Tel: (614) 291-3133 or 272-5678.

DAYTON
Olive Road Flea Market

DATES: Saturday and Sunday.
TIMES: 9:00 AM-5:00 PM.
ADMISSION: Free parking and admission.
LOCATION: 2222 N Olive. Approximately 5 miles NW of downtown Dayton. From I-75, take SR 35 W and go about 5 miles to James H McGee Blvd. Go north to Little Richmond, turn left (west) 2 miles south of SR 49 and 2 miles north on SR 35.
DESCRIPTION: Opened in 1989, this old-fashioned indoor/outdoor flea market of over 125 vendors sells antiques, collectibles, crafts, garage sale goodies, seasonal produce, and used and new merchandise. Their fully air-conditioned and heated 56,000-square-foot building houses 212

spaces and there is outside space as well. There is a concession stand and handicapped-accessible restrooms when you need them.

DEALER RATES: Inside: $35 per 10' × 14' space/booth weekly, $136.50 monthly. 14' × 14' space is $40 weekly, $156 monthly. Outside spaces are $10 per day. Reservations are preferred for inside; outside is first come, first served.

CONTACT: Olive Road Flea Market, PO Box 235, Brookville OH 45309-0235. Tel: (937) 837-3084 or (937) 833-3884. Fax: (937) 833-5122.

Paris Flea Market

DATES: Sunday, mid-April through mid-November.

TIMES: 7:00 AM-3:00 PM.

ADMISSION: $.50 per walk-in, $1 per car.

LOCATION: 6201 N Dixie Dr. Take Needmore Exit W off I-75.

DESCRIPTION: There are an average of 200 dealers in this outdoor market, a fixture here since 1966. There are plenty of antiques for sale, as well as collectibles, arts and crafts, produce in season, and new merchandise. The Air Force Museum is 3 miles down the road. Dayton is the home of the Wright Brothers. Concession stand and restrooms are on the premises. They have sister markets at Caesar Creek and Turtle Creek.

DEALER RATES: $12 per 19' × 25' area (between movie speaker posts). Reservations are not required; first come, first served.

CONTACT: Paris Flea Market, c/o Levin Associates, 111 W 1 St Ste 848, Dayton OH 45402. Tel: (937) 890-5513 (tape) or headquarters at (937) 223-0222. Fax: (937) 223-0154. Email: turtle848@aol.com.

DELAWARE

Kingman Drive-In Theatre Outdoor Flea Market

DATES: Every Sunday, April through October.

TIMES: 10:00 AM-2:00 PM.

ADMISSION: $.50 per carload, includes parking.

LOCATION: On Route 23 N at Cheshire Rd, 1 mile south of Delaware and 8 miles north of I-270.

DESCRIPTION: This outdoor market began in 1982 and currently attracts about 275 dealers selling a variety of collectibles, as well as fresh produce, handmade goods, and new merchandise. Food and restrooms are available.

DEALER RATES: $6 per 20' × 20' space. No advance reservations are required.

CONTACT: Dale Zinn, Rainbow Theatres, 865 King Ave, Columbus OH 43212. Tel: (614) 548-4227 or (614) 291-3133.

HARTVILLE
Hartville Flea Market

DATES: Every Monday and Thursday, year round.

TIMES: 7:00 AM-3:00 PM.

ADMISSION: Free. Parking available, $1 per car.

LOCATION: 788 Edison St NW; take Rt 77 to Exit 118 (Rt 241) to Rt 619 E. Go east on Rt 619, 6 miles to market.

DESCRIPTION: This market began in 1937 as a livestock auction; it currently draws up to 1,200 dealers during the summertime (Mondays tend to draw the largest crowds) and 200 in the winter. Indoor and outdoor selling spaces offer a place to find all sorts of antiques and collectibles, as well as local farm goods, craft items, and new merchandise. Food is available at the Hartville Kitchen and many food concessions around the market; handicapped-accessible restrooms are also available on the premises.

DEALER RATES: Mondays $6-$8 per 12' × 30' space, Thursdays $4, depending on location. Advance reservations are suggested. There is first-come, first-served space; be there between 6:00 AM-7:00 AM to claim a space.

CONTACT: Marion Coblentz, Hartville Flea Market 788 Edison St NW, Hartville OH 44632. Tel: (330) 877-9860. Fax: (330) 877-0961. Email: info@hartvillefleamarket.com. Web: www.hartvillefleamarket.com.

MONROE

Turtle Creek Flea Market

DATES: Saturday and Sunday, year round, also Memorial Day and Labor Day, and the Friday after Thanksgiving. Rain or shine.

TIMES: 9:00 AM-5:00 PM.

ADMISSION: Free. Free parking is available.

LOCATION: Just off I-75, Exit 29. Go west on Rt 63, right on Garver Rd. You can see the market from the highway.

DESCRIPTION: This flea market opened in 1992. It is held both indoors and outdoors and accommodates approximately 500 dealers during the summer and 300 dealers during the winter. From 9,000 to 12,000 people per weekend come here to shop. Items found here include tools, belts, Zippos, furniture, wood products, gifts, collectibles, craft items, as well as fresh produce. There are a number of food concessions dotted around the market and handicapped-accessible restrooms on site. Wheelchairs and strollers are available in Aisle 3.

DEALER RATES: Inside: $35 to $45 for smaller 10' × 13' booths. Outside space: uncovered $12 per 10' × 12' space on paved lot, or $16 per 10' × 14' covered space per day. Reservations are required for indoor space, while outside space is given out on a first-come, first-served basis.

CONTACT: Darren Foster, Turtle Creek Flea Market, 320 Garver Rd, Monroe OH 45050. Tel: (513) 539-4497 or the main office (937) 223-0222. Email: turtle848@aol.com. Web: www.turtlecreeks.com.

PROCTORVILLE
Proctorville Flea Market

DATES: Friday through Sunday.

TIMES: 8:00 AM-5:00 PM.

ADMISSION: Free. Parking is free.

LOCATION: 1 Shade Dr. Near the Huntington East End Bridge, 2 blocks off Rt 7. Follow the signs.

DESCRIPTION: Open since February 1991, this market is readily accessible to the many travelers going through three states: West Virginia, Kentucky, and Ohio. It has 185 inside dealer spaces and 60 outdoor spaces. Dealers sell antiques, collectibles, produce, coins, stamps, books, ceramics, crafts and supplies, carpeting, tapes and records, electronics, new and used clothing, tools, lots of new merchandise, garage sale goodies, and more. There is a restaurant with clean handicapped-accessible restrooms on site. There are 40 covered outside spaces. The state is constructing a highway by-pass which will bring in more business.

DEALER RATES: $7.50 per day inside or $15 for the weekend for a 10' × 14½' space; $3 a day outside for a 16' × 26' space. October through March is free outside setup, tables are $1 each. Reservations are suggested for inside; outside is first come, first served.

CONTACT: Proctorville Flea Market, 187 Township Rd 1280, Proctorville OH 45669. Tel: (740) 886-7606.

Know Your Stuff!
The story is told here of the dish marked for "40" purchased for $40. The seller thought she did really well as she had marked it for 40 cents, not $40. The pleased buyer later told the seller that it was actually a rare dish worth $250!

ROGERS
Rogers Community Auction and Open-Air Market

DATES: Every Friday. Rain or shine.

TIMES: 7:30 AM on to midnight? There isn't really a closing time.

ADMISSION: Free, with plenty of free parking.

LOCATION: At 45625 State Route 154, 8 miles east of Lisbon.

DESCRIPTION: This humongous market and auction has been operating on this site since 1955. A typical, local community-based market, it is mostly outdoors with over 3 miles of outside dealers under lights, and about 300 indoor traders under 90,000 square feet of roof. The 1,200 dealers sell antiques, collectibles, crafts, vegetables, fruit, meats and cheeses, the occasional alpaca or turtle, as well as new merchandise. On mid-summer peak weekends as many as 30,000 shoppers and browsers show up. There is a state park campgrounds nearby, and they have their own small restaurant serving plenty of homemade food, several good stands around the market and handicapped-accessible restrooms. The auction starts at 5:00 PM for eggs, produce, and miscellaneous items, and for poultry at 6:00 PM. You really have to see this one to believe it!

DEALER RATES: $13-$14 per 15' × 30' setup space per day. Reservations are required. However, if there is a vacant space available due to a cancellation, then it's first come, first served.

CONTACT: Manager, Open-Air Market, 45625 SR 154, Rogers OH 44455. Tel: (330) 227-3233. Fax: (330) 227-2074. Email: rogers@valunet.com. Web: fleamarkets.com/rogers.

SOUTH AMHERST
Jamie's Flea Market

DATES: Every Wednesday and Saturday, year round. Rain or shine. First Sunday in December is their Annual Christmas Special.

TIMES: 8:00 AM-4:00 PM.

ADMISSION: Free. Free parking.

LOCATION: On Rt 113, ½ mile west of Rt 58, 30 miles west of Cleveland.

DESCRIPTION: This market, opened around 1970, has 200 permanent dealers indoors and an average of 400 transient dealers outdoors. All types of goods are available here, both new and used, including books, tools, crystal, china, silver, glassware, jewelry, coins, stamps, handmade goods, baseball cards, floral displays, greenhouse plants and garden supplies, candles, Hummels and Goebbels collector plates, Amish crafts, clocks, lamps, music boxes, clothes, etc. One shopper even reported seeing a kitchen sink here ($50)! Claimed to be the largest and the oldest in Northeast Ohio, average daily attendance has been put at 6,000 in the summer and 2,500 in the winter. An annual Christmas special is held on the first Sunday in December from 10:00 AM-4:00 PM. Fresh farm produce featuring German, Amish, and American specialties are conveniently located for the hungry shopper. More variety of foods is available including bread, health food stands, candy and nuts. Food concessions and restrooms add to the amenities.

DEALER RATES: $26-$28 per 10' × 15' space indoors, $10 per 10' × 15' space per day outdoors. There is a waiting list for indoors; there are 300 outdoors first come, first served; 120 reserved outdoor spaces marked with "R." They tend to sell out of space early on Saturday.

CONTACT: Jamie's Flea Market, PO Box 183, Amherst OH 44001-0183. Day of show call Lolita Mock at: (440) 986-4402. Email: jamiesfleamarket@aol.com.

SPRINGFIELD
Springfield Antique Show and Flea Market

DATES: Friday through Sunday, usually the third weekend of every month except July. May and September shows are Extravaganzas. December's market is held the second weekend. Call for specific dates. 2002 Extravaganzas: May 1-19, July 5-7, September 20-22.

TIMES: Regular shows Friday 5:00 PM-8:00 PM, Extravaganza Fridays 12:00 PM-6:00 PM. Saturday 8:00 AM-5:00 PM, Sunday 9:00 AM-4:00 PM.

LOCATION: Clark County Fairgrounds, next to Exit 59 off I-70.

ADMISSION: $2. Extravaganzas $3. Parking is free. Early bird admission to Extravaganzas from Friday noon throughout the show $10.

DESCRIPTION: Started in 1971, this market attracts 1,500 dealers in summer and 600 indoors in winter selling quality antiques, collectibles, handmade craft items, and new merchandise. Several snack bars and handicapped-accessible restrooms add to the amenities.

DEALER RATES: Reserved asphalt spaces 15' × 20' are $30 per weekend; grass spaces 14' × 30' are $45 per weekend. First come, first served spaces $20 per day. Extravaganza rates: asphalt $45, grass $70 per weekend. For other building and long-term rates call. Reservations are required.

CONTACT: Steve and Barbara Jenkins, Managers, PO Box 2429, Springfield OH 45501-2429. Tel: (937) 325-0053.

TIFFIN
Tiffin Flea Market

DATES: Two shows May and October; one weekend each month, June through September. Call for exact dates. Generally the same weekend each time. 2002: May 4-5, 18-19 (first and last weekends), June 15-16 (3rd weekend), July 6-7 (1st weekend), August 17-18 (3rd weekend), September 7-8 (1st weekend), October 5-6, 19-20 (1st and 3rd weekends).

TIMES: 9:00 AM-4:00 PM.

ADMISSION: Free. Plenty of free parking.

LOCATION: Seneca County Fairgrounds, Hopewell Ave. Take SR 53 to Euclid Ave, then turn west; or, take SR E18 to Wendy's, then turn right; or, take SR 224 and turn east at Wolohan's.

DESCRIPTION: Started in 1977 and sponsored by the Seneca County Jr. Fair Foundation, this market operates from May through October with an average of over 200-400 dealers selling all types of antiques and collectibles, as well as fresh produce, crafts, tools, clothing, old jewelry, old glassware, and new merchandise. Proceeds go to promoting the welfare of the Seneca County Jr Fair and its activities. Overnight camping is available on the site for $10 per vehicle. Plenty of food concessions (serving breakfast, too) and handicapped-accessible restrooms add to the amenities. Sunday shows feature a dinner or barbecue put on by various organizations. July and August Sunday shows have Car and Truck Shows. Pets are discouraged.

The manager of the market, Don Ziegler, is a quadriplegic (from polio) who is around the market all the time. Do stop and say Hi! Without Don, there may not be a market. As June says, "He's the backbone."

DEALER RATES: $16 for the weekend, or $10 for the first day for a 10' × 10' space inside, additional day $8 if available, $2 for electric. Outside $8 per day for a 15' × 15' space, $2 for electric. Reservations are required for inside space only. Tables are available for a rental fee of $5 per table period; tables must be reserved in advance. Showers are available for campers.

CONTACT: Don and June Ziegler, Tiffin Flea Market, 6627 S TR 173, Bloomville OH 44818. Tel: (419) 983-5084. Email: fleamarket@tiffinohio.com. Web: www.tiffinohio.com/fleamarket.

Pets
Once a pet snake toured the market draped over his owner's shoulder. As he was upsetting too many people, he had to leave.

URBANA
Urbana Antiques and Flea Market

DATES: Saturday and Sunday, first full weekend monthly. Not in August because of the Fair.

TIMES: Saturday 9:00 AM-4:00 PM, Sunday 9:00 AM-3:00 PM.

ADMISSION: $1 adults, children free. Free parking is available.

LOCATION: Champaign County Fairgrounds, Park Ave.

DESCRIPTION: This very successful indoor/outdoor market, started in 1969, has a bit of everything available from over 200 indoor dealers alone. Weather permitting, from 100 to 200 dealers sell outside. There are antiques and collectibles, handicrafts and new merchandise, vegetables, meats, and cheeses. Refreshments and food are available on the premises. This is a growing market, full of very good antiques and collectibles. There are four heated buildings full of dealers year round. Two of the buildings are air-conditioned for summer.

DEALER RATES: $23 and up for a three 8' table setup per weekend. Reservations are required for inside sellers. This market is more than willing to work with their dealers.

CONTACT: Elizabeth and Steve Goddard, Urbana Antiques and Flea Market, 934 Amherst Dr, Urbana OH 43078-2212. Tel: (937) 653-6013 or (937) 788-2058.

WALNUT CREEK
Holmes Country's Amish Flea Market

DATES: Thursday through Saturday, March through December.

TIMES: 9:00 AM-5:00 PM.

ADMISSION: Free. Parking $1.

LOCATION: SR 39, 3 miles east of Berlin. Just about in the dead center of Ohio, in the heart of Amish country.

DESCRIPTION: Opened in 1990, this market has grown to a three-building complex of 500 booths in a 100,000-square-foot with a paved outside area, crammed with vendors selling everything from antiques to Amish woodcrafts, including lace, gifts, ironwork, furniture, jewelry and plenty more. There is a cafeteria which makes its own homemade ice cream in case you want a break from shopping, handicapped-accessible restrooms, and beat this: an escalator from the parking lot up to the market! The owners and manager of this market are quite considerate of their buyers as well as their sellers and plow their profits back into market improvements.

DEALER RATES: Outside: $6 per space. Inside: $35 for the weekend for a 10' × 10' space plus $5 for electric. Reservations are required for inside space. Outside is first come, first served.

CONTACT: Ben and Laura Mast, PO Box 172, Walnut Creek OH 44687-0172. Tel: (330) 893-2836. Email: jmast@amishfleamarket.com. Web: www.amishfleamarket.com.

WILMINGTON

Caesar Creek Flea Market

DATES: Saturday and Sunday, year round, also Memorial Day, Labor Day, and the Friday after Thanksgiving. Rain or shine.

TIMES: 9:00 AM-5:00 PM.

ADMISSION: $1 per carload.

LOCATION: 7763 SR 73 W at I-71, Exit 45. Five miles east of Caesar Creek Lake State Park on SR 73. Located only 19 miles north of Kings Island Amusement Park on I-71.

DESCRIPTION: This flea market first opened in 1979. It is held both indoors and outdoors and accommodates over 600 dealers. From 12,000 to 14,000 people per weekend come here to shop. Items found here include antiques, collectibles, craft items, dolls, furniture, mattresses, RV equipment, shoes, jewelry, Nascar collectibles, tools, kitchen utensils, and more. Five indoor restaurants and several concessions outside serve the hungry. Handicapped-accessible restrooms accommodate other needs. Wheelchairs and strollers are available in the office in Aisle 4.

DEALER RATES: Inside: $50 to $68 for smaller 10' × 12' booths; $130 per 20' × 25' booth per weekend. Outside space: uncovered $14, sheltered $18. Reservations are required for indoor space, while outside space is first come, first served.

CONTACT: Louis Levin, Caesar Creek Flea Market, 7763 SR 73 W, Wilmington OH 45177. Tel: (937) 382-1669 or (937) 223-0222. Fax: (937) 223-0154. Email: turtle848@aol.com. Web: www.caesarcreek.com.

OTHER FLEA MARKETS

We know or have heard about these markets, but have not personally contacted each one, as we have the markets with descriptions. If you plan to visit one of the markets listed below, *please call first* to make sure they are still open. Flea markets do come and go. While they were open when we went to press, they may not be later. We can't be responsible. *Call first!*

Akron: Fifth Ave Flea Market, 2301 Romig Rd. Tel: (330) 753-5530.

Ashtabula: Bargain Mart Flea Market, 2229 W Prospect Rd. Tel: (440) 992-9060.

Ashtabula: Flea Country USA, 3501 N Ridge Rd W. Tel: (440) 998-3177.

Athens: Athens Flea Market, 122 Columbus Rd. Tel: (740) 593-7626.

Barnesville: East Main Flea Market, 511 E Main St. Tel: (740) 425-4310.

Batavia: Red Barn Market, 50 W Main St. Tel: (513) 732-0515.

Bridgeport: Chapter Square Flea Market, 68210 Belmont Ave. Tel: (740) 635-0090.

Chesapeake: Chesapeake Flea Market, 10917 County Road 1. Tel: (740) 867-6355.

Chesapeake: Chesapeake Flea Market, 10949 County Road 1. Tel: (740) 867-9676.

Cincinnati: Elmwood Trading Post, 6015 Vine St. Tel: (513) 641-4414.

Cincinnati: Peddlers Flea Market, 4343 Kellogg Ave. Tel: (513) 871-3700.

Cleveland: Broadway Flea Market, 7640 Broadway Ave. Tel: (216) 341-0007.

Cleveland: Don's Garden Valley Flea Market, 7237 Kinsman Rd. Tel: (216) 341-1199.

Cleveland: Hopkins Flea Market, 12005 Buckeye Rd. Tel: (216) 752-0683.

Cleveland: Kinney Flea Market, 12514 Superior Ave. Tel: (216) 231-7227.

Columbus: Flealess Market, 4170 W Broad St. Tel: (614) 272-0177.

Columbus: Westland Flea Market, 4170 W Broad St. Tel: (614) 272-5678.

Columbus: Southland Expo Ctr, 3660 S High St. Tel: (614) 497-0200.

Dayton: West 3rd St Flee Market, 930 W 3rd St. Tel: (937) 461-3532.

Dayton: Berthel Briggs Flea Market, 3200 Oakridge Dr. Tel: (937) 268-7379.

Dayton: Forest Park Flea Market, 4444 N Main St. Tel: (937) 274-3983.

Dayton: Frank & Gladys Flea Market, 3700 Keats Dr. Tel: (937) 279-0947.

Dayton: Huber Heights Flea Market, 4434 Powell Rd. Tel: (937) 236-0028.

Dayton: Valley Street Flea Market, 1602 Valley St. Tel: (937) 222-1400.

Dover: Dover Flea Market, 120 S Tuscarawas Ave. Tel: (330) 364-3959.

Dundee: Garver's Flea Market, 7287 Dundee Strasburg Rd NW. Tel: (330) 878-5664.

Elyria: Hall's Trading Post, 41957 N Ridge Rd. Tel: (440) 233-8613.

Findlay: Sholiz Flea Market, 120 E Sandusky St. Tel: (419) 424-3881.

Franklin: Schomy's Flea Market, 100 Schomy Dr. Tel: (937) 746-0389.

Hartville: Byler's Flea Market, 900 Edison St NW. Tel: (330) 877-6433.

Lancaster: Dumontville Flea Market, 980 Ginder Rd NW. Tel: (740) 756-4457.

Mansfield: Lincoln Center Peddler's Market, 995 Ashland Rd. Tel: (419) 589-7785.

Mansfield: Teeter's Flea Market, 928 Springmill St. Tel: (419) 747-1818.

Massillon: Massillon Flea Market, 332 Erie St S. Tel: (330) 833-8457.

Navarre: Vavare Indoor Flea Market, 2 Main St N. Tel: (330) 879-0252.

Newark: 11th Street Flea Market, 50 N 11th St. Tel: (740) 349-9179.

Newark: Union St Flea Market, 34 Waterworks Rd. Tel: (740) 344-7774.

North Bloomfield: Bloomfield Flea Market Inc, 2211 S Rt 87 NW. Tel: (440) 685-9791.

Oberlin: East Oberlin Flea Market, 43433 Oberlin Elyria Rd. Tel: (440) 774-4312.

Painesville: Painesville Flea Market, 1301 Mentor Ave. Tel: (440) 352-7373.

Pataskala: Red Barn Flea Market, 10501 Columbus Expy Park. Tel: (740) 927-2276.

Piketon: Southbound Flea Market, 1439 US Hwy 23. Tel: (740) 289-4151.

Piqua: Piqua Flea Market, 8225 Looney Rd. Tel: (937) 778-2299.

Shelby: Jerry's Flea Market, 209 N Gamble St. Tel: (419) 342-4353.

Shelby: Paul & Thelma's Flea Market, 175 N Gamble St. Tel: (419) 342-3623.

Springfield: Village Trading Post, 2819 E Main St. Tel (937) 323-8164.

St Louisville: St Louisville Flea Market, 8291 Mount Vernon Rd. Tel: (740) 745-2550.

Tiffin: After Hours Flea Market, 281 N Sandusky St. Tel: (419) 448-0104.

Toledo: Flea Market, 3352 LaGrange St. Tel: (419) 243-1723.

Toledo: High-Level Flea Market, 523 Oak St. Tel: (419) 698-4481.

Toledo: Hidden Treasures Flea Market, 2001 Starr Ave. Tel: (419) 693-1307.

Warren: Warren Flea Market, 428 Main Ave SW. Tel: (330) 399-8298.

Waynesfield: Old Schoolhouse Flea Market, 20322 US Rt 33. Tel: (419) 568-4501.

West Jefferson: West 40 Flea Market, 4280 US Hwy 40. Tel: (614) 879-5801.

Westerville: 3-C Flea Market, 6950 Chandler Dr. Tel: (614) 882-5076.

Willoughby: Indoor Flea Market, 33180 Vine St. Tel: (440) 946-9726.

Xenia: Heartland Flea Market, 457 Dayton Ave. Tel: (937) 372-6699.

Youngstown: Austintown Flea Market, 5370 Clarkins Dr. Tel: (330) 799-1325.

Youngstown: Four Seasons Flea Market, 3000 McCartney Rd. Tel: (330) 744-5050.

Zanesville: Big Rock Flea Market, 5705 East Pike. Tel: (740) 872-4120.

OKLAHOMA

DEL CITY
Cherokee Flea Market and Swap Meet

DATES: Daily, year round.
TIMES: 7:00 AM-3:00 PM.
ADMISSION: Free. Parking is also free.
LOCATION: 3101 SE 15th St, corner of SE 15th and Bryant.
DESCRIPTION: Said to be one of the oldest flea markets in Oklahoma, and at the same location for 37 years, this market has over 40 dealers selling everything from antiques and collectibles to garage sale loads, attic finds, furniture, produce, new, used, and old merchandise, VCRs, TVs, and whatever. A snack bar on premises serves breakfast, lunch, and other treats. They invite you to drop in to watch the domino games in the Domino Room of the snack bar. There are handicapped-accessible restrooms on the premises.

DEALER RATES: $5 per outside table setup; building space starts at $45 and up per space. Reservations are not required. No peddler's license required as they are considered their own 8-block county.
CONTACT: KO Jose, Cherokee Flea Market and Swap Meet, 3101 SE 15 St, Del City OK 73115. Tel: (405) 677-4056.

LOCUST GROVE
Old Locust Grove Sale Barn Flea Market

DATES: Every Thursday. Weather permitting.
TIMES: Early morning until mid-day.
ADMISSION: Free. Parking is free.
LOCATION: East side of the grade school on the east side of Locust Grove. From the junction of Rts 82 and Scenic 412, it's 4 blocks north, 3 blocks west and 1 block south.
DESCRIPTION: Starting in the mid-1930s as an outdoor meeting, swapping, and visiting place, this market hosts 25 vendors in winter to 50 in summer selling musical instruments, tools, plants, antiques, collectibles, garage sale goodies, crafts, coins, stamps, cards, furniture, and "just about anything and everything." There are restrooms available, but no mention of food, aside from produce.

DEALER RATES: $5-$7.50 for 12' × 24' space outside. Some sheds are available for $6-$8. First come, first served.
CONTACT: Jerry Koelseh, HC 64 Box 100, Locust Grove OK 74352. Tel: (918) 479-5960 or 479-8257.

OKLAHOMA CITY
AMC Family Flea Market

DATES: Saturday and Sunday, year round.
TIMES: 9:00 AM-6:00 PM.
ADMISSION: Free. Free parking is available.
LOCATION: 1001 N Pennsylvania St.

DESCRIPTION: This indoor/outdoor market started in 1988 and has 600 booth spaces with over 250 dealers selling antiques, collectibles, baseball cards, coins, stamps, office supplies and furniture, new furniture, Indian art, garage sale treasures, 14-karat gold jewelry, and new merchandise among other things. Housed in a 135,000-square-foot building, with about 50 dealer spaces outside, this is probably the largest flea market in Oklahoma. Four concession stands selling Chinese and American foods and handicapped-accessible restrooms add to the amenities. There is a huge train exhibit taking up 1,000 square feet of space. They are expanding their outside area to hold 300 booths on the south end of the parking lot.
DEALER RATES: $50 per weekend; $184 per month. Reservations are not required. Daily rates also available: $10 per day outside. New spaces in the outdoor market will be $5 to start with.
CONTACT: Nick Adams, AMC Family Flea Market, 1001 N Pennsylvania St, Oklahoma City OK 73107. Tel: (405) 232-5061. Fax: (405) 232-0141.

Mary's Ole Time Swap Meet

DATES: Every Saturday and Sunday, year round. Rain or shine.
TIMES: Dawn to dusk.
ADMISSION: Free admission and parking.
LOCATION: 7905 NE 23 St. Northeast corner of 23rd St and Midwest Blvd.
DESCRIPTION: This market started in 1963. There are over 300 dealers selling both indoors and out. Lots of antiques, collectibles, primitives, and western curios complement an assortment of handmade items, produce, as well as new merchandise. Dennis has seen billy-goats to Rolls Royces sold here. One café and two concession stands provide eatables; handicapped-accessible restrooms provide relief. There is a Dodge City western town as part of the market where they hold music shows. It has a saloon, authentic old wagons and a jail, among other buildings (of course, if the kids get rowdy...).
DEALER RATES: $7 and up for 12' × 20' booths, plus electric. No advance reservations are required.
CONTACT: Dennis Sizemore, Mary's Ole Time Swap Meet, 7905 NE 23 St, Oklahoma City OK 73141-1430. Tel: (405) 427-0051.

Old Paris Flea Market

DATES: Every Saturday and Sunday, year round. Rain or shine.

TIMES: 9:00 AM-6:00 PM.

ADMISSION: Free admission and parking.

LOCATION: 1111 S Eastern Rd; access from I-40 and I-35.

DESCRIPTION: This indoor/outdoor show started January 3, 1976, and hosts 400-plus dealers selling everything from antiques, crafts, and collectibles to produce, meats, cheeses, and new merchandise. Close to a KOA campground and near the Baseball Hall of Fame. Two snack bars and handicapped-accessible restrooms add to the amenities.

DEALER RATES: $26.50 per 8' × 15' booth indoors per selling day. $12.50 for 10' × 20' outdoor space daily. Reservations are required by the Monday before the weekend requested. Monthly rate discounts available.

CONTACT: Brandi Duncan or Georgie Parker, Old Paris Flea Market, 1111 S Eastern Rd, Oklahoma City OK 73129. Tel: (405) 670-2611 or 670-2612.

TULSA

The Great American Flea Market and Antique Mall

DATES: Friday, Saturday and Sunday, year round.

TIMES: 10:00 AM-6:00 PM.

ADMISSION: Free. Parking is also free.

LOCATION: 9210-9244 E Admiral Pl.

DESCRIPTION: Opened in 1989, this market holds 500 dealers inside and up to 100 outside selling antiques, collectibles, glassware, jewelry, baseball cards, garage sale stuff, and more "from A to Z." A cafe provides meals. There is a mall and a produce market section adjacent to this market open daily.

DEALER RATES: Reasonable rates vary according to location, size and length of rental. Reservations are suggested.

CONTACT: Ty Hogan, The Great American Flea Market, 6019 S 66 E Ave, Tulsa OK 74145. Tel: (918) 834-6363 or 492-3476. Email: gamarket1@aol.com. Web: gamarket.com.

The Tulsa Flea Market

DATES: Saturday, closed during the fair and some holiday weekends.

TIMES: 8:00 AM-5:00 PM.

ADMISSION: $1. Parking is free.

LOCATION: Tulsa Fairgrounds at 21st and Yale.

DESCRIPTION: This indoor air-conditioned/heated market has been operated by the same family since 1972. From 235 booths, their dealers sell antiques, primitives and antique collectibles. Very little crafts or new merchandise. This is a dealer's paradise and people come from all over the country to buy here. One snack bar and handicapped-accessible restrooms add to the amenities. Described by a lot of dealers as "the best one."

DEALER RATES: $25 per space regardless of size; deposit required. $4 per table. Spaces are approximately 10' × 12' or larger. Table and chairs are available for rental. Reservations are requested.

CONTACT: Tulsa Flea Market, PO Box 4511, Tulsa OK 74159. Tel: (918) 744-1386. Office hours: Wednesday and Thursday, 8:00 AM-noon, Friday and Saturday 8:00 AM-5:00 PM.

YUKON
Route 66 Traders Market

DATES: Saturday and Sunday

TIMES: 9:00 AM-5:00 PM.

ADMISSION: Free. Parking is free.

LOCATION: IH-40 west just past Yukon to Exit 132, then 1/4 mile north, 1 mile back east to Rt 66 Traders sign and 1/4 mile south.

DESCRIPTION: Opened in March 2000, this indoor/outdoor market is housed in a 57,000-square-foot pavilion building with outside space on asphalt or grass, but under cover, with another area set aside for special events. They estimate that 75% of the goods sold are old with lots of flea market stuff to rummage through. The entire market is handicapped-accessible with three sets of restrooms and a dealers' restroom with lounge and shower. The Safari Grill (painted to look like a huge tiger by the owner's cousin) serves all sorts of goodies, including home-made cookies and breads. An ATM could come in handy, along with the courtesy phone, and color TV.

DEALER RATES: Per weekend: $43 per 10' × 15' space under roof with a parking space on the asphalt just behind. Outside space: $10 per day or $18 for the 2-day weekend.

CONTACT: Jerald, Marilyn Ashby or Julie McKenzie, 3201 N Richland Rd, Yukon OK 73099. Tel: (405) 350-3366, mobile Jerald (405) 417-4989, mobile Julie (405) 409-6159. Email: jashby@rt66traders.com or jmckenzie@rt66traders.com. Web: rt66traders.com.

Great Finds!

For only being open a year, they've had some serious successes! Witness these:

A regular customer found an ashtray for $2 and sold it on eBay for $90.

A dealer who also owns a franchise store, brought in a 6' × 10' trailer filled with goods his franchise wouldn't let him sell at the store. He sold all the merchandise before noon.

Tinker Bell, a longtime dealer, didn't sell anything on Saturday. Desperate, she borrowed money to pay for gas to get there the next day. Sunday afternoon she sold $1500 worth of collectibles and antiques to dealers from Kansas.

A vendor had a life-size Star Wars character in front of her booth to attract customers. The vendor didn't have a price on the character but the customer offered her $600. Sold.

OTHER FLEA MARKETS

We know or have heard about these markets, but have not personally contacted each one, as we have the markets with descriptions. If you plan to visit one of the markets listed below, *please call first* to make sure they are still open. Flea markets do come and go. While they were open when we went to press, they may not be later. We can't be responsible. *Call first!*

Afton: D & E Flea Market, 17 St 1st. Tel: (918) 257-8611.
Afton: Grand Lakes Swap Meet, 24861 E Hwy 59. Tel: (918) 786-8082.
Bartlesville: Ainesworth's Flea Market, 208 E 2nd St. Tel: (918) 338-2368.
Chelsea: Southern Belle Flea Market, 426 Walnut St. Tel: (918) 789-5212.
Claremore: Cowboy Trade Day, 4600 NE Sawyer Rd. Tel: (918) 341-6985.
Duncan: Chisholm Trail Flea Market, 2900 S Hwy 81. Tel: (580) 252-7200.
Eagletown: Lasch's Flea Market, Hwy 70. Tel: (580) 835-7443.
Edmond: Buchanan's Antique Flea Market, 3200 E Memorial Rd #700. Tel: (405) 478-4050.
Fairland: Fran's Flea Market, 110 N Main. Tel: (918) 676-3400.
Grove: Autry's Midway Flea Market, 33490 S 59 Hwy. Tel: (918) 786-4727.
Grove: Odds & Ends Flea Market, 5527 Hwy 59 N. Tel: (918) 786-7403.

Grove: Ned's Antique & Flea Market, 3638 Hwy 59 N. Tel: (918) 786-4409.
Guymon: Main Street Flea Market, 110 N Main St. Tel: (580) 338-8400.
Idabel: American Legion Flea Market, 16th & Indian St. Tel: (580) 286-9418.
Jay: R-U-Kiddin Flea Market, PO Box 264. Tel: (918) 253-8220.
Jet: Al's Flea Market, Main St. Tel: (580) 626-4633.
Kingston: 82 Flea Market. Tel: (580) 564-5348.
Mead: Mead Flea Market, State Hwy 70. Tel: (580) 924-7242.
Moore: Superflea Fleamarket, 2600 S Service Rd. Tel: (405) 794-2481.
Muskogee: Cherokee Flea Market, 1720 S Cherokee St. Tel: (918) 682-7594.
Muskogee: Oktaha Trader Market, 12501 Oktaha Rd. Tel: (918) 686-9925.
Oklahoma City: Golden Goose Flea Market, 2323 N Douglas Blvd. Tel: (405) 769-5442.
Okmulgee: K C's Flea Mart, 1303 N Wood Dr. Tel: (918) 756-2715.
Seminole: Seminole Flea Market, S of City. Tel: (405) 382-2659.
Shawnee: Ole Shawnee Town Flea Market, 1 W Main St. Tel: (405) 273-5044.
Tahlequah: Flea Market, 108 W 4th St. Tel: (918) 456-8724.
Tulsa: Admiral Flea Market, 9401 E Admiral Pl. Tel: (918) 834-9259.
Tulsa: L & B Flea Market, 1823 N Lewis Ave. Tel: (918) 587-1122.
Turpin: K/O Flea Market, Hwy 83. Tel: (580) 778-3339.
Wagoner: Main Street Flea Market, 108 S Main St. Tel: (918) 485-5496.
Wagoner: Pestolite Rd Flea Market, 1440 S Tyler Ave. Tel: (918) 485-9288.

OREGON

EUGENE
Picc-A-Dilly Flea Market

DATES: Sunday shows throughout the year, generally two per month excluding July and August. Call or write for 2002 and 2003 dates.

TIMES: 10:00 AM-4:00 PM.

ADMISSION: $1.50 per adult; children under 10 enter free. Early bird shoppers can get in at 8:00 AM for $7.50.

LOCATION: Lane County Fairgrounds, 796 West 13th (8 blocks west of city center).

DESCRIPTION: Claiming to be "Oregon's First Giant Flea Market," this indoor show has been going strong since February 1970 and draws 400 dealers set up at almost 500 tables and 2,000 to 3,000 customers depending on the season, making it one of the largest flea markets in the area. Among the items available are antiques and collectibles, handmade crafts, sports cards, coins, clocks, records, Indian artifacts, plants, gold, silver, toys, new merchandise, and fresh produce when in season. As Peggy says, "This is a family atmosphere, and most everyone appreciates that." Hot and cold lunches are available, and there are handicapped-accessible restrooms.

DEALER RATES: $19.50 per 8' × 2½' table and cloth and 1 chair provided. Reservations are recommended. Setup time begins at 8:00 AM on day of show.

CONTACT: Picc-A-Dilly, PO Box 2364, Eugene OR 97402-2364. Tel: (541) 683-5589. Phone open one week prior to each market or leave message. Email: jksonz@teleport.com. Web: www.picc-a-dillyfleamarket.com.

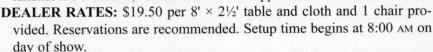

MEDFORD
The Original Medford Giant Flea Market

DATES: Monthly, Sunday only, varies each month. For 2002: January 13, February 17, March 10, April 7, May 19, June 9. Call for the rest of the year.

TIMES: 9:00 AM-4:00 PM.

ADMISSION: $.50 for anyone over 12. Parking is free.

LOCATION: 1701 S Pacific Hwy in the Medford National Guard Armory. Off I-5 Exit 27. Coming from the south turn left on Barnett; coming from the north turn right. Follow Barnett to S Pacific Hwy, turn left. Go 2 blocks; the market will be on your left.

DESCRIPTION: Since 1971, this market has been held inside the Armory, drawing 130 dealers filling the 184 spaces at the market. They cater to

antiques and collectibles, but try to have something for all the 1,000 to 3,000 shoppers. There are concessions and handicapped-accessible restrooms available.

DEALER RATES: $15 per table or same size space. Reservations are an excellent idea, as they are usually full. Wall spaces have electricity.

CONTACT: Dennis & Dee Nelson, The Original Medford Giant Flea Market, 1701 S Pacific Hwy, Medford OR 97504. Tel: (541) 772-8211. Email: nelson@ccountry.net.

Now Who Was That?
Once a dealer tried to sell a coffin with a human skeleton in it, but it caused so many complaints that it was removed.

ONTARIO
Flea Mart

DATES: Friday thru Sunday.

TIMES: 9:00 AM-5:00 PM.

ADMISSION: Free. Parking is free.

LOCATION: 1414 SE 5th Ave. I-84 exit (Ontario) east side of freeway, 1 block from Staples Office Supply, on SE 5th Ave.

DESCRIPTION: Opened since 1998, this market is composed of 20 permanent dealers in buildings and a bunch to 40 dealers outside selling "everything that's legal." Plenty of garage sale goodies, antiques, collectibles, and old merchandise. Food vendors offer sno-cones, tacos and burritos and the usual flea market fare, and there are restrooms when needed. Ladies, Uncle Bud is in need of companionship... Say Hi to Ray and Bud if you can find them.

DEALER RATES: Daily spaces $7 per day. 10' × 12' permanent booths with locking capability $100 a month.

CONTACT: Ray Miller, Owner, Flea Mart, 550 NW 3 St, Ontario OR 97914. Tel: (541) 889-2795.

PORTLAND
#1 Flea Market

DATES: Saturday and Sunday.

TIMES: 9:00 AM-5:00 PM.

ADMISSION: $.50, children under 12 free, seniors $.25. Parking is free.

LOCATION: At the D St Corral dance hall, 17119 SE Division St. From I-84 181st Exit, south to Division St, west to 17119 SE Division.

DESCRIPTION: Opened in 1989, this market hosts 150 dealers inside and out (in tents) selling antiques, collectibles, garage sale goodies, and about 33% new merchandise. There are three food vendors and handicapped-accessible restrooms.

DEALER RATES: $10 per table per day. Reservations are not required for outside tent space. There is a waiting list for inside space. If you want to reserve, you must pre-pay for your space.

CONTACT: #1 Flea Market, 17119 SE Division St, Portland OR 97236-1238. Tel: (503) 761-4646.

If I'd Only Known!
The owner once sold a painting for $75, only to learn it was worth $3,500!

"America's Largest" Antique & Collectible Sale

DATES: 2002: March 2-3, July 13-14, October 26-27. Watch for the same weekends in 2003.

TIMES: Saturday 8:00 AM-6:00 PM; Sunday 9:00 AM-5:00 PM.

ADMISSION: $5 per person, kids under 12 free, kids 12-17 $2. Parking is available (2,000 spaces) for $5 per vehicle, and free parking with a free shuttle service.

LOCATION: Multnomah County Expo Center aka Portland Expo. Take Exit 306B off I-5.

DESCRIPTION: This series of shows, which began operation in October 1981, is certainly one of the largest in the country, filling 1,325 dealer booths in March and October, and an additional 450 in July, in an impressive 240,000 square feet of indoor selling space devoted exclusively to antiques and collectibles. It is held three times each year in March, July, and October, and is so successful that the promoter runs similar events in Tacoma and San Francisco. Three snack bars and handicapped-accessible restrooms add to the amenities.

DEALER RATES: $150-$165 per 10' × 10' booth. Reservations are required well in advance of shows as they are sold out for the next 2 years in March and October. There is a lottery system to sell remaining spaces for the July show only.

CONTACT: Palmer/Wirfs Associates, 4001 NE Halsey #5, Portland OR 97232. Tel: (503) 282-0877. Fax: (503) 282-2953. Email: palmerwirfs@qwest.net. Web: www.palmerwirfs.com.

"America's Largest" Antique & Collectible Sale

DATES: November 23-24, 2002. Watch for the same weekend in 2003.
TIMES: Saturday 8:00 AM-6:00 PM, Sunday 9:00 AM-5:00 PM.
ADMISSION: $5, kids 12-17 $2, kids under 12 are free. Parking is $5.
LOCATION: Oregon Convention Center.

DESCRIPTION: This is the 12th show at this facility, which began operation in 1990. The Oregon Convention Center is one of the nicest in the country, and filling 600-plus booths you will find an excellent assortment of antiques and collectibles. Food is available on the premises, as well as handicapped-accessible restrooms.
DEALER RATES: $140 for a 10' × 10' booth. Reservations are required.
CONTACT: Palmer/Wirfs & Associates, 4001 NE Halley #5, Portland OR 97232. Tel: (503) 282-0877. Fax: (503) 282-2953. Email: palmerwirfs@qwest.net. Web: www.palmerwirfs.com.

"America's Largest" Christmas Bazaar

DATES: November 29-30, December 1, 6-8, 2002. Generally the same weekends every year.
TIMES: Friday and Saturday 10:00 AM-8:00 PM, Sunday 10:00 AM-6:00 PM.
ADMISSION: $5 per person, $2.50 under 17, free under 12. Parking at $5 per vehicle. Friday December 6, admission is free with 2 cans of donated food for the Oregon Food Bank.
LOCATION: Multnomah County Expo Center. Take Exit 306B off I-5.

DESCRIPTION: This annual indoor 6-day show began in 1983 and currently draws around 1,000 dealers selling mostly craft items, gifts, with some new merchandise and some antiques and collectibles. The shows draws over 40,000 shoppers buying stocking stuffers and gifts for the holidays. Food and handicapped-accessible restrooms are available on the premises.
DEALER RATES: $385 per 10' × 10' space for crafters, with one 8' bare table and 500 watts electricity, pipe and drape and a booth sign, per 6-day show. Reservations are required.
CONTACT: Palmer/Wirfs and Associates, 4001 NE Halsey, Portland OR 97219. Tel: (503) 282-0964 or fax: (503) 282-2953. Email: palmerwirfs@qwest.net. Web: www.palmerwirfs.com.

Catlin Gabel Rummage Sale

DATES: Annually, first weekend in November, Thursday through Sunday.
TIMES: Thursday 5:00 PM-9:00 PM, Friday, Saturday 10:00 AM-6:00 PM, Sunday 10:00 AM- 3:00 PM.
ADMISSION: Free. Parking is available at $4 per vehicle.
LOCATION: Portland Exposition Center. Off I-5, near Jantzen Beach.

DESCRIPTION: This indoor 88,000-square-foot "rummage sale" has been held annually since 1943 by the Catlin Gabel School, and certainly ranks among the largest markets of its type in the state of Oregon, with thousands of shoppers attending. The rummage sale benefits students on Financial Aid at the Catlin Gabel School, one of the finest independent schools on the West Coast. Material is donated locally and ranges from antiques and collectibles to books, hardware, furniture and even some new merchandise. In 1998 they sold a car, motorcycle and a 17' sailboat! In the past, they've sold a beer truck and a horse. Definitely a most unusual sale. This place is considered a treasure trove of goodies. Imagine, it takes 15-20 semi-trucks to deliver the goods to the Expo Center. This market will be written up in *Country Living's* U.S. flea and antique markets in the November 2001 issue. A snack bar and handicapped-accessible restrooms will come in handy.

DEALER RATES: All merchandise is donated. No independent dealers are admitted to sell, but certainly to buy.

CONTACT: Lesley Sepetoski, Catlin Gabel School, 8825 SW Barnes Rd, Portland OR 97225-6599. Tel: (503) 297-1894 × 423. Email: sepetoskil@catlin.edu. Web: www.catlin.edu.

> **Unusual Sale Items for 2001**
> A new iMac computer, windsurfers, collectible dolls, 1929 Martin guitar, porcelain (Royal Dalton and others), art deco, antique Waltham desk set, the list is endless. This is a great place to stock up. Lesley says that antique dealers are breaking down the doors on Thursday.

Fantastic Flea Market

DATES: Saturday and Sunday, year round.

TIMES: 9:00 AM-5:00 PM.

ADMISSION: $1, seniors $.50, children under 12 free with an adult. Parking is free.

LOCATION: 19340 SE Stark. On the light rail and bus lines.

DESCRIPTION: This market of 160 dealers is at their new location, 45,000 square feet indoors, selling Disney movies, antiques, primitives, computers and parts, groceries, new clothing, new and used items, as well as vendors selling and trading electronic games. There is an ATM on site, in case you need something badly. The inside concession stand serves "Carol's world-famous Biscuits and Gravy," and handicapped-accessible restrooms. There's an antique mall as part of the building housing 60 dealers, open daily.

DEALER RATES: Table rents start at $10 each table per day. There are discounts for vendors needing lots of tables. Reservations are recommended. If interested in showing in the mall, call.

CONTACT: Jim Brittan or Dave Newsom, Owners, Fantastic Flea Market, PO Box 1170, Fairview OR 97024-1170. Tel: (503) 618-9119. Email: jbrittan@prodigy.net.

Sandy Barr's Flea Market

DATES: Saturday and Sunday, year round.

TIMES: 8:00 AM-4:00 PM.

ADMISSION: $1; seniors and children $.50. Parking is free.

LOCATION: 711 SE MLK Blvd. Exit 300B off I-5.

DESCRIPTION: Originally opened in March 1969, this market moved in 2001 to the former Corno's Food Market, an historic landmark in Portland. This 36,000 square feet of retail space houses dealers selling everything: antiques, collectibles, office equipment, bulk food, shampoo, electronics, jewelry, dog clothes—you name it!

DEALER RATES: Tables are $12.50 per day, $20 for the weekend. Square footage is available at $.65/foot per weekend. Reservations are nice.

CONTACT: Sandy Barr's Flea-Mart, PO Box 17202, Portland OR 97217. Tel: (503) 283-9565. Email: sandybarrs@aol.com. Web: www.sandybarr.com.

SUMPTER
Sumpter Flea Market

DATES: Memorial Day, July 4 weekend, and Labor Day, usually Friday through Monday midday.

TIMES: 8:00 AM-5:00 PM. Really morning to evening, no set hours.

ADMISSION: Free. Free parking is also available.

LOCATION: Town of Sumpter. From I-84 or US 26, via Hwy 7, to Sumpter.

DESCRIPTION: Originating in the yard at the Black Market Antiques in 1971, this event has grown up to about 400 vendors during the Memorial Day weekend and stretches from one end of town to the other. The former SVD Grounds, with modern handicapped-accessible restrooms and coin-op showers, hosts about 45% of the vendors. Items sold include antiques, collectibles, new merchandise, crafts, and some produce. There are plenty of food vendors selling a variety of goodies. For entertainment, there is Bingo, an old-time Fiddler's show, and tours on the old Sumpter Valley narrow-gauge, steam-powered railroad, as well the old gold dredge at the State Park.

DEALER RATES: From $2.25 per frontage foot for a space 20' deep/wide, minimum space of 12', plus $20 for city vendor license. Reservations are required.

CONTACT: Toni Thompson, City Recorder, City of Sumpter, PO Box 68, Sumpter OR 97877-0213. Tel: (541) 894-2314. Fax: (541) 894-2329.

WALDPORT
Seamarket

DATES: Daily.
TIMES: Weekends: 9:00 AM-5:00 PM. Weekdays: 10:00 AM-5:00 PM.
ADMISSION: Free. Parking is free.
LOCATION: Hwy 101 at 260 SW Arrow. Literally right on the highway.
DESCRIPTION: Opened in the winter of 1994, this admittedly little indoor/outdoor market houses 30 dealers inside and as many as want to set up outside. The inside dealers are generally there all the time selling antiques, collectibles, "junk," just about everything, according to Pauline. The garage sale goodies come in mostly during the warmer weather outside. As this market is located right on a major tourist highway running along the Pacific coast, not only do the tourists stop for the market, but the views are "stunningly gorgeous." What an enticement!
DEALER RATES: From $80 monthly inside. Outside: $5 per day. Reservations are a good idea if you want inside space, as there is a waiting list. Otherwise, set up outside!
CONTACT: Pauline Gates, 2240 Crestline Dr, Waldport OR 97394. Tel: (541) 563-6436 or home (541) 563-2402. Email: pgates@harborside.com.

OTHER FLEA MARKETS

We know or have heard about these markets, but have not personally contacted each one, as we have the markets with descriptions. If you plan to visit one of the markets listed below, *please call first* to make sure they are still open. Flea markets do come and go. While they were open when we went to press, they may not be later. We can't be responsible. *Call first!*

Cloverdale: Red Barn Flea Mart, 33920 Hwy 101 S. Tel: (503) 392-3973.
La Pine: Highway 97 Flea Market, 52674 Hwy 97. Tel: (541) 536-2336.
Ontario: Flea Market, 1381 N Verde Dr. Tel: (541) 889-4570.
Portland: Skidmore Saturday Sunday Market, 50 SW 2nd Ave #200. Tel: (503) 228-2392.
St Helens: St Helens Flea Market, 50 Cowlitz St. Tel: (503) 366-5363.

PENNSYLVANIA

ADAMSTOWN
Renninger's #1 Antique Market
DATES: Every Sunday, year round.
TIMES: 7:30 AM-4:00 PM.
ADMISSION: Free. Free parking is available.
LOCATION: At 2500 N Reading Rd, on Rt 272, 1 mile north of Exit 21 (watch for new exit numbers!) on the Pennsylvania Tnpk, between Adamstown and Denver in Lancaster County.
DESCRIPTION: This indoor and outdoor market has operated since 1967 and houses up to 500 dealers in a huge, indoor building. They deal in fine antiques and all types of collectibles. No crafts or new merchandise are permitted. In fair weather, outdoor dealers number from 200 to 400. Stands are in a grove and lot behind the main market building. There is a sit-down restaurant and two snack bars, one specializing in funnel cakes, serving breakfast and lunches, and new handicapped-accessible restrooms.
DEALER RATES: $15 per day Saturday or Sunday, $25 for the weekend, except five special dates, when the fee is somewhat higher. Reservations for indoor stands, if available, are required. No reservations are needed for the outdoor section. Apply at the market office. Watch the website for special dates and times, plus rates. It is kept up to date.
CONTACT: Office: Renninger's Promotions, 27 Bensinger Dr, Schuylkill Haven PA 17972. Tel: (570) 385-0104 or toll-free (877) 385-0104, Monday through Thursday; Friday through Sunday at the market (717) 336-2177. Web: www.renningers.com.

> **I Declare—**
> It is said that the famous copy of the Declaration of Independence that was found behind an old picture frame, was found here. Smart buyer!

Stoudt's Black Angus Antique Mall
DATES: Every Sunday, year round.
TIMES: 7:30 AM-4:00 PM.
LOCATION: Rt 272, 1 mile north of Pennsylvania Tnpk, Exit 21.
ADMISSION: Free. Plenty of free parking is available.

DESCRIPTION: Over 33 years old, this Sunday market is part of a huge complex including Stoudt's Black Angus Restaurant, brewery, brewery hall, the Stoudtburg Village, and the Clock Tower Antique Mall (open daily except Wednesday 10:00 AM-5:00 PM). They hold a Beer Fest every weekend during August and every Sunday in October. Polka weekend is Labor Day weekend! They hold Antique Extravaganzas three times a year in April, June and September for the entire weekend. Only antiques and collectibles are sold at the Antiques Mall by 400 permanent indoor dealers year round, and another 200 dealers set up in four outdoor pavilions in the summer. One source tells me that the Black Angus Restaurant serves the best steak dinner he has ever eaten, and this man travels extensively! They built a Bavarian-style German village, called Stoudtsburg, with homes, an antique co-op, and five antique stores. The downstairs of each unit is a shop, and the owners live above on the second and third floor—like European villages.

DEALER RATES: Contact Carl Barto for rates. Reservations are required.

CONTACT: Carl Barto, Manager, Stoudt's Black Angus, PO Box 880, Rt 272, Adamstown PA 19501-0880. Tel: (717) 484-4385. Or call Carl directly at (717) 569-3536. Clock Tower tel: (717) 484-2757.

BENSALEM
Philadelphia Flea Market

DATES: Fridays, mid-March through December, weather permitting (very rare).

TIMES: 8:00 AM-2:00 PM.

ADMISSION: Free. Parking is free.

LOCATION: Philadelphia Park Race Track. Street Rd, Exit 37 off I-95.

DESCRIPTION: Open since 1993, or so, this outdoor market of 500 or so dealers sells more collectibles and antiques than new merchandise—making it quite popular. The crowds for the old stuff show up quite early. There are free wheelchairs available for those who need to use them at the market. There are 10 concession stands, 2 serve the famous Philadelphia Pretzel! After that, you'll need the handicapped-accessible restrooms. Arthur treats his vendors and customers as human beings, as he has 20 years experience as a vendor.

DEALER RATES: $30 per day, $80 per month. Reservations are needed depending on the season, so call.

CONTACT: Arthur, Philadelphia Flea Market, PO Box 1024, Somerset NJ 08873-1024. Tel: (856) 665-8558 or cell (732) 558-5016. Email: aeloudon@aol.com.

COLLEGEVILLE
Power House Antique and Flea Market

DATES: Every Sunday.

TIMES: 9:00 AM-5:00 PM.

ADMISSION: Free. Free parking available.

LOCATION: On Rt 29 N. From Philadelphia: take Rt 422 west to Collegeville, then north on Rt 29. From Reading: take Rt 422 east to Collegeville, then north on Rt 29.

DESCRIPTION: This indoor market has been functioning since 1970 in an old power house, and currently holds approximately 50 dealers who sell many antique items, a range of collectibles including coins, baseball cards, books, and jewelry, as well as new merchandise and crafts. Food is not served on the premises, although handicapped-accessible restrooms are available. For the record, they are only a few miles from Valley Forge Historical Park.

DEALER RATES: Call for rates, as they will change for 2002. Reservations are required, and rates for larger spaces are available on request. There is a waiting list, as their dealers tend to stay to the bitter end.

CONTACT: Janet McDonnell, Power House Antique and Flea Market, 45 First Ave, Collegeville PA 19426. Tel: (610) 489-7388.

EDINBURG
Michaelangelo's

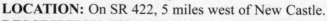

DATES: Sunday, year round.

TIMES: 6:00 AM-3:00 PM.

ADMISSION: Free. Parking is free.

LOCATION: On SR 422, 5 miles west of New Castle.

DESCRIPTION: This indoor/outdoor market, started in 1971, boasts 200-300 dealers offering antiques, handmades, musical greeting cards, floral arrangements, collectibles, cards, gifts, produce, meats, cheese, and new and used merchandise. Food is always available at the ground's concessions, Michaelangelo's Restaurant, and smorgasbord. Sisters Kathy and Brenda are running this market successfully after losing both parents to illness, and one of their buildings to fire in 2000. What a lovely tribute to their parents' hard work.

DEALER RATES: $7 per vehicle outside, $10 pavilion space, $10 for an 8' table space indoors or $27 for 3 tables inside. Reservations are not required outdoors, but are required for indoor selling.

CONTACT: Kathy Mike and Brenda Mellott, Michaelangelo's, RD 1 Box 211, Edinburg PA 16116. Tel: (724) 654-0382. Fax: (724) 658-1131.

EPHRATA
Green Dragon Farmers' Market and Auction

DATES: Every Friday (except Christmas). Rain or shine.

TIMES: 9:00 AM-9:00 PM.

ADMISSION: Free. Thirty acres of free parking.

LOCATION: 955 N State St, 1 mile north of Ephrata; also, ¼ mile off Rt 272. Look for the dragon.

DESCRIPTION: Green Dragon began in 1932 and now has over 400 merchants weekly, including 250 local growers and craftsmen. Meats, fish, poultry, cheeses, and sweets are among the fresh produce available, and all types of antiques and collectibles may be found at the market. The auction offers a range of products from dry goods to small animals—a real down-home country affair for the whole family. Food is served in five restaurants and seven snack bars; restroom facilities are available.

DEALER RATES: $27 per 20' × 20' space, but rates vary by which building and what facilities are available. Advance reservations are required.

CONTACT: Larry L Loose, Manager, The Green Dragon, 955 N State St, Ephrata PA 17522. Tel: (717) 738-1117. Email: info@greendragonmarket.com. Web: www.greendragonmarket.com.

FAYETTEVILLE
Fayetteville Antique Mall

DATES: Daily.

TIMES: 9:00 AM-5:00 PM.

ADMISSION: Free. Parking is also free.

LOCATION: I-81, Exit 16 on Rt 30, 18 miles west of Gettysburg, or 4 miles east of Chambersburg.

DESCRIPTION: This market, located in four buildings, has 320 dealers selling mostly antiques, collectibles, cast iron, depression glass, books, toys, dolls, china, tools, postcards, primitives, furniture, and more! Crafts are located in Building 4. A snack bar operates daily. Outside setups are available. There are six to eight smaller buildings rented by individuals selling even more items.

DEALER RATES: Call for more information.

CONTACT: L L Dymond, Jr, Fayetteville Antique Mall, 40 Dymond Ave, Fayetteville PA 17222. Tel: (717) 352-8485 or the office at (717) 352-2515.

Zern's Farmers' Market and Auction

DATES: Every Friday and Saturday, year round. Rain or shine.

TIMES: Friday 2:00 PM-10:00 PM; Saturday 11:00 AM-10:00 PM.

ADMISSION: Free. Free parking for 5,000 cars is available.

LOCATION: On Rt 73, 1 mile east of Boyertown.

DESCRIPTION: First opened in 1922, this market is one of the oldest and largest continuous farmers' markets in the country. And it's still with the same Lipton family, on the third generation now running the market. There are five auctions on Friday and Saturday. Their 400 dealers, both indoors (300) and out (100), sell a vast variety of antiques, collectibles, Amish crafts, and all types of produce, meats and cheeses, seafood, baked goods, poultry, plants, yard sculptures, new and vintage clothing, new and used books, musical instruments, and whatever. You could probably furnish a house and clothe your family from the markets and auctions here—from hearing aids and glasses to kitchens, hats and shoes. Located in the heart of "Amish Country," this market is self-billed as the "World's Largest Dutch Treat." It was once voted "Best of Philly" by *Philadelphia Magazine*. When the munchies get you, try the Coffee Café, the Philly cheese steak stand, the Carving Board, the pizza place; there's even a vegetarian lunch stand and a to-drop-for bakery, making the handicapped-accessible restrooms a necessity. One of the market favorites is Fried Chicken Gizzards and Mushrooms drawing in lines of drooling customers. Watch for the old Garage Sale weekend schedules, as they have changed.

As 2002 is their 80th birthday, they will be having whopping great ongoing celebrations. Watch for the festivals, auctions, craft shows, concerts, bazaars, and specials. Check out their website for future specials, as they have one generally every weekend.

DEALER RATES: Covered Flea Market: $32 per 8' × 9' outside space with 2 tables for Friday and Saturday. Midway: $27 for an 8' × 9' area with 2 tables. The fee covers both Friday and Saturday. Reservations are required. If you are interested in Market Stands, check in with the office.

CONTACT: Ms. Hinarapa Lipton, Zern's, PO Box 279, Gilbertsville PA 19525-0279. Tel: (610) 367-2461. Fax: (610) 367-2403. Web: www.zerns.com.

GREENSBURG
Greengate Flea Market

DATES: Sundays: April through October outdoors, open all holiday weekends.

TIMES: Outdoors 7:00 AM-3:00 PM.

ADMISSION: Free. Parking is free.

LOCATION: Rt 30 west of Greensburg, on the upper parking lot next to the Greengate Mall. From the turnpike take Exit 7 (Irwin), go east to market.

DESCRIPTION: Moved from Latrobe in 1991, this outdoor market has grown with their new space. They can accommodate 150 dealers and have come close in their first year. Their dealers sell antiques, collectibles, crafts, produce, household goods, garage sale finds, coins, stamps, loads of baseball cards, baked goods, furniture, new merchandise, whatever. I am assured that the snack concession serves the "best hot sausage sandwich in Pennsylvania." People drive from all over just to have a sandwich! Found among the Tupperware and stuff brought in: a hanging salt in blue spongeware (very rare item), and two beautiful handmade quilts. In 2001, someone bought a marble top washstand, in solid walnut with burled walnut fronts, drawers, and original pulls—in great condition. Definitely a place to check out!

DEALER RATES: Outdoors: $15 for a 21' × 14' space, room for your vehicle. Spaces always available on Sunday mornings. Dealers supply their own tables.

CONTACT: Carol J Craig, 214 Kenneth St, Greensburg PA 15601-1946. Tel: (724) 837-6881 evenings.

Hanna's Town

DATES: Second weekend Sunday and the previous Saturday afternoon of the month from May through September.

TIMES: Daybreak to 2:30 PM.

ADMISSION: Free. Parking is $2 per car.

LOCATION: Westmoreland County Historical Society, 951 Old Salem Rd. Just 3 miles north of Greensburg between Rts 119 and 819.

DESCRIPTION: Founded in 1974, this popular strictly antiques and collectibles market has 275 dealers selling on a wide-open grassy field. This historic site has a re-created 1773 log courthouse tavern, more log buildings, a fort, and an archaeological site. Ten snack bars will keep you energized and raring for more shopping. Their restrooms just may come in handy. Keep an eye out for the hot air balloons from a nearby business; they fly up in the mornings.

DEALER RATES: $40 per 24' × 20' space. Reservations are not required. There is a season pass rate for vendors wishing to sell the entire season.

CONTACT: Westmoreland County Historical Society, 951 Old Salem Rd, Greensburg PA 15601. Tel: (724) 836-1800. Fax: (724) 836-2702. Email: history@wchspa.com.

Advance Planning

When the market was about 10 years old, they had so many cars cramming every available inch of road that it created one serious traffic headache. So bad was it that the state police flew over the market in a helicopter and through a bullhorn requested the presence immediately of the owners of said event to meet a police car at a specific location. Gulp.

Things were sorted out with the police. Now the traffic runs smoothly and the market has plenty of parking space on two large hillsides.

HAZEN
Warsaw Township Volunteer Fire Company Flea Market

DATES: First Sunday of the month and preceding Saturday (even if it isn't the same month, i.e. July 31, August 1), May through October.

TIMES: Daybreak to around 4:00 PM, depending on weather.

ADMISSION: Free. $2 to park.

LOCATION: On Rt 28, ½ mile north of Hazen. Take I-80 to Exit 14, then north 6 miles on Rt 28. Located in northwest Pennsylvania near Brookville, Brockway and Dubois. Only 80 miles from the Ohio state line.

DESCRIPTION: This extremely successful outdoor market began in the early 1970s as a fundraiser for the fire house. They average 450 dealers selling a majority of antiques and collectibles, as well as farm produce and a few new items, mostly t-shirts and tools. This is truly a great place to find treasures. A violin went for $2,000. One customer was seen walking around with a boa constrictor around her neck. It is quite common for out-of-state dealers to fly to this area several times during the year, stock up on antiques, store them, then return later with a truck to collect their booty. Because of the success of this market, area motels and hotels have expanded to accommodate the influx of traffic. On the day of the flea market, the entire area becomes a giant yard sale. If you are a true-blue hunter of treasures and bargains, come in on Saturday when the dealers start setting up and start hunting. Food and toilet facilities are available.

DEALER RATES: $15 for 18' × 24' space outdoors. Call for reservation information. Dealers get discounts at local area hotels and motels. Just ask. All dealers must have a Pennsylvania sales tax number.

CONTACT: Warsaw Township Volunteer Fire Co, RD5 Box 146B, Brookville PA 15825. Call the Fire Hall at (814) 328-2528 or Clyde at (814) 328-2536.

Be Specific—

An out-of-state dealer asked the price of a butter churn and butter maker dish. "Two-fifty each." Thinking that $250 each was a bit steep, he continued browsing. The next buyer admired the pair and asked the price. "Five bucks for the pair." They were sold on the spot.

Later the dealer told Clyde that he really would have paid $250 each for the items, they were more than worth it.

Get Smart!
One woman held up a dish she was selling and asked fellow dealers what they thought it was worth, as she had it marked for $10. The others consulted and said it was a very good, expensive dish. The dealer promptly raised the price to $50. No one bought it—yet. When she checked into the matter with experts, she found the dish was worth $1200!

HULMEVILLE
Old Mill Flea Market

DATES: Thursday through Sunday, year round. Rain or shine.

TIMES: Thursday and Friday 6:00 PM-9:00 PM; Saturday 12:00 PM-9:00 PM; Sunday 12:00 PM-5:00 PM. They may be changing their hours, so check the website or call first.

ADMISSION: Free. Free parking is available.

LOCATION: Intersection of Hulmeville Rd/Bellevue and Trenton Aves; 2 miles from Exit 28 on the Pennsylvania Tnpk (US Rt 1); 2 miles from I-95 (US Rt 1) Exit 28 for Penndel/Langhorne.

DESCRIPTION: This small, year-round indoor market started in 1971 in a large, 1880s historic Bucks County grist mill. The market draws several hundred shoppers each weekend. A full range of antiques and collectibles is available, including dolls, books, china, textiles, jewelry, furniture, glassware, advertising, breweriana, photographica, pottery, etc. This place is a "haunt" for dealers and collectors, more so than the general public (who haven't caught on—yet), as the management buys out house contents and estates. No food is available on the premises. Restrooms are provided.

DEALER RATES: Currently there is no space available.

CONTACT: Kathy Loeffler, Old Mill Flea Market, PO Box 7069, Penndel PA 19047-7069. Tel: (215) 757-1777. Fax: (215) 860-4494. Email: glass@antiquesoldmill.com. Web: www.antiquesoldmill.com.

KUTZTOWN
Renninger's #2 Antique Market

DATES: Antique market every Saturday, year round. Extravaganzas in April, June, and September. Pennsylvania Dutch Farmers' market is open every Friday and Saturday.

TIMES: Saturdays 8:00 AM-4:00 PM. Pennsylvania Dutch Farmers' market is open every Friday 10:00 AM-7:00 PM.

ADMISSION: Free. There is an admission charge for Extravaganzas. Free parking is provided.

LOCATION: 740 Nobel St, 1 mile south from the center of town. Midway between Allentown and Reading on Rt 222.

DESCRIPTION: This indoor (outdoor for overflow) market has been in operation since 1955 and now ranks among the most popular markets in the Northeast. The market attracts approximately 300 dealers during regular weekends, and up to 1,500 during the Extravaganzas. A wide range of antiques and collectibles is featured along with craft items, new merchandise, and fresh foods including smoked and fresh meats, poultry, seafood, and baked goods. For the Extravaganzas, dealers are said to arrive from as many as 42 different states, as well as from Canada and Europe. There is no flea market on Extravaganza days. One restaurant and snack bars offer plenty of food, and restrooms are available.

DEALER RATES: $12 per 10' × 25' outdoor pavilion space per day, $10 for special outdoor section, during normal sale days. Check the website for information on particular shows, or call for Extravaganza rates. Reservations are required.

CONTACT: Renninger's Promotions, 27 Bensinger Dr, Schuylkill Haven PA 17972. Tel: toll-free (877) 385-0104 or (570) 385-0104 Monday through Thursday; Friday and Saturday call (610) 683-6848. Web: www.renningers.com.

LEEPER
Leeper Flea Market

DATES: Saturday and Sunday, from mid-April to mid-October, plus the holiday Mondays of Memorial Day and Labor Day.

TIMES: Dawn to dusk.

ADMISSION: Free. Parking is free.

LOCATION: At the intersection of Rts 66 and 36, 14 miles north on Rt 66 from Clarion, near Cooks Forest National Recreation Area.

DESCRIPTION: Open since 1975, this lively outdoor market averages 60-100 dealers (with 170 available spaces) selling just about everything. Antiques, garage sale goodies, crafts, and new and used hunting and fishing supplies are among the treasures mentioned by an enthusiastic shopper who sent in this listing of her favorite market. Fresh baked goods are sold by Amish vendors on Saturdays. They are located near Cooks Forest Recreational Area and the Allegheny National Forest with plenty of camps and weekend getaways around them.

DEALER RATES: $5 per day for 20' × 20' space, first come, first served. Find Helen at the Red & White Market located on the upper corner of the market area, daily until 4:00 PM.

CONTACT: Brian or Helen, Leeper Red & White Market, PO Box 150, Leeper PA 16233. Tel: (814) 744-8811.

> **The Bear Facts**
> This market is surrounded by woods. The Dumpsters are kept at the lower end of the market away from the crowds. Every fall, black bears come out of the woods to check out the tossed-in goodies. Labor Day 1996 saw a packed market—of shoppers—when the bears decided to pay a visit. "What an audience they had!"

LEESPORT
Leesport Farmers' Market

DATES: The flea market is every Wednesday year round, and the first and third Sunday of each month from April through the first Sunday in December; the farmers' market is held every Wednesday, year round.

TIMES: Wednesday flea market from 7:00 AM; first and third Sunday 7:00 AM-2:00 PM; farmers' market from 9:00 AM-8:00 PM.

ADMISSION: Free admission and free parking.

LOCATION: One block east off Rt 61; eight miles north of Reading.

DESCRIPTION: This family run market, operating since 1947, currently has over 600 dealers spaces both indoors and out. The complete farmers' market, with a livestock auction on Wednesday, is complemented by the collectibles, jewelry, clothing, crafts and new merchandise available in the flea market. Many items are supplied by neighboring Pennsylvania Dutch merchants. Food is available on the market grounds.

DEALER RATES: $10 per 12' × 35' unsheltered space, no tables; $10 per 10' × 10' space with 8' table. Some spaces are reserved for the season. Otherwise, first come, first served.

CONTACT: Daniel "Woody" Weist, PO Box 747, Leesport PA 19533. Tel: (610) 926-1307. Fax: (610) 926-2749. Email: info@leesportmarket.com. Web: www.leesportmarket.com.

LIMERICK
Limerick Flea Market

DATES: Friday, Saturday and Sunday, year round.

TIMES: Indoors: Friday 12:00 PM-9:00 PM; Saturday 9:00 AM-9:00 PM; Sunday 9:00 AM-5:00 PM. Outdoors: Saturday 7 AM-2:00 PM; Sunday 7:00 AM-2:00 PM.

ADMISSION: Free. Parking is free.

LOCATION: West Ridge Pike at Sunset Road. On old Route 422 between Collegeville and Pottstown.

DESCRIPTION: This 50-year-old outdoor market is now, with the construction of three buildings, an indoor market as well. There are 300 dealer spaces inside and growing. Fully wheelchair accessible, this market is growing to accommodate the needs of the local community. There are plenty of handicapped-accessible restrooms and one building is just for food!

DEALER RATES: Yard sale rates: $10 per day per table, maximum 2 tables. Inside: $60 per table for the three days or $25 for one day, courtyard spaces at $75 per weekend. Reservations are required for inside spaces, not for outside.

CONTACT: Limerick Flea Market, West Ridge Pike at Sunset Road, Limerick PA 19468. Tel: (610) 489-3338. Fax: (610) 489-9533. Email: kim@limerickfleamarket.com. Web: www.limerickfleamarket.com.

MARSHALLS CREEK
Pocono Bazaar Flea Market

DATES: Every Saturday and Sunday (except Christmas and New Year's Day if they fall on a weekend), also open major holidays (Presidents Day, Memorial Day, July 4, Labor Day and Thanksgiving Friday).

TIMES: 9:00 AM-5:00 PM.

ADMISSION: Free. Ample free parking is available.

LOCATION: On US Rt 209. Take Exit 309 off I-80 (1 mile west of the Delaware Water Gap toll bridge), then drive 5 miles north on US Rt 209.

DESCRIPTION: Located in the Pocono Mountains and started in 1983, this rapidly expanding indoor/outdoor complex currently supports 50 indoor dealers, 140 more under outdoor pavilions, and about 400 more located in an outdoor paved lot. The indoor market is known as the Pocono Bazaar, and the outdoor arrangements trade in a variety of collectibles, crafts, produce, and new merchandise. Food is available at a food court area with a picnic pavilion. Clean, modern restrooms are on site.

DEALER RATES: Antique/garage sale outdoor booths (no new merchandise) $10/day. $25-$40 for spaces depending on size and location. No reservations are required. Pennsylvania Sales Tax number required for vendors selling taxable items. Not required for one-time garage sale vendors or non-taxable items (like clothing).

CONTACT: Kevin Hoffman, Pocono Bazaar, PO Box 248, Marshalls Creek PA 18335-0248. Tel: (570) 223-8640. Email: office@poconofleamarket.com. Web: www.poconofleamarket.com or www.poconobazaar.com.

MECHANICSBURG
Silver Spring Flea Market

DATES: Every Sunday of the year. Rain or shine.

TIMES: 6:00 AM-2:00 PM.

ADMISSION: Parking and admission are free.

LOCATION: 6416 Carlisle Pk, 7 miles west of Harrisburg on US Rt 11.

DESCRIPTION: This flea market, founded in 1969, is the largest in the area, with 700 to 1,000 indoor and outdoor dealers attracting thousands of visitors each Sunday. Here you'll find antiques, collectibles, crafts, farm goods, and about 75% new merchandise. "You can find anything at this market." Ten restaurants, snack bars and food wagons quell any screaming munchies and when you need them, handicapped-accessible restrooms.

DEALER RATES: $12 per 10' × 10' outside space per day; $45 per 3' × 8' table monthly rental cost. First come, first served. There are some reserved outside spaces.

CONTACT: Alan Kreitzer, Silver Spring Flea Market, 6416 Carlisle Pk, Mechanicsburg PA 17055-2393. Tel: (717) 766-7215. Day of market call Mim Myers: (717) 766-9027.

MENGES MILLS
Colonial Valley

DATES: Every Sunday.

TIMES: 8:30 AM-4:30 PM. Special events last longer.

ADMISSION: Free. Free parking is available.

LOCATION: Colonial Valley Rd. Off Rt 116, 10 minutes west of York and 10 minutes east of Hanover.

DESCRIPTION: This market grew from a little flea market into a resort. It has 140 dealers indoors and more outdoors, covering over 140 acres. Antiques, collectibles, craft items, and new merchandise are offered. There is a haunted house for the six weekends up to Halloween. At Christmas, they really light up the whole town with 100,000 lights and have a variety of carriage and sleigh rides! They now have one building devoted to Christmas year round with animated scenes and characters among other goodies. They have a real camel (Bosco), and a petting zoo with white-tailed deer for Christmas. Auctions are held occasionally. Bus tours frequently stop here. Snack concessions feed the famished, and handicapped-accessible restrooms are available.

DEALER RATES: $10 per table inside; $8 outside. Reservations are required for inside spaces.

CONTACT: Judy Phillips or Herb Sterner, Owners, or Betty Staines, Manager, Colonial Valley Resorts, Box 3561 Colonial Valley Rd, Menges Mills PA 17362. Day of show call (717) 225-4811. Fax: (717) 225-4403.

History Lesson

This is the site of one of the oldest working post offices. Former President Richard Nixon grew up around here and was at the post office when he got the call to go to China, the first sitting president to do so.

They have over 60 Tennessee walking horses here. Many are trained for police departments all over the country.

MIDDLETOWN-ELIZABETHTOWN
Saturday's Market

DATES: Every Saturday. Rain or shine.

TIMES: Inside 8:00 AM-4:00 PM, but shop early! Outside 4:30 AM until ?—weather permitting.

ADMISSION: Free. Ample free parking is available.

LOCATION: 3751 E Harrisburg Pk, just off Rt 283, on Rt 230 between Middletown and Elizabethtown PA. Only minutes from Hershey Park and Amish country.

DESCRIPTION: This indoor/outdoor market opened in 1984 and claims to be the "largest indoor market in Pennsylvania" and home for 300-plus dealers indoors and hundreds outdoors. Items sold include antiques, arts and crafts and collectibles. New merchandise is also available. At the farmers' market there is always a large supply of fresh produce, bakery snacks, meats, a deli, candies, and sodas, along with the delicacies of 21 other eateries on the premises. After all that, you'll be glad there are handicapped-accessible restrooms. They are totally air-conditioned.

DEALER RATES: $50 per month for a 10' space inside. Outside special: two spaces for $20. Consult management; reservations are sometimes required.

CONTACT: Rod Rose or Peggy Beckley, Saturday's Market, 3751 E Harrisburg Pk, Middletown PA 17057. Tel: (717) 944-2555 or 944-9400. Fax: (717) 944-3232 or 944-1300. Email: rod@saturdaysmarket.com or peg@saturdaysmarket.com. Web: www.saturdaysmarket.com.

NEW HOPE
New Hope Country Market

DATES: Tuesday through Sunday, year round, weather permitting.

TIMES: 7:00 AM-5:00 PM.

ADMISSION: Free. Parking is free.

LOCATION: 463 York Rd. On Rt 202, ½ mile south of New Hope.

DESCRIPTION: This outdoor market (formerly Country Host) was formed in 1970 and is now under new management. Their 30-70 dealers sell primarily antiques and collectibles including books, new and vintage clothing, coins, stamps, crafts, fine art, new and used furniture, jewelry and silver, pottery, porcelain, toys, and new and used merchandise. They are located in beautiful Bucks County in "antique" country in the "center of Lambertville, NJ and Lahaska, PA" with buyers from New York City and Philadelphia. There is a diner open during market hours next door and handicapped-accessible restrooms.

DEALER RATES: $5 per space with two large tables weekdays, $20 on Saturday, $25 on Sunday. Reservations helpful.

CONTACT: Jack Artz, Manager, New Hope Country Market, 463 York Rd Rte 202, New Hope PA 18938. Tel: (215) 862-3111. Fax: (215) 862-9107.

Rice's Sale and Country Market

DATES: Every Tuesday. Rain or shine.

TIMES: 6:30 AM-2:00 PM.

ADMISSION: Free. Paid parking is available for $1.

LOCATION: 6326 Green Hill Rd, between Aquetong and Mechansville Rds, off Rt 263.

DESCRIPTION: This market is said to have started in 1857 selling cattle and farm goods, ranking it among the very oldest existing flea markets in the state of Pennsylvania (or in the USA for that matter). There are currently over 1,200 spaces each week at this indoor/outdoor event, selling "everything from A to Z," including antiques, collectibles, and fine art to new merchandise, fresh produce, meats, baked goods, and zucchini. Plenty of snack bars and concession stands feed the hungry; paved walkways and handicapped-accessible restrooms add to the amenities.

DEALER RATES: $25 per 8' × 3' table weekly; $100 monthly.

CONTACT: Chuck, 6326 Green Hill Rd, New Hope PA 18938. Tel: (215) 297-5993. Fax: (215) 297-8722.

NEWRY

Leighty's 29-Acre Indoor/Outdoor Flea Market

DATES: Saturday and Sunday, year round.

TIMES: Summer: 7:00 AM-5:00 PM. Winter: 8:00 AM-5:00 PM.

ADMISSION: Free, with ample free parking.

LOCATION: On old Rt 220 (I-99), take Roaring Spring Exit, turn left at light, go 1 mile; 7 miles south of Altoona.

DESCRIPTION: This show began 21 years ago and has from 60 dealers in the winter to 350 in the summer both indoor (130 tables) and out (575 tables) exhibiting antiques, collectibles, handmades, and new merchandise, as well as an assortment of yard sale items. Food vendors and a concession are on the property. This is a large, clean, well-managed market for the area and is located near the famous "horseshoe curve." They also have a large farmers' market across the street. There is a new sports shop in an 80,000-square-foot building, a golf range—just for fun.

DEALER RATES: $12 and up per 11' × 28' outdoor sales space. Indoor spaces vary in size and price. Reservations are suggested but not necessary. For walk-ins, the earlier you come the better the location for you.

CONTACT: Roger Azzarello, Leighty's Flea Market, PO Box 307, Newry PA 16665-0307. Daily information call (814) 695-5151. Weekends at the market call (814) 695-7520. Email: sacbud1@aol.com. Web: www.leightys.com.

PHILADELPHIA
Quaker City Flea Market

DATES: Every Saturday and Sunday. Rain or shine.

TIMES: 8:00 AM-4:00 PM.

ADMISSION: Free. Free parking nearby.

LOCATION: Tacony and Comly Sts, 3 blocks south of the Tacony-Palmyra Bridge. On I-95 N to Bridge St Exit, right onto Tacony St to 5th traffic light. From I-95 South, take Bridge St Exit, go left 1 block to Tacony St, left to the 3rd light.

DESCRIPTION: This market began operation in 1972 and currently attracts between 150 and 175 dealers on indoor and outdoor spaces selling a variety of items including antiques, collectibles, handmade crafts, fresh produce, and new and used merchandise. Quite a few "finds" have come from here (paintings, rare books, furniture, pottery, old jewelry), later to be sold at auction elsewhere for loads of money. Obviously, a good place to haunt. Food is served inside and outside, and handicapped-accessible restrooms are available.

DEALER RATES: Between $25 for an outside space; $50 and up for inside space. Reservations are required in advance for indoors. First come, first served outdoors.

CONTACT: Jim or Joan Aiello, Quaker City Flea Market, 5001 Comly St, Philadelphia PA 19135. Tel: (215) 744-2022. Fax: (215) 535-0395.

PHILADELPHIA/FT WASHINGTON
Philly Big Flea

DATES: For 2002: April 6-7, October 12-13. Call or visit website for 2003 dates.

TIMES: Saturday 10:00 AM-6:00 PM, Sunday 11:00 AM-5:00 PM.

ADMISSION: $5; children under 12 free. Parking is free.

LOCATION: Ft Washington Expo Center at 1100 Virginia Dr.

DESCRIPTION: This show has over 500 dealers from 20 states selling primarily antiques and collectibles. This market is billed to become the "largest antique market on the East Coast." Food concessions and handicapped-accessible restrooms add to the amenities.

DEALER RATES: $120 single space. Reservations are required. This facility does charge $65 for electrical hookup.

CONTACT: D'Amore Promotions, 2125 McComas Way Ste 102, Virginia Beach VA 23454. Tel: (757) 430-4735. Fax: (757) 430-4738. Email: sales@damorepromotions.com. Web: www.damorepromotions.com.

PITTSBURGH/NORTH VERSAILLES
Eastland Super Flea

DATES: Saturday and Sunday.

TIMES: 8:00 AM-4:00 PM.

ADMISSION: Free. Parking is free.

LOCATION: 833 E Pittsburgh-McKeesport Blvd #1. At New Eastland Mall and Marketplace, just off Lincoln Hwy, Rt 30, less than 5 miles east of Pittsburgh.

DESCRIPTION: Opened in 1988, this is an indoor/outdoor market of 300 inside spaces and 200 outdoor tables—with as few as 2 to as many as 150 outside dealers depending on the weather. The ratio of old to new is 60/40, making this a great place to cruise for treasures. A lot of garage sale goodies come in, as well as antiques, collectibles, clothing, crafts, new and used merchandise, furniture, jewelry, fresh produce, and even a specialty butcher shop. There are two food courts, food vendors outside, and handicapped-accessible restrooms.

DEALER RATES: $15 for outside space, $15 inside. Monthly rates: $80-$200 depending on location and size. You can make phone reservations, however, if you are not in your place by 8:00 AM you forfeit the space. Vendors should arrive by 8:00 AM weekends and can come Friday from 9:00 AM-3:00 PM.

CONTACT: Ed Williams, Eastland Flea Market, 833 E Pittsburgh McKeesport Blvd, North Versailles PA 15137. Tel: (412) 673-3532 or (412) 678-8050. Fax: (412) 678-5340.

PITTSBURGH/WILDWOOD
Wildwood Peddler's Fair

DATES: Every Sunday, year round. Rain or shine.

TIMES: 6:00 AM-4:00 PM.

ADMISSION: Free. Parking on premises is available at $1 per vehicle; free parking is also available nearby.

LOCATION: 2330 Wildwood Rd. From Pittsburgh: take Rt 8 to Wildwood Rd towards North Park (Yellow Belt).

DESCRIPTION: This indoor/outdoor market has operated year round since 1972 on the site of the Old Wildwood Coal Mine. The mine closed in the 1960s. It currently draws between 350 and 500 dealers in 600 booths, depending on the time of year. A wide variety of merchandise, including antiques and collectibles, unique crafts, tools, store close-outs, fresh produce, furniture, jewelry, clothes, baked goods, and sports items is offered here. They have grown substantially, having added 5 new rooms to the one-acre building, making a total of 300 indoor spaces, currently filled to capacity. Additional restrooms and another complete concession stand were added with the addition, making a total of two complete kitchens offering everything from homemade chili to cotton candy. There is a festive family atmosphere at this market.

DEALER RATES: Outside: $12 per 14' × 22' space, BYOT (bring your own tables). Inside: $18-$60 per space, with monthly discounts available. Sizes range from 6' × 11' to 20' × 20' in various buildings. Reservations are not required for outdoor space; they are for indoor.

CONTACT: Vince Rutledge, President, Peddler's Fair Inc, PO Box 248, Wildwood PA 15091. Tel: (412) 487-2200. Fax: (412) 487-4946. Email: wildwood@usaor.net. Web: www.wildwoodpa.com.

QUAKERTOWN
Quakertown Flea and Farmers' Market

DATES: Friday, Saturday and Sunday, year round. Rain or shine. Additional holiday dates and times, check with the market.

TIMES: Friday and Saturday 9:00 AM-9:00 PM; Sunday 10:00 AM-5:00 PM.

ADMISSION: Free. Ample free parking is provided.

LOCATION: 201 Station Rd, ¼ mile south of Quakertown, ¾ mile east of Rt 309.

DESCRIPTION: Originally established as a farmers' market in 1932 on the farm of Stanley Rottenberger, this indoor/outdoor market has been in operation as a flea market since 1970. The flea market is located in a building that holds 100 permanent vendors with 150,000 square feet of outside selling area for up to 400 dealers. There are several more buildings, including a 115,000-square-foot Farmer's Building, a main building, as well as a discount grocer and health club. Their dealers cover the gamut of antiques and collectibles, crafts, and new merchandise, as well as the traditional farmers' market fare. "Everything you can eat, wear or use!" They have plenty of restaurants, discount grocery stores, butchers/delis, bakeries and produce markets. Yes, they have food! They hold special events throughout the year with special seasonal events. Many of their vendors are third and fourth generations working the same booths.

DEALER RATES: $10 for 2 tables per day, or $15 per 16' × 20' tailgate area. Prime tailgate areas run $20 per day. $45 per 120-square-foot space indoors for three days. Reservations are accepted for outdoor space on a 4-week advanced pre-pay basis. Discounts on rentals are given for reserved space. Indoor space rents on a week-to-week advanced payment basis and starts at $30 per weekend for a 10' × 10' space. Indoor space is rented on an availability basis and requires a space application to be completed with ID. Vendors are permitted access to the market on Wednesday and Thursday to stock and set up their stands from 8:30 AM-4:30 PM each day, but must sign in and out at the Market Office. The market is closed Monday and Tuesday.

CONTACT: John Chism, Manager, Quakertown Flea and Farmers' Market, 201 Station Rd, Quakertown PA 18951. Tel: (215) 536-4115. Fax: (215) 536-9019. Email: jchism@quakertownfarmersmkt.com. Web: www.quakertownfarmersmkt.com.

Whoa!
This market used to hold auctions of livestock in the barns now housing the flea markets. One regular, Tex, attends this market with his cow. Once, he stopped a President from passing, blocking the road with himself and his companion.

SCIOTA
Collectors' Cove

DATES: Saturday and Sunday.
TIMES: 9:00 AM-5:00 PM.
ADMISSION: Free. Parking is free.
LOCATION: Rt 33 and 209.
DESCRIPTION: Started in 1977 and self-billed as the "Largest Antique and Farmers' Market in NE Pennsylvania," this indoor market's dealers sell antiques, collectibles, garage sale goodies, and whatever else shows up. There are 5 buildings connected by "an old-West style porch" arranged in a semi-circle with 2 large pavilions putting 40,000 square feet under roof on 38 acres. This place is known as another of those places where dealers scrounge for treasures. There are estate liquidators and dealers in the wholesale warehouses and transient dealers outside. The Country Cafe serves homemade meals and each of the five buildings has handicapped-accessible restrooms. For the record, NE Pennsylvania is the Poconos!

DEALER RATES: $10 to $50 per space.

CONTACT: Collectors' Cove, Ltd, Rt 33, Sciota PA 18354-0333. Tel: (570) 992-5110 or 421-7439 (business office). Fax: (570) 421-2783. Email: admin@covemarket.com. Web: www.covemarket.com.

TARENTUM
Flea-Tique at Bull Creek

DATES: Third Sunday of each month, May through October.
TIMES: Daybreak to 2:00 PM.
ADMISSION: Free. Parking is $2.
LOCATION: Route 28, Exit 14—Ridge Road.

DESCRIPTION: Opened in 1983, this market of 175 outdoor dealers specialize in just antiques and collectibles. Located on a large level field shaded by some trees, this market makes a pleasant summer visit with the historic coal mine tours. Specialty food vendors sell alongside of the usual concessions. Restrooms are on site.
DEALER RATES: $25 per 24' × 20' space. $125 for a full season. Payment at the gate or by mail. Reservations are not required. The Society does not supply electricity.
CONTACT: Cathy Wencel, Museum Manager, Allegheny-Kiski Valley Historical Society, 224 E 7 Ave, Tarentum PA 15084-1513. Tel: (724) 224-7666. Fax: (724) 224-7666.

WEST MIFFLIN
Woodland Flea Market

DATES: Weekends, April through October. Rain or shine. Also Memorial Day, July 4, and Labor Day.
TIMES: 6:00 AM-2:00 PM.
ADMISSION: Free. Parking is free.
LOCATION: 526 Thompson Run Rd, 1 mile from the Allegheny County Airport, 1½ miles from Kennywood Park and just 7 miles from downtown Pittsburgh.

DESCRIPTION: This indoor/outdoor market has been operating since 1962. It currently attracts between 250 to 500 sellers, and between 10,000 and 15,000 buyers. Antiques, collectibles, handmade and craft items, fresh produce, new merchandise and other items are sold. Food and clean restrooms are available on the premises.
DEALER RATES: Outdoors $10 per 10' × 23' space or 2 spaces for $15; indoors $10 per 8' × 3' table or 2 tables for $15; and garage rentals 10' × 25' at $100 per month. Reservations are required for indoor and garage rentals.
CONTACT: Bob Kranack, Woodland Flea Market, 526 Thompson Run Rd, West Mifflin PA 15122. Tel: (412) 462-4334. Fax: (412) 462-3616.

WIND GAP
Wind Gap Flea Market

DATES: Saturday and Sunday.
TIMES: 8:00 AM-4:00 PM.
ADMISSION: Free. Parking is free.
LOCATION: 316 North Broadway. Going North on 33, get off Wind Gap exit, bear to right (512). On the left after third light. Going South on 33, get off Wind Gap exit; bear to left (old 155). Located 1 mile on right.
DESCRIPTION: This two-story indoor market of 75 dealers sells just about everything. One vendor supplies the necessary eats to keep you going, another sells fresh produce, and restrooms on each floor with a ramp between floors makes this building fully handicapped-accessible.
DEALER RATES: Call for rates. Reservations are necessary.
CONTACT: Wind Gap Flea Market, 316 North Broadway, Wind Gap PA 18091. Tel: (610) 863-8534.

OTHER FLEA MARKETS

We know or have heard about these markets, but have not personally contacted each one, as we have the markets with descriptions. If you plan to visit one of the markets listed below, *please call first* to make sure they are still open. Flea markets do come and go. While they were open when we went to press, they may not be later. We can't be responsible. *Call first!*

Barto: Jake's Flea Market, 1380 Rt 100. Tel: (610) 845-7091.
Beaver Falls: Indoor Flea Market, 1410 7th Ave. Tel: (724) 847-9650.
Bird In Hand: Millcreek Market, 2557 Old Philadelphia Pike. Tel: (717) 299-9625.
Blairsville: Jonnet Flea Market, Rt 22 W. Tel: (724) 459-0143.
Chambersburg: Seven Acre Flea Market, 3893 Molly Pitcher Hwy. Tel: (717) 375-4055.
Claysville: Claysville's Big Flea Market, 24 Varner Dr. Tel: (724) 663-5337.
Corsica: Peddler's Ridge, RR 1. Tel: (814) 379-9743.
Cranberry Twp: Spot Light 88 Flea Market, Rt 65 & 588. Tel: (724) 538-4055.
Duncannon: Susquehanna Flea Market, RR 4. Tel: (717) 834-3391.
Farrell: Sara Hailstock Flea Market, 947 Hamilton Ave. Tel: (724) 342-6866.
Hatboro: Hatboro Flea Market, 53 S York Rd Rear. Tel: (215) 672-3511.
Jeannette: L & L Flea Market, Claridge Rd & Elliott Rd. Tel: (724) 527-2097.
Kulpsville: Kulpsville Flea Market, 1375 Forty Foot Rd. Tel: (215) 361-7910.
La Jose: Country Side Flea Market, RR 36. Tel: (814) 277-4452.
Lewisburg: Route 15 Flea Market, Rt 15 N. Tel: (570) 568-8080.
Lucinda: Midway Auction & Flea Market, Rt 66. Tel: (814) 226-6697.
Lykens: Lykens Valley Flea Market, 110 Main St. Tel: (717) 453-7474.

Mechanicsburg: Carter's Silver Springs Market, 22 Carlisle Pke. Tel: (717) 766-9032.

Nottingham: Nottingham Flea Market, 488 W Christine Rd. Tel: (610) 998-0960.

Oakdale: Trader Jack's Flea Market, Steen & Thoms Run Rd. Tel: (412) 257-8980.

Paxinos: Paxinos Flea & Farmers Market, SRt 61. Tel: (570) 648-6232.

Penns Creek: Walter's Market, 605 Market. Tel: (570) 837-1050.

Philadelphia: Big T Flea Market, 2600 E Tioga St. Tel: (215) 291-0280.

Philadelphia: Ontario Street Market, 2235 E Ontario St. Tel: (215) 288-7338.

Pocono Lake: Farmers Marketplace, 940 Hwy 115 N. Tel: (570) 646-7094.

Pulaski: Pulaski Flea Market, Rt 551 N. Tel: (724) 654-0531.

RHODE ISLAND

CHARLESTOWN
General Stanton Flea Market

DATES: Saturdays, Sundays and Monday holidays, April through November, weather permitting.

TIMES: Saturdays 7:00 AM-3:00 PM, Sundays and holiday Mondays 7:00 AM-4:00 PM.

ADMISSION: Free. Parking is $1.

LOCATION: 4115A Old Post Rd between Rts 1A and 1. From New York: I-95 N, Exit 92 (Rt 2) 3 miles to Rt 78, 4 miles to Rt 1, go north 12 miles to Charlestown. From Boston: I-95 south, Exit 9 to Rt 1, South Charlestown Beach Exit. They are 35 miles south of Providence and 40 miles northeast of New London CT.

DESCRIPTION: There is space for 200 dealers, with Sunday being the big day, at this outdoor market started in 1967. It is located on the property of The General Stanton Inn, one of America's oldest inns. There is everything from antiques and collectibles to handmade crafts, vegetables and new merchandise at this market. There is one restaurant and one snack bar on the premises. They are also conveniently located between Mystic and Newport, so there is plenty to do in the area. They are planning a Christmas in July event. Watch for it.

DEALER RATES: $25 for a 15' × 20' space, $35 for a space under tent. Reservations are not required. Canopies are available for $10 extra. There is security ($12 extra) for dealers who wish to leave their goods over Saturday night.

CONTACT: Janice Falcone, General Stanton Inn, Route 1A Box 222, Charlestown RI 02813. Tel: (401) 364-8888 or fax: (401) 364-3333.

EAST GREENWICH
Rocky Hill Flea Market

DATES: Every Sunday, April through November.

TIMES: 5:00 AM-4:00 PM.

ADMISSION: Free. Parking is $1.

LOCATION: 1408 Division Rd, corner of Division Rd and Rt 2. Take Exit 8 or 8A off I-95.

DESCRIPTION: This market has been around since 1960 and now attracts approximately 300-400 dealers with virtually all types of merchandise available, including crafts, collectibles, fresh produce, and new merchandise. Food is available on the premises.

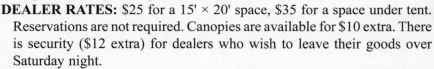

DEALER RATES: $20 per 20' × 25' space, corner spaces go for $25, smaller spaces are available for $15. Advance reservations are not required.

CONTACT: Gary Hamilton, Rocky Hill Flea Market, 1408 Division Rd, East Greenwich RI 02818. Tel: (401) 884-4114.

PROVIDENCE
Big Top Flea Market

DATES: Saturday and Sunday.

TIMES: 9:00 AM-5:00 PM.

ADMISSION: Saturday free, Sunday $.50. Parking is free.

LOCATION: 120 Manton Ave. Just one block from Rt 6, towards Olneyville.

DESCRIPTION: Opened in 1976 in a historic 1800s mill building, this market of 100-150 dealers sells antiques, collectibles, garage sale goodies, produce, used general merchandise, new merchandise, and crafts. There is food on the premises, served by a snack bar and handicapped-accessible restrooms when needed.

DEALER RATES: $25 per 8' × 10' booth per weekend. Reservations are suggested.

CONTACT: Sully or Howard, Big Top Flea Market, 120 Manton Ave, Providence RI 02909. Tel: (401) 274-0060. Fax: (401) 464-8666.

SOUTH CAROLINA

ANDERSON/BELTON
Anderson Jockey Lot and Farmers' Market

DATES: Saturday and Sunday. Rain or shine.

TIMES: Saturday 7:00 AM-6:00 PM; Sunday 9:00 AM-6:00 PM.

ADMISSION: Free. Parking is free.

LOCATION: Hwy 29 between Greenville and Anderson, 10 miles from Anderson.

DESCRIPTION: Opened in 1974, this huge market hosts between 1,500 and 2,000-plus dealers on 65 acres selling everything, quite literally. To prove their point, their crowds average 40-60,000! "If we don't have it, you don't need it." Just some of the items sold are: antiques, collectibles, tons of produce, clothing, comics, cleaning supplies, pantyhose, pharmaceuticals, office supplies, cologne, stamps, coins, garage sale goodies, and other new merchandise. There are "lots of restaurants and snack bars" and clean handicapped-accessible restrooms on site. So popular is this place that they once had 40 tour buses at once!

Just as an aside, they have an Anderson exchange telephone at the front of the market, a Williamston exchange telephone at the back of the market and a Belton address. That's what you get for operating at the junction of three separate entities.

DEALER RATES: Inside: $10 for one day with a wooden table. Outside, pick a vacant, non-reserved space; one of the owners will tap you for $6 for the space and one concrete table for each day. Reservations are required for inside space only. Those spaces can be hard to get. You must reserve in person. Watch for their website.

CONTACT: Anderson Jockey Lot and Farmers' Market, 120 W Whitner St, Anderson, SC 29621. Tel: (864) 224-2027. Fax: (864) 231-6927. Email: info@jockeylot.com. Web: www.jockeylot.com.

¿Que Pasa?

A group of tourists from Poland were visiting the market when one gent was separated from his group and got thoroughly lost. (This *is* a huge place.) One of the group was offered the PA system to call his pal to the office to rejoin the group.

That was cool. It seems there were other Polish visitors who also came to the office looking for their fellow countrymen!

CHARLESTON
Lowcountry Flea Market and Collectibles Show

DATES: Third Saturday and Sunday of each month, year round; except February and November, the second weekend.

TIMES: Saturday 9:00 AM-6:00 PM, Sunday 10:00 AM-5:00 PM.

ADMISSION: $2 per person, kids free. Parking is sometimes free, sometimes not.

LOCATION: At Gaillard Auditorium, 77 Calhoun St, in Charleston, near Meeting and Calhoun Sts.

DESCRIPTION: This show has been operating since 1973 in the historic downtown area. Over 50 dealers offer antiques, collectibles, estate merchandise and handcrafts from indoor stalls. This is mostly an antiques and collectibles show. A restaurant serves full meals, and there are handicapped-accessible restrooms.

DEALER RATES: $85 per 10' × 10' booth per weekend. Reservations are required in advance.

CONTACT: Donna Garrett Kidd, 605 Johnnie Dodds Blvd, Mount Pleasant SC 29464. Tel: (843) 849-1949.

COLUMBIA
Barnyard Flea Market

DATES: Saturday and Sunday. Rain or shine.

TIMES: 8:00 AM-5:00 PM and later in summer.

ADMISSION: Free. Paved parking is also free.

LOCATION: Between Lexington and Columbia on Hwy 1. Just 2.3 miles from Exit 58 off I-20; 3 miles from Exit 111A off I-26.

DESCRIPTION: Built as a new market in April 1988, this collection of 12 red-tin-roofed buildings houses 552 spaces for dealers. The number of dealers varies by how many spaces each dealer will rent. They are usually full. The buildings are lit inside and out, allowing late-evening shopping in summertime. There are 75-100 dealer tables outside without cover. Four restaurants, including a brand-new barbecue restaurant take care of hungry shoppers. Among the fares sold are antiques, collectibles, boiled peanuts, car stereos, t-shirts, sunglasses, hardware, fishing supplies, used appliances, fashion jewelry, handbags, clothes new and used, "and the usual generic flea market stuff." Also notable are air-conditioned restrooms and the Barnyard RV park next door. Their sister market is located in Fort Mill.

DEALER RATES: $10 per day for 4' × 8' tables undercover in a 10' × 10' space; $5 for 4' × 8' tables outside. Reservations are suggested, as they do fill up fast.

CONTACT: Manager, Barnyard Flea Market, 4414 Augusta Rd, Lexington SC 29073. Tel: 1-800-628-7496 or (803) 957-6570.

EDMUND
Smiley's Edmund Flea Market and Open Air Mall

DATES: Tuesday, Friday, Saturday and Sunday.

TIMES: 8:00 AM-5:00 PM.

ADMISSION: Free. Parking is free.

LOCATION: From Columbia, take Hwy 302 south (9 miles south of the airport). From Lexington, off I-20, Exit 55, take Hwy 6 south to Edmund. Only 7 miles north of Pelion on Hwy 302.

DESCRIPTION: Opened in November 1996, this is another of Smiley's successful flea markets dotting the South. There are over 500 outside spaces, most with tables and many more under cover. Considering that many dealers take several spaces (and at these prices who wouldn't?) they generally have over 100 dealers outside and 40-60 inside selling almost everything imaginable, including lots of garage sale goodies.

DEALER RATES: Outside: $3 per table, or 4 for $10. Inside: $5 per space. Reservations are suggested. There is a new full-service RV campground in the back with special deals for dealers who wish to stay. Watch for their website.

CONTACT: Pam and George Redick, Smiley's Flea Market, 5910 Edmund Hwy, Lexington SC 29073. Tel: (803) 955-9111. Fax: (803) 955-2829.

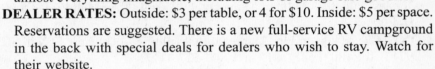

FLORENCE
Florence Flea Market

DATES: Saturday and Sunday, year round.

TIMES: 7:00 AM-6:00 PM.

ADMISSION: Free. Parking is free.

LOCATION: Corner of Rts 327 and 76 at 301 N. Exit 170 off I-95; go south 5 miles.

DESCRIPTION: Open since 1980, this indoor/outdoor market of 400 dealers sells crafts, produce, new merchandise, and garage sale goodies. Two snack bars and restrooms add to the amenities.

DEALER RATES: $8 per 10' × 10' yard space, $10 per 10' × 10' open shed space, $12 per 10' × 10' space in the main building. Reservations are recommended. Office is open Friday for rentals.

CONTACT: Florence Flea Market, 4001 E Palmetto St, Florence SC 29506-4205. Tel: (843) 667-9585.

FORT MILL
Flea Market at Pineville

DATES: Saturday and Sunday. Rain or shine.

TIMES: Saturday 7:00 AM-5:00 PM, Sunday 8:00 AM-5:00 PM.

ADMISSION: Free. Parking is free.

LOCATION: 3674 Hwy 51. Exit 90 (Carowinds Exit) off I-77.

DESCRIPTION: Built as a new market in June 1995, this collection of red-tin-roofed buildings houses over 500 spaces for dealers. The number of dealers varies by how many spaces each dealer will rent. The buildings are lit inside and out, allowing late evening shopping in summertime. There are dealer tables outside without cover. Two restaurants, including a pizza place, and canteen take care of hungry shoppers. Among the fares sold are antiques, collectibles, t-shirts, sunglasses, hardware, fishing supplies, used appliances, fashion jewelry, handbags, clothes new and used, "and the usual generic flea market stuff." Handicapped-accessible restrooms add to the amenities. Their sister market is located in Columbia.

DEALER RATES: $11 per day per 10' × 10' space inside with electricity, $10 for a covered area. $6 outside for a table per day. Reservations are required. Permanent warehouse facilities available. Office hours are also Monday 9:00 AM-12:00 PM, Thursday 9:00 AM-4:00 PM, and Friday 8:00 AM-4:00 PM.

CONTACT: Manager, Flea Market at Pineville, 3674 Hwy 51, Ft Mill SC 29715. Tel: (803) 548-1817 or 1-800-527-4117.

GREENVILLE
Fairgrounds Flea Market

DATES: Saturday and Sunday. Rain or shine.

TIMES: Saturday 5:00 AM-5:00 PM, Sunday 6:00 AM-5:00 PM.

ADMISSION: Free. Parking is also free.

LOCATION: 2600 White Horse Rd. From I-85 South, take the White Horse Rd Exit (Exit 44), turn right, go 1 mile to market.

DESCRIPTION: This market, opened in March 1990, hosts 800 to 1,000 dealers selling everything: some antiques and collectibles, lots of crafts and produce, garage sale goodies, some new merchandise, racing material, tools, pantyhose, and the occasional goat to chickens, rabbits, dogs and cats. Home-cooking and the usual snack bar fare feed the famished. There are plenty of restrooms, inside and out, just in case.

DEALER RATES: $9 under the shed, $7 outdoors, $9 for a 10' × 10' space inside. Reservations are required for all but a few outside spaces set aside for first come, first served.

CONTACT: Marvin Kelly or Monika Baker, Fairgrounds Flea Market, 2710 White Horse Rd, Greenville SC 29611. Tel: (864) 295-1183.

LADSON
Coastal Carolina Flea Market

DATES: Every Saturday and Sunday. Rain or shine.

TIMES: 8:00 AM-5:00 PM.

ADMISSION: Free. Free parking is available on 15 acres.

LOCATION: At the junction of College Park Rd and Hwy 78. Take I-26 to Exit 203 (College Park Rd); or take Hwy 78. Flea market is next door to the local fairgrounds. They are just minutes from the center of historic Charleston.

DESCRIPTION: This indoor/outdoor market started in June 1981 and now has over 500 indoor booths and 300 outside spaces available. In 2001, they added 114 spaces in a new covered area. It usually draws 400 to 450 dealers selling a full range of antiques and collectibles such as tools, jewelry, furniture, old and new clothing, baby items, pets and pet supplies, birds, as well as fresh produce, garage sale items and new merchandise. There are often local airbrush artists on hand for portraits. Computer portraits are also a draw. Their new air-conditioned/heated 100-seat restaurant, "Weekends" at the Flea Market, serves the starving shoppers.

DEALER RATES: $12 per 10' × 10' space per day inside. $6 per table outside. $10 per space for the new covered area outside. Reservations required for inside space and the covered outside space; first come, first served open-air outside.

CONTACT: Michael W Masterson, Coastal Carolina Flea Market Inc, PO Box 510, Ladson SC 29456-0510. Tel: (843) 797-0540. Fax: (843) 797-8995.

What a Comeback, the Rising Phoenix!
On Sunday, July 12, 1998, the flea market burned to the ground. Over 100,000 square feet of market and the merchandise of 250 vendors. Gone. The next day, 95% of their vendors, who had lost everything, as well as the owners pitched in to begin the clean up. Within a week, they had reopened, filling 300 outdoor spaces.

July 11, 1999 saw their grand reopening in a new state-of-the-art 100,000-square-foot complex. They would like to thank everyone who helped them rebuild, as well as their loyal patrons.

MYRTLE BEACH
Myrtle Beach Flea Market

DATES: Daily.

TIMES: 9:00 AM–6:00 PM.

ADMISSION: Free. Parking is free.

LOCATION: 3820 S Kings Hwy, Hwy 17 Bus.

DESCRIPTION: This market opened in 1993 with 120 vendors in four buildings selling one building's worth of antiques, some collectibles, garage sale goodies, and lots of used and new merchandise. This is a well-lit, air-conditioned market with wide aisles, and a food court serving full meals with handicapped-accessible restrooms. Plenty of giveaways (vacations and show tickets), magicians strolling the market, loaner wheelchairs and strollers, hourly prize drawings, three-times-a-week auction, a monthly antique auction, free blood pressure screenings every other Thursday, and scary ghosts and goblins (dealers in disguise) on Halloween.

DEALER RATES: $10-$25.50 per day depending on location of space. Monthly rates available. Reservations are suggested.

CONTACT: Myrtle Beach Flea Market, 3820 S Kings Hwy, Myrtle Beach SC 29577-4833. Tel: (843) 477-1550. Fax: (843) 238-2555. Web: www.americanparknswap.com.

> **Market Notes:**
> They sell a hot sauce here that is sooooo hot, you have to sign a release form to try it!
>
> One dealer in 50s-70s vintage clothing (heck! I remember that stuff) has a size 42 poodle skirt pinned up in her booth. It was used by a local male actor on stage.

NORTH MYRTLE BEACH
North Myrtle Beach Flea Market

DATES: Every Friday, Saturday and Sunday.

TIMES: 9:00 AM-4:00 PM.

ADMISSION: Free. Parking is free.

LOCATION: Hwy 17 at intersection with Hwy 9.

DESCRIPTION: Operating since 1984, this market is full most of the time (it is a tourist area!) with hundreds of dealers filling 350 booths (200 lockable sheds) or under cover. There are several antique dealers, loads of collectibles, crafts, new and used merchandise, tools, and garage sale goodies. The mix is roughly 50/50 old versus new according to management. There is a food court area with handicapped-accessible restrooms.

DEALER RATES: $22 for yard sale space outdoors, $200 per month for a lockable shed building. Reservations are required one week in advance.

CONTACT: North Myrtle Beach Flea Market, PO Box 3467, N Myrtle Beach SC 29582. Tel: (843) 249-4701.

Animal Tails
One season, they had a monkey at the market riding a bike. Another time, a bear got loose and was found behind the market in a wild grapevine. It wasn't after honey?

PICKENS
Pickens County Flea Market

DATES: Every Wednesday.
TIMES: 4:00 AM-2:00 PM.
ADMISSION: Free. Parking is free.
LOCATION: Hwy 183 W, 2 miles out of town of Pickens on Hwy 183 W.
DESCRIPTION: Operating since 1974, this market of 1,000 booths with 500-600 dealers in them sells antiques, collectibles, crafts, animals, new and used merchandise, produce, and almost anything you are looking for. There are food concessions and restrooms on site.
DEALER RATES: $5 per 10' × 12' outside space, $6 per 10' × 10' shed and space per day.
CONTACT: Pickens County Flea Market, 1427 Wahalla Hwy, Pickens SC 29671. Tel: (864) 878-9646.

PROSPERITY
Prosperity Jockey Lot

DATES: Saturday and Sunday, year round.
TIMES: Saturday 7:00 AM-5:30 PM, Sunday 8:00 AM-5:30 PM.
ADMISSION: Free. Parking is free.
LOCATION: 221 Hwy 773, off Exit 82 on I-26, between Prosperity and Clinton.
DESCRIPTION: Opened in 1989, this indoor/outdoor market of 350-400 dealers sells antiques and collectibles, chickens, ducks, geese, the occasional cow, peanuts, new merchandise, "a little bit of everything," as manager Wayne Owens describes it. There are two restaurants, plenty of concession stands, including one peanut stand—but he needs another; any takers? Call Wayne. After roaming and buying, the handicapped-accessible restrooms will come in handy! This is one of a number of Jockey Lots around three states. Their big "brother" market is in Anderson SC.
DEALER RATES: Outside under cover $7 per day, inside the building $8 per day. There are storage sheds available (occasionally someone will let one loose!) for $42 per weekend and up. All first-come, first-served.
CONTACT: Wayne Owens, Manager, Prosperity Jockey Lot, PO Box 870, Prosperity SC 29127-0870. Tel: (803) 276-0084. Web: www.jockeylot.com.

SPRINGFIELD
Springfield Flea Market

DATES: Saturday and Monday. Rain or shine.

TIMES: 5:00 AM until afternoon, generally around 2:00 PM. There is no set opening or closing times; however, most people work during these times.

ADMISSION: Free. Free parking is available nearby.

LOCATION: 9113 Neeses Hwy. At the intersection of Rts 3 and 4, approximately 1 mile east of Springfield.

DESCRIPTION: This market evolved from an auction held at a livestock market and has been running as a flea market since 1958. The farmers would often bring along farming tools and "whatever" to auction off as well. Soon, the auctioneer, Oscar Cooper, decided it was time the farmers sold their own stuff and sent them off to the "yard" adjacent to the Stockyard. At first, it was slow going with only ten "dealers," but in the mid-70s this market blossomed, turning sleepy Springfield into a lively town one day a week. The market moved to its current 35-acre location in 1983. It now accommodates between 750 and 1,000 dealers inside and outside, selling a varied selection of antiques and collectibles, fresh farm goods, and some new merchandise. According to its current owner, Oscar's son Henry, while there are many regular dealers, the "first-timers" cleaning out their houses generally bring in a wonderful variety of merchandise. Food is served by a concession stand and a convenience store is on the premises. Clean handicapped-accessible restrooms are available, and law enforcement officers patrol the grounds. It is said that many people come so early they must use flashlights to find their way to the bargains and treasures.

DEALER RATES: $5 for an open 12' × 12' space with table outdoors; $7 per 10' × 10' shed space with table. Advance reservations are not required.

CONTACT: Henry Cooper, Owner and Manager, PO Box 74, Springfield SC 29146-0074. Tel: (803) 258-3192.

SUMTER
The Market at Shaw

DATES: Every Friday, Saturday and Sunday.

TIMES: Friday and Sunday 10:00 AM-6:00 PM; Saturday 7:00 AM-6:00 PM.

ADMISSION: Free. Parking is free.

LOCATION: 5500 Broad St Ext. Hwy 378 E, across from Shaw Air Force Base, 30 miles east of Columbia.

DESCRIPTION: Operating since 1988, this market of 63 tables, some under cover and others in the open, and plenty of field space has 50 or so vendors selling antiques, collectibles, crafts, furniture, books, fresh produce, garage sale goodies, all manner of livestock, a woodshop, gifts, and lots of new merchandise. A snack bar quells the munchies, and there are handicapped-accessible restrooms when needed.

DEALER RATES: Field area, no cover: $2-$3 per space; uncovered tables $5 per day; monthly under cover $173 with electric and security. Reservations are required for monthly space, otherwise first come, first served.

CONTACT: Bob, The Market at Shaw, 5500 Broad St Ext, Sumter SC 29154. Tel: (803) 494-5500.

WEST COLUMBIA
US #1 Metro Flea Market

DATES: Friday, Saturday and Sunday. Rain or shine. Wednesday wholesale market only.

TIMES: Friday and Sunday 8:00 AM-5:00 PM; Saturday 6:30 AM-5:00 PM. Wednesday 7:00 AM-12:00 PM.

ADMISSION: Free. Free parking is available.

LOCATION: 3500 Augusta Rd, on US Hwy 1. From I-26, take US Hwy 1 south to Lexington (Exit 111A South) approximately 1½ miles; from I-20, take US Hwy 1 (Exit 58) to West Columbia, 4½ miles. Only 5 miles from the state capitol.

DESCRIPTION: This show began in March 1980 and currently draws 800 dealers inside (in permanent stalls) and outside peddling antiques, collectibles, crafts, fresh farm produce, and some new merchandise. They are the oldest and "most popular" market in the Columbia area, drawing between 5,000 and 15,000 per weekend depending on weather. There is even a vendor selling medical supplies—one wheelchair went for $2.95! This place is garage-sale heaven! Full of surprises. Food is available on the premises. Wednesday is open for a special wholesalers market only, open from 7:00 AM-12:00 PM.

DEALER RATES: Fridays are free—no reservations required; Saturday $15 per day under covered stalls, $10 in open space; and Sunday $12 per day for covered stalls and $8 per open outdoor stalls. Wednesday wholesale rate is $25 per day or $75 by the month. Advance reservations are recommended for Saturday and Sunday at least a week to two weeks in advance.

CONTACT: Richard Hook, US#1 Metro Flea Market, PO Box 1457, Lexington SC 29071-1457. Tel: (803) 796-9294. Email: help@us1fleamarket.com. Web: www.us1fleamarket.com.

OTHER FLEA MARKETS

We know or have heard about these markets, but have not personally contacted each one, as we have the markets with descriptions. If you plan to visit one of the markets listed below, *please call first* to make sure they are still open. Flea markets do come and go. While they were open when we went to press, they may not be later. We can't be responsible. *Call first!*

Beaufort: Laurel Bay Flea Market, 484 Laurel Bay Rd. Tel: (843) 846-2258.

Conway: Conway East Flea Market, 1080 Hwy 501 Bus. Tel: (843) 347-1414.

Fort Mill: Flea Market at Pineville, 3674 Hwy 51 N. Tel: (803) 548-1817.

Gaffney: Highway 18 Flea Market, 905 Shelby Hwy. Tel: (864) 488-1712.

Greenwood: Greenwood Trading Post & Flea Market Inc, 1428 S Main St. Tel: (864) 229-3791.

Hartsville: 151 Auction & Flea Market, 1427 E Bobo Newsom Hwy. Tel: (843) 383-4332.

Hartsville: Open House Flea Market, 1624 S 5th St. Tel: (843) 332-8557.

Hodges: Greenwood Flea Market & Jockey Lot, 111 Dixie Dr. Tel: (864) 223-3045.

Johnston: Margie's Flea Market, 1194 SC Hwy 191. Tel: (803) 275-3142.

Leesville: Trade Winds, 3967 Hwy 378. Tel: (803) 532-4841.

Lugoff: Kershaw County Flea Market, I-20 US Hwy 601. Tel: (803) 438-5488.

Moncks Corner: Garlands, South Live Oak Dr. Tel: (843) 761-8929.

Myrtle Beach: Hudson's Surfside Flea Market, 1040 Hwy 17 S. Tel: (843) 238-0372.

Myrtle Beach: Kings, 3820 S Kings Hwy. Tel: (843) 828-0323.

North Augusta: Mini Flea, 207 Belvedere Clearwater. Tel: (803) 441-0076.

Pageland: Watermelon Patch, 151 By Passage. Tel: (843) 672-5235.

Rock Hill: S & S Flea Market, 251 Albright Road. Tel: (803) 366-5412.

Ruby: Jewel City Flea Market. Tel: (843) 634-6290.

Spartanburg: Spartanburg Flea Market, 8010 Asheville Hwy. Tel: (864) 503-9026.

Sumter: Sumter County Flea Market, 2277 Myrtle Beach Hwy. Tel: (803) 495-2281.

Travelers Rest: Foothills Flea Market, 1131 North Hwy 25. Tel: (864) 834-2021.

Trenton: Three J Flea Market, 5156 Edgefield Road. Tel: (803) 275-9255.

Westminster: Traders Junction Flea Market, 4265 S Hwy 11. Tel: (864) 638-0100.

West Columbia: West Columbia Antique Mall, 205 Wattling Rd. Tel: (803) 794-7197.

SOUTH DAKOTA

SIOUX FALLS
Sioux Falls Flea Market

DATES: Saturday and Sunday, first weekend of every month. No shows May through August.

TIMES: Saturday 9:00 AM-5:00 PM; Sunday 11:00 AM-4:00 PM.

ADMISSION: $1 per person. Ample free parking.

LOCATION: Expo Building at 12th and Louise Ave Fairgrounds.

DESCRIPTION: This indoor market first opened in 1970. There are 250 dealers selling antiques, collectibles, arts and crafts items, as well as new merchandise. At least 70% of the items shown are antiques. The crowds keep growing every weekend and have more than doubled in size in this good, clean, smoke-free atmosphere. Handicapped access throughout the market is very easy, as this is a large well-lit building with wide aisles. Food is available on the premises.

DEALER RATES: $30 per 8' table and space per weekend; $95 for 4 tables. Advance reservations are required, as there is a waiting list.

CONTACT: Ed and Bonnie Benson, PO Box 236, Sioux Falls SD 57101-0236. Tel: (605) 334-1312. Email: bensfelix@aol.com.

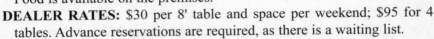

OTHER FLEA MARKETS

We know or have heard about these markets, but have not personally contacted each one, as we have the markets with descriptions. If you plan to visit one of the markets listed below, *please call first* to make sure they are still open. Flea markets do come and go. While they were open when we went to press, they may not be later. We can't be responsible. *Call first!*

Black Hawk: Black Hawk Flea Market, 5805 N Hwy 79. Tel: (605) 787-6402.

Madison: Four Seasons Flea Market, 223 N Egan Ave. Tel: (605) 256-6696.

Rapid City: Black Hills Flea Market, 909 Saint Francis St. Tel: (605) 343-6477.

Sioux Falls: Cliff Avenue Flea Market, 3515 N Cliff Ave. Tel: (605) 338-8975.

TENNESSEE

CROSSVILLE
Crossville Flea Market

DATES: Saturday and Sunday and Memorial Day and Labor Day holiday Mondays.

TIMES: 7:00 AM-3:00 PM.

ADMISSION: Free. Parking is free.

LOCATION: Hwy 70 N, midway between Knoxville and Nashville. Take I-40, Exit 317 towards Crossville, turn right at 4th traffic light. Right at the next traffic light. Market is about 1½ miles on the right.

DESCRIPTION: A flea market in the original sense, operating under covered sheds, this market has been running since 1970. Depending on the season, there are 200 to 400 dealers selling antiques, collectibles, furniture, dogs, coins, cats, cards, chickens, garage sale goodies, livestock, new merchandise, crafts, produce, stamps, and whatever else shows up. Because of the nature of this market, much of the merchandise is old and/or used. Think unfound treasures. There are 4 snack bars and a restaurant as well as handicapped-accessible parking and restrooms, and showers. Members of the Tennessee Flea Market Association.

DEALER RATES: $9 for a 12' × 14' covered space. Electricity is $3 per day extra, $10 per day for a camper or motor home. Reservations are suggested.

CONTACT: Mary Gunter or Lois Wilbanks, PO Box 3037, Crossville TN 38557-3037. Tel: (931) 484-9970.

HIGHWAY 127
Highway 127 Corridor Sale

DATES: August, from the Thursday before the third Sunday through Sunday for 4 days. Dates for 2002: August 15-18.

TIMES: Whenever.

ADMISSION: Free. Parking is wherever you can find it—off the road.

LOCATION: All along US Hwy 127 through three states: Kentucky, Tennessee, and Alabama. When you see a collection of sellers, it's there.

DESCRIPTION: Started in 1987 as a way to get travelers off the interstate and back onto the country roads by Fentress County's former County Executive Mike Walker and some of his friends, this market of thousands of dealers in "oddities and antiques," yard sale unloaders, and whoever and whatever else shows up, selling everything old and/or crafty. If you wish to travel the entire 450-mile route, start in Covington KY and work your way down to around Gadsden AL. There are plenty of food vendors. This has to be "the World's Longest Outdoor Sale."

Rules of the road: 1) Drive Cautiously—then you won't hit pedestrians or miss that goody you've been looking for. 2) Be extremely careful crossing the road! 3) Use your turn signals and don't stop suddenly for that goody (have a lookout who can give you ample warning). Otherwise, you may be dealing with insurance companies and wreckers rather than rare Ming.

DEALER RATES: Whatever the local landowner charges. Check out the website for a list of contacts in each state (it's huge) or call.

CONTACT: Fentress County Chamber of Commerce, PO Box 1294, Jamestown TN 38556-1294. Tel: (800) 327-3945 or (931) 879-9948. Web: http://jamestowntn.org/worlds.htm.

JACKSON
Friendly Frank's Flea Market

DATES: First weekend of every month, except September, from Friday night through Sunday.

TIMES: Friday evenings 6:00 PM-9:00 PM, Saturday 9:00 AM-6:00 PM and Sunday 9:00 AM-5:00 PM.

ADMISSION: Free. Parking is free.

LOCATION: Hwy 45 S.

DESCRIPTION: Opened in 1983, this indoor/outdoor market's 200-plus dealers sell a few antiques and collectibles, coins, stamps, cards, furniture, garage sale clean-outs, but mostly new merchandise and crafts. Two snack bars serve to quell the munchies. There are clean handicapped-accessible restrooms on site. Find Peggy and say Hi for me!

DEALER RATES: $60 for the weekend for a 9' × 10' space. Reservations are required.

CONTACT: Peggy Mullikin, Friendly Frank's Flea Market, PO Box 328, Cordova TN 38088-0328. Tel: (901) 755-6561.

KNOXVILLE
Esau's Antique and Collectible Market

DATES: Saturday and Sunday, third weekend of each month, except September when it is held the fourth weekend. October is a huge 3-day extravaganza.

TIMES: Saturday 9:00 AM-5:00 PM. Sunday 12:00 PM-5:00 PM.

ADMISSION: $3 per person for regular markets, $4 for extravaganza. Thirty acres of free parking is provided.

LOCATION: Take the Rutledge Pk Exit 392 off I-40 E.

DESCRIPTION: This indoor market has run since 1975 and now includes 300 dealers selling a range of antiques and collectibles, craft items, and new articles. (Antiques and collectibles account for about 70% of the merchandise.) Food is available on the premises. Members of the Tennessee Flea Market Association.

DEALER RATES: Outside: $40 for a 120 sq ft space. Inside: $70-90 per 9' × 10' space per weekend, plus City and County Business License fee.

CONTACT: Cindy Crabtree, Esau Inc, PO Box 50096, Knoxville TN 37950-0096. Tel: (423) 588-1233 or 1-800-588-ESAU (3728). Email: info@esaushows.com. Web: www.esaushows.com.

Knoxville Flea Market

DATES: For 2002: January 18-20, February 15-17, March 15-17, May 17-19, August 2-4, October 18-20, November 22-24.

TIMES: Friday 3:00 PM-7:00 PM, Saturday 10:00 AM-7:00 PM, Sunday 10:00 AM-4:00 PM.

ADMISSION: Free. Parking is free.

LOCATION: I-75 Expo. Take I-75 to Exit 108, on the corner of Clinton Hwy and Merchants Dr.

DESCRIPTION: Opened in 2001, this market boasts 500 dealers selling antiques, collectibles, and the usual flea market everything. Already it is quite successful. There is food available as well as handicapped-accessible restrooms.

DEALER RATES: $95 per 10' x 10.5' space, $143 per 15' x 10.5' space, $190 per 20' x 10.5' space. Reservations are required.

CONTACT: Stewart Promotions, 2950 Breckenridge Ln #4A, Louisville KY 40220. Tel: (502) 456-2244. Email: sp2950@home.com. Web: www.stewartpromotions.com.

KODAK

Great Smokies Craft Fair/Flea Market

DATES: Friday, Saturday, and Sunday, year round.

TIMES: 9:00 AM-6:00 PM.

ADMISSION: Free. Parking is also free.

LOCATION: 220 Dumplin Valley Rd W. Off I-40, Exit 407, turn onto Dumplin Valley Rd, about ¼ mile down the road. Sixteen miles from Gatlinburg. Only 12 miles from Dollywood.

DESCRIPTION: Ideally situated on 25 acres next to the Interstate, this very successful market opened on August 3, 1990. The dealers are housed in a 250-space air-conditioned building, with unlimited outdoor space. There are 250 dealers inside and at least another 250-plus outside under cover offering their goods to their 45,000 weekend visitors. They have a special section of wonderful antiques and collectibles, including player pianos! The dealers are noted for their friendliness, courtesy and helpfulness. They are more than willing to help each other and their customers out. There is a tremendous variety of superb crafts as well as manufacturer-direct booths. There is a food court selling homemade pizzas and corn bread, soup beans, gourmet burgers and regular burgers, hot dogs, and daily specials. A video arcade keeps the kids busy. The market is kept spotlessly clean. They hold dealer-only auctions every Thursday at 11:00 AM; every Friday they hold a public auction at 7:00 PM. They have added an Expo Center, new handi-capped-accessible restrooms and Juno's Pizza. They welcome RVs, tour buses and tractor-trailers. Ninety percent of their dealers are permanent; 80% have been here since they opened. Definitely a family market includ-ing vendors with kid's stuff. They choose their vendors to meet the wants and desires of all of their customers. The management strives to be the best market in the business and was chosen as one of the top 10 markets in the state by the Tennessee Flea Market Association. Nearby are 15,000 motels and hotel rooms and plenty of restaurants around the area. Members of the Tennessee Flea Market Association.

DEALER RATES: Winter: $60 per weekend, Friday through Sunday. Outside open spaces $12 a day, covered sheds $12 a day. Tables $2 a day. Summer rates can vary, but within this scale. Reservations are required because of a long waiting list.

CONTACT: Great Smokies Craft Fair and Flea Market, 220 Dumplin Valley Rd W, Kodak TN 37764. Tel: (865) 932-FLEA (932-3532). Fax: (865) 932-3534. Email: info@greatsmokiesfleamarket.com. Web: www.greatsmokiesfleamarket.com.

LEBANON
Parkland Flea Market

DATES: Every Saturday and Sunday, March 1 through December 15.

TIMES: 7:00 AM-dark.

ADMISSION: Free. Ample free parking is provided.

LOCATION: Across the street from the entrance to Cedars of Lebanon State Park. From I-40 take Exit 238, go 6 miles south. Between Lebanon and Murfreesboro on Hwy 231.

DESCRIPTION: This indoor/outdoor market has operated since 1977 near the center of the state of Tennessee. It has enjoyed steady growth with a "great group of family type dealers where 90% of the 300 are regulars." They are housed in a complex of seven buildings on ten acres of land, with another 40 acres available for further expansion. Large and small items, both new and used, can be found including boats, trailers, vans, and trucks, as well as the traditional flea market fare. Free weekend camping is available for dealers, and food is available at the site. Other attractions nearby are the Grand Olde Opry and Opry Mills only 30 miles away, and the new Nashville Super Speedway. Members of the Tennessee Flea Market Association.

DEALER RATES: $11 for 12' × 12' space under shed; $7 per 15' × 15' outside space. Reservations are strongly suggested.

CONTACT: Gwynn or Nancy Lanius, Parkland Flea Market, 403 Cambridge, Lebanon TN 37087-4207. Tel:(615) 449-6050.

LOUISVILLE
Green Acres Flea Market

DATES: Saturday and Sunday. Rain or shine.

TIMES: 6:30 AM-4:30 PM.

ADMISSION: Free. Plenty of free parking is available. Space is also available for vehicles such as motor homes and trailers.

LOCATION: On Alcoa Hwy 129 between Knoxville and the Knoxville Airport.

DESCRIPTION: Located on 13 acres at the foothills of the Great Smoky Mountains, this indoor/outdoor show has been in operation since 1976. It draws an average of 500 dealers in 400 available spaces outdoors and over 300 indoors selling miscellaneous antiques and collectibles, gold, furniture old and new, as well as new items and farm goods. There is a large restaurant and large breakfast bar on the premises selling yogurt, cotton candy, pork skins and corndogs. Members of the Tennessee Flea Market Association.

DEALER RATES: $12 per space, approximately 20' × 20'. Reservations are suggested. Dealers can come on Friday and stay overnight.

CONTACT: Green Acres Flea Market, 908 Hillside Dr, Louisville TN 37777. Tel: (865) 681-4433 or fax: (865) 681-1091.

MEMPHIS
Memphis Flea Market, The BIG One

DATES: Saturday and Sunday, the third weekend of each month.

TIMES: 8:00 AM-6:00 PM.

ADMISSION: $2 per vehicle.

LOCATION: Mid-South Fairgrounds at Central and East Pkwy.

DESCRIPTION: Opened in 1969, this indoor/outdoor market of 900 to 1,200 dealers sells anything from antiques, collectibles, crafts, produce, housewares, and clothing to new merchandise. Plenty of food concessions and handicapped-accessible restrooms are on premises.

DEALER RATES: $70-$75 for a 10' × 8' inside space per weekend, $40-$50 for a 10' × 12' outside space for the weekend. Covered outside spaces are available. Reservations are needed for inside and covered outside space.

CONTACT: Randa Kahn, Memphis Flea Market, 955 Early Maxwell Blvd, Memphis TN 38104. Tel: (901) 276-3532. Fax: (901) 276-0701. Email: memflea@aol.com or info@americanparknswap.com. Web: www.memphisfleamarket.com.

NASHVILLE
The Flea Market at the Nashville Fairgrounds

DATES: Weekend of the fourth Saturday of every month except December. One week earlier in December. Rain or shine.

TIMES: Saturday 7:00 AM-6:00 pm; Sunday 7:00 AM-4:00 PM. Friday (Early Bird Special) 12:00 pm-5:00 PM.

ADMISSION: Free. $2 per car for parking. There is a shuttle bus from the parking lot to the fairgrounds.

LOCATION: Tennessee State Fairgrounds, at Wedgewood and Nolensville Rd. Easy access from Nashville and middle Tennessee via Interstates 65, 440, and 24.

DESCRIPTION: The Flea Market at the Nashville Fairgrounds was established in 1969 and is now run by the Tennessee State Fair. The popular indoor/outdoor market has, on average, about 2,000 booths per month, with the April, May, and October markets being the largest shows of the year. The market contains a large section of antiques and collectible items. Also sold are handmade craft items and some new merchandise. There are a variety of delicious foods available. Member of the Tennessee Flea Market Association.

DEALER RATES: $60 for 10' × 10' outside shed space or 12' × 15' parking lot space; $75 for a 10' × 9' inside booth. Reservations and pre-payment are required.

CONTACT: Deborah Dornan, Manager, Nashville Fairgrounds Flea Market, PO Box 40208, Nashville TN 37204. Tel: (615) 862-5016. Office is open Monday through Friday 8:00 AM-4:30 PM and during show hours. Email: TSF@metro.nashville.org. Web: www.tennesseestatefair.org.

SMYRNA
Expo Flea Market

DATES: January 11-13, February 8-11, March 8-11, April 12-14, May 10-12, June 7-9, July 12-14, August 9-11, September 13-15, October 11-13, November 8-10, December 6-8, 2002. Call or check website for 2003 dates.

TIMES: Friday 3:00 PM-8:00 PM, Saturday 9:00 AM-6:00 PM, Sunday 10:00 AM-4:00 PM.

ADMISSION: Free. Parking is free.

LOCATION: I-24 Expo Center. Take a right off I-24 at Exit 66A.

DESCRIPTION: This new market offers over 500 dealers selling antiques, collectibles, and the usual flea market goodies. Food and handicapped-accessible restrooms are offered on site. This market is one of a series of successful markets in Kentucky, Tennessee, and Indiana presented by Stewart Promotions.

DEALER RATES: $85 per 10' × 10.5' space, $128 per 15' × 10.5' space, $170 per 20' × 10.5' space. Reservations are required.

CONTACT: Stewart Promotions, 2950 Breckenridge Ln #4a, Louisville KY 40220. Tel: (502) 456-2244. Email: sp2950@home.com. Web: www.stewartpromotions.com.

SWEETWATER
Fleas Unlimited

DATES: Saturday and Sunday, rain or shine.

TIMES: 8:00 AM-5:00 PM.

ADMISSION: Free. Parking is also free.

LOCATION: Directly off I-75 at Exit 60. Between Knoxville and Chattanooga.

DESCRIPTION: Opened in December of 1989, this indoor/outdoor market is housed in a 160,000-square-foot building. It attracts 500 dealers inside and there are another 50 spaces outdoors. There is a bit of everything here including plenty of antiques and collectibles, cards, coins, stamps, furniture, books, crafts, clothing, garage sale finds and some new merchandise. There are five stores on site that are open daily. They have an in-house deli, RV camping facilities with bath house, and handicapped-accessible restrooms. Members of the Tennessee Flea Market Association.

DEALER RATES: Main building: $22.50-$27.50 per day per 10' x 12' space or $19.50-$24.50 a day if paid monthly. North and South buildings: $20.50 per day per space or $17.50 per day if paid monthly. Outside spaces $15.50 per day per 9' x 18' space. Reservations are recommended.

CONTACT: Whittney, Fleas Unlimited, 121 County Rd 308, Sweetwater TN 37874. Tel: (423) 337-3532. Email: fleasunlimited@sweetwaterfleamarket.com. Web: www.sweetwaterfleamarket.com.

TELFORD (JONESBOROUGH)
Jonesborough Flea Market

DATES: Sunday, year round.

TIMES: 6:00 AM-4:00 PM.

ADMISSION: Free. Parking is free.

LOCATION: Five miles west of Jonesborough on State Hwy 11.

DESCRIPTION: This outdoor market boasts 200 dealers in summer and 50 in winter selling antiques, collectibles, crafts, produce, coins, stamps, cards, garage sale finds, furniture and new merchandise. Two snack bars and handicapped-accessible restrooms add to the amenities.

DEALER RATES: $8 per 12' × 20' per day, or $7.50 per day if paid by the month. Reservations are not required.

CONTACT: John Crawford or Alan Shelton, Jonesborough Flea Market, PO Box 413, Jonesborough TN 37659-0413. Tel: (423) 753-4241 or 753-4115 or 753-4999.

TRENTON
First Monday Trade Days

DATES: Saturday through Monday, the first Monday weekend of the month.

TIMES: Saturday 6:00 AM-11:30 PM, Sunday 6:00 AM-8:00 PM, Monday 6:00 AM-6:00 PM.

ADMISSION: Free. Parking is free.

LOCATION: Gibson County Fairgrounds. On Manufacturers Row, off Rts 54 and 367.

DESCRIPTION: Another of the original First Monday markets, this one started in 1856 as the Gibson County Agricultural and Mechanical Fair. They have between 100 and 200 dealers selling all sorts of stuff. There is food available as well as restrooms.

DEALER RATES: There are 4 locations for set up, per space from $12-$15 for 1-day; $20-$30 for 2 days; $25 per space for 3 days. Reservations are necessary. Set up starts on Thursday.

CONTACT: Gibson County Fair Association, 1252 Manufacturers Row, Trenton, TN 38382. Tel: (731) 855-2981. Email: trenton@firstmonday.com. Web: www.firstmonday.com.

OTHER FLEA MARKETS

We know or have heard about these markets, but have not personally contacted each one, as we have the markets with descriptions. If you plan to visit one of the markets listed below, *please call first* to make sure they are still open. Flea markets do come and go. While they were open when we went to press, they may not be later. We can't be responsible. *Call first!*

Ardmore: A & S Flea Market, 26649 Elk St. Tel: (931) 427-8424.
Arlington: Galloway Trading Post, 914 Hwy 70. Tel: (901) 867-7549.
Arrington: Triune Flea Market, 7960 Nolensville Rd. Tel: (615) 395-7140.
Baxter: Baxter Flea Market, 6051 Flea Market Rd. Tel: (931) 858-3111.
Bluff City: Tri-City Flea Market, 4571 Hwy 11 E. Tel: (423) 538-0584.
Camden: Medlin's Flea Market, 131 Robertson Ave. Tel: (731) 584-1852.
Clarksville: Carol's Flea Market, 1690 Wilma Rudolph Blvd. Tel: (931) 552-1952.
Clarksville: Country Junction, 140 Lafayette Rd. Tel: (931) 645-9349.
Clarksville: Davis Depot, 1154 Fort Campbell Blvd. Tel: (931) 552-3038.
Clarksville: Dean Drive Flea Market, 135 Dean Dr. Tel: (931) 553-0562.
Clarksville: Flea Market, 1214 College St. Tel: (931) 905-0023.
Clarksville: Flea World, 1114 Crossland Ave. Tel: (931) 645-6378.
Clarksville: Lisa's Flea Market, 1158 Fort Campbell Blvd. Tel: (931) 645-5888.
Clarksville: Queen City Flea Market, 1156 Fort Campbell Blvd. Tel: (931) 648-4174.
Clarksville: Treasure Chest Flea Market, 200 Providence Blvd. Tel: (931) 552-2987.
Cleveland: Trader's Swap & Shop, 5538 Georgetown Rd NW. Tel: (423) 472-5810.
Coalmont: Flea Market 56 Junction. Tel: (931) 692-4000.
Cornersville: Tennessee Flea Market & Mall, 9146 Lewisburg Hwy. Tel: (931) 424-8970.
Covington: A & B Flea Market, 1024 Hwy 51 N. Tel: (901) 476-4525.
Covington: Westside Flea Market, 3392 Hwy 59 W. Tel: (901) 476-8995.
Crump: Hilltop Flea Market, 3465 Hwy 64. Tel: (731) 632-0626.
Eads: Top Dog Trade Ctr, 11625 Hwy 64. Tel: (901) 867-3532.
East Ridge: Bitter Creek, 6725 Ringgold Rd. Tel: (423) 954-3039.
East Ridge: East Ridge Flea Market, 6725 Ringgold Rd. Tel: (423) 894-3960.
Elizabethton: Street's Flea Market, 1207 19E Byp. Tel: (423) 543-7515.
Gordonsville: Morning Star Flea Market, 16 Main St E. Tel: (615) 683-5132.
Gruetli Laager: Gruetli-Laager Flea Markets. Tel: (931) 779-3477.
Jacksboro: Coffey's Craft & Flea Market, 102 West St. Tel: (423) 562-6613.
Johnson City: U S Flea Market Mall, 3501 Bristol Hwy. Tel: (423) 854-4860.

Knoxville: Cawood Flea Market, 3610 E Magnolia Ave. Tel: (865) 633-9293.

Lawrenceburg: Deerfield Flea Market, 4140 Waynesboro Hwy. Tel: (931) 766-5908.

Louisville: Green Acres Flea Market, 908 Hillside Dr. Tel: (865) 681-4433.

Manchester: Johnson's Highway 55 Flea Market, 4683 New Tullahoma Hwy. Tel: (931) 723-0740.

Memphis: A & A Flea Market, 1436 Airways Blvd. Tel: (901) 324-4208.

Memphis: Airways Mini Flea Market, 1426 Airways Blvd. Tel: (901) 323-5505.

Memphis: C D Flea Market, 3340 Millington Rd. Tel: (901) 358-4092.

Memphis: Cleveland Street Flea Market, 438 N Cleveland St. Tel: (901) 276-3333.

Memphis: Frayser Flea Market, 3238 Millington Rd. Tel: (901) 353-3532.

Memphis: Lesa's Flea Market, 2992 Clearbrook St. Tel: (901) 362-9490.

Memphis: Memphis Flea Market, 2370 Kentucky St. Tel: (901) 274-6901.

Nashville: Big Jim's Trading Post, 707 Hart Ave. Tel: (615) 578-1655.

Nashville: Giant Flea Market, 2917 Nolensville Rd. Tel: (615) 333-8196.

Nashville: T & H Flea Market, 1999 Nolensville Pike. Tel: (615) 254-0331.

Parsons: Tennessee River Flea Market, 545 Pentecostal Camp Rd. Tel: (731) 847-9383.

Powell: Clinton Highway Flea Market, 7622 Clinton Hwy. Tel: (865) 947-4232.

Rockwood: Railroad Flea Market, 116 W Rockwood St. Tel: (865) 354-1005.

Rockwood: Rockwood Super Flea Market, 4380 Roane State Hwy. Tel: (865) 354-4066.

Sevierville: Flea Traders Paradise, 1939 Kyker Ferry Rd. Tel: (865) 429-2716.

Shelbyville: Hillis Auction, 1119 N Main St. Tel: (931) 685-9495.

Sparta: Cherry Creek Flea Market, 3007 Cherry Creek Rd. Tel: (931) 738-3440.

Tazewell: Giles Flea Market, Hwy 25 E. Tel: (423) 626-8983.

Union City: Giant Flea Market-Union City, 1700 W Reelfoot Ave. Tel: (731) 885-2377.

Walland: Hillbilly Flea Market, 4504 E Lamar Alexander Pkwy. Tel: (865) 983-2410.

Whiteville: Culver's Flea Market, 1815 Hwy 64. Tel: (731) 254-8321.

TEXAS

ALAMO
All Valley Flea Market

DATES: Thursday, Saturday and Sunday. Rain or shine.

TIMES: 4:30 AM to dark.

ADMISSION: $.25 per person. Parking is free.

LOCATION: Intersection of Cesar Chavez (formerly Morningside) Rd and Exp 83.

DESCRIPTION: Started in 1969 after a visit to another successful market elsewhere gave Mr Bruns the idea, he opened his first of four markets in Pharr. Also the first in the Valley area. When a highway was built through the market, they moved to Alamo. Now there are around 1,500 dealers presenting "everything!" And 20,000 to 30,000 buyers coming through every weekend buying everything including antiques, collectibles, used items, garage sale goodies, and some new merchandise. Food concessions and handicapped-accessible restrooms add to the amenities.

DEALER RATES: $4.50 per 10' × 18' space with 2 tables; Saturdays $5; Sundays $9. Reservations are strongly suggested if you are traveling from far away.

CONTACT: All Valley Flea Markets, 501 N Bridge St Ste 528, Hidalgo TX 78557. Tel: (956) 781-1911.

AMARILLO
T-Anchor Flea Market

DATES: Every Saturday and Sunday, year round.

TIMES: 9:00 AM-5:00 PM.

ADMISSION: Free. Free parking is available.

LOCATION: 1401 Ross St, off I-40.

DESCRIPTION: This indoor market began in 1978. Their 175 inside vendors come from all over the country to sell antiques, collectibles, crafts, produce, and new merchandise. Weather permitting, vendors rent space outdoors—almost year round. Produce vendors are furnished with a permit. One snack bar and handicapped-accessible restrooms add to the amenities. Think of this as a real "old-fashioned" flea market.

DEALER RATES: $8 per 10' × 20' space per day outside and $10-$12 inside. Reservations are not required for outside but definitely required for inside space.

CONTACT: HD and Claudia Blyth, T-Anchor Flea Market, PO Box 31182, Amarillo TX 79120. Tel: (806) 373-0430.

AUSTIN
Austin Country Flea Market

DATES: Saturday and Sunday, year round. Rain or shine.

TIMES: 10:00 AM-6:00 PM.

ADMISSION: $1 per car.

LOCATION: 9500 Hwy 290 E.

DESCRIPTION: This is central Texas' largest flea market, with over 500 selling spaces. Their dealers sell antiques, collectibles, crafts, vegetables, and new merchandise. Open every weekend, it offers good food (barbecue beef, and the usual snack bar fare), family fun, and big bargains. The entire market is covered. There are handicapped-accessible restrooms when the need arises.

DEALER RATES: $40 per 10' × 8' booth (20' dealer parking directly behind each space if desired, or dealer's vehicle may be moved to an authorized area and parking space can be used as additional selling area). One display table is provided. RV electricity is available in limited areas. Gates are open to dealers at 7:00 AM; gates close at 10:00 PM. Advance reservations required.

CONTACT: Buz Cook or David Ritter, Austin Country, 9500 Hwy 290 E, Austin TX 78724. Tel: (512) 928-2795. Office is closed Tuesday-Thursday.

BLANCO
Blanco Flea Market

DATES: Wednesday through Sunday.

TIMES: Wednesday and Thursday 10:00 AM-4:00 PM, Friday and Saturday 9:00 AM-5:00 PM, Sunday 1:00 PM-5:00 PM.

ADMISSION: Free. Parking is free.

LOCATION: 5th and Pecan Sts. One block north of the Courthouse. Blanco is on Hwy 281, 47 miles southwest of Austin or 47 north of San Antonio.

DESCRIPTION: Located in a 6,000-square-foot restored historic mohair warehouse, this market of 3 dealers, including Shandy Hale and his custom knives who can and does play any musical instrument brought in the store (and there are lots of them), sells antiques, collectibles, power tools, manual tools, used or custom-built furniture, musical instruments, and whatever else comes in. There is plenty of outside space available, 5 of which are covered, to set up what you will. Say Hi to Shandy and ask for a tune. He'd love to oblige you. The music is so popular that the market set up a place for musicians to play and entertain!

DEALER RATES: Inside: $1.15 per square foot, about $138 per month. Outside $15 per day covered or uncovered or about $85 per month. Outside, reservations are not necessary. Inside is another story—call.

CONTACT: Shandy Hale, Manager, Blanco Flea Market, 801 Darden Hill Rd, Driftwood TX 78619. Tel: (830) 833-5640.

BONHAM
Bonham Trade Days

DATES: Thursday through Sunday the weekend after the first Monday, year round.

TIMES: 7:00 AM-5:00 PM, mostly daylight to dusk.

ADMISSION: Free. Parking is free.

LOCATION: Fort Inglish Park. At the intersection of Hwy 56 and Hwys 121 and 82 By-pass.

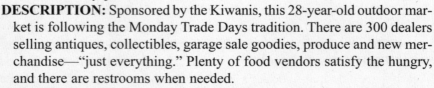

DESCRIPTION: Sponsored by the Kiwanis, this 28-year-old outdoor market is following the Monday Trade Days tradition. There are 300 dealers selling antiques, collectibles, garage sale goodies, produce and new merchandise—"just everything." Plenty of food vendors satisfy the hungry, and there are restrooms when needed.

DEALER RATES: $20 per 20' × 30' space per weekend. First come, first served.

CONTACT: Jo, Bonham Trade Days, Rt 4 Box 358, Bonham TX 75418. Tel: (903) 583-2367.

BOWIE
Second Monday Trade Days

DATES: Friday through Sunday before the second Monday of each month.

TIMES: 7:00 AM-dark.

ADMISSION: Free. Parking is free.

LOCATION: Rodeo grounds on E Wise St. Bus Hwy 287 and Hwy 81. Going north from Hwy 287, take the US 81 Waurika exit.

DESCRIPTION: Another Monday Court Day market! That judge, he did get around. Now in its second hundred years (started in 1893), this venerable market has approximately 400-plus dealers selling antiques, collectibles, livestock, crafts, electronics, and whatever comes in. This is the Northern Texas place to be on second Monday. They can easily boast they have 15-20,000 visitors each month. In addition to their current handicapped-accessible restrooms with showers for dealers, they have expanded their facilities with new paving, more water spouts and electric outlets, awnings on the 50' × 200' shed, a new RV septic dump and a new restroom with showers. Next door to the market is the Palham Park with an RV park, swimming pool, bath house, walking trail and game courts.

DEALER RATES: $20 per space for the weekend; electric is $4 extra per day, per connection. Reservations are recommended, because they do fill up.

CONTACT: Clyde Johnson, Parks & Recreation Director, Bowie City of Grounds Maintenance Dept, 304 Lindsey St, Bowie TX 76230. Tel: (940) 872-1680. Email: 2ndmonday@morgan.net. Web: www.morgan.net/~a2ndmonday.

> **From Bowie's History**
> Barter and trade was nothing new in the early days of Bowie. A group of interested livestockmen and dealers across Montague, Clay, and Wise counties conceived the need for a central trade market. In those early years, traders began arriving with their herds Friday evening, before the main trade day, and leaving out the following Tuesday evening. Medicine shows, novelty hawkers and peddlers would ply their "trade"—providing the entertainment. After WWI, commodities were added to the collection of goods.

BUFFALO GAP
Buffalo Gap Flea Market

DATES: Friday, Saturday, and Sunday, third Saturday of each month from February through December (weather permitting in December), except July when it's the fourth Sunday weekend.

TIMES: 7:00 AM until the customers mosey on.

ADMISSION: Free. Parking is available nearby.

LOCATION: In Buffalo Gap, 10 miles south of Abilene on Hwy 89.

DESCRIPTION: This outdoor market began in 1974 and currently draws around 150 dealers selling a wide range of antiques, collectibles, fresh produce, crafts, and new merchandise. This market is described by its owner as the "prettiest market in the west." Food and toilet facilities are available. If you see a six-foot Scot with a white ponytail, say Hi to John. He's either the City Councilman or Mayor of Buffalo Gap. John says, "Ya'll come!"

DEALER RATES: $15 per 12' × 18' space for a three-day weekend, plus electricity, $5 per day, if needed. All electric wiring has been updated. Reservations are required at least one week in advance, as they have had to turn away dealers before. A $2 city permit is required to sell.

CONTACT: John & Peggy Brolls, Buffalo Gap Flea Market, PO Box 575, Buffalo Gap TX 79508-0575. Tel: (915) 572-3327.

CANTON
First Monday Trade Days

DATES: Begins on Thursday before the first Monday of each month, and runs Thursday through Sunday and Labor Day Monday. Rain or shine.

TIMES: 7:00 AM-dark.

ADMISSION: Free. Parking is available for $3 per vehicle. RV spaces are available, with advance reservations and some first come, first served.

LOCATION: Two blocks north of downtown square. Easy access on Hwy 19, Hwy 64 and FM Rd 859. From I-20, Exit 526, 2 miles south on left.

DESCRIPTION: This is surely one of the most popular and well-known flea markets in the country, if not the world. Originating in 1876 as the town's court day, people at that time began to take care of their trading and purchasing of animals, produce, etc. while waiting for the judge. In 1965, the city of Canton acquired a six-acre plot of land two blocks north of the Court House which is now the Historic District. The dealers selling animals can be found four blocks east of the Court House on the property known as Curry's Trade Grounds or Dog Grounds. Since 1965, the number of available lots has grown from 150 to well over 4,000. The number of visitors is up to 300,000 per month! They now have covered pavilions and an indoor civic center. The heated/air-conditioned civic center is 34,000 square feet with a food concession and handicapped-accessible restrooms. From here all the best antique and collectible dealers sell. First Monday Trade Days began advertising its unique market in 1974, and since then has appeared on NBC's "Today Show," "Good Morning America," the front page of *The Wall Street Journal*, in *National Geographic, Smithsonian* and in several other local and national media. All kinds of antiques, collectibles, new merchandise, handmade crafts, and food are available. Restrooms with showers are provided.

DEALER RATES: $50 for each open-air lot. Dealer spaces are approximately 12' × 20'. Dealers who reserve in advance may renew for following sale. Unreserved lots are also available. Covered space is limited and ranges from $150-$225. Inside the Civic Center, space is available for $125 per 10' × 10', $150 per 10' × 12', $175 per 10' × 14' space.

CONTACT: City of Canton, PO Box 245, Canton TX 75103. Tel: (903) 567-6556. Fax: (903) 567-1753. Email: cityhall@vzinet.com. Web: www.firstmondaycanton.com.

Some Canton History

History relates one incident where a man was hanged for stealing his partner's wagon of goods for trading. He is buried facing south (not east) in Hillcrest Cemetery by the First Monday Park.

CHANNELVIEW
White Elephant, Inc

DATES: Every Saturday and Sunday. Rain or shine.

TIMES: 7:30 AM-5:30 PM.

ADMISSION: Free. Parking is free.

LOCATION: 15662 I-10 E. Take the Sheldon-Channelview exit; the market is on the Service Rd of I-10.

DESCRIPTION: Between 350 and 375 dealers show up each week for this indoor/outdoor market, which has been in operation since 1971. Articles for sale include antiques, collectibles, garage sale items such as tools, furniture, and jewelry, as well as some new items and fresh produce. A snack bar and handicapped-accessible restrooms are available on the premises.

DEALER RATES: From $13-$17 per space depending on location. Reservations not required.

CONTACT: Debby, White Elephant Inc, PO Box 209, Channelview TX 77530-0209. Tel: (281) 452-9022. Office is open Monday-Friday at (281) 452-1701.

DONNA
Don Wes Flea Market

DATES: Wednesday, Saturday and Sunday.

TIMES: 8:00 AM-4:30 PM.

ADMISSION: Free. Parking is free.

DIRECTIONS: Victoria Rd. Exit Victoria Rd in Donna, go South 1/4 mile on the left side (there are signs) located between Expwy and Old Bus 83.

DESCRIPTION: Opened over 25 years ago by Dee & Roy Thompson, it is now owned by the Fitzgeralds. Originally a dairy farm, it has since been converted into a Flea Market. There are 220 inside vendors and 350 outside vendors selling a wide variety of merchandise new and used, including hardware, tools, clothing, jewelry, household items, collectibles, crafts, coins, antiques, music, books, toys, fresh produce, bicycle shop, Indian jewelry, silver and gold, wooden items, pecans, peanuts, golf clubs, Avon, t-shirts and more. A full service restaurant serves breakfast and lunch to live music. There are several different food concessions as well, making the clean handicapped-accessible restrooms handy. Attracting approximately 10,000-15,000 visitors each day.

DEALER RATES: Inside: $60 per week, tables $25 per week. There are 100 RV spots with full hook-ups, at $3.50 per day plus electric and $5 per week garbage fee. There is a 10' × 20' selling space in front of RV.

CONTACT: Debbie & Jim Fitzgerald or Joshua Trevino, Don Wes Flea Market, PO Box 906 Donna TX 78537. Tel: (956) 464-3502. Email: Droobear4@aol.com.

GARLAND
Vikon Village Flea Market

DATES: Saturdays and Sundays, year round. Also the Friday after Thanksgiving and some extra dates in December, usually the weekdays before Christmas.

TIMES: 10:00 AM-7:00 PM.

ADMISSION: Free. Free parking for up to 750 cars is available nearby.

LOCATION: 2918 S Jupiter. Near the corner of Kingsley and Jupiter, 2 blocks north of Rt 635.

DESCRIPTION: This indoor market began in 1975 and averages around 350 booths with 175 dealers selling such items as books, baseball cards, coins, jewelry, furniture, clothing, and plants, with about 60% new merchandise. One large snack bar, a popcorn stand and handicapped-accessible restrooms add to the amenities. This is Texas' "oldest and largest" indoor flea market, according to Terry. They hold events all year long, including a Turkey Bowl before Thanksgiving, Harley-Davidson Show to benefit for St. Jude's Hospital, Santa and Halloween fun.

DEALER RATES: Lease available at $140 and up per month (minimum one month). Weekends are available. Reservations are required. Call for information Thursdays from 10:00 AM-5:00 PM or Fridays 10:00 AM-6:00 PM.

CONTACT: Vikon Village Flea Market, 2918 S Jupiter, Garland TX 75041. Tel/fax: (972) 271-0565. Web: www.vikonvillage.com.

> **Great Beginnings**
> The chap who started CD Warehouse (selling CDs) began as a vendor here at Vikon Village. Not bad!

GRAND PRAIRIE
Traders Village

DATES: Every Saturday and Sunday, year round. Rain or shine.

TIMES: 8:00 AM-dusk.

ADMISSION: Free. Parking for over 7,000 cars is available at $2 per vehicle. Handicapped parking is available.

LOCATION: 2602 Mayfield Rd in Grand Prairie. In the heart of the Dallas/Ft Worth area, 5 miles south of Six Flags Over Texas theme park off Hwy 360. Or, take Hwy 360 north 1 mile off I-20.

DESCRIPTION: Traders Village is a 106-acre complex, which opened in November 1973. Since that date, over 60 million people have visited this market, roughly 2.7 million a year. The market currently attracts between

1,500 and 1,800 dealers who set up on open, covered, and enclosed spaces. Crowds average 50,000-80,000 per weekend. Special events include a chili cook-off (April), Cajun Fest (May), an Antique Auto Swap Meet (June), Antique Tractor and Farm Implement Show (July), an authentic Indian Pow-wow (September), a Barbecue Cook-off (October), and more throughout the year. Most of the special events are open to the public for free. Traders Village runs its own food and beverage department, with over 30 stands selling everything from Mexican specialties to pizza by the slice, from chicken-fried steak to funnel cakes. Produce vendors and bulk-food dealers are also on hand. Other features include kiddie rides, an arcade, stroller and wheelchair rentals, shaded rest areas, two ATM machines and a first-aid room. There is also a sister market in Houston. Traders Village is a member of the National Flea Market Association.

DEALER RATES: $20 per 14' × 25' open lot per day. $25 per covered space per day. Reservations are required for two-day rentals only.

CONTACT: Allan Hughes, Director of General Services, Traders Village, 2602 Mayfield Rd, Grand Prairie TX 75051. Tel: (972) 647-2331. Email: tvgp@flash.net. Web: www.tradersvillage.com.

Local History

Traders Village is a continuing extension of the trading that went on between various Indian tribes over the centuries. An historical marker, dedicated in 1980, marks the site of the million-acre "Cross Timbers" area where Shoshone, rooted out by Apaches, in turn chased out by Comanches, traded until white man showed up in the 17th and 18th centuries. In the 1840s, white settlers stayed, leading to the Battle of Village Creek on May 24, 1841, marking the end of the Indian domination of the area.

HOUSTON
Traders Village

DATES: Every Saturday and Sunday, year round. Rain or shine.

TIMES: 8:00 AM-dusk.

ADMISSION: Free. Parking for over 4,000 cars is available at $2 per vehicle. Handicapped parking is available.

LOCATION: 7979 N Eldridge Rd. Off Northwest Fwy (Hwy 290), Eldridge Exit, 3/10 mile south.

DESCRIPTION: Traders Village is a 100-acre complex which opened in May 1989. More than one million people visit each year. The market

currently attracts over 600 dealers every weekend who set up on covered and enclosed spaces selling imports, antiques, collectibles, crafts, produce, garage sale merchandise, pets, clothes, furniture, auto parts, flowers and plants, electronics, music, toys and lots more. Crowds average 10,000-15,000 a weekend. Special events and festivals are held weekly throughout the year. Most of the special events are open to the public. There are over 30 stands selling everything from Mexican specialties to pizza by the slice, from chicken-fried steak to funnel cakes. Produce vendors and bulk-food dealers are also on hand. Other features include kiddie rides, live bands and entertainment, a traditional Texas ice house, stroller and wheelchair rentals, shaded rest areas, an ATM machine, and a first-aid room. There is also a sister market in Grand Prairie. Traders Village is a member of the National Flea Market Association.

DEALER RATES: $20 per day, or $41 for the weekend reserved. Reservations are required for two-day rentals only.

CONTACT: Michael Baxter or Ken Hinz, Traders Village—Houston, 7979 N Eldridge Rd, Houston TX 77041. Tel: (281) 890-5500. Fax: (281) 890-6568. Email: tvh@flash.net. Web: www.tradersvillage.com.

Trading Fair II

DATES: Every Friday, Saturday and Sunday. Rain or shine.

TIMES: 10:00 AM-6:00 PM.

ADMISSION: Free. Parking is free.

LOCATION: 5515 S Loop E. Midway between the Astrodome and the Galveston Fwy on Loop 610. Use the Crestmont Exit either way.

DESCRIPTION: This indoor market started in 1974 and currently draws over 400 dealers selling a wide range of new merchandise, including furniture, artifacts, and gift items. They are possibly the largest indoor market in the Houston area. Their building has two floors of 60,000 square feet each and an additional 30,000-square-foot annex in the back. The first floor and annex house the dealers. The second floor is now a convention center and is used as an entertainment center with mostly live shows, with the occasional merchandise shows. Their selection of sale items is described as "some of everything, a lot of some things." Two restaurants and one snack bar take care of hunger problems; handicapped-accessible restrooms provide relief. They do plenty of advertising as well as everything they can to gain the notice, goodwill, and support of the buying public. There's another five acres that is used for live entertainment when the temperatures fall to reasonable.

DEALER RATES: $275 monthly for a 11' × 15' space and up depending on size. Dealer reservations are suggested.

CONTACT: Trading Fair II, 5515 S Loop E, Houston TX 77033. Tel: (713) 731-1111. Fax: (713) 731-1121. Watch for their website and email.

LUBBOCK
National Flea Market

DATES: Every Wednesday through Sunday, except Thanksgiving Day and the week after Christmas.

TIMES: Wednesday-Friday 9:00 AM-5:00 PM, Saturday and Sunday 9:00 AM-6:00 PM.

ADMISSION: Free. Parking is also free.

LOCATION: 1808 Clovis Rd. One half block west of Ave Q.

DESCRIPTION: This market first opened in 1982. It is both an indoor and outdoor market attracting from 100 to 150 dealers selling everything from antiques and collectibles to crafts and vegetables. New merchandise, including clothing, tools and electronics, are also available. For your convenience, a snack bar and concession stand are on the premises. The original barn for weekend dealers burned down. They have rebuilt it housing 105 spaces inside with heating, air-conditioning and lovely clean handicapped-accessible restrooms.

DEALER RATES: There are two buildings and outdoor space available: weekly rates in the main building start at $45 and up for 10' × 10' booth depending on location; rates in the other building, which usually houses the weekend dealer, vary from $21-$53, while space varies from 10' × 10' to 10' × 20'. Storage sheds that can be sold from are $47 per week or $188 a month.

CONTACT: Debie Grant, National Flea Market, 1808 Clovis Rd, Lubbock TX 79415. Tel: (806) 744-4979. Fax: (806) 744-0164.

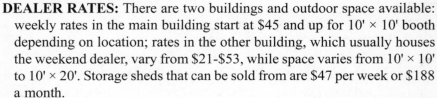

Wow!
A customer bought an antique doll here for literally "peanuts," then took it to an appraiser, who told him it was worth "thousands!"

MCKINNEY
Third Monday Trade Days

DATES: Saturday and Sunday preceding the third Monday each month. (It doesn't always fall on the third weekend.)

TIMES: 8:00 AM-4:00 PM. The deal is: all dealers must be open during these times. However, they can be open earlier or later. Earlier is the rule.

ADMISSION: Free. $2 parking.

LOCATION: Hwy 380, 2 miles west of US 75.

DESCRIPTION: Another fantastic court day market started when that circuit judge came around and did his job on Mondays (see Kentucky's markets). There are six in Texas: see Canton and Weatherford for First

Monday markets, Bowie and Bonham for Second Monday markets and Whitewright for a Fourth Monday market. Although there are 700 spaces here, usually all spaces are filled with at least 500 dealers (some use more space than others). This is a great place to find antiques, collectibles, crafts, produce, animals and new merchandise. There are plenty of food vendors; you won't starve.

DEALER RATES: $40 and up for open air, $50-$90 for sheds, $100-$180 in a building per space (single or double) per weekend. Reservations are necessary; they keep running out of room!

CONTACT: Darrell Lewis, Third Monday Trade Days, 4550 W University Dr, McKinney TX 75070. Tel: (972) 562-5466 or 542-7174. Web: www.tmtd.com.

MERCEDES
Mercedes Flea Market

DATES: Saturday and Sunday, year round.

TIMES: 4:30 AM to dusk.

ADMISSION: $.25. Parking is free.

LOCATION: Mile 2 W and Exp 83.

DESCRIPTION: Opened in 1973 as the second of the All Valley Flea Markets, this market attracts over 800 vendors under shelters selling fresh produce, odds and ends, garage sale goodies, tools, plants, used and new merchandise. From 8-10,000 local people come here each weekend. Thirteen concession stands provide a cure for the munchies, and handicapped-accessible restrooms provide relief.

DEALER RATES: Saturdays $5 per space; Sundays $9. Monthly reservations are strongly suggested. Daily, just show up.

CONTACT: Mercedes Flea Market, 501 N Bridge St Ste 528, Hidalgo TX 78557. Tel: (956) 565-2751 market. Or (956) 781-1911 during the week.

PEARLAND
Cole's Antique Village and Flea Market

DATES: Every Saturday and Sunday. Rain or shine.

TIMES: 6:30 AM-6:00 PM.

ADMISSION: Free. $1 for parking.

LOCATION: 1014-1022 N Main St, 4 miles south of the Hobby Airport on Telephone Rd (Hwy 35).

DESCRIPTION: This indoor/outdoor market started in 1969 and currently draws approximately 700 dealers selling a range of antiques and collectibles such as furniture, tools, and glassware; fresh produce and plants, crafts and new items are also sold. A full restaurant sells breakfasts and full lunches, and handicapped-accessible restrooms are available on the premises. The antique co-op is open every day but Wednesday, as is the office.

DEALER RATES: $43 per 10' × 10' space indoors per weekend; $46 per outdoor covered space per weekend. Reservations can be made for these spaces Fridays from 8:00 AM-5:00 PM.

CONTACT: Cole's Antique Village and Flea Market, 1014 N Main St, Pearland TX 77581-2208. Tel: (281) 485-2277. Fax: (281) 485-2581.

SAN ANTONIO
Eisenhauer Road Flea Market

DATES: Wednesday through Sunday. Rain or shine.

TIMES: Weekends 9:00 AM-7:00 PM; weekdays 12:00 PM-7:00 PM.

ADMISSION: Free. Parking is free.

LOCATION: 3903 Eisenhauer Rd.

DESCRIPTION: This market, started in 1979, operates 90% indoors in an air-conditioned space with over 200 steady dealers plus transients. A variety of antiques and collectibles is sold, along with crafts and new merchandise. Food is served at three snack bars on the premises, and there are handicapped-accessible restrooms just in case.

DEALER RATES: Outdoors: $7 per 8' table per day Saturday and $13 for Sunday. If you rent a table for the weekend, there is no charge for the other three days. Reservations are suggested. Indoors: $10 for Saturday, $20 for Sunday, and other days are free with weekend payment.

CONTACT: Harry Weiss or Mrs Pat Walker, Eisenhauer Road Flea Market, 3903 Eisenhauer Rd, San Antonio TX 78218. Tel: (210) 653-7592. Fax: (210) 657-1692.

Mission Open Air Market

DATES: Wednesday, Saturday and Sunday.

TIMES: 6:00 AM-4:00 PM.

ADMISSION: $.75 a walk-in or $1 a carload.

LOCATION: 207 W Chavaneaux Rd. Between I-35 and 37, Moursund Blvd Exit inside Loop 410 W.

DESCRIPTION: Started in 1985, this outdoor "real flea market" consists of 1,500 dealers under covered areas selling 90% used merchandise. They claim to be the "largest outdoor market in South Texas." Some of the items sold include antiques, collectibles, produce, garage sale goodies, furniture, and some new merchandise. When hunger hits, try the snack bar. There are handicapped-accessible restrooms on site. Watch for Swap-O the Clown as he greets visitors during the market. For a touch of excitement, they hold drawings and do cash giveaways every day. During Christmas and Thanksgiving holiday season, the prizes are turkeys or hams. This is not a dull place!

DEALER RATES: $18 on Wednesday, $15 on Saturday, $18 on Sunday. Reservations are not required.

CONTACT: Mission Open Air Market, 707 Moursund Blvd, San Antonio TX 78221. Tel: (210) 923-8131 (information), 921-1569 (administration). Fax: (210) 923-8004.

Northwest Flea Market

DATES: Saturday and Sunday.

TIMES: 7:00 AM-5:00 PM.

ADMISSION: Free. Parking is free.

LOCATION: 3600 Fredericksburg Rd. Off Loop 410 on north side of town. Go south toward the city 1½ miles to the Northwest Center on Fredericksburg Rd. The market is behind the mall.

DESCRIPTION: Open since 1973, this indoor/outdoor market of approximately 250 dealers sells antiques, collectibles, crafts, produce, coins, stamps, cards, garage sale goodies, furniture and new merchandise. "It has not been disputed that this is the first indoor flea market to set up in a modern air-conditioned building for the sole purpose of running a flea market, with permanent tables, storage and lock-up rooms. I have a dealer, Mr and Mrs Linderman, who have rented their tables and left them set up for 28 years 'straight!'" says Mr Markwell.

DEALER RATES: Outdoors: $15 Saturday, $20 Sunday per day for 20' × 20' space, table provided for $5 (first come, first served). Inside: $15 per day with 8' table. Rooms starting at $197 per month. Reservations are suggested one week in advance.

CONTACT: James C Markwell, Northwest Flea Market, 3600 Fredericksburg Rd, San Antonio TX 78201. Tel: (210) 736-6655.

SEVEN POINTS
Big Daddy's Trader Market

DATES: Saturday and Sunday.

TIMES: 8:00 AM-6:00 PM.

ADMISSION: Free. Parking is free.

LOCATION: Hwy 274, 1 mile south of Seven Points; near Cedar Creek Lake, 60 miles east of Dallas.

DESCRIPTION: Opened in 1991, this indoor and sometimes outside market of 150 vendor spaces (all full) sells lots of antiques and collectibles, books, clothing, crafts, jewelry, lots of garage sale goodies, specialty items, fresh produce and new and used merchandise. A snack bar and handicapped-accessible restrooms come in handy. They are noted for their cleanliness and accessibility—not bad!

DEALER RATES: $22 per 10' × 20' for the weekend. Permanent rates are $210 per month. Reservations are required, as they are usually full. They have an ongoing dealer-participation advertising that is included in the rates.

CONTACT: Larry Hart, Big Daddy's Trader Market, PO Box 43718, Seven Points TX 75143. Tel: (903) 432-4911. Fax: (903) 778-2887. Email: shartlhart@aol.com.

SCHERTZ
Bussey's Flea Market

DATES: Saturday and Sunday, year round.

TIMES: 7:00 AM to dusk.

ADMISSION: Free. $1 per car.

LOCATION: 18738 IH-35 N.

DESCRIPTION: This outdoor show began in 1979. There are 513 dealer spaces, with most of them filled on the weekends. Anything from antiques and collectibles to very little new merchandise and craft items are available. Generally 70% used, 30% new merchandise. Plenty of garage sale items. There are many Mexican imports and a variety of curios as well. Food is available on the premises, with eight fantastic snack bars and plenty of hamburgers, hot dogs, breakfast tacos and special hand-me-down recipes among other delights (hand-dipped ice cream). This is a family operated market. There are handicapped-accessible restrooms on site.

DEALER RATES: $10-$12 on Saturday, $18-$25 on Sunday per space. No reservations needed.

CONTACT: Harold Smith, General Partner, Bussey's Flea Market, 18738 IH-35 N, Schertz TX 78154. Tel: (210) 651-6830. Fax: (830) 609-0800, yes, the area code is different, but correct.

Tear Your Hair Out

A woman, cleaning out her attic, brought in a crystal punch bowl and cup set and put them out for $25. She was offered $15 by a professional dealer and refused it; another dealer offered her $20, which started a screaming match between the two dealers. Eventually one won, and 20 minutes later the victor sold the set for a 900% profit.

WEATHERFORD
First Monday Trade Days

DATES: Friday through Sunday, preceding the first Monday of the month.

TIMES: Daylight, from dawn until sundown—or so, at least 9:00 AM-6:00 PM.

ADMISSION: Free. Parking is free on the streets, some in lots isn't.

LOCATION: At the intersection of Santa Fe Dr and Fort Worth Hwy, approximately 20 miles west of the Fort Worth/Dallas Metroplex.

DESCRIPTION: Started in 1909, this First Monday market joined the legions of others as the judge came through doing his legal job. This market has 476 vendor spaces, frequently sold out, with dealers selling everything from junk to new merchandise, including some antiques and collectibles, household stuff, animals in their own lot, garage sale goodies, and whatever. There are plenty of food vendors and handicapped-accessible restrooms.

DEALER RATES: $13 per space, about 9½' × 11' space—non-reserved. If you reserve in advance, the rate is $10 per space.

CONTACT: First Monday Trade Days, 119 Palo Pinto, Weatherford TX 76086. Tel: (817) 598-4351. Day of event: (817) 598-4359. Web: www.ci.weatherford.tx.us.

WHITEWRIGHT
Whitewright Trade Days

DATES: The weekend before the fourth Monday of every month starting the preceding Friday through Sunday, technically Saturday and Sunday, but some dealers persist in setting up on Thursday and Friday!

TIMES: All day Friday through early afternoon Sunday, generally 6:00-7:00 AM until they drop late in the day.

ADMISSION: Free. Parking is free.

LOCATION: American Legion grounds on Sears St. From Hwy 69, turn right at the Y onto Grant St, then turn right on Sears.

DESCRIPTION: This 22-plus-year-old market is another of the judge's famous stops. Over 150 dealers set up selling antiques, collectibles, and all manner of items. Jim says there isn't much new here, making it a great place to find old treasures. There are 300 dealer spaces, so drop on down! This market is the fundraiser for the American Legion and other local efforts, including the park itself. Two food concessions and handicapped-accessible restrooms could come in handy! Do stop in at Caraway's Exxon and shout a Hi to Jim and Odell!

DEALER RATES: $10 per space for the weekend. Reservations are nice.

CONTACT: Odell Caraway, Whitewright Trade Days, c/o Caraway Exxon, Box 566, Whitewright TX 75491. Tel: (903) 364-2994.

WICHITA FALLS
Holliday Street Flea Market

DATES: Every Saturday and Sunday, year round.

TIMES: 7:00 AM-dark.

ADMISSION: Free, with free parking available.

LOCATION: 2820 Holliday St. Near Hwys 281 and 287 on Holliday Rd near Holliday Creek.

DESCRIPTION: This market runs both indoors and out. Under the same ownership as before, it began in 1966 and currently hosts 200 to 250 dealers. The property was originally an amusement park, swimming pool and trailer park before becoming a flea market. There are antiques, collectibles, and crafts for sale, alongside produce and new merchandise. In addition, there are Mexican imports, musical instruments, saddles, boots, clothes new and used, t-shirts, furniture, appliances and tack offered. There are 12 acres of selling space (as the city took 5 acres for flood control), including individual buildings with inside lockups. There are food concessions on the premises. As Vivian describes it, "As you know, every Saturday is like Christmas. You never know what will show up."

DEALER RATES: $8 per 12' × 30' space uncovered; $11 per 12' × 12' covered shed per day; $90 to $130 per lockup stall indoors per month. Reservations are required for indoor spaces and covered sheds.

CONTACT: Jim and Vivian Parish, Owners, 2820 Holliday St, Wichita Falls TX 76301. Tel: (817) 767-1712 or 767-9038 or 767-3571.

Is This Maine?
They tell of a dealer couple from Maine who visited several times selling lobster and bear traps—a bit unusual for Texas!

WINNIE
Old Time Trade Days Flea Market

DATES: The weekend following the first Monday, year round.

TIMES: Daylight to dusk.

ADMISSION: Free. parking is $2 a carload. Tour buses are free.

LOCATION: I-10, Exit 829 at Winnie. When you get off the Interstate, you are there. Between Beaumont and Houston.

DESCRIPTION: Formerly a part of Larry's Antique Mall and Flea Market in Beaumont, this market opened in 1992, taking the major part of the flea market with it. Housed in permanent shops, covered pavilions, or outdoors, it hosts 500 to 1,000 dealers specializing in antiques, collectibles and crafts. The crafters have their own space showing their wares from the Ozarks to the south Texas coast. Decorators come from all over the country to find those "special somethings" to furnish their jobs. There is a special designated place for garage sales and everyone is invited to use it. With the publicity from the move from Beaumont, this market put the

town of Winnie on the Texas map. So much so that all the major fast-food companies have space there including McDonald's, Burger King, Taco Bell, and plenty more. There are clean restrooms available. Very quickly, this market has become "family" to some and a capsule history of Texas in that there have already been at least one wedding, a two-foot flood, tornados, and hurricanes—"some real hair-raisers," says Mrs. Tinkle, one of the owners. "But our customers are loyal, our vendors are loyal, and somehow the market just keeps growing."

DEALER RATES: $30 and up depending on location and size: outdoors, covered pavilion, indoors, shop; 20' × 20' to 20' × 50'. Reservations are recommended.

CONTACT: Larry and Justine Tinkle, 14902 Hwy 1663, Winnie TX 77665. Tel: (409) 892-4000 or (409) 296-3300. Fax: (409) 296-3301.

Blowing in the Wind
Well, they had a "big top tent," but that "is somewhere blowing in the wind," according to Justine Tinkle.

OTHER FLEA MARKETS

We know or have heard about these markets, but have not personally contacted each one, as we have the markets with descriptions. If you plan to visit one of the markets listed below, *please call first* to make sure they are still open. Flea markets do come and go. While they were open when we went to press, they may not be later. We can't be responsible. *Call first!*

Abilene: Elmdale Flea Market, 5423 E Hwy 80. Tel: (915) 673-8623.
Abilene: Old Abilene Town Flea Market, 3300 E IH 20. Tel: (915) 675-6588.
Alice: Mary's Flea Market, 7146 Hwy 359. Tel: (361) 661-0272.
Alvarado: All American Texas Flea Markets, S IH 35 W. Tel: (817) 783-5468.
Amarillo: ICX Flea Market, 513 Ross St. Tel: (806) 373-3215.
Aransas Pass: Little Texas Flea Market, 2112 N Hwy 35. Tel: (361) 758-6367.
Arthur City: Arthur City Flea Market. Tel: (903) 732-4576.
Austin: Austin Country, 9500 E Hwy 290. Tel: (512) 928-2795.
Austin: Oakhill Flea Market, 5526 W Hwy 290. Tel: (512) 892-0402.
Avinger: B & J Outpost, RR 1 Box 393. Tel: (903) 755-4260.
Baytown: Main Flea Market, 1010 N Main St. Tel: (281) 427-5601.
Beaumont: Antique Mall and Flea Market, 7135 Concord Rd. Tel: (409) 892-4000.
Beaumont: King Mart Flea Market, 2655 S 11th St. Tel: (409) 842-5401.
Beaumont: Old Time Trade Days, IH 10 Exit 829. Tel: (409) 892-4000.
Beeville: Bush Country Flea Market, S Hwy 181. Tel: (361) 358-9111.

Beeville: F M 351 Flea Market, Hwy 351. Tel: (361) 358-7368.
Belton: Bell County Flea Market, George Wilson Rd. Tel: (254) 939-6411.
Belton: Centroplex Flea Market, 200 Whitsett St. Tel: (254) 939-5242.
Belton: Hwy 190 Flea Market, Hwy 190. Tel: (254) 939-9196.
Bridge City: Gulf Coast Flea Market, 3140 Texas Ave. Tel: (409) 735-5377.
Brownsville: Ashly Bazaar, 5968 N Expressway. Tel: (956) 350-3577.
Canton: Mill Creek Trade Ground. Tel: (903) 567-1177.
Channelview: Flea Market-East Freeway, 15660 East Fwy. Tel: (281) 452-9022.
Cleveland: Frontier Flea Market, 18431 Hwy 105. Tel: (281) 592-2101.
Cleveland: Olde Security Square Flea Market, 20024 Hwy 105. Tel: (281) 592-6017.
Comfort: Hwy 87 Flea Market, Hwy 87 N. Tel: (830) 995-2998.
Corpus Christi: Casa Linda Flea Market II, 1551 Baldwin Blvd. Tel: (361) 884-2264.
Corsicana: Cassel Flea Market, 708 S 7th St. Tel: (903) 872-7170.
Dallas: Bargin City Bazaar, 735 N Westmoreland Rd. Tel: (214) 330-8111.
Dallas: Gaston Bazaar, 3035 N Buckner Blvd. Tel: (214) 319-7600.
Dallas: Kleberg Flea Market, 13939 C F Hawn Fwy. Tel: (972) 557-1717.
Dayton: County Line Flea Market, Fm 1960. Tel: (936) 258-8251.
Del Rio: Flores Market, Hwy 277 S. Tel: (830) 774-6305.
Denton: Flea Market 380, 4200 E University Dr. Tel: (940) 566-5060.
Dickinson: Morgan Flea Market, 2802 Hwy 3. Tel: (281) 337-1290.
Dublin: 377 Swap Meet & Market, 16027 S U S 377. Tel: (254) 445-1840.
Eastland: Commerce Street Warehouse Flea Market, 307 E Commerce St. Tel: (254) 629-3199.
El Paso: Ascarate Drive In Swap, 6701 Delta Dr. Tel: (915) 779-2303.
El Paso: Country Flea Market, 14730 Montana Ave. Tel: (915) 855-7114.
El Paso: Bronco Swap Meet, 8408 Alameda Ave. Tel: (915) 858-5555.
Eldorado: Flea Market, 602 SW Main St. Tel: (915) 853-3796.
Fort Stockton: Inside Flea Market, 901 N Colpitts Blvd. Tel: (915) 336-8341.
Fort Worth: Henderson Flea Market, 1000 N Henderson St. Tel: (817) 877-3021.
Frost: Frost Flea Market & Furniture, 201 N Garitty St. Tel: (903) 682-3019.
Ganado: Ganado Flea Market, 106 S 3Rd St. Tel: (361) 771-3509.
Glen Flora: Bridge Street Flea Market, 115 Bridge Av. Tel: (979) 677-3676.
Granbury: Four Seasons II Flea Market, 4238 E Hwy 377. Tel: (817) 279-6888.
Granbury: Old Time Flea Market, 5830 E Hwy 377. Tel: (817) 326-6611.
Hereford: Chaves Flea Market, 225 Main St. Tel: (806) 364-4834.
Highlands: Browzer's Trading Village, 106 Harris Rd. Tel: (281) 426-6685.
Hooks: Fairground, 1 Hwy 82 W. Tel: (903) 223-7663.
Houston: 45 Flea Market Inc, 630 W Little York Rd. Tel: (281) 445-4566.
Houston: A-1 Flea Market, 1818 Gessner Dr. Tel: (713) 465-7759.

Houston: A-1 Flea Market, 717 Maxey Rd. Tel: (713) 451-4434.

Houston: Cheng's Flea Market, 10802 Airline Dr. Tel: (281) 445-5269.

Houston: Frank & AJ Super Flea Market, 7075 Bellfort St. Tel: (713) 644-2710.

Houston: Houston Flea Market, 6116 Southwest Fwy. Tel: (713) 780-0070.

Houston: Houston Indoor Flea Market, 6116 Windswept Ln. Tel: (713) 266-2785.

Houston: Kings Flea Market, 5100 Griggs Rd. Tel: (713) 747-9234.

Houston: New Flea Market, 8315 Long Point Rd. Tel: (713) 722-7122.

Houston: No 1 Flee Market, 9820 Gulf Fwy. Tel: (713) 910-5749.

Irving: Irving Flea Market, PO Box 154913. Tel: (972) 986-2508.

Jewett: Flea Market of Jowett, Hwy 79. Tel: (903) 626-5674.

Kemp: Big Daddy's Traders Market, Hwy 274 S. Tel: (903) 432-4911.

Killeen: Debra's Flea Market, 3301 Todd St. Tel: (254) 699-1666.

Kingsville: Kingsville Flea Market, 2420 E King Ave. Tel: (361) 516-0013.

Kyle: Kyle Flea Market. Tel: (512) 262-2351.

Kyle: Old Texas Trading Post. Tel: (512) 262-2351.

Laredo: Border Town Flea Market, Hwy 359. Tel: (956) 726-1186.

Littlefield: Littlefield Trade Days, 807 E Hwy 84. Tel: (806) 385-0088.

Livingston: Boyd Flea Market, W Hwy 190. Tel: (936) 967-0547.

Lubbock: Flea Market, 2323 Avenue K. Tel: (806) 747-8281.

Lubbock: Interstate Flea Market, 3418 I-27. Tel: (806) 765-7003.

Lufkin: Olde Frontier Town, Hwy 59 S. Tel: (936) 632-8696.

Mabank: Gun Barrel City Flea Market, 1307 W Main St. Tel: (903) 887-1000.

Marion: Interstate 10 Flea Market, 1819 W I-10. Tel: (830) 914-4447.

McAllen: Bargain Bazaar, 4400 N 23Rd St. Tel: (956) 631-7716.

Mercedes: Red Barn Flea Market & Mobile Home Park, 2 ½ Mile Rd. Tel: (956) 565-6566.

Midland: Rankin Flea Market, 2840 S State Hwy 349. Tel: (915) 684-5060.

Mineola: Armstrong Mineola Flea Market, NW Loop 564. Tel: (903) 569-6402.

Mission: Ochoas Flea Market, N Conway And Four Mile. Tel: (956) 580-1757.

Nacogdoches: Junction Indoor Flea Market, S Hwy 59. Tel: (936) 560-6365.

Nacogdoches: Nacogdoches Trade Days, 1304 NW Stallings Dr. Tel: (936) 564-2150.

Newton: Hwy 87 Flea Market, Hwy 87. Tel: (409) 379-5029.

Odessa: County Road Flea Market, 6410 W County Road. Tel: (915) 368-4305.

Odessa: Henry's Flea Market, 7715 Andrews Hwy. Tel: (915) 366-8189.

Orange: Maurceville Flea Market, Hwy 12. Tel: (409) 745-4534.

Pampa: Jim's Tradin City Flea Market, 918 E Frederic Ave. Tel: (806) 665-3620.

Paris: 3 D Flea, 2810 NE Loop 286. Tel: (903) 785-1851.

Paris: Gene's Flea Market, 2810 NE Loop 286. Tel: (903) 785-1851.

Pasadena: Grand Bazaar, 904 Main St. Tel: (713) 477-8192.

Pipe Creek: Pipe Creek Flea Market, State Hwy 16 S. Tel: (830) 535-4615.

Port Neches: Old Towne Flea Market, 1216 Port Neches Ave. Tel: (409) 721-9690.

Porter: Old World Flea Market, 88 Legion Rd. Tel: (281) 354-3477.

Post: Old Mills Trade Days, 318 S Ave F. Tel: (806) 495-3529.

Quinlan: Lake Tawakoni Trade Days. Tel: (903) 356-2520.

Rockport: Red Barn Flea Market, 6737 Hwy 35 N. Tel: (361) 729-5292.

San Antonio: Ballpark Market, 239 W Sunset. Tel: (303) 295-7059.

San Antonio: Flea Market Northwest Center, 3600 Fredericksburg Rd. Tel: (210) 736-6655.

San Antonio: Fleamarket San Antonio. Tel: (210) 624-2666.

San Antonio: Gibsons Flea Market, 1331 Bandera Rd. Tel: (210) 432-8200.

San Antonio: I-37 Flea Market, IH 37 At Southton Rd. Tel: (210) 633-2220.

San Antonio: Northwest Flea Market, 3600 Fredericksburg Rd. Tel: (210) 736-6655.

San Antonio: Palo Alto Flea Market, 1936 SW Loop 410. Tel: (210) 628-1896.

Stanton: Old Sorehead Trade Days, 301 N St Peter St. Tel: (915) 756-2006.

Stephenville: Chicken House Flea Market, Dublin Hwy. Tel: (254) 968-0888.

Sweetwater: Havner's Flea Market, 608 E Ave A. Tel: (915) 235-0399.

Texarkana: 67 Flea Market, 5605 W 7th. Tel: (903) 838-4663.

Texarkana: Berd's Book & Flea Market, Hwy 59 S. Tel: (903) 838-2594.

Texarkana: Flea Market, 3015 S Lake Dr. Tel: (903) 792-7939.

Texarkana: Great American Flea Market, 2615 New Boston Rd. Tel: (903) 793-7700.

Tyler: North Beckham Flea Market, 825 N Beckham Ave. Tel: (903) 593-6693.

Tyler: Downtown Flea Market, 302 E Locust St. Tel: (903) 592-7123.

Tyler: Ethel's Flea Market, 731 N Bois D Arc Ave. Tel: (903) 531-9955.

Tyler: Armory Flea Market, 2114 W Front St. Tel: (903) 593-0870.

Waco: Bargain Mart Flea Market, 1000 S New Rd. Tel: (254) 752-2235.

Wharton: Lee's Flea Market, 622 E Milam St. Tel: (979) 532-0777.

Whitesboro: 82 Flea Market. Tel: (903) 564-5348.

Winnie: Bridge City Flea Market, 1204 Campbell. Tel: (409) 792-0054.

UTAH

SALT LAKE CITY
Antique Collectors' Fair

DATES: 2002: February 2-3, May 4-5, November 16-17.
TIMES: Saturday 10:00 AM-6:00 PM; Sunday 10:00 AM-5:00 PM.
ADMISSION: $4, $3 with ad from local newspaper (in the classified section). Early bird admission for Saturday 9:00 AM-10:00 AM: $10.
LOCATION: South Towne Exposition Center, 9575 S State St.
DESCRIPTION: Limited to antiques and collectibles only, this market opened in 1986 and hosts 70 to 100 dealers during its three to four shows per year. Savvy shoppers and other dealers come from all over the west to restock their own inventory buying jewelry, vintage clothing, glassware, a huge variety of oak furniture, primitives, kitchenware, Mormon pine, prints, dolls, postcards, books, old tools, cowboy items, toys and more. Plenty of hotels, motels, and restaurants surround the Expo Center. This is the only market of its type between Denver and the West Coast. Food is available on the premises.
DEALER RATES: $150 for a 10' × 13' booth; 10% additional for a wall or aisle end position. Setup Friday 10:00 AM-7:00 PM. Security is provided by the Salt Palace. RV parking within 3 miles of site.
CONTACT: James Reece Antique Promotion, PO Box 510432, Salt Lake City UT 84151. Tel: (801) 532-3401. Email: utmart@earthlink.net. Web: www.utmart.com.

Redwood Swap Meet

DATES: Every Saturday and Sunday.
TIMES: Winters 9:00 AM-3:00 PM; summers 8:00 AM-3:00 PM.
LOCATION: 3688 S Redwood Rd. Take I-15 to 3300 S. Go west to 1700 W. Go south to Redwood Swap Meet.
ADMISSION: $.50 per person. Parking is free.
DESCRIPTION: This indoor/outdoor market started in 1972 and currently draws approximately 170 dealers in winter and up to 700 dealers in summer. The merchandise available includes antiques, collectibles, tools, electronics, hundreds of garage sales and new merchandise. Fresh farm goods and craft items are also available. Food is served on the premises and there are handicapped-accessible restrooms when the need arises.
DEALER RATES: $12 per dealer on Saturday; $15 and up per space on Sunday. Reservations are suggested. Showers and overnight parking are available.

CONTACT: Redwood Swap Meet, 3688 S Redwood Rd, West Valley UT 84119. Tel: (801) 973-6060. Fax: (801) 973-0644.

OTHER FLEA MARKETS

We know or have heard about these markets, but have not personally contacted each one, as we have the markets with descriptions. If you plan to visit one of the markets listed below, *please call first* to make sure they are still open. Flea markets do come and go. While they were open when we went to press, they may not be later. We can't be responsible. *Call first!*

Blanding: Ol'West Traders, 1949 S Main St. Tel: (435) 678-2568.

VERMONT

CHARLOTTE
Charlotte Flea Market

DATES: Saturday and Sunday, April through November, weather permitting.
TIMES: 6:00 AM-5:00 PM or later.
ADMISSION: Free. Parking is free.
LOCATION: Rt 7, just south of the Wildflower Farm, 10 miles south of Burlington. About 5 miles south of the Shelburne Museum.

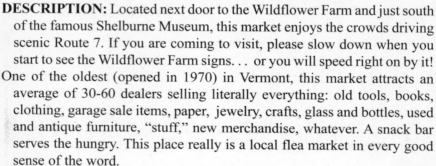

DESCRIPTION: Located next door to the Wildflower Farm and just south of the famous Shelburne Museum, this market enjoys the crowds driving scenic Route 7. If you are coming to visit, please slow down when you start to see the Wildflower Farm signs... or you will speed right on by it! One of the oldest (opened in 1970) in Vermont, this market attracts an average of 30-60 dealers selling literally everything: old tools, books, clothing, garage sale items, paper, jewelry, crafts, glass and bottles, used and antique furniture, "stuff," new merchandise, whatever. A snack bar serves the hungry. This place really is a local flea market in every good sense of the word.
DEALER RATES: For a 3-table setup, tables and canopies included: $15 a day. Essentially, $5 per table per day. Reservations are not required.
CONTACT: Larry Lavalette, 5665 Ethan Allen Hwy, Charlotte VT 05445. Tel: (802) 425-2844.

CHELSEA
Chelsea Flea Market

DATES: Second Saturday of July.
TIMES: 9:00 AM-4:00 PM.
ADMISSION: Free. Parking in designated areas for a small fee (fundraising!).
LOCATION: On the North and South Common of Chelsea, on Rt 110, south of Barre.

DESCRIPTION: Started in 1972 by the Ladies Service Guild of a local church, this show has grown to include 110-120 vendors from all over New England. Over 3,000 visitors choose from antiques, collectibles, and whatever, spread over Chelsea's two town commons (that is most uncommon). The Fish and Game Department runs the famous chicken barbecue (a special Vermont treat); hot dogs, homemade doughnuts, hamburgers, coffee and sodas are sold by the Ladies Service Guild. The Chelsea Library holds their annual Book Sale at the Town Hall during this show. Chelsea is another of Vermont's beautiful towns stretched along the back roads. Definitely worth the trip.

DEALER RATES: $20 per space. Call for reservations, as there is a long waiting list.

CONTACT: Elaine Braman, Flea Market Coordinator, 444 VT Rt 110, Chelsea VT 05038. Tel: (802) 685-3392.

Limed!
Each year, the Ladies reassess their planning and strategy. Years ago, ways to mark the dealer spaces came up regularly. One early year, two of the Ladies decided that using a lime spreader would work very well indeed—and be faster to boot. It did work—very well, indeed. Until it rained—the night before the show!

CRAFTSBURY COMMON
Craftsbury Antique and Unique Festival

DATES: Second Saturday in July, come heck or high water!

TIMES: 10:00 AM-4:00 PM.

ADMISSION: Free. Parking is $2—to benefit the Craftsbury Fire Department.

LOCATION: On Craftsbury Common itself. From the south: take Rt 100 heading north through Morrisville to Rt 15 east to Rt 14 north, follow the signs to Craftsbury, then Craftsbury Common. From the north: Rt 14 south from Newport and follow the signs.

DESCRIPTION: Set in the picturesque village of Craftsbury Common, this special market, started in 1970, helps raise funds for the Vermont Children's Aid Society. The dealers specialize in antiques, collectibles and unique crafts, including stuffed animals, jewelry, handmade wooden clocks, pottery, clothing, sculpture, soaps, and other treasures. Sterling College is next door and the local sports center is home to some wild mountain-bike races. Food is provided by local bakers. Food is provided by local bakers; mouthwatering baked goods, jams, relishes and breads are sold by community members. Live music is provided by Seth Eames Band to liven this already lively event. This is considered a "four-plunger day" by the two directors of the Festival. Relief facilities are available, for real now.

DEALER RATES: $75 for a 14' frontage and ample space behind. Three large tents are placed in the center of the common with 10' × 12' and 10' × 15' spaces, as well as open spaces along the outside of the common. Reservations are a must and should be in by sometime in January, as the invitations to sell are sent in February. There is a long waiting list for this event.

CONTACT: Gale Andreotta, VCAS, PO Box 127, Winooski VT 05404-0127. Tel: (802) 655-0006. Email: mainadmn@vtcas.org

MANCHESTER CENTER
Manchester Flea Market

DATES: Every Saturday and Sunday, May through October, weather permitting.

TIMES: 9:00 AM-5:00 PM.

LOCATION: Junction of Rts 11 and 30. Take Bromley Mountain Rd 3 miles from the center of Manchester.

ADMISSION: Free. Free parking is available.

DESCRIPTION: This popular outdoor show has operated since 1970 in the heart of the Green Mountains and ski country. Stratton, Magic and Bromley ski areas surround Manchester. It currently attracts 35 to 40 dealers of primarily antiques, with collectibles, crafts, with some farm goods also available. There is an exhibit of antique farm machinery here, and this is also the location of a locally well-known Saturday auction. Robert Todd Lincoln's historic home Hildene is nearby and open to the public. Wessners Surplus Store resides here, too. One snack bar and restrooms add to the amenities.

DEALER RATES: $15 per 20' × 15' space. Advance reservations are suggested.

CONTACT: Albert H Wessner, 2783 Depot St, Manchester Center VT 05255. Tel: (802) 362-1631.

NEWFANE
The Original Newfane Flea Market

DATES: Every Sunday, May through October. Rain or shine.

TIMES: 6:00 AM-5:00 PM.

ADMISSION: Free. Ample free parking is available.

LOCATION: On Rt 30, 1 mile north of Newfane Village.

DESCRIPTION: This outdoor market has been around since 1963 and is claimed to be the oldest and largest in Vermont. It is well known throughout the state, attracting between 100 and 150 dealers who come from near and far to exhibit such diverse items as antiques, collectibles, craft items, new merchandise, and fresh produce—in a word: "Everything that's legal." Three food concessions and an ice cream stand satisfy any hunger pangs you may suffer. Please leave your dogs at home.

DEALER RATES: $20 per space. No reservations period! Just show up. Dealers may camp free Saturday nights. Get there by 6:00 PM for sites.

CONTACT: Bill Morse, The Original Newfane Flea Market, Inc., PO Box 55, Newfane VT 05345-0055. Tel: (802) 365-4000, Sundays (802) 365-7771 at the market.

Find Bill at the market, he has some stories to tell!
"Being the oldest, and back in the 'Old Days' we had a dealer who sold Poison Ivy, when in season, and Vermont Rocks exclusively (from his driveway)—now known as Vermont Paperweights!"
"When someone asks for a little OFF®, we usually ask them, 'From the top or the bottom?'"

History Notes
When Teddy Roosevelt was President, he came through Newfane and had dinner at the hotel that was then attached to the local jail. The hotel has since been torn down, but the building's other half, still housing the now discontinued jail, is the Windham Co. Sheriff's office. In any case, when TR heard that the prisoners were fed the same food as the hotel guests, he volunteered to return after his term of office, break some minor law, and retire in bliss to the jail, where he could get the same wonderful meals for free.

From Archer Mayor

Some Mysterious Fiction
For those of you who read Archer Mayor's mystery series, starring Joe Gunther of the Brattleboro Police Department, this is just about where all his stories take place, in and around southeastern Vermont.

On the Subject of Breakfast
From Bill Morse, whose wife's grandmother served TR coffee at that hotel, it was TR who coined the phrase, "Good to the last drop," referring to his morning java.

WATERBURY
Waterbury Flea Market

DATES: Saturday, Sunday and holidays, weather permitting, May through October.

TIMES: Daybreak to exhaustion. Usually 6:00 AM to 6:00 PM, but things slow down in the afternoon.

ADMISSION: Free. Parking is free.

LOCATION: Rt 2, just north of Waterbury. Exit 10 W off I-89.

DESCRIPTION: Opened in 1979, this outdoor market attracts anyone and everyone with up to 100 vendors selling everything from classic antiques, attic treasures, ancient books and old magazines, new merchandise, jewelry, tools new and very old, furniture, yard-sale and house clean-outs, collectibles and "stuff." It's the locals clearinghouse. Great finds! A snack concession serves breakfast, hot dogs, cremies, and Benzies famous french fries sates hungry appetites. Then again, there is Ben & Jerry's Ice Cream and the Cider Mill around the corner and down Route 100.

DEALER RATES: $15 per day for a 20' × 25' space. Dealers may set up over the weekend for free and set up on Friday afternoon. All dogs must be on leases, please.

CONTACT: Reginald Erwin, Waterbury Flea Market, 71 N Main St, Waterbury VT 05676. Tel: (802) 244-5916. Fax: (802) 244-1574.

WATERBURY CENTER
Stowe Road Flea Market

DATES: Saturday and Sundays, May through October's fall foliage season. Weather permitting.

TIMES: 9:00 AM-5:00 PM. Could be earlier and later depending on weather, light and dealer inclination.

ADMISSION: Free. Parking is free.

LOCATION: Rt 100. Only 3.2 miles from I-89, Exit 10 Waterbury Stowe, on the road to Stowe. Not even 3 miles north of Ben & Jerry's Ice Cream Factory.

DESCRIPTION: This outdoor market, opened in 1971, has the unique distinction of being surrounded by some of Vermont's biggest attractions: Ben & Jerry's Ice Cream Factory (the largest tourist attraction in the state), the Cold Hollow Cider Mill across the street, and the resort town of Stowe just north on scenic Route 100. They host anywhere from 20 to 50 dealers selling loads of antiques, collectibles, Vermont crafts, glass, furniture, garage sale goodies and whatever turns up. New merchandise is very rare and discouraged. If you are hungry, try B&J's or the cider mill. Enjoy! Do find Walter and say Hello.

DEALER RATES: $15 for roughly a 25' × 20' space per day—in other words, for reasonable space you need, including parking your car; or $25 for the weekend. Reservations are not required. Tents (10' × 20') or 8' tables are available by advance reservation.

CONTACT: Col Walter Flatow, CAI, 3579 Waterbury Stowe Rd, Waterbury Center VT 05677. Tel: Walter or Marie at (802) 244-8817 or Barb at (802) 244-8879.

WILMINGTON
Wilmington Outdoor Antique and Flea Market

DATES: Saturday, Sunday and holiday Mondays, from the weekend before Memorial Day through the weekend after Columbus Day.

TIMES: No specific times, really. Say dawn on…

ADMISSION: Free. Parking is free.

LOCATION: Junction of Rts 9 and 100.

DESCRIPTION: Since 1982 this market has been located on a choice 10-acre lot at the junction of two heavily traveled scenic roads through Vermont. They do a lot of advertising and draw crowds. Up to 125 dealers sell antiques, collectibles, garage sale items, all manner of stuff. Food is available from a concession stand.

DEALER RATES: $20 per space. Reservations are not required.

CONTACT: Peter and Sally Gore, Wilmington Outdoor Antique and Flea Market, PO Box 22, Wilmington VT 05363-0022. Tel: (802) 464-3345.

VIRGINIA

ALTAVISTA
First Saturday Trade Lot

DATES: First Saturday of each month and the preceding Friday, year round.
TIMES: Friday noon until 4:00 PM on Saturday.
ADMISSION: Free. Parking is free, but limited.
LOCATION: On Seventh St, 1 block off Bus Hwy 29, between Lynchburg and Danville.

DESCRIPTION: This outdoor market first opened in 1911 and is one of the oldest flea markets in the East. There are more than 200 dealers selling mostly antiques, collectibles, crafts, new and secondhand merchandise, as well as some produce. There is also food available on the premises. Don't miss the hot dogs. I am assured they are terrific! The Altavista High School Band Boosters now run this show and man the concession stand to help pay their expenses. Uncle Billy's Day (the first Saturday weekend in June, Friday through Sunday) is a town-wide celebration that lasts three days centered around the Trade Lot and Riverfront Park. Uncle Billy started the Trade Lot by trading animals at the turn of the century. Fireworks, entertainment and more are featured on this weekend.
DEALER RATES: $10 per 9' × 20' space for the weekend. Six-month reservations are $8 per weekend paid in advance. Uncle Billy's Day space is $25 a space unless already reserved for six months. Reservations are strongly suggested, or else. Town permits are required and sold there for $1.50 a year. No telephone reservations are accepted.
CONTACT: Altavista Band Boosters, PO Box 333, Altavista VA 24517-0333. Tel: (804) 369-5001 (Town Hall).

ARLINGTON/CLARENDON
Clarendon Antiques and Collectibles Market

DATES: Saturday, year round.
TIMES: 9:00 AM-4:00 PM.
ADMISSION: Free. Parking is free at 3033 Wilson Blvd.
LOCATION: 2900 Wilson Blvd. Between Wilson and Clarendon Blvd. At North Fillmore St.
DESCRIPTION: This outdoor market is run by the same management as the Georgetown Flea Market in DC. Fifty dealers sell their wide selection of furniture and collectible goods in the middle of the eclectic neighborhood of Clarendon. Many of the dealers are regulars who sell fine antiques, collectibles, deco furniture, vintage clothing, antique silver,

handmade arts and crafts among their offerings. There are plenty of restaurants and shops in the neighborhood when the munchies strike.

DEALER RATES: $40-$50 depending on space and if you have our vehicle with you. Setup starts at 8:00 AM.

CONTACT: Michael Shahrabani, Arlington Flea Markets, 730 N Barton St, Arlington VA 22201. Tel: (703) 528-6748. Web: www.clarendon.org.

CHANTILLY/WASHINGTON DC
DC Big Flea

DATES: For 2002: January 12-13, March 2-3, July 13-14, September 14-15, November 16-17. Call or visit the website for 2003 dates.

TIMES: Saturday 10:00 AM-6:00 PM, Sunday 11:00 AM-5:00 PM.

ADMISSION: $5; children under 12 free. Parking is free. $6 in January and March.

LOCATION: Chantilly Convention Center.

DESCRIPTION: This show has over 500 dealers from 20 states in one huge building. During January and March they fill two buildings with over 1,100 booths. Their dealers sell primarily antiques and collectibles. It is claimed to be the "fastest-growing market on the East Coast." Food concessions and handicapped-accessible restrooms add to the amenities.

DEALER RATES: $120 single space. Reservations are required. This facility does charge $65 for electrical hookup.

CONTACT: D'Amore Promotions, 2125 McComas Way Ste 102, Virginia Beach VA 23456. Tel: (757) 430-4735. Fax: (757) 430-4738. Email: sales@bigfleamarket.com. Web: www.damorepromotions.com.

FREDERICKSBURG
Manor Mart Flea Market

DATES: Saturday and Sunday, year round.

TIMES: 7:00 AM-dusk.

ADMISSION: Free. Parking is free.

LOCATION: US Hwy 1, just south of Fredericksburg.

DESCRIPTION: An indoor/outdoor flea market established in 1983, the Manor Mart offers over 100 dealers selling antiques, collectibles, crafts, and new merchandise, as well as fresh produce. It is located near historic Fredericksburg, scene of much Civil War fighting and near other historic battlefields. Food is available on the premises, there are handicapped-accessible restrooms, and plenty of motels and campgrounds are nearby.

DEALER RATES: $10 per 16' × 10' booth (indoors and out). Reservations are not required. There are monthly rates for buildings; just call and ask for Chuck the Manager.

CONTACT: Nick or Jeannie Dommisse, Manor Mart Flea Market, 9040 Jeff Davis Hwy, Fredericksburg VA 22407. Tel: (540) 898-4685.

HARRISONBURG
Shenandoah Heritage Farmers' Market

DATES: Monday through Saturday.

TIMES: Weekdays 10:00 AM-6:00 PM. Saturday 9:00 AM-6:00 PM.

ADMISSION: Free. Parking is free and quite ample.

LOCATION: 121 Carpenter Ln. Take I-81 Exit 243, go south on Rt 11. Market is on the left.

DESCRIPTION: This market's dealers sell antiques, collectibles, garage sale goodies, crafts, home-canned goods, fresh produce, sports equipment, bulk foods, silk flowers, and plenty of new merchandise. There is a full-service restaurant and handicapped-accessible restrooms to satisfy your every need.

DEALER RATES: Please call for rates, as their dealers are permanent, but there may be openings.

CONTACT: Shenandoah Heritage Farmers' Market, 121 Carpenter Ln, Harrisonburg VA 22801. Tel: (540) 433-3929.

HILLSVILLE
VFW Labor Day Gun Show and Flea Market

DATES: Friday through Monday, Labor Day weekend. Rain or shine.

TIMES: 8:00 AM-6:00 PM.

LOCATION: At the VFW Complex. On US Rt 58-221 W (Galax Rd), 1 mile east of I-77.

ADMISSION: $1 per person; children under 12 admitted free. Parking is $3 a day; $10 a day for RVs.

DESCRIPTION: This market is one of the granddaddys of markets! The population of the town of Hillsville expands five-fold during this annual event sponsored by the Grover King Post 1115 Veterans of Foreign Wars. The show has been held each year since 1967, and in 2001 it brought over 350,000 shoppers despite rain and cold weather, according to local police records. There are over 2,450 spaces, but how many dealers depends on how many spaces a dealer nabs. Usually, 950-1,500 dealers set up selling a variety of items that goes beyond firearms and militaria to encompass all types of antiques and collectibles including coins, jewelry, glassware, tools, toys, and other Americana. For the 1990 show, visitors registered from 40 different states plus 4 foreign countries, and attendance is growing each year. Food is served on the premises.

DEALER RATES: $50 per 9' × 20' space plus vendor license fee, for four days. Space sizes are 9' × 20 or 10' × 20'. Dealer reservations are required. Dealers set up Thursday prior to the show.

CONTACT: VFW Flea Market, c/o Ray Chappell, 217 Ridgeview Dr, Mt Airy NC 27030. Tel: (336) 789-5347. Email: raychappell@advi.net.

OAK GROVE
Red Barn Flea Market

DATES: Friday through Sunday. "Absolute" auctions held on the first and third Saturdays. No buyers premium.

TIMES: Winter: Friday and Sunday 12:00 PM-4:00 PM, Saturday 9:00 AM-4:00 PM; Summer: Friday and Sunday 12:00 PM-5:00 PM, Saturdays 9:00 AM-5:00 PM.

ADMISSION: Free. Parking is also free.

LOCATION: Westmoreland County, 36 miles east of Fredericksburg on Rt 3. On left of road, look for the big red barn.

DESCRIPTION: This market started in August 1989 as an addition to an auction house, which started originally as a huge horse barn—"the size of a football field." Crammed with 52 dealers inside and growing, selling antiques, and baby booties to collectibles, glassware, toys, books, TVs, appliances, "everything." Carolyn loves old books and collects them; if you have any old books or stories, stop and chat. This is a friendly, old-fashioned country market the way flea markets used to be. They were written up in the July 1998 issue of *Mademoiselle* as a great place to shop. The outside is open to whoever wants to set up and sell family oriented goods.

DEALER RATES: $40 per month inside. $3 a day for outside table space. Reservations are suggested, as they have a waiting list.

CONTACT: Curtis and Carolyn Bartmess, Red Barn Flea Market, 430 Circle Ln, Colonial Beach VA 22443. Tel: (804) 224-1119.

Don't You Wish
The Bartmesses sold a set of candlesticks with hanging crystals on them for $20, then they saw them for sale at Christie's for $20,000.

PETERSBURG
South Side Station Market Place

DATES: Daily.

TIMES: Weekdays 10:00 AM-5:00 PM. Weekends 8:30 AM-5:00 PM.

ADMISSION: Free. Parking is free.

LOCATION: 5 River St, off I-95 Exit 52 to Washington St, follow Historic Olde Towne Petersburg signs to Visitors' Center. They are located just behind the farmers' market.

DESCRIPTION: Opened in 1993, this indoor/outdoor market's dealers sell antiques, collectibles, crafts, produce, cards, garage sale goodies, furniture, new merchandise, fabric, Old Mansion coffee, teas and spices, ceramics, fine jewelry, toys, and clothing. One coffee shop and handicapped-accessible restrooms add to the amenities. In the fall of 2001, a tornado leveled one of their two buildings, but the dealers are still working outside and in!

DEALER RATES: Building 1: $.75 per square foot. Building 2: $150 per 13' × 16' space, monthly. First come, first served. Outdoor sales: $5 per day. Due to the tornado everything is negotiable!

CONTACT: c/o Station Master, South Side Station Market Place, 7 River St, Petersburg VA 23804-2820. Tel: (804) 720-2323. Fax: (804) 733-0667.

RICHMOND
American Heritage Antique Jubilee

DATES: For 2002: October 25-27. Rain or shine.

TIMES: 9:00 AM-5:00 PM.

ADMISSION: Friday $10 (Early Buyers Pass for 3 days); Saturday and Sunday $5 per day. Parking is free.

LOCATION: Richmond State Fairgrounds at Strawberry Hill, 600 E Laburnum Ave.

DESCRIPTION: An annual, multi-dimensional show featuring indoor and outdoor spaces. Over 1,000 dealers come from 25 states. This is an antique and collectible show only with entertainment and specialty food vendors. Handicapped-accessible restrooms add to the amenities.

DEALER RATES: $110 per heated space, $90 for unheated space, $70 per outdoor space. Tents are available for outdoor vendors at affordable rates. Reservations and pre-payment are required.

CONTACT: D'Amore Promotions, 2125 McComas Way Ste 102, Virginia Beach VA 23456. Tel: (757) 430-4735. Fax: (757) 430-4738. Email: sales@bigfleamarket.com. Web: www.damorepromotions.com.

Bellwood Flea Market

DATES: Saturday and Sunday, year round. Weather permitting.

TIMES: 5:30 AM-4:00 PM.

ADMISSION: $1 per person. Free parking.

LOCATION: 9201 Jefferson Davis Hwy. Exit 64 off I-95 and Willis Rd, south of Richmond.

DESCRIPTION: This market has been run since 1970 outdoors on pavement. Between 150 and 400 dealers offer antiques, collectibles, handmades, produce, meats, musical instruments, auto parts, appliances, real estate, furniture, clothing and new merchandise, as well as tools and curios. A large air-conditioned food concession opens early and remains open all day. A handicapped-accessible restroom is on site. There are still reminders of the fierce Civil War battle fought on the Bellwood property as people are occasionally finding mini-balls and some trench-works are still visible. Dealers and buyers from as far away as Alaska and Florida come here for goodies!

DEALER RATES: $14 per 20' × 20' space. First come, first served.

CONTACT: Julie Kline Campbell, c/o Bellwood Flea Market, 9201 Jeff Davis Hwy, Richmond VA 23237. Tel: (804) 275-1187 or 1-800-793-0707.

What a Find

An old ugly wooden chair, with pegs, was purchased for $50 from an elderly couple. The young man knew it was worth something because of the pegs. It was sold in Pennsylvania at a big market for enough to buy a new truck!

One dealer cruising through the market found an inkwell base, with no vials or anything. He wasn't quite sure what it was. At another stall, he found the vials! He bought them all.

The Big Flea Market at the Richmond State Fairgrounds

DATES: For 2002: January 19-20, March 16-17, July 6-7, August 3-4, and 31-September 1, November 30-December 1. Call or visit their website for 2003 dates.

TIMES: Saturday 10:00 AM-6:00 PM; Sunday 12:00 PM-5:00 PM.

ADMISSION: $3; children under 12 free. Parking is free.

LOCATION: Richmond State Fairgrounds at Strawberry Hill, 600 E Laburnum Ave.

DESCRIPTION: Part of a series of shows started in 1977, this show has between 300 and 600 spaces filled with dealers from 15 states. They sell primarily antiques and collectibles and some new merchandise. This market is considered the largest antique flea market in the Mid-Atlantic region. Food concessions and handicapped-accessible restrooms add to the amenities.

DEALER RATES: $85 per space per show. $150 for two spaces per show. Reservations are required.

CONTACT: D'Amore Promotions, 2125 McComas Way Ste 102, Virginia Beach VA 23456. Tel: (757) 430-4735. Fax: (757) 430-4738. Email: sales@bigfleamarket.com. Web: www.damorepromotions.com.

SuperFlea Flea Market

DATES: Saturday and Sunday.

TIMES: 9:00 AM-6:00 PM.

ADMISSION: Free. Parking is free.

LOCATION: 5501 Midlothian Tnpk, (Rt 60) 1 mile east of Chippenham Pkwy.

DESCRIPTION: Open since 1988, this indoor market houses up to 260 dealers in a huge 120,000-square-foot heated and air-conditioned building, making them one of the largest markets around. Under new management this market has been cleaned up and is full of happy vendors. There are barbershops, beauty shops, largest wholesale flower market, a dollar store, Avon, a major salvage operation, clothing, electronics, computers, photo-art, African art, shoes, furniture, giftware, videos, groceries, with only 8% is garage sale goodies. All the rest is new merchandise. There is a "table" section with 100 tables There is a restaurant on site, as well as handicapped-accessible restrooms. This is a growing market.

DEALER RATES: 10' × 12' booth—$220 per month, 6' × 12' booth—$170 per month, $180 per 9' × 12' booth; $25 per weekend for the table section. Electricity is available in all booths. Reservations most necessary, as there is a waiting list for the booths; however, the table section is first-come, first-served.

CONTACT: SuperFlea Flea Market, 5501 Midlothian Tnpk, Richmond VA 23225. Tel: (804) 231-6687. Fax: (804) 598-5938.

ROANOKE

The Big Flea Market at the Roanoke Civic Center

DATES: For 2002: November 2-3. Call or visit their website for 2003 dates.

TIMES: Saturday 10:00 AM-6:00 PM; Sunday 11:00 AM-5:00 PM.

ADMISSION: $5; children under 12 free. Parking is free.

LOCATION: Roanoke Civic Center, Orange Ave. Follow I-64 W to 81 South, take the 2nd Roanoke Exit, Hwy 581 to the 460 East exit (also the second Orange Ave exit). Go 1 block and turn right. It's there!

DESCRIPTION: Part of a series of shows started in 1977, this show has between 300 to 600 spaces filled with dealers from 15 states. They sell primarily antiques and collectibles and some new merchandise. Food concessions and handicapped-accessible restrooms add to the amenities.

DEALER RATES: $90 per space per show. $40 for electric. Reservations are required.

CONTACT: D'Amore Promotions, 2125 McComas Way Ste 102, Virginia Beach VA 23456. Tel: (757) 430-4735. Fax: (757) 430-4738. Email: sales@bigfleamarket.com. Web: www.damorepromotions.com.

Happy's Flea Market

DATES: Tuesday through Sunday, year round.

TIMES: Tuesday through Friday 8:00 AM-5:00 PM; Saturday and Sunday 6:30 AM-5:00 PM.

ADMISSION: Free. Parking is free.

LOCATION: 5411 Williamson Rd NW (Rt 11). Hershberger Rd Exit off Rt 581.

DESCRIPTION: Obviously successful, this market has been open since 1978. There are 150 inside dealers, another 300 outside with 100 of those spaces permanently reserved. The dealers sell an endless variety of everything: antiques, batteries, collectibles, used and new merchandise, and much more. A restaurant is on the premises as well as handicapped-accessible restrooms. There are outlet stores as part of the scene.

DEALER RATES: $12 Saturday and Sunday; $3 Tuesday; $5 Wednesday through Friday. Monthly and yearly rates available. First come, first served.

CONTACT: Faith DeLong, Manager, Happy's Flea Market, 5411 Williamson Rd, Roanoke VA 24012. Tel: (540) 563-4473/4.

VIRGINIA BEACH
Virginia Beach Big Flea Market

DATES: May 24-26 and September 20-22, 2002.

TIMES: Friday 7:00 PM-10:00 PM; Saturday 10:00 AM-6:00 PM, Sunday 12:00 PM-5:00 PM.

ADMISSION: $5; children under 12 are free. Free parking.

LOCATION: Virginia Beach Pavilion Convention Center. Take Rt 64 to the end, Rt 44. Follow the signs.

DESCRIPTION: For 19 years this show has been attracting up to 300 dealers from 15 states selling antiques and collectibles, plus assorted crafts and new merchandise. This show is considered one of Virginia's largest antiques and collectibles shows and is part of a series of shows held in Richmond and the Washington DC area. Food concessions and handicapped-accessible restrooms add to the amenities.

DEALER RATES: $90 per single space; $170 per double space per show. Reservations and deposits are required. Dealer space sells out fast. Electric is $40.

CONTACT: D'Amore Promotions, 2125 McComas Way Ste 102, Virginia Beach VA 23456. Tel: (757) 430-4735. Fax: (757) 430-4738. Email: sales@bigfleamarket.com. Web: www.damorepromotions.com.

OTHER FLEA MARKETS

We know or have heard about these markets, but have not personally contacted each one, as we have the markets with descriptions. If you plan to visit one of the markets listed below, *please call first* to make sure they are still open. Flea markets do come and go. While they were open when we went to press, they may not be later. We can't be responsible. *Call first!*

Abingdon: Banner Star Flea Market, 550 Russell Rd NW. Tel: (540) 628-2937.

Aldie: Great Aldie Flea Market, 39359 John Mosby Hwy. Tel: (703) 327-4452.

Bassett: Billy's Flea Market, 6766 Fairystone Park Hwy. Tel: (540) 629-4114.

Calverton: Calverton Flea Market, 9646 Bristersburg. Tel: (540) 788-9150.

Chesapeake: Bypass Flea Market, 1325 Battlefield Blvd S. Tel: (757) 546-1584.

Chesapeake: DO Drop In Flea Market, 3020 S Military Hwy. Tel: (757) 485-8511.

Chesapeake: Park Place Flea Market, 1707 Park Ave. Tel: (757) 494-7845.

Edinburg: Flea Market, 164 Landfill Rd. Tel: (540) 984-8771.

Front Royal: Front Royal Flea Market, 409 N Commerce Ave. Tel: (540) 636-9729.

Gainesville: Park's Flea Market, 14221 Lee Hwy. Tel: (703) 754-4087.

Gordonsville: Gordonsville Antique & Flea, Rt 15 & Klockner Rd. Tel: (540) 832-7376.

Gretna: Gretna Flea Market, 101 N Main St # A. Tel: (434) 656-6902.

Hillsville: Bowman Fleamarket, 1024 W Stuart Dr. Tel: (540) 728-2340.

Hillsville: Howlett Street Flea Market, 1017 W Stuart Dr. Tel: (540) 728-0604.

Hinton: Rawley Springs Flea Market, 9871 Rawley Pike. Tel: (540) 867-5086.

Keller: South Star Flea Market, 30552 Lankford Hwy. Tel: (757) 787-4048.

Lancaster: Lancaster Market, 11480 Courthouse Rd. Tel: (804) 462-0373.

Luray: Luray Flea Market, Highway 211 E. Tel: (540) 743-7374.

Martinsville: Family Flea Market, 1319 Memorial Blvd S. Tel: (540) 666-1256.

Martinsville: Martinsville Mega Flea, Rt 220 S. Tel: (540) 638-1471.

Mechanicsville: Indoor Swapmart Inc, 7508 Mechanicsville Tpke. Tel: (804) 559-0500.

Newport News: Flea Market, 10171 Jefferson Ave. Tel: (757) 599-5565.

Newport News: King Flea, 9710 Jefferson Ave. Tel: (757) 595-9673.

Norfolk: Flea Market of Norfolk, 3416 N Military Hwy. Tel: (757) 857-7824.

Portsmouth: El Rastro, 3409 George Washington Hwy. Tel: (757) 399-1797.

Portsmouth: J & L Flea Market, 3709 Victory Blvd. Tel: (757) 485-3013.

Richmond: Azalea Flea Market, 5209 Wilkinson Rd. Tel: (804) 329-8853.

Richmond: Frances's Flea Market, 2701 Byron St. Tel: (804) 643-2140.

Richmond: Super Flea Mart, 5501 Midlothian Tpke. Tel: (804) 231-6687.

Rocky Mount: A 1 Flea Market, 21231 Virgil H Goode Hwy. Tel: (540) 334-2323.

Rustburg: Big B Flea Market, 74 Exchange Dr. Tel: (434) 821-1326.

Strasburg: Strassburg Flea Market, 390 E King St. Tel: (540) 465-3550.

Sutherland: Gary's Flea Market, 18303 Cox Rd. Tel: (804) 265-8489.

Temperanceville: Shore Flea Market, 12085 Lankford Hwy. Tel: (757) 824-3300.

Urbanna: Urbanna Flea Market, Lord Mott Rd. Tel: (804) 758-4042.

Virginia Beach: Bill's Flea Market, 4815 Virginia Beach Blvd. Tel: (757) 340-0233.

Virginia Beach: Aragona Trading Post, 1017 Aragona Blvd. Tel: (757) 473-3028.

Warsaw: Warsaw Flea Market, 401 Main St # B. Tel: (804) 333-4062.

Waynesboro: Waynesboro Flea Market, 121 E Broad St. Tel: (540) 943-8933.

Waynesboro: Waynesboro Flea Market, 205 8th St. Tel: (540) 943-8933.

White Post: Shen-Valley Flea Market. Tel: (540) 869-7858.

Winchester: Valley Avenue Flea Market, 1000 Valley Ave. Tel: (540) 722-6768.

WASHINGTON

EVERETT
Puget Park Swap-O-Rama

DATES: Saturday and Sunday, April through September. Into October, weather permitting.

TIMES: 9:00 AM-3:30 PM.

ADMISSION: $1 per person. Free parking is provided.

LOCATION: 13020 Meridian Ave S. The 128th St exit off I-5.

DESCRIPTION: Started in 1975, this market currently attracts up to 250 dealers who set up to sell a wide range of objects including antiques, collectibles, fine art, crafts, fresh produce, and some new merchandise. A snack bar with a full kitchen feeds the famished. This area is near the marina where the whale-watching boats take off for trips through the spectacular San Juan Islands. Not to be missed.

DEALER RATES: $15 for a 20' × 20' space per day; $18 for a 20' × 40' space with electricity. Advance reservations are advised, but not necessary, and can be made in person Fridays from 12:00 PM-3:30 PM or during market hours.

CONTACT: Valentine Reyes, Puget Park Swap-O-Rama, PO Box 91723, Bellevue WA 98009. Tel: (425) 337-1435 (market) or call Mike Lancaster at the head office (425) 455-8151. Fax: (425) 455-8165.

KENNEWICK
Cable Bridge Flea Market

DATES: Daily, except Tuesdays and Sunday mornings.

TIMES: 10:00 AM-5:00 PM, except Sunday morning.

ADMISSION: Free. Parking is free.

LOCATION: 433 E Columbia Dr. Find the cable bridge (it's hard to miss); they are below it.

DESCRIPTION: This four-year-old market may have only 6 dealers, but that's all they could stuff into a 4,000-square-foot building. According to Mary, this place is so crammed that first-time visitors stand in awe upon entering. They are especially loaded with collectibles and old jewelry; other items include lots of antiques, glassware, one dealer sells appliances, others housewares. Anyone can set up outside, there's always room. Say Hi to Mary, if you can find her among the treasures.

DEALER RATES: Outside: $10 per table, first come, first served. Inside, call first, as it is stuffed! However, Mary says she could make room for you if you wish to rent monthly. Then you would be charged by the square foot (not cubic foot).

CONTACT: Mary Scott, Cable Bridge Flea Market, 433 E Columbia Dr, Kennewick WA 99336. Tel: (509) 586-7413.

KENT
Midway Swap 'N Shop

DATES: Saturday and Sunday, year round.
TIMES: 8:00 AM-4:00 PM.
ADMISSION: $1 adults, children under 12 free. Parking is free.
LOCATION: 24050 Pacific Hwy S, 5 miles south of Sea-Tac Airport on Hwy 99.
DESCRIPTION: Opened in 1971, this large indoor/outdoor market hosts 200 dealers inside and 500 outside selling plenty of yard sale treasures, appliances, clothes, some antiques and collectibles (culled from the yard sale stuff), produce in season and new merchandise. The ratio of old to new is about 40/60 in the winter, but more old stuff comes in in the summer, bringing the ratio up considerably. There is plenty of food available from speed bars and snack bars, as well as a Polish barbecue. Handicapped-accessible restrooms are on site.

DEALER RATES: $16 per space per day, inside 9' × 9', outside 18' × 18'. Reservations are required in the summer as they get full. Pay in advance for the following weekend, or come in on Friday for that weekend to assure yourself a space.
CONTACT: Frank Wilson, Manager, Midway Swap 'N Shop, PO Box 3068, Kent WA 98032-3068. Tel: (206) 878-1990 (recording) or 878-1802.

LAKEWOOD
Starlite, Inc

DATES: Tuesday through Sunday.
TIMES: Tuesday-Friday 10:00 AM-6:00 PM inside, 8:30 AM-6:00 PM outside. Weekends 9:00 AM-6:00 PM inside, 7:30 AM-6:00 PM outside.
ADMISSION: Weekends only: $1 adults, $.75 seniors and juniors (12-15), under 12 free. Parking is free.
LOCATION: The Star-Lite Drive-In Theater, 8327 S Tacoma Way.
DESCRIPTION: This huge indoor/outdoor market hosts 50-plus dealers inside year round and 200 dealers outside in an old-fashioned flea market. Much of the merchandise is new, although there are some collectibles and other items, plenty of produce in season, and an auction every Sunday. There is a cafeteria, as well as a Polish smoothie stand. Handicapped-accessible restrooms on site.

DEALER RATES: Outside: weekdays $10 for space, weekends $13 for 10' × 20', $18 for 20' × 20' space. Inside: $200 per month full time, or $100 per month weekends only with a month-to-month agreement.

CONTACT: Star-Lite, Inc, 8327 S Tacoma Way, Lakewood WA 98499-4577. Tel: (253) 588-8090. Fax: (253) 588-8929.

PASCO
Pasco Flea Market

DATES: Every Saturday and Sunday, March through November.

TIMES: 6:00 AM-4:00 PM.

ADMISSION: $1 per carload.

LOCATION: Pasco Kahlotus Hwy. Jct of Hwy 12 and E Lewis St.

DESCRIPTION: Averages up to 300 vendors with antiques, collectibles, new and used merchandise, cars, crafts, books, clothing, new and used furniture, and lots of fresh produce. Snack bars and concessions feed the famished and there are restrooms when needed.

DEALER RATES: $7 per space, 20' × 25'. Reservations are nice, but not necessary.

CONTACT: Pasco Flea Market, PO Box 3845, Pasco WA 99302. Tel: (509) 547-5035 (market) or 547-7057 (home).

PROSSER
Prosser Harvest Festival

DATES: Friday and Saturday, the fourth full weekend of September.

TIMES: 10:00 AM-5:00 PM or later.

LOCATION: At the corner of 6th and Meade in downtown Prosser. Mostly downtown Prosser.

ADMISSION: Free. Free parking is available nearby.

DESCRIPTION: This outdoor market started in 1972 and is held in conjunction with the annual Great Prosser Balloon Rally. This is the annual Harvest Festival (formerly known as the Prosser Flea Market) that includes the entire town of Prosser. There are sidewalk sales, farmers' market stands and vendors everywhere. It currently attracts 30-45 outside dealers selling a variety of antiques and collectibles, arts and crafts, fresh herbs, new merchandise, and loads of freshly harvested produce. Food is available on the premises. There is entertainment for the children. The balloons go up early Saturday and Sunday morning and Saturday night they light the balloons up in a spectacular "night glow" display.

DEALER RATES: $15 per 10' × 10' space for the whole shebang. Reservations are required.

CONTACT: Prosser Chamber of Commerce Harvest Festival Chairman, 1230 Bennett Ave, Prosser WA 99350. Tel: (509) 786-3177 or 1-800-408-1517.

SEATTLE
Fremont Sunday Outdoor Flea Market

DATES: Sundays, in the summer.

TIMES: 10:00 AM-5:00 PM.

ADMISSION: Free. Parking is free.

LOCATION: At the corner of North 34th St and Evanston Ave N one block west of the Fremont Bridge. Just 1 mile from the Space Needle.

DESCRIPTION: Established in 1990, this popular Sunday market offers 120 dealers selling antiques, collectibles, world imports, and flea market treasures. The street market is held outdoors in the summer undercover November through April in the winter, accommodating about 100 dealers inside. Handicapped-accessible restrooms are at the market, and just outside the market are plenty of restaurants and European-style pubs and bistros in this creatively eccentric neighborhood and self-proclaimed "Center of the Universe," aka Seattle's Left Bank. They were recently featured on a PBS special, "Flea Market Directory."

DEALER RATES: $35 and up for 10' × 10' space. First come, first served. To set up, come between 6:30 AM-8:30 AM. Tables and chairs can be rented for $5 per day.

CONTACT: Jon, Sunday Markets, 319 Nickerson St PMB 189, Seattle WA 98109. Tel: (206) 781-6776. Web: www.fremarket.com.

SEATTLE/BALLARD
Ballard Sunday Market

DATES: Sunday, year round.

TIMES: 10:00 AM-5:00 PM.

ADMISSION: Free. Parking is free.

LOCATION: Old Ballard Ave. Corner of 20th Ave NW and Old Ballard Ave NW, ½ mile west of the Ballard Bridge.

DESCRIPTION: In the summer of 2001, the original grew too big for its spot and split, creating this market with 100 dealers in flea stuff and crafts, and a large portion is a farmers' market. They sell antiques and collectibles, crafts, no new merchandise other than the craft goods, making it an old-fashioned European-style street market. The produce is locally grown and organic, there is local seafood, exotic cheese and lots of apples—"billions of apples." Old Ballard Avenue a historic district filled with wonderful, eclectic restaurants and shops.

DEALER RATES: $35 per day per 10 × 10' space outdoors. Reservations are not required, just show up between 6:30 AM and 8:30 AM.

CONTACT: Jon, Sunday Markets, 319 Nickerson St PMB 189, Seattle WA 98109. Tel: (206) 781-6776. Web: www.fremarket.com.

TACOMA
"America's Largest" Antique and Collectible Sale

DATES: 2002: January 26-27, June 1-2, and September 28-29.

TIMES: Saturday 8:00 AM-6:00 PM; Sunday 9:00 AM-5:00 PM.

LOCATION: Tacoma Dome, Tacoma Dome Exit off I-5.

ADMISSION: $5, kids under 12 are free, kids 12-17 are $2. Parking is handled by the Tacoma Dome and costs about $5.

DESCRIPTION: The first Tacoma Dome market was held June 1989. This market and its more than 600 booths deal only in high-quality antiques and collectibles. Food is available on the premises.

DEALER RATES: $140 per 10' × 10' booth, $280 per 10' × 20' booth, $420 per 10' × 30' booth. Reservations are mandatory.

CONTACT: Palmer/Wirfs & Associates, 4001 NE Halsey #5, Portland OR 97232. Tel: (503) 282-0877 or fax: (503) 282-2953. Email: palmerwirfs@qwest.com. Web: www.palmerwirfs.com.

OTHER FLEA MARKETS

We know or have heard about these markets, but have not personally contacted each one, as we have the markets with descriptions. If you plan to visit one of the markets listed below, *please call first* to make sure they are still open. Flea markets do come and go. While they were open when we went to press, they may not be later. We can't be responsible. *Call first!*

Blaine: King's Flea Market & General Store, 2078 Peace Portal Dr. Tel: (360) 332-8278.

Edmonds: Doce's Mall, 24111 Hwy 99. Tel: (425) 775-7212.

Ephrata: Major Flea Market, 1884 Basin St SW. Tel: (509) 754-2788.

Lynden: FMI-More Than Antiques, 444 Front St. Tel: (360) 354-7576.

Monroe: Main St Garage Sale Store, 225 W Main St. Tel: (360) 863-0833.

Shelton: Jackson's Flea Market, 14848 N US Hwy 101. Tel: (360) 426-7282.

WEST VIRGINIA

BLUEFIELD
City of Bluefield Parking Facilities Flea Market
DATES: Every Saturday, March through November.
TIMES: 6:00 AM-2:00 PM.
ADMISSION: Free. Metered parking is available.
LOCATION: On Princeton Ave, 2 miles from the junction of Rts Bus 19 and 460, in the heart of Bluefield.
DESCRIPTION: This indoor market began in 1981, and now draws approximately 175 dealers selling a wide range of items, including antiques and collectibles, crafts, fresh produce, and new merchandise. Shopping can begin as early as 5:30 AM as people hurry to catch the best bargains. Two snack bars serve the hungry and handicapped-accessible restrooms are nearby.
DEALER RATES: $5 per 14' × 20' space. First come, first served for 6 ramps, with first 3 ramps reserved.
CONTACT: Sharon Leffel, City of Bluefield, Parking Commission, 514 Scott St, Bluefield WV 24701. Tel: (304) 323-2498 at City Hall.

FAYETTEVILLE
Bridge Day
DATES: Third Saturday in October (by state law!).
TIMES: 9:00 AM-3:00 PM.
ADMISSION: This may change, as they are planning a festival to coincide with Bridge Day. Parking along roadway and in Fayetteville.
LOCATION: New River Gorge Bridge, US 19 between Fayetteville and Lansing.
DESCRIPTION: Remember the TV ad where a "Jimmy" car was shoved over the side of a bridge attached to a bungee cord? This is the bridge; the longest single-arch bridge in the world, the second highest in the United States at 876 feet. Bridge Day is the celebration of the building of this bridge. One day a year, since 1980, the police close off the northbound lanes of this four-lane bridge and all traffic is narrowed down to the two remaining lanes. Tourists come from all over to watch the goings-on. Last year 42 vendors set up along the north end of the 3,030-foot-long bridge and the rest (total averages 200 vendors) on the south end, selling or performing West Virginia crafts, food, produce, tourism, gospel singing—whatever! Over 100,000 people invade the bridge on foot to participate. Parachutists fling themselves off the bridge trying to land on the "landing pad." Some don't make it onto the dry parts and have to be fished out of the

water. The dealers must meet and get organized starting at 6:30 AM and then line up in their assigned order of booth number. At the appointed moment, they charge the bridge to their space, set up and sell like mad until 3:00 PM, when the state police come by to tell them it's time to pack up. They must be off the bridge by 4:00 PM, otherwise they will be run over.

This event will coincide with Taste of Bridge Day, and a festival after the market with all sorts of music and events planned around it.

DEALER RATES: Out-of-state dealer rates: $110 before August 1, $200 for a 25' space after August 1, $150 for WV residents. Reservations are mandatory.

CONTACT: Executive Director, Bridge Day, 310 Oyler Ave, Oak Hill WV 25901. Tel: 1-800-927-0263. Fax: (304) 465-5618. Email: fayette@citynet.net. Web: www.fayettecounty.com (look under Links) or www.newrivercvb.com/bridge.cfm.

Market Tales

A couple married on the bridge during one Bridge Day, then "took the plunge," parachuting down the gorge. That year, they had about 210,000 visitors!

Ace Whitewater runs rafting trips with a special on Bridge Day. They stop under the bridge, serve a gourmet meal and watch, from safe river banks, the shenanigans of parachutists and bungee jumpers—plunging into space.

HARPERS FERRY
Harpers Ferry Flea Market

DATES: Saturday and Sunday, plus Memorial Day and Labor Day, from March to December.

TIMES: Dawn to dusk.

ADMISSION: Free. Parking is free.

LOCATION: On Dual Hwy Rt 340 at Bloomery Rd, about 1 mile from Harpers Ferry Historical Park. Only 60 miles from Washington DC and Baltimore.

DESCRIPTION: Started in 1983, this market hosts an average of 200-plus dealers selling collectibles, antiques, crafts, yard sale treasures, a veritable variety of goodies. This is definitely a family market! Burgers, chicken, fries, ice cream, and hot dogs as well as breakfast are sold at the various snack bars. Visitors come from all over the East Coast but mainly from Baltimore and Washington DC. Harpers Ferry is located where the

Potomac and Shenandoah Rivers converge, where John Brown led his famous raid on the Harpers Ferry Arsenal, with plenty of interesting outdoor activities (hiking, biking, etc.) as well as a National Park, the C&O Canal and a historical museum. It is truly a beautiful area to visit.

DEALER RATES: $11 per day per 20' × 24' space with a table. Reservations are not required. First come, first served. A limited number of pavilion spaces are also available.

CONTACT: Harpers Ferry Flea Market, 904 Oregon Trail, Harpers Ferry WV 25425. Tel: Ron at (304) 725-4141 or Dan (304) 725-0092. Email: info@harpersferryfleamkt.com. Web: www.harpersferryfleamkt.com.

Rare Treasure Found

One of their market vendors purchased a carton full of yard sale items, costume jewelry and household goods from someone cleaning out their house. The deal was so good, the vendor never bothered to look at his finds, he just forked over the cash.

Plowing through the goodies, there in one of the jewelry boxes was a *huge* ring. Upon inspection, the name on the side of the ring was "Dean." It was the 1983 Super Bowl Ring of Vernon Dean of the Washington Redskins.

Family History

A man from Washington DC, visiting the market and looking at old pictures, found a familiar photo. Taken 35 years before, it showed the fellow as a lad fishing with his father and grandfather, both of whom had since died. He was so excited to see the picture that the kind dealer gave it to him as a gift.

Just Hanging Around

Two older couples once asked if they could rent a space. No problem. They picked a nice grassy spot with a great view, laid out their blankets and then a grand picnic. For four hours they sat and watched the market and the view while enjoying their repast. They later thanked the owners for giving them such a lovely observation area.

MARTINSBURG
I-81 Flea Market

DATES: Friday, Saturday and Sunday, weather permitting, year round.
TIMES: 8:00 AM-6:00 PM.

ADMISSION: Free. Parking is free.

LOCATION: Off Exit 20, off I-81, Spring Mills area.

DESCRIPTION: Opened in 1989, this outdoor market has up to 140 outside dealers selling antiques, collectibles, crafts and new merchandise. Their building, housing the inside dealers and farmers' market, burned down on September 3, 1995, but the outside dealers have kept the market alive. A food wagon serves the standard snack bar fare and handicapped-accessible restrooms come in handy.

DEALER RATES: $5 Friday, $11 Saturday and Sunday per space, plus tax. Reservations would be nice, but are not necessary.

CONTACT: Betty Kline, I-81 Flea Market, 5292 Williamsport Pike, Martinsburg WV 25401. Tel: (304) 274-1313.

MILTON
Milton Flea Market

DATES: Friday, Saturday and Sunday.

TIMES: Friday 8:00 AM-4:00 PM, weekends 8:00 AM-5:00 PM.

ADMISSION: Free. Parking is free.

LOCATION: Take Exit 28 (Milton WV) off I-64, turn north to junction US 60, turn east ¼ mile. You can't miss it.

DESCRIPTION: Open since 1989, this indoor/outdoor market has 500 dealers inside and spaces for 100 outside (number of dealers depends on the weather!) selling "really old antiques," collectibles, crafts, tools, new and used clothing, musical instruments, baseball cards, books (you can trade in the ones you've read), trains, toys, comic books, fudge, woodwork, and a variety of other goods. One restaurant and two snack bars deal with the hunger not quelled by the fudge. There are handicapped-accessible restrooms on the premises. In 1993 they added roofs to the outside spaces as well as 60 new vendor spaces. The local Chamber of Commerce recommended this market and said it was one of the biggest around.

DEALER RATES: $33 and up for the weekend indoors (there is a waiting list) for a 10' × 14' space; $8 and up for 10' wide and whatever deep outside space (depends on the location of the space). First come, first served. Reservations are okay.

CONTACT: Boyd & Betty Meadows, PO Box 549, Milton WV 25541-0549. Tel: (304) 743-9862 or 743-1123.

MORGANTOWN
Blue Horizon Flea Market at the
Morgantown Auto Auction

DATES: Sunday, year round.

TIMES: 6:00 AM-1:00 PM (when people drift out).

ADMISSION: $1 per car.

LOCATION: Rt 19 north of Morgantown.

DESCRIPTION: Opened in 1989, this indoor/outdoor market houses about 400-500 dealers selling lots of "good old junk" as well as some antiques and collectibles, yard sale stuff, the occasional new merchandise, produce in season, household stuff, some live animals (rabbits), historic old newspapers, and whatever. There is a cafeteria serving breakfast, a hot dog stand, a corner meeting area especially adapted for the handicapped, as well as handicapped-accessible restrooms. In the past couple of years, they have grown from 100 dealers to over 400 covering 16 acres of land and inside a 20,000-square-foot building. Yikes!

They hold an Antique and Classic Auto Show in May and again in October. But call for dates, as these change yearly depending on other activities in town.

DEALER RATES: $7 per table inside, outside $5 per space. Reservations are needed inside (some dealers have been there for ages and reserve "their" spot). Outside is first come, first served.

CONTACT: Morgantown Auto Auction, Box 2118, Morgantown WV 26502. Tel: (304) 328-5851 or 1-800-443-7702. Fax: (304) 328-5854.

I Didn't Know That!
One of the owners of the Auto Auction found a 1948 phone book among the piles of stuff sold. It listed his then phone number as 3217. Weren't those the easy-to-remember days.

OTHER FLEA MARKETS

We know or have heard about these markets, but have not personally contacted each one, as we have the markets with descriptions. If you plan to visit one of the markets listed below, *please call first* to make sure they are still open. Flea markets do come and go. While they were open when we went to press, they may not be later. We can't be responsible. *Call first!*

Burnsville: Burnsville Flea Market, 430 Depot St. Tel: (304) 853-2400.
Chapmanville: Traders Town Flea Market, Corridor G. Tel: (304) 855-4259.
Charleston: Bill's Flea Market, 1457 Washington St W. Tel: (304) 344-4337.
Charleston: Capitol Flea Market, 24 Meadowbrook Dr. Tel: (304) 342-1626.
Elkins: Elkins Flea Market, 110 Poplar St. Tel: (304) 636-5823.
Falling Waters: I-81 Flea Market Inc, 1721 Robins Ln. Tel: (304) 274-3387.
Kermit: Corner Flea Market, Rt 52. Tel: (304) 393-3643.
Milton: Milton Flea Market, 1215 E US Rt 60. Tel: (304) 743-1123.
Moorefield: Frosty Hollow Flea Market, PO Box 4. Tel: (304) 434-2835.
Moorefield: J & K Flea Market, 222 Water Street Dr. Tel: (304) 538-3257.

Moorefield: Tony's Flea Market, 231 S Main St. Tel: (304) 538-7680.
Ripley: Fort Ripley Flea Market, 105 Miller Dr. Tel: (304) 372-3532.
Shinnston: Sunset Flea Market, Rt 19. Tel: (304) 592-0405.
Sistersville: Sistersville Flea Market, 225 Burt St. Tel: (304) 652-1766.
Yawkey: Midge's Flea Market, Rt 3. Tel: (304) 524-7639.

WISCONSIN

ADAMS
Adams Flea Market
DATES: Every Saturday and Sunday, May through October; also open Memorial Day, July 4, and Labor Day.
TIMES: 6:00 AM-4:00 PM.
ADMISSION: Free. Free parking available.
LOCATION: 556 S Main St, by the railroad tracks in Adams.
DESCRIPTION: This market has been operating since 1980 and growing each year. There are 57 permanent indoor dealers and 100 outdoors, with 15 acres of grounds on which to expand. This is a country market with plenty of trees, grass, wildflowers, birds and small animals around to awe the newcomers. There's a bit of everything here, from antiques, collectibles, and handcrafted items, to farm produce and a good mix of old and new merchandise. One dealer deals with sports cards, another is one of the largest suppliers of canopies around. For your convenience, there is a lunch wagon on the premises. A note: No dogs are allowed on the grounds; please leave them in your car if you bring them.
DEALER RATES: $7 or $10 per day for each table. There is reserved table space for the whole year, should you need it. No advance reservations are taken. No overnight camping.
CONTACT: Ms Irene Steffen, 2151 Hwy 13, Adams WI 53910. Tel/Fax: (608) 339-3079. Day of show call (608) 339-9223.

ANTIGO
Langlade County Fairgrounds Flea Market
DATES: Every Saturday, Memorial Day weekend through Labor Day weekend. Rain or shine.
TIMES: Dawn-4:00 PM.
ADMISSION: $1 per person. Free parking (200 spaces).
LOCATION: Langlade County Fairgrounds. On Hwy 45.
DESCRIPTION: This indoor/outdoor market opened in 2000 with hundreds of dealers featuring antiques, Wisconsin folk art, collectibles, bargains, close-outs and new merchandise. Food is available as well as handicapped-accessible restrooms.
DEALER RATES: $29 for a 25' × 15' space. Reservations are not required.
CONTACT: Zurko's Midwest Promotions, 211 W Green Bay St, Shawano WI 54166. Call Eileen Potasnik or Bob Zurko at (715) 526-9769. Fax: (715) 524-5675. Email: RobertZurko@aol.com. Web: www.zurkoantiquetours.com.

CALEDONIA
7 Mile Fair/Market Square

DATES: Saturday and Sunday, year round.

TIMES: Outdoors: April-October 7:00 AM-5:00 PM. Indoors year round: 9:00 AM-5:00 PM.

ADMISSION: $1.50 for adults, senior citizens $1. Children 11 and under free with an adult. Free parking.

LOCATION: 2720 W 7 Mile Rd. I-94 and 7 Mile Rd, Exit 326; 15 miles south of Milwaukee and 25 miles north of the Illinois-Wisconsin state line.

DESCRIPTION: This indoor/outdoor market began in 1961, adding a 45,000-square-foot building in 1989 and another 60,000-square-foot building in 1994. There are 600 outdoor spaces and 400 indoor spaces with dealers marketing a wide variety of merchandise, including some collectibles. The outdoor farmers' market sells fresh vegetables, fruits and flowers. Various restaurants and food concessions feed the famished. The entire market is handicapped-accessible.

DEALER RATES: Outdoor: $10 Saturday, $15 Sunday and holidays per 12' × 24' space, first come, first served. Indoors: $60-$90 per 8' × 10' booth inside per weekend, reservations required. Office hours are Monday through Friday 8:00 AM-4:00 PM.

CONTACT: Scott T Niles, 7 Mile Fair Inc, PO Box 7, Caledonia WI 53108-0007. Tel: (262) 835-2177. Fax: (262) 635-2968. Email: sevenmf@execpc.com. Web: www.7milefair.com.

CEDARBURG
Maxwell Street Days

DATES: Four shows a year. Always the last Sunday in May and July, Labor Day Monday, first Sunday in October. Rain or shine. For 2002: May 26, July 28, September 2, October 6.

TIMES: 6:00 AM to between 2:00-3:30 PM.

ADMISSION: Free. Parking $3 on the Park grounds.

LOCATION: Firemen's Park. 796 N Washington Ave. Follow the cars (or pedestrians) and if you find an empty parking space—grab it!

DESCRIPTION: This is an all-volunteer non-paid fire-department-run market and the main fundraiser for the Cedarburg Fire Department. (The American Legion gets the parking money as their fundraiser.) Opened in the 1960s, it is one of the largest markets in the Midwest. There are over 900 spaces for dealers. Representative of what is sold includes: lots of antiques and collectibles, junk, flea market goodies, fresh produce, plants, garage sales, a sign-maker, a construction company selling gazebos, and quality crafters, sports stuff, and fine artists. No animals, firearms or fireworks allowed. They are encouraging mostly antiques, collectibles, and used items rather than new. Some spaces have been property settlements in divorce cases! The firemen and firewomen handle all the food concessions, including specialties like bratwurst, sauerkraut, pizza (okay, this is the local Booster Club's effort), health food, ice cream, a pancake breakfast, and the usual fare.

DEALER RATES: $40 and up per space per event. There is a discounted rate for the season. Reservations are absolutely necessary. Call the number and follow instructions on the tape message.

CONTACT: Cedarburg Maxwell Street Days, PO Box 344, Cedarburg WI 53012-0344. Tel: (262) 377-8412. Email: maxstday@execpc.com. Web: www.cedarburgfiredept.com.

ELKHORN
Antique Flea Market

DATES: 2002: May 19, June 30, August 11, September 29.

TIMES: 7:00 AM to whenever.

ADMISSION: $3 per adult, children free. Parking is free.

LOCATION: Walworth County Fairgrounds, Hwy 11 E.

DESCRIPTION: Started in 1982, this indoor/outdoor market hosts 600-plus dealers selling almost entirely old stuff. The requirement is pre-1970. Ladies, here's your chance to unload your hot pants and poodle skirts. Plenty of garage sale goodies and attic clean-outs show up here, making it a good place to raid. There is plenty of good food, from turkey legs and buffalo burgers to cream puffs and cones. Handicapped-accessible restrooms are available when the need strikes.

DEALER RATES: $50 per outside space, $75 per inside space, sizes vary. Reservations are a darned good idea.

CONTACT: Nona, NL Promotions LLC, PO Box 544, Elkhorn WI 53121-0544. Tel: (262) 723-5651.

GRAYSLAKE
Grayslake Market

DATES: The second weekend, monthly: 2002: January 12-13, February 9-10, March 9-10, April 13-14, May 11-12, June 8-9, July 13-14, August 10-11, September 7-8, October 12-13, November 9-10, and December 7-8.

TIMES: Saturday: 11:00 AM- 4:00 PM, early buyer 9:00 AM-11:00 AM. Sunday: 7:00 AM-3:00 PM.

ADMISSION: Saturday: $4 per person, early buyer $15. Sunday: $4 per person. Free parking.

LOCATION: Lake County Fairgrounds, 4 miles W of Illinois Tollway, I-94 at the corner of Rt 120, (Belvedere Rd) and Rt 45.

DESCRIPTION: This huge indoor/outdoor market sells only antiques and collectibles by the 1,000s. Under new management since 2001, their dealers sell pottery, furniture, jewelry, art glass, primitives, old toys, linens, advertising, post cards—the list is endless. Over 200 dealers market their wares indoors, and hundreds do so outside. There is plenty of food available, and handicapped-accessible restrooms when needed.

DEALER RATES: Indoors: $100 for both days. Outdoors: both days $100, Sunday only $75 per space. Reservations are required for inside space only.

CONTACT: Zurko's Midwest Promotions, 211 W Green Bay St, Shawano WI 54166. Call Eileen Potasnik or Bob Zurko at (715) 526-9769. Fax: (715) 524-5675. Email: RobertZurko@aol.com. Web: www.zurkoantiquetours.com.

HATFIELD
Giant Flea Market and Crafts at Thunderbird Village

DATES: Memorial weekend, July 4 weekend, the second weekend in August, and Labor Day weekend. The holiday weekends are all three days.

TIMES: Sunup to sundown.

ADMISSION: Free. Parking is free.

LOCATION: N9517 Thunderbird Ln. Thunderbird Village behind the Museum in downtown Hatfield. Just 12 miles NE of Black River Falls on County Trunk E or 6 miles SE of Merrillan on County Trunk K.

DESCRIPTION: For more than 30 years the Thunderbird Museum has held this market for approximately 180 dealers on the grounds of their museum. Amid towering pines, shoppers can browse through loads of antiques, collectibles, crafts, in-season produce, garage sale goodies and some new merchandise. The Thunderbird Eatery, Brenda's Fry Bread and several other food concessions satisfy the hunger pangs. Restrooms add to the amenities. This market is in a summer resort area next to Lake Arbutus with plenty of camping, restaurants and an Indian casino nearby.

DEALER RATES: $40 per 3-day event with approximately 20' frontage. There are trees on most lots. Reservations are necessary.

CONTACT: Jerry Miller, Thunderbird Museum, 7621 Hwy 13N, Pittsville WI 54466. Tel: summer (715) 676-2838.

HAYWARD
Hayward Fame Flea Market

DATES: Every Tuesday and Wednesday during June, July and August. They have four special events: Memorial and Labor Day weekends, Log Rolling weekend; and the weekend of July 4 and July 4 itself. Call for dates.

TIMES: 7:30 AM-4:00 PM.

ADMISSION: Free admission and free parking.

LOCATION: Junction of Hwy 27 S and Hwy B.

DESCRIPTION: This outdoor flea market, started in 1978, is located across from the National Fishing Hall of Fame. It attracts between 70 and 80 dealers in the summer who sell antiques, collectibles, crafts, and new and used merchandise. A world log rolling contest is held two blocks down the street from this market. Food is available and there are handicapped-accessible restrooms.

DEALER RATES: $9 per 12' × 25' booth. Reservations are suggested.

CONTACT: Jan Thiry, 10556 N Sunnyside Ave, Hayward WI 54843. Tel: (715) 634-4794.

KENOSHA
Kenosha Flea Market

DATES: Friday, Saturday and Sunday, year round.

TIMES: Friday 10:00 AM-5:00 PM; Saturday and Sunday 9:00 AM-5:00 PM.

ADMISSION: Free. Parking is also free.

LOCATION: 5535 22nd Ave.

DESCRIPTION: Started in 1985, this small, but solid, "calm old-fashioned" indoor flea market has 40 vendors selling some antiques, collectibles, handmade decorated dolls and clothing, fresh produce, new appliances, more new merchandise, jewelry, household goods, electronics, junk, and more. The variety of items changes as dealers leave and are replaced with different dealers and merchandise. Restrooms are available upstairs.

DEALER RATES: $20 and up depending on booth, location and size. Reservations are required, as they are currently full.

CONTACT: Beth or Don Goll, Kenosha Flea Market, 5535 22nd Ave, Kenosha WI 53140. Tel: (262) 658-3532.

LADYSMITH
Van Wey's Community Auction and Flea Market

DATES: April 20-something through last weekend in October, plus two-day holiday markets. Now held on either Saturday or Sunday, two or three times a month. Do call or write for the dates.

TIMES: 6:30 AM-3:00 PM.

ADMISSION: Free. $.75 per vehicle parking.

LOCATION: On Hwy 8, 4½ miles west of Ladysmith.

DESCRIPTION: Now run by the third generation of the same family, this outdoor market began as a small community consignment auction on April 20, 1926, and had operated until 1996 on the fifth and twentieth of summer months, as these are the farmers' paydays from the local creamery. Now the market is held on weekends. The flea market originally developed beside the auction and now has grown to attract nearly 200 dealers at peak season, along with hundreds of shoppers from all over the country. As far as the range of items available, the managers have commented that "if you don't find it here you don't need it." Aside from the standard flea market fare, antiques, collectibles, autos, farm machinery, clothing, and fresh farm products are available, along with miscellaneous and new merchandise. Livestock is sold as well: poultry, rabbits, goats, pot belly pigs are among the offerings. Therefore, no dogs or cats are allowed. An auction starts at 10:00 AM on market days. A lunch stand and restrooms are available.

DEALER RATES: $9-$11 per 14' × 20' space. Reservations are not required.

CONTACT: Mark and Judy Van Wey, W10139 Van Wey Ln, Ladysmith WI 54848. Tel: (715) 532-6044. Send a self-addressed stamped envelope for a schedule card of dates. Email: van-weyauction@jrec.com.

MILWAUKEE
Rummage-O-Rama

DATES: The schedule generally follows these weekends depending on holidays: January 1st weekend, February 1st and 3rd, March 2nd, April 2nd, October 1st, November 3rd, December 1st and 3rd. Please call first! For 2002: January 5-6, February 2-3, 16-17, March 9-10, April 13-14, October 5-6, November 2-3, December 7-8, 21-22.

TIMES: 10:00 AM-5:00 PM.

ADMISSION: $2; seniors $1.75; children 12-16 $.50; under 12 is free. Parking is $3.

LOCATION: Wisconsin State Fair Park in Milwaukee. Off I-94, Exit 306.

DESCRIPTION: Started in 1973, classified as the "largest indoor show in the Midwest" and rated "one of the top ten in the USA," this market has 450 dealers selling antiques, collectibles, flea market treasures, new clothes, rummage goods, crafts, oak furniture, reproduction furniture, new merchandise and a bit of everything, including a kitchen sink. The dealers must stand behind their products, with a refund or replacement for new goods sold. This is such a family market/local affair that events are planned around these market dates, including weddings! Early birds come and line up their purses and bags to hold their places in line while they go chat and catch up on local gossip. An excellent biergarten restaurant serves luscious meals, including sauerkraut and sausages, and there are booths selling homemade sausages and cheeses and low-cholesterol cookies. *Candid Camera* made an appearance here in September 1992 for one of their shows.

DEALER RATES: $75-$90 for a 10' × 10' space per weekend. Additional rental fee for table and chairs. Reservations are required.

CONTACT: Rummage-O-Rama, PO Box 510619, New Berlin WI 53151-061969. Tel: (262) 521-2111. Email: rummagegal@mindspring.com.

OCONTO
Copperfest 2002 11th Annual Flea Market

DATES: The second Saturday and Sunday in June.

TIMES: 8:00 AM-4:00 PM, or exhaustion, whichever comes last.

ADMISSION: Free. Parking is free.

LOCATION: Copperfest Grounds. Watch for the signs. Oconto is 30 miles
north of Green Bay.

DESCRIPTION: This market of about 50 dealers is part of the annual
Copperfest celebrated by the entire town of Oconto. It consists of a parade, flea market, and the grand festival, which runs from late Thursday
through Sunday evening. The town is on Green Bay on the shores of
Lake Michigan. Over 12,000 people view the parade through downtown
Oconto. There's a craft show, Wisconsin State Lumberjack Contest, a
truck-pull, music, and other events as part of this festival. Dealers sell
handmade goods, antiques, collectibles, and garage sale stuff. There is
plenty of food and handicapped-accessible restrooms when needed.

DEALER RATES: From $25 for one day, $40 for two days, for a 20' × 20'
space. Reservations are required. The rates and sizes of spaces may be
changed by market time, so call for correct information.

CONTACT: Sharon Hickey, Copperfest, 3219 Airport Rd, Oconto WI
54153. Tel: (920) 835-3662.

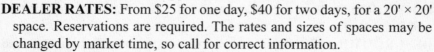

SHAWANO
Shawano County Fairgrounds Flea Market

DATES: Every Sunday, April through October, except Labor Day weekend (when they hold their Antigo market).

TIMES: Dawn-4:00 PM.

ADMISSION: $1 per person Sunday. Free parking (200 spaces).

LOCATION: Shawano County Fairgrounds. On Hwy 29, 30-minute drive west of Green Bay.

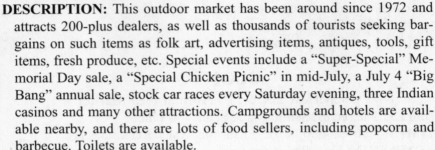

DESCRIPTION: This outdoor market has been around since 1972 and attracts 200-plus dealers, as well as thousands of tourists seeking bargains on such items as folk art, advertising items, antiques, tools, gift items, fresh produce, etc. Special events include a "Super-Special" Memorial Day sale, a "Special Chicken Picnic" in mid-July, a July 4 "Big Bang" annual sale, stock car races every Saturday evening, three Indian casinos and many other attractions. Campgrounds and hotels are available nearby, and there are lots of food sellers, including popcorn and barbecue. Toilets are available.

DEALER RATES: $29 per 20' × 15' space. Reservations are not required.

CONTACT: Zurko's Midwest Promotions, 211 W Green Bay St, Shawano WI 54166. Call Eileen Potasnik or Bob Zurko at (715) 526-9769. Fax: (715) 524-5675. Email: RobertZurko@aol.com. Web: www.zurkoantiquetours.com.

ST. CROIX FALLS
Pea Pickin' Flea Mart

DATES: Saturday and Sunday and holidays, starting the third weekend in April through the third weekend in October.

TIMES: 6:00 AM-5:00 PM.

ADMISSION: Free. Free parking is provided.

LOCATION: On Hwy 8, 5 miles east of St. Croix Falls near the junction of Rt 35 N.

DESCRIPTION: This indoor/outdoor market has been in business since 1968 selling a "good variety of things," including new and used merchandise, fresh produce, and "sophisticated junque." Dealers and shoppers come from all over, and camping space is provided for those who want to come on Friday afternoon and spend the night. There is plenty of food available, including a taco stand and snack bar with mini-doughnuts and popcorn. Toilet facilities are available.

DEALER RATES: $9 per day. Reservations are suggested.

CONTACT: Steve and Judy Hansen, Pea Pickin' Flea Mart, 1938 Little Blake Ln, Luck WI 54853. Tel: (715) 857-5479 (home) or 483-9460 (market).

Sad, but True

It was here that an 87-year-old dealer, a longtime fixture at the market, drove in to set up. Instead of his usual routine of driving directly to his spot, he drove around and through the market, everywhere, slowly. When he got to his spot, he stepped out of his car—and died.

OTHER FLEA MARKETS

We know or have heard about these markets, but have not personally contacted each one, as we have the markets with descriptions. If you plan to visit one of the markets listed below, *please call first* to make sure they are still open. Flea markets do come and go. While they were open when we went to press, they may not be later. We can't be responsible. *Call first!*

Janesville: Janesville Flea Market, 3030 S Cty Rd G. Tel: (608) 755-9830.
Shawano: Highway 47-55 Flea Market, W7563 Strauss Rd. Tel: (715) 524-8655.
Wild Rose: Wild Rose Flea Market & Craft, 350 Cty Rd G and H. Tel: (920) 622-4949.

WYOMING

CASPER
Antique Show and Sale
DATES: The first full weekend in June and October.
TIMES: Saturday 10:00 AM-5:00 PM; Sunday 10:00 AM-4:00 PM.
ADMISSION: $1.25 per person. Free parking is provided.
LOCATION: Central Wyoming Fairgrounds. Take CY Ave (Hwy 220) from downtown Casper.
DESCRIPTION: This indoor show began in 1971 and currently draws a select 40 dealers selling only antiques and collectibles. Run by a non-profit organization, The Casper Antique and Collectors Club, which donates to Wyoming museums and other charities, this show is said to be among the largest in the state. Food is served on the grounds.
DEALER RATES: $25 per 8' table, 4-table minimum. Reservations are required. There is a long waiting list.
CONTACT: Casper Antique and Collectors Club Inc, c/o Mr Bruce Smith, 1625 S Kenwood, Casper WY 82601-4049. Tel: (307) 234-6663.

Casper Flea Market
DATES: March, August and November. Call for dates.
TIMES: Saturday 10:00 AM-5:00 PM; Sunday 10:00 AM-4:00 PM.
ADMISSION: $.50. Parking is free.
LOCATION: Central Wyoming Fairgrounds. Take CY Ave (Hwy 220) from downtown Casper.
DESCRIPTION: Started in 1974, this indoor flea market is sponsored by the Casper Antique and Collectors Club, a non-profit organization. Forty-five dealers gather to trade in antiques, collectibles and miscellaneous items.
DEALER RATES: $20 per 8' table. Reservations are required.
CONTACT: Casper Antique and Collectors Club Inc, c/o Mr Bruce Smith, 1625 S Kenwood, Casper WY 82601-4049. Tel: (307) 234-6663.

CHEYENNE
Avenues Antiques and Collectibles
DATES: Daily.
TIMES: Monday through Saturday 10:00 AM-5:00 PM, Sunday 12:00 PM-5:00 PM.
ADMISSION: Free. Parking is free.
LOCATION: 315½ E 7th Ave, at Evans Ave.

DESCRIPTION: This indoor market opened in 1993 with 50 dealers selling high-quality antiques, collectibles, coins, books, clothing, used merchandise, furniture, Western memorabilia, "a great collection of Victorian glassware and estate jewelry," and furniture.

DEALER RATES: $1.49 per square foot, plus commission. Call to check on vacancies.

CONTACT: Avenues Antiques and Collectibles, 315½ E 7 Ave, Cheyenne WY 82001. Tel: (307) 635-5600.

Lincolnway Flea Market

DATES: Daily, except for holidays: July 4, Labor Day, Thanksgiving, Christmas and New Year's.

TIMES: 10:00 AM-8:00 PM.

ADMISSION: Free. Parking is free.

LOCATION: 2825 E Lincolnway. On US 30, or take Lincolnway Exit off I-80; turn north to Lincolnway, then west on Lincolnway to 2825.

DESCRIPTION: Opened in 1997, this climate-controlled over-21,000-square-foot indoor market of 150 dealers sells antiques, collectibles, coins, garage sale goodies, and furniture. No food, unless you are a termite, then they don't want you. There are handicapped-accessible restrooms on site.

DEALER RATES: Monthly rates from $1.60 per square foot and 9% commission. Call for rates and vacancies.

CONTACT: John Mason, Lincolnway Flea Market, 2825 E Lincolnway, Cheyenne WY 82001. Tel: (307) 634-1503. Fax: (307) 634-2615. Email: lincolnwayflea@aol.com.

JACKSON HOLE
Mangy Moose Antique Show and Sale

DATES: Annually, the second weekend in July. Rain or shine. Call for specific dates. They have added another show, Arts and Antiques at the Mangy Moose, the third weekend in August.

TIMES: 9:00 AM-6:00 PM.

ADMISSION: Free. Free parking is available.

LOCATION: In Teton Village, behind the Mangy Moose Restaurant and the Hostel at the base of the gondola to the Tetons.

DESCRIPTION: This outdoor show opened in 1985 and is considered Wyoming's biggest and best antique show. It currently accommodates approximately 95 dealers and is growing fast. This show specializes in fine antiques; dealers display furniture, carpets, jewelry, dolls, accessories, china, silver, Indian items, vintage clothes, books, and much more.

All of this is sponsored by the Mangy Moose Restaurant. Food is served on the premises. Jackson Hole, in the heart of the Tetons, offers gondola rides to the top, horseback riding, white-water trips, and "the greatest golf in the U.S."

DEALER RATES: $195 per 10' × 12' space for all three days. Reservations are required. Bring your own canopy, tables and chairs. If you wish to sell here, and come from far away, the Hostel comes highly recommended.

CONTACT: Jan Perkins or Jeffrey, 2902 Breneman St, Boise ID 83703. Tel: (208) 345-0755 or 368-9759. Day of show call (307) 733-4913 at the Hostel; leave a message.

CANADA
AND
INTERNATIONAL
MARKETS

CANADA

BRITISH COLUMBIA
SURREY
HiWay 10 Flea Market
DATES: Saturday and Sunday.
TIMES: 9:00 AM-5:00 PM.
ADMISSION: Free. Parking is free.
LOCATION: 17790 56th Ave Hwy 10.
DESCRIPTION: This market of 300 tables has dealers selling everything including antiques, collectibles, crafts, coins, cards, toys, clothing and new merchandise.
CONTACT: Larry Williams, HiWay 10 Flea Market, 17790 56 Ave Hwy 10, Surrey, British Columbia V3S 1E2. Tel and Fax: (740) 594-3808.

ONTARIO
BARRIE
The 400 Market, Inc
DATES: Saturday and Sunday.
TIMES: 9:00 AM-5:00 PM.
LOCATION: Exit 85 Innisfil Beach Road, Hwy 400.
DESCRIPTION: This market of 300 dealers, as per others, sells just about everything, including antiques, collectibles and new merchandise.
CONTACT: The 400 Market, PO Box 1312, Barre, Ontario, L4M 4V3. Tel: (705) 436-1010.

BROCKVILLE
The Market
DATES: Saturday and Sunday.
TIMES: 9:00 AM-4:00 PM.
ADMISSION: Free. Parking is free.
LOCATION: 175 King St W.
DESCRIPTION: This market of 10 vendors specializes in antique and collectibles. It is obviously a tiny but thriving local market. If you stop by, find and say "Hi" to Anna!
DEALER RATES: $25 per space.

Traders Post Flea Market

DATES: Saturday and Sunday.

TIMES: 9:00 AM-4:00 PM.

ADMISSION: Free. Parking is free.

LOCATION: 14 Courthouse Ave.

DESCRIPTION: This market of 10 vendors specializes in antiques and collectibles. Another thriving local market—Anna comes here, too.

DEALER RATES: $25 per space.

CONTACT: Traders Post Flea Market, 14 Courthouse Ave, Brockville, Ontario, Canada. Tel: (613) 342-0493.

Only the Lonely

Occasionally, a local gent feels lonely. His cure? He puts out a sign reading, "John's Flea Market." Within minutes, someone is bound to stop to chat. If you see the sign—stop and say "Hi!"

COURTICE
Courtice Flea Market

DATES: Saturday and Sunday.

LOCATION: Exit Hwy 401 at Courtice Rd (4 km east of Oshawa). Go north and follow the signs.

DESCRIPTION: A large country market in six buildings on 12 acres with a farmers' market and another for crafts.

CONTACT: Courtice Flea Market, 1696 Bloor St, Courtice, Ontario L1E2N1. Tel: (905) 436-1024. Fax: (905) 430-3270 Email: randih@istar.ca.

MISSISSAUGA
Fantastic Flea Market

DATES: Saturday and Sunday.

TIMES: 10:00 AM-5:00 PM.

ADMISSION: Free on Saturday, $.25 on Sunday (the money goes to local charity). Parking is free.

LOCATION: Dixie Mall, QEW and Dixie Rd.

DESCRIPTION: This market of 100 dealers is strictly a flea market in every sense of the word. They sell plenty of old goodies as well as new merchandise. Two small food concessions feed the famished. Its sister market is in North York.

CONTACT: Fantastic Flea Market, 1250 S Service Rd, Mississauga, Ontario O5E 1V4, Canada. Tel: (905) 274-9403. Email: fleaweb@idirect.com. Web: www.fantasticfleamarket.com.

NORTH YORK
Fantastic Flea Market

DATES: Saturday and Sunday for the flea market.

TIMES: 10:00 AM-6:00 PM for the flea market, every day but Monday 10:00 AM-6:00 PM as a regular retail outlet.

ADMISSION: Free. Parking is free.

LOCATION: 2375 Steels Ave W.

DESCRIPTION: On weekends, they open up folding doors and turn the place into a huge flea market with up to 150 dealers selling just about everything you can imagine. During the week they are the Steeles West Marketplace.

CONTACT: Fantastic Flea Market, 2375 Steeles Ave W, North York, Ontario M3J 3A8. Tel: (416) 650-1090. Email: fleaweb@idirect.com. Web: www.fantasticfleamarket.com.

STOUFFVILLE
Stouffville Country Flea Market

DATES: Saturday and Sunday.

TIMES: Saturday 8:00 AM-4:00 PM, Sunday 9:00 AM-4:00 PM.

ADMISSION: Free. Parking is free.

LOCATION: 12555 Tenth Line North (Hwy 47 N).

DESCRIPTION: Opened in 1952 as the Stouffville Stockyard selling livestock, this is a flea market in every sense of the word, with 300 dealers inside and out selling loads of stuff. In 1996 they opened a new building housing a food court and food vendors including a butcher, baker, and deli, selling fresh fruit and other goodies. I'm told the lasagna is superb.

DEALER RATES: From $20 per day for garage sale stuff, regular vendors $40 per 20' × 10' space; inside from $60 per space. Reservations are required for inside, outside is first come, first served.

CONTACT: Stouffville Country Flea Market, PO Box 399, Stouffville, Ontario L4A 7Z6. Tel: (905) 640-3813. Fax: (905) 640-3873. E-mail: info@stouffvillemarket.com. Web: www.stouffvillemarket.com.

TORONTO
Dr Flea's Hwy 27 and Albion Flea Market

DATES: Saturday and Sunday.

TIMES: 10:00 AM-5:00 PM.

ADMISSION: Free. Parking is free.

LOCATION: From Toronto take Hwy 401 to Dixon Rd. Exit (near the airport) to Hwy 27 N. From there it is about a 10-15-minute drive. It would be hard to miss with its 35-foot-tall flea on the top of the building.

DESCRIPTION: This market of 400 vendors sells everything including antiques, collectibles and new merchandise. There is a farmers' market outside. They average 15-20,000 visitors per weekend.

DEALER RATES: $410 per month and up.

CONTACT: Dr Flea's Hwy 27 & Albion Flea Market, 8 Westmore Dr, Rexdale, Toronto, Ontario. Tel: (416) 745-FLEA (3532). Fax: (416) 745-7193. Email: drflea@idirect.com. Web: www.dr-fleas.com.

QUÉBEC
BROMONT
Marché aux Puces de Bromont

DATES: First Sunday of May through second Sunday of November.

TIMES: 9:00 AM-5:00 PM.

ADMISSION: Free. Parking is free.

LOCATION: Motorway 10 at Bromont.

DESCRIPTION: This indoor market's 350 dealers sell crafts, produce, garage sale finds, furniture, coins, stamps, cards, and new merchandise.

CONTACT: Marché Aux Puces Bromont 5 Étoiles, 16 LaFontaine, Brmt, QC J2L 2S9. Tel: (450) 534-0440.

MONTREAL
Super Mercado

DATES: Thursday through Sunday, year round.

TIMES: 9:00 AM-5:00 PM.

ADMISSION: Free.

LOCATION: Brossard, just south of Montreal.

DESCRIPTION: This is the "hot" place to shop around Montreal— which means it is very crowded. While they don't sell antiques, per se, they do sell just about anything else.

CONTACT: Super Mercado Inc, 3710 Chambly, Longueuil, QC J4L 1N8 Tel: (514) 875-5500.

SAINT EUSTACHE
Marché aux Puces de Saint Eustache

DATES: Thursday through Sunday.

TIMES: 9:00 AM-5:00 PM.

ADMISSION: Free. Parking is free.

LOCATION: 640 W. Just north of Montreal, 3 miles before St Eustache.

DESCRIPTION: This year-round indoor/outdoor market's dealers sell antiques, collectibles, crafts, produce, garage sale finds, furniture, new merchandise, stamps, coins, and cards among other things. This is one of the biggest markets around and apparently crammed full of customers on Sundays. So beat the crowd and go another day.

CONTACT: Marché aux Puces du Ciné-Parc St-Eustache, 400 Hector Lanthier, Saint-Eustache, QC J7P 4C1. Phone: (450) 472-6660 or (800) 471-6660 or (514) 879-1707.

OTHER CANADIAN FLEA MARKETS

ALBERTA

Avenue Flea Market The, 8930 118 Ave NW, Edmonton, AB T5B 0T6. Tel: (780) 479-8640.

Crossroads Market, 1235 26 Av SE, Calgary, AB T2G 1R7. Tel: (403) 291-5208.

Flea Market-Dawnwood, 160 22 St, Fort Macleod, AB T0L 0Z0. Tel: (403) 553-2848.

Mini Crafts & Flea Market, 6315 Horn St, Red Deer, AB T4N 6H5. Tel: (403) 343-7998.

Purple House Antiques, 4801 1 St, Claresholm, AB T0L 0T0. Tel: (403) 625-4441.

Redwater Flee Market, 8928 152A Ave NW, Edmonton, AB T5E 5W1. Tel: (780) 942-3169.

Southside Crafts & Flea Market, 8170 50 St NW, Edmonton, AB T6B 1E6. Tel: (780) 469-7354.

Super Flea Market, 12011 111 Ave NW, Edmonton, AB T5G 0E7. Tel: (780) 413-8998.

Yellowhead Flea Market, 12112 67 St NW, Edmonton, AB T5B 1M7. Tel: (780) 477-7133.

BRITISH COLUMBIA

Cloverdale Flea Market, Aldergrove, BC V4W 1A3. Tel: (604) 856-1100.

Flea Dome, 2502 41 St, Vernon, BC V1T 6J9. Tel: (250) 558-3030.

Langley Flea Market, 20409 Imperial Ave, Langley, BC V3A 7S4. Tel: (604) 532-1324.

Liquidators Flea Market, 4050 Knight St, Vancouver, BC V5N 3M2. Tel: (604) 873-9050.

Riverside Flea Market, 290 Riverside Dr, Penticton, BC V2A 5Y5. Tel: (250) 490-2088.

Trading Post, 1034 Halston Ave, Kamloops, BC V2B 7L3. Tel: (250) 376-1888.

Trails Flea Market, 804 Rossland Ave, Trail, BC V1R 3N3. Tel: (250) 364-0200.

Vancouver Flea Market, 703 Terminal Ave, Vancouver, BC V6A 2M2. Tel: (604) 685-0666.

MANITOBA

Thrifty Tim's Antique Flea Market, Bonner & Hwy 59, Winnipeg, MB R2C 0A1. Tel: (204) 668-4325.

Winnipeg Flea Market Co-op Inc, 100 Mandalay Dr, Winnipeg, MB R2P 1V8. Tel: (204) 633-6658.

NEW BRUNSWICK

Flea Market, 9 Ch Cote, NB E3Y 2K4. Tel: (506) 473-6002.

Flea Market, 276 Av Marie, Bathurst, NB. Tel: (506) 546-3601.

Marché Aux Puces, 276 Av Marie, Bathurst, NB. Tel: (506) 546-3601.

Marche Aux Puces, 10 Ferry, Edmundston, NB E3V 1K4. Tel: (506) 735-6625.

Marche Idéal Market, 896 Bd des Acadiens, Bertrand, NB E1W 1A3. Tel: (506) 727-5522.

Meubles Chez Rita, 2800 Principale, Tracadie-Sheila, NB E1X 1A1. Tel: (506) 394-2589.

Rhoda's Market, 38 Coburg, Saint John, NB E2L 3J5. Tel: (506) 658-1232.

NOVA SCOTIA

Mont's Bill Flea Market, Halifax, Dartmouth, NS B3H 2P6. Tel: (902) 463-1406.

Station Street Flea Market, 1 Cresent Av, Amherst, NS B4H 4P7. Tel: (902) 667-2899.

ONTARIO

.747 Flea Market, 73 Parkhurst Sq, Brampton, ON L6T 5J2. Tel: (905) 790-3113.

Bayview Flea Market, 405 Dundas E, Belleville, ON K8N 1E7. Tel: (613) 962-9546.

Bentley Antiques & Collectibles Flea Market, 7 Cleopatra Dr, Nepean, ON K2G 3M9. Tel: (613) 225-5613.

Boa Valley Flea Market, Lakefield, ON. Tel: (705) 652-6660.

Bonville Flea Market, Hwy 138, ON. Tel: (613) 937-3532.

Calabogie Mall & Flea Market, Calabogie, ON. Tel: (613) 752-2468.

Cash Flea Market, 3 Brant School Rd, Brantford, ON N3T 5L4. Tel: (519) 753-7483.

Circle M Antique Flea Market, 367 Hwy 5 W, Flamborough, ON L0R 2H0. Tel: (905) 689-6492.

Cooper's Flea Market, RR 4, Trenton, ON K8V 5P7. Tel: (613) 394-0139.

Country Flea Market, 701 Powerline, Brantford, ON. Tel: (519) 750-0847.

Cowboy Bill's Flea Market, 8665 Hwy 11, Orillia, ON L3V 6H3. Tel: (705) 325-8321.

Crossroads Flea Market, 1146 Colborne E, Brantford, ON N3T 5M1. Tel: (519) 759-8960 or (877) 278-3423 or (519) 759-8960.

Deseronto Flea Market, 240 Main, Deseronto, ON K0K 1X0. Tel: (613) 396-2819.

Easton's Flea Market, RR 5, Bancroft, ON K0L 1C0. Tel: (613) 332-1669.

Elmvale Sales Barn & Flea Market, Hwy 92, Elmvale, ON. Tel: (705) 322-1633.

Family Flea & Farm Market, RR 5, Strathroy, ON N7G 3H6. Tel: (519) 246-1309.

Fenwick Flea Market, 878 Foss, Plhm, ON L0S 1C0. Tel: (905) 892-2525.

Firefly Flea & Farmers Market, 1720 Kirkfield, Kirkfield, ON K0M 2B0. Tel: (705) 438-5412.

Flea Market, RR 5, Perth, ON K7H 3C7. Tel: (613) 264-1999.

Flea Market 1221, 1221 Front St, Hearst, ON. Tel: (705) 362-8575.

Gananoque Flea Market, 145 River, Gananoque, ON K7G 2P8. Tel: (613) 382-8148.

Gerrard Main Flea Market, 145 Main, Toronto, ON M4E 2V9. Tel: (416) 691-1776.

Gibraltar Weekend Market, 1712 Dundas, London, ON N5W 3C9. Tel: (519) 659-8725.

Grand River Flea Market, 261 Hespeler Rd, Cambridge, ON N1R 3H8. Tel: (519) 623-0540.

Haggler's Market Place, 1565 Barton E, Hamilton, ON L8H 2Y3. Tel: (905) 545-4747.

Kingston 401 Flea Market, 751 Dalton Av, Kingston, ON K7M 8N6. Tel: (613) 549-6174.

London Sales Arena Ltd, RR 2, Thorndale, ON N0M 2P0. Tel: (519) 268-3840.

Madison Avenue Flea Market, 3855 County Hwy 121, Kinmount, ON K0M 2A0. Tel: (705) 488-2043.

Market Square Flea Market, 5669 Main, Osgoode, ON K0A 2W0. Tel: (613) 826-3907.

Market Square Trade Centre, 2109 Ottawa, Windsor, ON N8Y 1R8. Tel: (519) 977-7555.

Masson Flea Market, 110 Georges, Masson Angers, QC J8M 1A2. Tel: (819) 986-3552.

McHaffie Flea Market & Auction, Hwy 31, Morrisburg, ON K0C 1X0. Tel: (613) 543-2623.

Mega City Market Square, 30 Vice Regent Bl, Toronto, ON. Tel: (416) 740-4433.

Merchants' Market, 1921 Eglinton Av E, Scarborough, ON M1L 2L6. Tel: (416) 757-5698.

Meyersburg Flea Market & Antiques, 5082 Cty Rd 30, Campbellford, ON K0L 1L0. Tel: (705) 653-3979.

Millgrove Flea Market, Millgrove, Waterdown, ON L0R 2H0. Tel: (905) 689-8051.

Napanee Flea Market, 174 Robinson, Napanee, ON K7R 2S4. Tel: (613) 354-0163.

North Bay Flea Market, 134 McIntyre W, North Bay, ON P1B 2Y6. Tel: (705) 474-2457.

North Cobalt Flea Market, Hwy 11B North Cobalt, Hlyby, ON P0J 1R0. Tel: (705) 672-5848.

North York Jang Teo Market, 15 Grantbrook, North York, ON M2R 2E6. Tel: (416) 222-3896.

Olde Country Antiques & Flea Market, 4604 Erie, Nfls, ON L2E 3N4. Tel: (905) 356-5523.

OPS Flea Market, 554 Colborne W, Lindsay, ON K9V 4R1. Tel: (705) 878-5978.

Oshawa Festival Fleamarket, 500 Howard, Oshawa, ON L1H 8K3. Tel: (905) 579-3661.

Pinery Antique Flea Market, RR 2, Grand Bend, ON N0M 1T0. Tel: (519) 238-8382.

Port Elgin Flea Market, Port Elgin Beach, ON. Tel: (519) 389-5405.

Port Perry Country Flea Market, 19100 Hwy 12, Port Perry, ON L0C 1B0. Tel: (905) 985-8424.

Prudhommes Antique Market, 3319 North Service, Vnld, ON L0R 2C0. Tel: (905) 562-5187.

Red Roof Trading Post, RR 2, Arnprior, ON K7S 3G8. Tel: (613) 623-1148.

Rockford Flea Market, RR 4, Owen Sound, ON N4K 5N6. Tel: (519) 371-8333.

Scarboro Trade Centre, 4181 Sheppard Av E, Scarborough, ON M1S 1T4. Tel: (416) 291-0684.

Smiley's Flea Market, 6559 Bank, Greely, ON K0A 1Z0. Tel: (613) 821-0224.

Smiths Falls Market & Craft Barn, 65 Cornelia E, Smiths Falls, ON K7A 4Y1. Tel: (613) 283-8448.

Snelgrove Flea Market, 12231 Hurontario, ON L0P 1M0. Tel: (905) 846-0960.

St Clair Flea Market, 404 Old Weston, Toronto, ON M6N 3B1. Tel: (416) 654-6455.

Stittsville Market, 6176 Hazeldean Rd, Stittsvl, ON K0A 3G0. Tel: (613) 836-5612.

Towne And Country Flea Market, 1675 Cty Rd 26, Brighton, ON K0K 1H0. Tel: (613) 475-4828.

Trading Junction Dixie Value Mall, ON. Tel: (905) 891-1765.

Trailsend, RR 2, Thorndale, ON N0M 2P0. Tel: (519) 268-3840.

Trans Canada Flea Market, RR 5 Hwy 17, Thunder Bay, ON P7C 5M9. Tel: (807) 939-1522.

Uncle Richard's Flea Market, 2081 Hwy 17 E, Markstay, ON P0M 2G0. Tel: (705) 694-4499.

UxPort Country Market, 19100 Hwy 12, Port Perry, ON L0C 1B0. Tel: (905) 985-8424.

Vendor's Market, 53 Parkhurst Sq, Brampton, ON L6T 5H5. Tel: (905) 792-0666.

Village Barn The, RR 2, Kent Bridge, ON N0P 1V0. Tel: (519) 674-2317.

Woodstock Farmers Market Inc, 300 Main, Woodstock, ON N4S 1T3. Tel: (519) 537-6500.

PRINCE EDWARD'S ISLAND

Albrecht's Daily Flea Market, Mount Buchanan, Eldon, PE. Tel: (902) 659-2020.

QUEBEC MARKETS

Bentley Antiques & Collectibles Flea Market, 7 Cleopatra Dr, Nepean, ON K2G 3M9. Tel: (613) 225-5613.

Finnegan's Market, 775 Main Rd, Hud, QC J0P 1J0. Tel: (450) 458-4377.

Grand Marché Aux Puces Langelier (Le), 7455 Langelier, St-Léonard, QC H1S 1V6. Tel: (514) 252-0508.

Le Marché De La Place Enr, 1191 Galt O, Sher, QC J1H 2A5. Tel: (819) 822-2389.

Marché Au Puce Super Bazar Du Québec, 1500 Av D'Estimauville, Québec, QC G1J 5B8. Tel: (418) 661-2294.

Marché Aux Puce Dolbeau-Mistassini, 75 De Quen, Dolb Mistsn, QC G8L 4R8. Tel: (418) 276-9300.

Marché aux Puces Jean-Talon de Charlesbourg, 1750 du Périgord, Chsbrg, QC G1G 5X3. Tel: (418) 623-3424.

Marché aux Puces 5 Etoiles de Carignan, QC. Tel: (514) 861-5989.

Marché aux Puces Chez Dan, 385 Soumande, Vanier, QC G1M 1H5. Tel: (418) 687-4820.

M F Puce, 3355 Monselet, Montréal-Nord, QC H1H 1Z8. Tel: (514) 327-2427.

Marché Aux Puces le Toit Bleu, 1313 Ch Barrette, St Flx de V, QC J0K 2M0. Tel: (450) 889-4806.

Marché aux Puces les Encans St-Polycarpe, 1318 Ch de l'Eglise, St Polycarpe, QC J0P 1X0. Tel: (450) 265-3393.

Marché Aux Puces Lesage Inc, 2845 Bd du Curé Labelle, Prévost, QC J0R 1T0. Tel: (450) 224-4833 .

Marché Aux Puces Papa Jos, 2286 St Hubert, Jonquière, QC G7X 5N5. Tel: (418) 547-5005.

Marché Aux Puces, 70 Racine E, Chtmi, QC G7H 1P6. Tel: (418) 543-4380.

Marché Aux Puces, 3799 St-Félix, Jonq, QC G7X 3K2. Tel: (418) 695-0353.

Marché Aux Puces, 125 Rte 342, Pt Fort, QC J0P 1N0. Tel: (450) 451-5250.

Marché Aux Puces, 430 Latreille, Cap Mad, QC G8T 3G6. Tel: (819) 691-9994.

Marché aux Puces 5 Etoiles de Carignan, 2375 Chambly, Vl Carignan, QC J3L 4N4. Tel: (450) 658-6618.

Marché aux Puces A Et L, 680 Principale E, Cksr, QC J0B 1M0. Tel: (819) 875-3819.

Marché Aux Puces A Ponik, 2013 Principale, Pohénégamook, QC G0L 1J0. Tel: (418) 859-3133.

Marché Aux Puces Agapé, 3195 Loyola, Bprt, QC G1E 2R4. Tel: (418) 660-7086.

Marché Aux Puces Alexis Le Trotteur, 2345 Alexis Le Trotteur, Jonquière, QC G7X 9H8. Tel: (418) 542-8280.

Marché Aux Puces Angus, 23 Angus N, E Ang, QC J0B 1R0. Tel: (819) 832-3370.

Marché Aux Puces Au Grenier, 68 Notre Dame S, Thetford-Mines, QC G6G 1J3. Tel: (418) 335-5930.

Marché Aux Puces Aux 1001 Aubaines Enr, 272 Lafontaine, Rivière-du-Loup, QC G5R 3A8. Tel: (418) 862-1044.

Marché aux Puces Ben & Lison, 1251 5 Av, Ville de La Baie, QC G7B 1P5. Tel: (418) 697-1908.

Marché Aux Puces Boul Métropolitain Inc, 6245 Métropolitain E, St-Léonard, QC H1P 1X7. Tel: (514) 955-8989.

Marché Aux Puces Cacouna Enr, 303 Rte 132 E, Cacouna, QC G0L 1G0. Tel: (418) 867-1227.

Marché aux Puces Carignan, 2375 Chemin Chambly, Montréal, QC H3B 2M8. Tel: (514) 861-5989.

Marché aux Puces Carignan 1997 Inc, Montréal, QC. Tel: (514) 861-5989.

Marché Aux Puces Chez Clément Enrg, 502 Rte 386 O, Landrienne, QC J9T 3A1. Tel: (819) 732-4932.

Marché Aux Puces Ciné-Parc St-Eustache, 400 Hector Lanthier, St-Eustache, QC J7P 4C1. Tel: (450) 472-6660.

Marché Aux Puces d'Amos, 1161 Rte 111 E, Amos, QC J9T 4A5. Tel: (819) 727-5858.

Marché aux Puces de Gracefield, 161-A St Joseph, Gracefield, QC J0X 1W0. Tel: (819) 463-3645.

Marché Aux Puces De L'Isle Verte, 170 Seigneur Côte, L'Isle Verte, QC G0L 1K0. Tel: (418) 898-3025.

Marché Aux Puces De La Mauricie, Shawinigan, QC. Tel: (819) 537-3454.

Marché Aux Puces De La Mauricie, 1463 Cloutier, Shaw, QC G9N 8G7. Tel: (819) 537-4898.

Marché aux Puces de la Rive-Sud, 1845 Bd de la Rive Sud, St Rom, QC G6W 5M6. Tel: (418) 839-0548.

Marché aux Puces de la Ville de Sainte Foy, 936 Av Roland Beaudin, QC. Tel: (418) 654-4070.

Marché Aux Puces Des Encans St-Chrysostome Inc, 378 Rg Notre Dame, St Jean Chrysostome, QC J0R 1R0. Tel: (450) 826-0448.

Marché Aux Puces du lac à la Tortue, 950 70 Rue, Lac à la Tortue, QC G0X 1L0. Tel: (819) 538-3368.

Marché Aux Puces G L M, A-523 Rte Principale, Ste-Anne-du-Sault, QC G0Z 1C0. Tel: (819) 367-2024.

Marché Aux Puces Harrisson Enr, 481 Boul D'Alembert, D'Alemb, QC J9X 5A3. Tel: (819) 797-1005.

Marché Aux Puces J M C Inc, 230 Notre Dame, Tring Jct, QC G0N 1X0. Tel: (418) 426-2501.

Marché Aux Puces La Place À Pédro, 320 Rg des Ecossais, Ste Brig Iber, QC J0J 1X0. Tel: (450) 293-3442.

Marché Aux Puces La Rive Nord, 2145 Roussel, Chtmi, QC G7G 1W4. Tel: (418) 693-0505.

Marché aux Puces Lachute, 25 Principale, Lachute, QC J8H 3X2. Tel: (450) 562-2939.

Marché Aux Puces Le Bargainer, 206 Notre Dame, Black Lk, QC G6H 1T2. Tel: (418) 423-5771.

Marché aux Puces le Bazar, 1124 Rte Marie Victorin, Tracy, QC J3R 1L6. Tel: (450) 743-9873.

Marché Aux Puces Les Petits Cousins Enr, 476 Racine, St Rsli, QC J0H 1X0. Tel: (450) 799-1515.

Marché Aux Puces-Marchand Général, 200 Principale, Ayl, QC J9H 6J4. Tel: (819) 684-0012.

Marché aux Puces R P, 1811 Bd des Laurentides, Vimont, QC H7M 2P7. Tel: (450) 663-9117.

Marché Aux Puces Rg St-Pierre, 1725 Rg St-Pierre, Chtmi, QC G7H 5B3. Tel: (418) 545-1705.

Marché Aux Puces Saguenay Enr, 2015 St Dominique, Jonq, QC G7X 6N8. Tel: (418) 547-7823.

Marché Aux Puces St-Julien Enr, 2336 Rg 2 E, St-Julien, QC G0N 1B0. Tel: (418) 423-7451.

Marché aux Puces St Martin Laval Inc, 1550 Bd Daniel Johnson, Chomedey, QC H7V 3V7. Tel: (450) 686-9394.

Marché Aux Puces St Pascal, 260 Varin, St Pascal, QC G0L 3Y0. Tel: (418) 492-1221.

Marché Aux Puces Ste-Jeanne-d'Arc, 653 Rte 169, Ste-Jeanne-d'Arc, QC G0W 1E0. Tel: (418) 276-6096.

Marché aux Puces Sylvain Bergeron, 4620 Av Grande Décharge, Delisle, QC G0W 1L0. Tel: (418) 347-4182.

Marché aux Puces Terrebonne, 805 Mtée Masson, Lchnaie, QC J6W 2C7. Tel: (450) 471-9501.

Marché Aux Puces Tourville, 1200 Bd Tourville, Saint-Nicéphore, QC J2B 6V2. Tel: (819) 395-1195.

Marché Aux Puces Vertes, 322-B Principale, St Modeste, QC G0L 3W0. Tel: (418) 867-5793.

Marché Aux Puces Ville-Marie, 74 des Oblats N, Ville-Marie, QC J0Z 3W0. Tel: (819) 622-1709.

Marché Public Grenville, 427 Main, Grenville, QC J0V 1J0. Tel: (819) 242-0728.

Marchés Aux Puces, 315 Victoria, Thurso, QC J0X 3B0. Tel: (819) 985-9999.

Marchés Aux Puces 201, 2862 Rte 201, Ormstown, QC J0S 1K0. Tel: (450) 829-9848.

Marchés Aux Puces D M, 297 Bd Baril O, Princvl, QC G6L 3V8. Tel: (819) 364-2203.

Masson Flea Market, 110 Georges, Masson Angers, QC J8M 1A2. Tel: (819) 986-3552.

Puce de l'Ile, 684 Av Grande Ile, Grande Île, QC J6S 3N7. Tel: (450) 371-9868.

Puce du Haut-Richelieu (La), 353 Adrien Fontaine, St Athanase, QC J2X 4J3. Tel: (450) 346-4414.

Puces A Roger Enr (Les), 618 Ste Anne, Chtmi, QC G7J 2N9. Tel: (418) 543-6676.

Puces Chez André, 92 St Joseph O, Québec, QC G1K 1W9. Tel: (418) 522-5225.

Puces Chez Paulette (Les), 578-B Principale, St Donat, QC J0T 2C0. Tel: (819) 424-1241.

Stittsville Market, 6176 Hazeldean Rd, Stittsvl, ON K0A 3G0. Tel: (613) 836-5612.

Super Bazar, 1500 Av D'Estimauville, Québec, QC G1J 5B8. Tel: (418) 661-2294.

Témipuces, 115 Commerciale, Cabano, QC G0L 1E0. Tel: (418) 854-2904.

INTERNATIONAL

A note about European markets in the big cities: Generally everyone just walks about the market—no admission fees—and in the cities take the subway and save yourself a lot of aggravation.

In Paris, the market seems to run all daylight hours depending on whether you are visiting shops or wandering among the street vendors.

In England, all the markets I have personally visited or my friends have checked and visited lasted through the mornings only. Most of the fun and excitement was gone after lunch, although there may be a few stragglers.

In the provincal markets, Saturdays are the days—usually a farmers' market in season, like in the small town of Jonquières in Provence with the woman selling homemade goat's cheese out of the back end of a small pickup truck, or the occasional roving market like the one we happened upon in northern Germany.

I haven't put any times and admission information in with the listings, therefore, unless it was pertinent.

FRANCE
PARIS
Marché aux Puces

DATES: Saturday through Monday, year round.

TIMES: Daylight and then some; just get there.

LOCATION: Outside the Porte de Clignancourt Metro station (Line 4—Porte D'Orleans to Porte de Clignancourt). Just about due north at the edge of Paris.

DESCRIPTION: This market, started last century when people gathered to sell old clothes, is an institution. Visitors used to eat french fries and dance the polka. In the twenties, masterpiece paintings were found by chance here and made the market famous. Nowadays, it's practically its own village. You can find "anything you want, or don't want, or could ever dream about." You can find the most fabulous antiques and collectibles to the standard flea market t-shirts, bracelets, and whatnots. From food to junque. Vendors are all over the place—on the sidewalks, in shops, filling the streets, wherever. It's a treat. The atmosphere is electric, pulsing, bright, lively, and loud. Hold on to the kids and be prepared to use your elbows.

ENGLAND
LONDON
Bermondsey Market
(aka New Caledonia Market)

DATES: Sundays.

TIMES: 5:00 AM–6:00 AM for the serious dealings, but open all day.

LOCATION: Walk over Tower Bridge (heading south) to the crossroad (past the vinegar factory), turn right and you are there.

DESCRIPTION: This is *the* market in London. The serious antique deals are made here. Just be there very early. If you happen to watch *Lovejoy* on A&E, you'll understand. He mentions this market. It is also the one market where "unauthorized" goods get "legally" traded, according to my source.

Brick Lane Market

DATES: Sundays, year round, 9:00 AM–2:00 PM.

LOCATION: Shoreditch tube station, in the East End.

DESCRIPTION: Described as "straight out of Dickens," "with the best curry in town" by a London friend of mine, although he also describes the area as "Jack-the-Ripper-type." Everything here is second- to fourth-hand, at least.

Camden Lock Market

DATES: Sundays, year round.

LOCATION: Camden Town tube station (Northern Line).

DESCRIPTION: This is the current trendy market selling antiques, clothes, and jewelry. It is getting more popular every year. Traffic can get tricky, especially during excellent weather. Take the tube.

Camden Passage (or Walk) Market

DATES: Sundays, year round.

LOCATION: Outside the Angel tube station, turn right, then turn right again.

DESCRIPTION: This outdoor market is mostly shops selling antiques. But they are excellent antiques.

Petticoat Lane

DATES: Sundays, year round.

TIMES: Early to noon; after that the excitement is gone.

LOCATION: Middlesex Street in East End of London. Take the tube to Liverpool Street (take the road facing the station and the road will take you directly to the market), Aldgate or Aldgate East and follow the noise and crowd.

DESCRIPTION: All around the area, vendors are in a garage, on the streets, in shops, wherever. Hold on to anything of yours that you value. Better yet, don't take anything of value with you. This is the granddaddy of markets—full of new merchandise, used stuff, clothing of all sorts, dishes (you have to see the way the vendors display and demonstrate their wares to believe it—spinning, tossing, balancing—it's a performance!), electronics, the usual flea stuff, literally whatever. Called Petticoat Lane because petticoats were made here a very long time ago.

In the '70s when I was in London, there was a brass band made up of older gents (doing this to raise money for charity) who would play and entertain here. On Wednesdays they entertained us as we boarded the tube for work from the Earl's Court Station. Their band leader would recognize me from Wednesdays and always dance a little jig and wave to say "Hi." I have him immortalized on film.

Portobello Road

DATES: Saturdays, year round for the big market, daily for the shops.
TIMES: Morning is best.
LOCATION: West End of London. Take the tube to Notting Hill Gate.
DESCRIPTION: This was the classic antique and collectible market of London. If you ever saw the movie *Bedknobs and Broomsticks*, this is where the "market" part was filmed. Saturdays is the open-air market, otherwise the shops are open normal hours. Now it's rather "old hat."

THE NETHERLANDS

Queen's Birthday

DATES: April 30, every year.
TIMES: All day.
LOCATION: Everywhere.
DESCRIPTION: It's their beloved Queen's birthday, so everywhere and every place is suddenly a flea market, or a huge party or some sort of celebration. This is not to be taken heavily! Enjoy!

RUSSIA
MOSCOW
Ismailovsky Park Market

DATES: Saturday and Sunday.

TIMES: All day.

LOCATION: Ismailovsky Park in northeast Moscow. Take the blue Metro line to Ismailovsky Park station. Get out and follow the long lines ambling towards the market.

DESCRIPTION: Another mega market with hundreds and hundreds of vendors at the market, and more poorer vendors lining the way there, all selling everything, including nesting dolls, toys, art, Russian everything, wooden spoons and bowls, pins, amber, traditional clothing, and linen among others. Advice: take a Russian-speaking friend if you wish to haggle. And don't attempt to take any ancient religious icons with you; they can't leave the country. From an American who frequents this market, it is worth the trip to Moscow for all the sights, smells and sounds.

   A Russian friend gave this sage advice "from a Russian reality" for shopping in big Russian flea markets:
1. Never, ever flash any wads of money around. There are people watching foreigners, waiting for them to do this. When they find a mark—a quick push and the money disappears. It is better to stash small amounts in different pockets. Otherwise, as our friend says, "You'll reach for your key and all that's left will be dust and Moscow air."
2. Don't eat the food in these markets—it isn't always cooked thoroughly. The resulting food poisoning can be a serious problem.
3. If not buying souvenirs keep this in mind: "People do not sell things because they are tired of seeing them, they sell them because something is really wrong with their things. So, keep your eyes open and double-check everything you buy."

RUSSIAN FAR EAST—MAGADAN
Street Market of Magadan

DATES: Saturday and Sunday.

TIMES: Daylight.

LOCATION: 1,000 miles west of Anchorage, Alaska.

DESCRIPTION: This market of maybe 40-50 dealers is the equivalent of the Super Bowl in Magadan. This is the place to shop. Although originally it was illegal to hold this market, the police patronized it too. Dealers sell clothing, hardware, and stuff you'd expect to find in a supermarket. Much of the wares come from China and Japan. Americans are welcome.

SPAIN
MADRID
Coin and Stamp Market

DATES: Sundays.
TIMES: Mornings.
LOCATION: Plaza Major (the main Plaza of Madrid).
DESCRIPTION: If you are looking for any type of coin or stamp, this is the place to come. The columns surrounding the plaza are filled with dealers who have hundreds or more items on display. The collection blows the mind.

Rastro

DATES: Every Sunday, forever.
TIMES: Early morning until around 2:00 PM when the place empties.
LOCATION: The Rastro secton of Madrid, on the main road to Toledo.
DESCRIPTION: This monster market has easily thousands of dealers and even more thousands of shoppers spread over miles of main and side roads, up and down the hilly road. It is quite a sight.

CAYMAN ISLANDS

In the Cayman Islands, British West Indies, an unofficial national sport—known locally as Garage Sailing—is trolling the "Leaving the Island Sales." You can snag some real bargains. My friends picked up a $70 dive mask for $5. Start out Saturday morning and cruise through George Town, South Sound, and West Bay or grab a copy of the *Caymanian Compass* and check the listings for lawn sales. Trouble is getting the goodies back home, which is why the stuff is being sold in the first place!

HOW TO BE INCLUDED
IN THIS DIRECTORY

If you own or operate a flea market and would like to have your market considered for inclusion in the next edition of *The Official® Directory to U.S. Flea Markets*, either write us a letter requesting a questionnaire form or send complete information corresponding to the format currently employed in this directory. Market listings must be complete in order to be considered for publication. For a full explanation of the acceptable format for market listings, refer to the section entitled "How to Use This Book."

Address all mail to:

House of Collectibles
Editorial Department
299 Park Avenue 7ᵗʰ Floor
New York NY 10171